Managing Escalation While Competing Effectively in the Indo-Pacific

BRYAN FREDERICK, KRISTEN GUNNESS, BONNY LIN, CORTEZ A. COOPER III,
BRYAN ROONEY, JAMES BENKOWSKI, NATHAN CHANDLER,
CRISTINA L. GARAFOLA, JEFFREY W. HORNUNG, KARL P. MUELLER,
PAUL ORNER, TIMOTHY R. HEATH, CHRISTIAN CURRIDEN, EMILY ELLINGER

Prepared for the Department of the Air Force
Approved for public release; distribution unlimited

RAND PROJECT AIR FORCE

For more information on this publication, visit **www.rand.org/t/RRA972-1**.

About RAND

The RAND Corporation is a research organization that develops solutions to public policy challenges to help make communities throughout the world safer and more secure, healthier and more prosperous. RAND is nonprofit, nonpartisan, and committed to the public interest. To learn more about RAND, visit www.rand.org.

Research Integrity

Our mission to help improve policy and decisionmaking through research and analysis is enabled through our core values of quality and objectivity and our unwavering commitment to the highest level of integrity and ethical behavior. To help ensure our research and analysis are rigorous, objective, and nonpartisan, we subject our research publications to a robust and exacting quality-assurance process; avoid both the appearance and reality of financial and other conflicts of interest through staff training, project screening, and a policy of mandatory disclosure; and pursue transparency in our research engagements through our commitment to the open publication of our research findings and recommendations, disclosure of the source of funding of published research, and policies to ensure intellectual independence. For more information, visit www.rand.org/about/research-integrity.

RAND's publications do not necessarily reflect the opinions of its research clients and sponsors.

Published by the RAND Corporation, Santa Monica, Calif.
© 2022 RAND Corporation
RAND® is a registered trademark.

Library of Congress Cataloging-in-Publication Data is available for this publication.

ISBN: 978-1-9774-1038-2

Cover: Duncan Bevan/U.S. Air Force.

About This Report

In response to the recent growth in Chinese military activity and capabilities, the United States has undertaken its own increase in military activity in the Indo-Pacific over the past decade. Increasing tensions between China and the United States and the increasing military capabilities of both sides make it essential for the United States to identify ways to continue to safeguard its interests in the region while managing the risk of escalation with China. The authors of this report explored the factors and characteristics of U.S. military activities that have the greatest potential to contribute to the risk of escalation with China and developed a framework to help U.S. military planners limit these risks.

The research reported here was commissioned by Pacific Air Forces (PACAF) and conducted within the Strategy and Doctrine Program of RAND Project AIR FORCE as part of a fiscal year 2021 project, "Managing Escalation While Competing Effectively in the Indo-Pacific."

RAND Project Air Force

RAND Project AIR FORCE (PAF), a division of the RAND Corporation, is the Department of the Air Force's (DAF's) federally funded research and development center for studies and analyses, supporting both the United States Air Force and the United States Space Force. PAF provides the DAF with independent analyses of policy alternatives affecting the development, employment, combat readiness, and support of current and future air, space, and cyber forces. Research is conducted in four programs: Strategy and Doctrine; Force Modernization and Employment; Resource Management; and Workforce, Development, and Health. The research reported here was prepared under contract FA7014-16-D-1000.

Additional information about PAF is available on our website:
www.rand.org/paf/

This report documents work originally shared with the DAF on September 22, 2021. The draft report, issued on September 29, 2021, was reviewed by formal peer reviewers and DAF subject-matter experts.

Acknowledgments

The authors wish to thank several people without whom this report would not have been possible. To begin, we wish to thank the sponsors of the project that produced the report, Brigadier General Christopher J. Niemi and Brigadier General (Ret.) Michael P. Winkler of PACAF. We are also greatly indebted to other members of the PACAF team, including David J. Borbley, Lt. Col. Zofia A. Plummer, Maj. Derek C. Cox, and Capt. Jovan Popovich. We also wish to thank Rod Laszlo at U.S. Army Pacific, who enabled us to collaborate closely with a related project under his sponsorship. This report also benefited from the insights of several government attendees at our workshop to identify potential U.S. military activities in the Indo-Pacific. Lyle Morris of RAND and Dean Cheng of the Heritage Foundation provided reviews that substantially improved the document. All remaining errors are the responsibility of the authors alone.

At RAND, we are indebted to the contributions and collegiality of numerous colleagues, including particularly Raphael S. Cohen, the director of the Strategy and Doctrine Program within Project AIR FORCE where this project was conducted. Laura Poole provided invaluable administrative and logistical support. Stacie Pettyjohn gave us important initial guidance and mentorship. Jennifer Kavanagh, the director of the Strategy, Doctrine, and Resources Program within the Arroyo Center, enabled close collaboration between this project and another in that program.

Summary

The expansion of Chinese military activity and capabilities in the Indo-Pacific region has led the United States to undertake its own increase in activity in the region over the past decade, and additional increases in activity are under consideration. As the United States expands its military activities to safeguard its regional interests, the potential reactions of China are a crucial consideration. This report provides U.S. military planners and policymakers with guidance regarding how the characteristics of different potential U.S. military activities may affect Chinese perceptions and reactions, either in ways that the United States may prefer, such as by enhancing deterrence of People's Republic of China (PRC) aggression against U.S. allies and partners, or in ways the United States may wish to avoid, such as by increasing the risk of aggression and escalation.

Assessing China's Reactions to U.S. Military Activities

This report develops and presents a framework for assessing likely Chinese reactions to U.S. military activities. The framework is intended to help guide the thinking of U.S. military planners and policymakers that may be considering shifting or expanding existing activities or implementing new activities in the Indo-Pacific region by identifying the conditions under which a U.S. military activity is likely to result in an aggressive or escalatory PRC response. It does so by highlighting and encouraging consideration of a number of issues and factors that have a demonstrated link with Chinese perceptions and reactions.

Approach

This report has two main sections. In the first section, we develop our framework for assessing likely Chinese reactions to U.S. military activities. Our framework has three main components. First, it identifies the key factors that drive Chinese thinking and reactions. Second, it assesses how the characteristics of U.S. activities—their location, the U.S. allies or partners involved, their military capabilities, and the public profile or messaging that accompanies them—have the potential to affect Chinese reactions through each of the key factors. Third, the framework provides a typology of potential Chinese reactions organized by their level of intensity.

In the second section of the report, we develop a comprehensive set of potential military activities that the United States could undertake in the Indo-Pacific. We then evaluate the implications of our framework for this diverse set of potential activities, highlighting how China would likely perceive and react to different types of activities.

Key Findings

- *China assumes that most U.S. military activities in the region are hostile to China.* While U.S. policymakers can likely assume a negative Chinese reaction to most U.S. military activities in the region, the questions of the degree or intensity of those reactions, rather than just their direction, remain crucial.
- *China's level of concern for a U.S. military activity does not directly correlate with the near-term aggressiveness of its responses.* China will assess the leverage and capabilities it has against a specific country in addition to the escalatory potential in selecting a response. China's responses to activities it finds highly concerning could involve a mixture of political or economic inducements or coercion, in addition to or instead of military responses.
- *China's clear "redlines" appear to be limited in number.* Our analysis highlighted only a handful of activity characteristics likely to be associated with the most escalatory types of PRC responses, including proximity to or involvement of Taiwan or capabilities that threaten PRC command and control, nuclear, or regime targets.
- *However, Chinese sensitivities regarding Taiwan are likely to continue to complicate efforts to better defend the island while avoiding escalation.* Chinese "redlines" generally do touch directly on capabilities and locations that would be of substantial utility for the defense of Taiwan. This highlights the challenge that U.S. military planners face in identifying ways to enhance the defense of Taiwan.
- *U.S. activities that pose acute concerns for China are more likely to trigger consequential changes in longer-term PRC policies.* The immediately observable set of Chinese reactions to U.S. activities of particular concern may be followed by longer-term changes that may be more consequential.
- *China is now more likely to use lower-level military responses to signal disapproval or apply pressure than in the past.* China's recent development of less escalatory military options increases the likelihood that it would incorporate a lower-level military action into its response to a concerning U.S. military activity.

Recommendations

- U.S. military planners should utilize the considerations highlighted in this report to balance different activity characteristics to reduce the likelihood of an escalatory PRC response while accomplishing key objectives.
- U.S. military activities that directly involve Taiwan or that incorporate capabilities that could enable U.S. strikes on PRC regime or nuclear targets should be scrutinized with particular care.
- U.S. military planners should focus on aggregating lower-risk activities involving Taiwan to enhance the defense of the island. Smaller-scale or otherwise less-risky activities could potentially enhance Taiwan's defense, in larger numbers or over time, with less likelihood of leading to a disproportionately aggressive PRC response.

Contents

Figures and Tables

Figures

Tables

Chapter 1. Introduction

This report provides U.S. military planners and policymakers with a guide to understanding how China is likely to react to U.S. military activities in the Indo-Pacific. It does so by developing a framework that shows how Chinese perceptions and reactions are likely to be affected by the particular characteristics of U.S. military activities, and then summarizing the implications of this framework for different types of these activities. The framework does not provide precise guidance regarding specific Chinese responses, because Beijing's calculations in these matters will be highly context dependent. However, the framework does provide a detailed set of considerations for U.S. policymakers to take into account. The framework, therefore, is designed to work as a valuable guide or support for subject-matter experts tasked with anticipating China's perceptions and thinking.

The Challenge of an Increasingly Assertive China

China's military activities in the Indo-Pacific pose a number of challenges for the United States and its allies and partners in the region.[1] These activities may serve to pressure U.S. allies or partners to acquiesce to Chinese demands in territorial or other disputes, indicate improved Chinese military capabilities that could raise concerns in U.S. allies and partners that they may become increasingly vulnerable to a Chinese attack, or spread a narrative and impression that China is in the process of taking its place as the dominant power in the region.

In response to this growth in Chinese military activity and capabilities, the United States has undertaken its own increase in activity in the Indo-Pacific over the past decade. Since the 2011 "rebalance" to the Asia-Pacific was announced, the United States has gradually expanded its military posture in the region, increased the frequency and size of joint exercises, and energetically sought opportunities to further develop its presence and visibility in the region with a broader set of partners, including the emerging Quad framework.[2]

---

[1] On the growth in Chinese military capabilities, see, for example, Eric Heginbotham, Michael Nixon, Forrest E. Morgan, Jacob L. Heim, Jeff Hagen, Sheng Tao Li, Jeffrey Engstrom, Martin C. Libicki, Paul DeLuca, David A. Shlapak, David R. Frelinger, Burgess Laird, Kyle Brady, and Lyle J. Morris, *The U.S.-China Military Scorecard: Forces, Geography, and the Evolving Balance of Power, 1996–2017*, Santa Monica, Calif.: RAND Corporation, RR-392-AF, 2015.

[2] For a discussion of how the United States has used the Quad framework to expand regional partnerships, see Richard Rossow and Sarah Watson, "China Creates a Second Chance for the 'Quad,'" Asia Maritime Transparency Initiative, Center for Strategic and International Studies, March 14, 2016; and Evan A. Feigenbaum and James Schwemlein, "How Biden Can Make the Quad Endure," Carnegie Endowment for International Peace, March 11, 2021.

These increases in U.S. military activities may have served to enhance deterrence of threats to U.S. allies and partners or other goals, but they have not corresponded with any diminution in People's Republic of China (PRC) military activity.[3] Instead, China has continued to expand the frequency, scope, and, in some cases, the aggressiveness of its own military activities.[4] Particularly since the 2018 National Defense Strategy, U.S. policymakers have signaled an interest in more assertively and expansively responding to Chinese military activities to put China "into unfavorable positions, frustrating their efforts, precluding their options while expanding our own, and forcing them to confront conflict under adverse conditions."[5]

Notwithstanding any of these potential benefits, expanded U.S. military activities in the Indo-Pacific can also pose risks for the United States, most notably the risk of how China may respond. U.S. policymakers may wish to use military activities in the region to put China on the defensive, but doing so could also inadvertently increase the potential for escalation if China becomes so threatened by U.S. actions that it assesses that it needs to react aggressively to forestall further U.S. pressure that could undermine key Chinese goals or regime security.[6] Furthermore, Chinese reactions could involve changes to future PRC investments and defense spending, potentially worsening the security situation that the United States faces in the region over the long term.[7] It is therefore essential that expanded U.S. military activities in the region be informed by a deep and nuanced understanding of the types of U.S. military activities that could trigger escalatory or otherwise unwelcome Chinese responses.

---

[3] In general, if China assesses that U.S. capabilities and resolve to defend an ally or partner have been increased by a U.S. military activity, then it is likely to assess that the risks and costs for China of a potential attack on that ally or partner have also increased (John J. Mearsheimer, *Conventional Deterrence*, Ithaca, N.Y.: Cornell University Press, 1985, pp. 14, 28; and Robert Jervis, "Rational Deterrence: Theory and Evidence," *World Politics*, Vol. 41, No. 2, 1989, pp. 190–191). However, recent assessments of the state of deterrence over Taiwan suggest a mixed assessment of the ability for recent U.S. increases in activity to offset the substantial expansion in PRC capabilities. See Michael J. Mazarr, Nathan Beauchamp-Mustafaga, Timothy R. Heath, and Derek Eaton, *What Deters and Why: The State of Deterrence in Korea and the Taiwan Strait*, Santa Monica, Calif.: RAND Corporation, RR-3144-A, 2021.

[4] For example, China has become increasingly assertive in maritime territorial disputes in the East and South China Seas, using an array of gray zone capabilities that it has developed over the last decade. See Lyle J. Morris, Michael J. Mazarr, Jeffrey W. Hornung, Stephanie Pezard, Anika Binnendijk, and Marta Kepe, *Gaining Competitive Advantage in the Gray Zone: Response Options for Coercive Aggression Below the Threshold of Major War*, Santa Monica, Calif.: RAND Corporation, RR-2942-OSD, 2019.

[5] Jim Mattis, *Summary of the 2018 National Defense Strategy of the United States of America*, Washington, D.C.: U.S. Department of Defense, 2018, p. 5. Note that this quote refers to U.S. adversaries in general, while the National Defense Strategy names China and Russia as the two predominant U.S. adversaries.

[6] Stephen Van Evera, *Causes of War: Structures of Power and the Roots of International Conflict*, Ithaca, N.Y.: Cornell University Press, 1999, pp. 35–44. The Cuban Missile Crisis represents perhaps the most famous example of a state (in this case, the United States) threatening military action before an adversary could complete a military activity that it assessed to be threatening. See, for example, Len Scott and R. Gerald Hughes, *The Cuban Missile Crisis: A Critical Reappraisal*, New York: Routledge, 2015.

[7] Robert Jervis, "Cooperation Under the Security Dilemma," *World Politics*, Vol. 30, No. 2, January 1978.

Building on Prior Insights

Despite the importance of this issue, there have been only limited prior efforts in the public domain to understand how and why China is likely to respond to U.S. military activities in the Indo-Pacific. While we believe that this report develops the first rigorous and comprehensive framework for anticipating Chinese responses to U.S. military activities, it does so by building on previous research in three key areas: China's interests and strategies, China's signaling behavior, and Sino-American escalation dynamics.

A wide variety of recent studies examine China's interests, threat perceptions, security strategies, and approach to regional competition. For example, one study outlines China's grand strategy and China's approach to managing relations with the United States while still achieving its strategic objectives.[8] Others assess how Chinese perceptions of threats and interests evolve over time, how U.S. activities can impact the development of the People's Liberation Army (PLA), and how Chinese policymakers seek to combine various elements of national power together to achieve their long-term regional and global visions.[9] We draw on the findings of such works throughout the report, but they typically adopt a strategic-level view of Sino-American competition and do not attempt to identify the specific ways in which China might react to particular U.S. military activities.

A second body of research explores the drivers of Chinese aggression abroad. These studies have produced a number of useful insights regarding Chinese behavior that are incorporated into the development of key factors affecting Chinese responses to U.S. military activities found in Chapter 2 of this report.[10] Notably, however, these works typically concentrate on explaining China's behavior in territorial and maritime disputes, which, although important, represents only one channel through which U.S. activities can drive Chinese responses. They also often focus

---

[8] Andrew Scobell, Edmund J. Burke, Cortez A. Cooper III, Sale Lilly, Chad J. R. Ohlandt, Eric Warner, and J. D. Williams, *China's Grand Strategy: Trends, Trajectories, and Long-Term Competition*, Santa Monica, Calif.: RAND Corporation, RR-2798-A, 2020.

[9] Timothy R. Heath, Kristen Gunness, and Cortez A. Cooper III, *The PLA and China's Rejuvenation: National Security and Military Strategies, Deterrence Concepts, and Combat Capabilities*, Santa Monica, Calif.: RAND Corporation, RR-1402-OSD, 2016; and Nadège Rolland, *China's Vision for a New World Order*, Seattle, Wash.: National Bureau of Asian Research, NBR Special Report, No. 83, January 27, 2020.

[10] See, inter alia, Alastair Iain Johnston, "China's Militarized Interstate Dispute Behaviour 1949–1992: A First Cut at the Data," *China Quarterly*, Vol. 153, 1998; M. Taylor Fravel, "Regime Insecurity and International Cooperation: Explaining China's Compromises in Territorial Disputes," *International Security*, Vol. 30, No. 2, Fall 2005; M. Taylor Fravel, "Power Shifts and Escalation: Explaining China's Use of Force in Territorial Disputes," *International Security*, Vol. 32, No. 3, Winter 2007/2008; Andrew Chubb, "PRC Assertiveness in the South China Sea: Measuring Continuity and Change, 1970–2015," *International Security*, Vol. 45, No. 3, Winter 2020/2021; Ketian Zhang, "Cautious Bully: Reputation, Resolve, and Beijing's Use of Coercion in the South China Sea," *International Security*, Vol. 44, No. 1, 2019; and Michael Green, Kathleen Hicks, Zack Cooper, John Schaus, and Jake Douglas, *Countering Coercion in Maritime Asia: The Theory and Practice of Gray Zone Deterrence*, Washington, D.C.: Center for Strategic and International Studies, May 2017.

only on China's military or gray zone responses, to the exclusion of its political and economic policies.

Equally useful are studies that evaluate China's approach to deterrence signaling and provide a more granular window into Beijing's decisionmaking. Some even develop typologies or frameworks for understanding China's behavior.[11] Lessons drawn from those studies inform our own analysis, particularly in Chapter 4, which examines patterns in China's near- and longer-term responses to different U.S. actions. A subset of this research focuses on analyzing Chinese behavior in crises and conflicts and has significantly enhanced our understanding of China's evolving approach to using military force to control escalation,[12] as well as the escalation risks associated with a U.S.-China conflict.[13] This work informs our analysis of potential high-intensity PLA responses but is less helpful for understanding how and why U.S. military activities might cause China to adopt lower-intensity and nonmilitary forms of aggression, particularly in peacetime.

It is also worth noting a fourth and more limited body of research that has sought to identify the ways in which other states might respond to different U.S. military activities. For example, we leverage methodological insights from a previous effort to predict potential Russian responses to U.S. posture changes.[14] Unpublished RAND research assesses potential Chinese responses to U.S. Army posture options. It focuses on the degree to which China might view a U.S. posture shift as provocative, as well as how effectively China might be able to counter or oppose it. Although that research is more narrowly focused than our own, it has conceptual similarities to this report, and we have built on that research's findings.

Taken together, these studies help to reveal China's interests, as well as the ways in which it might use its military coercively in both peacetime and during crises. However, they do not seek to identify the most influential or important drivers of Chinese aggression or provide a tool for predicting how China might respond to specific U.S. actions.

This report therefore fills an important gap by providing a substantially more detailed, comprehensive open-source framework to anticipate likely Chinese reactions to U.S. military

---

[11] Nathan Beauchamp-Mustafaga, Derek Grossman, Kristen Gunness, Michael S. Chase, Marigold Black, and Natalia D. Simmons-Thomas, *Deciphering Chinese Deterrence Signalling in the New Era: An Analytic Framework and Seven Case Studies*, Santa Monica, Calif.: RAND Corporation, RR-A1074-1, 2021; and Paul H. B. Godwin and Alice L. Miller, "China's Forbearance Has Limits: Chinese Threat and Retaliation Signaling and Its Implications for a Sino-American Military Confrontation," *China Strategic Perspectives*, No. 6, Washington, D.C.: Institute for National Strategic Studies, April 2013.

[12] Burgess Laird, *War Control: Chinese Writings on the Control of Escalation in Crisis and Conflict*, Washington, D.C.: Center for a New American Security, April 2017.

[13] Caitlin Talmadge, "Would China Go Nuclear? Assessing the Risk of Chinese Nuclear Escalation in a Conventional War with the United States," *International Security*, Vol. 41, No. 4, 2017; and Fiona S. Cunningham and M. Taylor Fravel, "Dangerous Confidence? Chinese Views on Nuclear Escalation," *International Security*, Vol. 44, No. 2, 2019.

[14] Bryan Frederick, Matthew Povlock, Stephen Watts, Miranda Priebe, and Edward Geist, *Assessing Russian Reactions to U.S. and NATO Posture Enhancements*, Santa Monica, Calif.: RAND Corporation, RR-1879-AF, 2017.

activities than previously available. However, our framework retains relatively modest goals. It offers a method for ensuring careful consideration of a number of key issues that can be shown to affect Chinese perceptions and reactions, but it does not on its own provide a comprehensive assessment of costs and benefits. Furthermore, the framework is not intended to provide recommendations for whether the United States should or should not undertake specific activities based solely on possible PRC responses. In some cases, for example, it may be prudent for the United States to conduct certain activities in the Indo-Pacific region with the knowledge or expectation that those activities would create countervailing actions by the PRC. Our framework is therefore best used to support ongoing analysis of U.S. military activities, but not as a replacement for other efforts that may also consider, for example, the costs and feasibility of different options for the United States, the trade-offs if capabilities are relocated from other regions, or the reactions of other U.S. allies and partners to U.S. activities, issues that are not covered in detail in this report.

Structure of This Report

This report has two main parts. In the first part, consisting of the next three chapters, we develop a framework to assess likely PRC reactions to U.S. military activities. Chapter 2 identifies the six key factors that we have assessed are most essential in understanding PRC perceptions and reactions. Chapter 3 outlines the linkages we have identified between these key factors and the particular characteristics of U.S. military activities. Chapter 4 presents a typology of potential Chinese reactions to U.S. military activities.

In the second part, we develop a menu of potential U.S. military activities for competing with China in the Indo-Pacific and identify how these activities could be varied to have different effects on Chinese thinking and reactions, including particularly the implications of different activities for the risk of escalation. Chapter 5 contains a detailed typology of U.S. military activities, including both those that have been used in the competition with China since 2011 or those that have been employed against other U.S. adversaries since 1945. This typology therefore provides a list of potential types of activities that the United States might consider undertaking in the competition with China, as well as a discussion regarding how the characteristics of different activities might be varied for meaningful effects on PRC reactions. Chapter 6 then summarizes the implications of the framework developed in the first part of the report for the different activity types developed in Chapter 5. It does so by providing a brief overview of the characteristics of different U.S. activity types that are likely to have the most escalatory effects on PRC perceptions and reactions. Chapter 7 concludes and summarizes the implications from our analysis and identifies recommendations for U.S. policymakers and the U.S. Air Force (USAF) in particular.

This report also has three appendixes. Appendix A discusses key factors considered for inclusion for our framework in Chapter 2 but ultimately omitted. Appendix B provides the full text of the case studies used to inform our analysis throughout the report. Appendix C outlines the procedure for applying the framework at a higher level of detail to a particular U.S. military activity and includes an example of such an application.

Chapter 2. Key Factors That Affect Chinese Responses to U.S. Military Activities

The first part of our framework identifies the key factors that are the most reliable and influential in affecting Chinese reactions to U.S. military activities in the Indo-Pacific region. Our research highlighted six such factors that appear to most directly affect Chinese thinking and perceptions and, in turn, Chinese responses. Taken together, they form the basis for our framework to assess how PRC thinking might be affected by a U.S. military activity and the resulting potential nature and scale of Chinese responses. Table 2.1 summarizes these key factors.

Table 2.1. Key Factors That Affect Chinese Responses to U.S. Military Activities

Key Factors
1. China's perceptions of the potential military threat from U.S., allied, and partner capabilities
2. China's perceptions of U.S., allied, and partner hostile intent
3. China's perceptions of threats to its regime legitimacy
4. China's perceptions of threats to its economic development
5. China's perceptions of threats to its regional influence
6. China's perceptions of U.S. commitment to the defense of U.S. allies or partners

The significance of these six factors was validated through a survey of existing international relations research and 18 case studies of China's reactions to specific events or U.S. activities. Two other potential factors were initially identified and tested but were ultimately excluded because of either a lack of evidence or because of difficulties in applying them in a predictive capacity. Appendix A contains analysis of these excluded factors, which are China's internal instability and its own perceptions of its reputation for resolve. The case studies used to test the framework factors are presented in Appendix B.[15] We also wish to emphasize that our discussion of these factors in this chapter is meant primarily to establish how and why these factors affect PRC perceptions and concerns. It is not meant to imply that China worries equally or substantially about every U.S. military activity that touches on any of these key factors. Indeed, the *degree* to which U.S. military activities may affect Chinese thinking through these key factors is the central consideration of the remainder of our analysis, particularly in Chapters 3

---

[15] Although discussed in more detail in Appendix B, we would briefly note that the cases were selected on the basis of four considerations: recency (within the past 10–20 years), diversity (to capture a wide range of U.S., allied, and partner activities), applicability to each of the specific factors we were evaluating, and information availability. The full list of cases is presented in Table B.1.

and 6. This chapter focuses first on identifying and justifying our selection of these key factors, to set the stage for later discussions.

The remainder of this chapter explains and analyzes the framework factors in detail. Each factor begins with a summary of the principal conclusions and implications regarding the potential effect of the factor on Chinese responses. It then assesses the general level of theoretical and empirical support for the factor in existing research, as well as historical evidence from modern Chinese history. It proceeds to briefly examine key cases that validate the role of the factor in shaping Chinese reactions to U.S. and allied and partner activities. Finally, it offers a synopsis of the implications for Chinese behavior derived from the preceding analysis. Following discussions of all six factors, the chapter concludes with a brief survey of key conclusions regarding the framework factors as a whole.

Factor 1: China's Perceptions of the Potential Military Threat from U.S., Allied, and Partner Capabilities

China's perceptions of the potential threat that U.S. and partner and allied military capabilities could pose to its regime or physical security appear to strongly shape Chinese reactions, with aggressive Chinese responses more likely the greater the perceived threat. Such threats could include the potential for foreign military forces to directly attack Chinese territory, China's nuclear command and control (C2) and deterrence capability, domestic military and civilian infrastructure and facilities, or its leadership. The Chinese response to such potential threats is likely to be relatively aggressive in order to signal China's resolve to defend itself and deter such attacks from occurring.[16] Chinese investments in new military capabilities, which are themselves driven by Chinese perceptions of the threats posed by competitors' military capabilities, enable and may embolden more aggressive Chinese responses to activities seen as threatening.

All states carefully monitor their potential adversaries' development of military capabilities. They adapt their defense postures and responses on the basis of the perceived threats that these capabilities may pose to their regime and physical security. Control of their physical territory is a key security interest of all states, and threats against territorial integrity are particularly likely to result in an aggressive response.[17] Conventional military threats to the security of nuclear forces

---

[16] Glenn H. Snyder, *Deterrence and Defense*, Princeton, N.J.: Princeton University Press, 1961; Paul K. Huth, "Extended Deterrence and the Outbreak of War," *American Political Science Review*, Vol. 82, No. 2, 1988; and Daryl G. Press, *Calculating Credibility: How Leaders Assess Military Threats*, Ithaca, N.Y.: Cornell University Press, 2005.

[17] Stacie E. Goddard, "Uncommon Ground: Indivisible Territory and the Politics of Legitimacy," *International Organization*, Vol. 60, No. 1, Winter 2006; Paul R. Hensel and Sara McLaughlin Mitchell, "Issue Indivisibility and Territorial Claims," *GeoJournal*, Vol. 64, No. 4, 2005; Paul F. Diehl, "Geography and War: A Review and Assessment of the Empirical Literature," *International Interactions*, Vol. 17, No. 1, 1991; Paul R. Hensel, "Charting

are also considered to be highly likely to produce aggressive responses by states. When states face an adversary with similar nuclear capabilities, both states realize that nuclear strikes against the other would be accompanied by a risk of costly retaliation, incentivizing both to act with more restraint.[18] However, should the nuclear deterrent of either side be threatened by other means, including conventional capabilities that a potential aggressor might not necessarily assume would prompt nuclear retaliation, states have a strong incentive to act aggressively to signal their concerns and maintain their assured nuclear deterrent and second strike capability.[19] Finally, state leaders are naturally highly concerned with physical threats to the leadership itself—often referred to as *decapitation strikes*—although this has not largely featured in Chinese writings.[20]

China's past actions illustrate the care with which Beijing tracks potential threats to its regime and physical security from foreign military capabilities, as well as its willingness to respond aggressively if it perceives that U.S. or allied forces may be threatening those interests. For example, China's nuclear weapons program, which began in 1955 following the Korean War, is believed by both Chinese and American scholars to have been a response to the threat posed by U.S. nuclear weapons to China as well as China's changing relationship with the Soviet Union.[21] A decade later, China reacted strongly to American deployments into South Vietnam because of concerns about an American proxy on China's southern border or a potential invasion of the PRC from the south.[22]

More-recent Chinese literature and statements paint a similar picture. Chinese discussions regarding its "core interests" emphasize sovereignty and territorial integrity as critical to China's security, and official Chinese statements over the past decade indicate a growing willingness on Beijing's part to impose costs to deter countries from impinging on its territorial and sovereignty

---

a Course to Conflict: Territorial Issues and Interstate Conflict, 1816–1992," *Conflict Management and Peace Science*, Vol. 15, No. 1, 1996; and John A. Vasquez, "Why Do Neighbors Fight? Proximity, Interaction, or Territoriality," *Journal of Peace Research*, Vol. 32, No. 3, 1995.

[18] Robert Jervis, *The Meaning of the Nuclear Revolution: Statecraft and the Prospect of Armageddon*, Ithaca, N.Y.: Cornell University Press, 1990.

[19] There is evidence both that the United States has taken efforts to make the second-strike capabilities of other states more vulnerable and that China has responded to perceived threats to its nuclear capacity (Thomas J. Christensen, "The Meaning of the Nuclear Evolution: China's Strategic Modernization and U.S.-China Security Relations," *Journal of Strategic Studies*, Vol. 35, No. 4, 2012; and Austin Long and Brendan Rittenhouse Green, "Stalking the Secure Second Strike: Intelligence, Counterforce, and Nuclear Strategy," *Journal of Strategic Studies*, Vol. 38, Nos. 1–2, 2015).

[20] On the relationship between military capability development and leadership concerns over decapitation strikes, see Caitlin Talmadge, "Emerging Technology and Intra-War Escalation Risks: Evidence from the Cold War, Implications for Today," *Journal of Strategic Studies*, Vol. 42, No. 6, 2019, pp. 873–876.

[21] Jeffrey Lewis, *Paper Tigers: China's Nuclear Posture*, New York: Routledge, 2015, p. 16.

[22] Xiaoming Zhang, *Deng Xiaoping's Long War: The Military Conflict Between China and Vietnam, 1979–1991*, Chapel Hill, N.C.: University of North Carolina Press, 2015, p. 21.

claims.[23] The inclusion of "sovereignty claims" in official statements indicates that China conceives of its territorial integrity as also including its claimed maritime territorial waters (TW) in the East China Sea (ECS) and South China Sea (SCS).[24]

China also views its nuclear forces as critical to regime and physical security and would likely perceive the development of foreign military capabilities that pose a particular threat to its nuclear deterrent as justifying a potentially aggressive response. Chinese analysis and official Chinese statements from the past decade hold that China views nuclear weapons as valuable tools for deterring nuclear attack, protecting national security interests, and cementing China's great-power status.[25] Although China publicly adheres to a No First Use policy, Chinese writings and Western analysis highlight concern about the ability of U.S. conventional precision strike weapons to hold China's nuclear forces at risk.[26] China has responded in various ways to this concern—for example, by investing in conventionally armed short-, medium-, and long-range ballistic and cruise missiles and developing its own boost-glide systems that allow the Chinese military to target U.S. forces further afield. This suggests that U.S. or allied capabilities that can threaten China's nuclear deterrent could be met with an aggressive response, including one that could utilize these newer capabilities.[27]

Two additional more-recent cases provide further support for this factor. First, Chinese reactions to the U.S. hypersonic missile program and its potential deployment to the Indo-Pacific

---

[23] Core interests include (1) security: preserving China's basic political system and national security; (2) sovereignty: protecting national sovereignty, territorial integrity, and national unification; and (3) development: maintaining international conditions for China's economic development. See Andrew Scobell, Edmund J. Burke, Cortez A. Cooper III, Sale Lilly, Chad J. R. Ohlandt, Eric Warner, and J. D. Williams, *China's Grand Strategy: Trends, Trajectories, and Long-Term Competition*, Santa Monica, Calif.: RAND Corporation, RR-2798-A, 2020, pp. 12–14.

[24] China's most recent national defense white paper states that "[d]isputes still exist over the territorial sovereignty of some islands and reefs, as well as maritime demarcation. Countries from outside the region conduct frequent close-in reconnaissance on China by air and sea, and illegally enter China's territorial waters and the waters and airspace near China's islands and reefs, undermining China's national security." "Countries from outside the region" is a clear reference to the United States. See State Council Information Office of the People's Republic of China, *China's National Defense in the New Era*, July 24, 2019.

[25] See "Xi Calls for Powerful Missile Force," *China Daily*, December 5, 2012; and Wei Fenghe and Zhang Haiyang, "Diligently Build a Powerful, Informatized Strategic Missile Force" ["努力打造强大的信息化战略导弹部队"], *People's Daily*, December 13, 2012. The 2019 Chinese defense white paper reiterated that China views nuclear weapons as a key capability for maintaining national security and deterring aggression from outside powers (State Council Information Office of the People's Republic of China, *China's National Defense in the New Era*, July 24, 2019).

[26] Jeffrey Lewis, *Paper Tigers*: *China's Nuclear Posture*, New York: Routledge, 2015, p. 36. Another author notes that the United States' expanding precision strike arsenal means that China must develop the capability to penetrate these systems to ensure a second-strike capability—even if the new U.S. missile-defense systems are not aimed at reducing China's second-strike capabilities—because they impact China's capacity for nuclear retaliation (He Qisong [何奇松], "Trump Administration (Missile Defense Assessment)" ["特朗普政府(导弹防御评估)"], *International Forum* [国际论坛], No. 4, 2019).

[27] Jeffrey Lewis, *Paper Tigers*: *China's Nuclear Posture*, New York: Routledge, 2015, p. 37.

region illustrate China's concern over physical and regime security threats.[28] China worries that U.S. hypersonic weapons could negate China's anti-access/area denial (A2/AD) bubble and could target China's C2 and nuclear forces.[29] China has responded to the U.S. development of this capability by investing in its own hypersonic weapons program, bolstering its nuclear deterrent posture, and potentially revisiting its No First Use policy to deter the use of U.S. conventional weapons against China's nuclear forces.[30] Chinese analysis directly ties these reactions to the PRC's view that U.S. deployment of hypersonic weapons could threaten China's nuclear forces and thus its ability to defend the mainland.[31] Although China's direct military response has not been aggressive so far, the United States has yet to deploy hypersonic weapons into the region, making this only a partial test of the hypothesis.

Second, following the 2016 announcement of the deployment of a U.S. Terminal High Altitude Area Defense (THAAD) system to South Korea, Beijing appears to have perceived several military threats to its physical security, including most notably that THAAD would weaken China's nuclear deterrent due to THAAD's highly advanced X-band radar, which could potentially be used to target Chinese intercontinental ballistic missiles (ICBMs), as well as the expansion of U.S. and allied regional missile defense architecture.[32] China responded with an

---

[28] Case 1 in Appendix B explores this in greater detail. The U.S. Department of Defense (DoD) is developing hypersonic weapons as part of its conventional prompt global strike program. There has been increased discussion of deploying long-range hypersonic weapons (LRHWs) to the Indo-Pacific region, as well as discussions on where to base the new capability. See John T. Watts, Christian Trotti, and Mark J. Massa, *Primer on Hypersonic Weapons in the Indo-Pacific Region*, Washington, D.C.: Atlantic Council, August 2020.

[29] Yong Zhao [赵永], Weimin Li, Chenhao Zhao, and Xu Liu, "U.S. Global Prompt Strike System Development Status and Trend Analysis" ["美国全球快速打击系统发展现状及动向分析"], *Cruise Missile* [飞航导弹], Vol. 1, No. 3, 2014; and Tong Zhao, *Conventional Challenges to Strategic Stability: Chinese Perception of Hypersonic Technology and the Security Dilemma*, Washington, D.C.: Carnegie Endowment for International Peace, 2016.

[30] For a description of China's efforts to develop hypersonic weapons, see Office of the Secretary of Defense, *Annual Report to Congress: Military and Security Developments Involving the People's Republic of China 2019*, Washington, D.C., 2019, p. 44; and Office of the Secretary of Defense, *Annual Report to Congress: Military and Security Developments Involving the People's Republic of China 2020*, Washington, D.C., 2020, p. 65. Some Western scholars assert that China's No First Use policy could become more ambiguous to account for China's potential nuclear retaliation after a conventional strike on its nuclear forces. See Fiona S. Cunningham and M. Taylor Fravel, "Assuring Assured Retaliation: China's Nuclear Posture and U.S.-China Strategic Stability," *International Security*, Vol. 40, No. 2, October 2015.

[31] Yong Zhao [赵永], Weimin Li, Chenhao Zhao, and Xu Liu, "U.S. Global Prompt Strike System Development Status and Trend Analysis" ["美国全球快速打击系统发展现状及动向分析"], *Cruise Missile* [飞航导弹], Vol. 1, No. 3, 2014; and Xu Liu [刘旭], Weimin Li, Zhipeng Jiang, and Wenjing Song, "Thoughts on Hypersonic Cruise Missile Combat Characteristics and Offense-Defense Model" ["高超声速巡航导弹作战特点及攻防模式思考"], *Cruise Missile* [飞航导弹], No. 9, 2014.

[32] Case 7 in Appendix B explores this in greater detail. See Li Bin, "The Security Dilemma and THAAD Deployment in the ROK," *China-U.S. Focus*, March 6, 2017. Chinese analysis cited the X-band radar, which Chinese missile defense experts argued could detect most Chinese missile tests in northeast China and strategic ICBMs in the western part of the country, as well as allowing the United States to detect the radar signature from the back of the warhead, and could differentiate between a real Chinese warhead and a decoy, imperiling China's

aggressive diplomatic, economic, and media campaign that had substantial effects on the South Korean economy, eventually leading to promises by Seoul to limit future similar collaboration with the United States, although the THAAD deployment itself went forward.[33] China's military response was generally more restrained, including the cancellation of some military-to-military engagements, but other aspects were likely intended to signal serious concern, including a PLA Rocket Force combined ballistic and cruise missile exercise in the Bohai Sea, likely with the DF-26 intermediate-range ballistic missile (IRBM), which simulated a strike on a THAAD battery and a mock F-22 aircraft.[34] These events illustrate that while China does react aggressively to U.S. capabilities that it perceives as threatening to Chinese physical or regime security, the response may not necessarily be military in nature. In this instance, China likely believed that nonmilitary levers would be more likely to achieve Chinese goals.[35]

China's perception of the threats generated by new U.S., allied, and partner capabilities has pushed it to develop its own new capabilities. These expand the range of PLA responses and

nuclear deterrent capability. Effective missile defense systems of even relatively modest scale could affect China's perception of the security of its nuclear response. The PLA's inventory of nuclear warheads on ICBMs is expected to grow to 200 in the next five years. By contrast, the United States has 1,550 deployed warheads across its delivery platforms and an inventory of 3,750 warheads. See Office of the Secretary of Defense, *Military and Security Developments Involving the People's Republic of China 2020*, Washington, D.C., 2020, p. viii; U.S. Department of State, "Transparency in the U.S. Nuclear Weapons Stockpile," fact sheet, October 5, 2021; and U.S. Department of State, "New START Treaty Aggregate Numbers of Strategic Offensive Arms of the United States and the Russian Federation, February 2011–March 2022," fact sheet, March 1, 2022.

[33] See Ministry of Foreign Affairs of the People's Republic of China, "Foreign Ministry Spokesperson Hong Lei's Regular Press Conference on July 8," July 8, 2016. Chinese officials frequently condemned the deployment. According to one study, China's Ministry of Foreign Affairs spoke out on the issue more than 50 times in 2016 and 2017 and conducted an extensive media campaign against the deployment (Ethan Meick and Nargiza Salidjanova, *China's Response to U.S.-South Korean Missile Defense System Deployment and Its Implications*, Washington, D.C.: U.S.-China Economic and Security Review Commission, July 26, 2017). Beijing's economic coercion efforts cost South Korea at least $7.5 billion in economic losses. See "When China and U.S. Spar, It's South Korea That Gets Punched," *Los Angeles Times*, November 20, 2020. The crisis eased in May 2017, after the inauguration of President Moon Jae-in. The new government made considerable effort to restore the relationship with China. Beijing responded positively, and, on October 31, Beijing and Seoul announced a joint statement on their rapprochement.

[34] See Ethan Meick and Nargiza Salidjanova, *China's Response to U.S.-South Korean Missile Defense System Deployment and Its Implications*, Washington, D.C.: U.S.-China Economic and Security Review Commission, July 26, 2017; Ai Jun, "New Missile Signals China's Resolve to Counter THAAD," *Global Times*, May 10, 2017; and Deng Xiaoci, "China's Latest Missile Test Shows Country Can Respond to Aircraft Carriers, THAAD," *Global Times*, May 10, 2017.

[35] Chinese experts recommended numerous military countermeasures against THAAD, although the extent to which the PLA considered implementing them is unclear. A PLA Academy of Military Science expert recommended the use of jamming and EW against the THAAD radar in the event of conflict. He also suggested using stealth and maneuvering technologies to enable Chinese missiles to evade the defense. He further recommended striking the deployment base with cruise missiles in the event of war. See "Major General Zhu Chenghu: To Respond to THAAD, China Must Be Fully Prepared" ["朱成虎少将: 应对美国 '萨德' 中国要未雨绸缪"], *Bauhania* [紫荆网], August 2, 2016. The crisis eased in May 2017, after the inauguration of President Moon Jae-in. who worked to restore the relationship with China. Beijing and Seoul announced a joint statement on their rapprochement in October 2017. See Ministry of Foreign Affairs of the People's Republic of China, "China and South Korea Communicate on Bilateral Relations and Other Issues" ["中韩双方就中韩关系等进行沟通"], October 31, 2017.

increase China's confidence in its ability to respond with military means while controlling escalation.[36] In some areas, China's development of new military capabilities has likely emboldened it to behave more aggressively.[37] Such capabilities include high-end systems, such as China's expanding A2/AD umbrella, as well as "gray zone" forces that operate below the threshold of armed conflict.[38]

Extensive literature and multiple cases therefore support the hypothesis that China is more likely to react aggressively when it perceives U.S., allied, and partner capabilities as posing greater threats to its regime or physical security. It will probably often try to do so in ways that are sensitive to escalation risks. However, China's perceptions of threats have encouraged it to develop more military options, which enables, and perhaps emboldens, it to undertake more aggressive responses to U.S. actions than in the past.

Factor 2: China's Perceptions of U.S., Allied, and Partner Hostile Intent

Whereas Factor 1 focuses on the potential threat posed to PRC regime and physical security from shifts in foreign military capabilities, Factor 2 focuses on China's perceptions of the hostility of U.S., allied, and partner intent. These two factors are closely related, as the interaction of Beijing's concern over U.S., allied, and partner capabilities with its perceptions of their intent informs how threatened it feels.[39] The greater the perceived hostility of the United States' intent toward China, the more threatening U.S. military capabilities come to seem by Chinese leaders. Similarly, the greater U.S. military capabilities with the potential to attack China, the more sensitive Beijing will be to indicators of U.S. hostility. Taken together, Factors 1

---

[36] David M. Finkelstein, "Breaking the Paradigm: Drivers Behind the PLA's Current Period of Reform," in Phillip C. Saunders, Arthur S. Ding, Andrew Scobell, Andrew N. D. Yang, and Joel Wuthnow, eds., *Chairman Xi Remakes the PLA: Assessing Chinese Military Reforms*, Washington, D.C.: National Defense University Press, 2019. China's 13th Five Year Plan (2015–2020) stated that by 2020 the PLA should have achieved mechanization and made progress in applying information technology and developing strategic capabilities. At the 19th Party Congress in 2017, Xi Jinping reiterated these goals, stating that by 2035, national defense modernization should be complete and the PLA should be a "world-class force." See "Full Text of Xi Jinping's Report at the 19th CPC National Congress," Xinhua, November 3, 2017; and "CMC Opinions on Deepening National Defense and Military Reforms" ["中央军委关于深化国防和军队改革的意见"], Xinhua, January 1, 2016.

[37] Lyle J. Morris, Michael J. Mazarr, Jeffrey W. Hornung, Stephanie Pezard, Anika Binnendijk, and Marta Kepe, *Gaining Competitive Advantage in the Gray Zone: Response Options for Coercive Aggression Below the Threshold of Major War*, Santa Monica, Calif.: RAND Corporation, RR-2942-OSD, 2019, pp. 27–42.

[38] China's gray zone capabilities include paramilitary maritime forces—the Chinese Coast Guard and the People's Armed Forces Maritime Militia (PAFMM)—and nonconventional capabilities, including information operations, cyber, space, and electronic warfare. See Lyle J. Morris, "Gray Zone Challenges in the East and South China Sea," *Maritime Issues*, January 7, 2019; and Andrew S. Erickson, "Maritime Numbers Game," *Indo-Pacific Defense Forum*, January 28, 2019.

[39] For a general discussion of the interrelationship of perceptions of state intentions and capabilities, see Charles L. Glaser, "The Security Dilemma Revisited," *World Politics*, Vol. 50, No. 1, October 1997, p. 178.

and 2 form the core of Chinese assessments regarding the threat that they may face from the United States and its allies and partners.

A significant body of international relations literature discusses states' tendencies to react assertively to adversary actions when their intent is perceived to be certainly or potentially hostile.[40] Furthermore, states often rely on limited or false information or past experiences to make inferences about the intent of their adversaries—sometimes leading to misperceptions and subsequent aggressive or escalatory behavior—such that initial perceptions of hostile intent can be difficult to change in the future.[41] Past crises, which states factor into current and future assessments of intent, also heighten suspicions between adversaries while increasing the influence of hard-liners and hawks on each side.[42] Adversary alliances or coalitions can further enhance perceptions of hostility, particularly if the states involved share a history of negative relations with the target state.[43]

Chinese perceptions of U.S. and allied hostile intent in the Indo-Pacific region are well documented. For many years, the Chinese leadership's assessments of U.S. objectives and intentions toward China have assumed a high level of hostility toward the Chinese Communist Party (CCP). These assessments include that the United States intends to "strategically contain" China's rise, keep Taiwan separated from the mainland, challenge the legitimacy of the CCP, use military alliances to encircle China, and impinge on other Chinese "core interests."[44] U.S. military deployments to the region, particularly when combined with broader shifts in U.S. policy that indicate greater focus on the region, tend to exacerbate Chinese concerns about hostile U.S. intent, as does U.S. security cooperation with regional states.[45]

For example, some Chinese concerns about the U.S. rebalance to the Asia-Pacific in 2012 focused on the increased potential for the United States to interfere in territorial disputes in the SCS. According to Chinese statements, the rebalance heralded "the watershed of the South China Sea issue and the U.S. acted as the driving force and root cause behind the tension in the South

---

[40] James D. Fearon, "Rationalist Explanations for War," *International Organization*, Vol. 49, No. 3, Summer 1995; and Stephen M. Walt, *The Origins of Alliances*, Ithaca, N.Y.: Cornell University Press, 1987.

[41] Robert Jervis, *Perception and Misperception in International Politics*, Princeton, N.J.: Princeton University Press, 2017.

[42] John A. Vasquez, *The War Puzzle*, New York: Cambridge University Press, 1993; and Paul R. Hensel, "An Evolutionary Approach to the Study of Interstate Rivalry," *Conflict Management and Peace Science*, Vol. 17, No. 2, 1999.

[43] Glenn H. Snyder, "The Security Dilemma in Alliance Politics," *World Politics*, Vol. 36, No. 4, 1983, p. 470.

[44] David M. Finkelstein, "The Chinese View of Strategic Competition with the United States," testimony before the U.S.-China Economic and Security Review Commission, June 24, 2020. These are several of the primary complaints one sees in Chinese statements and literature, but there is a broader mistrust of the United States as a founder of the current liberal order, which Beijing views as antithetical to China's national interests. See Nadège Rolland, *China's Vision for a New World Order*, Seattle, Wash.: National Bureau of Asian Research, NBR Special Report, No. 83, January 27, 2020.

[45] Case 11 in Appendix B examines the strengthening of U.S.-India ties as a particular example of this dynamic.

China Sea."[46] The Chinese Ministry of Foreign Affairs stated that the region was peaceful prior to U.S. interference, and then the introduction of "the so-called Rebalance to Asia strategy" led to increased regional tensions.[47] Beyond the SCS issue, Chinese commentary indicated that the rebalance was viewed as an encirclement of China, specifically engineered by the United States and its allies to hinder China's rise.[48]

Chinese literature also indicates that the PRC tends to view the primary purpose of the United States' regional alliances, partnerships, and military capabilities as the containment of China. This perception undergirds Chinese reactions to shifts in U.S. regional capabilities, particularly if those changes suggest closer relations between the United States and one of China's neighbors or the strengthening of what China sees as a U.S.-led coalition intended to balance against China's rise. Chinese reactions to the deployment of THAAD to South Korea in 2017, which consisted of diplomatic, media, and economic pressure and some low-level military activities, are one example of Beijing regarding the deployment of a new U.S. capability that threatened China's physical and regime security as also signaling the United States' increasingly hostile intent.[49] China reacted aggressively as a result. Similarly, U.S. initiatives meant to strengthen regional partnerships, such as the 2016 Maritime Security Initiative, led to accusatory statements in Chinese media about the United States provoking a security dilemma in the region, followed by Chinese naval exercises in the SCS.[50]

In addition to these examples, two cases we examined provide support for this factor. First, increased security cooperation since 2019 undertaken by the United States, India, Japan, and Australia within the framework of the Quadrilateral Security Dialogue (the Quad) has provoked a stern diplomatic protest from China.[51] U.S.-Quad activities have included the November 2020

---

[46] Xu Bu, "U.S. 'Rebalancing' Is Fishing in S. China Sea's Troubled Waters," *Straits Times*, May 19, 2016; and Zhao Beibei, "The South China Sea Issue and Sino-U.S. Relations Under the Background of U.S. 'Return to Asia'" ["美国'重返亚洲'背景下的南海问题与中美关系"], *Journal of the Party School of CPC Jinan Municipal Committee*, Vol. 5, 2014.

[47] Ministry of Foreign Affairs of the People's Republic of China, "Foreign Ministry Spokesperson Lu Kang's Regular Press Conference on May 11, 2016," May 11, 2016.

[48] Many Chinese scholars stated that the rebalance had two main objectives: to strengthen the encirclement of China while containing China's rise and to weaken China's influence in the region while maintaining U.S. hegemony. See Zhu Lu-ming and Zhang Wen-wen, "The Causes and Influences of Strengthening the American-Japan Ally Under the Background of the Asia-Pacific Rebalancing Strategy" ["美国'亚太再平衡'背景下美日同盟的强化原因及影响"], *Journal of Lanzhou University of Arts and Science* [兰州文理学院学报], Vol. 4, 2014.

[49] Zhong Sheng [钟声], "The U.S. and South Korea Must Understand the Deep Meaning Behind China and Russia's Warnings—Deployment of THAAD Threatens Peace in Northeast Asia" ["美韩须领会中俄严正警告的深意—部署'萨德'威胁的是东北亚和平"], *People's Daily* [人民日报], August 4, 2016.

[50] Zhao Minghao, "Washington Adds to U.S.-China Security Dilemma," *Global Times*, July 24, 2016. The Maritime Security Initiative began in 2016 as a maritime capacity building program for states in Southeast Asia.

[51] The growth of the Quad is discussed in more detail in Case 9 in Appendix B. In 2019, senior leaders from all four countries stated that the Quad would support "rules-based order in the region that promotes stability, growth, and

Malabar exercises in the Indian Ocean, followed by Quad Plus naval exercises in the Bay of Bengal in April 2021, which included France as well as the four Quad nations.[52] In March 2021, the Quad nations announced a collective plan to produce coronavirus disease 2019 (COVID-19) vaccines in large number for distribution throughout Southeast Asia.[53]

China has responded to the increased activity of the Quad with vigorous protests and criticisms in official statements and media commentary—directed both at the United States and at other Quad members.[54] However, China's military responses to Quad activities have been relatively muted. In March 2021, the People's Liberation Army Navy (PLAN) held major combat–oriented exercises in the North, East, and South China Seas, with PRC media stating that the naval exercises occurred as the U.S. Secretary of Defense visited the Indo-Pacific to "'foster credible deterrence' against China."[55] More aggressive have been Chinese actions against individual Quad members, such as the June 2020 Chinese-Indian border clash and increased Chinese military incursions into Japanese maritime and airspace near the Senkaku Islands. Although not a direct response to Quad activities, these are likely meant to signal that Beijing will not be intimidated by the Quad or by increased U.S. activities with its members.[56]

---

economic prosperity," and discussed cooperation on "counter-terrorism, cyber, development finance, maritime security, humanitarian assistance, and disaster response" (U.S. Department of State, "Media Note: U.S.-Australia-India-Japan Consultations ['The Quad']," November 4, 2019; Tanvi Madan, "The Rise, Fall, and Rebirth of the 'Quad,'" *War on the Rocks*, November 16, 2017; and Jeff M. Smith, "Democracy's Squad: India's Change of Heart and the Future of the Quad," *War on the Rocks*, August 13, 2020).

[52] Kunal Purohit, "India Joins French-Led Naval Exercise, Revealing Clues About Quad's Plans to Contain China in Indo-Pacific," *South China Morning Post*, April 4, 2021.

[53] Salvatore Babones, "The Quad's Malabar Exercises Point the Way to an Asian NATO," *Foreign Policy*, November 25, 2020; and David Brunnstrom, Michael Martina, and Jeff Mason, "U.S., India, Japan and Australia Counter China with Billion-Dose Vaccine Pact," Reuters, March 12, 2021.

[54] Chinese media commentary on the Quad's naval exercises has focused on the increased security cooperation between the four nations, accusing the United States of forming a "clique," and its destabilizing effects on the region. Foreign Minister Wang Yi, for example, called the Quad a "so-called Indo-Pacific new NATO." He accused the Free and Open Indo-Pacific strategy of seeking to "trump an old-fashioned Cold War mentality" and "stoke geopolitical competition" in a bid to "maintain the dominance and hegemonic system" of the United States. Ministry of Foreign Affairs of the People's Republic of China, "Jointly Safeguarding Peace, Stability and Development in the South China Sea with Dialogue, Consultation and Win-Win Cooperation," September 2, 2020. See also "Commentary: Forming Clique and Flexing Muscles Only to Shake Regional Peace, Stability," Xinhua, October 23, 2020; and Zhang Yanping [张燕萍], "Can the U.S., Japan, India and Australia Quad Group Contain China? Expert: There Is Not Much the United States Can Give to Its Allies" ["美日印澳'四方安全对话'牵制中国？专家：美国能给盟国的已经不多了"], *Global Times* [环球时报], February 19, 2021.

[55] Liu Xuanzun, "China Holds Naval Drills in Three Maritime Areas amid US Military Threats," *Global Times*, March 15, 2021. Notably, an article in the *Global Times* reported that sailors participating in the SCS exercise paid respects to "heroes who emerged victorious" in one of China's most recent clashes involving Vietnam in 1988.

[56] Yun Sun, "China's Strategic Assessment of the Ladakh Clash," *War on the Rocks*, June 19, 2020; Saibal Dasgupta, "China's Move to Empower Coast Guard Stirs Tensions," *Voice of America*, February 11, 2021; and Zachary Haver, "China Begins Month of Military Exercises in South China Sea," *Radio Free Asia*, March 1, 2021. China has so far refrained from economic retaliation against the Quad, although Beijing has employed economic coercion against individual member countries over separate issues, but Chinese commentators warned that Beijing

The evidence therefore suggests that China views the Quad's development as an indicator of its members' hostile intents.[57] It behaves more aggressively in response for two reasons. First, signs of the Quad's closer military and diplomatic cooperation stir fears that the United States is carrying out a containment strategy targeted against China that would require Chinese activism to overcome.[58] Second, China appears to see the United States as harboring particularly malign intentions regarding China's security and development interests. Therefore, U.S. success in building a coalition of countries that appears designed to oppose Chinese power reinforces the perception that hostile intent toward China is growing and requires an aggressive response.[59]

The second case we examined involved Chinese reactions to increasing levels of U.S. support to Taiwan during the Trump administration in 2019–2020.[60] During that time, the Trump administration, following the passage of the Taiwan Travel Act, sent several high-level U.S. officials to Taiwan and significantly increased the quantity and quality of arms it sold to Taipei and the frequency of its naval patrols around Taiwan.[61] These actions took place during a period of heightened cross-strait tensions that followed the electoral victories of Taiwan President Tsai Ing-wen and her Democratic Progressive Party (DPP) in 2020, which raised concerns in Beijing that Taiwan could take steps toward independence.

---

could retaliate economically against Quad countries if the cooperation continued. One commentary in the *Global Times* claimed that China's economic pressure against Australia was an example of the types of instruments that could be employed. See Wang Qi, "China Can Retaliate Economically If Red Line Crossed: Experts," *Global Times*, February 18, 2021.

[57] Of course, a viable Quad alliance may also alter Chinese perceptions of the military capabilities possessed by the United States and its allies if the states engage in joint exercises or other planning that would enhance their ability to fight together.

[58] Fear of U.S. efforts to contain China and thereby prevent its ability to achieve the CCP's goal of national revitalization pervades Chinese commentaries. See Zhong Sheng [钟声], "Accumulating Damage to the Strategy to Contain China" ["对华遏制战略蓄患积害"], *People's Daily* [人民日报], August 31, 2020.

[59] Chinese security assessments point to concern about the United States using coalitions of allies or partners to block China's access to key energy sea lines of communication (SLOCs), for example. See Hu Bo, "Three Major Maritime Security Issues Pose a Test for 'One Belt, One Road'" ["三大海上安全问题考验'一代一路'"], in Zhang Jie, ed., *Assessment of China's Peripheral Security Situation 2016* [中国周边安全形势评估 2016], Beijing: Social Sciences Academic Press, 2016.

[60] Case 10 in Appendix B addresses U.S. support for Taiwan under the Trump administration in greater detail.

[61] Ralph Jennings, "U.S. Speeds Arms Sales for Taiwan as Island Revamps China Strategy," *Voice of America*, November 6, 2020. Arms sales in 2019 totaled more than $10 billion, and those in 2020 totaled more than $5 billion, significantly higher than had been extended in 2017 or 2018. See Ben Blanchard, "Timeline: U.S. Arms Sales to Taiwan in 2020 Total $5 Billion amid China Tensions," Reuters, December 7, 2020. For the increase in U.S. freedom of navigation operations (FONOPs) and Taiwan Strait transits, see Lolita C. Baldor, "Sharp Jump in U.S. Navy Transits to Counter China Under Trump," Associated Press, March 15, 2021. In addition, several officials in the Trump administration made speeches indicating a turn toward a more hawkish approach to China. See Michael R. Pompeo, "Remarks at the Richard Nixon Presidential Library and Museum: 'Communist China and the Free World's Future,'" U.S. Department of State, July 23, 2020.

China responded to these increased U.S. expressions of support for Taiwan by condemning the actions in official Chinese media and levying sanctions on American companies involved in arms sales to Taiwan.[62] The People's Liberation Army Air Force (PLAAF) increased airspace incursions, crossing the median line of the Taiwan Strait 40 times in 2020.[63] In addition, that year China conducted several military exercises, including naval exercises involving carrier operations, near Taiwan.[64] Beijing has also engaged in a variety of broader economic and subversive actions against Taiwan since Tsai's first election in 2016.[65] China's reactions were likely driven by Beijing's perceptions of increased hostility from the Trump administration's support to Taiwan, as well as other bilateral tensions, such as the Sino-U.S. trade war.[66] Chinese literature and commentary further suggest that Beijing viewed increased U.S. FONOPs and Taiwan Strait transits, arms sales, and other actions in support of Taiwan as potentially emboldening President Tsai on the issue of Taiwan's independence.[67] This encouraged China to increase incursions into Chinese airspace, increase military exercises, and enact a range of punitive economic measures against the United States and Taiwan.

The literature and cases we examined support the hypothesis that China is more likely to respond aggressively to U.S. actions that it perceives as indicating heightened levels of U.S. and allied hostility. Chinese responses to particular instances of perceived hostility have varied in intensity and involved a range of economic, diplomatic, and military measures, with the most potentially escalatory being the increased PLAAF incursions into Taiwan's airspace.

---

[62] RAND researchers conducted a search of Chinese publications during this time period, which found that the volume of articles in *Qiushi*, the official bimonthly publication of the CCP Central Committee, condemning American and Taiwanese actions increased significantly in 2019 relative to 2018 or 2020. See David Brunnstrom, Mike Stone, and Krisztina Than, "China to Impose Sanctions on U.S. Firms That Sell Arms to Taiwan," Reuters, July 12, 2019.

[63] In 2020, PLA warplanes conducted more flights into Taiwan's Air Defense Identification Zone (ADIZ) than at any time since 1996, and by late 2020, such incursions had become an almost daily occurrence. See John Xie, "China Is Increasing Taiwan Airspace Incursions," *Voice of America*, January 6, 2021.

[64] Liu Xuanzun, "PLA Carrier, Warplanes Surround Taiwan in Drills, in Show of Capability to Cut Off Foreign Intervention," *Global Times*, April 6, 2021.

[65] These have included actions to restrict the number of Chinese tourists in 2016 and strengthened tourist restrictions in 2019, as well as sanctions against Taiwanese pineapples in early 2021. See "China to Stop Issuing Individual Travel Permits to Taiwan," *BBC News*, July 31, 2019; and Helen Davidson, "Taiwanese Urged to Eat 'Freedom Pineapples' After China Import Ban," *The Guardian*, March 2, 2021.

[66] By 2019, official CCP publications accused Trump of "seeing China as an enemy in all respects." See Zhang Hongyi [张宏毅], "America's Ability to Read China Once Again Put to the Test" ["美国再次面临是否'读懂中国'的考验"], *Qiushi* [求是], November 7, 2019.

[67] Ren Chengqi [任成琦], "Playing the 'Taiwan Card' Is a Dangerous Game" ["大'台湾牌'是一场危险游戏"], *Qiushi* [求是], July 10, 2019.

Factor 3: China's Perceptions of Threats to Its Regime Legitimacy

China's perception of how U.S. military actions threaten PRC regime legitimacy plays an important role in shaping Chinese reactions. The CCP legitimizes itself as the driving force behind China's rising economic and social prosperity as well as its defender against the foreign imperialists that have sought to exploit or divide China since its century of humiliation. The Chinese leadership is highly sensitive to foreign efforts that appear to challenge its ability to fulfill these roles, including U.S. military activities that support independence or pro-democracy movements in Taiwan, Xinjiang, Tibet, and Hong Kong. China is therefore more likely to respond aggressively to U.S. actions that it perceives as threats to Chinese regime legitimacy.

The CCP seeks to legitimize its rule over China in two main ways. The first is by sustaining China's economic growth through party-driven market reforms that have led to rapid economic growth, alleviated poverty, and created substantial wealth for Chinese citizens.[68] The second is by portraying itself as the defender and promoter of Chinese interests and the driver of China's rise as an internationally powerful and respected country. This includes the Chinese leadership portraying itself as helping China overcome its "century of humiliation" (1840–1949) from foreign imperialist forces and the introduction of CCP policies such as Xi Jinping's Chinese Dream, which outlines the steps toward "national rejuvenation" of the Chinese nation. The Chinese Dream includes continued Chinese economic development and social progress. unity (unification with Taiwan and full implementation of the "one country, two systems" policies for Hong Kong), building a world-class military, and "pursuing an independent foreign policy of peace."[69] Chinese reactions to threats to its economic development are addressed in a different factor below because they touch on a broader range of sensitivities beyond concerns of regime legitimacy. This factor focuses primarily on the Chinese leadership's long-running concern over external actors challenging the other pillar of the regime's legitimacy: the CCP's ability to promote and defend China's national territory, unity, and reputation.

Concerns over perceived threats to these issues are far from unique. Foreign activities perceived as undermining state legitimacy can act as both near- and longer-term drivers of

---

[68] Since Deng Xiaoping's economic reforms and opening up of China in 1978, the CCP has deemphasized the Party's focus on central planning and state allocation of resources to allow for market reforms and economic liberalization. See Jacque deLisle and Avery Goldstein, "Introduction: China's Economic Reform and Opening at Forty," in Jacque deLisle and Avery Goldstein, eds., *To Get Rich Is Glorious*, Washington, D.C.: Brookings Institution Press, 2019.

[69] Qu Qingshan [曲青山], "Chinese Communist Party's 100 Year Major Contribution"
["中国共产党百年大贡献"], *Renmin News*, March 30, 2021; "Xi Stresses Unity, Striving for National Rejuvenation at PRC Anniversary Reception," Xinhua, September 30, 2019; and Elizabeth C. Economy, *The Third Revolution: Xi Jinping and the New Chinese State*, New York: Oxford University Press, 2018.

conflict for many states, and particularly authoritarian regimes.[70] This risk is compounded because the sources of China's legitimacy are particularly prone to generating aggressive behavior. For example, China's persistent territorial disputes with other countries—which lie at the heart of the CCP's efforts to cast itself as the rectifier of China's "century of humiliation"—are not only the most common driver of interstate conflict but tend to be especially escalatory if they involve historical rivalries, as many of China's disputes do.[71] Moreover, most states are deeply concerned about their reputations for national greatness or international prestige; studies suggests that competition over prestige shapes state behavior and can influence the likelihood of conflict.[72] Adjacent to these concerns are the legacies of perceived national humiliation, which may also fuel aggression in interstate disputes.[73] Chinese leaders' concerns over territorial issues, prestige, and historical humiliation coalesce in their tolerance for (if not embrace of) expressions of popular nationalism that appear to help legitimate the CCP.[74]

China has reacted to concerns that foreign actors—foreign countries, transnational networks, and terrorist groups—may undermine these sources of its regime legitimacy in several ways.[75]

---

[70] Brian Lai and Dan Slater, "Institutions of the Offensive: Domestic Sources of Dispute Initiation in Authoritarian Regimes, 1950–1992," *American Journal of Political Science*, Vol. 50, No. 1, 2006. Note that personalistic regimes may be especially likely to initiate conflicts, whereas one-party states are typically less likely to do so, which suggests that China's changing domestic political institutions may influence this factor. See Jessica L. Weeks, "Strongmen and Straw Men: Authoritarian Regimes and the Initiation of International Conflict," *American Political Science Review*, Vol. 106, No. 2, 2012.

[71] Dan Altman, "The Evolution of Territorial Conquest After 1945 and the Limits of the Territorial Integrity Norm," *International Organization*, Vol. 74, No. 3, Summer 2020; and John Vasquez and Christopher S. Leskiw, "The Origins and War Proneness of Interstate Rivalries," *Annual Review of Political Science*, Vol. 4, 2001.

[72] This reflects both an innate desire for status and the strategic value of gaining others' voluntary deference regarding issues of national importance. See Deborah Welch Larson, T. V. Paul, and William C. Wohlforth, "Status and World Order," in T. V. Paul, Deborah Welch Larson, and William C. Wohlforth, eds., *Status in World Politics*, Cambridge, UK: Cambridge University Press, 2014; Jonathan Mercer, "The Illusion of International Prestige," *International Security*, Vol. 41, No. 4, 2017; Emilie M. Hafner-Burton and Alexander H. Montgomery, "Power Positions: International Organizations, Social Networks, and Conflict," *Journal of Conflict Resolution*, Vol. 50, No. 1, 2006; and Yuen Foong Khong, "Power as Prestige in World Politics," *International Affairs*, Vol. 95, No. 1, January 2019.

[73] Robert E. Harkavy, "Defeat, National Humiliation, and the Revenge Motif in International Politics," *International Politics*, Vol. 37, No. 3, 2000; and Oded Löwenheim and Gadi Heimann, "Revenge in International Politics," *Security Studies*, Vol. 17, No. 4, 2008.

[74] On debates over the prominence of Chinese nationalism, see Alastair Iain Johnston, "Is Chinese Nationalism Rising? Evidence from Beijing," *International Security*, Vol. 41, No. 3, 2017; and Jessica Chen Weiss, "How Hawkish Is the Chinese Public? Another Look at 'Rising Nationalism' and Chinese Foreign Policy," *Journal of Contemporary China*, Vol. 28, No. 119, 2019. Additionally, speeches by U.S. officials that challenge China's views of these issues can also spark reactions from Chinese officials. For an example, see White House, "Remarks by Deputy National Security Advisor Matt Pottinger to the Miller Center at the University of Virginia," May 4, 2020.

[75] In terms of concern over transnational actors, for example, Chinese leaders are concerned about the potential connections between the Uyghurs diaspora and radical Islamist militant groups and the risk that these groups could infiltrate into China. See Sheena Chestnut Greitens, Myunghee Lee, and Emir Yazici, "Counterterrorism and Preventive Repression: China's Changing Strategy in Xinjiang," *International Security*, Vol. 44, No. 3, Winter 2019/2020.

First, Beijing requests that all countries with which it has diplomatic relations acknowledge there is only one China. The CCP has repeatedly identified, warned, and, in some cases, punished foreign actors for supporting what it perceives to be separatist activities.[76] Second, China has ramped up PLA military coercion of Taiwan and frozen diplomatic relations with states that challenge its positions on Hong Kong or Tibet.[77] Third, the CCP has drastically curbed freedoms inside China in areas that it fears may have separatist tendencies, including arresting masses of pro-democracy protesters in Hong Kong and significantly expanding its security presence in Tibet and Xinjiang.[78]

We examined several cases that support the hypothesis that China would likely respond more aggressively when it perceives its regime legitimacy is threatened. The 1962 Sino-Indian border conflict provides some insight into Chinese behavior under these circumstances. India's sympathy for Tibetans and New Delhi's sheltering of the Dalai Lama and the Tibetan government in exile played a part in fueling and escalating past China-India border tensions. One of the main drivers of China's decision to attack India in 1962 was Chairman Mao Zedong and the Chinese leadership's incorrect assessment that India was about to seize Tibet as a buffer zone. Mao and the CCP had arrived at this error in judgment for a variety of reasons, including misinterpreting Indian leader Jawaharlal Nehru's Forward Policy as a sign of aggressiveness toward China.[79] Another reason that Beijing launched the 1962 China-India war was Mao and the CCP's belief that India was responsible for inflaming and sustaining strong Tibetan resistance to the CCP. The CCP's assessments and responses in the 1962 China-India war provide a caution regarding how aggressively China could respond given perceived challenges to its regime legitimacy.

---

[76] China's history and the CCP's anxieties have caused Beijing to, at times, be more paranoid and aggressive than warranted in accusing other countries of seeking to divide China. Beijing has also at times sought to scapegoat foreign countries for its own domestic problems.

[77] Thomas Carothers, "The Backlash Against Democracy Promotion," *Foreign Affairs*, March/April 2006; and Dingding Chen and Katrin Kinzelbach, "Democracy Promotion and China: Blocker or Bystander?" *Democratization*, Vol. 22, No. 3, 2015.

[78] The 2019 China national defense white paper lists separatism as "becoming more acute." It names Taiwan and the DPP's views on "Taiwan independence" as well as "external separatist forces" pushing for "Tibet independence" and the creation of "East Turkistan" as posing threats to China's national security and social stability. See State Council Information Office of the People's Republic of China, *China's National Defense in the New Era*, July 24, 2019.

[79] Instead, the Indian policy of deploying small numbers of lightly armed Indian infantry deep into unoccupied disputed border areas was implemented to allow Nehru to maintain his overall less confrontational policy toward China but appease his domestic opponents who criticized him as weak on China. The policy was based on the belief among Indian leadership that China would abstain from conflict. See John W. Garver, "China's Decision for War with India in 1962," in Alastair Iain Johnston and Robert S. Ross, eds., *New Directions in the Study of China's Foreign Policy*, Stanford, Calif.: Stanford University Press, 2006, p. 103; and Johan Skog Jensen, "A Game of Chess and a Battle of Wits: India's Forward Policy Decision in Late 1961," *Journal of Defence Studies*, Vol. 6, No. 4, October 2012.

U.S. support for Taiwan is another case that provides insight into Chinese reactions to threats to its regime legitimacy. Over the past several decades, Beijing has viewed the United States as Taiwan's primary backer and accused it of engaging in a range of efforts to support Taiwan's independence, including a perceived U.S. willingness to militarily support Taiwan in the event of a PRC attack of the island.[80] Chinese leaders, including President Xi Jinping and military leaders, have warned of the possibility of using military force against Taiwan should it move toward independence.[81]

China has responded more aggressively against increased U.S. naval transits of the Taiwan Strait since Taiwan's DPP assumed power in 2016.[82] In 2020, the frequency of American naval transits through the Taiwan Strait increased significantly.[83] American warships transited the strait 13 times that year, up from nine times in 2019 and three times in 2018.[84] In 2020 and early 2021, China increased its military actions in the Taiwan Strait in response, particularly with the PLAAF, whose fighters crossed the median line of the Taiwan Strait in 2019, after avoiding doing so for nearly 20 years.[85] By late 2020, such incursions had become an almost daily

---

[80] Since 2008, there have been increasing Chinese concerns that "the U.S. has provided support to separatist forces in China's Taiwan, Tibet, Xinjiang and Hong Kong using the excuse of human rights, religion, democracy and freedom. China viewed the United States and U.S. social media platforms as enabling instability in Tibet and Xinjiang and blocked YouTube after unrest in Tibet in 2008 and banned Facebook and Twitter after riots in Xinjiang in 2009. According to a recent Chinese report, examples of U.S. support to Xinjiang also include providing funding to the World Uyghur Congress and related individuals through the U.S. Congressionally funded National Endowment for Democracy (NED) and U.S. 'think tanks' or 'scholars' manipulating reports on 'oppression' in the region, media covering 'sad stories of victims,' and the U.S. government or the Congress backing bills and other political interference to pressure China." See Liu Xin and Lin Xiaoyi, "U.S. Supports Separatism in Rivals, Upholds Territorial Integrity in Allies: Report," *Global Times*, November 10, 2020.

[81] China's willingness to use force to prevent separatism and against "secessionist forces" was further codified into domestic law when Beijing passed the 2005 Anti-Secession Law. Article 8 of the law specifically states: "In the event that the 'Taiwan independence' secessionist forces should act under any name or by any means to cause the fact of Taiwan's secession from China, or that major incidents entailing Taiwan's secession from China should occur, or that possibilities for a peaceful reunification should be completely exhausted, the state shall employ non-peaceful means and other necessary measures to protect China's sovereignty and territorial integrity." See "Chinese General Says Force an Option to Stop Taiwan Independence," *Nikkei Asia*, May 29, 2020.

[82] The issue of U.S. activity in the Taiwan Strait in 2020 is explored in Case 14 in Appendix B.

[83] FONOPs were halted for the prior three years (2017–2020) by the Obama administration. While some of China's reaction might be explained by the resumption of the FONOPs program under the Trump administration, the additional context of the Trump administration's increased support to Taiwan also likely added to China's aggressive response.

[84] Most of these transits were by single destroyers, though they occasionally involved more ships. Such U.S. operations were always roundly condemned in Chinese official statements and media, and the U.S. ships were often tailed by Chinese vessels or aircraft. See Lolita C. Baldor, "Sharp Jump in U.S. Navy Transits to Counter China Under Trump," Associated Press, March 15, 2021; Caitlin Doornbos, "Navy Ties Record with Its 12th Transit Through the Taiwan Strait This Year," *Stars and Stripes*, December 19, 2020; Ben Blanchard and Reuters Beijing Newsroom, "U.S. Warships Transit Taiwan Strait, China Denounces 'Provocation,'" Reuters, December 30, 2020; and Ben Blanchard and Idrees Ali, "U.S. Warship Sails Through Taiwan Strait, Second Time in a Month," Reuters, April 23, 2020.

[85] "Chinese Incursions Highest Since 1996," *Taipei Times*, January 4, 2021.

occurrence to the south of the island, between Taiwan and the Taiwan-controlled Pratas Islands.[86] Most of these incursions involved surveillance aircraft, but they occasionally included flights of a dozen or more warplanes, including fighters, bombers, and airborne early warning systems.[87] These air exercises were sometimes conducted in conjunction with PLAN carrier operations and naval exercises near the island.[88] The more-aggressive Chinese military response is likely due to a combination of Beijing's concerns over increased U.S. support for Taiwan and the DPP from the Trump administration, which had signaled support for Taipei throughout 2020. This support included arms sales packages, high-level visits of U.S. officials, and passage of legislation such as the Taiwan Travel Act, along with increased U.S. naval activities and transits near the island. The Trump administration's actions against China in other areas, such as the trade war, might have also played a role in China's more aggressive response because the PRC likely perceived the United States' intent as increasingly hostile during this period (see Factor 2).[89]

The literature and cases we examined support the hypothesis that China is more likely to respond aggressively to U.S. actions that it perceives as threatening to Chinese regime legitimacy. China conducted more-aggressive military actions near Taiwan when it perceived increased U.S. support for Taipei in the aftermath of an electoral win for the pro-independence DPP combined with expanded U.S. naval actions in 2020. Although a historical case, China's reaction to India's support of Tibet and the Dalai Lama was a driver of Beijing's decision to attack India in 1962, illustrating that Beijing could respond aggressively to perceived challenges to its legitimacy and territory.

Factor 4: China's Perceptions of Threats to Its Economic Development

China's perception of the threat that U.S. military actions constitute to PRC economic development or access to resources appears to play an important role in shaping Chinese reactions. These perceived threats could be driven by U.S. capabilities that could impede China's access to key SLOCs or posture enhancements that could hamper China's ability to protect its regional economic interests. Chinese reactions to these concerns have recently ranged from nonaggressive activities, such as diversifying energy partnerships and access options, to more-

---

[86] John Xie, "China Is Increasing Taiwan Airspace Incursions," *Voice of America*, January 6, 2021; and Ben Blanchard, "Taiwan Reports Large Incursion by Chinese Air Force," Reuters, January 23, 2021.

[87] Liu Xuanzun, "PLA Carrier, Warplanes Surround Taiwan in Drills, in Show of Capability to Cut Off Foreign Intervention," *Global Times*, April 6, 2021.

[88] Liu Xuanzun, "PLA Prepared as US, Secessionists Provoke," *Global Times*, April 8, 2021.

[89] The PLA has continued these incursions, most recently sending 77 PLAAF aircraft into Taiwan's ADIZ. See Eric Cheung and Brad Lendon, "China Sends 77 Warplanes into Taiwan Defense Zone over Two Days, Taipei Says," *CNN*, October 3, 2021.

aggressive reactions that include developing the military capability to protect SLOCs or deny U.S. forces access to critical chokepoints.[90]

China is far from unique in its concern over economic interests. States typically consider economic threats to be one of their primary national security concerns. Trade, access to resources, and risks to economic development are generally regarded by international relations experts as common motivations for interstate war.[91] Economic growth and the need to protect it also play a role in many states' political and domestic stability, including China, where the CCP relies on economic growth to underpin its political power.[92] Economic interests also provide an additional venue for competition between states, which can make states more antagonistic toward one another and increase the risk of escalation to conflict.[93] There are numerous examples throughout history of nations responding aggressively when economic interests are severely threatened. In perhaps the most infamous example, Japan's 1941 attack on Pearl Harbor was largely in response to U.S. economic sanctions, asset freezes, and the U.S. oil embargo, rather than any direct military threat the United States posed to Japanese territory.[94]

The Chinese leadership has devoted significant effort to expanding access to resources and markets necessary to sustain continued economic growth—both regionally and overseas. This prioritization has been driven by many factors, including the Chinese need for raw materials and energy imports, especially crude oil and natural gas, to fuel domestic economic growth.[95] As a result, Chinese leaders have expressed increasing concern that Chinese energy shipments are vulnerable to piracy or interdiction by foreign navies, especially in maritime "chokepoints."[96]

---

[90] Jeffrey Becker, *Securing China's Lifelines Across the Indian Ocean*, Newport, R.I.: U.S. Naval War College, China Maritime Studies Institute, China Maritime Report No. 11, December 2020.

[91] Robert Gilpin, *War and Change in World Politics*, Cambridge, UK: Cambridge University Press, 1981, p. 69; Edward D. Mansfield and Brian M. Pollins, "The Study of Interdependence and Conflict," *Journal of Conflict Resolution*, Vol. 45, No. 6, 2001; and United States Institute of Peace, *Natural Resources, Conflict, and Conflict Resolution*, Washington, D.C., 2007.

[92] For a discussion of Chinese leadership economic priorities, see Nicholas R. Lardy, *The State Strike Back: The End of Economic Reform in China?* Washington, D.C.: Peterson Institute for International Economics, 2019.

[93] A recent assessment of economic tools in national competition is Robert D. Blackwill and Jennifer M. Harris, *War by Other Means: Geoeconomics and Statecraft*, Cambridge, Mass.: Harvard University Press, 2016.

[94] John M. Schuessler, "The Deception Dividend: FDR's Undeclared War," *International Security*, Vol. 34, No. 4, Spring 2010.

[95] U.S. Energy Information Administration, "Country Analysis Executive Summary: China," September 30, 2020.

[96] In 2003, Hu Jintao labeled this the "Malacca Dilemma," after the strait through which around 80 percent of Chinese oil imports flow. This issue is explored in greater detail in Case 2 in Appendix B. See Hu Bo, "Three Major Maritime Security Issues Pose a Test for 'One Belt, One Road'" ["三大海上安全问题考验'一代一路'"], in Zhang Jie, ed., *Assessment of China's Peripheral Security Situation 2016* [中国周边安全形势评估 2016], Beijing: Social Sciences Academic Press, 2016, p. 193; Huang Xiaoyong, "Promote Collective Asian Energy Security Through 'One Belt, One Road'" ["以'一带一路'促进亚洲共同能源安全"], *Foreign Affairs Observer* [外交观察], August 7, 2015; and Erica Downs, Mikkal E. Herberg, Michael Kugelman, Christopher Len, and Kaho Yu, *Asia's Energy Security and China's Belt and Road Initiative*, Seattle, Wash.: National Bureau of Asian Research, 2017.

Chinese writings also express concern that instability in the SCS could affect China's access to energy and resources, as well as disrupt shipping in general.[97] While the United States has not explicitly threatened Chinese access to the Malacca Strait or other strategic waterways, U.S. military capabilities—particularly those that could be used to protect or defend key regional SLOCs—and increased U.S. Navy (USN) presence in the SCS (e.g., carrier strike group [CSG] deployments) have exacerbated Chinese worries that these U.S. capabilities could also be used to restrict Chinese access to resources and investments.[98]

China has responded to these concerns by

1. developing partnerships through the BRI for overland pipeline construction—for example, with Russia and other Central Asian countries, as well as Pakistan—as a means of enhancing energy security[99]

2. prioritizing port construction and access agreements, particularly in the Indian Ocean, to increasing access to strategic waterways[100]

3. upgrading PLAN capabilities focused on counterpiracy and SLOC protection, including shipboard missile defense and ASW capabilities[101]

---

[97] Zhang Jie, "Assessment of China's Surrounding Security Environment in the New Era" ["新时期中国周边安全环境评估"], Beijing: Institute of Asia-Pacific and Global Strategy, Chinese Academy of Social Sciences, February 16, 2019.

[98] Some Chinese literature speculates, for example, that the United States will use "diplomatic resistance" and military tools to frustrate China's plans, including by inciting tensions in the SCS to complicate the development of the Belt and Road Initiative (BRI) maritime silk road. Other analyses speculate that increased U.S.-Indian maritime security cooperation and joint statements on the SCS have been intended as a response to the maritime silk road. See Hu Bo, "Three Major Maritime Security Issues Pose a Test for 'One Belt, One Road'" ["三大海上安全问题考验'一代一路'"], in Zhang Jie, ed., *Assessment of China's Peripheral Security Situation 2016* [中国周边安全形势评估 2016], Beijing: Social Sciences Academic Press, 2016, p. 193; and Fu Mengzi and Liu Chunhao, "Some Thoughts on Building the 21st Century 'Maritime Silk Road'" ["关于21世纪'海上丝绸之路'建设的若干思考"], *Contemporary International Relations* [现代国际关系], No. 3, 2015, p. 2. In addition, there is a substantial amount of U.S. military literature that discusses the use of blockades or distant blockades, indicating that the U.S. military would potentially consider such actions against China in a regional conflict. See T. X. Hammes, "Offshore Control: A Proposed Strategy for an Unlikely Conflict," *Strategic Forum*, Vol. 278, June 2012.

[99] MSCConference, "Maritime Security Challenges Virtual—Session 1—Ms. Nadège Rolland on China's BRI," video, YouTube, October 21, 2020.

[100] Li Jian, Chen Wenwen, and Jin Jing, "Overall Situation of Sea Power in the Indian Ocean and the Expansion in the Indian Ocean of Chinese Sea Powers" ["印度样海权格局与中国海权的印度洋扩展"], *Pacific Journal*, Vol. 22, No. 5, 2014, p. 75; and Fu Mengzi and Liu Chunhao, "Some Thoughts on Building the 21st Century 'Maritime Silk Road'" ["关于21世纪'海上丝绸之路'建设的若干思考"], *Contemporary International Relations* [现代国际关系], No. 3, 2015, p. 2.

[101] For an overview of the PLAN's capability development, see Office of the Secretary of Defense, *Annual Report to Congress: Military and Security Developments Involving the People's Republic of China 2020*, Washington, D.C., 2020; Jeffrey Becker, *Securing China's Lifelines Across the Indian Ocean*, Newport, R.I.: U.S. Naval War College, China Maritime Studies Institute, China Maritime Report No. 11, December 2020; and Kristen Gunness, "The China Dream and the Near Seas," in Roy Kamphausen, David Lai, and Tiffany Ma, eds., *Securing the China Dream*, Seattle, Wash.: National Bureau of Asian Research, 2020.

4. opening the PLAN base in Djibouti, which gives China closer proximity to energy-rich countries in Africa and the Middle East and provides a permanent naval presence overseas.[102]

Although many of these actions are not militarily aggressive—diversifying energy access and expanding port agreements are political and economic activities—the rationale behind them reflects deep concern over U.S. and allied intent and anxiety about the potential for U.S. naval interdiction of Chinese shipping should relations deteriorate more. The development of PLAN capabilities for SLOC protection and to secure maritime approaches is directly tied to China's perception that this access is essential for its economic survival. For example, the PLAN's modernization program has focused on enhancing China's A2/AD bubble, which includes building the capabilities to secure China's maritime approaches in the Near Seas (the East, South, and Yellow Seas), and key SLOCs. The counterpiracy operations that started in 2009 were a direct result of pressure on the PLA by the Chinese leadership to develop more capacity to protect Chinese shipping from security threats. The base in Djibouti represents a broader strategy of building overseas maritime power and protecting Chinese interests through a larger PLA presence. While the base in its current form has limited capabilities and represents little threat to the United States or its allies or partners, it is possible that this or other future bases could be expanded alongside the growth in PLAN capabilities to enable more-aggressive Chinese responses to perceived threats to PRC access to economic resources in the future.

The Chinese literature and examples discussed above support the hypothesis that China is likely to react more aggressively to U.S. actions that it perceives as threatening to Chinese economic development or access to vital resources. But it is also important, especially in the near term, not to overstate the acuteness of Chinese concerns. Threats to China's ability to access resources and maintain its economic growth are generally longer-term concerns for China. While some of China's responses—such as diversifying energy sources—reflect short-term efforts to improve energy access, its other reactions are largely about mitigating the longer-term potential for U.S. or allied capabilities to restrict access to key waterways and shipping, should relations continue to deteriorate. The aggressiveness of Chinese reactions to threats to economic resources and assets are therefore likely to reflect, and are likely to track, broader concerns about U.S. and allied hostile intent. If overall Chinese perceptions of U.S. hostility continue to increase, so too will Chinese sensitivity over potential threats to economic resources and the likely aggressiveness with which China may respond.

Factor 5: China's Perceptions of Threats to Its Regional Influence

China's perception of the threat that U.S. operations, activities, and policies constitute to PRC regional influence appears to strongly shape Chinese reactions, although the nature of its

---

[102] "Commentary: China's Djibouti Base Not for Military Expansion," Xinhua, July 13, 2017.

reactions can be complex. China can react aggressively if it believes that doing so will help advance its regional influence and position—for example, by coercing regional states to not pursue closer partnerships with the United States—but China may also act less aggressively when its leaders believe that they can garner greater regional influence over time by tempering their reactions to activities that concern them or by co-opting regional leaders through incentives. Therefore, Beijing's responses to U.S. and allied regional activities that it perceives as undermining its regional influence have included both coercive measures and incentives to shape the regional status quo in Beijing's favor and limit the risk of escalation.

International relations scholarship suggests that states are likely to respond aggressively when they believe that their influence in the international community is inconsistent with the influence to which they feel they are entitled.[103] When a state's position in the regional order does not reflect its relative power, moreover, the state may take action to enhance its regional role and influence by force.[104] States will also use incentives to build regional influence or counter the effects of an adversary's attempts to undermine its regional standing.[105] This can include the cultivation of economic ties with neighboring countries through trade agreements, infrastructure investments, or other forms of foreign direct investment.[106]

China perceives a range of challenges to its efforts to expand its regional influence. These include threats to Chinese sovereignty over disputed waters and territory that, if successful in challenging PRC claims, would undermine Chinese prestige and credibility; challenges to economic strategies for expanding China's influence, such as the BRI; threats to regional diplomatic initiatives designed to assert China's position as Asia's central power; and threats to domestic stability that could accrue from regional political, economic, and security developments that would, in turn, undermine China's ability to project power and influence abroad. China is also concerned with U.S. regional democracy promotion and other aspects of American soft power, which it sees as potential drivers of destabilization that could reduce China's regional influence or even spill over into China itself. These threats are interlinked and coalesce around a

[103] Thomas J. Volgy and Stacey Mayhall, "Status Inconsistency and International War: Exploring the Effects of Systemic Change," *International Studies Quarterly*, Vol. 39, No. 1, March 1995; and Douglas Lemke and Suzanne Werner, "Power Parity, Commitment to Change, and War," *International Studies Quarterly*, Vol. 40, No. 2, June 1996.

[104] Suzanne Werner, "Choosing Demands Strategically: The Distribution of Power, the Distribution of Benefits, and the Risk of Conflict," *Journal of Conflict Resolution*, Vol. 43, No. 6, December 1999.

[105] Todd S. Sechser, "Reputations and Signaling in Coercive Bargaining," *Journal of Conflict Resolution*, Vol. 62, No. 2, 2018.

[106] Ludger Kühnhardt, *Region-Building*: Vol. I, *The Global Proliferation of Regional Integration*, New York: Berghahn Books, 2010, p. 52.

perception that the United States seeks to contain or block Chinese long-term strategic objectives.[107]

These concerns often prompt China to carefully scrutinize U.S. influence activities in its burgeoning regional "partnerships" or with countries with which Beijing has exerted particular effort to sway to its side. One example is Vietnam. One Chinese scholar notes that the USS *Carl Vinson* aircraft carrier port call in Vietnam in 2018 was likely a manifestation of U.S. "naval diplomacy," signaling to China that the United States stands with states that have territorial disputes with China and will be stepping up its defense cooperation and presence in the neighborhood.[108] Chinese scholars see these activities not only as a U.S. effort to warn China against taking aggressive action in the region but also as a way to increase U.S. influence with allies and partners in the region.[109] By taking steps to counter or minimize the effects of U.S. activities, China seeks both to increase its own regional influence relative to the United States and to secure China's core interests of national sovereignty, security, and development, as discussed above in Factors 1 and 4.[110]

China's responses to U.S. activities that it perceives as threatening to its regional influence have ranged from the relatively aggressive, when Beijing perceives that its core interests are at stake, to a more constrained mixture of coercive measures and incentives when China perceives that it can press an advantage in the diplomatic or economic realms or diffuse the potential for escalation. Its reactions to challenges to its maritime claims in the SCS illustrate Beijing's tendency to shape regional states' actions with both "carrots," involving economic incentives and

---

[107] Andrew Scobell, Edmund J. Burke, Cortez A. Cooper III, Sale Lilly, Chad J. R. Ohlandt, Eric Warner, and J. D. Williams, *China's Grand Strategy: Trends, Trajectories, and Long-Term Competition*, Santa Monica, Calif.: RAND Corporation, RR-2798-A, 2020.

[108] Zhu Feng [朱 锋], "What Did 'Carl Vinson's' Trip to the South China Sea Reveal?" ["'卡尔·文森'号南海之行透射出什么"], *World Affairs* [世界知识], No. 7, 2018.

[109] Zhu Feng [朱 锋], "What Did 'Carl Vinson's' Trip to the South China Sea Reveal?" ["'卡尔·文森'号南海之行透射出什么"], *World Affairs* [世界知识], No. 7, 2018, p. 32.

[110] China's 2019 foreign policy white paper provided the rationale for this goal, marking the Asia-Pacific as the "foundation of China's development and prosperity" and stating an intention to "lead regional cooperation and safeguard regional peace and development." See State Council Information Office of the People's Republic of China, "China and the World in the New Era," September 27, 2019; and Andrew Scobell, Edmund J. Burke, Cortez A. Cooper III, Sale Lilly, Chad J. R. Ohlandt, Eric Warner, and J. D. Williams, *China's Grand Strategy: Trends, Trajectories, and Long-Term Competition*, Santa Monica, Calif.: RAND Corporation, RR-2798-A, 2020. See also Timothy R. Heath, Derek Grossman, and Asha Clark, *China's Quest for Global Primacy: An Analysis of Chinese International and Defense Strategies to Outcompete the United States*, Santa Monica, Calif.: RAND Corporation, RR-A447-1, 2021.

joint energy exploration agreements, and "sticks," including paramilitary forces and other gray zone activities meant to coerce other claimants and solidify China's claims.[111]

China's BRI, meanwhile, exemplifies PRC efforts to gain influence using carrots by building regional economic dependencies with preferential trade conditions and free trade agreements.[112] China's strong-arm tactics in the SCS have somewhat mitigated the successfulness of its economic endeavors, however, as China has tended to prioritize its security objectives—in this case, standing firm on territorial claims—over opportunities to expand its economic and diplomatic influence with claimant states (a tendency discussed in the case of the Philippines below). Taken together, these examples illustrate China's tendency to calibrate its responses to be less aggressive in one domain if it thinks it can advance its regional influence but to maintain its military pressure in sovereignty disputes.

We examined two cases that support the hypothesis that China is more likely to respond aggressively to perceived U.S. threats to its regional influence. The first case examines the growth of U.S.-Vietnam security relations from 2013 to 2016.[113] China clearly perceived U.S.-Vietnamese ties as threatening its regional influence, and Beijing employed both carrots and sticks in response. China's reactions to deepening U.S.-Vietnam security ties included criticizing U.S. involvement in the SCS while seeking to further deepen PRC economic and political ties with Hanoi in an attempt to ensure that Vietnam did not further tilt toward the United States.[114] Chinese analysts and scholars discussed the benefits of strengthening economic ties with Vietnam as well as improving China's position in the region by partnering with Russia against the United States.[115] Chinese literature also highlighted concerns that a stronger U.S.-

---

[111] For an overview of China's activities in the SCS, see Ronald O'Rourke, *U.S.-China Strategic Competition in South and East China Seas: Background and Issues for Congress*, Washington, D.C.: Congressional Research Service, March 18, 2021.

[112] Christopher K. Johnson, *President Xi Jinping's "Belt and Road" Initiative: A Practical Assessment of the Chinese Communist Party's Roadmap for China's Global Resurgence*, Washington, D.C.: Center for Strategic and International Studies, March 28, 2016.

[113] The expansion of U.S.-Vietnam security ties is addressed in greater detail in Case 5 in Appendix B.

[114] One Chinese analyst described the recommended approach toward Vietnam as "promot[ing] the positive development of bilateral relations and reduc[ing] the negative effects brought about by South China Sea disputes" (Wang Zheng [王峥], "The Interaction Between Politics and Security: Perspectives on China-Vietnam Relations Under the South China Sea Disputes" ["政治与安全的互动: 南海争端下中越关系透视"], *Southeast Asian Studies* [东南亚研究], No. 6, 2018, p. 130). See also Cui Haoran [崔浩然], "The Adjustment of Vietnam's South China Sea Policy Under the New Situation and China's Response Strategy" ["新形势下越南南海政策的调整及中国的应对策略"], *Issues of Contemporary World Socialism* [当代世界社会主义问题], No. 4, 2018, pp. 163–164; "Xi Calls for Mended China-Vietnam Ties," Xinhua, August 28, 2014; and Robert S. Ross, "China-Vietnamese Relations in the Era of Rising China: Power, Resistance, and Maritime Conflict," *Journal of Contemporary China*, Vol. 30, No. 130, 2020.

[115] Luo Huijun [罗会钧], "U.S.-Vietnam Defense and Security Cooperation and Its Influence on China" ["美越防务安全合作及其对中国的影响"], *Journal of International Security Studies* [国家安全研究], No. 3, 2017, p. 147.

Vietnam relationship could weaken China's relations with the Association of Southeast Asian Nations (ASEAN), a key target for and means of furthering China's influence in southeast Asia.[116] These reactions suggest that Beijing was concerned that closer U.S.-Vietnam security ties could weaken China's bilateral relationship with Vietnam, which would, in turn, both directly and indirectly risk reducing its regional influence.

A second case explores the first several years of the Duterte administration in the Philippines, to assess whether China reacts less aggressively when it believes that there may be an opportunity to expand its regional influence.[117] Duterte's first major decision as president in 2016 was to not press Manila's victory over China at the Permanent Court of Arbitration ruling on resource rights claims in the SCS. The Duterte government instead signaled its openness to warmer relations with China, publicly suggesting bilateral SCS talks with Beijing even though China showed no softening in its SCS position.[118] A Chinese diplomatic charm offensive ensued that included economic aid, military assistance, and praise for Duterte's policies, but these policies persisted alongside continued PRC militarization of the SCS features under dispute and intermittent clashes between Chinese and Philippine forces.[119] This suggests that China will be pragmatic and strategically opportunistic when it sees a window of opportunity to build influence in the diplomatic and economic domain but that pursuing such opportunities is likely to remain secondary to staunchly defending territorial issues.

Although the literature and cases provide some evidence that China will react more aggressively when it feels that its regional influence is threatened, PRC responses frequently combined economic inducements and diplomatic initiatives with military activities primarily involving China's paramilitary maritime forces. When motivated by concerns regarding its regional influence, China's economic and diplomatic responses have tended to be conciliatory toward regional partners. However, there appear to be clear limits to the use of such carrots. China's perception that losing ground in the pursuit of its territorial claims would damage its influence and credibility can drive it to undertake aggressive military responses despite the fact that such responses risk limiting or undermining China's efforts to improve its relations with regional claimants—although China remains sensitive to escalation risks and, as a result, mainly responds through paramilitary maritime forces or other gray zone capabilities. This suggests that

---

[116] Luo Huijun [罗会钧], "U.S.-Vietnam Defense and Security Cooperation and Its Influence on China" ["美越防务安全合作及其对中国的影响"], *Journal of International Security Studies* [国家安全研究], No. 3, 2017.

[117] Chinese reactions to the Duterte administration are explored in Case 8 in Appendix B.

[118] Asia Maritime Transparency Initiative, "China's New Spratly Island Defenses," webpage, Center for Strategic and International Studies, December 13, 2016; and Michael Martina, "China Welcomes Manila's Offer for South China Sea Talks," Reuters, June 1, 2016.

[119] Wang Yi [王毅], "China Firmly Supports the Philippines in Pursuing an Independent Foreign Policy" ["中方坚定支持菲律宾奉行独立自主外交政策"], Ministry of Foreign Affairs of the People's Republic of China, July 25, 2017; and Manuel Mogato, "China Offers $14 Million Arms Package to the Philippines: Manila's Defense Minister," Reuters, December 20, 2016.

Beijing's efforts to enhance its regional influence are pursued through a combination of conciliatory and aggressive actions according to whether a targeted state might threaten other Chinese interests that could affect China's regional standing beyond their bilateral relationship.

Factor 6: China's Perceptions of U.S. Commitment to the Defense of U.S. Allies or Partners

China's perceptions of how committed the United States is to the defense of its allies and partners likely shape Beijing's reactions to U.S. posture enhancements. International relations literature suggests that states can deter attacks on their allies and partners by making credible commitments to come to their defense in the event that they are attacked.[120] States considering aggression against these allies or partners would then assess higher potential costs of doing so because they may need to risk fighting both the ally or partner and its protector.[121] These "extended deterrence" commitments rely on their credibility to be effective.[122] Credibility can be enhanced in numerous ways, including formal defense pacts, the forward stationing of military forces, or heightened levels of peacetime military coordination with the ally or partner.[123]

Although the primary goal of the United States' policies toward its regional alliance and security partner relationships may be to enhance the perceived credibility of its extended deterrence commitments, China has tended to adopt more-aggressive interpretations of U.S. behavior. It generally views the U.S. alliance structure in the Indo-Pacific region as a means by which the United States can expand its military capabilities and influence while balancing against China and checking Chinese power.[124] This perception has only grown as the U.S.-China competition has evolved, with the result that even when U.S. posture changes in the region involving allies have not been focused on China (such as the 2016 decision to deploy THAAD in South Korea), Beijing considers these actions as aimed at least in part at China and intentionally

---

[120] Paul K. Huth, "Extended Deterrence and the Outbreak of War," *American Political Science Review*, Vol. 82, No. 2, 1988; Jesse C. Johnson, Brett Ashley Leeds, and Ahra Wu, "Capability, Credibility, and Extended General Deterrence," *International Interactions*, Vol. 41, No. 2, 2015; and James D. Fearon, "Rationalist Explanations for War," *International Organization*, Vol. 49, No. 3, Summer 1995.

[121] Alexander L. George and Richard Smoke, *Deterrence in American Foreign Policy: Theory and Practice*, New York: Columbia University Press, 1974.

[122] Adversaries would, of course, not be unduly concerned by defense commitments that do not appear to be serious or that the state shows no signs of preparing to uphold. See Bruce M. Russett, "The Calculus of Deterrence," *Journal of Conflict Resolution*, Vol. 7, No. 2, 1963.

[123] Bruce M. Russett, "The Calculus of Deterrence," *Journal of Conflict Resolution*, Vol. 7, No. 2, 1963; Jesse C. Johnson, Brett Ashley Leeds, and Ahra Wu, "Capability, Credibility, and Extended General Deterrence," *International Interactions*, Vol. 41, No. 2, 2015; and Vesna Danilovic, "The Sources of Threat Credibility in Extended Deterrence," *Journal of Conflict Resolution*, Vol. 45, No. 3, June 2001.

[124] Adam P. Liff, "China and the U.S. Alliance System," *China Quarterly*, Vol. 233, March 2018. The author draws from numerous Chinese sources when assessing China's views of the U.S. alliance structure.

damaging to Chinese security interests and regional influence.[125] China also regarded South Korea's decision to accept the deployment as an insulting disregard for Beijing's preferences and as a betrayal of what China regarded as a friendly relationship. Beijing therefore saw the move as a sign of potential U.S. success in strengthening U.S. regional influence.[126]

Similarly, China views the U.S.-Japan alliance as enabling Japanese remilitarization and allowing Japan to have a stronger regional security role, which China opposes.[127] Inclusion of new partners into U.S. defense policies or posture also concerns Beijing. For example, Australia's expanded military cooperation with the United States and other regional partners, such as Japan, has increased China's concerns over the multilateralization of the U.S. alliance system, which Beijing fears might allow the United States and other regional countries to hamper China's regional goals in a coordinated manner, particularly those goals related to sovereignty and territorial disputes in the ECS and SCS.[128] The recent reinvigoration of the Quad has also been concerning to China for similar reasons.[129] These dynamics highlight how U.S. efforts to enhance deterrence may be interpreted by Beijing as signs of hostile intent, as discussed above.

With respect to the deterrent value of U.S. presence in the region, there is some evidence to suggest that Beijing proceeds more cautiously in its responses to U.S. allies and partners' actions when the United States signals strong defense commitments to them. The 2011 rebalance to the Asia-Pacific, for example, certainly heightened Chinese concern about the United States developing a balancing coalition against China and augmenting U.S. military capability in the region. However, the Chinese reaction to the rebalance was relatively muted, consisting mainly of diplomatic protest and warnings.[130] Following the announcement of the U.S. Marine deployment to Australia, for example, the Chinese Ministry of Defense warned that it "is overreaction toward China's normal military moves and it might result in China's overreaction in

---

[125] "Wang Jisi: A 'New Norm' in U.S.-China Relations" ["王缉思: 中美关系进入一个 '新常态'"], *Global Times* [环球时报], August 19, 2016; and Li Bin, "The Security Dilemma and THAAD Deployment in the ROK," *China-U.S. Focus*, March 6, 2017.

[126] Greg Torode and Michael Martina, "Chinese Wary About U.S. Missile System Because Capabilities Unknown: Experts," Reuters, April 3, 2017.

[127] Sun Jianguo, "Use History as a Mirror: Beware the Return of Japanese Militarism"
["以史为鉴：警惕日本军国主义的死灰复燃"], *PLA Daily*, June 23, 2014.

[128] Fang Xiaozhi [方晓志], "U.S.-Australia Expand Military Cooperation: New Variable in Asia-Pacific Security Structure," *Contemporary World* [当代世界], Vol. 11, 2013, pp. 61–64.

[129] The Quad comprises the United States, Japan, India, and Australia. China has responded to the Quad's development with vigorous protests and criticisms in official statements and media commentary, as well as some naval and air exercises. See "Commentary: Forming Clique and Flexing Muscles Only to Shake Regional Peace, Stability," Xinhua, October 23, 2020.

[130] Bonnie Glaser, "U.S. Pivot to Asia Leaves China Off Balance," *Comparative Connections*, Vol. 13, No. 3, 2011.

the near future. This security dilemma, if it escalates, might lead to another Cold War."[131] China's relatively restrained immediate military reactions to the deployment of THAAD is another example in which the U.S. alliance commitment to South Korea, as well as Beijing's desire to maintain relations with Seoul, likely factored into China's decision to respond mainly with diplomatic protests and economic pressure.[132]

China's responses to Japan's nationalization of the Senkaku Islands provide a useful case to test this hypothesis given Beijing's concerns over the U.S.-Japan alliance.[133] In 2011, the governor of Tokyo entered into talks with the private Japanese owner of three of the Senkaku Islands to use official funds of the Tokyo metropolitan government and to build a dock on the islands.[134] Hoping to block this effort but wary of provoking a backlash from China, Prime Minister Noda Yoshihiko decided to purchase the three islands on September 11, 2012.[135] In April 2014, President Barack Obama—in the first public statement by a sitting U.S. president on the issue—said in a joint press conference with Japanese Prime Minister Abe Shinzō, "our treaty commitment to Japan's security is absolute, and Article 5 covers all territories under Japan's administration, including the Senkaku Islands."[136] This clarified that the United States backed Japan over the islands and that any efforts by China to counter Japan's administrative control risked involving the United States.[137]

---

[131] Li Xiaokun and Li Lianxing, "U.S. Military Base in Australia Shows 'Cold War Mentality,'" *China Daily*, December 1, 2011.

[132] Ethan Meick and Nargiza Salidjanova, *China's Response to U.S.-South Korean Missile Defense System Deployment and Its Implications*, Washington, D.C.: U.S.-China Economic and Security Review Commission, July 26, 2017. China's near-term military responses were muted. It should be noted, however, that China's longer-term military responses have likely included an acceleration of the PLA's own hypersonic weapons program, as well as development of other precision strike capabilities.

[133] This is explored in greater detail in Case 4 of Appendix B.

[134] Until that time, a Japanese government ministry had been leasing three of the islands—Uotsuri, Kita-kojima, and Minami-kojima—to prevent conservative elements in Japan from developing the islands in any way. See "Japan Government 'Reaches Deal to Buy' Disputed Islands," *BBC News*, September 5, 2012; and Yoko Wakatsuki, "Tokyo Governor Outlines Plan to Buy Islands Claimed by China," *CNN*, April 17, 2012.

[135] The purchase included Uotsuri, Kita-kojima, and Minami-kojima. The United States still leases the other two islands—Kuba and Taisho. The three remaining islets/rocks remain in the ownership of the central government. For a full explanation of the incident, see Michael Green, Kathleen Hicks, Zack Cooper, John Schaus, and Jake Douglas, "Counter-Coercion Series: Senkaku Islands Nationalization Crisis," Asia Maritime Transparency Initiative, Center for Strategic and International Studies, June 14, 2017.

[136] White House, "Joint Press Conference with President Obama and Prime Minister Abe of Japan," Office of the Press Secretary, April 24, 2014; and White House, "U.S.-Japan Joint Statement: The United States and Japan: Shaping the Future of the Asia-Pacific and Beyond," Office of the Press Secretary, April 25, 2014.

[137] While the level of authority was the highest that could be given, it was not the first time a U.S. official made this declaration. For example, prior to Obama's statement, on January 18, 2013, Secretary of State Hillary Clinton said that although the United States did not take a position on the sovereignty of the islands, Washington opposed "any unilateral actions that would seek to undermine Japanese administration." See Hillary Clinton, "Remarks with Japanese Foreign Minister Fumio Kishida After Their Meeting," Washington, D.C., January 18, 2013.

China reacted with strong diplomatic protest and economic reprisals, including through Beijing supporting or allowing boycotts against Japanese goods and protests against Japanese companies, resulting in both property damage and revenue loss for Japanese companies.[138] Militarily, incursions into Japanese TW by Chinese paramilitary forces such as the Chinese Coast Guard and the maritime militia increased, and in November 2013 China unilaterally declared the creation of an ADIZ over the ECS that covered the Senkaku Islands.[139]

Although President Obama's statement reiterating the U.S. commitment to the defense of Japan did not appear to reduce China's military responses, China did continue to follow a predictable pattern of behavior with regard to maritime incursions, relying primarily on paramilitary and civilian capabilities to send its message to Japan rather than escalating to the use of PLA Navy or air assets.[140] Direct evidence of PRC motivations is not available, but this likely reflected Beijing's concern over potential U.S. involvement or the risk of escalation to armed conflict should China employ military force. A recent RAND report on Chinese gray zone aggression examined the deterrent effects of U.S. commitments to Japan for countering Chinese actions toward the Senkaku Islands. The authors assessed that the level of deterrence is strong when the United States and Japan are aligned in messaging commitments (in Japan's case to the Islands and in the United States' case to the defense treaty) and when the United States has regional support from other countries for deterrence actions and capabilities.[141]

This suggests that U.S. signaling of a strong defense commitment to Japan can deter Chinese aggression. For example, China exhibits more caution in its ECS gray zone operations than in SCS activities—with Beijing generally avoiding in the ECS some of the more escalatory actions it has taken in the SCS, including frequent ramming and overt harassment of other countries'

---

[138] For example, China's Ministry of Foreign Affairs issued a statement that said, "The Chinese government solemnly states that the Japanese government's so-called 'purchase' of the Diaoyu Island is totally illegal and invalid. It does not change, not even in the slightest way, the historical fact of Japan's occupation of Chinese territory, nor will it alter China's territorial sovereignty over the Diaoyu Island and its affiliated islands." See Ministry of Foreign Affairs of the People's Republic of China, "Statement of the Ministry of Foreign Affairs of the People's Republic of China," September 10, 2012. For economic reprisals, see Richard Katz, "Mutual Assured Production," *Foreign Affairs*, July/August 2013.

[139] For the last four months of 2012, suddenly an average of 102 Chinese ships appeared in the Senkakus' contiguous zone (CZ), while an average of 17 ships appeared in the TW. In 2013 and for the first four months of 2014, these trends continued. In 2013, on average, 68 ships sailed in the CZ and 16 ships sailed in the TW. And in the first four months of 2014, prior to Obama's statement, on average, 65 ships sailed in the CZ and 7 ships in the TW. See Japan Coast Guard, "Trends in Chinese Government and Other Vessels in the Waters Around the Senkaku Islands, and Japan's Response"
["尖閣諸島周辺海域における中国海警局に所属する船舶等の動向と我が国の対処"], undated.

[140] Edmund J. Burke, Timothy R. Heath, Jeffrey W. Hornung, Logan Ma, Lyle J. Morris, and Michael S. Chase, *China's Military Activities in the East China Sea: Implications for Japan's Air Self-Defense Force*, Santa Monica, Calif.: RAND Corporation, RR-2574-AF, 2018, p. 9.

[141] Michael J. Mazarr, Joe Cheravitch, Jeffrey W. Hornung, and Stephanie Pezard, *What Deters and Why: Applying a Framework to Assess Deterrence of Gray Zone Aggression*, Santa Monica, Calif.: RAND Corporation, RR-3142-A, 2021, p. 50.

ships by Chinese Coast Guard and naval vessels.[142] The more predictable and slightly less aggressive approach likely reflects China's concerns over U.S. involvement in a Japan-China clash given the close U.S.-Japan defense relationship, as well as the strong military capabilities of the Japan Coast Guard and the Japan Self Defense Forces in general.[143]

Conversely, China seems less inclined to moderate its behavior where U.S. defense commitments appear weaker. China has employed aggressive tactics against the Philippines in and around disputed maritime territory in the SCS, for example, despite the U.S. defense commitment to Manila.[144] U.S.-Philippine bilateral relations have been rocky at times, and defense cooperation is less institutionalized than in the U.S.-Japan alliance, which includes American bases and troops on Japanese soil, as well as more-institutionalized security cooperation, reflecting Japan's importance to U.S. regional strategy. This difference between the U.S. approach toward Japan versus the Philippines may have led Beijing to perceive the U.S.-Philippine alliance as relatively weaker and, therefore, to perceive the risk of disputes involving the Philippines escalating into a conflict with the United States as lower than in comparable disputes involving Japan. Similarly, Chinese behavior toward U.S. partners that lack formal defensive commitments also appears to be more aggressive than it has been toward Japan. Deepening U.S.-Vietnam security cooperation from 2013 to 2016, for example, did not deter China from sending a state-owned enterprise's oil rig into Vietnam's Exclusive Economic Zone (EEZ) near the Paracel Islands in 2014, which resulted in a standoff between Chinese Coast Guard and naval vessels and Vietnamese ships.[145] These two examples suggest that China may behave more aggressively in response to a U.S. ally or partner when it perceives U.S. defensive

---

[142] In addition to an increased presence of Chinese Coast Guard vessels in the SCS, China has increased its PLA Navy and air presence. Furthermore, China has pursued land reclamation projects to create artificial islands in both the Spratly and Paracel Islands, on which it has built runways, hangars, radars, and missile batteries. See Michael J. Mazarr, Joe Cheravitch, Jeffrey W. Hornung, and Stephanie Pezard, *What Deters and Why: Applying a Framework to Assess Deterrence of Gray Zone Aggression*, Santa Monica, Calif.: RAND Corporation, RR-3142-A, 2021, pp. 24–26.

[143] Japan has the most capable navy and coast guard in the region, which has also likely affected Beijing's calculations with regard to response. See Lyle J. Morris, "Gray Zone Challenges in the East and South China Sea," *Maritime Issues*, January 7, 2019.

[144] China has become more assertive in territorial disputes with the Philippines in recent years, including around Second Thomas Shoal, Thitu Island, and Whitsun Reef, where the Philippines recently observed more than 200 presumed Chinese maritime militia vessels in March 2021. See Rene Acosta, "Persistent Chinese Maritime Militia Presence off Philippines Raises Concerns in Manila," *USNI News*, April 12, 2021.

[145] When Vietnam sent vessels to the rig, China quickly sent dozens of China Coast Guard (CCG) and maritime militia vessels, supported by PLAN vessels in overwatch and military aircraft flights over the rig area, while rumors spread about PLA ground troops operating on the land border with Vietnam. As the paramilitary vessels harassed the Vietnamese ships, China also pressured Vietnam to back down by breaking off diplomatic discussions, restricting border trade and tourism, and targeting Hanoi with cyberattacks. See Carlyle A. Thayer, "China's Oil Rig Gambit: South China Sea Game-Changer?" *The Diplomat*, May 12, 2014; and Bonny Lin, Cristina L. Garafola, Bruce McClintock, Jonah Blank, Jeffrey W. Hornung, Karen Schwindt, Jennifer D. P. Moroney, Paul Orner, Dennis Borrman, Sarah W. Denton, and Jason Chambers, *Competition in the Gray Zone: Countering China's Coercion Against U.S. Allies and Partners in the Indo-Pacific*, Santa Monica, Calif.: RAND Corporation, RR-A594-1, 2022.

commitments to that state as relatively weak, although other factors, such as the level of military capability of the regional country involved, likely also play important roles in China's calculations.[146]

These cases and examples suggest that China is more likely to respond aggressively to U.S. actions that involve allies or partners to whom the perceived U.S. defense commitment is weak and less likely to respond aggressively when the perceived U.S. defense commitment is strong. China did react to the rebalance to Asia, the deployment of THAAD, and the nationalization of the Senkaku Islands, but its concern over U.S. involvement and the risk of escalation appears to have tempered its responses. In contrast, China appears to have been less restrained in its dealings with U.S. allies or partners in the region seen as having weaker defense commitments, such as Vietnam or the Philippines.

Conclusion

Taken together, two aspects of these framework factors deserve special consideration. First, each of the factors focuses on Chinese perceptions of U.S. and allied and partner activities, rather than the activities themselves. How such perceptions might change as a result of U.S., allied, or partner activities is difficult to anticipate, or even to retrospectively assess, but it is nonetheless essential to try to do so. This means that careful attention needs to be paid to signals indicating Chinese leadership views on events. Failing to anticipate Chinese perceptions risks U.S., allied, or partner actions being misinterpreted—potentially driving more-aggressive Chinese responses and increasing the risk of inadvertent escalation.

Second, most of the factors shape, whether directly or indirectly, how intensely and the ways in which China feels threatened. Implicit is the assessment, well grounded in international relations and history, that China is likely to react more aggressively when it perceives greater threats. Less obvious is that actions taken by the United States and its allies and partners that do not directly threaten China's interests today may nonetheless change its perceptions of the threats that it will face in the future. China may therefore adopt near-term responses to those perceived longer-term threats that appear surprisingly or even unjustifiably aggressive in the present, a possibility explored in greater detail in Chapter 4.

In sum, a complex mix of variables informs China's conduct; attempts to flatten these variables into a single variable, or even a handful of variables, risks oversimplification or misleading predictions. Taken together, however, these six factors are particularly critical predictors. They are associated with a broad range of drivers of Chinese aggression and capture a range of indicators of historically aggressive Chinese responses. They therefore serve as a

---

[146] The Japan Self Defense Forces, for example, have more capabilities than the Philippine military and, in theory, are therefore more capable of unilaterally deterring Chinese aggression. Despite Japan's overall higher level of military capability, U.S. commitment to the defense of Japan as well as the U.S. forces and capabilities based there certainly adds to Beijing's calculations as to whether to pursue an aggressive response.

foundation for a framework able to assess the potential nature and scale of Chinese reactions to a given U.S., allied, or partner action. The next two chapters of this report develop the remainder of that framework.

Chapter 3. Linking Factors and Activity Characteristics

The second part of our framework involves identifying the linkages between the key factors in Chapter 2 and the characteristics of U.S. military activities. Put more simply, how do U.S. military activities have the potential to affect these key factors? What are the ways in which they may affect Chinese perceptions and thinking through these key factors, and how might they motivate China to pursue different responses? To address these questions, we considered how four different characteristics of potential U.S. military activities—the geographic location, the U.S. ally or partner involved, the military capabilities involved, and the profile or messaging accompanying the activity—could affect each of the key factors.

Characteristics of U.S. Military Activities

We focus on these four characteristics—location, U.S. ally or partner involvement, capabilities, and profile—because we assessed that they were likely to have the greatest salience and influence for China as it evaluates its level of concern with particular U.S. military activities.[147] Below we briefly summarize each of these four characteristics together with illustrations for how they might vary in practice.

Location: The United States can choose to engage in activities in areas of greater or lesser concern to the PRC. Activities that bring U.S. capabilities or forces closer to areas that are militarily or politically sensitive to China, such as key forces or regime targets, would likely be more concerning than deploying such capabilities farther away. For example, a U.S. deployment of strike capabilities to Taiwan would increase China's concern over the proximity of these capabilities to Chinese forces and bases across the Taiwan Strait, as well as to the Chinese mainland. Deployment of U.S. troops or a larger U.S. shift in military resources to Australia, however, would be of less concern given the larger geographic distance from Chinese forces and interests. While of less overall concern than the Taiwan Strait, U.S. deployments to the SCS, where China has heightened concerns over U.S. involvement in territorial disputes, would be of greater concern than deployments to the Indian Ocean, which are farther away from disputed territory.

Ally or partner involvement: The United States can also meaningfully expand its suite of activities by altering who participates. The United States can choose to engage in activities that

---

[147] We carefully considered a fifth potential characteristic: continuity. That is, does whether U.S. military activities constitute a break with past patterns of U.S. activity independently affect PRC thinking and reactions? We ultimately assessed that while China may take note of changes in U.S. patterns, ultimately the other four characteristics would likely have a substantially greater effect on Chinese perceptions. As such, in the name of parsimony, we incorporated some aspects of continuity that also overlapped with other characteristics into the analysis below, but we did not retain continuity as an independent fifth characteristic in our framework.

are consistent with its long-standing military commitments and agreements and previous levels of cooperation in the region. For example, U.S. activities with Australia and Singapore are consistent with both outstanding security commitments and ongoing levels of cooperation and should therefore be expected by the PRC. On the other hand, enhanced cooperation with states that fall outside of these expectations, such as Indonesia or Malaysia, may generate an entirely different response, potentially one of alarm, if they are seen to indicate closer cooperation or to build interoperability between nations. The United States can also engage in activities with countries that the PRC pays special attention to, such as India and Vietnam, or multilateral entities, such as the Quad. The United States can also expand its activities by including out-of-region partners, increasing their regional operational awareness in the event of a contingency, which also might provoke concern from China.

Capabilities: DoD can also alter the use of its activities in competition with the PRC by varying the capabilities and capacity included in each military action. U.S. capabilities vary in terms of lethal potential and application during a military conflict with the PRC. U.S. operational concepts also vary in terms of their usefulness in the event of a wartime contingency against the PRC. For instance, when the United States varies its military exercises to include capabilities to conduct antisubmarine warfare and island seizing, this sends a much different signal to the PRC than when the United States deploys humanitarian assistance and disaster relief capabilities in regional exercises. The United States can also increase the level of technological sophistication of the capabilities utilized in its activities. The use of advanced capabilities such as hypersonics in missile defense may threaten PRC military missions or defenses, prompting a different response than previously utilized capabilities. The size and composition of the U.S. force can also be varied. A U.S. military activity involving just a few destroyers is clearly of a much different scale than one that involves multiple CSGs.

Profile: The USAF and joint force can also take steps to adjust the profile of their military actions. The United States can also vary the optics of its activities through their timing. If U.S. military actions follow PRC or PRC-led regional initiatives, they will be seen as directly responding to these activities. The same may also be true if the United States acts on dates that are politically sensitive to China. If U.S. military actions correspond to other U.S. regional initiatives, such as negotiations with the Democratic People's Republic of Korea, they may be viewed as serving an ulterior motive, such as demonstrating strength to gain more favorable terms. The United States can also alter the signal sent by its activities through the associated government and DoD rhetoric. Rhetoric that frames U.S. action as a broader response to China's deployment of weapons, construction projects on islands and reefs in the SCS, or militarization in the SCS could result in an activity being received as more hostile, whereas accompanying statements that discuss other U.S. interests in conducting the activity or emphasize the limited nature of the activity would likely have the opposite effect.

These characteristics are summarized in Table 3.1.

Table 3.1. Key Characteristics of U.S. Military Activities

Characteristic	Examples
Location	• Proximity to PRC or PRC forces • Proximity to politically, economically, or militarily sensitive areas
Ally or partner involvement	• Number, importance, and political disposition of allies/partners • Consistency with previous cooperation with allies/partners
Capabilities	• Novelty of capabilities in activity • Lethal potential and wartime usefulness of activity • Technological level employed in activity
Profile	• Timing of activity in relation to PRC or regional events • Visibility of activity • Associated U.S. rhetoric

Identifying Linkages

To identify how these U.S. military activity characteristics could affect Chinese thinking, we next reviewed each combination of key factor and activity characteristic individually and identifying the most plausible or likely linkages between the two, based on the subject-matter expertise of the authors and the research conducted into each of the key factors summarized in Chapter 2. Our identification of these linkages is therefore not exhaustive, though it is extensive and covers a wide range of key issues likely to drive PRC perceptions and, ultimately, reactions.

Below we summarize our identification of the linkages between activity characteristics and key factors in two ways. First, we provide a detailed discussion of the most important linkages we identified organized by key factor. Second, at the conclusion of this chapter, in Table 3.2, we provide a table summary of the main points identified in these discussions.

Potential Military Threat

The PRC will choose how to respond to U.S. activities based, in part, on the military threat it believes that they could pose. We expect that China's perception of the potential military threat is likely to vary depending on the geographic location of the military action, the partners cooperating with the United States in the activity, and the capabilities involved in the activity. The potential military threat posed by the U.S. or allied capabilities involved in an activity, as perceived by the PRC, will vary based on the location of the U.S. military action in relation to PRC areas of interest. U.S. military actions that bring military capabilities closer to PRC forces, bases, or other militarily sensitive areas near mainland China have the potential to increase PRC threat perceptions. When U.S. or allied capabilities move within range of striking these targets, they become capable of inflicting significant damage that is more likely to prompt an aggressive PRC response. The same will also hold true for important domestic military and civilian infrastructure and facilities. If instead the United States conducts activities outside of this range, the United States will not hold China's militarily sensitive areas at risk and the PRC is less likely to respond aggressively. Likewise, if the United States shifts resources on a sustained basis away from areas that are militarily sensitive to China, this will reduce the potential military threat posed to the PRC and decrease the likelihood of an aggressive Chinese response.

The extent of allied and partner involvement can also affect the potential military threat posed by a U.S. military activity. When the United States includes partners with greater military capabilities in an activity, their combined effect is potentially more threatening to the PRC by virtue of being able to inflict greater damage on the PRC, its forces, or its areas of interest. If the partner also allows U.S. access to locations of high military utility for operations against China or its forces, the potential military threat posed by the activity may greatly increase, and the PRC is more likely to respond aggressively. This may be especially the case if the PRC believes that these partners may support the United States by granting access or committing capabilities in the event of a military conflict. The level of cooperation between the United States and the ally or partner could also magnify the effects of these capabilities. Interoperability of capabilities and command structure enhances the warfighting ability of the United States and its allies, posing a larger potential threat to the PRC in the event of a conflict.

In addition to the overall capabilities demonstrated or enabled by an activity, the nature of the capabilities involved will also help determine the extent of the potential military threat perceived by the PRC. Capabilities that could be used to threaten the CCP regime itself will likely be of foremost concern. China will therefore take careful note of capabilities that could target the PRC's second-strike nuclear capabilities or enable a decapitation strike of Chinese leadership, such as high-technology, novel capabilities like hypersonic weapons. Capabilities with a high utility in a conflict scenario with China, such as coordinated joint air-sea weapons platforms, may also be more likely to be met with an aggressive, escalatory response, as such capabilities, if left unchecked by China, could grant the United States a significant advantage in a conflict.

More generally, the PRC is more likely to respond aggressively if U.S. and partner capabilities involved in an activity increase PRC concern over its own ability to execute key military missions. However, if the capabilities involved in an activity are such that the PRC questions its own ability to manage escalation, it may instead choose not to respond in aggressive fashion, fearing that any resulting crisis could spiral out of control. This was potentially the case during the 1995/1996 Taiwan Strait Crisis, in which the PRC had few options to respond to a dual U.S. carrier presence short of opening fire, leading China to ultimately de-escalate the crisis.

Hostile Intent

PRC perceptions of hostile U.S. intent are likely to differ based on the location of the U.S. activity, in similar fashion to Chinese perception of the potential military threat that such activities pose. When U.S. or allied capabilities move within range of striking militarily sensitive targets, they may increase PRC belief that the United States intends on using its forces and capabilities for aggressive purposes. The same will also be true for U.S. activities that occur in proximity to politically sensitive areas for China. U.S. military actions in or near the SCS may be viewed by the PRC as indicative of U.S. intent to interfere in ongoing territorial disputes and an unwillingness to allow the PRC freedom of action in its sphere of influence. More broadly, activities that take place in a new politically or militarily sensitive location demonstrate that the United States is willing to push further against PRC redlines.

The partners that engage in an activity with the United States may be seen as a clear indicator of the level of U.S. hostility. As we have noted, cooperating with states that have a history of adverse interactions with the PRC is likely to increase perceptions of hostility. Any activity that involves U.S. allies and partners that the PRC believes to be firmly anti-China, such as Japan and Taiwan, is likely to be seen as anti-China in nature. Cooperation with certain partners may also reinforce the message that the United States seeks to build an anti-China coalition. When the United States engages in cooperation with states that the PRC believes the United States is recruiting to become more-anti China, such as Vietnam or India, this may increase fears of strategic containment in China. As the United States engages in deeper cooperation with such states, these fears are likely to only grow. This may increase the likelihood of an aggressive PRC response to attempt to deter or counter U.S. actions.

As we have noted, cooperation within the Quad could also stoke these fears by suggesting that a coalition is emerging to contain Chinese regional power. Similarly, the involvement of U.S. partners and allies that had previously played little role in the region, such as the UK and France, might increase China's perception that the United States seeks to expand a U.S.-led partnership to contain China.[148] As this is a major PRC concern, China is likely to attribute the expanded participation of extra-regional allies in such activities as evidence of U.S. hostility.

However, U.S. military actions that include a broader range of partners may not always increase Chinese fears of strategic containment. The involvement of partners with close, durable ties to China could actually lessen these concerns. For example, the engagement of states such as Laos and Pakistan could indicate that the U.S. activity entails a more superficial level of cooperation or has other goals than the containment of China. Furthermore, these states may be willing to share intelligence with the PRC about the content of these activities, further reducing the risk that China will perceive hostile intent from the activity.[149] In this case, we would expect a lower likelihood of an escalatory response from China.

PRC perceptions of hostile intent will also differ based on the capabilities involved in the U.S. military action in a similar fashion to its perception of the potential military threat. Activities that involve capabilities that could be of military utility directly against the PRC may

---

[148] Ding Duo, "European Countries Warships in S China Sea Undermine Stability," *China Daily*, March 18, 2021; and South China Sea Strategic Situation Probing Initiative [南海战略态势感知] (SCSPI), "2019 U.S. Military Exercises in the South China Sea and Neighboring Areas," December 27, 2019.

[149] It is possible that China could see an expansion of U.S. activities to include these states as increasing the threat of encirclement. However, we argue that this result is less likely.

be seen as a sign that the United States is preparing to engage the PRC in military conflict. If the United States demonstrates capabilities or concepts that are primarily or solely useful for combat with the PRC, Beijing may assume that the United States is preparing to use them. This is especially true if these capabilities are best used aggressively, such as for a preemptive strike on key PRC military targets. China will again be particularly concerned when activities include or enable capabilities that could threaten the PRC's second-strike nuclear capabilities or enable a decapitation strike of Chinese leadership. Military activities that involve such capabilities are therefore more likely to raise perceptions of hostility and lead to an escalatory PRC response.

U.S. activities that demonstrate U.S. capabilities more frequently or at a larger scale than in the past may suggest to the PRC that the United States is seeking to assert its influence in the region. If the United States instead chooses to decrease the size or scale of its activities in a way that reduces U.S. capabilities that have previously elicited Chinese concern, this is likely to lead to a decrease in PRC motivations for an aggressive response.

The profile of each U.S. activity can also send a signal that the PRC may take as an indicator of U.S. hostility. Highly visible or public displays, particularly when they involve military capabilities in or near areas of PRC political sensitivity, such as a U.S. carrier presence in the Taiwan Strait, may increase PRC perceptions of U.S. hostility and a disregard for PRC interests. U.S. activities will also more likely be seen as deliberately hostile when they coincide with politically sensitive dates for the PRC, such as multilateral activities with Taiwan that take place close to Taiwanese elections.

The United States and its partners can also alter the messaging surrounding military activities in ways that would impact PRC perceptions of hostile intent. If U.S. and multilateral military activities are accompanied by heated rhetoric from U.S. or allied and partner policymakers, the military activities themselves will be seen as a greater sign of hostility even if the other characteristics of the activity itself do not change. If instead the United States seeks to de-escalate a potential PRC response, including through outreach and transparency with the PRC in advance of the military activity, this could reduce concerns that the PRC would otherwise have about the purpose of the activity and make an aggressive response less likely, provided that China finds U.S. assurances to be credible.

Regime Legitimacy

U.S. actions that could pose a threat to Chinese regime legitimacy are a central concern for PRC leaders. A number of activity characteristics could alter PRC perceptions of this threat by affecting perceptions of the regime's role as the defender of Chinese interests and the sustainability of China's rise as a great power. For the CCP, regime legitimacy is intrinsically tied to defending the territorial integrity of China. Beijing will be highly sensitive to any U.S. military actions that appear to threaten its territorial interests. Because the CCP has historically seen the United States as engaging in efforts to support Taiwan's independence, any U.S. activities on or near Taiwan are more likely to be met with an aggressive response. Threats to other Chinese regional territorial claims may not risk undermining PRC regime legitimacy as directly, but as U.S. military actions become more proximate to other PRC territorial or maritime claims, such as those in the SCS or ECS, they may still be seen as challenging PRC claims, holding at risk a pillar of CCP legitimacy.

Similarly, U.S. military activities that involve allies and partners whose cooperation with the United States threatens the PRC's perceived territorial integrity may be more likely to be met with an escalatory response. Primarily, this means any U.S. cooperation directly with Taiwan. However, because the PRC has territorial and maritime disputes with states throughout the region, cooperation with other claimants may also trigger a PRC perception of the U.S. threat to its regime legitimacy should the U.S. activities appear to obstruct China's objectives to claim disputed territory.

When U.S. activities display capabilities that may have military utility for the defense of what the PRC sees as separatist actors, perceptions of the threat to regime legitimacy are likely to increase. For example, if the United States adds capabilities in the region whose primary utility would appear to be the interdiction of a PRC attempt to invade Taiwan, the PRC might interpret these as a sign that the United States plans to take active steps to undermine its territorial integrity, a key pillar of PRC regime legitimacy.

The United States might also pose a threat to CCP regime legitimacy through the rhetoric associated with its military activities. For example, if the United States were to accompany its activities with Taiwan with firmer rhetorical commitments to its defense in the event of an armed conflict or issue statements that call into question the One China principle, Beijing would likely respond with greater escalation than if these accompanying statements had been absent. If instead U.S. military activities with Taiwan were accompanied by statements that reinforced a U.S. commitment to the political status quo or statements that sought to restrain Taiwan from moves toward independence, China might be less likely to escalate in response.

Economic Development

The geographic location of a U.S. military action will be vital to understanding how China perceives the threat that the activity holds for its economic development. The PRC requires access to external markets and resources to maintain its economic growth. Any U.S. activities that threaten to close off access to these markets and resources are therefore likely to be perceived as a threat to PRC economic development. All else being equal, U.S. military activities near key SLOCs rather than alternative locations may reinforce concern over the potential obstruction or interdiction of Chinese shipping in the event of a conflict. If U.S. activities approach other areas that the PRC deems as vital for its economy, such as overland pipelines, or that could prove vital in the future, such as the location of potential natural resources, this would also increase Chinese concerns.

Similarly, U.S. activities that involve allies and partners that have the ability to restrict PRC access to key resources and markets could have the same impact. If the United States is seen to be increasing cooperation with partners that can exert control over these key maritime access points, Beijing may see this as evidence that the United States is attempting to recruit these states to engage in efforts that could in the future hamper PRC economic activity.

Specific capabilities involved in a U.S. activity may also trigger these concerns. If the United States demonstrates capabilities that appear designed to allow it to interdict PRC trade or otherwise interrupt PRC access to resources and markets, Beijing may see this as a direct threat to its economic development. For instance, when the United States masses significant capabilities such as CSGs along regional SLOCs, the PRC may assess that it could become the target of a potential blockade and act to counter the U.S. military action in an aggressive fashion to deter or prevent the United States from taking such actions.

The United States can also alter the likelihood of an escalatory PRC response through the messaging surrounding a U.S. military action. If the United States accompanies its military activities with statements calling into question PRC economic practices, the perceived threat posed to China's economic development might be heightened only to a small degree or not at all. If the United States instead spoke of how the PRC economy thrived only because the United States allowed it to do so, the potential for escalation should be higher. If the United States suggests that it may engage in economic coercion in the event of conflict, such as a blockade, this sends a clear signal that any subsequent activity demonstrating these capabilities poses a threat to PRC economic development. If instead U.S. messaging highlights that U.S. military activities with the potential to threaten PRC economic interests are in reality aimed at addressing nontraditional security threats, such as reducing piracy, or other shared regional security goals between the United States and China, then they may reduce the likelihood of an aggressive PRC response.

Regional Influence

Chinese reactions to U.S. military activities are also likely to be affected by characteristics of these activities that signal threats to Beijing's efforts to expand its regional influence. In the case of regional influence, we may see the PRC respond with either the carrot or the stick. U.S. activities may be seen as a threat to PRC regional influence by encroaching on geographical areas of PRC interest. U.S. activities that occur in proximity to or in influential states or regions of interest, such as Southeast Asia, may be seen as an attempt to shift influence toward the United States. In this case, the PRC might be more likely to respond with inducements toward these states to shift the balance back toward PRC influence or to discourage them from engaging in future U.S. activities. U.S. activities may also support efforts within the region to challenge perceptions of PRC credibility in defending its territorial claims, undermining perceptions of China's authority throughout the region as a whole. In this case, the PRC might respond in a more aggressive fashion to undermine U.S. efforts.

Beijing will likely also be concerned with specific types of ally and partner involvement due to the implications for PRC regional influence. The involvement of states that may themselves be competitors for regional influence, such as Japan, further threatens to challenge China's regional position. The involvement of states that China sees as important bellwethers for China's regional influence, such as Vietnam and Indonesia, may be more likely to draw a PRC response. China is more likely to respond with the stick if U.S. activities support efforts within the region to challenge PRC territorial claims. For example, if the United States were to engage with the Philippines following a dispute with the PRC over the Spratly Islands or with India following a dispute in the Galwan Valley, Beijing may believe that the United States seeks to undermine the legitimacy of its regional influence by lending support to direct challenges to that influence.

Multilateral participation in U.S. activities can also increase China's perceptions of challenges to its regional influence. The involvement of transnational organizations, whether ad hoc or more formal, such as the Quad and ASEAN, would add greater legitimacy to U.S. actions while simultaneously increasing the regional influence of these groupings, competing with China's own clout. The PRC may act aggressively to push back against an increased U.S. presence and demonstrate the consequences of this support. The involvement of large numbers of allies and partners may also signal broad regional support for U.S. military presence and activities, however. If U.S. activities have broad support, the PRC may be reluctant to go against the region and challenge the U.S. military action, fearing loss of regional influence if it should do so. It may instead attempt to offer inducements—likely economic—to ensure that these activities do not have a cascading impact on its influence.

If the United States accompanies its activities with rhetoric suggesting that they are intended to challenge PRC influence and interests, it could increase the risk of an aggressive PRC response. Additionally, if the United States includes messaging surrounding the activity that runs counter to PRC narratives, the likelihood of an aggressive PRC response may increase. The same may be true for statements issued by U.S. allies and partners. If allies and partners insist that the PRC narrative that the United States has no staying power in the region has no merit, the PRC may feel the need to respond in an assertive fashion to buttress this narrative. If U.S. activities are timed such that they coincide with or follow PRC regional initiatives, Beijing may believe that the U.S. activities will undermine those initiatives or minimize their impact. Of course, the United States can also reduce China's perceptions of threats to its regional influence by doing the reverse—acknowledging Chinese interests and setting firm limits on the intent and scope of U.S. activities or citing motivations for them that are not contrary to Chinese interests.

U.S. Commitment

Finally, China's perceptions of how committed the United States is to the defense of its allies and partners may shape Beijing's reactions to U.S. military activities. When the United States engages in activities with allies to which it has a formal defensive commitment, this may be a signal that further increases Chinese perceptions of U.S. commitment to the defense of these allies. Furthermore, increasing PRC perceptions of U.S. resolve to defend one ally may bolster a reputation of U.S. commitments to other allies. When the United States engages in cooperative activities with states with whom its military relationship has been growing, the PRC may also believe that the U.S. commitment to defend these partners is growing. If the PRC believes that the United States is firmly committed to the defense of its allies or partners, it may be less likely to challenge that commitment, at least in ways that it perceives would increase the risk of conflict.

Transitory or one-off activities are unlikely to dramatically change perceptions of U.S. commitment or resolve. Consistent U.S. activities demonstrate a sustained interest in a particular partner. A permanent U.S. presence is likely to send the strongest signal of commitment. For example, a shift from a rotational presence to a permanent presence in the Philippines would suggest a higher likelihood that the United States is willing to be involved in the defense of the Philippines. As a result, we would expect the PRC to respond more cautiously in threatening the security of the Philippines, though it may respond aggressively at lower levels if it believes that doing so could help to undermine the Washington-Manila relationship.[150]

Alternatively, certain U.S. activities may make the PRC question U.S. commitment to its allies and partners. Perceptions of U.S. commitment may decline if an activity entails a shift of forces and resources away from allies to which the United States was previously perceived to have clear defensive commitment. For example, if the United States reduced its presence in Japan to increase its footprint in the South Pacific, the PRC may be emboldened by this apparent shift in priorities away from the long-standing allies of the United States, unless the shift included bolstering Japan's military capabilities.

U.S. activities can also increase Chinese perceptions of U.S. commitment to the defense of these allies and partners by demonstrating the capabilities necessary to defend those allies and partners.[151] If U.S. military actions increase the level of interoperability between U.S. and Taiwan military forces, it could send a signal that the United States may be willing and more able to use its capabilities in the defense of Taiwan, giving China pause if it were considering aggressive actions against Taiwan.[152]

The United States can make its intent clear by making public statements or sending other signals that indicate that its military activities are designed to improve the ability of the United States to defend the ally or partner. Furthermore, when such statements and messaging are reciprocated by the partner and affirm the common interests of the United States and its partner, this shows a high level of alignment that should reduce the risk of PRC misperception regarding U.S. commitments. However, statements by U.S. government actors that question whether allies are sharing an appropriate amount of the burden of the U.S. security commitment might imply

---

[150] Such a presence may also increase PRC perceptions of U.S. hostile intent, which would be expected to have a more escalatory effect.

[151] We note that an increase in certain capabilities may also increase Chinese perceptions of the threat posed by the United States and its allies.

[152] Of course, this improvement in perceptions of U.S. commitment to Taiwan would be in tension with threats that such actions could pose to PRC regime legitimacy, which would be expected to have a more escalatory effect.

that the value and importance of these alliance commitments is low, leading the PRC to revise its beliefs about U.S. commitment and leading to a greater willingness to respond aggressively against the ally or partner.

The key aspects of the foregoing discussion are also summarized in table form for quicker reference in Table 3.2. In this table, we have added a simplified notation regarding whether the linkage noted is more likely to lead to more or less aggressive PRC responses. However, as the discussion above hopefully clarifies, in many cases the nature of PRC responses may be conditional and therefore might not reflect these binary codings. The primary value of the table, then, is in its summary of the issues involved, and not in the indicated direction of the potential effects on PRC behavior.

Table 3.2. Links Between U.S. Military Activity Characteristics and Key Factors Affecting Chinese Responses

Key Factor	Location	U.S. Ally or Partner Involved	Capabilities	Profile
1. China's perceptions of the potential military threat from U.S., allied, and partner capabilities	+ Proximity to militarily sensitive areas, bases, or forces of the PRC, adjusted for range – Shift of U.S. activity or resources away from militarily sensitive areas, bases, or forces of the PRC, adjusted for range	+ Capabilities of U.S. allies/partners involved + Interoperability of U.S. and allied/partner capabilities and command structure + Demonstrated U.S. access to allied/partner locations of high military utility for operations against China or Chinese forces	+ Overall military utility or potential against the PRC of U.S. capabilities involved + High-technology, novel capabilities that could undermine PRC defenses + Demonstrated capabilities that increase PRC concern over its own ability to execute key military missions – Demonstrated capabilities that reduce PRC confidence in ability to manage escalation	
2. China's perceptions of U.S., allied, and partner hostile intent	+ Proximity to militarily sensitive areas, bases, or forces of the PRC, including especially those that are novel, adjusted for range + Proximity to politically sensitive areas in or near the PRC	+ Involvement of allies/partners that the PRC believes to be anti-China (e.g., Japan) + Involvement of allies/partners that the PRC believes the United States is recruiting to be more anti-China or to encircle China (e.g., Vietnam, India) + Involvement of comparatively new allies/partners outside of the region (e.g., France, Germany) + Depth of U.S. cooperation/engagement demonstrated with allies/partners – Involvement of partners with close, durable ties to China could lessen concern (e.g., Laos)	+ Military utility or potential of U.S. capabilities involved against the PRC + Particular concern for high-technology, novel capabilities that could undermine PRC defenses + Demonstration of capabilities or concepts perceived to be primarily useful for conflict vs. the PRC + Activity demonstrates relevant capabilities more frequently or at a larger scale – Decrease in frequency or reduction in scale of activities of prior Chinese concern + Sustained program of activities that suggests U.S. efforts to prepare for conflict	+ Highly visible, public displays of military capabilities in or near areas of political sensitivity to the PRC + Timing of activities appearing to coincide with politically sensitive dates for the PRC + Heated rhetoric from U.S. or allied/partner policymakers that might accompany the activity – Outreach and transparency with the PRC in advance could reduce concerns

Key Factor	Location	U.S. Ally or Partner Involved	Capabilities	Profile
3. China's perceptions of threats to its regime legitimacy	+ Proximity to Taiwan + Proximity to other PRC territorial claims	+ Involvement of allies/partners whose cooperation with the United States threatens the PRC's perceived territorial integrity (e.g., Taiwan)	+ Military utility or potential to defend against PRC actions against perceived separatist actors (Taiwan)	+ Accompanying statements that imply U.S. activities may challenge to PRC legitimacy – Accompanying statements of commitment to status quo or respect for PRC interests
4. China's perceptions of threats to its economic development	+ Proximity to SLOCs (especially energy) or maritime chokepoints	+ Involvement of allies/partners that have the ability to restrict PRC economic access to resources or markets	+ Demonstrated capabilities that enable the United States to interdict or otherwise interrupt PRC access to resources or markets	+ Accompanying messaging that U.S. capabilities may be employed to threaten the PRC economy in conflict
5. China's perceptions of threats to its regional influence	+ Proximity to influential states or regions of interest to PRC (Southeast Asia) + Proximity to disputed territories or other areas that could undermine regional perceptions of China's clout	+ Involvement of allies/partners that the PRC believes may undermine its regional influence if they become closer to the United States (Vietnam, Indonesia) – Involvement of large numbers of allies/partners that may signal broad regional support for U.S. military presence and activities + Involvement of allies/partners that may themselves be competitors for regional influence (e.g., Japan) + Involvement of transnational organizations/ groupings (e.g., ASEAN, Quad) in U.S. activities		+ Accompanying statements that explicitly challenge PRC influence or interests – Accompanying statements that acknowledge Chinese interests and describe limits to U.S. intent and scope + Timing of activities to coincide with or undermine PRC initiatives + Accompanying U.S., allied, or partner messaging that counters PRC regional narratives

50

Key Factor	Location	U.S. Ally or Partner Involved	Capabilities	Profile
6. China's perceptions of U.S. commitment to the defense of U.S. allies or partners		– Involvement of allies to which the United States has a formal defensive commitment – Involvement of allies/partners with whom the United States has increasing engagement + Shift of forces or resources away from allies/partners to which the United States previously had a clear defensive commitment – Activities that signal permanent presence or commitment, rather than transitory U.S. involvement	– Demonstrated capabilities that could be used to defend allies and partners	– Accompanying political statements and signaling that activities are intended to better defend U.S. ally/partner – Alignment of political statements and messaging with those of U.S. ally/partner + Recent U.S. political statements that question the value or importance of U.S. alliance commitment

+ indicates characteristics of U.S. activities that may make a near-term aggressive PRC response more likely.
– indicates characteristics of U.S. activities that may make a near-term aggressive PRC response less likely.

51

Chapter 4. Typology of PRC Responses

The third part of our framework provides a typology for the types of responses that China might make in response to U.S. military activities, organized by the approximate level of intensity of those responses. China may respond in a more or less aggressive manner based on the considerations discussed in previous chapters. As it makes a decision to respond, it may choose among a number of different policy options that it believes will send relatively similar messages to the United States or other regional actors as it seeks to manage escalation risks while seeking to address concerns that may be raised by U.S. activities. We argue that the choice among these different intensity levels is relatively more predictable than the choice of specific responses within these levels themselves. That is, selecting a more or less intensive or escalatory response is likely to be a decision that China makes carefully, driven by the considerations discussed in the prior two chapters. But having decided how strong a signal to try to send, the specific choice of policy response is likely to be highly dependent on context and difficult to predict in advance. Our typology is therefore intended to give U.S. policymakers a rough sense of the potential range of Chinese policy responses that they may encounter in response to the military activities they undertake.

China's responses can also vary along two other important dimensions: their time horizons and the types of state power that they employ. China may undertake both near-term and longer-term responses, some of which might not be immediately visible to U.S. observers. It could decide not to change its near-term policies or could change them only marginally, even as it begins to make significant changes to its longer-term policies. Chinese responses may also vary across different domains, incorporating political, economic, or military actions. While the choice of specific actions within these domains is likely to be context dependent, below we identify four general behavioral patterns in China's responses that may help U.S. policymakers better prepare.

Near-Term PRC Policy Responses

China's near-term responses can occur at a spectrum of intensity that ranges from very low, or virtually indistinguishable from commonplace behavior, to very high, or virtually indistinguishable from war. Although divisions along the continuum of potential responses from more to less aggressive are in one sense arbitrary, we believe it is useful to classify potential PRC responses according to a typology of five intensity levels. Table 4.1 presents these intensity levels, as well as two key dimensions along which the responses within them tend to vary. "Visibility" captures how clear it is that a Chinese response is to a specific U.S. action and how public China's response is likely to be. "Escalation risk" describes the possibility of a Chinese response generating inadvertent escalation or otherwise resulting in a conflict.

Table 4.1. Key Dimensions of the Intensity-Level Typology

Intensity Level	Relative Visibility	Relative Escalation Risk
Level 1: No/minor response	Low	Low
Level 2: Notable response	Medium	Low
Level 3: Elevated response	High	Medium
Level 4: Severe response	High	High
Level 5: Maximal response	Highest	Highest

Table 4.2 contains potential near-term PRC responses to U.S. actions organized along this intensity-level typology. Within each intensity level, the responses are categorized according to their functional area (i.e., according to whether they are primarily military, diplomatic, or economic in character). This approach builds on previous analysis classifying China's approach to coercive signaling.[153] The specific actions that populate Table 4.2 were generated through the study of historical cases—including those presented in Appendix B of this report—which were also used to validate the overall typology itself.

Table 4.2. Near-Term PRC Responses

Level 1: No or minor response		
Political options	Economic options	Military options
• Negative but routine public statements, media criticism • Formal diplomatic protest/demarche	• Isolated protests of U.S., allied, or partner companies • Warnings of possible damage to regional or global economy	• Increase intel collection on U.S., allied, or partner activities • Formal diplomatic protest/demarche • Display Chinese military capabilities

---

[153] Examples of such work include Paul H. B. Godwin and Alice L. Miller, "China's Forbearance Has Limits: Chinese Threat and Retaliation Signaling and Its Implications for a Sino-American Military Confrontation," *China Strategic Perspectives*, No. 6, Washington, D.C.: Institute for National Strategic Studies, April 2013; Andrew Chubb, "PRC Assertiveness in the South China Sea: Measuring Continuity and Change, 1970–2015," *International Security*, Vol. 45, No. 3, Winter 2020/2021; and Nathan Beauchamp-Mustafaga, Derek Grossman, Kristen Gunness, Michael S. Chase, Marigold Black, and Natalia D. Simmons-Thomas, *Deciphering Chinese Deterrence Signalling in the New Era: An Analytic Framework and Seven Case Studies*, Santa Monica, Calif.: RAND Corporation, RR-A1074-1, 2021.

Level 2: Notable response

Political options	Economic options	Military options
• Concerted campaign of criticism in domestic media and associated international channels • Public or backchannel warning of escalation risk • Cancel or reschedule key meetings or engagements	• Limit Chinese tourism to United States, ally, or partner • Limit Chinese students studying in United States, ally, or partner • Limit select trade/aid/investment to United States, ally, or partner • Limit availability of international or public resources to United States, ally, or partner	• Limit military-to-military exchanges with United States, ally, or partner • Test new military capabilities targeted at United States, ally, or partner • Invest in new capabilities or strategies to counter United States, ally, or partner • Increase military engagement with third-party countries • Increase activities to challenge or block U.S., allied, or partner military activity

Level 3: Elevated response

Political options	Economic options	Military options
• Explicit threat to use force • Attempt political interference in United States or allied/partner state • Halt cooperation with United States • Deepen PRC support for U.S. adversaries • Close U.S. consulate or send back U.S. diplomats • Anti–United States, ally, or partner activity in United Nations (UN) and other international fora	• Widespread harassment of U.S., allied, or partner businesses operating in China • Boycott or destroy U.S., allied, or partner goods • Hamper production or export of U.S., allied, or partner goods made in China; restrict U.S., allied, or partner access to Chinese-controlled or dominated supply chains • Sharply constrain international or public resources to United States, ally, or partner	• Explicit threat to use force • Engage in targeted cyber ops vs. United States, ally, or partner • Aggressive response to U.S., allied, or partner reconnaissance activity and forces transits • High-profile posturing/exercises/signaling (major change to PLA status quo posture and activity)

Level 4: Severe response

Political options	Economic options	Military options
• Close United States, ally, or partner embassy • Proposed anti–United States, ally, or partner resolution in UN; broad condemnation and call for anti-U.S. action in China-dominated fora	• Full boycott or trade cutoff of United States, ally, or partner • Effort to build anti-U.S. trade movement in China-dominated blocks	• Direct use of force against United States, ally, or partner • Paramilitary action against United States, ally, or partner • Large-scale cyber campaign against critical targets of United States, ally, or partner

Level 5: Maximal response

Political options	Economic options	Military options
• Declaration of war vs. United States, ally, or partner • Detain/intern U.S., allied, or partner nationals in China	• Seize/appropriate U.S., allied, or partner firm assets • Interdict U.S., allied, or partner trade beyond PRC borders	• High-intensity strikes against U.S., allied, or partner targets • National mobilization • Heightened nuclear alert status • Invasion/seizure of contested ally or partner territory

PRC leaders tend to respond to U.S., allied, and partner activities by adopting one or more responses from an intensity level, mixing options from across functional areas depending on both the specifics of the action as well as the political-strategic context. As a result, responses are very difficult to anticipate in the abstract. Moreover, in some circumstances, China may choose to undertake a relatively low-intensity response in the near term even as it prepares or executes a higher-intensity but slower-to-manifest or longer-term response. In such cases, China's initial response may appear less aggressive than it really is. How the United States or its allies and partners react in turn may change how, and even whether, China implements higher-intensity follow-on actions. In other words, Chinese responses at different intensity levels are often the result of a stepwise signaling process as China adopts increasingly high-intensity policy changes to compel recalcitrant adversaries. The remainder of this section examines the PRC responses associated with each of the intensity levels in more detail.

At Level 1, "no or minor response," Chinese behavior can appear equivalent to routine activities that might have occurred even absent a U.S. or allied and partner action. Such signals may therefore be difficult to separate from the noise of common political conduct or military operations. This intensity level can also include more-visible responses, however, including diplomatic demarches, governmental permission for or even facilitation of small-scale protests against foreign diplomatic stations or companies, and general demonstrations of military strength. These activities are typically limited in not just their intensity but also their scope and duration, as they are intended more to warn other states about PRC dissatisfaction than to directly coerce them into changing their behavior.

Examples of policy responses are Level 1 are ubiquitous. In September 2015, for example, during a period of highly strained Sino-Japanese relations associated with Japan's nationalization of the Senkaku Islands, China held a military parade in Beijing's Tiananmen Square to commemorate the 70th anniversary of the end of World War II. The parade, which displayed a variety of military equipment, including ICBMs and anti-ship ballistic missiles, served in part as a warning to regional actors (such as Japan) regarding China's development of the types of military capabilities necessary to defend its interests in the ECS.[154] At the same time, however, China's response was limited in intensity and duration, and although it helped demonstrate China's displeasure, it did not significantly increase the risk of escalation.

Level 2, or "notable," responses tend to be more visible than Level 1 responses. They are intended, in other words, to send clearer and more overt signals to foreign actors that China has changed its behavior in response to foreign activities. Although this means that Level 2 responses are often public, they can still be delivered privately. For example, whereas displays of Chinese military capabilities that fall into Level 1 might include media coverage detailing an already-known Chinese weapon system, a Level 2 equivalent might include an unpublicized

---

[154] Chris Buckley, "Military Parade in China Gives Xi Jinping a Platform to Show Grip on Power," *New York Times*, September 3, 2015.

military test of novel capabilities conducted in a way that is likely to be detected by U.S. or allied and partner intelligence, surveillance, and reconnaissance (ISR) capabilities. These responses also tend to be of longer duration or involve PRC policy changes that, by their nature, tend to take longer to implement than Level 1 responses.

Level 2 responses are prominent in the cases presented in Appendix B. For example, China's approach to the revival of the Quad included a variety of Level 2 responses.[155] Politically, China mounted a concerted campaign of protests and criticism using official statements up to the ministerial level, as well as through media commentary. Economically, China's approach has been to allow the media to issue veiled threats about the imperiled economic interests of Quad member states should they follow the United States' anti-China line. It has also used various forms of Level 2 economic coercion against Quad member states, including Australia, although it is worth noting that it has also sought to employ economic means as a carrot rather than a stick to entice greater bilateral cooperation between China and regional Quad member states. Finally, the PLA has conducted some new exercises described in press reports as responding to Quad activities.

Level 3, or "elevated," responses tend to make more explicit threats, to cause greater diplomatic or economic harm, and to run greater risks of escalation than Level 2 responses. Regarding threats, Level 3 is marked by relatively clear signaling of political-strategic redlines and the consequences for violating them. Such threats can be specific and detailed, or they can describe ambiguous consequences, but, regardless, they will overtly describe China's willingness to use force in response to a U.S., allied, or partner action. Whereas Level 2 responses tend to suggest the potential for long-term political and diplomatic costs if the United States or its allies and partners do not modify their activities, Level 3 responses typically inflict real costs in order to demonstrate the credibility of China's deterrent or compellent threats to inflict even greater costs in the future. Such cost imposition can involve diplomatic measures (e.g., reducing the U.S. diplomatic and intelligence-gathering footprint in China or by attacking U.S. interests in international organizations), economic punishment (e.g., disrupting U.S. businesses in China or restricting U.S. access to Sinocentric supply chains), and military activities (e.g., utilizing tailored cyber operations against military targets or aggressively challenging the transit of other states' ships and aircraft). By their nature, such Level 3 responses tend to run greater risks of generating escalation than Level 1 or 2 responses. This is often by intent: The risk of escalation associated with more-intense responses, like targeted cyber options or aggressive responses to U.S. reconnaissance activities, serves as a source of coercive leverage with which China can attempt to shift U.S., allied, and partner behavior.

Of course, the risk of escalation also means that China is less likely to adopt Level 3 responses unless it perceives relatively serious threats. It also means that in some circumstances China may prioritize political and economic rather than military measures, because it may see

---

[155] More details about China's responses to the Quad are available in Case 9.

the former as less likely to trigger an armed conflict. Beijing's response to the deployment of a THAAD missile system in South Korea serves as a case in point.[156] After the United States and South Korea agreed to deploy a THAAD battery to defend against North Korea in July 2016, Beijing quickly implemented a variety of Level 1 and 2 diplomatic protests that rapidly metastasized into threats of retaliation in media commentary. Militarily, China froze cooperation and engagement with South Korea, carried out missile exercises that included simulated strikes on the THAAD battery, and appears to have also increased cyber espionage on the South Korean government.[157] Its most intense responses, however, were economic. Korean celebrities disappeared from Chinese airwaves; China reduced the flow of Chinese tourists to South Korea; and Chinese officials punished Korean companies through formal and informal punitive measures that cost Korea an estimated $7.5 billion in economic losses.[158] Most prominently, it cracked down on grocery conglomerate Lotte for providing part of a golf course as THAAD's deployment sight by embroiling it in tax and safety inspections that eventually erased much of its footprint in China at great expense.

Level 4, or "severe," responses lie between peacetime crisis and the opening stages of a conflict. They are so serious as to be very rare in the history of post-opening U.S.-China relations—but they are more common in China's relations with regional states, especially in response to perceived challenges to China's territorial integrity. In general, Level 4 responses are intended not just to inflict costs, but also to significantly increase the risk of war in order to coerce other states' behaviors. It is worth noting that even though Level 4 responses occur in the near term, they are likely to have significant long-term effects on China's relations with both the United States and its allies and partners. Diplomatic responses such as embassy closures, economic responses such as across-the-board boycotts of foreign companies, and military actions such as the direct use of force can not only leave deep, lingering damage in bilateral and multilateral relationships but also shape future diplomatic, economic, and military patterns of behavior. As a result, Level 4 responses are very likely to occur alongside longer-term Chinese policy changes.

China has not undertaken a Level 4 responses to U.S., allied, or partner activities since the Cold War. The closest China has come over the last three decades is the Taiwan Strait Crisis of 1995–1996, during which China test-fired missiles, conducted live-fire exercises, and simulated amphibious landings off of the Taiwanese coast to coerce Taiwan and shape its presidential

---

[156] The deployment of THAAD to South Korea from 2016 to the present is explored in more detail in Case 7 of Appendix B.

[157] Jonathan Cheng and Josh Chin, "China Hacked South Korea over Missile Defense, U.S. Firm Says," *Wall Street Journal*, April 21, 2017.

[158] "When China and U.S. Spar, It's South Korea That Gets Punched," *Los Angeles Times*, November 20, 2020.

elections.[159] However, even these uses of force straddle the line between Level 3 and Level 4 responses, as the PLA did not directly target Taiwanese or U.S. forces. China's relative restraint since then, moreover, appears to have two primary causes. First, Beijing has developed a wide range of political, economic, and military tools with which it can achieve coercive goals at lower levels of intensity. Second, neither the United States nor its allies and partners have taken actions provocative enough to justify true Level 4 responses.

Finally, the Level 5, or "maximal," responses constitute the most intense that China is able to exert against the United States or its allies and partners. Maximal political and economic responses—like interning U.S. or allied and partner nationals in China or seizing foreign financial and economic assets within China—may be intended as last plays for victory short of war in disputes that Chinese leaders perceive as critically important. Maximal military responses constitute direct preparations for the immediate outbreak of war, as well as precipitating acts of war. In this sense, Level 5 responses represent either the failure of deterrence or the culmination of compellence. Over the past 30 years, there are no examples of China undertaking Level 5 responses to U.S. actions. However, each of China's two largest foreign wars since 1949—its interventions in Korea against the UN forces from 1950 to 1953, and its invasion of Vietnam in 1979—involved Level 5 responses to perceived threats that its leaders judged unresolvable absent the direct, large-scale use of force.

Longer-Term PRC Policy Responses

As previously noted, in some cases China's near-term responses may be quite limited and its longer-term policy changes more pronounced; in other cases, China may utilize only near-term responses. This is because China can choose to respond on different time horizons in order to address different problems posed by U.S. and allied and partner activities. China might judge nearer-term responses to be sufficient if they allow it to address whatever concerns are raised by U.S. actions. However, it might also adopt longer-term responses intended to improve China's future strategic position by altering the political, economic, and military foundations of U.S.-Chinese competition. The likelihood that it does so depends in part on U.S. and allied and partner activities. In general terms, the greater the impact of those activities on China's expectations regarding its ability to achieve its long-term goals, including maintaining political stability and realizing the "China dream" of national rejuvenation, the more Chinese leaders will be motivated to react through longer-term changes in PRC policy.[160] Additionally, the more important the

---

[159] An overview of the crisis is provided in John W. Garver, *Face Off: China, the United States, and Taiwan's Democratization*, Seattle, Wash.: University of Washington Press, 2011.

[160] China's most important policy goals and strategies for achieving them are analyzed in Andrew Scobell, Edmund J. Burke, Cortez A. Cooper III, Sale Lilly, Chad J. R. Ohlandt, Eric Warner, and J. D. Williams, *China's Grand Strategy: Trends, Trajectories, and Long-Term Competition*, Santa Monica, Calif.: RAND Corporation, RR-2798-A, 2020. Its assessments of the international environment and threats to its interests are also explored in Timothy R.

policy goal threatened by U.S. activities, the more likely China is to change its longer-term policies in response.[161] China will probably often respond to threatening U.S. activities through a mixture of both near- and longer-term responses that it views as complementary. Its near-term responses may serve as signaling devices or might be used to address pressing threats and seize immediate opportunities, for example, while its longer-term measures improve China's strategic position by altering the political, economic, and military foundations of U.S.-Chinese competition. For example, China studied the U.S. and Iraqi militaries' performances in the first Gulf War closely and concluded that dangerous gaps in the PLA's capabilities threatened China's ability to achieve its future strategic goals, including its ability to prevent Taiwanese independence. As a result, the PLA adopted a variety of near-term policies alongside a multidecade military modernization effort that has yielded a range of new capabilities, including A2/AD systems.[162] More recently, U.S. development of ballistic missile defense systems has encouraged China to increase funding for systems intended to defeat such defenses, including hypersonic glide vehicles.[163] Longer-term responses can also be economic or political. The BRI was a response to both the global financial crisis, which seemed to signal the irreversible end of U.S. primacy, and the Obama administration's "pivot to Asia," which many Chinese observers interpreted as a U.S. commitment to containing China.[164] Similarly, the PLA's development of capabilities that could be used to protect or control key SLOCs is a response to Chinese perceptions of the threat that U.S. military capabilities pose to PRC economic development or access to resources.[165]

Heath, Kristen Gunness, and Cortez A. Cooper III, *The PLA and China's Rejuvenation: National Security and Military Strategies, Deterrence Concepts, and Combat Capabilities*, Santa Monica, Calif.: RAND Corporation, RR-1402-OSD, 2016.

[161] These two dimensions taken together suggest a framework similar to the realist "balance of threat" theory, which combines both the perceived seriousness of potential threats as well as the importance of the interests threatened to anticipate when states will take aggressive actions in response. See Stephen M. Walt, *The Origins of Alliances*, Ithaca, N.Y.: Cornell University Press, 1987; and Scott Cooper, "State-Centric Balance-of-Threat Theory: Explaining the Misunderstood Gulf Cooperation Council," *Security Studies*, Vol. 13, No. 2, December 30, 2003.

[162] Dean Cheng, "Chinese Lessons from the Gulf Wars," in Andrew Scobell, David Lai, and Roy Kamphausen, eds., *Chinese Lessons from Other Peoples' Wars*, Carlisle, Pa.: U.S. Army War College, 2012.

[163] As the 2020 DoD report on China states, Chinese efforts to develop hypersonic weapons and other advanced technologies such as directed energy weapons are driven in part by the desire to achieve the "defeat of missile defense systems." See Office of the Secretary of Defense, *Annual Report to Congress: Military and Security Developments Involving the People's Republic of China 2020*, Washington, D.C., 2020, p. 148.

[164] Weifeng Zhou and Mario Esteban, "Beyond Balancing: China's Approach Towards the Belt and Road Initiative," *Journal of Contemporary China*, Vol. 27, No. 112, 2018; and Michael Clarke, "Beijing's Pivot West: The Convergence of Innenpolitik and Aussenpolitik on China's 'Belt and Road'?" *Journal of Contemporary China*, Vol. 29, No. 123, 2020.

[165] Jeffrey Becker, *Securing China's Lifelines Across the Indian Ocean*, Newport, R.I.: U.S. Naval War College, China Maritime Studies Institute, China Maritime Report No. 11, December 2020.

Like the near-term responses analyzed above, longer-term responses can therefore be disaggregated into political, economic, and military categories. Table 4.3 does so.

Table 4.3. Potential Longer-Term PRC Policy Responses

Political	Economic	Military
<ul><li>Prioritizing relations with particular countries</li><li>Becoming more or less aggressive or friendly toward particular countries</li><li>Emphasizing or deemphasizing certain interests (territorial disputes)</li><li>Changing intensity of ideological competition</li></ul>	<ul><li>Altering BRI or other investment levels in particular countries</li><li>Modulating PRC openness to certain external investments</li><li>Moving supply chains or sourcing of goods or resources to or from particular countries</li></ul>	<ul><li>Adjusting spending levels</li><li>Shifting spending for different capabilities</li><li>Investing in militarily supportive infrastructure</li><li>Modifying PLA force posture</li><li>Revising military strategic guidelines or strategic direction</li><li>Updating PLA doctrine and operational concepts</li><li>PLA reorganization</li></ul>

NOTE: Policies may shift slightly or substantially depending on the level of PRC concern generated by the U.S. activity.

Longer-term responses can also vary in their intensity. However, we did not disaggregate the responses in Table 4.3 across intensity levels because we have less publicly available information about what might distinguish different intensities of longer-term responses than we do about near-term responses. Moreover, many of those distinctions would simply involve stating that China is doing relatively "more" or "less"—such as spending more on the PLAN or making larger investments in military infrastructure abroad—in intuitive ways.

Patterns in PRC Responses

The preceding sections addressed the intensity levels and time horizons of Chinese responses. We also carefully examined the case studies presented in Appendix B for patterns in China's behavior: how and when it typically pairs different functional types of responses together (e.g., military, political, and economic), how it sequences responses, and how its behavior tends to change across different intensity levels. We identified four important patterns, which are presented below.

Pattern 1: China Adopts Multilayered Responses

China's responses to U.S. activities that it finds particularly concerning tend to involve a multilayered mixture of diplomatic, economic, and military policy changes that Beijing calibrates—and integrates—depending on the situation. For example, the 2012 U.S. rebalance to Asia, which China perceived as an attempt to increase U.S. influence in the region and to refocus U.S. military capabilities on countering China's rise, helped motivate it to undertake the BRI, which seeks to grow China's regional influence through economic incentives. The rebalance also pushed Beijing to increase its own investments in military capabilities to address perceived threats, including in its SCS maritime disputes, and to adopt more-forceful rhetoric denouncing the United States as a destabilizing actor in the region.[166]

China appears especially likely to adopt multilayered responses when it perceives threats to its regime security and legitimacy or its territorial integrity. The case studies we examined that touched on these concerns and in which China used diplomatic, economic, and military actions include those related to Taiwan; the U.S. deployment to THAAD, which was perceived as physically threatening to China's regime security; and those related to territorial disputes in the ECS and SCS. In most instances, Chinese messaging and warnings through media and official statements were followed by some type of economic threat or action combined with a military response.

Three cases serve to illustrate this tendency. The first is the Trump administration's increased support for Taiwan between 2019 and 2020.[167] China responded first by condemning the actions in official Chinese media and then levying sanctions on American companies involved in arms sales to Taiwan. This was followed by the PLAAF increasing its incursions into Taiwanese airspace, as well as PLA exercises near Taiwan.[168] The second is the Scarborough Shoal incident in 2012. China responded by publicly criticizing the Philippines' incursions into Chinese waters, which was followed by customs restrictions to tie up imports of bananas from the Philippines restricting Chinese tourism.[169] Militarily, China deployed the maritime militia and Chinese Coast Guard to coerce Manila, while PLAN vessels were stationed nearby.[170] The third is the 2016 deployment of THAAD to South Korea.[171] China first relied on diplomatic pressure and public statements, followed by economic measures targeting tourism to South Korea and South Korean businesses in China. Upon news of the deployment, Beijing immediately canceled high-level military engagements. PLA exercises simulating the targeting of THAAD and related systems

---

[166] Zhu Lu-ming and Zhang Wen-wen, "The Causes and Influences of Strengthening the American-Japan Ally Under the Background of the Asia-Pacific Rebalancing Strategy"
["美国'亚太再平衡'背景下美日同盟的强化原因及影响"], *Journal of Lanzhou University of Arts and Science* [兰州文理学院学报], Vol. 4, 2014.

[167] David Brunnstrom, Mike Stone, and Krisztina Than, "China to Impose Sanctions on U.S. Firms That Sell Arms to Taiwan," Reuters, July 12, 2019. U.S. policy toward Taiwan under the Trump administration is addressed in more detail in Cases 10 and 14 of Appendix B.

[168] In 2020, PLA warplanes conducted more flights into Taiwan's ADIZ than at any time since 1996, and by late 2020, such incursions had become an almost daily occurrence. See John Xie, "China Is Increasing Taiwan Airspace Incursions," *Voice of America*, January 6, 2021.

[169] The 2012 Scarborough Shoal incident is the focus of Case 3 in Appendix B.

[170] Michael Green, Kathleen Hicks, Zack Cooper, John Schaus, and Jake Douglas, "Counter-Coercion Series: Scarborough Shoal Standoff," Asia Maritime Transparency Initiative, Center for Strategic and International Studies, May 22, 2017.

[171] THAAD deployment to South Korea is analyzed in detail in Case 7 of Appendix B.

began later, in August 2017.[172] These cases illustrate China's tendency to use the full spectrum of its diplomatic, economic, and military power to respond to U.S. and allied and partner activities that it perceives as especially significant or threatening to its core interests.

Pattern 2: Diplomatic and Political Responses Are Always Present

In the cases we examined, China's initial response to U.S. actions that it regarded as serious almost always began with political signaling of Chinese interests and displeasure. This signaling was conducted through a range of public and private channels, including media commentary and propaganda dissemination, official statements, and diplomatic protests such as demarches or suspension of high-level civilian or military visits. China's military reactions, particularly the more provocative ones, were all preceded and accompanied by extensive media commentary and sometimes by official statements that aimed to build domestic and international political support for China's position and demonize any potential target of China's actions. This pattern is particular apparent in China's responses to the THAAD deployment, the China-Vietnam standoff over Haiyang 981, and the China-Philippines standoff over Scarborough Shoal.[173]

But China occasionally deviates from this pattern, particularly when it hopes to de-escalate a crisis or dispute. For example, the China-India clash in 2020 erupted suddenly, and authorities appeared eager to de-escalate tensions and reduce risks of conflict.[174] China's media downplayed the military developments and frequently echoed the messages of officials who called for de-escalation. Additionally, in the cases of Chinese economic retaliation and coercion, officials sometimes downplayed direct linkage between coercive economic practices such as tourism restrictions and increased import inspections and a particular U.S. military action. Examples of this pattern include the China-Philippines standoff near Scarborough Shoal, the restriction of banana imports from the Philippines, and the THAAD case in South Korea when China targeted South Korean businesses and restricted tourism.[175]

This aversion to directly linking economic coercion to a specific military activity in public statements likely reflects China's desire to maintain its reputation as a business-friendly country. An exception to this pattern is China's sanctions of U.S. defense companies, which it explicitly links to U.S. arms sales to Taiwan.[176] The difference is likely due to China's view of Taiwan as a

---

[172] Ethan Meick and Nargiza Salidjanova, *China's Response to U.S.-South Korean Missile Defense System Deployment and Its Implications*, Washington, D.C.: U.S.-China Economic and Security Review Commission, July 26, 2017.

[173] For specific examples of such signaling, see Cases 3, 7, and 12 in Appendix B.

[174] The 2020 China-India border clash is addressed in Case 13 in Appendix B.

[175] Ethan Meick and Nargiza Salidjanova, *China's Response to U.S.-South Korean Missile Defense System Deployment and Its Implications*, Washington, D.C.: U.S.-China Economic and Security Review Commission, July 26, 2017; and Xinhua, "Philippines Claim Illegal—Beijing," *Manila Times*, April 28, 2012.

[176] Yew Lun Tian, Gabriel Crossley, and Stella Qiu, "China to Impose Sanctions on U.S. Firms over Taiwan Arms Sales," Reuters, October 26, 2020.

core interest and the arms sales as a particularly sensitive issue on which Beijing seeks to send a forceful message.

Pattern 3: China Responds Militarily to Low-Intensity Military Activities

Although China's responses to U.S. military activities of relatively high concern tend to be multilayered across multiple dimensions of Chinese power, its responses to less-concerning U.S. military activities tend to remain military in nature and tend not to include corresponding sustained economic or diplomatic responses. Furthermore, in responding, the PLA generally tailors the capabilities demonstrated, exercise location, and tempo to signal ability to counter a specific U.S. activity.

Two recent examples help illustrate this tendency. The first is China's response to dual U.S. aircraft CSG operations in the SCS, which involved PLA fighter aircraft conducing live-fire drills in the SCS and deploying fighters to the Paracel Islands.[177] The PLA Rocket Force also launched one anti-ship DF-26 IRBM in an exercise in the SCS.[178] At the end of July 2020, PLAAF and PLAN Aviation bombers drilled over the SCS.[179] Although Chinese media condemned U.S. military operations during the PLA drills, China's main response was military and specific to U.S. activities. The second example is the increase in USN Taiwan Strait transits near Taiwan in 2020.[180] China responded by boosting PLAAF incursions into Taiwan's ADIZ.[181] By late 2020, such incursions had become an almost-daily occurrence.[182] However, Beijing took few associated political or economic responses.

Pattern 4: China Uses a Spectrum of Military and Paramilitary Options

China's responses reflect its growing ability to conduct military and paramilitary operations at the lower end of the intensity spectrum. Its approach to territorial disputes in the ECS and SCS, for example, has evolved as China's gray zone capabilities have increased and now emphasizes the use of paramilitary and cyber forces whose use is either deniable or would not cross the threshold of armed conflict. Over the past decade, moreover, China's responses to

---

[177] Minnie Chan, "South China Sea: Chinese Air Force 'Sends Warning' to U.S. Navy with Live-Fire Drills," *South China Morning Post*, July 21, 2020; and Brian W. Everstine, "B-1Bs Fly Through South China Sea Sending Message to Beijing," *Air Force Magazine*, July 23, 2020.

[178] David Lague, "Special Report: Pentagon's Latest Salvo Against China's Growing Might—Cold War Bombers," Reuters, September 1, 2020; and Liu Xuanzun, "PLA Rocket Force Launches DF-26 'Aircraft Carrier Killer' Missile in Fast-Reaction Drills," *Global Times*, August 6, 2020.

[179] Mathieu Duchâtel, "China Trends #6—Generally Stable? Facing U.S. Pushback in the South China Sea," Institut Montaigne, August 6, 2020; and Brian W. Everstine, "B-1Bs Fly Through South China Sea Sending Message to Beijing," *Air Force Magazine*, July 23, 2020.

[180] China's response to U.S. FONOPs in the Taiwan Strait in 2020 is the subject of Case 14 in Appendix B.

[181] "Chinese Incursions Highest Since 1996," *Taipei Times*, January 4, 2021.

[182] John Xie, "China Is Increasing Taiwan Airspace Incursions," *Voice of America*, January 6, 2021; and Ben Blanchard, "Taiwan Reports Large Incursion by Chinese Air Force," Reuters, January 23, 2021.

maritime territorial disputes have involved fewer PLAN ships and more Chinese Coast Guard and maritime militia forces. It appears that China is also employing more-coercive cyber capabilities, although information gaps make this difficult to analyze.

Examples from the case studies include China's response to Japan's nationalization of the Senkaku Islands in 2012, which involved regular incursions into Japan's EEZ with CCG ships and fishing vessels.[183] Even though China had the capability to deploy naval vessels, it primarily used the less escalatory paramilitary forces during this time period.[184] This might also have been a result of the strong U.S. defense commitment to Japan, which likely made China wary of potentially escalating the issue to armed conflict involving the United States. Another example is the 2019 Vanguard Bank incident involving China's response to Vietnamese-approved drilling operations by the Russian firm Rosneft.[185] In response, China dispatched a maritime research vessel and several CCG vessels to the area, with one vessel reportedly intimidating Vietnamese vessels with high-speed maneuvers performed close to nearby vessels.[186] There are numerous other instances of China using paramilitary forces around disputed TW to increase its presence and coerce regional nations. This prevalence probably also reflects China's belief that these types of capabilities have been very effective in enforcing its territorial claims.

---

[183] Case 4 in Appendix B analyzes Chinese responses to Japan's nationalization of the Senkaku Islands.

[184] Michael Green, Kathleen Hicks, Zack Cooper, John Schaus, and Jake Douglas, *Countering Coercion in Maritime Asia: The Theory and Practice of Gray Zone Deterrence*, Washington, D.C.: Center for Strategic and International Studies, May 2017, pp. 80–81; and Japan Coast Guard, "Trends in Chinese Government and Other Vessels in the Waters Around the Senkaku Islands, and Japan's Response" ["尖閣諸島周辺海域における中国海警局に所属する船舶等の動向と我が国の対処"], undated.

[185] The 2019 Vanguard Bank incident is the focus of Case 12 in Appendix B.

[186] Lye Liang Fook and Ha Hoang Hop, "The Vanguard Bank Incident: Developments and What Next?" *ISEAS Perspective*, No. 69, 2019, p. 6.

Chapter 5. U.S. Military Activities to Compete with China

The second part of this report identifies potential military activities that the United States could employ in its ongoing strategic competition with China and highlights the characteristics of those activities that are likely to lead to more or less escalatory Chinese reactions. In this chapter, we develop a comprehensive set of military activities the United States could employ in the competition, drawing on both historical examples and potentially novel options. In Chapter 6, we then highlight the characteristics of different categories of U.S. military activities likely to have the most escalatory effect on Chinese reactions. Appendix C provides an alternate, more-detailed approach to applying the framework to a specific U.S. military activity that may be of particular interest.

The Pentagon has a sweeping range of activities to choose from to compete effectively with China in the Indo-Pacific over the next decade. DoD could, for instance, maintain or modify its current set of activities. It could resurrect or retool activities that it tried in the past against peer or nonpeer adversaries, particularly the Soviet Union and its proxies, but has not yet tried against China in the past decade. Or it could devise entirely new and innovative activity types altogether. Each of these choices could potentially influence escalation dynamics differently. Currently, however, no menu of U.S. military activities exists to help defense planners and policymakers methodically navigate this range of potential options.

This chapter is organized into three sections. First, we explain our overall methodology and approach. Second, we develop an original typology covering the continuum of activity types available to U.S. defense planners. Third, we discuss the broader implications of our findings, focusing on opportunities for U.S. defense planners to manage escalation and compete more effectively in the future by varying existing or ongoing activity types.

Identifying Potential U.S. Military Activities

To develop a representative typology of potential U.S. military activities to compete with China, the RAND team performed an inductive, four-step research process:

Review of baseline U.S. activities versus China. We began building the typology by conducting a comprehensive review of the spectrum of recent and ongoing (unclassified) military activities that the United States has pursued to compete with China. To do so, we surveyed a variety of scholarly works,[187] data sets on U.S. military activities and interventions,[188] recent DoD public affairs notices and news media reports, and capstone DoD/joint strategy and doctrine publications.[189] We then sorted (and resorted) the resulting list of varied activity types into categories to shape the conceptual building blocks of the typology.

Review of historical U.S. activities versus the Union of Soviet Socialist Republics (USSR). To attain a more comprehensive list of the universe of possible activities, we then supplemented this foundation by identifying activities that the United States has *not* yet pursued against China since 2011. Namely, we widened our research aperture to also examine a representative set of military actions that the United States pursued in competition with the Soviet Union and its client regimes and proxies during the Cold War. This process drew heavily upon past RAND research and data on U.S. military interventions.[190] We also analyzed more-detailed anthologies and histories of U.S. military activities since World War II.[191]

---

[187] See, for instance, Hu Bo, "Six Categories of U.S. Military Operations in the South China Sea and Their Tendencies," South China Sea Strategic Situation Probing Initiative, August 29, 2019; Yong Chen, "Strengthening Peripheral Bases, Promoting Forward Deterrence—The Analysis and Prediction of Recent U.S. Military Operations in the South China Sea," South China Sea Strategic Situation Probing Initiative, 2019; National Institute for South China Sea Studies, *The U.S. Military Presence in the Asia-Pacific 2020*, Beijing, June 2020; National Institute for South China Sea Studies, *Report on the Military Presence of the United States of America in the Asia-Pacific Region*, Beijing, November 2016; and SCSPI, *An Incomplete Report on U.S. Military Activities in the South China Sea in 2020*, Beijing: Peking University, March 12, 2021.

[188] Data sets consulted on recent activities included the International Crisis Behavior data set, the International Peace Institute Peacekeeping database, the Correlates of War Militarized Interstate Disputes database, and multiple data sets compiled by the Uppsala Conflict Data Program and the Peace Research Institute Oslo program.

[189] For instance, we considered the theoretical spectrums of activities presented in capstone documents such as Joint Publication 1, *Doctrine for the Armed Forces of the United States*, Washington, D.C.: Joint Chiefs of Staff, July 12, 2017; Joint Publication 3-0, *Joint Operations*, Washington, D.C.: Joint Chiefs of Staff, October 22, 2018; Joint Publication 3-57, *Civil-Military Operations*, Washington, D.C.: Joint Chiefs of Staff, July 9, 2018; and Joint Publication 3-16, *Multinational Operations*, Washington, D.C.: Joint Chiefs of Staff, March 1, 2019.

[190] See, for instance, Alan J. Vick, David T. Orletsky, Abram N. Shulsky, and John Stillion, *Preparing for U.S. Air Force Military Operations Other Than War*, Santa Monica, Calif.: RAND Corporation, MR-842-AF, 1997; Eric V. Larson, Gustav Lindstrom, Myron Hura, Ken Gardiner, Jim Keffer, and William Little, *Interoperability of U.S. and NATO Allied Air Forces: Supporting Data and Case Studies*, Santa Monica, Calif.: RAND Corporation, MR-1603-AF, 2003; and Jennifer Kavanagh, Bryan Frederick, Alexandra Stark, Nathan Chandler, Meagan L. Smith, Matthew Povlock, Lynn E. Davis, and Edward Geist, *Characteristics of Successful U.S. Military Interventions*, Santa Monica, Calif.: RAND Corporation, RR-3062-A, 2019.

[191] See, for instance, Larissa Forster, *Influence Without Boots on the Ground: Seaborne Crisis Response*, Newport, R.I.: Naval War College Press, 2013; Barbara Salazar Torreon and Sofia Plagakis, *Instances of Use of United States Armed Forces Abroad, 1798–2020*, version 31, Washington, D.C.: Congressional Research Service, July 20, 2020; Eugene Cobble, H. H. Gaffney, and Dmitry Gorenburg, *For the Record: All U.S. Forces' Responses to Situations, 1970–2000 (with Additions Covering 2000–2003)*, Alexandria, Va.: CNA, 2005; Timothy A. Warnock, ed., *Short of War: Major USAF Contingency Operations, 1947–1997*, Maxwell Air Force Base, Ala.: Air University Press, 2000; David E. Johnson, *Doing What You Know: The United States and 250 Years of Irregular Warfare*, Washington, D.C.: Center for Strategic and Budgetary Assessments, 2017; U.S. Navy, "Appendix A," in U.S. Navy, *2007 Program Guide to the U.S. Navy: Sea Power for a New Era*, Washington, D.C., 2007; Daniel Haulman, *One Hundred Years of Flight: USAF Chronology of Significant Air and Space Events, 1903–2002*, Maxwell Air Force Base, Ala.: Air University Press, 2003; Bruce A. Elleman and S. C. M. Paine, eds., *Naval Coalition Warfare: From*

Analysis of new and innovative activities to compete with China. To understand the potential value of expanding our typology moving forward, we identified a series of novel and innovative activities the United States could use in competition with China. These activities were derived from several sources. We conducted a literature review of scholarly works and commentary from China security studies experts and analysts focusing on strategic competition, deterrence activities, and escalation dynamics. This literature is comprised primarily of Western, English-language material focused on delineating U.S. policy options for managing the U.S.-PRC strategic competition; however, we also derived some options from analysis of Chinese literature that examines U.S. activity and indicates the level and type of Chinese response to this activity.[192] In addition, we drew from the aforementioned historical data on previous operations against the USSR and its proxies to derive potential options that might be adapted or revised to advance U.S. interests in the Indo-Pacific.

Validation of typology with a Pacific Air Forces–sponsored (PACAF-sponsored) workshop. Finally, we sought to validate our resulting typology by hosting a PACAF-sponsored workshop on May 12, 2021. The event convened a group of some 40 defense planners from across the joint force, who were challenged with answering whether the typology omitted any large and important (unclassified) ongoing or historical U.S. activities. Military leaders were also asked to consider which types of existing activities should be expanded, terminated, or otherwise modified to better compete with China and to comment on what factors or concerns DoD should weigh when considering U.S. military activities vis-à-vis China. Finally, workshop participants were asked to help brainstorm new or innovative actions that could be considered in future competition with China.

Napoleonic War to Operation Iraqi Freedom, New York: Routledge, 2007; Robert B. Mahoney, Jr., *U.S. Navy Responses to International Incidents and Crises, 1955–1975*: Vol. II, *Summaries of Incidents and Responses*, Arlington, Va.: Center for Naval Analyses, 1977; and Adam B. Siegel, *Use of Naval Forces in the Post-War Era: U.S. Navy and U.S. Marine Corps Crisis Response Activity, 1946–1990*, Alexandria, Va.: Center for Naval Analyses, February 1991.

[192] Chinese open sources speak in vague generalities, if at all, about potential Chinese responses to future U.S. and allied military operations. However, evaluations of past U.S. activities and ongoing operations in the U.S.-PRC competition give some insight into what likely figures into elite Chinese decisionmaking regarding deterrence and escalation calculations. See, for example, Yong Ceng, "Viewing the Trend of China's South China Sea Policy from the 'Huangyan Island Model'" ["从'黄岩岛模式'看中国南海政策走向"], *Forum of World Economics & Politics* [世界经济与政治论坛], No. 5, 2014; People's Daily [人民网], "China's Core Interests Are Not to Be Challenged" ["中国核心利益不容挑战"], May 25, 2015; Zhicheng Wu and Yiyi Chen, "What Is the Difference Between the U.S. Position on Huangyan Island and the Diaoyu Islands Issue?" ["美国在黄岩岛与钓鱼岛问题上的立场缘何不同?"], *Xiandai Guoji Guanxi* [现代国际关系], No. 4, 2013; and Zhu Feng [朱 锋], "What Did 'Carl Vinson's' Trip to the South China Sea Reveal?" ["'卡尔·文森'号南海之行透射出什么"], *World Affairs* [世界知识], No. 7, 2018, pp. 30–32.

Typology of U.S. Military Activities

The resulting typology distilled the range of potential U.S. activities into five top-level categories: strategic and doctrinal-level activities, posture enhancement and theater-setting activities, presence and theater-shaping activities, security cooperation activities, and military operations and kinetic activities. As summarized in Table 5.1, our analysis further ordered this menu around 19 second-level activity types. As discussed below, these types further include 83 third-level activity subtypes, of which at least 60 (72 percent) have been utilized to some degree in the Indo-Pacific since 2011.

Table 5.1. Simplified Typology of Possible U.S. Military Activities to Compete with China

Activity Category (Level 1)	Activity Type (Level 2)
Strategic- and doctrinal-level activities	1. Changes to U.S. national security and defense policy 2. Changes to DoD strategy and doctrine
Posture enhancement and theater-setting activities	3. Changes to enabling agreements 4. Changes to deployed force structure 5. Changes to theater infrastructure 6. Changes to theater equipment set
Presence and theater-shaping activities	7. Expeditionary shaping activities and declaratory actions 8. Garrisoned presence and force protection activities 9. ISR activities 10. Unilateral exercises and training activities
Security cooperation activities	11. Combined exercises and training activities 12. Materiel military assistance 13. Foreign military exchanges and military diplomacy
Military operations and kinetic activities	14. Direct military interventions 15. Proxy warfare operations 16. Deterrence operations 17. Crisis responses and demonstrations of force 18. Soft power and civil-military operations 19. Asymmetric, irregular, or covert warfare activities

In the sections that follow, we expand upon the simplified version presented above by detailing these 83 third-level activity subtypes. For each, we identify examples of specific actions since 2011 relevant to the U.S. competition with China, as applicable. In categories in which we were unable to identify publicly known examples, we offer examples in the text of historical activities that were either conducted against the Soviet Union during the Cold War or that have only been conducted against nonpeer adversaries since World War II.

Strategy and Doctrine

The first activity-type category in our typology distinguishes between two major types of strategic- and doctrinal-level activities—changes to guiding U.S. national security and defense policy, and changes to DoD's own strategy and capstone doctrine—as well as seven key activity subtypes. The U.S. experience conducting this range of activities to compete in the Indo-Pacific region since 2011 is summarized in Table 5.2.

Table 5.2. Detailed Typology of U.S. Strategic- and Doctrinal-Level Activities

Activity Type (Level 2)	Activity Subtype (Level 3)		Examples Since 2011 Relevant to the Competition with China
Changes to U.S. grand strategy and national security or defense policy	Publication of new guiding strategy documents	✓	Trump's National Security Strategy (2017) and National Defense Strategy (2018); Obama's Asia Pivot (2011)
	Formation of new mutual defense treaties	✗	—
	Creation of new international legal and security agreements; norm-building activities	✓	Code for Unplanned Encounters at Sea (2014)
	Shifts in leadership rhetoric and informal security commitments	✓	Shangri-La Dialogue forum declarations; symbolic support to Taiwan in 2018–2021 National Defense Authorization Acts
Changes to DoD strategy and doctrine	DoD and Joint Staff strategic reviews	✓	DoD's Indo-Pacific Strategy Report (2019), Global Defense Posture Review (2021)
	Service-level, capstone doctrinal reviews	✓	The Army Strategy (2020); USAF's AFDP-1 (2021)
	Concept of operations (CONOP) shifts; updated field manuals, joint publications (JPs), etc.	✓	USAF's "Dynamic Force Employment"

Activity Type 1: Changes to U.S. Grand Strategy and National Security or Defense Policy

Our analysis identified at least four major types of potential changes to U.S. grand strategy and national security and defense policy and doctrine, three of which have been executed in the Asia-Pacific region to compete more effectively with China since 2011:

- The National Security Council (NSC) and Interagency can implement realignments in the **policy documents (and underlying strategic theses) that guide U.S. national security and defense strategy**. Major examples in the past decade aimed at U.S.-PRC competition include the Obama administration's 2011 Asia-Pacific rebalance strategy and the Trump administration's 2017 National Security Strategy and 2018 National Defense Strategy.
- The United States can form **new mutual defense treaties**. While there have been no new U.S. mutual defense treaties signed in the Indo-Pacific region since 2011, updates have

been made to existing treaties (e.g., the 2015 update to the U.S.-Japan Mutual Defense Treaty).[193]

- The United States can create (or terminate) **new international security and legal agreements and/or engage in new norm-building activities**. For instance, in the past decade, progress has been made with China on new agreements to reduce the risk of miscommunication or miscalculation, as with the signing of the Code for Unplanned Encounters at Sea in 2014.[194]

- Defense leaders can also signal shifts to U.S. national security strategy, policy, and doctrine through **changes in leadership rhetoric and new informal security commitments**. Recent examples targeting China are numerous. For instance, DoD and U.S. lawmakers have utilized symbolic language in the 2018–2021 National Defense Authorization Acts to propose Taiwanese participation in the joint forces' biennial Rim of the Pacific (RIMPAC) exercise and USAF's annual Red Flag–Alaska Exercise, expand military-to-military joint training in the continental United States (CONUS) at the National Training Center, and reaffirm U.S. commitment to the Taiwan Relations Act and Six Assurances.[195]

Activity Type 2: Changes to DoD Strategy and Doctrine

U.S. defense planners can make at least three types of changes to DoD's existing military strategy and doctrine to enhance competitive dynamics in the Indo-Pacific:

- Driving changes to military activities and investments in virtually all other categories in this typology, the Joint Staff can conduct and adopt the **recommendations of periodic strategy reviews**—such as the 2021 Global Defense Posture Review or DoD's 2019 *Indo-Pacific Strategy Report*.

- The individual military branches also conduct periodic **service-level, capstone doctrinal reviews**. For instance, to codify strategic changes to compete more effectively against China, USAF released the Air Force Doctrine Publication 1 (AFDP-1) in 2021.[196]

- Relatedly, DoD makes periodic **changes to CONOPs, field manuals, and JPs**. For instance, to adjust to the era of renewed interstate competition, the Air Force has embraced the new CONOP of Dynamic Force Employment, while the Marines have

---

[193] By contrast, the United States signed numerous new multilateral and bilateral mutual defense treaties in the Indo-Pacific region early in the Cold War, including the Australia–New Zealand–U.S. Treaty (ANZUS, 1951), the U.S.-Philippines Mutual Defense Treaty (1951), the U.S.–South Korea Mutual Defense Treaty (1953), and the U.S.-Japan Mutual Defense Treaty (1960).

[194] However, recent U.S. government activities to compete with China have arguably focused as much on withdrawing from such international agreements as building new ones. For instance, in 2019, the Trump administration withdrew from the Intermediate-Range Nuclear Forces Treaty as it sought to deploy land-based, medium-range missiles to Asia.

[195] National Institute for South China Sea Studies, *The U.S. Military Presence in the Asia-Pacific 2020*, Beijing, June 2020, p. 90; and Susan Lawrence and Wayne Morrison, *Taiwan: Issues for Congress*, Washington, D.C.: Congressional Research Service, October 30, 2017, p. 28.

[196] Notable examples from the other service branches include U.S. Marine Corps, *United States Marine Corps Service Campaign Plan*, Washington, D.C., 2014; U.S. Army, *The Army Strategy 2020*, Washington, D.C., 2020; and U.S. Department of the Navy, U.S. Marine Corps, and U.S. Coast Guard, *Advantage at Sea: Prevailing with Integrated All-Domain Naval Power*, Washington, D.C., December 2020.

adopted Expeditionary Advance Base Ops, the Navy has adopted Distributed Lethality, and the Army has adopted Multi-Domain Operations (MDO).[197]

Posture and Theater-Setting

The second activity-type category in our typology (posture enhancement and theater-setting) distinguishes between four major types of activities—changes to enabling agreements, changes to deployed force structure, changes to theater infrastructure, and changes to deployed equipment sets—as well as 19 key activity subtypes, summarized in Table 5.3.

Table 5.3. Detailed Typology of U.S. Posture Enhancement and Theater-Setting Activities

Activity Type (Level 2)	Activity Subtype (Level 3)		Examples Since 2011 Relevant to the Competition with China
Changes to enabling agreements	Status of forces agreements (SOFAs)	✓	U.S.-Australia 25-year SOFA (2011)
	Basing and access agreements	✓	U.S.-Philippines Enhanced Defense Cooperation Agreement (EDCA) (2014)
	Overflight and transit rights agreements	✗	—
	Mutual logistics support agreements	✓	U.S.-India Logistics Exchange Memorandum of Agreement (2020)
	Acquisition and cross-servicing agreements (ACSAs)	✓	16 existing bilateral ACSAs in the area of responsibility (AOR) (2020)
	Information-sharing and intelligence-sharing agreements	✓	U.S.–Japan–Republic of Korea (ROK) General Security of Military Information Agreement (2016)
	Other defense agreements and memoranda of understanding (MOUs)	✓	U.S.-Singapore defense MOU (2019)
Changes to deployed force structure	Force strength augmentations	✓	MRF-Darwin authorized to 2,500 (2012)
	Unit type augmentations	✓	Aegis-capable destroyers to Japan (in 2019)
	Unit deployment model changes	✓	Rotational model changed for bombers forward deployed to Guam (2020)
	Unit composition augmentations (active, reserve, guard)	✓	Activation of 658th Regional Support Group, Army Reserves, to run base operations in South Korea (2011)
	C2 realignments	✓	Development of Joint All Domain Command & Control (2020–)
	Contractor force augmentations	✗	—[a]

---

[197] Hu Bo, "Six Categories of U.S. Military Operations in the South China Sea and Their Tendencies," South China Sea Strategic Situation Probing Initiative, August 29, 2019.

Activity Type (Level 2)	Activity Subtype (Level 3)		Examples Since 2011 Relevant to the Competition with China
Changes to theater infrastructure	Military construction (MILCON) for U.S. bases, facilities	✓	USMC Base Camp Blaz opening (Guam)
	MILCON for host nation logistics and AOR support infrastructure	✓	Palau runway expansion project (2020)
Changes to theater equipment set	Amount and mix of prepositioned equipment and stocks in theater	✓	~26% of Pacific Deterrence Initiative (PDI) allocated to expanding prepositioning and logistics in the AOR
	Public demonstrations of new weapons technologies and research and development (R&D)	✓	DoD hypersonic weapons systems tests (2020–ongoing)
	Next-generation capability procurement in theater	✓	USN installing more directed energy weapons on 7th Fleet guided missile destroyers (DDGs) (2021)

a We have not identified instances of significant contractor augmentations, although we note that minor fluctuations are likely to have occurred and that it is possible that our data are incomplete.

Activity Type 3: Changes to Enabling Agreements

Our analysis identified seven major types of enabling agreements, at least six of which have been executed in the Asia-Pacific region since 2011:

- The United States has completed **new SOFAs**, such as the 25-year U.S.-Australia SOFA signed in November 2011, providing the legal basis for new USMC and USAF rotations to the continent.[198]
- DoD has recently completed other types of **basing access and visiting forces agreements** in the U.S. Indo-Pacific Command (INDOPACOM) since 2011, such as the EDCA signed with Singapore in December 2015 providing increased access to Changi Naval Base and Paya Lebar Air Base.[199]
- To ensure lines of communication (LOCs) to overseas bases and austere deployment locations, DoD also routinely seeks **overflight and transit rights agreements** from friendly countries in the event of contingency operations. Our research did not uncover any examples of new overflight or transit agreements signed in the AOR since 2011.
- To help sustain U.S. forward-deployed posture in the Indo-Pacific, DoD has also recently signed **mutual logistics support agreements** with new partners in the theater. For instance, in 2020, Washington and New Delhi completed the U.S.-India Logistics Exchange Memo of Agreement guaranteeing U.S. aircraft and ships access to Indian ports and airports for supplies and maintenance if necessary (and vice versa).

---

[198] The United States has also recently updated decades-old SOFAs with Japan in 2016 and South Korea in 2014 and 2019. As of 2020, the United States maintained 14 SOFAs in the theater. In the past, Washington has had SOFAs with Bangladesh and Nepal, though these are no longer in effect.

[199] Likewise, Washington and Manila signed a new EDCA in April 2014, providing the United States with access to five new air and training bases in the Philippines. More recently, the United States and Australia have made progress in negotiations with Papua New Guinea over access to Lombrum Naval Base and Momote Airport on Manus Island.

- To build partnerships and allow commanders to obtain and provide bilateral logistics support, supplies, and services to and from eligible countries and international organizations in the theater, DoD has signed a number of **ACSAs**. As of 2020, DoD maintained 16 such ACSAs with countries in INDOPACOM, compared with 46 in the U.S. European Command and more than 100 worldwide.[200]
- Washington has also completed multiple new **intelligence-sharing and information-sharing agreements** in the Indo-Pacific region since 2011. For instance, in November 2016, the United States, Japan, and South Korea signed the General Security of Military Information Agreement to foster trilateral military intelligence sharing.[201]
- Since 2011, DoD has completed multiple **other defense agreements and MOUs** to deepen ties with partners in the AOR. For instance, Washington signed updated defense MOUs with India and Singapore in 2015 and 2019, respectively.[202]

Activity Type 4: Changes to Deployed Force Structure

Building on enabling agreements, the U.S. defense posture in the Indo-Pacific can be enhanced by four types of changes to the deployed force structure:

- The United States can bolster **the authorized end strength and/or temporary deployed force strength** in the theater. Since the start of the Obama administration's Asia-Pacific rebalance in 2011, however, muscle movements of troops in INDOPACOM have been relatively minor by historical standards. The largest of these have numbered in the hundreds or low thousands, such as the incremental buildup of marines rotationally deployed to MRF-Darwin (from 200 in 2012 to 2,500 in 2019) or the Army's addition of a 400-person Multiple Launch Rocket System battalion to its 28,500-strong baseline posture in Korea in 2015.[203]
- DoD can also enhance its deployed force structure by altering **the mix of unit types (and capabilities) deployed to the theater**. For instance, for the first time, DoD deployed Navy Littoral Combat Ships and PA-8 anti-submarine Naval patrol aircraft to Singapore (in 2013 and 2017, respectively), Aegis-capable destroyers to Japan (in 2019), and fast-response Coast Guard Cutter Ships and two Triton drone units to Guam (in 2020).[204]

---

[200] U.S. Government Accountability Office, "Defense Logistics Agreements: DoD Should Improve Oversight and Seek Payment from Foreign Partners for Thousands of Orders It Identifies as Overdue," Washington, D.C., March 2020.

[201] Ju-Min Park, "South Korea, Japan Agree Intelligence-Sharing on North Korea Threat," Reuters, November 22, 2016.

[202] Likewise, in 2011, Washington and Hanoi signed an MOU regarding medical cooperation, the first bilateral military cooperation agreement between the two nations since the beginning of normalized relations in 1995; in 2012, the United States completed a new defense MOU with Mongolia; and in 2012, Washington and Bangkok signed (and later renewed in 2020) the Joint Vision Statement for the Thai-U.S. Defense Alliance.

[203] Megan Eckstein, "Marines Reach 2011 Goal of 2,500 in Darwin, with Addition of HIMARS Platoon, More to Current Rotation," *USNI News*, July 25, 2019; and Carla Babb, "U.S. Adds Rocket Launch Unit in South Korea," *Voice of America*, March 20, 2015.

[204] Gerry Doyle, "Maritime Patrol Aircraft Seen as Key in Asia, but Buyers Elusive," Reuters, February 28, 2018; Franz-Stefan Gady, "U.S. Navy Littoral Combat Ship Arrives in Singapore for Rotational Deployment," *The Diplomat*, July 9, 2019; Wyatt Olson, "A Third Fast-Response Coast Guard Cutter Heads to Guam as Tensions

- The individual services can also change their **unit deployment models within the AOR**. For example, in 2020, the 5th Security Forces Assistance Brigade became permanently assigned to the AOR, ending the previous rotational model that at times suffered from continuity problems, while in 2015, the Army's 2nd Infantry Division, which had been deployed Korea since 1965, shifted to a rotational model.[205]

- The joint force can augment the **forward-deployed mix of active duty (COMPO 1), national guard (COMPO 2), and reserve (COMPO 3) units** in INDOPACOM. For instance, in late 2011 the 658th Regional Support Group, U.S. Army Reserves, was activated and assigned permanently to Korea to relieve the Active Component (AC) from the duties of running base operations, in line with the Army Total Force Policy.[206]

- The U.S. military can pursue **changes to its C2 systems**. For instance, in recent years, INDOPACOM has reportedly been working with the Defense Advanced Research Program Agency on experimental technologies to implement the Joint All Domain Command and Control system as to command the joint force in the highly automated, fast-paced, and globalized battlefields of the future.

- To supplement the authorized end strength of U.S. military personnel assigned to INDOPACOM, DoD can alter **the levels of U.S. and foreign contractors employed** in the theater. We have found no evidence to suggest that the theater has seen a major shift in the ratio of contractors to military since 2011, and for key regional allies like Japan, for example, this ratio remains a fraction of that in U.S. Central Command.[207]

Activity Type 5: Changes to Theater Infrastructure

The U.S. defense posture in INDOPACOM can be enhanced by two types of changes to theater infrastructure:

- DoD can make **expansions and MILCON upgrades to U.S. bases and facilities**. Major projects in the AOR since 2011 include the opening of USMC Base Camp Blaz in 2020 and MILCON investments to USMC, USAF, and USN facilities in Australia.[208]

- DoD can also invest in **improvements to theater and host nation infrastructure**, including C2 nodes, airports, ports, and roads. For instance, in late 2020, a U.S. civil-military engineer joint task force completed a runway reconstruction and expansion project at Angaur Airfield, Palau, enabling the landing of C-17 aircraft.[209]

Simmer with China," *Stars and Stripes*, April 22, 2021; and Oriana Palwyk, "Navy's New Triton Maritime Surveillance Drones Arrive in Guam for 1st Deployment," *Military.com*, February 3, 2020.

[205] Sean Kimmons, "South Korea Rotations Give Soldiers Deployment, Cultural Experience," *Army.mil*, August 24, 2018.

[206] Brandon Balestrieri, "Reserves Guarantee Continuity to U.S. Operations," *Korea JoongAng Daily*, April 1, 2013.

[207] U.S. Forces Japan, "About USFJ," webpage, undated; and Mark Cancian, "U.S. Military Forces in FY 2020: SOF, Civilians, Contractors, and Nukes," Center for Strategic and International Studies, October 24, 2019.

[208] "Marine Corps Activates Camp Blaz in Guam," *Marines.mil*, October 1, 2020; and Colin Packham, "Australia Says U.S. Plans to Build Military Infrastructure," Reuters, July 30, 2019.

[209] Diehl estimates that about 35 percent of PDI funding will support regional infrastructure. See Justin Diehl, "Indo-Pacific Deterrence and the Quad in 2030," *Journal of Indo-Pacific Affairs*, Vol. 4, No. 2, Spring 2021, p. 111;

Activity Type 6: Changes to Theater Equipment Set

Finally, the U.S. military can enhance its defense posture through at least three activities related to changes in its theater equipment set:

- The joint force can reduce or expand **the amount and mix of prepositioned stocks and equipment** that it permanently maintains in theater. For instance, the head of Army Materiel Command recently stated that Army prepositioned stocks in INDOPACOM were inadequate, while Diehl estimates that about a quarter of near-future PDI funding will go to enhancing prepositioned stocks and theater logistics.[210]
- The U.S. military can conduct **public demonstrations of new capabilities and weapons systems** in the Asia-Pacific region. For instance, the United States has recently conducted highly publicized tests on hypersonic missiles, including from Hawaii in March 2020.[211]
- DoD can enhance its defense posture through **acquisition and deployment of next-generation weapons capabilities**. As one example, in 2021, the Navy reported installing directed-energy weapons in its DDGs in the Asia-Pacific theater, which could be used for jamming and lasing Chinese aircraft and vessels.[212]

Presence and Theater-Shaping

The third activity-type category in our typology (presence and theater-shaping) distinguishes between four major types of activities—expeditionary and declaratory activities; garrisoned presence activities; intelligence, reconnaissance, and surveillance activities; and unilateral exercises and training activities—as well as 19 key activity subtypes, summarized in Table 5.4.

Table 5.4. Detailed Typology of U.S. Theater Presence and Shaping Activities

Activity Type (Level 2)	Activity Subtype (Level 3)		Examples Since 2011 Relevant to the Competition with China
Expeditionary and declaratory activities	FONOPs	✓	SCS FONOPs (10) and Taiwan Strait transits (13) broke records in 2020
	Long-range bomber and fighter aircraft overflight missions	✓	SCS bomber overflights in 2020 (~17) down steeply from 2018 (~30)
	Intercept and interdiction missions	✓	USCS cutter patrol of ECS claiming embargo enforcement of the Democratic People's Republic of Korea (2019)
	Escort and asset protection missions	✓	Manned and unmanned close air support for ISR missions

---

and Meghann Myers, "Small Rotations to Far-Flung Southeast Asian Countries Are Likely the Future of INDO-PACOM Assignments," *Military Times*, October 8, 2020.

[210] Jen Judson, "US Army Wants to Expand Pre-Positioned Stock in Pacific," *Defense News*, February 4, 2020; and Justin Diehl, "Indo-Pacific Deterrence and the Quad in 2030," *Journal of Indo-Pacific Affairs*, Vol. 4, No. 2, Spring 2021, p. 111.

[211] Sam LaGrone, "Pentagon Test Launches Prototype Hypersonic Weapon," *USNI News*, March 20, 2020.

[212] Megan Eckstein, "Navy Installing More Directed Energy Weapons on DDGs, Conducting Land-Based Laser Testing This Year," *USNI News*, April 7, 2021.

Activity Type (Level 2)	Activity Subtype (Level 3)		Examples Since 2011 Relevant to the Competition with China
	Commercial and environment protection patrols and missions	✓	Routine USN, USAF patrols of illegal fishing in SCS; securing maritime LOCs for trade
	Naval port visits	✓	First CSG to Vietnam since 1970s (2019)
Garrisoned presence activities	Continuous bomber presence missions (CBPMs)	✓	Guam CBPM (2004–2020)
	Ground-based air defense monitoring, A2/AD activities	✓	THAAD batteries shifted to INDOPACOM (2020)
	Strategic deterrence; ICBM, nuclear triad readiness activities	✓	Ground-Based Strategic Deterrent contract awarded (2020) to start replacing aging Minutemen III ICBM system by 2029
	Strategic airlift and rapid mobility readiness activities	✓	Army airlift training to overcome AOR's unique tyranny of distance (vs. roads/rails)
	Theater sustainment and support logistics	✓	8th Theater Sustainment Command's embrace of "predictive logistics" to prepare for large-scale combat operations (2019)
	Theater force protection and basing security activities	✓	Establishment of Joint Counter–Small Unmanned Aerial Systems (C-sUAS) Office (2019)
	Operational security, cyberspace defense, electronic protection activities	✓	U.S. Cyber Command expanded "hunt forward ops" aimed at PRC hackers (2020)
ISR activities	Overflight and naval surface ISR patrols (manned, unmanned)	✓	1,000+ annual in-close coastal ISR sorties
	Submarine oceanographic data collection and survey missions	✓	~10 major vessels from Military Sealift Command in SCS (2019)
	Launch of satellite constellations, semi-autonomous spying assets, and other space-based ISR assets	✓	Proposed PDI funding for space-based persistent radar constellation
	Private contractor ISR overflight missions	✓	Dozens of reported annual sorties over SCS, ECS, Yellow Sea
Unilateral exercises and training activities	Annual or periodic deployed joint force training exercises	✓	Defender Pacific Exercise; 7th Fleet alone conducts hundreds of drills in and around SCS annually
	Routine unit-level training programs	✓	Forward deployed train-ups at Rodriguez Live Fire Complex (Korea)

Activity Type 7: Expeditionary Activities and Declaratory Actions

Our analysis identified six types of expeditionary theater-shaping activities and declaratory actions regularly conducted by the joint force—primarily in the air and naval domains (but often supported by units and logisticians in the ground, space, and cyber domains):

- The USN and USAF both conduct routine **FONOPs**. In INDOPACOM, the United States has been steadily increasing the frequency and varying the characteristics of its SCS, ECS, and Yellow Sea FONOPs—as well as Taiwan Strait transits—over the past decade.
- The USAF performs **long-range bomber and fighter aircraft overflights** to assert its airspace rights. Since 2004, rotating bombers have often conducted dozens of sorties annually over strategic waterways and disputed maritime areas, including some 30 B-52 sorties in the SCS in 2018, a level "which has rarely been seen since the end of the Cold War."[213]
- The USN, U.S. Coast Guard (USCG), and USAF conduct **intercept and interdiction missions and patrols** throughout INDOPACOM. This line of efforts includes countering transnational criminal activities such as piracy, weapons smuggling, human trafficking, narcotics trafficking, and other maritime crimes, though these activities have not targeted the Chinese navy or maritime militia.
- The USN, USCG, and USAF conduct **escort and asset protection missions** throughout INDOPACOM, including manned and unmanned close air support for ISR and other mission sets. Notably, in recent years, this activity subtype has become a new area of bilateral cooperation. Between 2019 and 2020, for instance, the number of combined asset protection missions conducted by the United States and Japan grew from 14 to 25 missions in defense of U.S. ships or planes.[214]
- The USN, USCG, and USAF conduct persistent **commercial and environmental protection patrols and missions**, such as monitoring offshore competition for fisheries, energy, and minerals; securing vital maritime trade routes from piracy, smuggling, and trafficking; and assisting in laying and protecting commercial underwater cables.
- DoD utilizes symbolic **naval port visits** to exercise power and increase U.S. influence in the theater. In March 2018, for instance, the USS *Carl Vinson* carrier paid a port call to Vietnam—the first carrier visit since the end of the Vietnam War.[215]

Activity Type 8: Garrisoned Presence and Force Protection Activities

Our analysis further identified seven primary types of garrisoned presence and force protection activities conducted across multiple domains:

- Related to expeditionary overflights, the Air Force has at times maintained **CBPMs** as "a cornerstone of U.S. power projection and deterrence capabilities" in the Asia-Pacific.[216] Recently, the USAF deployed a CBPM to Guam and Diego Garcia from 2004 until April

---

[213] Hu Bo, "Six Categories of U.S. Military Operations in the South China Sea and Their Tendencies," South China Sea Strategic Situation Probing Initiative, August 29, 2019.

[214] Brad Lendon, "Japan Increases Protection for US Military amid 'Severe Security Environment,'" *CNN*, February 24, 2021.

[215] Jim Garamone, "Aircraft Carrier USS *Carl Vinson* Makes Vietnam Port Call," U.S. Department of Defense, March 5, 2018.

[216] Joseph Trevithick, "The Air Force Abruptly Ends Its Continuous Bomber Presence on Guam After 16 Years," *The Drive*, April 17, 2020.

2020, when these strategic bombers were withdrawn to CONUS to improve resilience and operational unpredictability, per the new Dynamic Force Employment CONOP.[217]

- The Army maintains primary responsibility for **enhancements to ground-based air defense and A2/AD readiness activities**. Expanded activities in this area have included the shift of THAAD batteries to Guam in 2013 and to South Korea in 2017.[218]

- The joint force can also make enhancements to its **strategic deterrence and nuclear triad activities**, including enhancements to its intercontinental and medium-range ballistic and conventional missile capabilities (i.e., ongoing upgrades from the aging LGM-30 Minutemen III ICBM system to the future Ground-Based Strategic Deterrent system) and nuclear submarine fleet.[219]

- The joint force regularly conducts **strategic airlift and rapid mobility readiness activities**, training to overcome the AOR's unique mobility challenges in which materiel and personnel must be moved without roads or rails.

- As a broad garrisoned presence activity, the Army builds resilience to **theater sustainment activities and logistics support to the joint force**. In preparing for "logistics under attack," this enduring Army requirement entails not only lifelining materiel such as weapons, equipment, food, and fuel but also responsibility for sustainment activities in support of the joint force, such as postal services, medical services, mortuary affairs, signals, engineering, ammunition resupply, and Joint Reception, Staging, Onward Movement, and Integration Plan activities.

- Enhancing **theater force protection** is another essential garrisoned presence activity to compete effectively in the future. For instance, DoD recently deployed new counter–unmanned aerial systems (C-UAS) technologies to INDOPACOM as well as establishing the Joint C-sUAS Office (JCO) in 2019 to lead, synchronize, and direct DoD's C-sUAS activities in the Asia-Pacific and other theaters.[220]

- Relatedly, **enhancements to cyber security and operational security activities** are vital activities to maintain competitive advantages in other areas. Indeed, U.S. Cyber

---

[217] Brian Everstine, "Air Force Ends Continuous Bomber Presence in Guam," *Air Force Magazine*, April 17, 2020; and Brian Everstine, "AFGSC's New Plan to Deploy Bombers Across the Globe," *Air Force Magazine*, April 29, 2020.

[218] Malcolm Cohens-Ashley, "U.S. Army's Only Forward-Stationed Multi-Component Air Defense Task Force," U.S. Indo-Pacific Command, February 7, 2019; and Jonathon Daniell, "THAAD Battery Reflags to Align with Air Defense Artillery Brigade in South Korea," U.S. Indo-Pacific Command, October 23, 2017. In addition, the United States has pulled multiple Patriot batteries and a THAAD battery from U.S. Central Command between 2018 and 2021 as part of a shift in focus toward China and Russia. See Nancy A. Youssef and Gordon Lubold, "On Iran, White House Criticism Grows, but U.S. Military Posture Recedes," *Wall Street Journal*, October 1, 2018; Daniel Cebul, "U.S. to Remove Several Missile Defense Systems from the Middle East," *Defense News*, September 26, 2018; Gordon Lubold, Nancy A. Youssef, and Michael R. Gordon, "U.S. Military to Withdraw Hundreds of Troops, Aircraft, Antimissile Batteries from Middle East," *Wall Street Journal*, June 18, 2021; and Rebecca Kheel, "Pentagon Pulling 'Certain Forces and Capabilities,' Including Air Defense, from Middle East," *The Hill*, June 18, 2021.

[219] Nick Adde, "Minuteman III Replacement Program Moves Toward Next Phase," *National Defense Magazine*, November 2, 2018.

[220] DoD, *Counter-Small Unmanned Aircraft Systems Strategy*, Washington, D.C., 2021.

Command took a much more aggressive posture ahead of the 2020 elections, expanding its "hunt forward ops" aimed hackers from China and elsewhere.[221]

Activity Type 9: Intelligence, Surveillance, and Reconnaissance Activities

We distinguish between four general subcategories of ISR activities:

- The United States conducts frequent **manned and unmanned overflight ISR patrols** in the Indo-Pacific. According to public estimates, in recent years the United States has typically conducted 1,000 to 1,200 in-close ISR sorties of China's coast—the most of any area in the world—compared with only about 260 in 2009.[222]
- The USN also routinely conducts **manned and unmanned submarine and surface ISR and data-collection missions**. This includes deployment of missile range instrumentation ships and oceanographic survey and surveillance ships focused on "research and hydrological survey to obtain accurate and detailed battlefield information like submarine topography, shallow seabed sections, and seabed surface geology, as well as temperature, density, and salinity of sea water."[223]
- To become more competitive operating in the gray zone, DoD has increasingly employed **private contractors to conduct ISR overflight patrols** in the Asia-Pacific theater. In 2020, for instance, at least 200 of these civilian ISR sorties were reported over the SCS, ECS, Yellow Sea, and Taiwan Strait.[224]
- We also include in this category theater-level activities to **maintain and support space-based ISR assets**, such as additions of new ground-based radars and sensors like those that have been proposed in Palau and Guam under the PDI.

Activity Type 10: Unilateral Exercises and Training Activities

The fourth and final category under theater presence and shaping activities includes two subtypes of unilateral exercises and training:

- The United States conducts **periodic deployed joint training exercises and wargames**. For instance, the Defender Pacific Exercise is one of the joint force's largest annual training exercises designed to demonstrate strategic readiness.
- The joint force also shapes the theater to compete with China by conducting **routine unit train-ups and exercises** while forward-deployed to the AOR. Regular in-theater training occurs, for instance, at the Rodriguez Live Fire Complex (South Korea), Pilsung Range

---

[221] Zachary Cohen, "U.S. Cyber Command Expands Operations Against Russia, China and Iran," *CNN*, November 3, 2020.

[222] SCSPI, "60 Sorties of U.S. Surveillance Planes Flew 'Upwind' to Spy on China in September," October 12, 2020; SCSPI, *An Incomplete Report on U.S. Military Activities in the South China Sea in 2020*, Beijing: Peking University, March 12, 2021, pp. 12–21; National Institute for South China Sea Studies, *Report on the Military Presence of the United States of America in the Asia-Pacific Region*, Beijing, November 2016, pp. 28–36; and Hu Bo, "Six Categories of U.S. Military Operations in the South China Sea and Their Tendencies," South China Sea Strategic Situation Probing Initiative, August 29, 2019.

[223] Hu Bo, "Six Categories of U.S. Military Operations in the South China Sea and Their Tendencies," South China Sea Strategic Situation Probing Initiative, August 29, 2019.

[224] SCSPI, "U.S. Flying Civilian Contractor Aircraft to Monitor China," November 18, 2020.

(South Korea), Joint Iwakuni Training Range (Japan), and Draughon Range (Japan), as well as major ranges in Misawa and Okinawa.

Security Cooperation

The fourth activity-type category in our typology (security cooperation) distinguishes between three major types of activities—combined exercises and training, materiel military assistance, and foreign military exchanges—as well as 11 activity subtypes, shown in Table 5.5.

Table 5.5. Detailed Typology of U.S. Security Cooperation Activities

Activity Type (Level 2)	Activity Subtype (Level 3)		Examples Since 2011 Relevant to the Competition with China
Combined exercise and training activities	Annual or periodic bilateral or multilateral training exercises	✓	RIMPAC, Cobra Gold; 1st U.S.-UK combined naval exercise in SCS (2019)
	Persistent or routine allied or partner technical training	✓	USAF–Royal Australian Air Force Enhanced Air Cooperation (2017); MRF-Darwin (2012)
	Military-to-military trust-building exercises with adversary	✓	U.S.-PRC drug interdiction and other programs under cooperative threat reduction program (ended in 2015)
Materiel military assistance	Arms and equipment sales and donations (foreign military sales [FMS], Excess Defense Articles)	✓	$8B deal w/ Taiwan (2019), end of Vietnam embargo (2016)
	Foreign military financing (FMF)	✓	~$640M FMF to AOR annually (fiscal year [FY] 2012–2018 average)
	Other military assistance programs and accounts	✓	~$760M other to AOR annually (FY 2012–2018 average)
	Cooperative R&D programs	✓	U.S.-India Defense Trade and Technology Initiative
Foreign military exchanges	High-level military diplomacy	✓	Quad; U.S.-Japan "2+2"
	Combined military command arrangements	✓	Combined Space Operations Center (2018)
	Officer educational exchange programs (international military education and training [IMET], service academies)	✓	~$105M IMET to AOR annually (FY 2012–2018 average)
	Officer exchange tours; ship-rider and flight-rider programs	✓	USCG's Shiprider program (since 2010)

Activity Type 11: Combined Exercises and Training Activities

We first distinguish between three major types of bilateral or multilateral training exercises:

- The United States conducts dozens of **major annual or periodic wargames and exercises with partners and allies in foreign theaters** to increase security cooperation, prepare for large-scale combat operations and contingencies, and build regional influence.[225] This activity subtype includes major annual or biennial multilateral and bilateral exercises, such as the biennial RIMPAC exercise involving some ten nations and the annual U.S.-Thai Cobra Gold exercise. It also includes periodic (nonrecurring) combined training activities in the theater, such as the first U.S.-British combined naval exercises conducted in the SCS in January 2019 and the first U.S.-ASEAN combined naval exercise held in September 2019.[226]

- The United States also conducts smaller **persistent, targeted technical training programs** with partners and hosts. For instance, in 2019, U.S. Forces Korea and ROK forces conducted nearly 100 conventional training exercises together.[227] DoD has also begun major new long-term technical training programs in recent years, like the USAF–Royal Australian Air Force's Enhanced Air Cooperation program launched in 2017.[228]

- To potentially de-escalate strategic competition, the Pentagon can also conduct **military-to-military trust-building exercises with adversaries**. While the United States has not done much in this area over the last decade vis-à-vis China, it did pursue a few such activities during the Obama administration. For instance, until 2015, Washington and Beijing cooperated on drug interdiction operations funded by the Cooperative Threat Reduction program account.[229] Likewise, in 2014 and 2016, the Obama administration invited China to participate in RIMPAC to help build mutual military-to-military trust, but China was subsequently disinvited by the Trump administration in 2018.[230]

Activity Type 12: Materiel Military Assistance

The second major type of U.S. security cooperation—materiel military assistance—consists of four subtypes:

- The United States can increase or decrease its **arms sales and donations to regional partners and allies,** namely through DoD's FMS account and, to a much lesser extent, its Excess Defense Articles account. For instance, in the past decade of competition with

---

[225] According to National Institute for South China Sea Studies estimates, for instance, in 2015 the U.S. Pacific Command conducted some 175 bilateral and multilateral exercises across all domains. See National Institute for South China Sea Studies, *Report on the Military Presence of the United States of America in the Asia-Pacific Region*, Beijing, November 2016, pp. 45–60.

[226] Tim Kelly, "U.S., UK Conduct First Joint Drills in Contested South China Sea," Reuters, January 16, 2019; and Dzirhan Mahadzir, "Inaugural AUMX Exercise Seeks to Deepen U.S.-ASEAN Maritime Cooperation," *USNI News*, September 3, 2019.

[227] National Institute for South China Sea Studies, *The U.S. Military Presence in the Asia-Pacific 2020*, Beijing, June 2020, p. 49.

[228] The Enhanced Air Cooperation program, for instance, is designed to help integrate fifth-generation fighters, C-17 aircraft repair and maintenance, C-130J aeromedical evacuation, refueling of F-16D and F-22 fighters, and other logistics training.

[229] Yong-an Zhang, "Asia, International Drug Trafficking, and U.S.-China Counternarcotics Cooperation," Washington, D.C.: Brookings Institution, February 10, 2012.

[230] John Hudson, "Congressman: Obama Is Letting China Steal U.S. Military Secrets," *Foreign Policy*, June 4, 2013; and Helene Cooper, "U.S. Disinvites China from Military Exercise amid Rising Tensions," *New York Times*, May 23, 2018.

China, the largest single such activity, by far, was DoD's $8 billion sale of fighter jets to Taiwan in 2019.[231]

- The United States also **directly funds partner defense ministries** through the State Department's FMF program. Between FY 2012 and 2019, FMF obligated to the AOR averaged about $91 million annually.[232]
- The United States **provides other types of materiel military and security assistance to regional partners** through a host of smaller DoD accounts, such as the Cooperative Threat Reduction Account. Between FY 2012 and FY 2019, cumulative military assistance in these programs flowed to the AOR at rate of about $125 million annually.[233]
- The United States provides (and accesses) materiel military assistance through the **conduct of cooperative R&D programs**, both through government agencies and private contractors. For instance, in 2012, DoD created the U.S. Defense Technology and Trade Initiative as a mechanism to deepen defense R&D cooperation with India by reducing bureaucratic impediments.[234]

Activity Type 13: Foreign Military Exchanges

The third and final major type of U.S. security cooperation—foreign military exchanges—consists of four subtypes:

- The United States can leverage **high-level military diplomacy** to manage escalation and compete effectively. In recent years, for example, such exchanges have included the Quad, the U.S.-Japan Security Consultative Committee (U.S.-Japan 2+2), and the U.S.-India 2+2 Ministerial Dialogue.
- DoD can enhance its use of **combined military commands**. Recent examples affecting the Asia-Pacific AOR include the 2018 creation of the Combined Space Operations Center (in CONUS); the planning of a future U.S.-Japan "command center for space,

---

[231] Not surprisingly, the top recipients of FMS in INDOPACOM, as measured by five-year annual average amounts (FY 2016–FY 2020), include the AOR's more advanced militaries: Japan ($3.9 billion), Taiwan ($3.3 billion), South Korea ($2.0 billion), Australia ($1.5 billion), India ($1.1 billion), New Zealand ($0.4 billion), and Singapore ($0.4 billion), followed by 15 other nations at $0.1 billion or less. Data are from Defense Security Cooperation Agency, *Historical Sales Book: Fiscal Years 1950–2020*, 2020.

[232] The list of top FMF recipients is notably different than top FMS recipients, with some 88 percent obligated to just three nations during this period, all bordering the SCS: the Philippines ($417 million), Indonesia ($130 million), and Vietnam ($94 million). Obligated dollars are measured in constant 2019 U.S. dollars. Data are from U.S. Agency for International Development, *U.S. Overseas Loans and Grants: Obligations and Loan Authorizations, July 1, 1945–September 30, 2019*, Washington, D.C., 2021.

[233] Over FY 2012–FY 2019, some 80 percent of "other military aid" obligated to the AOR was obligated to a similar list of SCS countries as the top FMF recipients: the Philippines ($418 million), Malaysia ($175 million), Vietnam ($116 million), and Indonesia ($92 million). Obligated dollars are measured in constant 2019 U.S. dollars. Data are from ForeignAssistance.gov, homepage, 2021.

[234] Office of the Executive Director for International Cooperation, "U.S.–India Defense Technology and Trade Initiative (DTTI)," U.S. Department of Defense, undated.

cyberspace, and electronic warfare"; and ongoing progress toward transitioning to a ROK-led future combined forces command in Korea.[235]

- The Pentagon can alter trends in **officer educational exchanges**, including offering of service academy scholarships and foreign military exchanges falling under the IMET program. For instance, each year between FY 2012 and FY 2019, hundreds of foreign officers hailing from some 22 Asia-Pacific countries (including China) received an annual average of about $16 million in IMET scholarships and funding, according to ForeignAssistance.gov data.[236]

- DoD can increase or change patterns in **officer exchange tours and programs**. For instance, the Coast Guard's Shiprider program, which has been ongoing with some 11 Pacific Island nations since 2010, stands as a notable model for future efforts to expand security cooperation and law enforcement activities.[237]

Military Operations and Kinetic Activities

The fifth and final top-level activity-type category in our typology (military operations and kinetic activities) distinguishes between six major types of activities—direct U.S. and coalition military interventions; proxy warfare operations; kinetic deterrence operations; demonstrations of force and crisis response operations; soft power and civil-military operations; and irregular, covert, and asymmetric warfare operations—as well as 28 activity subtypes. Unlike the previous four top-level categories, U.S. activities in the Indo-Pacific region since 2011 have not included most of these, as summarized in Table 5.6. While many of the subtypes omitted in this table involve higher-intensity conflict and have clearly not been utilized in the competition with China since 2011, other options involving more-covert actions may be more difficult to fully assess at the unclassified level, such as cyber or military deception (MILDEC) operations. Given the absence of acknowledged operations in these areas, we mark these as omitted in this table as well.

---

[235] Joint Force Space Component Command, "Combined Space Operations Center Established at Vandenberg AFB," July 19, 2018; Brian Everstine, "US, South Korea Prepare for Transfer of Wartime Operational Control," *Air Force Magazine*, March 18, 2021; and National Institute for South China Sea Studies, *The U.S. Military Presence in the Asia-Pacific 2020*, Beijing, June 2020, p. 63.

[236] ForeignAssistance.gov, homepage, 2021 (accessed August 8, 2021).

[237] Warren N. Wright, "Shiprider Program," *Indo-Pacific Defense Forum*, January 27, 2020.

Table 5.6. Detailed Typology of U.S. Military Operations and Kinetic Activities

Activity Type (Level 2)	Activity Subtype (Level 3)		Examples Since 2011 Relevant to the Competition with China
Direct U.S. and coalition military interventions	High-intensity warfare	✗	—
	Counterinsurgency-centric (COIN-centric) or counterterrorism-centric (CT-centric) warfare	✗	—
	Limited air and naval strikes	✗	—
Proxy warfare operations	Support to nonstate actors	✗	—
	Military advisory and assistance group (MAAG) support to states	✗	—[a]
	Employment of private military corporations (PMCs)	✗	—
Kinetic deterrence operations	No-fly zones and air policing missions	✗	—
	Military blockades	✗	—
	Interpositional ground deployments	✗	—
	Missile/fires warning shots	✗	—
	Military use of space	✗	—
Demonstrations of force and crisis response operations	CSG movements	✗	—
	Air armada movements	✗	—
	Ground force amassing on borders	✗	—
	Defense readiness condition (DEFCON) status changes	✗	—
Soft power and civil-military operations	Peacekeeping, peace enforcement, and stability operations	✗	—
	Military observer and arms control verification missions	✓	Strategic Arms Reduction Treaty and Intermediate Range Nuclear Forces Treaty verification missions
	Emergency humanitarian and disaster relief operations	✓	Earthquake and typhoon relief in the Philippines (2012, 2013)
	Enduring medical and humanitarian assistance programs	✓	Pacific Partnership mission (2006–); Civic Action Team Palau (1970–)
	Search-and-rescue (S&R) missions	✓	Thailand cave S&R (2018); Japanese F-35A pilot S&R (2019)
	Noncombatant evacuation operations (NEOs) and other civilian airlift/sealift	✗	—
Irregular, covert, and asymmetric, warfare operations	Military coups, assassination plots, kidnappings, and hostage-taking	✗	—
	Information, influence, psychological operations, and other political warfare	✓	JTF Indo-Pacific program to counter PRC disinformation campaigns
	MILDEC activities	✗	—

Activity Type (Level 2)	Activity Subtype (Level 3)		Examples Since 2011 Relevant to the Competition with China
	Lawfare operations	✓	Legal action to counter Chinese industrial espionage of U.S. defense industrial base
	Counter-economic military activities abroad, offensive intellectual property theft, etc.	✗	—
	Electronic warfare (EW), artificial intelligence operations	✗	—
	Cyber warfare operations	✗	—

[a] In 2017, a U.S. advisory group returned to the Philippines as part of Operation Pacific Eagle—Philippines to help counter terrorist/separatist groups. Although this is an example of MAAG support, because the target of the operation was the Islamic State in Iraq and Syria, rather than a Chinese-backed proxy, we did not identify this as an example of this activity being used in the competition with China. See Sean W. O'Donnell, Matthew S. Klimow, and Ann Calvaresi Barr, *Operation Pacific Eagle—Philippines: Lead Inspector General Report to the United States Congress*, Washington, D.C.: U.S. Department of Defense, U.S. Department of State, and U.S. Agency for International Development, July 1– September 30, 2020.

Activity Type 14: Direct U.S. and Coalition Military Interventions

The first category of operational and kinetic activities covers direct U.S. and coalition military interventions, broken into three primary subtypes. At least since the end of hostilities in the Korean War in 1953, DoD has not conducted any of these activities against a great power (including China and the USSR):

- The United States can conduct **high-intensity warfare**, including the spectrum ranging from conventional warfare to sustained air and naval bombing campaigns to chemical, biological, radiological, and nuclear warfare. During the Cold War, the Pentagon launched high-intensity conventional operations against Soviet partners and client states (e.g., the Soviet-backed Viet Cong, 1962–1975).
- The Pentagon can also use combat forces to conduct **lower-intensity COIN or CT operations**. Both during and after the Cold War, the United States occasionally conducted kinetic COIN and CT operations against insurgent and terrorist groups supported by peer or near-peer adversaries (e.g., Iranian-backed insurgents in Iraq, 2003– ongoing).
- Short of high- or low-intensity combat operations, DoD can also conduct **limited kinetic air and naval strikes**, either with manned or unmanned assets. The only precedents for limited U.S. strikes have been against the territory or military assets of less-capable rivals, such as Syria (1983), Libya (1986), and Sudan/Afghanistan (1998).

Activity Type 15: Proxy Warfare Operations

The Pentagon can also conduct indirect military operations (offensive and defensive) through foreign proxies. Though the United States has not conducted any (known) proxy warfare operations against China since 2011, it made extensive use of this activity category during the Cold War, with historical examples falling into three broad categories:

- Washington has conducted offensive proxy warfare by providing **direct or indirect military support (advising, equipment, cash, etc.) to violent nonstate actors** engaged in political conflict (insurgencies, terrorism) against a third-party regime aligned with or supported by a major U.S. adversary. For instance, U.S. Central Intelligence Agency (CIA) and DoD support to the Afghan Mujahideen and Nicaragua Contras in the 1980s was largely designed to contain the expansion of Soviet influence in those regions.

- The United States can also conduct defensive proxy warfare campaigns by providing **direct or indirect military support to partner states or client regimes** that may be confronted by domestic political violence/opposition supported by a major U.S. adversary. Historically, these programs have taken the form of MAAGs, such as the ones deployed to counter Soviet/communist influences in Greece (1947–1950) and Indochina (1950–1962).[238]

- DoD can also operate in the gray zone by conducting **contract warfare operations through PMCs**. In the past decade, Washington has extensively utilized PMCs (e.g., DynCorp, Blackwater) for defensive security operations as well as training and advising in other theaters, but it has not used PMCs in activities in INDOPACOM.

Activity Type 16: Kinetic Deterrence Operations

While the Pentagon has conducted a wide range of deterrence activities since 2011 designed to discourage China from taking unwanted military or political actions, it has not conducted what we more narrowly define as *kinetic deterrence operations*, including the following:

- The United States can conduct **air policing missions or enforcing no-fly zones** to reinforce redlines in the theater—as it did with the establishment of the North Atlantic Treaty Organization's (NATO's) first Air Policing mission in 1961 designed to preserve the integrity of allied airspace, or in no-fly zones executed in Iraq and Yugoslavia during the 1990s.

- As a form of kinetic deterrence, DoD can enforce **military blockades, primarily in the naval domain**. The United States deployed naval assets to blockade Soviet client states and kinetically enforce embargoes multiple times during the Cold War (e.g., the Cuban Missile Crisis).

- In the ground domain, DoD's menu of kinetic deterrence options primarily includes the **deployment of interpositional ground forces**. Historical examples against lesser adversaries include the deployment of U.S. troops to Multinational Force and Observers Sinai to Egypt since 1982 and the rapid buildup of U.S. forces along the Saudi-Iraq border in 1990–1991.[239]

- At potentially lower escalatory levels, commanders can conduct **warning shots/missile fires** as acts of kinetic deterrence. Unlike China, DoD has not done so in the Indo-Pacific since 2011, but it has done so recently to deter less capable rivals (i.e., Iran in May 2021).

- DoD can also use space to conduct military activities as a means of kinetic deterrence, including terrestrial-based activities that target space-based assets such as anti-satellite (ASAT) weapons tests. If DoD has pursued any such activities designed to compete with

---

[238] While the United States has not deployed any MAAGs since 2011 aimed directly at countering regional Chinese influence in the Asia-Pacific, we note that in 2017 the Pentagon resumed its "MAAG-like" support for ongoing COIN/CT operations in the Philippines under Operation Pacific Eagle.

[239] Because of the force protection and escalatory risks involved, the Pentagon never deployed large interpositional formations to conflict fault lines to directly block Red Army movements.

China since 2011, they would likely be classified and limited by international treaties and law (i.e., the Outer Space Treaty of 1967).[240]

Activity Type 17: Crisis Response Demonstrations of Force

DoD planners' toolbox also includes mass demonstrations of force in all domains, particularly in the context of crisis responses. Since 2011, DoD has not conducted any such maneuvers in the Indo-Pacific to communicate resolve, but Cold War precedents abound:

- In part to contain Soviet influence globally, the USN repeatedly conducted **rapid carrier battle group movements and other warship buildups** near the littorals of an international crisis to send political signals not only to the conflict participants, but also to Moscow. For instance, the USN deployed multiple CSGs to assert U.S. resolve during the Tanchen Islands incident (1955) and the Suez Crisis (1956).
- Less frequently, USAF conducted **rapid air armada movements** in moments of Cold War crisis, such as aerial demonstrations of force during Operation Paul Bunyan (1976).
- Also relatively infrequently, the Army conducted **rapid ground force buildups or border amassments** to counter communist threats in moments of Cold War crisis, including landings during the Lebanon Crisis of 1958 and the Thailand-Laos Crisis of 1962.
- As a final crisis response activity, DoD can alter **DEFCON levels**, as in the Cuban Missile Crisis (1962).

Activity Type 18: Soft Power and Civil-Military Operations

Unlike the preceding types of military operations, the United States has conducted some limited civil-military and soft power operations in the Indo-Pacific region since 2011, which may improve its competitive standing vis-à-vis PRC regional influence by increasing the appeal of American culture, policies, and political ideals:

- While the United States has not deployed troops to any civil-military **peacekeeping and stabilization operations** in INDOPACOM since 2011, it has contributed to regional peacekeeping via the State-DoD Global Peace Operations Initiative, training peacekeepers from more than a dozen Indo-Pacific states since 2004.[241]
- DoD also often provides military observers and DoD civilians for more-limited **military observer and arms control verification missions**.
- The interagency routinely conducts civil-military operations in the form of **humanitarian and disaster relief missions** (e.g., Philippines typhoon relief in 2012, Indonesia earthquake and tsunami relief in 2018, and Mariana Islands typhoon relief in 2018).

---

[240] The last (publicly known) American ASAT test was conducted in 2008, in direct response to a Chinese ASAT test conducted in 2007. Beyond ASAT capabilities, in the future such activities could include the deployment of DoD (or private-sector) satellites armed with directed-energy or other kinetics weapons; semiautonomous orbital platforms armed with nonkinetic jamming, lasing, and EW/electromagnetic spectrum; or other cyberattack capabilities.

[241] Nina M. Serafino, "The Global Peace Operations Initiative: Background and Issues for Congress," Washington, D.C.: Congressional Research Service, June 11, 2009.

- DoD also has assisted with recent **S&R missions**, such as the Thailand cave rescue in 2018 and the search for missing pilot of Japanese F-35 in 2019.
- Beyond disaster relief and emergency aid, the U.S. military can further wield soft power by conducting **routine and ongoing medical, engineering, and humanitarian assistance operations** in the region. For instance, since 2007, the USAF has led Pacific Angel, an annual event offering "general health services (such as dental, optometry and pediatrics), engineering programs, as well as various exchanges among subject matter experts."[242]
- The Pentagon—often in coordination with the State Department—conducts **NEOs, medical evacuation missions, and other civilian repatriation and airbridge/sealift missions**, including hostage rescue operations and transport of refugees and the displaced. While DoD has not conducted any major NEOs in the Indo-Pacific since 2011, it regularly trains for large-scale future NEOs in the theater (i.e., evacuating 150,000 Americans from South Korea).

Activity Type 19: Asymmetric, Irregular, and Covert Warfare Activities

The ongoing and historical records of potential asymmetric, irregular, and covert activities are necessarily opaque and possibly largely classified. Unless otherwise noted, we assume that the following activity subtypes have not been conducted against China in the past decade.

- Throughout the early Cold War, the United States affected regime change by providing covert (namely, CIA) support **to military coups and assassination plots** in states threatened by Soviet influence or leftist ideologies (e.g., Guatemala in 1954, Congo in 1961).
- Covertly or overtly, the United States can conduct **information/influence/psychological operations and other forms of political warfare**. To these ends, U.S. Special Operations Command has recently acknowledged the creation of a Joint Task Force Indo-Pacific team "focused on information and influence operations in the Pacific theater."[243]
- Closely related to disinformation, DoD can invest in **MILDEC activities** designed to cause the enemy to use its finite resources unwisely or uneconomically. However, since the days of Patton's Ghost Army in World War II, U.S. MILDEC capabilities have atrophied while becoming more difficult technologically.
- The United States (namely the Department of Justice) has increasingly **employed rule-based "lawfare"** in a defensive capacity—for instance, to prosecute Chinese industrial espionage. However, it has not yet embraced (more-provocative) offensive lawfare operations, nor has the Joint Chiefs yet codified the use of lawfare in DoD doctrine and strategy.
- Similarly, U.S. defense planners can embrace **offensive economic warfare operations**. Our analysis found no publicly known examples of recent such activities against China.

---

[242] National Institute for South China Sea Studies, *The U.S. Military Presence in the Asia-Pacific 2020*, Beijing, June 2020, p. 53.

[243] Mark Pomerleau, "Special Operations Team in Pacific Will Confront Chinese Information Campaigns," *Army Times*, March 25, 2021.

- Either in isolation or as part of larger kinetic operations, DoD can conduct asymmetric or irregular activities related to **control of the electromagnetic spectrum, EW, and other uses of artificial intelligence**. Indeed, electronic attack assets for jamming and lasing are increasingly being integrated into the joint force in all theaters, as, for instance, with the new creation of Terrestrial Layer System Brigade Combat Teams.[244]
- Finally, DoD and other civilian agencies can also conduct **offensive cyber warfare** activities. Cyber Command has recently acknowledged increasingly aggressive offensive activities aimed at cyber criminals from China, Russia, North Korea, and Iran.

Typology Summary and Findings

Based on our typology development and comparative analysis of U.S.-Soviet versus U.S.-China activity sets, we arrived at three main conclusions. First, DoD has already covered much of the range—roughly three-quarters—of possible activity types identified in competition with China since the start of the Obama administration's Asia-Pacific rebalancing strategy. The major exception has been in operational and kinetic activities. In the other four top-level activity bins, our analysis identified only scattered gaps. Importantly, we note that the locus of most of this recent U.S.-PRC competition has been in the Indo-Pacific rather than across theaters, as in the Cold War.

Second, most of the activity types that have recently gone unutilized have seemingly been avoided out of concern for the risks of escalation involved. Many of the activities that DoD has not conducted against China in the past decade—such as engaging in proxy warfare or advancing space weaponization—might invite steeper escalatory risks than U.S. defense planners are currently willing to bear, particularly given China's more advanced capabilities and less bellicose behavior than that of the Soviet Union during the early Cold War. In the future, however, depending on the trajectory of the ongoing U.S. strategic competition with China, utilizing these more escalatory activity types may (or may not) become more acceptable.

Third, and perhaps most significantly, our comparative analysis between America's Cold War activity set and its post-2011 "return to great power competition" activity set found that more significant historical differences exist between *how* similar activity types have been conducted, rather than between *which* activity types have been conducted. In general, many activity types were conducted on a larger scale and signaled more-hostile intent during U.S.-Soviet Cold War competition. This statement covers activity types across the full spectrum of our typology. For instance, at the strategic level, during the Cold War, the United States took a much stronger position against the Soviet Union in its guiding national security documents. NSC 20/4 in 1948 specified the strategy of containing the USSR, while NSC 68 in 1950 called for the rollback of communism more broadly. This raised the profile of U.S. strategic behavior and military actions. In terms of posture and theater-setting activities, force strength augmentation

---

[244] Mark Pomerleau, "U.S. Army to Upgrade Bigger Units with New Electronic Warfare Gear," *C4ISRNet*, October 1, 2020.

was often conducted on a much greater scale, as with the roughly 100,000-troop increase in West Germany in 1951. In the category of U.S. presence and theater-shaping activities, the USAF engaged in more intercept and interdiction activities against the Soviet Union in geographic areas of strategic interest to the USSR, leading to air-to-air losses on both sides.[245] In the area of security cooperation, NATO's command structure provided a more expansive integrated military C2 arrangement with a broader array of treaty allies than U.S. alliances and partnerships in the Indo-Pacific. Finally, in the category of military operations and kinetic activities, we have already noted that the United States has not engaged in many activities in this area against the PRC in the past decade; in terms of covert and asymmetric activities, the U.S. commitment and use of capabilities occurred on a much greater scale, such as programs like Radio Free Europe and other Cold War programs run by the U.S. Information Agency to direct covert political support to underground, nonviolent movements throughout Europe.

Drawing on an example of a U.S.-led multilateral exercise highlights the differences in characteristics between similar activity types conducted during the Cold War and the recent past. The Return of Forces to Germany (REFORGER) exercises began in January 1969. The exercises tested the ability of the United States to rapidly reinforce its forces and those of its NATO allies in the event of conflict mobilization. As part of the exercises, the United States deployed one or two divisions—up to 35,000 soldiers—alongside associated materiel.[246] The scale of the exercises increased throughout the Cold War, with more than 100,000 American and European troops participating by the late 1980s, eventually ensuring the ability to deploy ten divisions to the U.S. European Command in ten days.[247]

By contrast, the plan for the RIMPAC exercise—even before it was reduced due to concerns about the COVID-19 virus—was to include 25,000 personnel, its largest iteration to date.[248] Similarly, plans for Defender Pacific in 2021 called for a division-sized exercise.[249] While plans for exercises in the region are expanding, the scope and capacity of the REFORGER exercises during the late Cold War dwarf those in the Indo-Pacific today.[250] Furthermore, the United States has not demonstrated its ability to rapidly reinforce existing forces in support of allies in the region in such a manner. By following cues from its Cold War behavior, the United States can

---

[245] For example, see Paul Glenshaw, "Secret Casualties of the Cold War," *Air & Space Magazine*, December 2017.

[246] Robert D. Blackwill and Jeffrey W. Legro, "Constraining Ground Force Exercises of NATO and the Warsaw Pact," *International Security*, Vol. 14, No. 3, 1989.

[247] Susanne M. Schafer, "Reduced REFORGER Exercise Announced," Associated Press, August 7, 1991.

[248] Megan Eckstein, "Scaled-Back, At-Sea RIMPAC 2020 Exercise Kicks Off Near Hawaii," *USNI News*, August 18, 2020.

[249] Jen Judson, "US Army Wants $364 Million for Defender Pacific in FY21," *Defense News*, February 25, 2020.

[250] This is not to suggest that the way the PRC interprets RIMPAC is based on differences between the exercise and Cold War activities, but rather to demonstrate the scope of exercises the United States has undertaken in the past and may undertake in the future.

drastically change the character of even existing activities. Activities like Defender Pacific could be built up over time in a fashion similar to the REFORGER exercises.

As these examples show, U.S. defense planners looking for additional options in the intensifying competition with China may wish to look primarily at changes in the characteristics of existing activities, rather than searching for entirely new options, with some possible exceptions discussed below. Reviving potentially escalatory, so-far-unutilized Cold War activity types may someday be necessary, but in the near term the joint force may be better served by varying existing activity types to achieve U.S. goals.

Options for U.S. Planners

Our findings suggest that areas in which DoD and USAF could broaden the activities they undertake in the Indo-Pacific over roughly the next decade will likely not come primarily from completely novel activities, but from varying the characteristics of ongoing activities. In this section, we draw on our framework to highlight how defense planners can use variations in the four dimensions highlighted in Chapter 3 to meaningfully alter the nature of the activity in the strategic competition with China. Each of the activities we have identified could be meaningfully varied along the dimensions of location, ally and partner involvement, capabilities, and profile to expand the tools that the USAF and joint force have at their disposal, all of which may have different implications for Chinese reactions, as we discussed in Chapter 3. We demonstrate how the range of options the USAF and the joint force have in competition with the PRC can be expanded tremendously when we consider this axis of variation.

Applied Examples of Variation in U.S. Activities

The dimensions of variation discussed in great detail in Chapter 3 can be broadly applied to any of the 83 activity subtypes identified in the preceding typology to generate novel U.S. activities that may advance U.S. interests and have higher (or lower) degrees of escalation. Recognizing that U.S. objectives might fall into several categories—from enhancing U.S. regional influence to deterring specific Chinese actions to compelling changes in Chinese behavior—we examined a range of possible activities for U.S. planners and strategists to consider with varying levels of escalatory potential. In this section, we delineate a set of activities within our typology that the United States has not pursued as part of its competitive toolkit to this point—but that it could pursue by changing the location, involvement of allies and partners, capabilities, and/or profile of existing activities.

At the strategic and doctrinal level, the United States could change its policies regarding Chinese regional territorial and maritime disputes. One example would be for Washington to clarify its policy position on SCS disputes by backing the sovereignty claims of allies and partners against China in specific cases.[251] The U.S. State Department's statement on July 13, 2020, is an example of a strategic change. While the statement did not explicitly support the sovereignty claims of U.S. allies and partners, it did clarify U.S. policy on the maritime claims in the SCS by stating that the United States supports the July 2016 Arbitral Tribunal ruling that struck down all of China's maritime claims in the SCS.[252] The United States could also consider the merits of specific claims by the Philippines, Vietnam, and Malaysia and establish a U.S. policy position that supports respective sovereignty claims based on current administrative control, geographic proximity, and/or legal precedent, such as the 2016 ruling supporting Manila against China's SCS resource rights claims.[253] This higher-profile action should improve relations with partners and allies and, while possibly being quite escalatory, would convey to Beijing that using the PLA to resolve differences with China's neighbors would likely come at an increased cost.

Also at the strategic level, Washington could vary ally and partner involvement in security agreements—for instance, by establishing a new, formal security agreement in the Quad between the United States, Australia, Japan, and India.[254] Such changes could both cement U.S. regional leadership in a free and open Indo-Pacific and send a strong message to China regarding behavioral norms in the region. Despite the difficulties associated with expanding the Quad's remit into security commitments, any Quad defense agreement would significantly impact Chinese calculations for using force to resolve regional disputes by enhancing the capabilities and interoperability of a potential balancing coalition. Such an agreement would increase U.S. military and nonmilitary support in the region, though it likely would elevate Chinese fears of the United States using its Indo-Pacific strategy to undermine Chinese regional interests as part of a larger containment strategy that stresses the two-oceans aspect of this strategy.[255]

---

[251] Colm Quinn, "The U.S. Declared China's South China Seas Claims 'Unlawful. Now What?" *Foreign Policy*, July 14, 2020.

[252] Michael R. Pompeo, "U.S. Position on Maritime Claims in the South China Sea," press statement, U.S. Department of State, July 13, 2020.

[253] This may pose legal and political challenges given that the various SCS disputants disagree among themselves, as well as with China, in certain cases.

[254] Assuming, of course, that such an agreement would be of interest to all parties. See John Grady, "Biden Admin Wants to Expand Pacific 'Quad' Relationship," *USNI News*, January 30, 2021; Lindsey W. Ford and James Goldgeier, *Retooling America's Alliances to Manage the China Challenge*, Washington, D.C.: Brookings Institution, January 25, 2021; Justin Diehl, "Indo-Pacific Deterrence and the Quad in 2030," *Journal of Indo-Pacific Affairs*, Vol. 4, No. 2, Spring 2021; and Aaron Bartnick, *Asia Whole and Free? Assessing the Viability and Practicality of a Pacific NATO*, Cambridge, Mass.: Belfer Center, March 2020.

[255] Lin Zhiyuan [林治远], "New Changes in U.S. Military Strategy and Combat Theory" ["美国军事战略和作战理论新变化"], *Military Digest* [军事文摘], No. 1, 2019.

The recent strengthening of the U.S.-Taiwan relationship also offers the potential for innovative strategic activities, albeit with significant escalatory implications.[256] Within the construct of the American Institute on Taiwan, the establishment of more-formal structures for managing the security aspects of the relationship and expanding uniformed and civilian American Institute on Taiwan staff could lay the groundwork for greater U.S.-Taiwan defense cooperation at strategic, operational, and even tactical levels, improving the ability of the United States and Taiwan to act in a contingency. The United States could also improve defense cooperation through engaging in more senior military visits to Taiwan. More provocatively, but still remaining within the bounds of stated U.S. policy, Washington could still revamp the Taiwan Relations Act to explicitly provide a strong security guarantee, leaving little or no ambiguity regarding U.S. response to Chinese use of force against Taiwan.[257]

Not all strategic options under consideration need bear the potential escalatory weight of activities such as those to enhance the U.S.-Taiwan security relationship. One cooperative rather than competitive option that has attracted support in recent years would be for the United States and China to pursue a strategic and/or conventional forces treaty—as the United States and the Soviet Union did.[258] China has remained free to pick and choose if, when, and how it might enter into international protocols that limit the scope of its military expansion. Although most analysts agree that China has little to gain from entering into arms control dialogue with the United States, the option remains viable for consideration if only as a means to exert international pressure on Beijing to reduce concerns about its comprehensive, and somewhat unprecedented, military modernization program.

While posture enhancement and theater-setting activities are already underway in a number of areas across the Indo-Pacific, innovative options remain to improve the competitive position of the United States by varying location, the partners involved, and the capabilities and capacities deployed. Of note is the potential value provided by enhanced first and second island chain prepositioning that might be afforded by agreements with Palau, Palawan, and even Taiwan.[259] Improvements to U.S. infrastructure in theater to facilitate prepositioned equipment sets and logistical stocks would introduce significant uncertainty into Chinese plans to deny or limit U.S.

---

[256] Walker Mills, "Deterring the Dragon: Returning U.S. Forces to Taiwan," *Military Review*, September–October 2020.

[257] Bonny Lin, "U.S. Allied and Partner Support for Taiwan: Responses to a Chinese Attack on Taiwan and Potential U.S. Taiwan Policy Changes," testimony presented before the U.S.-China Economic and Security Review Commission on February 18, 2021, Santa Monica, Calif.: RAND Corporation, CT-A1194-1, 2021. The United States would still need to include wording to deter Taiwanese provocation.

[258] Tong Zhao, *Practical Ways to Promote U.S.-China Arms Control Negotiations*, Washington, D.C.: Carnegie Endowment for International Peace, October 7, 2020.

[259] Andrew Rhodes, "The Second Island Cloud: A Deeper and Broader Concept for American Presence in the Pacific Islands," *Joint Force Quarterly*, Vol. 95, No. 4, 2019.

access and freedom of maneuver in a regional contingency and may come in concert with the establishment of a new, major headquarters in Palau, for example.

Along the same lines, basing and access agreements between the United States and new, geo-strategically important regional partners, such as Singapore and Palau, could provide the United States with improved posture to control key regional SLOCs and, at minimum, would indicate to China that U.S. influence is not limited to treaty allies alone. This would be particularly true if the negotiations were aimed at establishing a major new U.S. air or naval headquarters.[260] This would undermine China's military and political efforts to keep the United States at a distance in a regional conflict and reinforce U.S. deterrence objectives. However, this might therefore also increase concerns among the Chinese leadership regarding the PLA's ability to prosecute a regional conflict.[261]

With the demise of the Intermediate Range Nuclear Forces Treaty, plans to deploy U.S. ground-based intermediate-range missile capabilities have focused largely on issues over agreements for allies and partners in the Indo-Pacific to host these systems. Such plans require resolution of a number of political, legal, and operational issues; but progress toward dispersed, regional deployment would likely complicate PLA targeting calculations and introduce doubt into PLA operational plans.[262] In the same vein, public demonstrations of new operational capabilities could serve U.S. deterrence objectives, particularly new integrated air and missile defense capabilities that underscore coordination and interoperability with Japan, Australia, and/or South Korea.[263] Demonstrations of advanced weapons such as hypersonic surface-to-surface missiles in the region could likewise complicate Chinese military plans and risk assessments.[264]

Variance in the dimensions of ongoing security cooperation activities with allies and partners also offer a range of possibilities for increasing U.S. regional influence, strengthening interoperability with allies and partners, and improving U.S. regional deterrence posture. In keeping with the strategic-level enhancements in the U.S.-Taiwan relationship, DoD could expand the footprint of security assistance and uniformed liaison personnel on Taiwan, and USAF and other U.S. services could weigh options for formal service-to-service training program agreements with Taiwan counterparts. Options also include new, combined bilateral and multilateral exercises, such as conducting a major annual exercise with Quad partners in the

---

[260] Gordon Lubold, "U.S. Military Is Offered New Bases in the Pacific," *Wall Street Journal*, September 8, 2020.

[261] Derek Grossman, "America Is Betting Big on the Second Island Chain," *RAND Blog*, September 8, 2020.

[262] Eric Gomez, "Are America's East Asia Allies Willing and Able to Host U.S. Intermediate-Range Missiles?" *Asia Pacific Bulletin*, No. 522, August 19, 2020.

[263] Ryo Nakamura, "U.S. to Build Anti-China Missile Network Along First Island Chain," *Nikkei Asia*, March 5, 2021.

[264] John T. Watts, Christian Trotti, and Mark J. Massa, *Primer on Hypersonic Weapons in the Indo-Pacific Region*, Washington, D.C.: Atlantic Council, August 2020.

Indian Ocean that includes SCS transits. Another option in this area would be to initiate an annual program of USCG training and exercise programs with regional partners.[265] Foreign military exchanges might expand to include new flight- and ship-rider programs between USAF and USN organizations and allied and partner counterparts in the SCS and ECS. Combined naval and Special Operations Forces programs could be developed with regional partners to mirror existing joint air patrol activities, while existing activities could be expanded in scope. For example, joint air patrols with Japan could be increased and extended beyond the ECS. One potential departure from current activities could be to focus on more allied and partner-led (as opposed to U.S.-led) bilateral and multilateral activity to improve partner equities.[266]

Military operations and kinetic activities conducted against Chinese forces or targets would of course be accompanied by significant escalatory risk. We sought in our analysis to include options that might meet U.S. objectives in response to heightened PRC aggression or coercive actions and that would require preparations in the steady-state environment for later execution by the United States and its partners. These options could include direct actions taken against China or Chinese forces or actions taken by or against a proxy.

In terms of direct interventions, activities in support of SCS partners confronting Chinese incursions and gray zone operations could be considered. The United States could take more-direct actions in support of Japan to confront PRC activities in the ECS—such as actions taken against Chinese coast guard or maritime militia forces operating in the vicinity of the Senkaku Islands (known in China as the Diaoyu Islands). Blockade or embargo operations could also be included in these courses of action or executed separately to deter further Chinese aggression or coercion. Less escalatory deterrence operations could be considered and planned as well, including imposition of no-fly zones or air policing operations in support of allies in the SCS and/or ECS.

In terms of proxy warfare operations, the United States could work with regional allies and partners to develop indirect support options for SCS and ECS partners confronting Chinese incursions and gray zone operations. Support could range from improving partner coast guard capabilities (both lethal and nonlethal capabilities) to equipping partner forces with advanced ground- and/or air-launched anti-ship missiles. In any case, proxy actions such as these would be reinforced and enabled by development and activation of an integrated sensor fusion network for maritime and air situational awareness and targeting.[267] Given the growing nature of China's

---

[265] Michael Sinclair and Lindsey Ford, "Stuck in the Middle with You: Resourcing the Coast Guard for Global Competition," Brookings Institution, October 16, 2020; and Blake Herzinger, "Reorienting the Coast Guard: A Case for Patrol Forces in the Indo-Pacific," *War on the Rocks*, November 5, 2019.

[266] One model that may be followed is the Indo-Pacific Jet Training Program. This program includes fighter jet training detachments from India, Japan, and Australia on Guam and is designed to enhance interoperability between the four nations. Leadership of the program rotates between the participating states.

[267] Deon Canyon, Wade Turvold, and Jim McMullin, "A Network of Maritime Fusion Centers in the Indo-Pacific," *Security Nexus*, Vol. 22, 2021.

drive to establish overseas basing infrastructure and access agreements, proxy actions could also be developed and planned for support of nonstate actors or opposition groups opposing PRC regional and/or global basing agreement efforts. This would entail a whole-of-government approach by the United States to enable such groups to impact national-level decisionmaking within a given country.[268]

While the list of new or innovative options discussed in this section is by no means comprehensive, it leverages our typology to recommend areas and activities for consideration by U.S. planners as they think through options based on the evolving competition with China—both for current operations and for future plans and preparations on a dynamic playing field. Table 5.7 summarizes the activities discussed.

Table 5.7. Examples of Potential Varied U.S. Military Activities to Compete with China

Activity Category	Examples of Modified or Varied U.S. Activities
Strategic- and doctrinal-level activities	• New Taiwan Relations Act with stronger security guarantee • Strategic and/or conventional forces arms control treaty with PRC • Formal Quad security agreement
Posture enhancement and theater-setting activities	• Larger security assistance and uniformed liaison presence on Taiwan (enlarged American Institute on Taiwan) • Public demo of new integrated air and missile defense capability (coordinated with Japan, Australia, and/or ROK) and/or hypersonic surface-to-surface missile capability • New basing/prepositioning arrangements (major headquarters) with Singapore and Palau
Theater presence and shaping activities	• Formal training program with Taiwan (service-to-service agreements) • Ground-based intermediate-range missile basing agreements with regional allies/partners • Quad major annual exercise in Indian Ocean w/ SCS transits • Annual program of USCG exercises with regional partners
Security cooperation activities	• More partner-led (rather than U.S.-led) bilateral and multilateral regional training and exercises • New combined naval and Special Operations Forces programs like existing Air Force joint patrols
Military operations and kinetic activities	• Activation of integrated sensor fusion network (maritime and air domain awareness) with SCS partners during PRC gray zone operations • Proxy or direct actions (blockade, no-fly zone, etc.) in support of SCS partners confronting Chinese incursions/gray zone operations • Proxy or direct actions in support of Japan confronting Chinese incursions in ECS • Proxy actions in support of nonstate actors or opposition groups opposing PRC basing agreement efforts (regional and global)

---

[268] For a discussion of potential U.S.-PRC proxy conflict, see Dominic Tierney, "The Future of U.S.-PRC Proxy War," *Texas National Security Review*, Vol. 4, No. 2, Spring 2021.

Having developed this menu of U.S. military activity options, in the next chapter we return to the framework presented in the first half of this report, pulling together these analytical tasks by applying the framework to activities in all five categories to assess likely Chinese reactions and identify the characteristics of particular U.S. military activities that have increased escalation potential.

Chapter 6. Anticipating the Escalation Risks of Different Types of U.S. Military Activities

This chapter illustrates how the characteristics of different types of U.S. military activities can lead to either more- or less-escalatory Chinese responses, as informed by the framework developed in the first part of this report. It does so by discussing examples drawn from each of the five top-level categories of U.S. military activities developed in Chapter 5 that are likely to be associated with each level of potential intensity of Chinese reactions, as outlined in Chapter 4. While certainly not exhaustive of the types of activities that U.S. military planners may consider in the Indo-Pacific, these illustrations provide shorthand examples of the types of activities likely to be associated with different levels of escalation risks. We also highlight the specific characteristics of each activity that have the greatest influence over the likely escalation level of PRC responses. At the end of this chapter, we aggregate our analysis of these characteristics across activity types to identify those with the overall greatest potential to increase the escalation risk of PRC responses.

While the analysis in this chapter is intended to provide a shorthand look at the implications of our framework for particular U.S. military activities, it is important to note that our framework can also be applied in a more detailed, comprehensive manner to a specific U.S. military activity. This more detailed application of the framework, discussed in Appendix C, requires substantial prior knowledge of China and regional security issues, in addition to a substantial investment of time to complete, and may not be required for all planning purposes. However, for activities of particular importance or escalation risk, the more detailed approach discussed in Appendix C may be advisable. To assist military planners in undertaking the detailed approach, Appendix C also contains a full-length example of the application of our framework to a specific hypothetical U.S. military activity: a set of enhanced-access agreements negotiated with India.

Strategic and Doctrinal-Level Activities

This section illustrates how U.S. strategic and doctrinal activities may vary in their risk of escalatory Chinese reactions. It reviews examples of activities in this category that would be likely to be associated with each different level of PRC reaction intensity, as described in Chapter 4. Table 6.1 summarizes the activities discussed and highlights how their characteristics affect PRC reactions through the key factors of our framework. Subsequent sections repeat this illustrative exercise for the other top-level activity categories.

Table 6.1. Summary of Potential Escalation Risks of Varied Strategic and Doctrinal Activities

Potential Intensity of PRC Response	Activity Description	Anchoring Activity Characteristics
No/minor	U.S. informal security commitment to Nauru	• Involvement of Nauru illustrates U.S. interests in countering China in Pacific Islands, could increase PRC perception of hostile intent, threat to regional influence • PRC aggressive reaction deterred by increased perception of U.S. commitment to defense of Nauru, limited size of the country
Notable	New U.S. security agreements with several ASEAN members that increase naval and air training	• Enhanced U.S. military cooperation with regional states, involvement of SCS claimants could increase PRC perception of threat to regional influence, hostile intent • PRC reaction limited because although indicative of expanding U.S. political ties, naval training exercises of little military concern given limited capabilities of most ASEAN states
Elevated	Army's development of MDO in the Indo-Pacific	• MDO would be primarily used in conflict with China, increasing PRC perception of military threat, hostile intent • PRC reaction limited because some U.S. capabilities already in theater, not novel
Severe	Defense policy shift that signals intent to move U.S. troops, capabilities into Taiwan	• U.S. support for Taiwan increases PRC perception of threat to regime legitimacy • Future U.S. capabilities and troops on Taiwan would increase China's perception of military threat, hostile intent • PRC reaction tempered by increased U.S. defense commitment to Taiwan, concerns for escalation risk
Maximal	New mutual defense treaty with Taiwan that recognizes Taiwan's de facto independence	• Formal U.S. defense commitment with Taiwan substantially raises PRC perception of threat to regime legitimacy • Likely indication that substantial U.S. military forces in Taiwan may follow, increasing PRC perception of military threat, hostile intent • Formal U.S. defense commitment to Taiwan, risks of escalation insufficient to limit PRC reaction given acute threats to PRC interests

While strategic and doctrinal activities may appear to raise fewer direct concerns for China, as they do not incorporate immediate military changes in the region, we still identified hypothetical activities in this category for which the likely Chinese response would vary widely in intensity. At the lowest end of the spectrum, the no/minor category, an example could include the United States making informal defense commitments to states that are farther away from China's borders, sensitive political or military areas, and forces and are not U.S. allies and partners that are known to be anti-China. The United States making an informal defensive commitment to the Pacific Island nation of Nauru, for example, would likely cause no or minor PRC reaction. This is not to say that China would have no concerns with the activity. China would likely view an informal defense commitment as evidence of U.S. interests in countering China's presence in the Pacific Islands, which could raise PRC perceptions of threats to its regional influence. In addition, China might perceive an increase in U.S. hostile intent given that the U.S. defense commitment to Nauru, even if informal, could circumvent China's attempts to gain military access to the Pacific Island nations. However, PRC reactions would be tempered by the fact that Nauru is a small country with no domestic military capabilities, remote from any areas of acute PRC concern. While unlikely in response to such an activity, the risk of direct Chinese aggression against Nauru would also likely be reduced by the increased perception of U.S. commitment to the defense of Nauru, and potentially the Pacific Island region in general.

China's reaction might fall into the notable category if the United States reached security agreements with states that are located closer to China, Chinese forces, or Chinese interests or that involved influential regional states that China is attempting to build relationships with. For example, new U.S. security agreements with several ASEAN members, such as Vietnam or Indonesia, that increase naval and air training led by U.S. forces could cause China to react at this intensity level, as these agreements would enhance U.S. military cooperation and potentially military interoperability with regional states, increasing China's perception of threats to its regional influence and expansion of U.S. political ties with key Southeast Asian states. In addition, the involvement of SCS claimants in the agreements could increase PRC perception of U.S. hostile intent, particularly if China believes that the increases in partner air and naval capabilities could affect these disputes. That said, China's reactions would be comparatively restrained because naval and air training exercises are of minor military concern given the limited capabilities of most ASEAN states in these domains. In addition, the United States already conducts some training exercises with several ASEAN states, such as Singapore, so this would likely limit Chinese concerns.

An activity that might cause China to react in the elevated category could be the formulation of new operational concepts that would augment U.S. capabilities in the Indo-Pacific region against China in a conflict. For example, the Army's MDO concept in the Indo-Pacific is meant to augment U.S. ability to counter China's military capabilities across domains, enabling the United States to better sustain operations against China in the region. Chinese responses to this change may also be more likely to be long term in nature, if China assessed that it needed to shift resources and investments to better counter U.S. capabilities, with short-term, more immediately visible Chinese responses more limited. Because MDO is primarily aimed at countering Chinese military capabilities and would be mainly used in a conflict against China, this would likely increase PRC perception of the military threat posed by U.S. capabilities as well as the perception of U.S. hostile intent. However, China might not pursue even more escalatory reactions because the capabilities required for MDO are largely not new or novel, and many of them are already being used by various U.S. forces in the region. Furthermore, it is likely that China is already reacting to the MDO concept by incorporating potential PLA responses into the current Chinese defense planning cycle.

U.S. strategic and doctrinal activities that could potentially spur a severe PRC reaction are likely to involve Taiwan and herald the movement of U.S. capabilities and forces onto the island. A shift in U.S. defense policy that signals the intent to move U.S. troops and capabilities into Taiwan, for example, would cause China to perceive significant threat to its regime legitimacy and would lead to a severe reaction. In addition, the prospect of a future U.S. military footprint on Taiwan would substantially increase China's concerns over the U.S. military threat to Chinese forces should the PRC attack Taiwan, as well as the level of U.S. hostile intent. All of these factors would likely contribute to a severe PRC reaction. China's reactions could be somewhat constrained by the increased U.S. defense commitment to Taiwan, which would raise China's concerns about risking escalation to direct conflict with the United States.

However, a new U.S.-Taiwan mutual defense treaty that de facto recognizes Taiwan and clearly indicates U.S. commitment to defend Taiwan's independence has the potential to spur a maximal PRC reaction. China would perceive an immediate, acute threat to its regime legitimacy by de facto U.S. recognition of Taiwan's independence and willingness to put U.S. forces on Taiwan to protect the island from Chinese attack. Additionally, the mutual defense treaty would signal the potential for the United States to have a sizable military presence on Taiwan in the future, heightening China's fears over the military threat as well as U.S. hostile intent. Because a U.S. defense treaty with Taiwan poses serious threats to China's interests, the formal U.S. defense commitment to Taiwan and China's concerns of escalation to direct conflict with the United States would likely be insufficient to limit China's reactions.

Posture Enhancement and Theater-Setting Activities

Next, we assess how the characteristics of U.S. posture enhancement and theater-setting activities may be most likely to affect Chinese reactions and the risk of escalation. Table 6.2 provides examples of U.S. posture enhancement and theater-setting activities that may cause PRC reactions in each of the escalation categories. A more detailed discussion of these dynamics follows.

Table 6.2. Summary of Potential Escalation Risks of Varied Posture Enhancement and Theater-Setting Activities

Potential Escalation Risk	Activity Description	Anchoring Activity Characteristics
No/minor	New mutual logistics support agreement with India that provides expanded access to an Indian port	• Increased U.S. access to an Indian port signals closer U.S.-India relationship, could increase PRC perception of threat to regional influence • More U.S. logistics capability to assist operations near South Asian SLOCs potentially heightens PRC perception of threat to economic development • PRC reactions limited because agreement does not involve new capabilities and is limited in scale and scope, and USN already operates extensively in Indian Ocean
Notable	Expansion of existing SOFA with Australia to provide more access to U.S. forces, personnel	• Demonstrates more U.S. access to Australian military sites and facilities, potentially paving the way for increased U.S.-Australian military interoperability, potentially raising PRC concerns over U.S. military threat, hostile intent • Likely increased PRC concerns over threats to regional influence as demonstrates Australian willingness to form closer defense relations with United States, move away from PRC influence • PRC reaction limited as does not involve new U.S. capabilities or forces in Australia
Elevated	Public demonstration of U.S. LRHWs in region	• Demonstration of new U.S. capability that can target PRC mainland likely increases China's concern over potential military threat • LRHWs demonstrate U.S. investment in capability that would be primarily used against China in conflict, raising China's fears of hostile intent • However, PRC reaction limited because LRHWs not actually deployed in region
Severe	Deploying long-range fires to Japan, including in locations that can range Taiwan, with U.S.-Japan statements on concerns over stability in Taiwan Strait	• Expanded/additional capabilities, potential use for Taiwan increase PRC perception of military threat, hostile intent, threat to PRC regime legitimacy • Enhanced U.S. ability to defend Japan likely limits higher PRC response
Maximal	Deploy THAAD plus supporting U.S. troops to Taiwan	• Capabilities enable targeting of PRC C2, enhanced missile defense increases PRC perception of military threat • Taiwan willingness to host U.S. capabilities/troops, U.S. commitment to defense of Taiwan increases PRC perception of hostile intent • U.S. presence signals increased support for Taiwan, PRC concerns of threats to regime legitimacy

As discussed in Chapter 5, posture and theater-setting activities include changes to enabling agreements, deployed force structure, theater infrastructure, and theater equipment. We identified several hypothetical activities in these categories that would potentially lead to a PRC response at each escalation level. For the no/minor category, the United States forming an enabling agreement that is limited in scale and scope and is located farther from sensitive areas to China but that signals U.S. desire for a stronger defense relationship with key states might cause China to react in a minor way. For example, the United States forming a mutual logistics agreement with India that would expand U.S. access to an Indian port would likely be of minor concern to China. The primary PRC concern would likely focus on threats to China's regional influence, as the agreement would signal a move toward a stronger U.S.-India defense relationship. In addition, the agreement would enable more U.S. logistics capability to assist with operations near South Asian SLOCs, potentially heightening China's perception of threat to economic development given concerns over U.S. ability to interdict Chinese shipping in key maritime chokepoints in a conflict. However, China's reactions would be limited because the agreement does not involve new military capabilities and is limited in scale and scope. In addition, the USN already has the logistics capacity to operate extensively in the Indian Ocean, so this agreement would not lead to a new capability.

A Chinese reaction in the notable category might be spurred by, for example, an expansion of existing agreements with key regional states that increase U.S. military access or interoperability but do not involve new U.S. or allied military capabilities directly threatening to China. An expansion of the existing U.S.-Australia SOFA agreement that provides more access for U.S. personnel and forces would potentially lead to a PRC reaction in the notable category. The expanded agreement would demonstrate increased U.S. access to Australian military sites and facilities, potentially allowing for increased military interoperability between U.S. and Australian forces. This would likely increase PRC concerns over the threat posed by the U.S. military presence in Australia and in the region more broadly, as well as raise Chinese fears over U.S. and Australian hostile intent. In addition, an expanded SOFA agreement would potentially increase China's concerns over threats to its regional influence because it demonstrates Australia's willingness to have a closer defense relationship with the United States, as well as U.S. ability to convince Australia to move away from China's influence. China's reaction would not be more aggressive because the SOFA agreement is an expansion of one that already exists and would not involve new U.S. capabilities or forces based in Australia.

China might react in the elevated category if the United States demonstrates capabilities that are new, that involve high technology, and that could undermine China's defenses and be used primarily against the PRC in a conflict. Demonstrating these capabilities but not deploying them in theater would likely keep China's reaction in the elevated category instead of a more escalatory response. For example, a public, visible demonstration of U.S. LRHW capabilities in the Indo-Pacific region would likely lead to an elevated PRC reaction. The U.S. demonstration would illustrate a new capability that could potentially target the Chinese mainland and undermine China's C2, which would increase China's concern over the potential military threat posed by this capability should the United States deploy it in the region. In addition, China's concerns about U.S. hostile intent would likely increase because LRHWs are meant to be primarily used against China in a conflict, so the demonstration signals U.S. investment in capabilities to counter China's forces. China's reaction would remain in the elevated category because the United States has not actually deployed LRHWs in the region.

For the severe category, China might react to posture enhancement and theater-setting activities that involve the United States deploying new or enhanced capabilities close to China's borders, forces, or sensitive political areas, such as Taiwan, and where the capabilities are intended to directly target and counter Chinese forces in a conflict. An example could be if the United States deployed long-range fires to Japan, including in locations that can range Taiwan, with accompanying U.S.-Japan statements on concerns over stability in the Taiwan Strait. The expanded U.S. strike capabilities in Japan that are primarily meant to be used against China in a conflict would increase China's perception of the military threat posed by the United States. In addition, that the capability could potentially be used in a Taiwan contingency would raise PRC concerns about regime legitimacy and U.S. support for Taiwan. China would also likely perceive an increase in hostile intent from the U.S. and Japan, because deploying long-range fires in Japan demonstrates Japan's willingness to host additional U.S. capabilities that could target Chinese forces in a conflict. China's reactions would be limited by increased U.S. ability to defend Japan, which would likely deter more-severe Chinese responses.

China's reactions in the maximal category would likely be preceded by theater-setting and posture enhancement activities that involve the U.S. placing capabilities and forces directly on Taiwan and where the capabilities deployed could affect China's military capabilities and defenses, including the PRC's C2 and nuclear deterrent, in addition to augmenting Taiwan's defenses against Chinese attack. For example, the United States deploying THAAD to Taiwan along with a supporting contingent of troops would likely result in a maximal Chinese response. THAAD capabilities would enable targeting of China's C2 and would augment Taiwan's missile defense capabilities, increasing China's perception of the military threat posed by the United States. In addition, Taiwan willingness to host U.S. capabilities and troops, and the signal of U.S. commitment to Taiwan's defense that this activity would send, would heighten Chinese concerns over threats to regime legitimacy and fears over U.S. and Taiwan hostile intent. China's response would not be deterred by U.S. commitment to defend Taiwan in this case because the deployment of U.S. high-end capabilities and troops on Taiwan would pose serious threats to China's interests.

Theater Presence and Shaping Activities

In this section, we assess how the characteristics of U.S. theater presence and shaping activities may be most likely to affect Chinese reactions and the risk of escalation. Table 6.3 summarizes the U.S. activity and characteristics that potentially could result in a PRC response at each escalation level.

Table 6.3. Summary of Potential Escalation Risks of Varied U.S. Theater Presence and Shaping Activities

Potential Escalation Risk	Activity Description	Anchoring Activity Characteristics
No/minor	Annual joint force training exercises in the Indian Ocean	• Indian Ocean location demonstrates potential increase in U.S. presence in that area, possibly raising Chinese concerns of U.S. threats to China's access to SLOCs, economic development • PRC reaction limited by routine nature of exercises, no new capabilities, distance from more acute areas of PRC concern
Notable	Air and Naval FONOPs in ECS	• Proximity to disputed islands in ECS potentially raises PRC concerns over U.S. hostile intent, threats to China's regional influence • China's reaction limited as FONOPs are routine, U.S. naval/air capabilities for these operations of limited concern
Elevated	Conducting overflight and naval surface ISR patrols (manned, unmanned) out of the Philippines to assist in SCS surveillance	• Enhanced ISR near SCS territorial disputes could raise PRC concerns over the potential U.S. military threat • Signals U.S. interest in helping regional states resist PRC coercion, increasing China's perception of U.S. hostile intent • PRC reaction limited as capabilities restricted to ISR/nonkinetic
Severe	U.S. bomber task force missions in SCS and around Taiwan that simulate targeting PRC forces around disputed territories and mainland China	• Proximity to Taiwan, SCS would heighten China's perception of U.S. military threat, hostile intent • Demonstrated capabilities would raise China's concerns over possibility that U.S. forces could be practicing for a precipitous attack on Chinese targets, signaling potential military threat and hostile intent • Missions near Taiwan signal increased U.S. support for defense of Taiwan, likely increasing PRC perception of threat to regime legitimacy • PRC reaction limited by fear of escalation to direct conflict with the United States
Maximal	Expanded A2/AD activities in Japan including LRHWs with explicit demonstrations of U.S. capability to strike PRC C2, nuclear and regime targets	• Explicit demonstration of capability to strike PRC C2, nuclear and regime targets would substantially increase China's perception of imminent U.S. military threat • Japan's willingness to host capability and demonstrations would increase China's perception of U.S.-Japan hostile intent • Would raise PRC concerns over threats to regime legitimacy as capability could be used in a Taiwan conflict, signals U.S. support for defense of Taiwan • Given serious threats to PRC regime, nuclear deterrent, and C2, PRC reactions likely not limited by increased U.S. capabilities to defend Japan or by fear of escalation

We identified theater presence and shaping activities that could potentially result in Chinese reactions in each of the escalation categories. An activity that would lead to no or minor reaction from China in this activity category could include annual U.S. military training exercises that take place in an area farther from China's borders or politically sensitive areas, that are routine, and that do not involve new or high-end capabilities or shows of force. An example might be an annual joint force training exercise in the Indian Ocean, which would likely lead to little or no reaction from China. The location of the exercises in the Indian Ocean, near key maritime SLOCs, demonstrates the potential for U.S. military presence to increase in that area in the future. This could potentially raise Chinese concerns of U.S. threats to PRC access to SLOCs, which could heighten concerns of threats to China's economic development. However, a more aggressive PRC response would be limited because the exercises are annual and routine and involve no new capabilities or novel demonstrations of force. In addition, the exercises would take place in the Indian Ocean, which is a sizable distance from more acute areas of PRC concern such as the SCS or Taiwan.

A notable Chinese reaction for theater presence and shaping activities might occur if the United States were to conduct naval and air FONOPs in the ECS, near the Senkaku Islands, for example. The location of the operations close to disputed islands in the ECS and the signal it sends of increased U.S. support for defending Japan from Chinese coercion would likely raise China's concerns over U.S. hostile intent. In addition, visible, increased U.S. military presence around disputed maritime territory might heighten China's perception of threats to its regional influence if other states in the SCS, for example, would be emboldened by the demonstration of U.S. support. China's reaction would be limited because FONOPs are routine and the U.S. naval and air capabilities deployed for these operations are of minor concern to China.

China might react in the elevated category if the activity included enhanced U.S. capabilities and/or increased U.S. military presence near China's borders or forces, near areas of political concern, or where the activity might contribute to regional states being emboldened by U.S. support. For example, the United States conducting overflight and naval surface ISR patrols (including manned and unmanned) out of the Philippines to assist in SCS surveillance would likely contribute to an elevated Chinese response. The patrols would enhance Philippine and regional ISR near the SCS territorial disputes, which could raise China's concerns over the potential U.S. military threat as the ISR could be used to detect Chinese forces. Similarly, flying patrols out of the Philippines demonstrates increased U.S. willingness to assist regional states in countering PRC coercive actions in disputed waters, which would likely increase China's perception of U.S. hostile intent. However, China's reaction would not be more escalatory as the U.S. capabilities used for this activity are limited to ISR and are nonkinetic in nature.

China's reactions in the severe category might be induced by U.S. theater shaping and presence activities that occur near or in politically or militarily sensitive areas such as Taiwan or the SCS or where the capabilities demonstrated could be primarily used to attack China in a conflict. An example that might result in a severe PRC response is if the United States were to deploy bomber task force missions in the SCS and around Taiwan that simulate the targeting of Chinese forces around disputed territories and mainland China. The location of the bombing demonstrations close to Taiwan and in the SCS would substantially raise China's perception of military threat from the United States. In addition, the capabilities demonstrated would significantly raise China's concerns over the possibility that U.S. forces could be practicing for a precipitous attack on Chinese targets, also contributing to China's perception of military threat as well as increasing concerns of U.S. hostile intent. In addition, the bombing missions near Taiwan demonstrate increased U.S. support for the defense of Taiwan, which would likely heighten China's perception of the activity as posing a threat to its regime legitimacy. China's reactions could be limited somewhat by fear that an aggressive response would escalate to direct conflict with the United States.

Activities that would potentially lead China to have a maximal response include those that involve high-end capabilities that could augment U.S. or allied ability to target China's C2, nuclear, or regime capabilities and that are located near Taiwan or other politically or militarily sensitive areas. For example, should the United States expand A2/AD activities in Japan, including deploying LRHWs accompanied by public demonstrations of U.S. capability to strike PRC C2, nuclear, and regime targets, this would likely precipitate a maximal response from China. The explicit U.S.-Japan demonstration of a high-end capability LRHW to strike critical targets in China would substantially increase China's perception of imminent U.S. military threat. In addition, Japan's willingness to host the LRHW capability and U.S. demonstrations would increase China's perception of hostile intent on the part of Japan and the United States. China would also perceive threats to its regime legitimacy because LRHWs could be used to target Chinese capabilities in a conflict over Taiwan, and the United States demonstrating the capability would signal U.S. support for defense of Taiwan and Japan in a regional conflict. Because this would represent a serious threat to China's regime, nuclear deterrent, and C2 capabilities, China's reactions would likely not be limited by increased U.S. capabilities to defend Japan or by fear of escalation.

Security Cooperation Activities

There are a number of ways in which the characteristics of U.S. security cooperation activities may affect Chinese reactions. Table 6.4 provides examples of U.S. security cooperation activities and their characteristics that could potentially lead to varying PRC responses in the different escalation tiers.

Table 6.4. Summary of Potential Escalation Risks of Varied U.S. Security Cooperation Activities

Potential Escalation Risk	Activity Description	Anchoring Activity Characteristics
No/minor	Expanded foreign military exchanges with Singapore	• Expansion of military exchanges with Singapore could increase PRC concerns about threats to China's regional influence • PRC reaction limited by existing robust U.S.-Singapore defense relations; no new or kinetic capabilities involved
Notable	Involving new regional partners such as Indonesia or Vietnam in annual exercises near the SCS or involving states from outside the region in exercises near Taiwan	• Expanded partners in region and exercises in SCS increase PRC perception of hostile intent, threats to regional influence • Involvement of external partners in exercises near Taiwan increases China's perception of hostile intent • However, PRC reaction limited as exercises are routine and do not involve high-end capabilities
Elevated	Foreign military financing and donations to Vietnam of advanced military platforms (fighter aircraft, ISR, and EW capabilities)	• Donations would enhance Vietnam capabilities to patrol the SCS, defend territory, potentially increasing PRC perception of military threat from Vietnam, United States • Demonstrates closer U.S.-Vietnam security relations and increased U.S. support for SCS states, likely raising PRC concerns of hostile intent • PRC reaction limited by relatively small scope of assistance package, limited existing Vietnam military capabilities
Severe	Large-scale arms sales containing LRHWs to Japan	• LRHWs in Japan could be used to target Chinese forces in regional conflict, TW contingency, likely increasing PRC perception of U.S. and Japanese military threat, threats to PRC regime legitimacy • Japan purchasing LRHWs demonstrates willingness to host capability that would be primarily used in conflict with China, likely raising PRC concerns about U.S. and Japanese hostile intent • China's reaction could be limited by increased capabilities for defense of Japan, potential for escalation with United States
Maximal	Cooperative R&D program with Taiwan to develop nuclear deterrent	• Potential for nuclear weapons on Taiwan substantially increases China's concerns about U.S., Taiwan military threat, hostile intent • U.S. support for Taiwan obtaining nuclear capabilities makes PRC perception of threat to regime legitimacy acute • China might also perceive threats to its regional influence given that other states might also wish to work with the United States on nuclear R&D • PRC concerns for escalation risks, U.S. involvement insufficient to restrain PRC responses given acute threats to vital national interests

Security cooperation activities, which include combined exercises and training, materiel military assistance, and foreign military exchanges, can also precipitate a range of Chinese responses at various escalation tiers. Security cooperation activities that might cause no or minor PRC response could include new or expanded foreign military exchanges with regional states. Particularly if the United States already has a security relationship with the country engaging in the exchanges, China is likely to have little reaction to these types of cooperative activities. For example, the United States and Singapore expanding their existing foreign officer exchange program would likely result in no or only a minor reaction by China. The expansion of military exchanges with Singapore could increase Chinese concerns about threats to regional influence, as it signals a closer relationship with a key regional state, Singapore, that China is also trying to build influence with. However, China's reaction would be tempered by the existing robust U.S.-Singapore defense relationship and the fact that the activity does not involve new or kinetic capabilities.

For the notable category, security cooperation activities that might cause China to react in this manner include expanding routine military exercises near China's borders or politically or militarily sensitive areas to involve new partners. For example, involving new regional partners such as Indonesia or Vietnam in routine U.S. military exercises that take place in the SCS might cause China to have a notable reaction. Similarly, expanding U.S. exercises taking place near Taiwan that includes partners from outside of the region, such as Germany or France, might also lead to a notable PRC response. In these examples, the participation of new partners from the SCS region could potentially increase China's perception of threat to its regional influence as China has also sought to woo these states from becoming closer to the United States. Involving partners from outside of the region in exercises near Taiwan might increase China's perception of U.S. and allied hostile intent, as this activity would potentially signal increased U.S. willingness to counter China's coercion of Taiwan as well as an expanded set of states outside of the region that might support Taiwan independence. However, China's reaction would be limited by the routine nature of the exercises and the fact that they do not involve high-end or new capabilities.

China's reactions might fall into the elevated category if the United States conducts security cooperation activities that enhance the capabilities of regional states that could be used to counter Chinese actions in politically sensitive areas such as the SCS. For example, the United States providing FMF and donations to Vietnam of advanced military platforms, to include fighter aircraft, ISR and EW capabilities, would likely lead to an elevated PRC response. The donations of military platforms would enhance Vietnam's capabilities to patrol its littoral and disputed TW in the SCS, as well as increase the capabilities to defend Vietnamese territory. This would likely raise China's perception of military threat from Vietnam and the United States, the supplier of the capabilities. In addition, the military assistance demonstrates closer U.S.-Vietnam security relations and signals increased U.S. support for SCS states and countering Chinese coercive actions. This would likely increase China's concerns of U.S. hostile intent. Despite these concerns, PRC reaction would be limited by the small scope of the assistance package to Vietnam, as well as Vietnam's limited existing military capabilities.

Severe Chinese reactions might occur when a security cooperation activity results in the deployment or development of a capability in a U.S. ally or partner that could significantly undermine China's defenses or target key capabilities such as China's C2 or nuclear forces. A hypothetical example might be the United States selling a large-scale arms package to Japan with high-end missile systems, including LRHWs. Selling these types of systems to Japan could be used to target Chinese forces in regional conflict, which would significantly increase China's perception of the military threat posed by both the United States and Japan. In addition, offensive strike and LRHW capabilities could be used in a Taiwan contingency, which would heighten China's fears of threats to its regime legitimacy. Japan purchasing these types of high-end systems from the United States demonstrates its willingness to host capabilities that would be primarily used to target Chinese forces in a conflict, which would also raise PRC concerns about the level of hostile intent from the United States and Japan toward China. Although China's reactions would be severe in this example, the PRC could be deterred from even more-escalatory responses by the increased capabilities for the defense of Japan that the LRHW and missile strike systems represent, as well as the potential for escalation to a larger conflict involving the United States.

China might consider a maximal reaction if U.S. security cooperation activities involve assisting Taiwan in developing capabilities that would seriously threaten China's physical and regime security as well as its ability to attack the island. For example, a cooperative R&D program with Taiwan to develop nuclear weapons technologies for deterrent purposes would potentially lead China to react in this category. In this case, the potential that Taiwan would eventually have nuclear weapons would substantially increase China's concerns about the military threat from the United States and Taiwan. In addition, security cooperation on nuclear weapon technologies between the United States and Taiwan would certainly heighten China's perception of U.S. and Taiwan hostile intent. U.S.-Taiwan security cooperation on nuclear technologies would also signal U.S. support for Taiwan obtaining nuclear weapons to deter Chinese attack, which would make China's perceptions of threat to regime legitimacy particularly acute. Finally, China might also perceive threats to its regional influence given that other states in the region, such as Japan, might also wish to work with the United States on nuclear weapon R&D. Given the acute threats to vital national interests, China's concerns over escalation risks with the United States are unlikely to constrain PRC responses.

Military Operations and Kinetic Activities

Finally, there are a number of ways in which the characteristics of U.S. military operations and kinetic activities may affect Chinese reactions. Table 6.5 provides examples of U.S. activities in this category and their characteristics that could potentially lead to PRC responses in the different escalation tiers.

Table 6.5. Summary of Potential Escalation Risks of Varied U.S. Military Operations and Kinetic Activities

Potential Escalation Risk	Activity Description	Anchoring Activity Characteristics
No/minor	Multilateral S&R operations or exercises with Vietnam, Philippines, and Indonesia near disputed SCS territory	• Involvement of SCS claimants could increase PRC perception of threat to regional influence • PRC reaction limited because capabilities demonstrated are not of military concern and not in themselves indicative of anti-China activities
Notable	CSG transits through the Taiwan Strait, with accompanying U.S. statements emphasizing legal use of international waters, not specifically directed against PRC	• Proximity to Taiwan would likely increase PRC concern over potential U.S. military threat, U.S. hostile intent • Strait transits signal U.S. support for Taiwan, heightening PRC concerns over threats to regime legitimacy • PRC reaction limited because United States not deploying capabilities to Taiwan, only transiting Strait; statements de-emphasize threats to China from transit, ostensible non-China rationales
Elevated	Deploy UAVs to surveil SCS and provide intel to partners along with aircraft that use EW to disrupt the communications capabilities of PRC forces in disputed waters	• Proximity to SCS territorial disputes and disruption of PRC forces' communications increase PRC concern over potential U.S. military threat • Intel-sharing signals increased support for regional states, raising China's concern about hostile intent, threats to PRC regional influence • China's reaction limited by lack of kinetic capabilities used, preexisting U.S. ISR in the SCS
Severe	United States establishes no-fly zone in Taiwan Strait to prevent Chinese aircraft from incursions into Taiwan's territory	• Location of no-fly zone in Taiwan Strait and U.S. ability to potentially shoot down PRC aircraft violating the zone significantly increase China's perception of U.S. hostile intent, military threat • Signals U.S. willingness to defend Taiwan, prevent PRC forces from coercing Taiwan, raising acute PRC concerns over threats to regime legitimacy • PRC reaction limited by lack of high-end capabilities deployed, fear of escalation to larger conflict with the United States
Maximal	United States implements a comprehensive military blockade in key maritime chokepoints in the SCS, ECS, and other regions farther from China to strangle PRC economy, with accompanying statements about deterring PRC aggression against Taiwan	• U.S. operations restricting key SLOCs, maritime chokepoints raise acute PRC concerns over threats to economic development • Statements on countering PRC aggression against Taiwan signals increased U.S. support for Taiwan independence and defense of Taiwan, substantially raising PRC concerns over threats to regime legitimacy • Threats to economy and ability to coerce Taiwan mean that PRC reactions not limited by fear of escalation to direct conflict with United States

NOTE: UAV = unmanned aerial vehicle.

U.S. military operations and kinetic activities could lead to PRC responses in each of the escalation tiers, depending on the activity and context. PRC reaction in the no or minor category could occur in response to military soft power activities that are conducted farther away from China's borders or sensitive political areas and that do not involve kinetic or high-end military capabilities. For example, a multilateral S&R operation led by the United States that includes Vietnam, the Philippines, and Indonesia, even if it takes place near disputed territory in the SCS, could lead to this level of response. The involvement of other SCS claimants in a U.S.-led exercise could increase China's perception of threat to regional influence, because China has made efforts to woo many of these states away from closer cooperation with the United States. However, China's reactions would be limited because the capabilities used for the exercise are not of military concern and the exercise is not in and of itself indicative of anti-China motivation.

In the notable category, Chinese responses might stem from limited or temporary U.S. military operations that occur close to China's borders or forces, close to Taiwan, or close to other politically sensitive areas to China, even if they involve demonstrations of U.S. capabilities that could be directed against the PRC in conflict. U.S. CSG transits through the Taiwan Strait, for example, if accompanied by U.S. statements emphasizing that the transits were conducted to uphold the legal use of international waters and were not specifically directed against China or timed to coincide with any sensitive developments on Taiwan, could result in a notable PRC reaction. The location of the transits in the Taiwan Strait would likely increase China's concern over the potential U.S. military threat and hostile intent. In addition, China's concerns over threats to its regime legitimacy would be heightened by the signal that the transits send about U.S. support for Taiwan. In this case, China's reactions would be limited because the United States would be transiting the Strait a single time, rather than making a more durable change to U.S. posture or activities in the region, and U.S. statements and timing took pains to de-emphasize the threats to China from the transits.

China's reactions in the elevated category could occur in response to U.S. military operations or kinetic activities that are threatening to Chinese forces, that occur in politically or military sensitive areas to China, and that demonstrate support for regional states in countering Chinese coercion. For example, U.S. deployment of capabilities such as UAVs to augment surveillance of the SCS and provide intelligence to regional states, along with U.S. military aircraft that would use EW to disrupt the communications capabilities of PRC forces around disputed waters, would likely result in an elevated response by China. The location of the UAVs and aircraft in the SCS and around the disputed territory, plus disruption of local Chinese forces' communications, would increase China's concerns over the potential U.S. military threat. In addition, the United States sharing its intelligence and ISR with SCS states signals increased U.S. support for other claimants, raising China's concern about hostile intent and threats to PRC regional influence. China's reactions would likely be limited by the lack of kinetic capabilities used by the United States for these operations, in addition to the ISR capability not being new, because there are already preexisting U.S. ISR capabilities in the SCS.

U.S. military operations or kinetic activities that might lead China to react severely could include those that occur near Taiwan, that have the potential to directly target Chinese forces in a conflict, or that would increase China's concern over its ability to conduct key military missions. An example might be if the United States were to establish a no-fly zone in the Taiwan Strait to prevent Chinese aircraft from incursions across the median line and into Taiwan's TW. Establishing a no-fly zone in the Taiwan Strait and deploying the capabilities to potentially fire on PRC aircraft violating the no-fly zone would significantly increase China's perception of the military threat posed by the United States, as well as the level of U.S. hostile intent toward China. In addition, the establishment of a no-fly zone in the Taiwan Strait signals increased U.S. willingness to defend Taiwan and prevent PRC forces from coercing Taiwan, which would raise acute Chinese concerns over threats to PRC regime legitimacy. China's reactions would be limited by their concerns over the potential for escalation to a larger conflict with the United States.

A maximal Chinese response might occur if the United States conducted military operations that are meant to counter Chinese aggression against Taiwan or PRC coercive actions against regional states. For example, China might respond in this category if the United States were to implement a comprehensive military blockade to restrict Chinese shipping through key maritime chokepoints in the SCS, ECS, and other regions farther from China, such as the Indian Ocean or Persian Gulf, to strangle China's economy, along with accompanying statements about the blockade being motivated by a need to prevent Chinese aggression against Taiwan. In this example, U.S. operations restricting key SLOCs and maritime chokepoints would raise acute concerns by China over threats to its economic development and indicate acute U.S. hostile intent. In addition, the statements on countering China's aggression against Taiwan signals increased U.S. support for Taiwan's independence and U.S. willingness to defend Taiwan, which would substantially raise China's concerns over threats to its regime legitimacy. Because of the acute threats to its economy and ability to coerce Taiwan if the blockade were left unchecked, PRC reactions would likely not be limited by fear of escalation to direct conflict with the United States.

Activity Characteristics and Escalation Potential

While escalation risks should ideally be considered holistically, incorporating all activity characteristics and context, our analysis of the escalation risks of numerous potential U.S. military activities highlights several specific characteristics that are likely to be associated with particular degrees of escalation from China across most activities and conditions. This final section in the chapter provides a summary of several noteworthy specific activity characteristics and the escalation risk of China's responses with which they are most likely to be associated. These estimates are general and approximate and could well vary in different circumstances. They are also cumulative, as military activities invariably have some characteristics across all of the listed categories, and, as such, no characteristic is ever really present in isolation from others. But the analysis below does provide U.S. military planners with useful "rules of thumb" regarding how China may respond to particular characteristics of activities that they may be considering undertaking. The discussion following provides an explanation and examples for each activity characteristic category and the potential escalation risk of China's responses.

Location

At the lower end of the escalation risk spectrum, U.S. activities that are near to key SLOCs or maritime chokepoints could increase China's concerns about U.S. and allied ability to interdict Chinese shipping resulting in threats to PRC economic development. For example, conducting U.S.-led multilateral exercises with India and Australia in the Indian Ocean could raise China's concerns that these countries could restrict China's movement through South Asian SLOCs. Similarly, U.S. naval ships transiting through the SCS could also raise Chinese concerns that the United States might use these capabilities to restrict China's access to resources in that area. But in most circumstances, the escalation risks associated with such locations are likely to be more limited than two others.

First, activities that occur close to China's borders, that occur near Chinese military forces or facilities, or that are proximate to politically sensitive areas such as Taiwan, the SCS, or ECS, would likely result in a higher risk of a more escalatory Chinese response. For example, conducting air and naval surveillance patrols near disputed territory in the SCS would likely increase China's concerns over U.S. hostile intent and threats to regional influence and might result in a more aggressive response. Likewise, an activity that demonstrates a new U.S. capability to target China would have a higher likelihood of leading to an aggressive PRC response if the demonstration occurs in the ECS as opposed to a less sensitive area to China, such as the Indian Ocean.

Last, activities that are close to or on Taiwan, as well as those that are proximate to China's borders and military forces and facilities, carry the highest risk of an escalatory PRC response. Increased U.S. security cooperation with Taiwan that could potentially lead to the United States deploying forces or capabilities to Taiwan, for example, would result in an aggressive Chinese response because it would lead to heightened fears of PRC regime legitimacy and U.S. hostile intent. Figure 6.1 summarizes the relative escalation risks of these noteworthy locations.

Figure 6.1. Potential Escalation Risk of Noteworthy Locations of U.S. Military Activities

Location

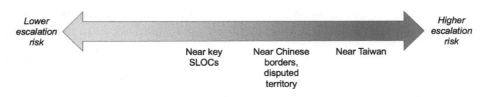

Lower escalation risk ⟵———————————————⟶ *Higher escalation risk*

Near key SLOCs   Near Chinese borders, disputed territory   Near Taiwan

Placement of characteristics intended to be approximate.
Ordering of characteristics can easily change in different context and circumstances.

Allies/Partners Involved

For this characteristic, U.S. activities that involve smaller or less influential states in the region, particularly those with limited military capabilities, would likely present a comparatively low escalation risk for China's response. Conducting security cooperation activities with a Pacific Island nation, for example, would potentially increase China's concerns about threats to its regional influence given that the Pacific Islands are viewed by Beijing as an area of growing competition with the United States. However, this concern alone likely presents very little risk of an aggressive Chinese response.

Similarly, substantial expansion of military exchanges or defense ties with existing U.S. allies or partners (with the exception of what China perceives to be clearly anti-China countries, as discussed below) could elicit a more aggressive Chinese response and heighten the escalation risk, though it still would remain comparatively low. The United States substantially expanding military exchanges with Singapore, for example, might increase China's concerns over its regional influence because the PRC has tried to bolster its own relationship with Singapore. However, the existing robust U.S.-Singapore defense relationship would likely limit China's response to any moderate expansion of those defense ties.

The involvement of U.S. partners in the region that are new to a U.S. activity, such as including Indonesia in a U.S.-led large-scale joint maritime exercises in the SCS, could lead to a somewhat more escalatory PRC response. China might perceive heighted threats to its regional influence from Indonesia's decision to participate in the exercise. Similarly, including a U.S. ally or partner from outside of the region that is new to an activity can also lead to a more escalatory Chinese response. For example, the United States coordinating a series of FONOPs in the ECS with the French and German navies would likely increase China's concerns over U.S. and allied hostile intent, as well as the potential future military threat, though the level of coordination and nature of the operations would also play a role in China's level of reaction.

The involvement of allies and partners in a U.S. military activity that signals that the United States is forming or attempting to form a more robust anti-China coalition could contribute to a more escalatory PRC response. U.S. leadership statements with various ASEAN countries that emphasize the development of collective capabilities to counter Chinese coercive actions in the SCS, for example, would potentially elicit a more escalatory PRC response. U.S. activities involving countries that are clearly anti-China and supportive of U.S. actions and objectives, such as Japan and Australia, would likely involve additional escalation risk because China's perception of U.S. and allied hostile intent would increase. Finally, activities involving Taiwan carry the highest risk of escalation, as China would likely perceive heightened threat to its regime legitimacy as well as an increase in U.S. hostile intent. These characteristics are summarized in Figure 6.2.

Figure 6.2. Potential Escalation Risk of Noteworthy U.S. Ally and Partner Involvement with U.S. Military Activities

U.S. Ally and Partner Involvement

Placement of characteristics intended to be approximate.
Ordering of characteristics can easily change in different context and circumstances.

Capabilities

We identified five noteworthy capabilities that are likely to be associated with different escalation levels of PRC responses. U.S. activities involving capabilities that substantially increase interoperability between the U.S. military and allies or partners have some potential escalation risk, depending on the ally or partner and capabilities involved. Establishing new information-sharing or intelligence-sharing agreements that could assist U.S. and allied or partner forces in coordinating operations to counter China is one example. In this case, China might perceive an increase in U.S. and allied hostile intent.

U.S. activities that deploy capabilities to allies and partners (excluding those perceived to be clearly anti-China, as discussed below) or augment existing allied and partner ability to threaten China's borders, forces, or other Chinese interests likely pose a higher escalation risk. An example includes donating U.S. ISR platforms for use by the Philippine military that could be used to detect Chinese forces in the SCS and increase the Philippines' ability to respond. This could heighten China's perception of military threat and U.S. and Philippine hostile intent and lead to a more escalatory PRC response.

U.S. exercise or deployment of capabilities that would be primarily or only used in a conflict with China could lead to a greater escalation risk. Deploying LRHWs to Japan, for example, would substantially increase China's perception of the military threat from the United States and

Japan, as well as China's concerns about U.S. and Japanese hostile intent. U.S. activities that would deploy capabilities to substantially increase Taiwan's defenses, such as high-end missile defense platforms, long-range radars, or offensive strike weapons that can target the Chinese mainland, would potentially lead to a highly escalatory Chinese response. At the highest end of the escalation spectrum, U.S. capabilities that can target China's C2, nuclear forces, or leadership would be highly escalatory. In both examples, China would perceive acute threats to its regime legitimacy, significantly increased level of military threat from the United States, and increased hostile intent from the United States and Taiwan and would likely respond in a disproportionately escalatory manner. These noteworthy capabilities are summarized in Figure 6.3.

Figure 6.3. Potential Escalation Risk of Noteworthy Capabilities Involved in U.S. Military Activities

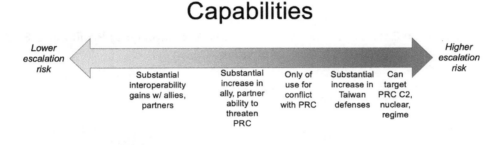

Placement of characteristics intended to be approximate.
Ordering of characteristics can easily change in different context and circumstances.

Profile

U.S. statements or other aspects of profile that accompany activities can also affect escalation risk. U.S. statements or leadership rhetoric that generally challenge China's regional influence or objectives—for example, broad statements on countering China's regional military power—represent a relatively lower escalation risk because China might perceive a slight increase in U.S. threat to its regional influence, but this would likely not be so concerning as to spur much of a reaction. Statements on closer defense relationships with U.S. allies or partners could present a slightly higher escalation risk, particularly if the statements involve partners that China has been trying to form a closer relationship with, such as Vietnam or Indonesia. Again, China might perceive an increase in threat to its regional influence as well as greater U.S. and partner hostile intent; however, these types of statements would still likely not lead to a highly aggressive Chinese reaction.

Statements that indicate specific support for SCS claimants, however, could lead to a higher escalation risk as China would perceive increased threat to its regional influence, an increased level of hostile intent, and potentially greater military threat from the United States depending on whether the statements also involve signaling future U.S. force or capabilities deployments to the region. An even higher escalation risk would be present for U.S. statements that challenge China's claim to Taiwan or that discuss countering China's coercion of Taiwan. In this case, China would perceive an increase in threat to its regime legitimacy, in addition to increased U.S. hostile intent, and could respond in a more escalatory manner.

Explicit U.S. or allied or partner threats to use force to counter China's actions would likely further increase the risk of escalation, as China would perceive a heightened level of U.S. military threat and hostile intent. For example, threatening to fire on Chinese maritime or air forces in the SCS would likely encourage a more aggressive PRC response. The highest risk of escalation from profile would come from U.S. statements directly supporting Taiwan's independence. This would lead to acute concerns over U.S. threats to China's regime legitimacy, substantially increase China's perception of military threat and hostile intent from the United States, and increase PRC concerns over regional influence if other states back U.S. support of Taiwan. These characteristics are summarized in Figure 6.4.

Figure 6.4. Potential Escalation Risk of Noteworthy Accompanying Profile of U.S. Military Activities

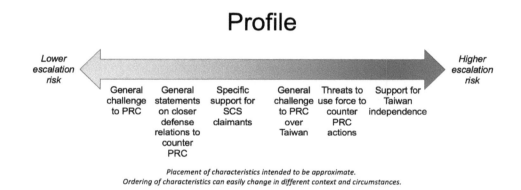

In conclusion, the U.S. activity characteristics we assessed to be most associated with the greatest risk of an escalatory PRC response include activities located near China's borders, near disputed territory in the SCS, or in or around Taiwan. Activities that signal that the United States is forming or attempting to influence countries to form an anti-China coalition or that involve anti-China countries that strongly support U.S. objectives would also likely lead to an aggressive PRC response, while activities that involve Taiwan carry the greatest risk of escalation.

The U.S. deploying or augmenting substantial regional capabilities that would be primarily or only used in conflict against China would also potentially risk escalation, as would capabilities that substantially increase Taiwan's ability to defend itself. The most significant escalation risk would come from U.S. activities resulting in deployment of capabilities in the region that could undermine China's C2, nuclear deterrent, or regime targets. An activity profile that includes U.S. statements challenging China's claim to Taiwan and statements that explicitly indicate threats to use force to counter coercive Chinese actions could also lead to higher risks of escalatory PRC responses.

Chapter 7. Conclusion

Military activities are an important lever for U.S. policymakers in the ongoing strategic competition with China in the Indo-Pacific. But the use of these levers has inherent risks and costs, most notably the possibility that China may take highly escalatory or otherwise unwelcome actions in response. This report has focused on providing U.S. military planners and policymakers with guidance regarding how the characteristics of different U.S. military activities may affect Chinese perceptions and reactions, either in ways that the United States may prefer—such as by enhancing deterrence of PRC aggression against U.S. allies and partners—or in ways the United States may wish to avoid—such as by increasing the risk of such aggression. This concluding chapter summarizes the main findings from the report, highlights a series of cross-cutting implications of particular importance, and identifies recommendations for U.S. policymakers that emerge from our analysis.

Summary of Findings

The primary contribution of this report is the development of a detailed, open-source framework that U.S. military planners or others interested in the topic can use to anticipate likely Chinese reactions to U.S. military activities in the Indo-Pacific region. While the framework does not provide precise guidance regarding specific Chinese responses, as Beijing's calculations in these matters will be highly context dependent, it does provide a detailed set of considerations for U.S. policymakers to take into account. The framework therefore is designed to work as a valuable guide or support for subject-matter experts tasked with anticipating China's perceptions and thinking, but it is not a replacement for their expertise.

The framework also makes a number of substantive contributions to the study of China's likely reactions to U.S. military activities in the Indo-Pacific. The heart of the framework is the six key factors we identified as most central to informing Chinese perceptions and reactions, summarized in Table 7.1.

Table 7.1. Key Factors That Affect Chinese Responses to U.S. Military Activities

Key Factors
1. China's perceptions of the potential military threat from U.S., allied, and partner capabilities
2. China's perceptions of U.S., allied, and partner hostile intent
3. China's perceptions of threats to its regime legitimacy
4. China's perceptions of threats to its economic development
5. China's perceptions of threats to its regional influence
6. China's perceptions of U.S. commitment to the defense of U.S. allies or partners

Among these six factors, the first three—dealing with Chinese perceptions of the military threat it faces from the United States and its allies and partners, PRC perceptions of U.S. and allied hostile intent, and broader threats to its regime legitimacy—are the most likely to lead to acute PRC regime or national security concerns and, in turn, the most likely to lead to highly escalatory PRC responses. While this report does not identify a specific list of Chinese "redlines," as these may be difficult to identify precisely and may change over time, China's greatest concerns with U.S. activities in the region are likely to be driven by these factors, particularly if they are combined. Chinese concerns over economic development and regional influence, in most circumstances, are likely to be less acute, though they can still motivate aggressive reactions.

Restraining the potential for aggressive Chinese reactions, of course, is Chinese concern over the costs it may face should it become involved in a direct military conflict with the United States. While China is likely to believe that such a conflict is a near-certainty should it take direct military action against the United States itself, its calculations regarding under what circumstances and to what extent the United States will intervene militarily to defend the wide range of U.S. allies and partners in the region are more complex. How China assesses U.S. willingness and, of course, ability to defend different allies and partners constitutes the sixth and final of our key factors. Many U.S. military activities in the region are intended precisely to reinforce China's perception that the United States will uphold the explicit defense commitments that it has made, in particular to Japan, the ROK, the Philippines, and Australia. But the United States also undertakes military activities that appear to be intended to signal to China that the United States *may* be willing to intervene militarily in the event of a Chinese attack on other states to whom the United States has not made such commitments, ranging from Vietnam to, most crucially, Taiwan. Understanding how China is likely to perceive these more nuanced signals is therefore vital to understanding their utility.

In selecting these six key factors, we have also excluded other factors that are sometimes cited as important in analyses of Chinese behavior. Two of the most commonly referenced of these—Chinese internal instability and Chinese concerns for its reputation for resolve—are discussed in detail in Appendix A. While we ultimately assessed that they were less essential than the six factors we did select for understanding Chinese behavior, we acknowledge that other analyses may have different perspectives, and so we include our full analyses of them to contribute to this broader debate.

Having established our six key factors, our framework then identifies the ways in which these factors may be affected by four characteristics of U.S. military activities, which are summarized in Table 7.2.

Table 7.2. Key Characteristics of U.S. Military Activities

Characteristic	Examples
Location	• Proximity to PRC or PRC forces • Proximity to politically, economically, or militarily sensitive areas
Ally or partner involvement	• Number, importance, and political disposition of allies/partners • Consistency with previous cooperation with allies/partners
Capabilities	• Novelty of capabilities in activity • Lethal potential and wartime usefulness of activity • Technological level employed in activity
Profile	• Timing of activity in relation to PRC or regional events • Visibility of activity • Associated U.S. rhetoric

These four characteristics—location, U.S. ally or partner involvement, capabilities, and profile—were judged to be the characteristics of U.S. military activities that most directly and consistently affected Chinese perceptions and behavior through the six key factors.[269] As we evaluated the ways in which each activity characteristic may affect each of the key factors, we identified 54 potential linkages that analysts should consider for a given U.S. military activity. These linkages were summarized in Table 3.2, but they incorporate a wide range of considerations, from how the capabilities demonstrated in an activity might affect Chinese perceptions of the potential military threat posed by the United States and its allies and partners to how the timing or messaging accompanying particular activities might serve to reinforce deterrence.

The final aspect of our framework consists of a rough typology and related observations regarding the form that Chinese reactions to particular U.S. military activities might take. While the relationship between the first two parts of the framework—assessments of key factors and linkages with activity characteristics—and this third—potential PRC reactions—is by no means

---

[269] We carefully considered a fifth potential characteristic: continuity. That is, does whether U.S. military activities constitute a break with past patterns of U.S. activity independently affect PRC thinking and reactions? We ultimately assessed that while China may take note of changes in U.S. patterns, ultimately the other four characteristics noted above would likely have a substantially greater effect on Chinese perceptions.

mechanistic, the typology of potential PRC reactions that we developed does help to understand what types of specific PRC reactions might occur in response to different aggregate levels of PRC concern, ranging from quite minor concerns to those sufficient to motivate a precipitous Chinese attack on U.S. or allied or partner forces. The analysis in Chapter 4 also highlights the importance of considering both short-term and long-term Chinese reactions, as the most durable or problematic ways in which China reacts, from a U.S. perspective, may not be those that are most immediately apparent. From our case studies and literature review, we also made four broader observations regarding patterns in Chinese reactions to U.S. military activities that are worth highlighting here.

- **Pattern 1: China adopts multilayered responses.** China's responses to U.S. activities that it finds particularly concerning tend to involve a multilayered mixture of diplomatic, economic, and military policy changes that Beijing calibrates—and integrates—depending on the situation.

- **Pattern 2: Diplomatic and political responses are always present.** In the cases we examined, China's initial response to U.S. actions that it regarded as serious almost always began with political signaling of Chinese interests and displeasure. China's military reactions, particularly the more provocative ones, were all preceded and accompanied by extensive media commentary and sometimes by official statements that aimed to build domestic and international political support for China's position and demonize any potential target of China's actions.

- **Pattern 3: China responds militarily to low-intensity military activities.** Although China's responses to U.S. military activities of relatively high concern tend to be multilayered across multiple dimensions of Chinese power, its responses to less concerning U.S. military activities tend to remain military in nature and tend not to include corresponding sustained economic responses, for example. Furthermore, in responding, the PLA generally tailors the capabilities demonstrated, exercise location, and tempo to signal ability to counter a specific U.S. activity.

- **Pattern 4: China uses a spectrum of military and paramilitary options.** China's responses reflect its growing ability to conduct military and paramilitary operations at the lower end of the intensity spectrum. Its approach to territorial disputes in the ECS and SCS, for example, has evolved as China's gray zone capabilities have increased, and this approach now emphasizes the use of paramilitary and cyber forces whose use is either deniable or would not cross the threshold of armed conflict.

Having developed this framework, the second part of this report explored what implications the framework has for particular U.S. military activities. We began by developing a relatively comprehensive set of potential U.S. military activities in the Indo-Pacific, based on the record of what activities the United States has undertaken recently in the region, as well as what activities it has undertaken in other historical or geographic contexts, including, most notably, during the

Cold War against the Soviet Union. Overall, our typology of U.S. military activities covered five main categories and 19 subcategories, as shown in Table 7.3. We also identified a third level of more specific activity subtypes, of which there were 83, as discussed throughout Chapter 5.

Table 7.3. Simplified Typology of Possible U.S. Military Activities to Compete with China

Activity Category (Level 1)	Activity Type (Level 2)
Strategic- and doctrinal-level activities	1. Changes to U.S. national security and defense policy 2. Changes to DoD strategy and doctrine
Posture enhancement and theater-setting activities	3. Changes to enabling agreements 4. Changes to deployed force structure 5. Changes to theater infrastructure 6. Changes to theater equipment set
Presence and theater-shaping activities	7. Expeditionary shaping activities and declaratory actions 8. Garrisoned presence and force protection activities 9. ISR activities 10. Unilateral exercises and training activities
Security cooperation activities	11. Combined exercises and training activities 12. Materiel military assistance 13. Foreign military exchanges and military diplomacy
Military operations and kinetic activities	14. Direct military interventions 15. Proxy warfare operations 16. Deterrence operations 17. Crisis responses and demonstrations of force 18. Soft power and civil-military operations 19. Asymmetric, irregular, or covert warfare activities

Our consideration of this set of U.S. activities led to three initial insights.

- DoD has already covered much of the range—roughly three-quarters—of possible activity types identified in competition with China since the start of the Obama administration's Asia-Pacific rebalancing strategy.
- Most of the activity types that have recently gone unutilized have seemingly been avoided out of concern for the risks of escalation involved. Many of the activities that DoD has not conducted against China in the past decade—such as engaging in proxy warfare or advancing space weaponization—might invite steeper escalatory risks than U.S. defense planners are currently willing to consider.
- Finally, and perhaps most significantly, our analysis found that more-significant historical differences exist between *how* similar activity types have been conducted in the past rather than between *which* activity types have been conducted. In general, many activity types were conducted on a larger scale and signaled more-hostile intent during U.S.-Soviet Cold War competition. As such, U.S. defense planners looking for additional options in the intensifying competition with China may wish to look

primarily at changes in the characteristics of existing activities, rather than searching for entirely new options.

We then examined the types of activities, and more specifically the characteristics of those activities, that are likely to lead to PRC responses at different levels of escalation. We discussed examples of activities in each escalation tier—no/minor, notable, elevated, severe, and maximal—and then highlighted noteworthy characteristics from these activities that are likely to be associated with different levels of escalation or intensity in Chinese responses. These characteristics, summarized above in Figures 6.1 through 6.4, provide U.S. military planners with a number of rules of thumb that can be used in designing U.S. military activities in ways that limit escalation risks. Our analysis also highlighted several potential activity characteristics that are likely to be associated with the highest levels of escalatory response by China. These include the following:

- **Location:** Activities located near Chinese borders, disputed territory, or in or around Taiwan
- **Allies/partners involved:** Activities that signal the formation of an anti-China coalition, involve anti-China countries that strongly support U.S. objectives, or involve Taiwan
- **Capabilities:** Capabilities that would be primarily or only used in conflict against China; capabilities that substantially increase Taiwan's ability to defend itself; and capabilities that could undermine China's C2, nuclear deterrent, or regime targets
- **Profile:** Statements challenging China's claim to Taiwan and statements that explicitly indicate threats to use force to counter coercive Chinese actions.

Insights for the Conduct of U.S. Military Activities in the Indo-Pacific Region

Our research highlights six broader insights for U.S. policymaker consideration.

1. **China assumes that most U.S. military activities in the region are aggressive and hostile to China.**

China is likely to perceive most U.S. military activities in the Indo-Pacific region as aggressive actions by the United States, intended to counter or target China's military capabilities and, more broadly, hinder China's regional ambitions. The Chinese leadership's assessments of U.S. objectives and intentions toward China have come to assume a high level of U.S. hostility toward the CCP. However, while U.S. planners should be aware of China's perceptions that most U.S. military activities are meant to threaten Chinese forces, there is still a wide range in terms of the levels of threat or concern that China may perceive from a given activity. So, while U.S. policymakers can likely assume a negative Chinese reaction to most U.S. military activities in the region, the important questions of the degree or intensity of those reactions, rather than just their direction, are crucial.

2. China's level of concern for a U.S. military activity does not translate directly into the aggressiveness of its response.

Our evaluation of recent Chinese behavior highlights that China's level of concern about a military activity does not directly correlate with the aggressiveness of its responses. Rather, China will assess the leverage and capabilities it has against a specific country, in addition to the escalatory potential of a response, in deciding how to react. In some cases, China may be highly concerned by a U.S. military activity, but its response may include nonaggressive actions such as economic or political inducements to a U.S. partner. China may also choose not to respond immediately if it assesses that the risk of escalation is too high or that its actions might erode PRC advantages in other areas, such as its regional influence. U.S. military activities that occur on U.S. territory would have perhaps the highest barriers to consideration of a direct, military response by China given China's perceptions of the risk of direct military confrontation with the United States. Military activities that occur on or near the territory of U.S. allies and partners, however, may provide more opportunities for Chinese pressure or coercion if China believes the likelihood of direct U.S. involvement is reduced, or the ally or partner involved lacks native capabilities to credibly escalate in a potential conflict or crisis that may result.

China's responses to U.S. military activities it finds particularly concerning tend to involve a multilayered mixture of political, economic, and military policy changes that Beijing calibrates—and integrates—depending on the situation and the leverage that it assesses it has over a host nation. For example, U.S. allies and partners that are economically closer to China and that agree to host U.S. posture enhancements are likely to face more pressure from China in various domains because Beijing might view its ability to coerce those countries into changing course as plausible given its economic leverage. This was the case with the THAAD deployment, where China used primarily diplomatic, political, and economic levers to punish South Korea and attempt to prevent the deployment of the capability. Where U.S. capabilities are less directly threatening to China, Beijing might consider a combination of carrots and sticks to alter the willingness of U.S. allies and partners to host U.S. capabilities, until such point where the posture enhancement directly impinges on China's redlines or core objectives. Several cases involving the Philippines that are discussed in Chapter 2 also show how China may continue to use inducements in the diplomatic or economic realms while it simultaneously applies military pressure where core issues such as territorial integrity are at stake.

3. China's clear "redlines" appear to be limited in number.

Our analysis highlighted only a handful of activity characteristics likely to be associated with the most escalatory types of PRC responses, including proximity to or involvement of Taiwan or capabilities that threaten PRC C2, nuclear, or regime targets. While this report outlines a large number of additional characteristics likely to concern China to a lesser degree, U.S. military activities with these other characteristics are unlikely to lead to immediate escalation. Instead, they may lead to Chinese responses short of conflict with which U.S. policymakers will need to contend, and they may contribute to a gradual ratcheting up of tensions between the two states that may increase escalation risks across the board over the long term, if the current more-conflictual trajectory of the U.S.-China relationship continues.

4. **However, Chinese sensitivities regarding Taiwan are likely to continue to complicate efforts to better defend the island while avoiding escalation.**

While Chinese "redlines" may be comparatively few in number, they generally do touch directly on capabilities and locations that would, in operational terms, be of substantial utility for the defense of Taiwan. Capabilities such as long-range precision strike and locating forces and capabilities directly on Taiwan could have substantial operational value for the defense of the island, but they are also (not unrelatedly) the types of U.S. military activities most likely to lead to highly aggressive PRC responses. While this is not a novel observation, it does highlight the challenge that U.S. military planners face in identifying ways to enhance the defense of Taiwan without precipitating an unwanted Chinese reaction. Threading this needle for other U.S. goals in the region, including enhancing the security of other U.S. allies and partners, is likely to be comparatively easier.

5. **China is now more likely to use lower-level military responses to signal disapproval or apply pressure than in the past, having better developed such capabilities.**

China's recent development of less escalatory military options—such as paramilitary forces or other "gray zone" capabilities—increases the likelihood that China would incorporate a lower-level military action into its response to a concerning U.S. military activity. For the past decade, Chinese leaders have directed the PLA to develop a greater range of military options that fall below the threshold of armed conflict. As a result, a U.S. military activity that generates a heightened level of Chinese concern is now less likely to present China with a choice between escalating to conflict or essentially backing down, as it did in the 1996 Taiwan Straits crisis. Instead, China is now more able to pursue a combination of lower-level responses, including military, to signal its concerns and resolve in its own efforts to deter further U.S. action.

6. **U.S. military activities that pose acute concerns for China are more likely to trigger consequential changes in longer-term PRC policies.**

A final point to consider when assessing likely PRC reactions is that China may also respond to U.S. military activities with longer-term changes to Chinese policy, including economic initiatives and military investments. These responses may not be immediately visible, because they take place over a longer time horizon and are meant to address larger issues in the regional military balance or the U.S.-China strategic competition and are more likely in response to U.S. military activities that pose acute concerns for Beijing. In the past, China's longer-term military responses have generally focused on addressing key capabilities gaps vis-à-vis the U.S. military. These shifts have also included significant changes to China's military doctrine and operational concepts—such as revising the military strategic guidelines—as well as far-reaching changes to the PLA's structure and institutions, as is visible with the current PLA reform effort, and investments to counter specific U.S. capabilities, such as China's development of LRHWs. U.S. analysts and policymakers should therefore be mindful that the immediately observable set of

Chinese reactions to U.S. military activities may not be the end of the story and, indeed, the longer-term changes may prove to be the more consequential.

Policy Recommendations

- **U.S. policymakers and military planners, including particularly those in the USAF, seeking to enhance deterrence or expand the set of U.S. activities employed in the region should consider utilizing notable changes in the scale or scope of existing military activities in the Indo-Pacific rather than explore entirely novel means of signaling U.S. capabilities and commitment to China.** Our analysis of U.S. military activities in the Indo-Pacific in Chapter 5 highlighted how over the past decade the United States has conducted a relatively comprehensive set of military activities in the region. Potential activities that the United States has not recently conducted, but that the United States has conducted vis-à-vis other adversaries such as the Soviet Union during the Cold War, tended to be substantially more escalatory. At the same time, many of the recent set of U.S. activities in the Indo-Pacific have been notably smaller in scale than their counterparts in earlier historical periods. If U.S. policymakers assess that deterrence of Chinese aggression against U.S. allies and partners is eroding, then exploring notable increases to the size and scale of joint exercises, forward deployments, or other ongoing military activities in the region may be a more promising way to respond.

- **U.S. military planners should balance different activity characteristics to reduce the likelihood of an escalatory PRC response while accomplishing key objectives.** When designing a military activity, military planners should balance activity characteristics that are more or less likely to lead to an aggressive Chinese response in order to enable the execution of the activity while limiting escalation risks. If some characteristics of the activity are judged to be both mission essential and potentially escalatory, then planners should consider altering other characteristics of the activity to reduce PRC concerns. For example, should the United States decide to undertake military exercises in a highly sensitive area for China in order to improve U.S. ability to operate in that location, then U.S. planners should consider designing the exercise to avoid other characteristics with substantial escalatory potential, such as the inclusion of highly threatening capabilities. Military planners may also consider incorporating other characteristics that may reduce PRC concerns, such as increased transparency and outreach to PRC military counterparts.

- **U.S. military planners should carefully consider activities that directly involve Taiwan, as these have the most potential to lead to an escalatory response by China.** While this report does not identify a comprehensive set of Chinese "redlines" that U.S. military planners should avoid in U.S. activities in the Indo-Pacific, as such lines may shift or be context dependent in ways described in our framework, there are still three potential characteristics of U.S. military activities that have the greatest escalatory potential and are therefore worth emphasizing, though these concerns are of course well-established in prior research as well. U.S. military activities that take place on Taiwan, with Taiwan forces, or that involve capabilities that substantially enhance the defense of Taiwan have perhaps the greatest potential to trigger a highly escalatory PRC response. Furthermore, while the profile or messaging accompanying many U.S. activities may be a more limited factor in determining PRC responses than their capabilities or location, this is likely not the case for activities directly involving Taiwan, where any such statements would be carefully scrutinized for signals that the United States was encouraging Taiwanese independence.

- **U.S. military planners should focus on aggregating lower-risk activities involving Taiwan to enhance the defense of the island.** While military planners should be extremely cautious in undertaking activities at the higher end of the escalation risk spectrum with respect to Taiwan, those at the lower end could potentially enhance Taiwan's defense, in larger numbers or over time, with less likelihood of leading to a disproportionately aggressive PRC response. While any activities involving Taiwan would raise China's level of concern, judicious use of lower-risk activities could still enable the United States and Taiwan to substantially augment defense cooperation.

- **U.S. activities that incorporate capabilities that could enable U.S. strikes on PRC regime or nuclear targets should be scrutinized with particular care.** U.S. military activities with the potential to directly threaten PRC regime survival or the PRC nuclear deterrent, including particular types of exquisite ISR and long-range strike capabilities, could lead to similarly aggressive reactions. China views its nuclear forces as critical to regime and physical security and would likely perceive threats to its nuclear deterrent as justifying an aggressive response. Chinese analysis highlights concern about the ability of U.S. conventional precision strike weapons to hold China's nuclear forces at risk and has already responded in various ways to this concern—for example, by investing in conventionally armed short-, medium-, and long-range ballistic and cruise missiles and developing its own boost-glide systems that allow the Chinese military to target U.S. forces outside of the region. This suggests that U.S. or allied capabilities that can threaten China's nuclear deterrent could be met with a potentially escalatory response.

Appendix A. Excluded Factors

The main body of this report identified six factors that are associated with a greater likelihood of aggressive Chinese responses to U.S., allied, and partner activities. As noted in the framework factor chapter, however, other factors were considered but excluded from the report. Appendix A addresses two of these factors: China's internal instability and its own perceptions of its reputation for resolve. Each offers a conceptually attractive hypothesis regarding the drivers of Chinese aggression. However, we found insufficient support to include either in our framework. The reasons for their exclusion are summarized below. The factor analyses are then presented in their entirety.

Insufficient Evidence to Include in the Framework

It is often argued that China is more likely to respond aggressively to U.S. and allied and partner actions when it is experiencing greater domestic political unrest or turmoil. Certainly, the CCP is highly sensitive to public opinion and uses nationalism to strengthen its grip on power. There is significant evidence, moreover, that governments occasionally use "diversionary" external aggression to boost their domestic popularity. Nonetheless, a careful analysis of both the historical record and more-contemporary events finds little support for this factor. Since 1949, China has not systematically behaved more aggressively abroad during periods of acute internal instability than during periods of relative domestic tranquility. During the 1980s and into the early 1990s, for example—the most politically unstable period in China's post–Cultural Revolution history—the CCP exhibited significant restraint in its foreign policy. In more-recent crises that came during a period of intense unrest in Hong Kong, including China's reaction to Vietnamese-Russian oil exploration in waters claimed by China in 2019, the evidence suggests that domestic unrest may have actually motivated China to adopt *less* aggressive policies, as China did not want to encourage foreign support for or exploitation of its protest movements.[270] Under different internal and external circumstances in the future, Chinese leaders may respond to internal unrest aggressively. However, our analysis makes clear that other factors are currently much more useful predictors of the likelihood of aggressive Chinese responses.

Similarly, we examined whether China is more likely to behave aggressively if it believes that its competitors question its willingness to defend its interests, as aggressive responses may help it establish a reputation for resolve that deters future challenges, but we found inadequate evidence to include this as a framework factor. China has historically paid careful attention to its reputation for resolve—and to this day it devotes considerable attention to managing foreign

---

[270] Cases 12 and 13 in Appendix B explore this finding.

perceptions of China's willingness to defend its key interests—but the salience of reputational concerns to the aggressiveness of China's policy responses appears to have decreased over time. In particular, its burgeoning capabilities and power have reduced its need to respond to perceived challenge to its resolve aggressively. Moreover, even in cases in which reputational concerns appear most likely to have influenced the aggressiveness of Chinese behavior, it is not clear that they did so.[271] This reflects, in part, the challenge of information gaps. Fully analyzing and applying this factor requires a depth of knowledge regarding Chinese leaders' beliefs and decisionmaking processes that is rarely attainable. The available evidence, which is for the most part indirect or circumstantial, provides moderate support for the conclusion that Chinese concern over its reputation for resolve can influence Chinese policy. However, it is insufficient to conclude that reputational concerns are a core driver of the aggressiveness of Chinese responses to U.S. and allied and partner actions.

Excluded Factor 1: Internal Unrest and External Aggression

"Winning or losing public support," Xi Jinping remarked in 2013, concerns "the survival or extinction" of the CCP and is thus a central consideration in CCP decisionmaking.[272] Historically, however, China has often responded to domestic unrest by adopting conciliatory approaches in its disputes in order to focus on domestic problems. There are also few clear connections between domestic political unrest and its aggression abroad in recent crises. We therefore found insufficient evidence to conclude that China will be more likely to respond aggressively to U.S. and allied and partner actions in the future if it is experiencing greater domestic political unrest or turmoil.

A significant body of research has examined whether regimes use external aggression or even start "diversionary" wars to buttress their popularity when they face heightened levels of internal unrest. Some studies find that the risk of diversionary aggression is greater under personalistic or military regimes than under single-party regimes and higher under a range of conditions, including during economic troubles and when states can exploit territorial disputes or long-standing rivalries.[273] However, other work has found that the connections between domestic

---

[271] See especially Case 3 in Appendix A.

[272] Chun-yue Chang, "Study History, Be Close to the People," *China Daily*, July 9, 2013.

[273] Relevant literature includes George W. Downs and David M. Rocke, "Conflict, Agency, and Gambling for Resurrection: The Principal-Agent Problem Goes to War," *American Journal of Political Science*, Vol. 38, No. 2, May 1994; Brian Lai and Dan Slater, "Institutions of the Offensive: Domestic Sources of Dispute Initiation in Authoritarian Regimes, 1950–1992," *American Journal of Political Science*, Vol. 50, No. 1, 2006; Jaroslav Tir, "Territorial Diversion: Diversionary Theory of War and Territorial Conflict," *Journal of Politics*, Vol. 72, No. 2, 2010; Jeffrey Pickering and Emizet F. Kisangani, "Diversionary Despots? Comparing Autocracies' Propensities to Use and to Benefit from Military Force," *American Journal of Political Science*, Vol. 54, No. 2, April 2010; and Sara McLaughlin Mitchell and Brandon C. Prins, "Rivalry and Diversionary Uses of Force," *Journal of Conflict Resolution*, Vol. 48, No. 6, December 2004.

unrest and a state's aggressiveness are tenuous or nonexistent.[274] As one review concludes, it is likely that internal instability influences states' foreign policies but does not do so "in the same way in every instance and not in every state in the international system."[275]

The imperative to maintain public support has consistently shaped the CCP's approach to foreign affairs. In the 1958 Taiwan Strait Crisis, for example, Mao Zedong used the threat of war to mobilize the Chinese people behind the Great Leap Forward's ultimately disastrous economic and social policies.[276] This is not an example of internal instability leading to external aggression, as Mao sought to build elite and popular support for his revolutionary program rather than to distract from ongoing domestic unrest, but it demonstrates the close connection between the CCP's foreign and domestic policies. That the CCP remains highly sensitive to public opinion and internal stability today is clear in the amount of effort that it dedicates to internal security and population management.[277] Many analysts argue that China's efforts to manage public unrest intensify during crises. Moreover, some suspect that the rising nationalism or hawkishness of the Chinese people will shape these efforts in the future, as the CCP employs nationalism to bolster domestic support for its foreign policy goals.[278] Nonetheless, there are thus far no examples of rising nationalism pushing Beijing into a more aggressive stance abroad.

---

[274] Giacomo Chiozza and H. E. Goemans, "Peace Through Insecurity: Tenure and International Conflict," *Journal of Conflict Resolution*, Vol. 47, No. 4, 2003; Brett Ashley Leeds and David R. Davis, "Domestic Political Vulnerability and International Disputes," *Journal of Conflict Resolution*, Vol. 41, No. 6, December 1997; James Meernik and Peter Waterman, "The Myth of the Diversionary Use of Force by American Presidents," *Political Research Quarterly*, Vol. 49, No. 3, September 1996; and M. Taylor Fravel, "The Limits of Diversion: Rethinking Internal and External Conflict," *Security Studies*, Vol. 19, No. 2, 2010.

[275] Benjamin O. Fordham, "More Than Mixed Results: What We Have Learned from Quantitative Research on the Diversionary Hypothesis," in William R. Thompson, ed., *The Oxford Encyclopedia of Empirical International Relations Theory*, New York: Oxford University Press, 2018.

[276] Thomas J. Christensen, *Useful Adversaries: Grand Strategy, Domestic Mobilization, and Sino-American Conflict, 1947–1958*, Princeton, N.J.: Princeton University Press, 1997.

[277] China established the People's Armed Police in 1982 as a paramilitary force tasked with protecting the CCP and ensuring domestic stability and has subsequently built a sophisticated system to regulate information flows and monitor citizens' behavior. It has nonetheless experienced considerable instability, including in Tibet in 2008 and Xinjiang in 2009. Controlling more-ubiquitous acts of unrest, such as the 180,000 cases of domestic "mass incidents" that "disturbed" social stability in 2010, according to the Chinese government, is also a fixation of the CCP. See Joel Wuthnow, "China's Other Army: The People's Armed Police in an Era of Reform," *China Strategic Perspectives*, No. 14, August 2019; Frank Langfitt, "In China, Beware: A Camera May Be Watching You," *NPR*, January 29, 2013; Simon Denyer, "China's Scary Lesson to the World: Censoring the Internet Works," *Washington Post*, May 23, 2016; U.S.-China Economic and Security Review Commission, *2014 Report to Congress*, Washington, D.C., November 2014; and Sheena Chestnut Greitens, Myunghee Lee, and Emir Yazici, "Counterterrorism and Preventive Repression: China's Changing Strategy in Xinjiang," *International Security*, Vol. 44, No. 3, Winter 2019/2020.

[278] Scholars have argued that increasing hawkishness or nationalism will shape China's foreign policy (Jessica Chen Weiss, "How Hawkish Is the Chinese Public? Another Look at 'Rising Nationalism' and Chinese Foreign Policy," *Journal of Contemporary China*, Vol. 28, No. 119, 2019; and Suisheng Zhao, "Foreign Policy Implications of Chinese Nationalism Revisited: The Strident Turn," *Journal of Contemporary China*, Vol. 22, No. 82, 2013), that China's political instability may increase pressure on the regime to adopt a more nationalist and aggressive foreign

It is also not clear that China's propensity for external aggression increases in periods of heightened internal instability. The period from the inflationary late 1980s through the Tiananmen protests was the most politically unstable in China's post–Cultural Revolution history, for example, but, even so, the CCP did not behave more aggressively abroad during or immediately after it.[279] This does not appear to have been a historical aberration. One review of China's conflicts between 1949 and 1992 identified no systematic relationship between domestic instability and Chinese adventurism abroad.[280] Another analysis concluded that, with rare exceptions, Chinese leaders have actually been *less* likely to escalate crises when they confront heightened internal instability, as their desire to focus on resolving internal threats creates the "conditions for cooperation, producing a 'diversionary peace' instead of war."[281] A follow-on study of China's border disputes found that although internal unrest may "exacerbate perceptions of [China's] declining bargaining power" in interstate disputes and encourage Chinese aggression as a result, it has not "provided an independent incentive for escalation."[282]

Two recent cases cast additional doubt on whether China's internal unrest is a predictor of its external aggressiveness. Both occurred in the shadow of recent instability in Hong Kong. From March 2019 into 2020, resistance to a proposed law that would allow the extradition of criminal suspects to the mainland coalesced into mass public protests. Because China's leadership expressed heightened concern over internal unrest during these protests, we would expect to find evidence of heightened Chinese external aggression if this factor's hypothesis is correct.[283]

The first case occurred from mid-May to October 2019 after the Russian oil firm Rosneft, with Vietnamese support, began drilling in maritime territory claimed by China near Vanguard

---

policy to win public support (Robert S. Ross, "The Domestic Sources of China's 'Assertive Diplomacy,' 2009–2010," in Rosemary Foot, ed., *China Across the Divide: The Domestic and Global in Politics and Society*, New York: Oxford University Press, 2013), and that Chinese use of popular nationalism to strengthen its bargaining positions in crises may also constrain China's ability to compromise in foreign policy disputes (Jessica Chen Weiss, *Powerful Patriots: Nationalist Protest in China's Foreign Relations*, New York: Oxford University Press, 2014).

[279] There is also little evidence that China's political instability in the late 1980s had any direct influence on Chinese decisionmaking during the 1995–1996 Taiwan Strait Crisis.

[280] Alastair Iain Johnston, "China's Militarized Interstate Dispute Behaviour 1949–1992: A First Cut at the Data," *China Quarterly*, No. 153, 1998.

[281] M. Taylor Fravel, "Regime Insecurity and International Cooperation: Explaining China's Compromises in Territorial Disputes," *International Security*, Vol. 30, No. 2, Fall 2005.

[282] M. Taylor Fravel, "Power Shifts and Escalation: Explaining China's Use of Force in Territorial Disputes," *International Security*, Vol. 32, No. 3, Winter 2007/2008, p. 80.

[283] A communiqué drafted during the fourth plenary session of the 19th CCP Central Committee in late October 2019 noted that China faced "complicated situations marked by increasing risks and challenges at home and abroad" and highlighted the importance of "maintaining lasting prosperity and stability in Hong Kong." Chinese leaders may have also been worried about increased unrest in Xinjiang. See "19th CPC Central Committee Concludes Fourth Plenary Session, Releases Communiqué," Xinhua, October 31, 2019; Ministry of Foreign Affairs of the People's Republic of China, "Foreign Ministry Spokesperson Hua Chunying's Regular Press Conference on July 30, 2019," July 30, 2019; and Mamatjan Juma, Shohret Hoshur, Kurban Niyaz, and Ekrem Hezim, "10th Anniversary of Urumqi Unrest Brings Protests over Internment Camps, Accountability Demands," *Radio Free Asia*, July 5, 2019.

Bank, about 230 miles southeast of Vietnam.[284] Even though the 2019 standoff happened during intense unrest in Hong Kong, China's response was more restrained than it had been in 2014. It reiterated its territorial claims but did not dispatch ships to challenge or disrupt Vietnamese activities for approximately a month. Chinese paramilitary vessels gradually concentrated near Vanguard Bank to escort Chinese survey ships and harass Vietnamese vessels, and many stayed until the conclusion of the standoff in late October.[285] Although the PLA conducted drills around the Paracel Islands in both early June and early August and test-fired anti-ship ballistic missiles from the mainland into the SCS for the first time even as the United States signaled its direct and indirect support for Vietnamese claims, neither China nor Vietnam took punitive diplomatic or economic measures against the other.[286] Indirect evidence suggests that one reason for this may have been China's desire to discourage Vietnam and ethnic Vietnamese people living in Hong Kong from supporting the Hong Kong protest movement.[287] It therefore appears that internal

---

[284] China viewed this as just the latest in a string of Vietnamese challenges to its claims. This incident also followed a 2014 standoff near the Paracel Islands triggered by Chinese oil exploration in Vietnam's exclusive economic zone. That earlier crisis, which had occurred during Hong Kong's "Umbrella Movement" protests, had rapidly escalated as Vietnam and China massed forces and took coercive economic and diplomatic measures against one another. See Michael Green, Kathleen Hicks, Zack Cooper, John Schaus, and Jake Douglas, *Countering Coercion in Maritime Asia: The Theory and Practice of Gray Zone Deterrence*, Washington, D.C.: Center for Strategic and International Studies, May 2017, pp. 202–223.

[285] Each side's deployed maritime forces varied. Vietnamese Major General Nguyen Minh Hoang claimed that there were 40 Chinese and 50 Vietnamese vessels operating in the vicinity of Block 06-01; other sources estimate that 80 Chinese vessels simultaneously operated in the area. See Laura Zhou, "As Coastguard Boats Circle, Vietnam Prepares for Bigger Challenge in South China Sea," *South China Morning Post*, October 12, 2019; and Carlyle A. Thayer, "Will Vanguard Bank Ignite Vietnamese Nationalism?" Australian Naval Institute, August 4, 2019.

[286] Laura Zhou, "Beijing Starts Military Exercise in Disputed South China Sea as Tensions with Vietnam Rise," *South China Morning Post*, August 15, 2019; Jim Gomez, "U.S. Carrier Sails into Disputed Waters amid New Flare-Ups," Associated Press, August 6, 2019; and Jesse Johnson, "Japan-Based U.S. Aircraft Carrier in South China Sea Ahead of Key Chinese Anniversary," *Japan Times*, September 29, 2019. U.S. freedom of navigation operations are reported in Ronald O'Rourke, *U.S.-China Strategic Competition in South and East China Seas: Background and Issues for Congress*, Washington, D.C.: Congressional Research Service, March 18, 2021, p. 35. Chinese experts tracked U.S. activities in the SCS during this crisis and noted exercises and exchanges involving the Vietnamese military. See SCSPI, *Incomplete Report on U.S. Military Activities in the South China Sea in 2019* [2019 年美军南海军事活动不完全报告], Beijing: Peking University, March 28, 2020, pp. 7, 16–23.

[287] In 2014 and 2019, ethnic Vietnamese people living in Hong Kong had protested there, and many Vietnamese citizens supported the protest movement. In 2019, however, the Chinese government worked to suppress or contradict public blame on Vietnam for Hong Kong's unrest. This suggests a desire by China to focus popular attention on the threat posed by the United States, which Beijing claimed to be behind the protests, while decoupling territorial disputes with Vietnam from China's internal instability. See Marianne Brown, "Hong Kong Protesters 'Inspire' Vietnam Activists," *Voice of America*, October 2, 2014; Consulate General of the People's Republic of China in Ho Chi Minh City, "Consul General Wu Jun Engage in Discussions and Exchanges with Hong Kong Police Wanchai District Junior Youth Call" ["吴骏总领事与香港警务处湾仔警区少年警讯代表团座谈交流"], July 30, 2019; De Ling [凌德] and Fengxiang Li [李风向], "Forgetting Family and Ethnic History, Leading Hong Kong Troublemakers Bring in External Forces" ["忘祖籍抛民族身份，乱港头目成外部势力'带路党'"], *Global Times*, August 21, 2019; and "The Worst HK Troublemakers Are Ethnic Vietnamese? Media Refute Allegations" ["香港闹得最凶的是越南裔？媒体驳斥"], *Sina News*, August 21, 2019.

instability may, if anything, have reduced China's appetite for external aggression during the Vanguard Bank standoff.

The second case began in May 2020, when a series of skirmishes broke out in disputed territory along the Sino-Indian border's Line of Actual Control (LAC). These reached an apex in the middle of June, when fighting claimed the lives of at least 20 Indian and four Chinese troops and wounded significantly more.[288] Indian and Chinese troops also fired on one another on September 7, 2020, marking this crisis as both the most intense and the first to claim life on the LAC in more than four decades.[289] Notably, however, it happened as China's internal unrest appeared to be declining. By June 2020, COVID-19 restrictions and tightening security measures had largely suppressed protests in Hong Kong and suffocated opposition in Xinjiang.[290] China also did little to enflame or exploit popular nationalism around the border clash. Its early interest in de-escalating the crisis suggests that it was more interested in refocusing on higher-priority challenges, such as unrest linked to Hong Kong and COVID-19, than exploiting a foreign crisis to build additional popular support for the regime.[291]

Across the broader literature and both older and more-recent cases, we therefore found insufficient evidence to conclude that China is more likely to respond aggressively to U.S. and allied and partner actions when it faces more domestic political unrest or turmoil. Indeed, to the extent that internal instability has had any effect at all, since 2019 it appears that internal instability may have had a de-escalatory effect on China's external uses of force. Although Chinese leaders could potentially respond to domestic unrest with external aggression in the future under a different set of circumstances or different leadership, at present other factors are more reliable and useful predictors of the likelihood of aggressive Chinese responses.

---

[288] These reflect official statements of losses from each side. Other estimates have ranged much higher. India, for example, claims that China suffered at least 20 fatalities. See Steven Lee Myers, "China Acknowledges 4 Deaths in Last Year's Border Clash with India," *New York Times*, March 1, 2021.

[289] The escalation followed years of rising tensions between China and India caused in part by each state's construction on disputed territory, burgeoning security partnerships (between China and Pakistan, as well as between India and the United States), and competition for influence across much of Asia. Chinese statements and commentaries tend to blame the crisis on Indian incursions into Chinese territory, but some also highlight India's cooperation with the United States and its competition with the BRI. See Yun Sun, "China's Strategic Assessment of the Ladakh Clash," *War on the Rocks*, June 19, 2020.

[290] Polling data suggest that the central government had weathered the worst of both internal challenges with its general popularity largely intact. See Ken Moritsugu, "AP Interview: China Signals Shift but No Letup in Xinjiang," Associated Press, December 21, 2020; Primrose Riordan and Nicolle Liu, "Hong Kong Protesters Defy Ban to Show Support for Detained Leaders," *Financial Times*, March 1, 2021; and Edward Cunningham, Tony Saich, and Jessie Turiel, *Understanding CCP Resilience: Surveying Chinese Public Opinion Through Time*, Cambridge, Mass.: Ash Center for Democratic Governance and Innovation, July 2020.

[291] Yew Lun Tian and Sanjeev Miglani, "China-India Border Clash Stokes Contrasting Domestic Responses," Reuters, June 23, 2020.

Excluded Factor 2: Chinese Perceptions of U.S. and Allied and Partner Views of Chinese Resolve

A state's concerns over its reputation for resolve—that is, whether it thinks that other states see it as willing to pay costs, whether in blood or treasure, to defend its interests—can be important drivers of its behavior.[292] However, we found insufficient support to conclude that China is more likely to respond to U.S. and allied and partner actions aggressively when it believes that its reputation for resolve is being or has been undermined. The available evidence suggests that China has become less sensitive to reputational concerns as it has grown more powerful. Moreover, there are few recent cases in which Chinese concerns over whether other states view its past actions as lacking resolve played a clear role in shaping the aggressiveness of China's policy responses.

Many scholars argue that states are very concerned over their reputations—for resolve, risk acceptance, sensitivity to threats, commitment, and other characteristics—and modify their behavior accordingly.[293] All states have an incentive to develop reputations for being willing to defend their interests against future challenges. States worry that without such a reputation, or if they acquire a reputation for irresoluteness, they may appear more vulnerable to foreign coercion and thus more likely to face attempts at coercion in the future.[294] In contrast, states that have reputations for resolve may be able to more easily deter or compel others.[295] Evidence suggests that states tend to be more sensitive to their perceived reputations if they think that they have

---

[292] *Reputation* refers to the subjective beliefs about a state's behavior held by other states. *Resolve* refers to a state's willingness to bear costs, and even to risk or initiate wars, in order to achieve its objectives. See Allan Dafoe, Jonathan Renshon, and Paul Huth, "Reputation and Status as Motives for War," *Annual Review of Political Science*, Vol. 17, 2014; and Danielle L. Lupton, *Reputation for Resolve: How Leaders Signal Determination in International Politics*, Ithaca, N.Y.: Cornell University Press, 2020, pp. 2–3.

[293] Work on such topics includes Mark J. C. Crescenzi, Jacob D. Kathman, Katja B. Kleinberg, and Reed M. Wood, "Reliability, Reputation, and Alliance Formation," *International Studies Quarterly*, Vol. 56, No. 2, 2012; Gregory D. Miller, *The Shadow of the Past: Reputation and Military Alliances Before the First World War*, Ithaca, N.Y.: Cornell University Press, 2011; Barbara F. Walter, *Reputation and Civil War: Why Separatist Conflicts Are So Violent*, New York: Cambridge University Press, 2009; Anne E. Sartori, *Deterrence by Diplomacy*, Princeton, N.J.: Princeton University Press, 2005; Robert Jervis, "Signaling and Perception: Drawing Inferences and Projecting Images," in K. R. Monroe, ed., *Political Psychology*, Mahwah, N.J.: Lawrence Erlbaum, 2002; Paul K. Huth, "Reputations and Deterrence: A Theoretical and Empirical Assessment," *Security Studies*, Vol. 7, No. 1, 1997; Scott Wolford, "The Turnover Trap: New Leaders, Reputation, and International Conflict," *American Journal of Political Science*, Vol. 51, No. 4, October 2007; and Joe Clare and Vesna Danilovic, "Multiple Audiences and Reputation Building in International Conflicts," *Journal of Conflict Resolution*, Vol. 54, No. 6, December 2010.

[294] Alex Weisiger and Keren Yarhi-Milo, "Revisiting Reputation: How Past Actions Matter in International Politics," *International Organization*, Vol. 69, No. 2, 2015.

[295] One way of winning a contest of expectations is to establish a reputation for having a greater risk tolerance than an opponent. As Thomas Schelling argued, reputation might be "one of the few things worth fighting over." See Thomas C. Schelling, *Arms and Influence*, New Haven, Conn.: Yale University Press, 1966, p. 124.

failed in previous disputes or judge the future to be increasingly dangerous.[296] In such situations, they may become more likely to engage in signaling behaviors that they think will demonstrate their resolve to other states, ranging from externally focused public statements and internally focused propaganda efforts to military mobilizations and even initiating or escalating conflicts.[297]

Certainly, China has historically paid close attention to what it perceives as its reputation for resolve, particularly among its neighbors and potential adversaries.[298] There is evidence that China has employed this tactic in its more recent territorial disputes. During tensions over its border with India in 1959, for example, China crushed armed resistance in Tibet and deployed military forces against Nepal, Burma, and India itself, in part to demonstrate its resolve.[299] Reputational concerns also informed China's use of force following major failures of deterrence or coercive diplomacy since 1949, including its wars in Korea, against India, against the Soviet Union, and against Vietnam. In each, evidence suggests that China escalated not only to achieve its proximate political objectives but also to establish a reputation for resolve in order to deter adversaries in the future.[300] Because Beijing has favorably assessed its conflict termination strategies in these conflicts, there is reason to believe that its behavior in a future conflict may be similar.[301]

A variety of Chinese sources suggest that China remains committed to managing foreign perceptions of China's resolve. Official government statements and expert commentary frequently declare China's willingness and ability to use force in order to defend its core interests

---

[296] Todd S. Sechser, "Reputations and Signaling in Coercive Bargaining," *Journal of Conflict Resolution*, Vol. 62, No. 2, 2018.

[297] James D. Fearon, "Signaling Foreign Policy Interests: Tying Hands Versus Sinking Costs," *Journal of Conflict Resolution*, Vol. 41, No. 1, February 1997; Joe Clare and Vesna Danilovic, "Multiple Audiences and Reputation Building in International Conflicts," *Journal of Conflict Resolution*, Vol. 54, No. 6, December 2010; Kai Quek, "Four Costly Signaling Mechanisms," *American Political Science Review*, Vol. 115, No. 2, May 2021; and Alexandre Debs and Jessica Chen Weiss, "Circumstances, Domestic Audiences, and Reputational Incentives in International Crisis Bargaining," *Journal of Conflict Resolution*, Vol. 60, No. 3, 2016.

[298] Indeed, China has leveraged reputational concerns to influence its competitors' behaviors since at least since the early Warring States period; an old Chinese idiom, to "kill the chicken to warn the monkeys" ["杀鸡儆猴"], refers in contemporary Chinese strategic discourse to the targeted use of aggression against a weaker state in order to shape other states' future actions by changing their perceptions of Chinese behavior. See Ketian Zhang, "Cautious Bully: Reputation, Resolve, and Beijing's Use of Coercion in the South China Sea," *International Security*, Vol. 44, No. 1, 2019; Jifeng Liu [刘载锋], "Being in a Period of Nonphysical Warfare Is Far from Secure" ["身处非物理战时期远未居安"], *Guangming Daily* [光明日报], March 11, 2015; and Shiping Tang, "Reputation, Cult of Reputation, and International Conflict," *Security Studies*, Vol. 14, No. 1, 2005, p. 47.

[299] Krista E. Wiegand, "Militarized Territorial Disputes: States' Attempts to Transfer Reputation for Resolve," *Journal of Peace Research*, Vol. 48, No. 1, 2011, p. 105.

[300] Korea and the Sino-Soviet border conflict are especially salient examples of this behavior. See Sijin Cheng, *Fighting for Reputation: China's Deterrence Policy and Concerns About Credibility*, dissertation, Boston: Boston University, 2014; and Michael S. Gerson, *The Sino-Soviet Border Conflict: Deterrence, Escalation, and the Threat of Nuclear War in 1969*, Arlington, Va.: CNA, 2010.

[301] Oriana Skylar Mastro, "How China Ends Wars: Implications for East Asian and U.S. Security," *Washington Quarterly*, Vol. 41, No. 1, 2018, p. 47.

and function as a form of reputation management.[302] Chinese professional military writings on escalation management, or "war control," emphasize the use of different forms of signaling to demonstrate the credibility of China's coercive threats, including use of propaganda, raising military readiness levels, "displaying strength" by publicizing capabilities, deploying forces, and conducting exercises.[303] Although much of this work indicates a preference for resolving crises using nonmilitary means, there is a common understanding in PLA literature that China must demonstrate not just its capability but also its willingness to employ force in order to deter adversaries.[304]

Two post–Cold War cases suggest that perceptions of its reputation for resolve played at least a minor role in China's decisions to behave more aggressively in the relatively recent past. The first is the 1995–1996 Taiwan Strait Crisis. By the mid-1990s, Beijing feared that U.S. actions had emboldened Taiwan's pro-independence forces, and some Chinese officials began to argue that China should use more-forceful measures to demonstrate its determination to prevent Taiwanese independence.[305] In this context, Chinese leaders interpreted Taiwanese President Lee Teng-hui's 1995 visit to the United States to mean that the United States and Taiwan saw China's previously restrained approach to signaling resolve regarding unification—which

---

[302] A *Global Times* editorial states that China "needs to make the US be increasingly sure that if the US launches a war with the People's Liberation Army in China's adjacent waters, it will be defeated. . . . And China has a strong will to use these [military] forces to defend its core interests." The most recent defense white paper says that "China has the firm resolve and the ability to safeguard national sovereignty and territorial integrity" and the "determination, confidence, and capability to prevail over all threats and challenges" (State Council Information Office of the People's Republic of China, *China's National Defense in the New Era*, July 24, 2019), and Chinese military experts have stressed the need for either resolve or the reputation for resolve for deterrence to be effective. See "Chinese Mainland to Firmly Handle Chaos at Sea," *Global Times*, May 12, 2021; Xixin Wang [王西欣], "A Further Discussion on War Control" ["再论控制战"], *China Military Science* [中国军事科学], Vol. 64, 2014; and Chen Hu [陈虎], "Colonel Chen Hu: China Needs to Have the Ability to 'Resist' Wars," *Tencent Net* [腾讯网], 2010.

[303] Recent analyses of Chinese thinking on deterrence and escalation management include Nathan Beauchamp-Mustafaga, Derek Grossman, Kristen Gunness, Michael S. Chase, Marigold Black, and Natalia D. Simmons-Thomas, *Deciphering Chinese Deterrence Signalling in the New Era: An Analytic Framework and Seven Case Studies*, Santa Monica, Calif.: RAND Corporation, RR-A1074-1, 2021; Burgess Laird, *War Control: Chinese Writings on the Control of Escalation in Crisis and Conflict*, Washington, D.C.: Center for a New American Security, April 2017; Alison A. Kaufman and Daniel M. Hartnett, *Managing Conflict: Examining Recent PLA Writings on Escalation Control*, Arlington, Va.: CNA, February 2016; and David C. Gompert, Astrid Stuth Cevallos, and Cristina L. Garafola, *War with China: Thinking Through the Unthinkable*, Santa Monica, Calif.: RAND Corporation, RR-1140-A, 2016.

[304] As the 2013 edition of *The Science of Military Strategy* states, "when crises, especially major military crises erupt, we should . . . show a strong resolve of willingness to fight and powerful real strength to force an opponent to promptly reverse course." See Xiaosong Shou [寿晓松], ed., *The Science of Military Strategy* [战略学], 3rd ed., Beijing: Military Science Press [军事科学出版社], 2013, p. 119.

[305] The most significant U.S. actions in shaping Chinese perceptions were probably the George H. W. Bush administration's 1992 sale of 150 F-16 multirole fighters to and the Clinton administration's 1994 elevation of diplomatic contacts with Taiwan. Many Chinese leaders and experts interpreted these two events as signaling greater U.S. support for Taiwanese independence. See Robert S. Ross, "The 1995–96 Taiwan Strait Confrontation: Coercion, Credibility, and the Use of Force," *International Security*, Vol. 25, No. 2, 2000, p. 92.

emphasized economic and diplomatic tools—as a sign of weakness.[306] In order to demonstrate its ability and resolve to prevent Taiwanese independence, Beijing began a series of military demonstrations. These climaxed in large-scale exercises and missile tests in March 1996, even as the United States deployed two carrier groups to the Western Pacific and threatened grave consequences for Chinese aggression.[307] The seriousness of the U.S. response may have inadvertently encouraged China to continue its military exercises in order to demonstrate its resolve, although the evidence therein is not dispositive.[308] China's aggressive military activity during the 1995–1996 Taiwan Strait Crisis therefore appears to have been motivated in part by a desire to correct what it perceived as a lack of Taiwanese and U.S. respect for its resolve to prevent Taiwanese independence.

The second case is the 2012 standoff over Scarborough Shoal. Beginning around 2009, China perceived the United States and the Philippines as more actively challenging China's claims in the SCS.[309] A standoff between China and the Philippines over Scarborough Shoal escalated in April 2012 after a Philippine naval ship attempted to arrest the crew of a Chinese fishing boat. In response, China used a range of political, economic, and military tools to coerce the Philippines, and evidence suggests that it sought to use the crisis to signal its commitment to defending its maritime claims to other states.[310] A settlement reached between China, the Philippines, and the United States resulted in China effectively controlling the waters around the shoal. There is relatively weak indirect evidence that China escalated the standoff in part because it thought that the United States and its allies and partners perceived China as lacking resolve due to its comparative restraint in the 2000s. In the run-up to the Scarborough crisis, for example, Chinese governmental mouthpieces had begun to express concern that the Philippines did not find

---

[306] Andrew Scobell, "Show of Force: Chinese Soldiers, Statesmen, and the 1995–1996 Taiwan Strait Crisis," *Political Science Quarterly*, Vol. 115, No. 2, 2000.

[307] Arthur S. Ding, "The Lessons of the 1995–1996 Military Taiwan Strait Crisis: Developing a New Strategy Toward the United States and Taiwan," in Laurie Burkett, Larry M. Wortzel, and Andrew Scobell, eds., *The Lessons of History: The Chinese People's Liberation Army at 75*, Carlisle, Pa.: U.S. Army War College Press, 2003, pp. 381–383.

[308] Note that China reduced the risk of escalation by warning Taiwan ahead of its activities, tailoring its deployments and exercises so that they did not suggest an imminent invasion, and avoiding U.S. assets. See John W. Garver, *Face Off: China, the United States, and Taiwan's Democratization*, Seattle, Wash.: University of Washington Press, 2011, pp. 109–110; and Robert S. Ross, "The 1995–96 Taiwan Strait Confrontation: Coercion, Credibility, and the Use of Force," *International Security*, Vol. 25, No. 2, 2000, p. 111.

[309] Authoritative sources suggest China grew more sensitive to challenges to its maritime claims between 2008 and 2012. The 2010 defense white paper, for example, warned that "pressure builds up in preserving China's territorial integrity and maritime rights and interests," sharper language than that employed previously. See Information Office of the State Council of the People's Republic of China, *China's National Defense in 2010*, Beijing, March 31, 2011.

[310] Chinese coercive actions included reducing fruit imports from and tourism to the Philippines, as well as deploying PLAN and paramilitary ships to support its maritime militia vessels. See Ketian Zhang, "Cautious Bully: Reputation, Resolve, and Beijing's Use of Coercion in the South China Sea," *International Security*, Vol. 44, No. 1, 2019.

China's warning credible.[311] Beginning in 2012, some Chinese experts also began to argue that China had not sufficiently signaled its resolve on maritime territorial issues prior to the Scarborough standoff and embraced China's new assertiveness.[312]

A pattern emerges from these cases, as well as from Chinese behavior since 2013. Reputational concerns appear to have played a larger role in shaping Chinese behavior in the 1995–1996 Taiwan Strait Crisis, during which China's military capabilities were relatively weak in comparison with those of Taiwan and the United States, than during the Scarborough Shoal crisis, when China's military capabilities were relatively more powerful. Since then, in the shadow of China's growing strength, there has been even less evidence that reputational concerns have played a major role in driving the aggressiveness of Chinese reactions. What evidence does exist, moreover, is largely indirect or circumstantial.

Examples from the literature and the cases therefore provide limited evidence that this factor influenced Chinese behavior in the past. However, there is insufficient support to conclude with any confidence that reputational concerns play a key role in shaping the aggressiveness of Chinese responses to U.S. and allied and partner actions today or are likely to do so in the near future. China appears to have grown less sensitive to whether other states see it as lacking commitment or resolve as it has grown more powerful. It is worth acknowledging that this factor may become more important as the result of adverse shocks to what China perceives as the threats facing it—which suggests that the degree to which reputational concerns influence the aggressiveness of China's responses therefore depends in large part on the interaction of the framework factors developed in this report.

---

[311] See Ketian Zhang, "Cautious Bully: Reputation, Resolve, and Beijing's Use of Coercion in the South China Sea," *International Security*, Vol. 44, No. 1, 2019, pp. 147–149.

[312] A Chinese National Defense University–affiliated researcher argued in 2013 that other states had seen China as "trading territory for peace" and that the shift to a "tough approach" had helped China "clearly state to the international community that . . . China will never compromise and retreat" on its core interests. See Huang Yingying [黄莹莹], "Meng Xiangqing: Large Breakthroughs Have Already Been Made in Crisis Management and Control on China's Periphery" ["孟祥青: 中国周边危机管控已有大突破"], *International Herald Tribune* [国际先驱导报], November 6, 2012. Also see Xingang Long [龙心刚] and Dongxing Liang [梁东兴], "On the U.S. Factor in the South China Sea Issue" ["论南海问题中的美国因素"], *Around Southeast Asia* [东南亚纵横], Vol. 9, 2010.

Appendix B. Case Selection Methodology, Design, and Results

In order to validate the six factors central to shaping Chinese reactions to U.S. military activities that are presented in the main volume, the research team identified recent test cases. We then analyzed these cases to examine our hypotheses regarding how U.S. activities might affect each of these factors. This appendix presents 14 of these cases in chronological order.

We selected the cases on the basis of four considerations. The first was recency. We limited our cases to those that had occurred within the past two decades, and, when possible, the most recent decade, to have the greatest similarity between the underlying regional and structural conditions in the cases and those present today. The second was diversity. These cases capture a wide range of U.S., allied, and partner activities—with variance in their type, scale, scope, location, timing, intensity, and political context—which allows for a more robust evaluation of the explanations for China's divergent reactions to them. The third was their applicability to each of the specific factors: their ability to test widely held assumptions about the drivers of Chinese aggressiveness. Exploring cases that appear most likely to support those assumptions can suggest their plausibility if the cases provide confirmatory evidence, but it can also call them into serious question if the cases generate little or no support for them. The final consideration was information availability. Although we have often-limited understanding of internal Chinese decisionmaking across our cases, the cases we selected are all relatively well documented in terms of the public and visible reactions of the two sides. Information gaps persist—particularly regarding the crucial issues of China's perceptions of foreign threats and its internal security, as well as its decisionmaking processes—which require a degree of modesty regarding the strength of the conclusions that can be derived from them. By exploring multiple cases for each factor and hypothesis, we hope to offset this limitation to some degree.

Because the cases are intended to test hypotheses regarding the motivations for Chinese responses, they are focused on identifying the drivers of behavior rather than providing an exhaustive account of events. To do so, each case follows the same five-section structure. The first section summarizes the case, the tested hypothesis, and the key results. The second section examines key actions taken by the United States and its partners and allies, including any actions intended to manage escalation risks, and provides a brief explanation of the political and strategic context in which those actions were taken. The third section, titled "Chinese Reactions," explains (to the extent possible, given information constraints) how China perceived U.S. and allied and partner actions. It then analyzes the specific political, economic, and military policy changes that China implemented in response. The fourth section, "Explanations for Chinese Reactions," weighs the evidence for and against the tested hypothesis. In doing so, it also often examines alternative, and potentially contradictory, explanations for China's behavior. This is key, as for some of the cases more than one framework factor appears to have been important.

The final section highlights conclusions from the analysis, with a focus on the amount of support that the case provides for the hypothesis and, when applicable, implications for our understanding of China's behavior.

A summary of the cases, including their dates, the primary factor that they were intended to test, and the level of evidentiary support that each case provides for the tested factor(s), is provided in Table B.1.[313] As the table indicates, the cases provide significant evidence for the six hypotheses that form the basis of the framework factors developed in the main report. Although not listed in Table B.1, several of the cases also provided secondary support to other hypotheses, as discussed in the individual case studies themselves. The levels of primary and secondary support for each factor taken together are synthesized in Table B.2. Notably, we found little to no support for the hypothesis that greater Chinese internal instability increases the likelihood of it responding to U.S. and allied and partner actions aggressively—and we found weak evidence that, in certain cases, internal instability might actually *reduce* the likelihood of Chinese aggression. We also found only weak support for the hypothesis that Chinese perceptions that the United States and its allied and partner doubt China's resolve increase the aggressiveness of its policy responses. For these reasons, while we continue to present our analysis of these two factors in the report, we did not include them in our framework.

Table B.1. Summary of Cases

Case	Dates	Primary Tested Factor	Level of Support Found and Key Takeaways
1 U.S. hypersonic weapons programs	2000s to present	Chinese perceptions of military threat posed by U.S. or allied capabilities	**Strong:** China is concerned about the threat of U.S. hypersonic weapon systems and has undertaken a range of very intense (if not immediately aggressive) policy responses
2 U.S. naval capabilities and the Malacca Dilemma	Late 2000s to present	Chinese perceptions of threat to PRC economic development	**Moderate:** Chinese sensitivity to threats to its economic development, including its access to energy imports, fuels wide-ranging but not necessarily aggressive reactions
3 China-Philippines Scarborough Shoal standoff	2012 to present	Chinese perceptions that U.S. and allies/partners doubt Chinese resolve	**Weak:** Sources suggest that China thought that its past restraint had emboldened the Philippines and necessitated an aggressive response, but there are gaps in the evidence
4 Japanese nationalization of the Senkaku Islands	2012 to 2016	Chinese perceptions of U.S. commitment to the defense of allies or partners	**Weak to moderate:** China cut back its economic coercion following a strong and clear U.S. defensive commitment to the Senkaku Islands, but it remained aggressive in other ways, and additional factors may have mattered at least as much

---

[313] "Strong" support indicates that the case provides evidence of a very clear link between the U.S. or allied actions taken and a change in PRC perceptions and thinking through the noted factor. "Moderate" support indicates that the case provides more-limited, potentially indirect evidence of such a link, while "weak" support indicates limited evidence that may be circumstantial. "None" indicates that we identified no real plausible evidence or that the relationship may actually be in the opposite direction to that originally hypothesized.

Case		Dates	Primary Tested Factor	Level of Support Found and Key Takeaways
5	Expansion of U.S.-Vietnam defense and security ties	2013 to 2016	China's perceptions of threats to its regional influence	**Moderate:** China took aggressive actions against Vietnam but also implemented softer policies to entice Vietnam into acting more favorably toward Chinese interests
6	U.S. bomber overflights of the SCS	2015 and 2020	Chinese perceptions of military threat posed by U.S. or allied capabilities	**Moderate:** China was more aggressive in 2020 despite having more capabilities but likely saw U.S. intent as more hostile
7	THAAD deployment to South Korea	2016 to present	Chinese perceptions of military threat posed by U.S. or allied capabilities	**Moderate:** China acted politically and economically aggressively but was militarily restrained; other factors complicate analysis
8	Chinese reactions to the Duterte administration	2016 to 2018	China's perceptions of threats to its regional influence	**Strong:** The Duterte administration reduced Chinese concerns about threats to its regional influence, and China reduced political and economic aggressiveness
9	The Quad	2017 to present	Chinese perceptions of U.S. and allied hostile intent	**Strong:** Overlapping disputes obscure links between aggressive Chinese reactions and specific aspects of the Quad, but there is evidence that China's perceptions of the Quad's hostile intent influenced its behavior
10	U.S. support for Taiwan under the Trump administration	2018 to 2020	Chinese perceptions of threats to regime legitimacy	**Strong:** Chinese perceptions of threats to its legitimacy from the interplay of Trump administration hostility and Tsai administration political popularity appear to have motivated Chinese aggression
11	Strengthening of U.S.-India ties	2018 to present	Chinese perceptions of U.S. and allied hostile intent	**Moderate:** Anxiety about India's hostile intent, aggravated by U.S.-Indian security cooperation, may have been a significant driver of Beijing's aggressive reaction in the 2020 Sino-Indian border clash
12	Hong Kong and the Vanguard Bank dispute	2019	Internal Chinese political instability	**None:** China may have actually been reluctant to escalate the dispute out of concern that doing so would embolden Vietnamese or ethnic Vietnamese people to support the Hong Kong protests
13	Hong Kong and the China-India border clash	2020	Internal Chinese political instability	**Weak:** Hong Kong protests may have played an indirect role in the clash, but other factors appear to have been much more important
14	U.S. FONOPs in the Taiwan Strait	2020	Chinese perceptions of threats to regime legitimacy	**Strong:** The increased tempo of operations against Taiwan in 2020 most likely resulted from Beijing's sensitivity to the threat that Taiwanese independence poses to the CCP's political legitimacy

Table B.2. Overall Levels of Support for Hypothesized Framework Factors Found in Case Studies

Hypothesized Factor	Overall Level of Support Found
Chinese perceptions of the military threat posed by U.S. or allied capabilities	Strong
Chinese perceptions of threats to its regional influence	Strong
Chinese perceptions of U.S. and allied hostile intent	Strong
Chinese perceptions of threats to its regime legitimacy	Strong
Chinese perceptions of threats to its economic development	Moderate
Chinese perceptions of U.S. commitment to the defense of allies or partners	Weak to moderate
Chinese perceptions that U.S. and allies/partners doubt Chinese resolve	Weak
Chinese perceptions of its internal instability	Weak

Case 1: PRC Reactions to U.S. Hypersonic Weapons Programs

Case 1 tests the hypothesis that China is more likely to respond aggressively to U.S. or allied actions or capabilities that it perceives constitute a threat to the PRC regime or physical security by examining Chinese reactions to the U.S. development of LRHWs. Chinese experts, as well as the PLA, have watched this development closely. They express significant concern over two threats that LRHWs could pose to China in the future: First, Chinese sources argue that LRHWs could negate China's counter-intervention or A2/AD bubble, thus threatening China's ability to win future wars. Second, they warn that LRHWs could potentially degrade China's C2 and nuclear forces during a conflict. China has taken a number of steps in response. First, it is developing its own hypersonic weapons. Second, it is bolstering its nuclear deterrent posture. Third, it appears to be leveraging deliberate ambiguity about the parameters of its No First Use policy in order to deter conventional attacks on its nuclear forces. Chinese analysis directly ties these reactions to China's perceptions of the threat that U.S. deployment of LRHWs would pose to nuclear stability and the regional military balance. This provides strong support for the hypothesis.

U.S. Hypersonic Weapons Development and Potential Deployment to the Indo-Pacific

DoD is developing hypersonic weapons as part of its conventional prompt global strike program.[314] There has been increased discussion of deploying LRHWs to the Indo-Pacific region, as well as discussions on where to base the new capability.

The Army plans to integrate hypersonic weapons into its Long-Range Precision Fires capability set, which could be useful for penetrating and disintegrating A2/AD bubbles in accordance with MDO doctrine. LRHWs' combination of ballistic missile-like speed, cruise missile-like maneuverability, and accuracy give the United States new abilities to strike critical targets, and their relatively low detectability and high survivability allow for a more assured response. Long-range fires also increase the United States' ability to threaten punishment if an adversary action is taken. These are also theater-level hypersonic weapons that can be visibly emplaced in the region beforehand, which can be used to signal intent and resolve.[315] By threatening to defeat the primary means of potential Chinese aggression, the U.S. military considers LRHWs to serve as a strategic deterrent in peacetime. However, some experts worry about the implications of LRHWs for strategic stability because of their incredible speed, which compresses the time available for decisionmaking and, therefore, complicates deterrence.[316]

---

[314] John T. Watts, Christian Trotti, and Mark J. Massa, *Primer on Hypersonic Weapons in the Indo-Pacific Region*, Washington, D.C.: Atlantic Council, August 2020.

[315] Alan Cummings, "Hypersonic Weapons: Tactical Uses and Strategic Goals," *War on the Rocks*, November 12, 2019.

[316] John T. Watts, Christian Trotti, and Mark J. Massa, *Primer on Hypersonic Weapons in the Indo-Pacific Region*, Washington, D.C.: Atlantic Council, August 2020, p. 14.

Chinese Reactions

Chinese reactions have been primarily in the military sphere. Three are particularly notable.

Military

First, China has been working to develop its own boost glide weapons and hypersonic cruise missiles. Chinese authors argue that China's A2AD capability is facing a threat from hypersonic weapons and that China needs the same technology in order to develop the necessary countermeasures and "regain strategic balance."[317] China has already successfully tested its own hypersonic glide vehicles. In August 2018, China tested the XINGKONG-2 (Starry Sky-2), which it publicly described as a hypersonic waverider vehicle.[318]

In addition, the perceived threat to China's nuclear forces and C2 by advanced precision-strike capabilities has encouraged China to bolster its nuclear deterrent posture in response. While it is difficult to directly attribute the PLA's response to a competitor's deployment of a particular capability, it has continued to improve its ground- and submarine-based nuclear capabilities, including a new generation of mobile missiles, with warheads consisting of multiple independently targetable reentry vehicles, which it states are intended to ensure the viability of its strategic nuclear forces in the face of continued advances in U.S. precision-strike and missile defense capabilities.[319] The PLAN has also launched the JIN-class nuclear-powered, ballistic missile–carrying submarine, which represents China's first viable sea-based nuclear deterrent.[320]

Finally, in response to the possibility of an adversary launching a conventional strike against its nuclear forces, China's No First Use policy has become somewhat ambiguous. Western scholars believe that this is partly to account for China's potential nuclear retaliation after a conventional strike on its nuclear forces.[321]

Explanations for Chinese Reactions

Greater U.S. assurance of striking critical targets (e.g., Chinese A2/AD systems designed to hold a U.S. fleet at standoff range) has affected China's perceptions about their ability to carry

---

[317] Tang Huaiyu [汤怀宇] and Liu Jie [刘婕], "Media Reports and China's Hypersonic Weapon" ["从媒体报道看我国高超音速武器"], *Ordnance Knowledge* [兵器知识], No. 5, 2014.

[318] Office of the Secretary of Defense, *Annual Report to Congress: Military and Security Developments Involving the People's Republic of China 2020*, Washington, D.C., 2020, p. 44.

[319] Office of the Secretary of Defense, *Annual Report to Congress: Military and Security Developments Involving the People's Republic of China 2020*, Washington, D.C., 2020, p. 65.

[320] Office of the Secretary of Defense, *Annual Report to Congress: Military and Security Developments Involving the People's Republic of China 2020*, Washington, D.C., 2020, p. 66.

[321] Fiona S. Cunningham and M. Taylor Fravel, "Assuring Assured Retaliation: China's Nuclear Posture and U.S.-China Strategic Stability," *International Security*, Vol. 40, No. 2, October 2015.

out a first strike and inflated Chinese fears regarding the United States' intention to target China's C2 and nuclear forces.[322] PRC views are that the following:

- Hypersonic weapons will make the United States capable of preemptively striking China's nuclear forces—posing a threat to China's nuclear arsenal and C2 structure.[323]

- Because these weapons could be launched from far away, the United States would no longer need to use vulnerable military platforms to put China's nuclear and strategic targets at risk. Chinese experts warn that the "emergence of hypersonic weapons has completely removed the boundary between the frontline and the rear area" and that "the strategic rear area will become the frontline."[324] This implies that LRHWs provide more freedom of maneuver for the United States and may even reduce U.S. dependence on foreign bases.

- The increased freedom of maneuver and the ability to conduct precision strike without bringing forces close to the region means that an adversary's target list for a first strike could expand to "strategic command and control centers, nuclear weapons bases, aerospace launch facilities, and critical economic infrastructures."[325]

- The PLA justifies development of its own hypersonic glide vehicles as necessary to counter other countries' ballistic missile defense systems, suggesting that in the future China may use hypersonic glide vehicles to carry nonconventional payloads and to strike targets outside of the region.[326]

---

[322] The Chinese have a broad definition of advanced U.S. conventional prompt strike weapons. From the Chinese perspective, such weapons not only include U.S. conventional prompt global strike weapons, such as boostglider vehicles, but other conventional weapons that are perceived as having strategic military significance, such as the planned new strategic bomber B-21, space-based kinetic bombardment projectiles, and even high-speed unmanned aerial vehicles. See Tong Zhao, *Conventional Challenges to Strategic Stability: Chinese Perception of Hypersonic Technology and Security*, Washington, D.C.: Carnegie Endowment for International Peace, 2016, pp. 2–3.

[323] Yong Zhao [赵永], Weimin Li, Chenhao Zhao, and Xu Liu, "U.S. Global Prompt Strike System Development Status and Trend Analysis" ["美国全球快速打击系统发展现状及动向分析"], *Cruise Missile* [飞航导弹], Vol. 1, No. 3, 2014.

[324] Yong Zhao [赵永], Weimin Li, Chenhao Zhao, and Xu Liu, "U.S. Global Prompt Strike System Development Status and Trend Analysis" ["美国全球快速打击系统发展现状及动向分析"], *Cruise Missile* [飞航导弹], Vol. 1, No. 3, 2014, p. 9.

[325] Xu Liu [刘旭], Weimin Li, Zhipeng Jiang, and Wenjing Song, "Thoughts on Hypersonic Cruise Missile Combat Characteristics and Offense-Defense Model" ["高超声速巡航导弹作战特点及攻防模式思考"], *Cruise Missile* [飞航导弹], No. 9, 2014.

[326] Lora Saalman, "China's Calculus on Hypersonic Glide," Stockholm International Peace Research Institute, August 15, 2017.

While China's response has not been "aggressive" per se, the United States has not yet deployed LRHWs into the Indo-Pacific theater. The initial PRC reaction to date suggests a high level of concern with two aspects of LRHWs in particular: (1) the ability for these weapons to burst China's A2/AD bubble and therefore negate the PLA's regional defenses and (2) the potential for these weapons to target China's C2 and nuclear capability from a distance. China's investment into its own hypersonic weapons capability reflects Beijing's desire to have a similar capability that can hold U.S. forces at risk without having to send PLA assets into conflict, as well as presenting the United States with a deterrent. The discussion in Chinese literature of increasing the ambiguity of China's No First Use policy directly reflects Chinese assessments that the United States could target China's nuclear forces with conventional weapons, after which China could respond with a nuclear weapon.

Conclusion

The case provides strong support for a variant of the tested hypothesis: The intensity, if not necessarily the immediate aggressiveness, of China's policy responses to U.S. actions increases when it perceives those actions as threatening its regime or physical security. Over the longer term, this can also manifest in what appears to be more aggressive Chinese behavior. China's investments in its own hypersonic weapons and its modification of other aspects of its military posture reflect its perceptions of current and future military threats and its desire to even the military balance. Chinese perceptions of the risk of nuclear instability appear to be particularly significant drivers, as Chinese sources note with particular concern the risk that U.S. LRHWs could potentially target Chinese nuclear forces. An aggressive Chinese response to U.S. deployment of a LRHW system to the Indo-Pacific theater in the future would serve as additional confirmatory evidence for this hypothesis.

Case 2: U.S. Naval Capabilities and China's Malacca Dilemma

China may be more likely to respond aggressively to U.S. actions that it perceives as threatening its economic growth—including its access to vital resources. To test this hypothesis, Case 2 examines Chinese reactions to U.S. naval capabilities in the context of its growing dependence on resources imported over SLOCs. Chinese leaders attach great importance to maintaining China's development and are therefore very sensitive to threats that could derail it. This insecurity has manifested in a number of reactions to the vulnerability of key Chinese SLOCs to interdiction or blockade by hostile foreign forces, including diversification of its energy imports and transportation networks by investing in overland pipelines, increasing access to ports in the Indian Ocean and other strategic locations, upgrading PLAN capabilities for counterpiracy and SLOC protection, and opening an overseas base in Djibouti to expand the PLAN's presence and ability to conduct expeditionary operations in the western Indian Ocean. Some of these responses are marginally aggressive, and others are not aggressive at all. However, they collectively reflect the salience of concerns over the threat that the United States and its allies and partners might post to Chinese economic interests in China's policy responses to U.S. actions. As a result, this case provides mixed support for the tested hypothesis. Chinese concerns about protecting its economic development are clearly significant drivers of its external behavior but do not necessarily generate visibly aggressive reactions to U.S. activities.

China's Dependence on Energy Imports and the U.S. Naval Threat

China's economic growth over the past several decades has led Beijing to increasingly rely on energy imports, especially crude oil and natural gas. As a result, Chinese energy shipments are vulnerable to interdiction or blockade by foreign navies, especially in maritime "chokepoints," which Hu Jintao labeled the "Malacca Dilemma" after the strait through which around 80 percent of Chinese oil imports flow.[327] Beyond the issue of maritime chokepoints,

---

[327] Hu Bo, "Three Major Maritime Security Issues Pose a Test for 'One Belt, One Road'" ["三大海上安全问题考验'一代一路'"], in Zhang Jie, ed., *Assessment of China's Peripheral Security Situation 2016* [中国周边安 全形势评估2016], Beijing: Social Sciences Academic Press, 2016, p. 193; and Huang Xiaoyong, "Promote Collective Asian Energy Security Through One Belt, One Road" ["以'一带一路'促进亚洲共同能源安全"], *Foreign Affairs Observer* [外交观察], August 7, 2015. DoD reports that 10 percent of China's natural gas and 77 percent of its petroleum imports came through the strait. See Office of the Secretary of Defense, *Annual Report to Congress: Military and Security Developments Involving the People's Republic of China 2020*, Washington, D.C., 2020, p. 133; and Erica Downs, "China's National Oil Companies Return to the World Stage: Navigating Corruption, Low Oil Prices, and the Belt and Road Initiative," in Erica Downs, Mikkal E. Herberg, Michael Kugelman, Christopher Len, and Kaho Yu, *Asia's Energy Security and China's Belt and Road Initiative*, Seattle, Wash.: National Bureau of Asian Research, 2017.

Chinese writings express concern that instability in the SCS could affect China's access to energy and resources, as well as disrupt shipping.[328]

While the United States has not explicitly threatened Chinese access to the Malacca Strait or other strategic waterways, U.S. naval capabilities—particularly those that could be used to protect or defend key regional SLOCs, U.S. FONOPs, and increased USN presence in the SCS (e.g., CSG deployments)—have exacerbated Chinese concerns over the possibility that the United States could use these capabilities to restrict Chinese access to crucial energy resources needed for economic growth.[329]

Chinese Reactions

China has reacted to these concerns by trying to mitigate the security risk that the Malacca Dilemma presents through four measures: (1) expanding energy security by developing partnerships through the BRI for overland pipeline construction—for example, with Russia and other Central Asian countries, as well as Pakistan;[330] (2) increasing access to strategic waterways by prioritizing port construction and access agreements, particularly in the Indian Ocean;[331] (3) upgrading PLAN capabilities focused on counterpiracy and SLOC protection, including shipboard missile defense and ASW capabilities;[332] and (4) opening the PLA base in Djibouti, which serves as a strategic location for access to energy-rich countries in Africa and the Middle East and provides the PLAN a permanent presence in the Gulf of Aden/Arabian Sea from which to deploy expeditionary maritime operations.

---

[328] Zhang Jie, "Assessment of China's Surrounding Security Environment in the New Era" ["新时期中国周边安全环境评估"], Beijing: Institute of Asia-Pacific and Global Strategy, Chinese Academy of Social Sciences, February 16, 2019.

[329] Zhang Jie, "Assessment of China's Surrounding Security Environment in the New Era" ["新时期中国周边安全环境评估"], Beijing: Institute of Asia-Pacific and Global Strategy, Chinese Academy of Social Sciences, February 16, 2019.

[330] MSCConference, "Maritime Security Challenges Virtual—Session 1—Ms. Nadège Rolland on China's BRI," video, YouTube, October 21, 2020.

[331] Li Jian [李剑], Chen Wenwen [陈文文], and Jin Jing [金晶], "The Pattern of Indian Ocean Power and the Expansion of China's Sea Power in the Indian Ocean" ["印度洋海权格局与中国海权的印度洋拓展"], *China's Foreign Policy* [中国外交], 2015, p. 75; and Fu Mengzi and Liu Chunhao, "Some Thoughts on Building the 21st Century 'Maritime Silk Road'" ["关于21世纪'海上丝绸之路'建设的若干思考"], *Contemporary International Relations* [现代国际关系], No. 3, 2015, p. 2.

[332] Office of the Secretary of Defense, *Annual Report to Congress: Military and Security Developments Involving the People's Republic of China 2020*, Washington, D.C., 2020; and Jeffrey Becker, *Securing China's Lifelines Across the Indian Ocean*, Newport, R.I.: U.S. Naval War College, China Maritime Studies Institute, China Maritime Report No. 11, December 2020.

Explanations for Chinese Reactions

China's reactions reflect several concerns: First, Chinese analyses point to anxieties about ways in which the United States could actively attempt to counter the BRI, including blocking China's access to sea lanes. Some of this literature speculates, for example, that the United States will use "diplomatic resistance" and military tools to frustrate China's plans, including by inciting tensions in the South China to complicate the development of the BRI maritime silk road.[333]

A second concern articulated in the literature is that the United States will collaborate with regional allies and partners to obstruct the BRI and China's access to partner countries. For example, some Chinese scholars assert that the United States and Japan have colluded to oppose the BRI by refusing to join the Asian Infrastructure Investment Bank and "stirring up trouble" in the SCS.[334] Others speculate that increased U.S.-Indian maritime security cooperation and joint statements on the SCS have been intended as a response to the maritime silk road. One researcher describes the U.S.-Japan-India *Malabar* naval exercise as a demonstration of the United States' commitment to safeguarding sea lanes in the Indian Ocean given China's increasing naval presence.[335]

These concerns have likely driven Chinese reactions in the first two categories listed above: expanding energy access through overland pipelines and increasing access to strategic ports. The second two categories—the development of more-advanced and longer-range PLAN capabilities and the opening of an overseas base in Djibouti—reflect China's desire to both address maritime security threats (such as those from piracy and foreign navies in critical SLOCs) and become a strong maritime power that is regionally self-sufficient, free from encirclement from foreign powers, and capable of protecting Chinese economic and political interests overseas.[336]

For example, the PLAN's modernization program has focused on enhancing China's A2/AD bubble, which includes building the capabilities to secure China's maritime approaches in the

---

[333] Hu Bo, "Three Major Maritime Security Issues Pose a Test for 'One Belt, One Road'" ["三大海上安全问题考验'一代一路'"], in Zhang Jie, ed., *Assessment of China's Peripheral Security Situation 2016* [中国周边安 全形势评估2016], Beijing: Social Sciences Academic Press, 2016, p. 193.

[334] Zhang Jie, "Regional Security Issues in Constructing 'One Belt, One Road'" ["'一带一路' 建设 中的周边安全问"], *World Affairs* [世界知识], No. 9, 2017, pp. 22–23.

[335] Fu Mengzi and Liu Chunhao, "Some Thoughts on Building the 21st Century 'Maritime Silk Road'" ["关于 21世纪'海上丝绸之路'建设的若干思考"], *Contemporary International Relations* [现代国 际关系], No. 3, 2015, p. 2.

[336] MSCConference, "Maritime Security Challenges Virtual—Session 1—Ms. Nadège Rolland on China's BRI," video, YouTube, October 21, 2020; and Li Jian, Chen Wenwen, and Jin Jing, "Overall Situation of Sea Power in the Indian Ocean and the Expansion in the Indian Ocean of Chinese Sea Powers" ["印度样海权格局与中国海权的印度洋扩展"], *Pacific Journal*, Vol. 22, No. 5, 2014, p. 75.

Near Seas (the East, South, and Yellow seas), as well as protecting key regional SLOCs.[337] Beyond the regional SLOCs, the PLA has been developing expeditionary capabilities to protect Chinese interests overseas. The counterpiracy operations that started in 2009 were a direct result of pressure on the PLA by the Chinese leadership to develop more capacity to protect Chinese shipping from security threats, and the base in Djibouti provides a location for China to expand its military presence for the protection of shipping and energy interests in Africa, as well as build on its maritime expeditionary capabilities.[338]

The first two categories of reactions are not particularly aggressive—developing overland pipelines and expanding access to ports is something that any country in China's position is likely to do, and China has been open about the development of these projects through the BRI. However, the rationale behind these reactions reflects a deeper concern over U.S. and allied intent (in the SCS, for example) and anxiety about the potential for USN interdiction of Chinese shipping should relations deteriorate to that point. The second two categories constitute a more aggressive response to these concerns because the development of PLAN capabilities for SLOC protection and to secure maritime approaches is directly tied to China's perception that it needs to ensure its access to key waterways essential for its economic survival. The base in Djibouti represents a broader strategy of building overseas maritime power and protecting Chinese interests through a larger PLA presence, which—according to the standard set by China's own judgments regarding the United States' overseas basing infrastructure—is itself a somewhat aggressive response.

Conclusion

The case study illustrates that the potential for U.S. or allied actions to restrict access to key waterways and SLOCs influences China's approach to defending maritime approaches and shipping, as well as the level of aggressiveness with which it seeks to protect its overseas economic interests. Chinese behavior reflects a set of broad apprehensions about the future— although the United States has not undertaken directly aggressive actions toward Chinese maritime commerce in recent decades, Chinese leaders are concerned about the combination of the United States' ability to hold Chinese shipping at risk and are concerned about what they see as its increasingly hostile intent. China's responses range from the less aggressive diversification of energy access through overland pipelines and pursuing port agreements in the Indian Ocean to the more aggressive development of PLAN capabilities and opening of an overseas base in Djibouti. Given China's concerns about access to strategic chokepoints and maritime routes for shipping and resources, the case provides moderate support for the hypothesis that China is

---

[337] Kristen Gunness, "The China Dream and the Near Seas," in Roy Kamphausen, David Lai, and Tiffany Ma, eds., *Securing the China Dream*, Seattle, Wash.: National Bureau of Asian Research, 2020.

[338] "Commentary: China's Djibouti Base Not for Military Expansion," Xinhua, July 13, 2017.

likely to respond aggressively should the United States or its allies or partners directly threaten PRC economic interests.

Case 3: Scarborough Shoal and the 2012 Shift in Chinese Behavior in the South China Sea

Deterrence theory suggests that determination or resolve is a crucial factor in shaping a competitor's behavior and that states will go to great lengths to establish their reputations for resolve. Case 3 therefore tests the hypothesis that China is more likely to respond aggressively to activities that cause China to worry that the United States and its allies and partners doubt Chinese resolve. In order to do so, this case examines the 2012 Scarborough Shoal standoff between China and the Philippines. The CCG rapidly supported Chinese maritime militia vessels early in the standoff and aggressively countered Philippine ships in the area. Despite "negotiating" a resolution with the United States, China was able to strengthen its presence at the Scarborough Shoal. CCG vessels have since become a constant fixture there and deny Philippine fishing vessels entry.[339] Our examination of the events before, during, and after this incident provides weak support for the hypothesis. Evidence suggests that a perception had developed among Chinese experts and leaders that China had not been responding aggressively enough, either to what Beijing saw as a U.S. policy shift toward the SCS or to activities by emboldened rival claimants. Chinese sources from after the incident also reference the utility of a "Scarborough Shoal model" that leverages nonmilitary instruments of power to advance China's claims in the SCS. In tandem, this provides indirect and limited support for the hypothesis; information gaps preclude a more confident assessment. Moreover, the evidence also suggests that other factors likely informed Chinese behavior, including a growth in Chinese perception of the threat posed to China's physical and regime security, as well as its regional influence, by the United States. China's own expanding military and paramilitary capabilities, particularly in the maritime domain, also enabled its more-robust responses.

U.S. and Philippine Military Activities in the South China Sea

Amid the U.S. rebalance to Asia formally announced in 2011, U.S. policy focus increased on China's efforts to advance its territorial and maritime claims in the SCS.[340] Major U.S. activities from 2009 to 2012 included increasing focus on U.S. military capabilities in the Western Pacific, diplomatic engagement on maritime security and the SCS with Southeast Asian countries,

---

[339] Sofia Tomacruz and J. C. Gotinga, "List: China's Incursions in Philippine Waters," *Rappler*, August 22, 2019; and Carmela Fonbuena, "Video Captures China Coast Guard Taking PH Fishermen's Catch," *Rappler*, June 8, 2018.

[340] Mark E. Manyin, Stephen Daggett, Ben Dolven, Susan V. Lawrence, Michael F. Martin, Ronald O'Rourke, and Bruce Vaughn, *Pivot to the Pacific? The Obama Administration's "Rebalancing" Toward Asia*, Washington, D.C.: Congressional Research Service, March 28, 2012.

emphasis on building the maritime capacity of SCS claimants, growing focus on SCS FONOPs, and enhanced maritime components of regional exercises.[341]

During this period, the Philippines—a key claimant to features in the Spratly Islands and the only U.S. treaty ally among the SCS claimants—issued a National Security Policy in 2011 stating that the Aquino administration would work to "develop a defense capability to protect our sovereignty and strategic maritime interests," including regarding disputes in the SCS.[342] The Philippines undertook the following actions in the security realm, some in concert with the United States: It increased its defense budget; improved its maritime capabilities, including maritime domain awareness; upgraded bilateral security discussion with the United States; and sought to raise and criticize China's behavior in regional and international fora, including by countering China's claims in international court.[343]

---

[341] Five main lines of effort included (1) increased prioritization of U.S. military weapon system and platform acquisition, posture, and presence relevant for or located in the Western Pacific; (2) increased diplomatic engagement on maritime security and the SCS with Southeast Asian countries, including SCS claimants, and regional fora such as ASEAN, ASEAN Defense Ministers' Meeting Plus, ASEAN Regional Forum, and the East Asia Summit; (3) increased focus on security cooperation in building the maritime capacity of SCS claimants, including equipment transfers; (4) increased the number of SCS claimants subject to U.S. FONOPs (note that information on how many FONOPs have been conducted against each country are not available, but descriptions of the types of FONOPs conducted against China during this period include a greater variety over time, suggesting an increase in overall FONOPs and/or sophistication of challenges vis-à-vis China. In FYs 2008 and 2009, FONOPs were conducted against three SCS claimants—China, Malaysia, and the Philippines—as well as Indonesia, which has overlapping claims with China but does not consider itself a claimant. In FY 2010, Vietnam was added to that list, and in FYs 2011 and 2012, Taiwan was additionally added); and (5) enhanced maritime components of regional exercises, such as Cooperation Afloat Readiness and Training with multiple ASEAN members and Balikatan with the Philippines. See Mark E. Manyin, Stephen Daggett, Ben Dolven, Susan V. Lawrence, Michael F. Martin, Ronald O'Rourke, and Bruce Vaughn, *Pivot to the Pacific? The Obama Administration's "Rebalancing" Toward Asia*, Washington, D.C.: Congressional Research Service, March 28, 2012, pp. 2, 4–5, 20; DoD, *Asia-Pacific Maritime Security Strategy*, Washington, D.C., 2015, p. 27; DoD, "Challenges to Excessive Maritime Claims 1 October 2007–30 September 2008," undated; DoD, "Challenges to Excessive Maritime Claims 1 October 2008–30 September 2009," undated; DoD, "Challenges to Excessive Maritime Claims 1 October 2009–30 September 2010," undated; DoD, "Challenges to Excessive Maritime Claims 1 October 2010–30 September 2011," undated; DoD, "U.S. Department of Defense (DOD) Freedom of Navigation (FON) Report for Fiscal Year (FY) 2012," January 4, 2013; and Thomas Lum, *The Republic of the Philippines and U.S. Interests*, Washington, D.C.: Congressional Research Service, April 5, 2012, p. 15.

[342] Government of the Philippines, *National Security Policy 2011–2016: Securing the Gains of Democracy*, Manila, 2011, p. 30.

[343] Six main lines of effort included the following: The Philippines (1) increased the defense budget of the Armed Forces of the Philippines; (2) established a National Coast Watch Center beginning in 2011 with U.S. and Australian support; (3) established and held a bilateral dialogue series with the United States beginning in 2011, continued on an annual basis as a 2+2 foreign and defense ministerial dialogue since 2012 and including discussion on maritime security issues; (4) led efforts to develop a binding code of conduct between ASEAN and China on the SCS; (5) voiced concerns about China's behavior in ASEAN fora and solicited support within ASEAN for a unified approach to the SCS; and (6) pursued a legal case against China's historic rights claims to the SCS via the United Nations International Tribunal on the Law of the Sea, eventually filed in 2013. See Thomas Lum, *The Republic of the Philippines and U.S. Interests*, Washington, D.C.: Congressional Research Service, April 5, 2012, pp. 2, 26; Jonathan V. Zata, "National Coast Watch System Moves Forward," *Indo-Pacific Defense Forum*, December 5, 2016; Embassy of the Philippines, "Newsletter," Washington, D.C., No. 2, 2012, p. 1; Gregory B. Poling,

U.S. and Philippines Measures to Manage Escalation

The United States likely sought to manage escalation during the standoff by not directly challenging China's claims over Scarborough Shoal via a public assertion of its alliance commitment to defending them on behalf of the Philippines. In other words, the United States did not establish a clear redline that a Chinese attack against Philippine forces in the Scarborough Shoal would invoke an alliance response under the provisions of the Mutual Defense Treaty. It is worth noting that Secretary of State Pompeo would later make this assertion in 2019.[344] More broadly, the Obama administration refrained from endorsing any country's sovereignty claims in the SCS vis-à-vis China. Likewise, the Philippines may have initially delayed consultations with Washington because of past threats from China on bringing the United States into what Beijing frames as bilateral disputes between the Philippines and China.[345]

Chinese Reactions

Chinese sources typically date a shift in U.S. policy toward the SCS to policy announcements by Washington in between 2009 and 2011, which led to a number of Chinese responses.[346] A Western scholar notes that under Xi Jinping, between 2012 and the summer of 2013, Chinese leaders decided to compromise with fellow claimants less and assertively advance Chinese interests more in the SCS.[347] This view is summarized in an August 2013 speech by Xi Jinping

---

"Implications and Results: United States–Philippines Ministerial Dialogue," Center for Strategic and International Studies, May 4, 2012; U.S. Department of State, "Joint Statement of the United States–Philippines Bilateral Strategic Dialogue," Washington, D.C., January 27, 2012; Julio Amador III, "National Security of the Philippines Under the Aquino Administration: A Human Security Approach," *Korean Journal of Defense Analysis*, Vol. 23, No. 4, December 2011, p. 525; and Sheena Chestnut Greitens, "The U.S.-Philippines Alliance in a Year of Transition: Challenges and Opportunities," working paper, Washington, D.C.: Brookings Institution, May 2016, pp. 1–11.

[344] Julian Ku, "Does the U.S. Have a Legal Obligation to Defend the Scarborough Shoal for the Philippines? Not Until It Decides Who Owns It," *Lawfare*, April 27, 2016; Walter Lohman, "Scarborough Role for U.S.?" *The Diplomat*, June 2, 2012; and Karen Lema and Neil Jerome Morales, "Pompeo Assures Philippines of U.S. Protection in Event of Sea Conflict," Reuters, March 1, 2019.

[345] Michael Green, Kathleen Hicks, Zack Cooper, John Schaus, and Jake Douglas, *Countering Coercion in Maritime Asia: The Theory and Practice of Gray Zone Deterrence*, Washington, D.C.: Center for Strategic and International Studies, May 2017, pp. 101–102.

[346] Fang Xiaozhi [方晓志], "A Geo-Security Analysis of U.S. South China Sea Policy"

["对美国南海政策的地缘安全解析"], *Pacific Journal* [太平洋学报], Vol. 20, No. 7, 2012; Chen Cihang, "Changes of U.S. Stance on the South China Sea Issue Since 2009," South China Sea Strategic Situation Probing Initiative, May 27, 2021; Dai Zheng [戴正] and Zheng Xianwu [郑先武], "China's Security Strategy in the South China Sea Dispute in Recent Years: 'Differential Treatment and a Two-Pronged Approach'"
["中国近年南海争端安全战略: '区别对待，双管齐下'"], *Indian Ocean Economic Studies* [印度洋经济体研究], No. 5, 2019; and Zeng Yong [曾勇], "Research on Three Struggles for Rights Protection in the South China Sea Since 2012" ["2012年来三次南海维权斗争研究"], *Pacific Journal* [太平洋学报], Vol. 27, No. 5, 2019.

[347] Ryan D. Martinson, *Echelon Defense: The Role of Sea Power in Chinese Maritime Dispute Strategy*, Newport, R.I.: China Maritime Studies Institute, February 2018, p. 56.

regarding how to handle China's maritime disputes: "We love peace, and will continue to take the path of peaceful development, but we absolutely cannot give up our legitimate rights and interests, much less sacrifice core national interests."[348] Chinese academic analyses appear to bolster the view that Chinese responses changed notably in this period. Scholars from the Chinese Academy of Social Sciences and other institutions cowrote a 2013 article that viewed 2012 as a "turning point" for Chinese maritime policy transitioning from Deng Xiaoping's "keeping a low profile" [韬光养晦] to "taking the initiative" [主动作为].[349] Similar assessments about China's approach becoming more active and assertive in 2012 are echoed in a 2012 interview with a PRC scholar of Sino-U.S. relations following the Scarborough Shoal incident and a 2014 interview with the president of a Chinese national-level research organization on the SCS.[350]

Political Responses

During the Scarborough Shoal incident itself, China leveraged statements from its foreign and defense ministries and called on Washington and other parties not to "internationalize" the situation.[351] On a number of occasions, China's negative reaction illustrated that it may not have felt in control of escalation dynamics. For example, Beijing responded particularly negatively to the Philippines' April 17 announcement that Manila would seek international arbitration over the Scarborough Shoal dispute, with a senior Chinese MOFA official summoning the Philippine chargé d'affairs and PLAN ships reportedly sent to the shoal to monitor Chinese paramilitary

---

[348] Xi Jinping, "We Need to Do More to Take Interest in the Sea, Understand the Sea, and Strategically Manage the Sea, and Continually Do More to Promote China's Efforts to Become a Maritime Power" ["进一步关心海洋认识海洋经略海 洋推动海洋强国建设不断取得新成就"], *People's Daily*, August 1, 2013, referenced in Ryan D. Martinson, *Echelon Defense: The Role of Sea Power in Chinese Maritime Dispute Strategy*, Newport, R.I.: China Maritime Studies Institute, February 2018, p. 56.

[349] Zhang Jie [张洁], Li Zhifei [李志斐], Zhu Fenglan [朱凤岚], Yang Danzhi [杨丹志], Wu Zhaoli [吴兆礼], Li Chengri [李成日], Chen Chunhua [陈春华], and Fan Lijun [范丽君], "Maritime Disputes and Sino-U.S. Contests—China's Peripheral Security Situation" ["海上纷争与中美 博弈—中国周边安全形势"], *World Affairs* [世界知识], No. 2, 2013. We were not able to access the full article, but it is discussed in Mathieu Duchâtel, "China Trends #6—Generally Stable? Facing U.S. Pushback in the South China Sea," Institut Montaigne, August 6, 2020.

[350] "China Shifts Its Maritime Strategy," *People's Daily*, July 16, 2012, referenced in Ryan D. Martinson, *Echelon Defense: The Role of Sea Power in Chinese Maritime Dispute Strategy*, Newport, R.I.: China Maritime Studies Institute, February 2018, p. 56; and Wang Xiaofeng [王晓枫], "China's Maritime Patrols Cover All of the South China Sea and Maritime Rights Protection Is More Proactive Than in the Past" ["中国海上巡航覆盖整个南海海上维权更主动"], *People's Daily Online* [人民网], August 27, 2014, referenced in Ryan D. Martinson, *Echelon Defense: The Role of Sea Power in Chinese Maritime Dispute Strategy*, Newport, R.I.: China Maritime Studies Institute, February 2018, p. 56.

[351] Michael Green, Kathleen Hicks, Zack Cooper, John Schaus, and Jake Douglas, *Countering Coercion in Maritime Asia: The Theory and Practice of Gray Zone Deterrence*, Washington, D.C.: Center for Strategic and International Studies, May 2017.

vessels in overwatch.[352] When the Philippines bypassed the Chinese embassy in Manila a week later to lodge a complaint directly with Beijing, the embassy responded in "shock" and accused the Philippines of slighting the Chinese ambassador.[353]

Economic Responses

A 2012 *People's Daily* article described China's actions at Scarborough as "using non-military confrontation as the bottom line and exerted pressure on the Philippines through various administrative, diplomatic and economic means, and finally achieved control of Scarborough Shoal and nearby waters."[354] Key economic actions during the standoff included cutting banana imports from the Philippines and reducing Chinese tourism to the Philippines.[355] At that time, China was the Philippines' third-largest trading partner, importing over 30 percent of the Philippines' total banana exports, and ranked as the Philippines' fourth-largest source of international tourists.[356]

Military Responses

China used maritime assets, including maritime militia vessels and ships from the China Marine Surveillance and Fisheries Law Enforcement Command (predecessors to the CCG) to seize physical control of Scarborough Shoal. At various points, PLAN ships were reportedly stationed over the horizon in overwatch, and a PLAN flotilla later conducted an exercise between Taiwan and Luzon.[357] During the incident, China also warned that the PLA could conduct "joint

---

[352] Michael Green, Kathleen Hicks, Zack Cooper, John Schaus, and Jake Douglas, *Countering Coercion in Maritime Asia: The Theory and Practice of Gray Zone Deterrence*, Washington, D.C.: Center for Strategic and International Studies, May 2017, pp. 105–107. It is not known how close to the Chinese paramilitary vessels the PLAN vessels were operating, but the PLAN ships were likely stationed within a rapid steaming distance of the paramilitary vessels.

[353] Michael Green, Kathleen Hicks, Zack Cooper, John Schaus, and Jake Douglas, *Countering Coercion in Maritime Asia: The Theory and Practice of Gray Zone Deterrence*, Washington, D.C.: Center for Strategic and International Studies, May 2017, p. 109.

[354] Wang Xiaofeng [王晓枫], "China's Maritime Patrols Cover All of the South China Sea and Maritime Rights Protection Is More Proactive Than in the Past" ["中国海上巡航覆盖整个南海 海上维权更主动"], *People's Daily Online* [人民网], August 27, 2014.

[355] Kesha West, "Banana Crisis Blamed on Philippines-China Dispute," *ABC News*, June 28, 2012; and Aurora Almendral, "Philippines Feels Force of China Travel Warning," *BBC News*, October 22, 2014.

[356] "The China-Philippine Banana War," *Asia Sentinel*, June 6, 2012; and "Philippines Seeks New Markets amid Sea Dispute with China," Reuters, May 17, 2017.

[357] Michael Green, Kathleen Hicks, Zack Cooper, John Schaus, and Jake Douglas, *Countering Coercion in Maritime Asia: The Theory and Practice of Gray Zone Deterrence*, Washington, D.C.: Center for Strategic and International Studies, May 2017, pp. 106, 114.

efforts" with civilian maritime agencies if necessary.[358] We did not see reports of Chinese aircraft activities during the standoff; in general, overwater operations by Chinese military aircraft ramped up beginning in 2013, and flights leveraging Spratly Island airfields began in 2016.[359] Multiple cyber incidents targeting the Philippines have coincided with bilateral maritime incidents in the SCS or perceived changes to Philippine attitudes toward disputed territory.[360] In 2012, this included cyberattacks targeting a University of the Philippines website.[361]

Measures to Manage Escalation

During the early stages of the standoff, Beijing may have undertaken some tactical efforts to minimize escalation that were either not understood or not reciprocated by Manila, such as the withdrawal of two paramilitary ships on April 20–22, 2012, that left only one ship on patrol around Scarborough Shoal.[362] After tensions escalated to the point that dozens of Chinese government and fishing vessels were located near the shoal—vastly outnumbering Philippine ships—and accompanied by PRC economic actions mentioned above, Chinese representatives sought to negotiate a compromise involving the United States. After the Philippine ships withdrew, however, some Chinese ships remained near the shoal, and the lead Chinese interlocutor denied that an agreement had been reached.[363]

Explanations for Chinese Reactions

Two streams of analytical thought relating to SCS policy and Scarborough Shoal bolster the hypothesis that China is more likely to respond aggressively if it perceives that the United States and its allies and partners doubt China's resolve. First, prior to mid-2012, some Chinese analysts called on China to do more to counter the United States and the support it was providing to other claimants in the SCS. For example, a 2010 article on the U.S. role in the SCS written by PLA Navy Engineering University analysts argues that China needed to comprehensively increase its

---

[358] Michael Green, Kathleen Hicks, Zack Cooper, John Schaus, and Jake Douglas, "Counter-Coercion Series: Scarborough Shoal Standoff," Asia Maritime Transparency Initiative, Center for Strategic and International Studies, May 22, 2017; and Xinhua, "Philippines Claim Illegal—Beijing," *Manila Times*, April 28, 2012.

[359] Drake Long, "China's Naval Aviation Force Shows up at Fiery Cross Reef," *Benar News*, May 13, 2020; and Derek Grossman, Nathan Beauchamp-Mustafaga, Logan Ma, and Michael S. Chase, *China's Long-Range Bomber Flights: Drivers and Implications*, Santa Monica, Calif.: RAND Corporation, RR-2567-AF, 2018.

[360] Mark Manantan, "The Cyber Dimension of the South China Sea Clashes," *The Diplomat*, August 5, 2019; and FireEye, *Southeast Asia: An Evolving Cyber Threat Landscape*, Milpitas, Calif., March 2015, p. 3.

[361] Paolo Passeri, "Philippines and China, on the Edge of a New Cyber Conflict?" *Hackmageddon*, May 1, 2012.

[362] Michael Green, Kathleen Hicks, Zack Cooper, John Schaus, and Jake Douglas, *Countering Coercion in Maritime Asia: The Theory and Practice of Gray Zone Deterrence*, Washington, D.C.: Center for Strategic and International Studies, May 2017, pp. 107–108.

[363] Richard McGregor, *Asia's Reckoning: China, Japan, and the Fate of U.S. Power in the Pacific Century*, New York: Penguin, 2017, pp. 286–287. For two versions of the negotiations, see Michael Green, Kathleen Hicks, Zack Cooper, John Schaus, and Jake Douglas, *Countering Coercion in Maritime Asia: The Theory and Practice of Gray Zone Deterrence*, Washington, D.C.: Center for Strategic and International Studies, May 2017, pp. 117–119.

naval military power in order to meet Hu Jintao's call to protect maritime sovereignty and to support maritime rights and interests protection.[364] A 2012 article by a PLA scholar focuses on the shift in the U.S. position on the SCS in 2010–2011 and implies that U.S. efforts and encouragement of allies and partners will undermine China's position by "internationalizing" this issue unless addressed by additional countermeasures from Beijing.[365] Analysis by Chinese academics also identified China's position in the SCS as eroding between 2009 and 2010 as the United States increased its focus on the region and other disputants "internationalized" the issue, with one researcher noting that "with the actual support of the United States, in 2011, China . . . faced a situation in which Vietnam and the Philippines attacked the South China Sea."[366]

Second, multiple Chinese analytic communities and media sources discuss new Chinese approaches from 2012 onward, including the use of a "Scarborough Shoal model" [黄岩岛模式]. One 2012 article referred to China's successful layering of diplomatic, administrative, economic, and "non-governmental" activities, supported by military deterrence against the Philippines, as a "model" that China may harness elsewhere in the future to "protect Chinese maritime rights and interests" in other places like the Senkaku Islands.[367] Another article contrasted China's historical policy on the SCS—which it categorized as focusing in the 1970s and 1980s on military power—with the current strategy of mixing elements of both cooperation and coercion.

---

[364] Long Xingang [龙心刚] and Liang Dongxing [梁东兴], "On the U.S. Factor in the South China Sea Issue" ["论南海问题中的美国因素"], *Around Southeast Asia* [东南亚纵横], Vol. 9, 2010, p. 19.

[365] Fang Xiaozhi [方晓志], "A Geo-Security Analysis of U.S. South China Sea Policy" ["对美国南海政策的地缘安全解析"], *Pacific Journal* [太平洋学报], Vol. 20, No. 7, 2012, especially pp. 46–47 and 50–52.

[366] Zeng Yong [曾勇], "Research on Three Struggles for Rights Protection in the South China Sea Since 2012" ["2012年来三次南海维权斗争研究"], *Pacific Journal* [太平洋学报], Vol. 27, No. 5, 2019, p. 48; and Dai Zheng [戴正] and Zheng Xianwu [郑先武], "China's Security Strategy in the South China Sea Dispute in Recent Years: 'Differential Treatment and a Two-Pronged Approach'" ["中国近年南海争端安全战略: '区别对待，双管齐下'"], *Indian Ocean Economic Studies* [印度洋经济体研究], No. 5, 2019, p. 124.

[367] "Qin Hong: Facing the Philippines, We Have Sufficient Means" ["秦宏: 面对菲律宾我们有足够手段"], Xinhua, May 9, 2012; and Zhang Jie [张洁], "The Scarborough Shoal Model and the Shift in China's Maritime Strategy" ["黄岩岛模式与中国海洋维权政策的转向"], *Southeast Asian Studies* [东南亚研究], No. 4, June 2013. For additional information, see Andrew S. Erickson, "The South China Sea's Third Force: Understanding and Countering China's Maritime Militia," testimony before the House Armed Services Committee Seapower and Projection Forces Subcommittee, Washington, D.C., September 21, 2016. See also Zeng Yong [曾勇], "Viewing Trends in China's South China Sea Policy Trends from the 'Scarborough Shoal Model'" ["从'黄岩岛模式'看中国南海政策走向"], *Forum of World Economics & Politics* [世界经济与政治论坛], No. 5, 2014.

It attributed this new strategy to China's greater economic power and the array of tools available to it, as well as its ability to maintain a stronger maritime patrol presence in the region.[368]

In 2013, a PLA analyst from National Defense University stated that China's situation in the SCS had improved because of "the series of tough measures we have taken. In the past . . . we have always been passive. Neighboring countries felt that China was trading territory for peace, and that maintaining stability was greater than safeguarding rights, so they all dared to casually invade our territory. Now that we have strengthened our own maritime power and rights protection strength . . . neighboring countries . . . have gradually adapted" to Beijing's new approach.[369] The same analyst explained this "tough approach" more specifically in a 2012 interview:

> The South China Sea issue and the Diaoyu Islands issue are the thresholds that we must cross to take advantage of and seize the period of strategic opportunity. . . . To maintain the period of strategic opportunity, we must take the initiative to attack. . . . We must [also] clearly state to the international community that . . . if any force or any country . . . dares to use force on China's sovereignty issues, China will never compromise and retreat, and will make tough countermeasures.[370]

This analyst noted that China may not follow a "Scarborough Shoal model" in all disputes going forward because of unique factors in play for Scarborough Shoal,[371] but it is worth noting that subsequent periods of tensions in the SCS, such as the 2014 oil rig standoff with Vietnam, have often witnessed China layering paramilitary and military forces, as well as economic, political, and cyber/informational pressure against other claimants.

Although Chinese analysts writing in the academic literature tend to identify 2009 as the year when China's policy transitioned from "setting aside disputes" to "sovereignty belongs to China," they also typically cite China's actions at the Scarborough Shoal in 2012 as the first example of Beijing's new policy approach in action.[372] One of the academics finds that China's

---

[368] Mathieu Duchâtel, "China Trends #6—Generally Stable? Facing U.S. Pushback in the South China Sea," Institut Montaigne, August 6, 2020, quoting Dai Zheng [戴正] and Zheng Xianwu [郑先武], "China's Security Strategy in the South China Sea Dispute in Recent Years: 'Differential Treatment and a Two-Pronged Approach'" ["中国近年南海争端安全战略: '区别对待，双管齐下'"], *Indian Ocean Economic Studies* [印度洋经济体研究], No. 5, 2019.

[369] Huang Yingying [黄莹莹] and Sun Si [孙思], "Can the 'Scarborough Shoal Model' Be Copied?" ["'黄岩岛模式'是否可复制"], *International Herald Tribune* [国际先驱导报], April 12, 2013.

[370] Huang Yingying [黄莹莹], "Meng Xiangqing: Large Breakthroughs Have Already Been Made in Crisis Management and Control on China's Periphery" ["孟祥青: 中国周边危机管控已有大突破"], *International Herald Tribune* [国际先驱导报], November 6, 2012.

[371] Huang Yingying [黄莹莹] and Sun Si [孙思], "Can the 'Scarborough Shoal Model' Be Copied?" ["'黄岩岛模式'是否可复制"], *International Herald Tribune* [国际先驱导报], April 12, 2013.

[372] Zeng Yong [曾勇], "Research on Three Struggles for Rights Protection in the South China Sea Since 2012" ["2012年来三次南海维权斗争研究"], *Pacific Journal* [太平洋学报], Vol. 27, No. 5, 2019, pp. 42–44; and Dai

"struggles for safeguarding rights in the South China Sea" since 2012 "demonstrated the policy of the 'sovereignty of SCS islands belonging to China.'" This analyst notes that "specific rights protection struggles will focus on specific goals (such as restoring control of Scarborough Shoal)" and that Scarborough and other Chinese responses during 2014 and 2015 "did not involve the use of force, with the ultimate result of achieving the goal [of demonstrating China's sovereignty in the SCS] without causing the situation to further expand."[373]

While we therefore do find some support for the hypothesis that China's greater assertiveness in the SCS after 2012 was driven by Chinese concerns that the United States and other regional claimants viewed it as irresolute, there is also evidence for several alternative hypotheses to explain the change in PRC approach. First, China may have perceived that U.S. presence and capabilities, including support to allies and partners, were both increasing the threat to China's regime and physical security as well as eroding China's regional influence. As one PLA analyst stated in 2012, "if the status quo of the partition of the Spratly Islands continues and the United States' strong involvement in the South China Sea cannot be properly resolved, China will lose its 500–600 nautical mile-deep maritime strategic defense barrier in the South China Sea, and it will also lose its advantageous position in controlling South China Sea channels. This will be extremely detrimental to China's construction of a southern maritime defense force."[374] Likewise, "the 'active involvement' of the United States in the South China Sea dispute," both through its direct actions and through its incitement of other claimants to more vigorously challenge Chinese claims, "has posed a serious threat and challenge to China's national security and maritime rights and interests, and is a great constraint on China becoming a maritime power in the 21st century."[375]

Second, growth in China's military and paramilitary capabilities, particularly in the maritime domain, may have provided China's leaders with confidence to adopt a more aggressive

---

Zheng [戴正] and Zheng Xianwu [郑先武], "China's Security Strategy in the South China Sea Dispute in Recent Years: 'Differential Treatment and a Two-Pronged Approach'" ["中国近年南海争端安全战略: '区别对待，双管齐下'"], *Indian Ocean Economic Studies* [印度洋经济体研究], No. 5, 2019, p. 111. See also Zeng Yong [曾勇] and Wang Xuefei [万雪飞], "On China's Two Rights Protection Struggles Against the Philippines in the South China Sea" ["论中国两次对菲南海维权斗争"], *Indian Ocean Economic and Political Review* [印度洋经济体研究], No. 5, 2019, p. 130.

[373] Zeng Yong [曾勇], "Research on Three Struggles for Rights Protection in the South China Sea Since 2012" ["2012年来三次南海维权斗争研究"], *Pacific Journal* [太平洋学报], Vol. 27, No. 5, 2019, pp. 41–42.

[374] Fang Xiaozhi [方晓志], "A Geo-Security Analysis of U.S. South China Sea Policy" ["对美国南海政策的地缘安全解析"], *Pacific Journal* [太平洋学报], Vol. 20, No. 7, 2012, p. 50. This article was completed in May 2012 while events were unfolding at Scarborough Shoal and does not appear to reflect insights regarding events at the shoal.

[375] Fang Xiaozhi [方晓志], "A Geo-Security Analysis of U.S. South China Sea Policy" ["对美国南海政策的地缘安全解析"], *Pacific Journal* [太平洋学报], Vol. 20, No. 7, 2012, p. 51.

approach. A Western scholar traced a series of Chinese leadership policy decisions in the mid-2000s to early 2010s to increase ship patrols and presence in Chinese-claimed waters, grow the inventory and capabilities of Chinese maritime vessels, and convert increasing presence to control or enforcement of claims.[376]

Conclusion

There is only weak evidence to support the hypothesis that concerns over U.S. and allied and partner views of Chinese resolve encouraged China to act more aggressively in the SCS in the run-up to the Scarborough Shoal standoff. At least some Chinese analysts, mostly writing after the fact, argue that China had not acted aggressively enough prior to 2012 and that this may have emboldened regional actors as well as the United States to challenge Chinese claims. Starting with Scarborough Shoal in 2012, however, these analysts argue that China's embrace of a more assertive policy approach and the more aggressive actions that resulted from it began to reshape the SCS in its favor. That this shift was publicly acknowledged by Xi Jinping by August 2013 suggests that it had probably been adopted within at least some parts of the Chinese government well before then.[377] However, this represents mostly indirect and circumstantial evidence, which precludes a more confident assessment of this factor's validity.

---

[376] Ryan D. Martinson, *Echelon Defense: The Role of Sea Power in Chinese Maritime Dispute Strategy*, Newport, R.I.: China Maritime Studies Institute, February 2018, pp. 53–55.

[377] It is important to note that Xi was not in the top party leadership position during the Scarborough Shoal incident in spring 2012, as he did not become general secretary of the CCP until November 2012.

Case 4: Japanese Nationalization of the Senkaku Islands

Case 4 examines Chinese responses to the 2012 Japanese nationalization of three of the Senkaku Islands (known in China as the Diaoyu Islands) and the subsequent declaration by U.S. President Barack Obama in 2014 that they all fell under the U.S.-Japan security treaty in order to evaluate the hypothesis that China is less likely to respond aggressively to U.S. actions that involve allies or partners perceived as having strong U.S. defense commitments. Looking at the period from 2010 to 2016, we find only moderate support for the hypothesis.[378] The U.S. defensive commitment to Japan is long-standing. It is embodied in a formal security treaty, a permanent U.S. military presence in Japan, and extensive cooperation between the armed forces of both states. China is likely to have assessed that the U.S. defense commitment to Japan was strong during this period, particularly in comparison with the U.S. commitment to other U.S. regional partners and allies. Despite this, Japan's nationalization of the Senkaku Islands and the U.S. affirmation of its defense commitment plausibly generated a degree of variation in Chinese perceptions of the strength and credibility of the U.S.-Japan alliance. This appears to have had only a marginal effect on most aspects of Chinese policy. Beijing continued to use the same rhetoric against Japan and the United States as it had prior to nationalization and to employ PLA and paramilitary units in the same provocative ways following Obama's declaration. Although China did stop some forms of Chinese economic coercion against Japan, it is unclear whether that change was specifically tied directly to the U.S. declaration.

Japanese and U.S. Activities Regarding the Senkaku Islands

In 2011, then-governor of Tokyo Ishihara Shintarō entered into talks with the private Japanese owner of three of the Senkaku Islands. Until that time, a Japanese government ministry had been leasing three of the islands—Uotsuri, Kita-kojima, and Minami-kojima—to prevent conservative elements in Japan from developing the islands in any way. In April 2012, Governor Ishihara's plan was publicly made known, including his intention to use official funds of the Tokyo metropolitan government and to build a dock on the islands.[379] Hoping to block Ishihara's effort but wary of provoking a backlash from China, Prime Minister Noda Yoshihiko decided to purchase the three islands.[380] On September 11, 2012, his government bought the three islands.[381] Although Japan refers to this action as "acquisition and retention" (取得・保有),

---

[378] This time frame takes into consideration two years of activity prior to Japan's nationalization and two years following Obama's statement.

[379] "Japan Government 'Reaches Deal to Buy' Disputed Islands," *BBC News*, September 5, 2012; and Yoko Wakatsuki, "Tokyo Governor Outlines Plan to Buy Islands Claimed by China," *CNN*, April 17, 2012.

[380] For a full explanation of the incident, see Michael Green, Kathleen Hicks, Zack Cooper, John Schaus, and Jake Douglas, "Counter-Coercion Series: Senkaku Islands Nationalization Crisis," Asia Maritime Transparency Initiative, Center for Strategic and International Studies, June 14, 2017.

[381] The purchase included Uotsuri, Kita-kojima, and Minami-kojima. The United States still leases the other two islands—Kuba and Taisho. The three remaining islets/rocks remain in the ownership of the central government.

outside of Japan this has been commonly referred to as *nationalization*, which is the term that we use here.[382]

Roughly a year and a half afterward, in April 2014, President Barack Obama—in the first public statement by a sitting U.S. president on the issue—said in a joint press conference with Japanese Prime Minister Abe Shinzō that "our treaty commitment to Japan's security is absolute, and Article 5 covers all territories under Japan's administration, including the Senkaku Islands."[383] This was important because it clarified, in no uncertain terms, that the United States opposed any efforts by China to counter Japan's administrative control and that any conflict that might result risked involving the United States.

Although the level of authority was the highest that could be given, it was neither the first time a U.S. official made this declaration nor a clarification of U.S. policy.[384] For example, prior to Obama's statement, on January 18, 2013, Secretary of State Hillary Clinton said that although the United States did not take a position on the sovereignty of the islands, Washington opposed "any unilateral actions that would seek to undermine Japanese administration."[385] And in response to China's establishment of an ADIZ in November 2013, Secretary of Defense Chuck Hagel said, "The United States reaffirms its longstanding policy that Article V of the U.S.-Japan Mutual Defense Treaty applies to the Senkaku Islands."[386] Nevertheless, Obama's declaration was made because Tokyo was strongly urging Washington to take steps to help Japan shore up its position with the islands.

Beyond the declaration, the United States appears to have done nothing different vis-à-vis Japan or China following the statement. Bilateral exercises, for example, continued unchanged with no noticeable change in the number held. In addition to an annual joint exercise, each of the Japan Self Defense Forces services held a regular set of several bilateral exercises with their U.S.

---

[382] Japanese Prime Minister's Office, "Meeting of Related Cabinet Officials Regarding the Acquisition and Retention of the Senkaku Islands" ["尖閣諸島の取得・保有に関する関係閣僚会合"], September 10, 2014; and Japanese Prime Minister's Office, "Mutual Agreement Among Related Cabinet Officials Regarding the Acquisition and Retention of the Senkaku Islands" ["尖閣諸島の取得・保有に関する関係閣僚申し合わせ"], September 10, 2014.

[383] White House, "Joint Press Conference with President Obama and Prime Minister Abe of Japan," Office of the Press Secretary, April 24, 2014; and White House, "U.S.-Japan Joint Statement: The United States and Japan: Shaping the Future of the Asia-Pacific and Beyond," Office of the Press Secretary, April 25, 2014.

[384] Perhaps the earliest public declaration occurred in 2004 when Deputy Secretary of State Richard Armitage made an ambiguous reference, saying that the security treaty "would require any attack on Japan, or the administrative territories under Japanese control, to be seen as an attack on the United States." See Richard L. Armitage, "Remarks and Q & A at the Japan National Press Club," Department of State Archives, February 2, 2004.

[385] Hillary Clinton, "Remarks with Japanese Foreign Minister Fumio Kishida After Their Meeting," Washington, D.C., January 18, 2013.

[386] Chuck Hagel, "Statement on the East China Sea Air Defense Identification Zone," *Real Clear Defense*, November 23, 2013.

service counterparts.[387] Similarly, in addition to continued diplomatic engagement that included summits and ministerial-level meetings, U.S. officials' comments regarding U.S. commitment to defend the Senkaku Islands did not change from their pre-2014 statements. For example, a joint statement that followed a meeting in April 2015 stated that U.S. commitments "extend to all the territories under the administration of Japan, including the Senkaku Islands. In that context, the United States opposes any unilateral action that seeks to undermine Japan's administration of the Senkaku Islands."[388] Arguably, the only significant change that the United States pursued after 2014 was a revision of the *Guidelines for U.S.-Japan Defense Cooperation* in April 2015, the first time they had been revised since 1997.[389] While the contents of the revision were important for clarifying new roles and missions for the allies against a backdrop of increasing Chinese provocations, a link to the revision to Obama's 2014 statement is difficult to support, particularly since application of the security treaty to the Senkaku Islands was not a change in U.S. government policy.[390]

Chinese Reactions

Political Responses

China strongly opposed Japan's nationalization. China's Ministry of Foreign Affairs issued a statement saying that the "Chinese government solemnly states that the Japanese government's so-called 'purchase' of the Diaoyu Island is totally illegal and invalid. It does not change, not even in the slightest way, the historical fact of Japan's occupation of Chinese territory, nor will it alter China's territorial sovereignty over the Diaoyu Island and its affiliated islands."[391] And at the UN, China's ambassador declared the following:

> The recent so-called "island purchase" by the Japanese government is nothing different from money laundering. Its purpose is to legalize its stealing and occupation of the Chinese territory through this illegal means and to confuse international public opinion and deceive people in the world. This action of Japan constitutes a serious encroachment upon China's sovereignty and intends to continue and legalize the result of Japan's colonial policy. It is an open denial of the outcomes of victory of the world anti-fascist war, and a grave challenge to the

---

[387] Jeffrey W. Hornung, *Japan's Potential Contributions in an East China Sea Contingency*, Santa Monica, Calif.: RAND Corporation, RR-A314-1, 2020, p. 56.

[388] White House, "Remarks by President Obama and Prime Minister Abe of Japan in Joint Press Conference," Washington, D.C., April 28, 2015.

[389] Japanese Ministry of Foreign Affairs, *The Guidelines for Japan-U.S. Defense Cooperation*, April 27, 2015.

[390] For a summary of the revisions, see Jeffrey W. Hornung, *Japan's Potential Contributions in an East China Sea Contingency*, Santa Monica, Calif.: RAND Corporation, RR-A314-1, 2020, pp. 89–91.

[391] Ministry of Foreign Affairs of the People's Republic of China, "Statement of the Ministry of Foreign Affairs of the People's Republic of China," September 10, 2012.

post-war international order and the purposes and principles of the Charter of the United Nations.[392]

Obama's explicit support to defend the Senkaku Islands did not visibly change China's position, though of course how it may have changed Chinese thinking and perceptions is a more difficult question. Like in statements from prior years, Foreign Ministry spokesperson Qin Gang's response first conveyed tropes about the islands being China's inherent territory and Japan's occupation of them being illegal and invalid. It also criticized Japan by calling out its "provocative behavior" as "conclusive and unreasonable."[393] Qin then took aim at the alliance and the United States itself, saying that

> the Japan-US alliance is a bilateral arrangement formed during the Cold War and should not harm China's territorial sovereignty and legitimate rights and interests. China firmly opposes the use of the Diaoyu Islands as the target of the Japan-U.S. Security Treaty. The United States should respect the facts, take a responsible attitude, abide by its promise not to stand on the sidelines on the issue of territorial sovereignty, be cautious in its words and deeds, and effectively play a constructive role in regional peace and stability.[394]

Economic Responses

In response to Japan's nationalization in 2012, China took some economic actions to express its opposition. This was largely passive in nature, with Beijing supporting or allowing boycotts against Japanese goods and protests against Japanese companies that resulted in both property damage and revenue loss.[395] After Obama's statement, however, no similar responses were apparent. Instead, it appears that China did not take any additional economic responses against either Japan or the United States. This post-declaration cessation of economic responses is notable given that, after a 2010 incident in which a Chinese fishing trawler rammed Japan Coast Guard vessels, China reduced its exports of rare earth metals to Japan. While there is evidence to suggest that China may have initially implemented these export restrictions prior to the incident,[396] after the collision China apparently stepped up the enforcement of these restrictions,

---

[392] Permanent Mission of the People's Republic of China to the United Nations, "Remarks of Rebuke Against Japan's Statement on Diaoyu Dao by Ambassador Li Baodong During the General Debate of the 67th Session of the UN General Assembly," October 16, 2012.

[393] Qin Gang, "Foreign Ministry Spokesperson Qin Gang's Routine Press Conference on April 23, 2014" ["2014年4月23日外交部发言人秦刚主持例行记者会"], Ministry of Foreign Affairs of the People's Republic of China, April 23, 2014.

[394] Qin Gang, "Foreign Ministry Spokesperson Qin Gang's Routine Press Conference on April 23, 2014" ["2014 年 4 月 23 日外交部发言人秦刚主持例行记者会"], Ministry of Foreign Affairs of the People's Republic of China, April 23, 2014.

[395] Richard Katz, "Mutual Assured Production," *Foreign Affairs*, July/August 2013.

[396] Phil Taylor, "Rush on for Rare Earths as U.S. Firms Seek to Counter Chinese Monopoly," *New York Times*, July 22, 2010.

leading to the view that they were deliberate.[397] There is also some evidence that China manipulated tourism to Japan following both the 2010 and 2012 events; Chinese tourism to Japan rapidly fell and other cultural exchanges were canceled, leading analysts to believe that Beijing may have at least informally applied pressure.[398] Although there is no evidence to suggest that China's lack of economic responses after Obama's declaration was directly tied to Obama's statement, at the very least this pattern of Chinese behavior is consistent with the hypothesis examined in this case.

Military Responses

Obama's declaration had little apparent effect on Chinese activities in the waters around the Senkaku Islands. As Figure B.1 shows, CCG and other state-owned ships had already become a regular presence in the islands' CZ and TW after Japan's nationalization of the islands. Prior to Japan's nationalization, Chinese ships neared the islands on a handful of occasions. According to Japan Coast Guard data, the most such incidents (24 of them) occurred in 2010 after a Chinese fishing trawler rammed two Japan Coast Guard vessels.[399] After nationalization, Chinese activity increased and continued at an increased level through the end of 2017. Obama's declaration does not appear to have changed that in any way.

---

[397] Peter Harrell, Elizabeth Rosenberg, and Edoardo Saravalle, *China's Use of Coercive Economic Measures*, Washington, D.C.: Center for a New American Security, June 2018, pp. 9, 13–14, 42.

[398] Michael Green, Kathleen Hicks, Zack Cooper, John Schaus, and Jake Douglas, *Countering Coercion in Maritime Asia: The Theory and Practice of Gray Zone Deterrence*, Washington, D.C.: Center for Strategic and International Studies, May 2017, pp. 80–81.

[399] Japan Coast Guard, "Trends in Chinese Government and Other Vessels in the Waters Around the Senkaku Islands, and Japan's Response" ["尖閣諸島周辺海域における中国海警局に所属する船舶等の動向と我が国の対処"], undated.

Figure B.1. Chinese Vessels Around Senkaku Islands (2010–2017)

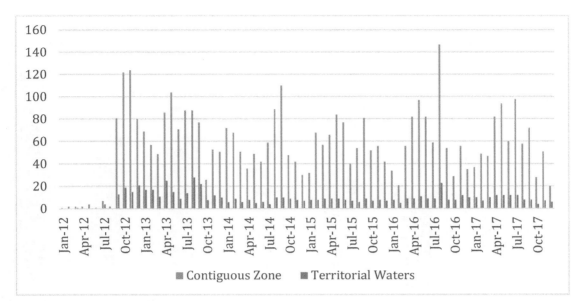

SOURCE: Japan Coast Guard, "Trends in Chinese Government and Other Vessels in the Waters Around the Senkaku Islands, and Japan's Response" ["尖閣諸島周辺海域における中国海警局に所属する船舶等の動向と我が国の対処"], undated.

Similarly, Obama's declaration did not change Chinese military activities in the waters and air around Japan. Instead, following a trend in place since Japan's nationalization, not only has Chinese military activity gradually increased, in November 2013 it unilaterally declared the creation of an ADIZ over the ECS that covered the Senkaku Islands. Over this time period, Chinese air assets increased in air patrols and transits near Japan's main territory and the Senkaku Islands.[400] One indicator that demonstrates that Chinese air activity has increased is the number of scrambles conducted by the Japan Air Self-Defense Forces to intercept these Chinese air assets. While not all scrambles are responses to illegal Chinese activity, the number of scrambles is positively correlated with the amount of air activity in or near Japanese airspace. Data collected by Japan's Joint Staff presented in Figure B.2 show that the number of Japan Air Self-Defense Forces emergency fighter scrambles increased over time, with no indication that Obama's declaration moderated behavior. For all of 2010, 96 scrambles against Chinese aircraft were reported, and the number of scrambles increased almost every year after this. 2016 saw a record-number 851 scrambles.

---

[400] It is difficult to determine with certainty the precise amount of Chinese air activity because the Japanese government does not publish the details of all activity.

Figure B.2. Japan Air Self-Defense Forces Emergency Fighter Scrambles, 2010–2016

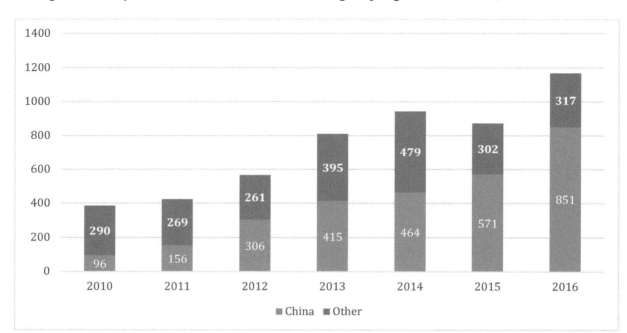

SOURCES: Joint Staff Japan, "About the Emergency Scramble Situation in FY 2017" ["平成２９年度の緊急発進実施状況について"], press release, April 13, 2018, p. 3; and Joint Staff Japan, "About the Emergency Scramble Situation in FY 2014" ["平成２６年度の緊急発進実施状況について"], press release, April 15, 2015, p. 3.

Similar trends are seen in Chinse naval activity.[401] Prior to nationalization, most PLAN activity occurred far from Japanese territory, such as transiting to the south of Okinawa prefecture or through the Miyako Strait. While most activity remains concentrated in the ECS and Miyako Strait area, after the 2012 nationalization, PLAN ships began appearing in other parts of Japan, such as the Tsushima Strait in the west and the Ōsumi Strait in its southwest. Then, two years after Obama's declaration, in 2016, PLAN vessels began to appear regularly throughout all of Japan, including the Tsugaru Strait in the north. And these vessels are sailing closer to Japanese territory, including Japan's undisputed TW. For example, in June 2016, a *Dongdiao*-class electronic reconnaissance ship sailed into Japanese TW around Kuchinoerabu Island and Yakushima Island and the CZ of Kitadaitō Island, marking the first PLAN ship to enter undisputedly Japanese TW since 2004.[402] These naval ships have even appeared around the Senkaku Islands. About a year and a half after Obama's statement, in November 2015, a

---

[401] PLAN activity is also difficult to determine with certainty because Japan's Joint Staff only provides details of activity deemed unusual.

[402] In November 2004, a nuclear submarine transited through Japanese TW. See Japanese Ministry of Defense, *Defense of Japan 2019*, Tokyo, 2019, p. 72.

Dongdiao-class reconnaissance ship went in and out of the Senkaku's CZ.[403] Then, in June 2016, a *Jiangkai I*–class frigate fully entered that CZ, the first for a PLAN ship.[404]

Explanations for Chinese Reactions

The historical record therefore provides limited evidence, at most, that China has responded less aggressively to U.S. and Japanese actions in the wake of an explicitly strong and clear statement of U.S. defensive commitment. There are several possible alternatives that may provide stronger explanations than this case's central hypothesis. It is possible that some combination of all three of the following are at play.

One possible explanation is that China is engaging in reactive assertiveness. As articulated by the International Crisis Group, this explanation posits that China is exploiting "perceived provocations in disputed areas by other countries to take strong countermeasures to change the status quo in its favor."[405] The increasingly robust Chinese reactions suggest that China purposefully interpreted Tokyo's nationalization and Obama's declaration as provocative and leveraged these to execute a series of preplanned actions as a means by which to question Japan's claim to the islands, to get it to recognize the existence of a dispute, or to change the facts on the ground in its favor.[406] Beijing stands to gain from this, if successful, as it would challenge not only the credibility of the U.S.-Japanese alliance, and U.S. commitment to Japan, but also the principles informing the maritime rules–based order.[407] Therefore, by making Tokyo and Washington look like provocateurs, China can induce costs on both the United States and Japan.

A second possible explanation is that Chinese leadership cannot back down in its responses because the issue threatens the legitimacy of the CCP, as it is tied directly to a core Chinese interest: territorial integrity. The CCP views the Diaoyu Islands as an inherent sovereignty issue and part of the CCP's long-term project of overcoming the century of humiliation. China's Ministry of Foreign Affairs spokesperson Hua Chunying, for example, said that "Diaoyu Island

---

[403] See Japanese Ministry of Defense, *Defense of Japan 2019*, Tokyo, 2019, p. 72.

[404] "Senkaku Islands: Chief Cabinet Secretary Suga 'Rising Tensions Extremely Regrettable,' Chinese Naval Ship Enters Area" ["尖閣諸島 菅官房長官 「緊張高め深刻に懸念」 中国軍艦入域"], *Mainichi Shimbun*, June 9, 2016.

[405] International Crisis Group, *Dangerous Waters: China-Japan Relations on the Rocks*, New York, Asia Report #245, April 8, 2013.

[406] Japan's Ministry of Foreign Affairs states that "there is no doubt that the Senkaku Islands are clearly an inherent part of the territory of Japan, in light of historical facts and based upon international law. Indeed, the Senkaku Islands are under the valid control of Japan. There exists no issue of territorial sovereignty to be resolved concerning the Senkaku Islands." See Japanese Ministry of Foreign Affairs, "About the Senkaku Islands," webpage, April 13, 2016.

[407] Doing so could be part of a long-term strategy by China to normalize Chinese presence, exercise law-enforcement rights, and take over exclusive control of the islands. See Alessio Patalano, "What Is China's Strategy in the Senkaku Islands?" *War on the Rocks*, September 10, 2020.

and its affiliated islands have been China's inherent territory since ancient times, and China has sufficient historical and legal basis for this claim. No matter what method Japan adopts to promote its illegal claims, it cannot change the objective fact that the Diaoyu Islands belong to China."[408] Similarly, Ministry of Foreign Affairs spokesperson Hong Lei argued that "Diaoyu Island and its affiliated islands are China's inherent territory. No matter what anyone says or does, it cannot change the fact that the Diaoyu Islands belong to China. The Chinese government and people will resolutely defend national sovereignty and territorial integrity."[409] Comments like these suggest that China may not have moderated its behavior because Beijing believes that it must continue to assert its indisputable sovereignty over the islands, which, in turn, requires it to demonstrate its resolve to defend the islands.[410] As such, it is unrelenting in pressuring Japan and the United States to deter them from defending the Senkaku Islands. And because this dispute is linked to China's territorial integrity, actions like Japan's nationalization and commitments of U.S. defense require strong responses to prevent encroachment by any foreign power.

A third possibility is that Chinese behavior has not changed because the purpose behind China's increasing provocations is to probe alliance responses. According to this thinking, it is natural that China's increasingly sophisticated capabilities and ambitions are matched by increasing probes of Japanese defenses and U.S. responses.[411] The PLA is growing and training for a potential conflict involving the United States and possibly Japan. Continued provocations against the allies are simply a means to see how the allies may react in a regional scenario as well as wear down their military response capabilities in the process.[412] Whether it be PLA activity in the waters or air surrounding Japan or the CCG and maritime militia activity around the Senkaku Islands, these are all useful means by which Chinese military planners can study allied defenses.

---

[408] "China Responds to Japan's Video on the Senkaku Islands and Urges It to Stop Provocative Words and Actions" ["中方回应日本涉钓鱼岛视频 促其停止挑衅言行"], *Sina*, October 23, 2013.

[409] Ministry of Foreign Affairs of the People's Republic of China, "Foreign Ministry Spokesperson Hong Lei's Routine Press Conference on April 28, 2015" ["2015年4月28日外交部发言人洪磊主持例行记者会"], April 28, 2015.

[410] Michael J. Mazarr, Joe Cheravitch, Jeffrey W. Hornung, and Stephanie Pezard, *What Deters and Why: Applying a Framework to Assess Deterrence of Gray Zone Aggression*, Santa Monica, Calif.: RAND Corporation, RR-3142-A, 2021.

[411] David Axe, "China Is Probing Japan's Defenses over the Disputed Senkaku Islands," *Forbes*, August 19, 2020; and Adam Liff, *China, Japan, and the East China Sea: Beijing's "Gray Zone" Coercion and Tokyo's Response*, Washington, D.C.: Brookings Institution, December 2019.

[412] Edmund J. Burke, Timothy R. Heath, Jeffrey W. Hornung, Logan Ma, Lyle J. Morris, and Michael S. Chase, *China's Military Activities in the East China Sea: Implications for Japan's Air Self-Defense Force*, Santa Monica, Calif.: RAND Corporation, RR-2574-AF, 2018.

Conclusion

Overall, our analysis of PRC reactions to Obama's declaration of U.S. commitment to defend the Senkaku Islands provides at best moderate support to the hypothesis that China is less likely to respond aggressively to U.S. actions that involve an ally to whom the perceived U.S. defensive commitment is strong. Looking at the period from 2010 to 2016, when compared with the period before Obama's declaration, we find evidence that China continued to use the same rhetoric against Japan and the United States and continued the same provocative military and paramilitary behavior against Japan after the United States emphasized its defensive commitment to the Senkaku Islands. At the same time, there appears to have been a cessation of economic coercion against Japan after 2014. It is unclear whether this change was a direct consequence of Obama's declaration, but the timing suggests that they are related. Although the rationale for China's behavior is uncertain, there are three possible alternative explanations that may provide stronger explanations than the current hypothesis. One is that China is engaging in reactive assertiveness. A second is CCP concern over political legitimacy leading China's leadership to need to defend what it has defined as a core interest. A final possibility is that Chinese provocations are meant to probe alliance reactions. Some combination of all three possibilities could be in play.

Case 5: Expansion of U.S.-Vietnam Defense and Security Ties, 2013–2016

Case 5 tests whether China is more likely to respond aggressively to U.S. actions that it perceives as threats to its regional influence by examining Chinese responses to the growth of U.S.-Vietnam security ties between 2013, when the two countries announced a comprehensive partnership, and 2016, when President Obama visited Vietnam. We find mixed support for this hypothesis. China clearly judged that closer U.S.-Vietnamese ties might harm its bilateral relations with Hanoi, threaten its territorial claims in the SCS, and reduce its influence within the ASEAN grouping, at the cost of its ability to shape political, economic, and security developments in southeast Asia, but its response was not always aggressive. Beijing denounced U.S. support for Vietnam during tensions in the SCS as provocative while seeking to balance what it perceived to be a growing U.S. presence in the region by building up its military capabilities and deepening its "comprehensive strategic partnership" with Russia. It employed a mixture of carrots and sticks, pursuing deeper ties with Vietnam while also selectively attempting to coerce it. Additionally, although Chinese sources identify the United States as the most problematic actor, it is not the only one of concern—Chinese experts also see Japan and others as potential spoilers. Vietnam's efforts to "internationalize" its SCS disputes with China through international and regional fora, as well as stronger bilateral security relations with regional states, concern Beijing and have contributed to its attempts to erode Vietnam's position via diplomatic, economic, military, cyber, and other means.

Deepening U.S.-Vietnam Security Relations

After the United States and Vietnam normalized relations in 1995, the two countries expanded diplomatic, trade, defense, and cultural ties over the ensuing decades, with new levels of defense cooperation reached during the Obama administration.[413] Priority areas for defense cooperation laid out in a 2011 bilateral memorandum included regular high-level dialogues and maritime security.[414] During Vietnam President Truong Tan Sang's trip to the United States in 2013, Truong and Obama announced an upgrade in bilateral relations to a "comprehensive partnership," with focus areas including political and diplomatic ties, defense and security cooperation, and addressing legacy issues from the Vietnam War.[415]

The 2014 oil rig standoff between China and Vietnam in the SCS appeared to crystallize Vietnamese perceptions that Hanoi needed to strengthen its efforts to counter Chinese coercion.

---

[413] U.S. Embassy and Consulate in Vietnam, "U.S.-Vietnam Relations," December 11, 2017. This is not long after Sino-Vietnamese relations were normalized in 1991. See also Huong Le Thu, "Rough Waters Ahead for Vietnam-China Relations," Carnegie Endowment for International Peace, September 30, 2020.

[414] This was the MOU on Advancing Bilateral Defense Cooperation. See Carlyle A. Thayer, "Vietnam Gradually Warms Up to U.S. Military," *The Diplomat*, November 6, 2013.

[415] White House, "Joint Statement by President Barack Obama of the United States of America and President Truong Tan Sang of the Socialist Republic of Vietnam," Washington, D.C., July 23, 2013.

During that incident, China sent a state-owned enterprise's oil rig into Vietnam's EEZ near the Paracel Islands, in waters that China also claims.[416] When Vietnam sent vessels to the rig, China quickly sent dozens of CCG and maritime militia vessels, supported by PLAN vessels in overwatch and military aircraft flights over the rig area, while rumors spread about PLA ground troops operating on the land border with Vietnam. As the paramilitary vessels harassed the Vietnamese ships, China also pressured Vietnam to back down by breaking off diplomatic discussions, restricting border trade and tourism, and targeting Hanoi with cyberattacks.[417] Vietnamese analysts characterized the standoff as a "wake-up call," and Hanoi announced a new foreign policy concept in August 2014 that emphasized "proactive contribution to shape regional policies and institutions" in order to deepen engagement with other countries.[418] Vietnam also viewed with concern China's dismissal of the 2016 arbitral tribunal ruling that rejected the basis for China's SCS claims.[419]

A 2015 Joint Vision Statement marked a new high point in U.S.-Vietnam defense relations, stating mutual interests in protecting the free flow of commerce by land, sea, and air, as well as the intent to increase bilateral collaboration on maritime security, training, and defense equipment transfers.[420] From 2013 to 2016, areas of growing security partnership included military sales or Excess Defense Article transfers, including to enhance the Vietnam Coast Guard's capability; port and maintenance visits by USN vessels; S&R and HA/DR exercises; support for Vietnamese UN peacekeeping operations; and partial lifting of restrictions on the sale of lethal U.S. arms to Vietnam (in 2014) followed by full lifting of restrictions announced during

---

[416] Carlyle A. Thayer, "China's Oil Rig Gambit: South China Sea Game-Changer?" *The Diplomat*, May 12, 2014.

[417] See Bonny Lin, Cristina L. Garafola, Bruce McClintock, Jonah Blank, Jeffrey W. Hornung, Karen Schwindt, Jennifer D. P. Moroney, Paul Orner, Dennis Borrman, Sarah W. Denton, and Jason Chambers, *Competition in the Gray Zone: Countering China's Coercion Against U.S. Allies and Partners in the Indo-Pacific*, Santa Monica, Calif.: RAND Corporation, RR-A594-1, 2022.

[418] Huong Le Thu, "Rough Waters Ahead for Vietnam-China Relations," Carnegie Endowment for International Peace, September 30, 2020; and Ha Hoang Hop, "The Oil Rig Incident: A Line Has Been Crossed in Vietnam's Relations with China," *ISEAS Perspective*, No. 61, November 18, 2014.

[419] Huong Le Thu, "Rough Waters Ahead for Vietnam-China Relations," Carnegie Endowment for International Peace, September 30, 2020.

[420] Aaron Mehta, "New U.S.-Vietnam Agreement Shows Growth, Challenges," *Defense News*, June 1, 2015. Presidential-level joint statements followed in 2015 and 2016. See Carlyle A. Thayer, "Vietnam's Foreign Policy in an Era of Rising Sino-U.S. Competition and Increasing Domestic Political Influence," *Asian Security*, Vol. 13, No. 3, 2017, p. 188.

President Obama's visit to Vietnam in 2016.[421] Since then, U.S.-Vietnam defense relations have continued to deepen.[422]

Measures to Manage Escalation

Both Vietnam and the United States have refrained from directly referencing China in leadership statements or speeches regarding growing bilateral defense ties.[423] Vietnamese analysts are wary of provoking Beijing, but officials also have broader concerns about irrevocably siding with Washington over Beijing, due to concerns that in the future Washington might seek to undermine Communist Party rule in Vietnam or increase pressure for Hanoi to improve its human rights record.[424]

Chinese Reactions

China's reactions to deepening U.S.-Vietnam security ties have included criticizing U.S. and others' involvement in SCS issues, while seeking to expand its own ties with Hanoi. Chinese analysts and scholars have also discussed the benefits of strengthening the Sino-Vietnamese economic relationship, as well as improving China's position in the region by partnering with Russia against the United States. These reactions are linked to concerns about Hanoi's approach toward the SCS, as well as China's relations with ASEAN and across Southeast Asia more broadly.[425] One Chinese analyst noted that the United States can influence Beijing's and Hanoi's

---

[421] Carlyle A. Thayer, "Obama's Visit to Vietnam: A Turning Point?" *The Diplomat*, May 31, 2016; and Congressional Research Service, "U.S.-Vietnam Relations," *In Focus*, February 16, 2021. Dang Cam Tu and Hang Thi Thuy Nguyen, "Understanding the U.S.-Vietnam Security Relationship, 2011–2017," *Korean Journal of Defense Analysis*, Vol. 31, No. 1, March 2019, notes that from "FY2012 to FY2017, Hanoi received over $55 million in bilateral State Department–funded security assistance" via the FMF program.

[422] Notable examples have included the first U.S. aircraft carrier port visits since the Vietnam War in 2018 and 2020.

[423] See, for example, White House, "Remarks by President Obama in Address to the People of Vietnam," Hanoi, Vietnam, May 24, 2016.

[424] Mark E. Manyin, *U.S.-Vietnam Relations in 2014: Current Issues and Implications for U.S. Policy*, Washington, D.C.: Congressional Research Service, June 24, 2014; and Dang Cam Tu and Hang Thi Thuy Nguyen, "Understanding the U.S.-Vietnam Security Relationship, 2011–2017," *Korean Journal of Defense Analysis*, Vol. 31, No. 1, March 2019.

[425] On U.S.-Vietnam ties and the South China Sea, see Derek Grossman and Paul S. Orner, "Tracking Chinese Perceptions of Vietnam's Relations with China and the United States," *Asia Policy*, Vol. 16, No. 2, April 2021, pp. 116–122; and Li Chunxia [李春霞], "From Enemy to Comprehensive Partner: Strategic Considerations Regarding Vietnam's Development of Relations with the United States" ["从敌人到全面伙伴: 越南发展对美关系的战略考量"], *International Forum* [国际论坛], Vol. 16, No. 4, 2014, p. 14. On ASEAN, see Cheng Hanping [成汉平], "The Strategic Interaction of U.S. and Vietnam in the South China Sea in the Perspective of Indo-Pacific Strategy: Path, Goal and Effect" ["印太战略视域下美越围绕南海问题的战略互动: 路径, 目标与影响"], *Asia-Pacific Security and Maritime Affairs* [亚太安全与海洋研究], No. 2, 2019, p. 83. On the importance of the SCS in shaping overall Chinese

dispute by adjusting its own policies toward the SCS and by strengthening relations with Vietnam. For "external involvement" to impact the dispute, not only must external powers be willing to intervene, but Hanoi must also be receptive to their actions.[426] Another analyst writing in 2016 attributed Vietnam's resistance in 2014 to U.S. and Japanese support, judging Vietnam as likely to tilt away from China in the future.[427]

Political Responses

China has pushed back against U.S. support to Vietnam during specific incidents. China publicly criticized U.S. remarks regarding the 2014 oil rig incident, urging third countries to remain neutral.[428] During a speech at the 2014 Shangri-La Dialogue, China's representative also pushed back against U.S. and Japanese criticism.[429] Meeting with a Vietnamese special envoy following the standoff, General Secretary Xi Jinping also appeared to warn Hanoi about partnering more closely with others at Beijing's expense: "A neighbor cannot be moved away and it is in the common interests of both sides to be friendly to each other," calling for both to "make correct political decisions at critical moments."[430]

---

security attitudes toward Vietnam, see Wang Zheng [王峥], "The Interaction Between Politics and Security: Perspectives on China-Vietnam Relations Under the South China Sea Disputes" ["政治与安全的互动: 南海争端下中越关系透视"], *Southeast Asian Studies* [东南亚研究], No. 6, 2018, pp. 108–130, 151.

[426] Wang Zheng [王峥], "The Interaction Between Politics and Security: Perspectives on China-Vietnam Relations Under the South China Sea Disputes" ["政治与安全的互动: 南海争端下中越关系透视"], *Southeast Asian Studies* [东南亚研究], No. 6, 2018, p. 121.

[427] Zeng Yong [曾勇], "South China Sea '981' Oil Platform Stand-Off and Its Impact on Vietnam's South China Sea Policy" ["南海 '981' 钻井平台冲突折射的越南南海政策"], *Journal of Contemporary Asia-Pacific Studies* [当代亚太], No. 1, 2016, pp. 124–153, 158–159. Only a portion of this article was available to us.

[428] Michael Green, Kathleen Hicks, Zack Cooper, John Schaus, and Jake Douglas, *Countering Coercion in Maritime Asia: The Theory and Practice of Gray Zone Deterrence*, Washington, D.C.: Center for Strategic and International Studies, May 2017, p. 212. On Japan, see Qin Gang, "Foreign Ministry Spokesperson Qin Gang's Regular Press Conference on May 27, 2014," Ministry of Foreign Affairs of the People's Republic of China, May 27, 2014.

[429] Zeng Yong [曾勇], "South China Sea '981' Oil Platform Stand-Off and Its Impact on Vietnam's South China Sea Policy" ["南海 '981' 钻井平台冲突折射的越南南海政策"], *Journal of Contemporary Asia-Pacific Studies* [当代亚太], No. 1, 2016, pp. 129–131.

[430] "Xi Calls for Mended China-Vietnam Ties," Xinhua, August 28, 2014; and Robert S. Ross, "China-Vietnamese Relations in the Era of Rising China: Power, Resistance, and Maritime Conflict," *Journal of Contemporary China*, Vol. 30, No. 130, 2020.

China has also sought to further deepen its ties with Vietnam, likely in an attempt to ensure that Vietnam does not further tilt toward others.[431] In 2013, the two countries upgraded their relationship to a "comprehensive strategic cooperative partnership," at that point the highest level of Vietnam's partnership with another country.[432] By 2015, some Chinese analysts assessed that bilateral relations had "recovered to a certain extent" from 2014, in no small part as the result of a 2015 trip to China by the General Secretary of the Communist Party of Vietnam, Nguyen Phu Trong, and one-third of Vietnam's Politburo members, which resulted in a joint communiqué agreeing to use bilateral mechanisms to discuss maritime issues rather than "actions that can further complicate and expand disputes."[433] This trip was later followed by a trip by Xi Jinping to Vietnam. Since 2016, official Chinese government statements have reaffirmed the need to follow the "correct path" of bilateral relations by building on the "comprehensive strategic cooperative partnership" agreed upon in 2013.[434]

Economic Responses

Although Chinese analysts focusing on Vietnam rarely mention specific actions in the economic sphere to counter growing U.S.-Vietnamese relations, Chinese experts note Vietnam's

---

[431] One Chinese analyst described the recommended approach toward Vietnam as "promot[ing] the positive development of bilateral relations and reduc[ing] the negative effects brought about by South China Sea disputes" (Wang Zheng [王峥], "The Interaction Between Politics and Security: Perspectives on China-Vietnam Relations Under the South China Sea Disputes" ["政治与安全的互动: 南海争端下中越关系透视"], *Southeast Asian Studies* [东南亚研究], No. 6, 2018, p. 130). See also Cui Haoran [崔浩然], "The Adjustment of Vietnam's South China Sea Policy Under the New Situation and China's Response Strategy" ["新形势下越南南海政策的调整及中国的应对策略"], *Issues of Contemporary World Socialism* [当代世界社会主义问题], No. 4, 2018, pp. 163–164.

[432] Carlyle A. Thayer, "Vietnam's Foreign Policy in an Era of Rising Sino-U.S. Competition and Increasing Domestic Political Influence," *Asian Security*, Vol. 13, No. 3, 2017, p. 187.

[433] "China Is Not Afraid of Making Waves in the South China Sea" ["南海，中国不怕兴风作浪"], *China National Defense News-Military Special Issue* [中国国防报-军事特刊], April 21, 2015; and "Vietnam, China Issue Joint Communiqué," *Vietnam Plus*, April 8, 2015.

[434] In the defense realm, during a January 2017 summit, both China and Vietnam committed to implementing a joint vision statement on defense cooperation by 2025, the specifics of which are not publicly available. See "China-Vietnam Joint Announcement" ["中越联合公报"], *People's Daily* [人民日报], January 15, 2017. On overall relations since 2016, see State Council of the People's Republic of China, "Xi Jinping with Vietnamese Communist Party's General Secretary and President Nguyen Phu Trong's Mutual Sent Congratulatory Telegrams on the 70th Anniversary of China and Vietnam Establishing Diplomatic Relations" ["习近平就中越建交70周年同越共中央总书记、国家主席阮富仲互致贺电"], January 18, 2020.

rapidly growing trade relationship with the United States.[435] One analyst highlights that countries such as "Japan, Russia and other countries, together with the United States, constitute an external factor system that affects the China-Vietnam maritime dispute . . . by adjusting their South China Sea policies and strengthening political, economic and security cooperation with Vietnam."[436]

Overall, Chinese experts cite Vietnam's economic dependance on China as a key element in the asymmetric relationship between the states.[437] One Chinese analyst recommends strengthening cooperation with Vietnam, including economic and cultural exchanges, to improve Sino-Vietnamese ties.[438] Chinese experts have also seen opportunities for greater Chinese economic integration with ASEAN, such as to condemn and counter trade protectionism during the Trump administration.[439]

---

[435] Li Chunxia [李春霞], "From Enemy to Comprehensive Partner: Strategic Considerations Regarding Vietnam's Development of Relations with the United States" ["从敌人到全面伙伴: 越南发展对美关系的战略考量"], *International Forum* [国际论坛], Vol. 16, No. 4, 2014, pp. 15–16.

[436] Wang Zheng [王峥], "The Interaction Between Politics and Security: Perspectives on China-Vietnam Relations Under the South China Sea Disputes" ["政治与安全的互动: 南海争端下中越关系透视"], *Southeast Asian Studies* [东南亚研究], No. 6, 2018, p. 122.

[437] Li Chunxia [李春霞], "From Enemy to Comprehensive Partner: Strategic Considerations Regarding Vietnam's Development of Relations with the United States" ["从敌人到全面伙伴: 越南发展对美关系的战略考量"], *International Forum* [国际论坛], Vol. 16, No. 4, 2014, pp. 15–16; and Wang Zheng [王峥], "The Interaction Between Politics and Security: Perspectives on China-Vietnam Relations Under the South China Sea Disputes" ["政治与安全的互动: 南海争端下中越关系透视"], *Southeast Asian Studies* [东南亚研究], No. 6, 2018, p. 124.

[438] Cheng Hanping [成汉平] and Ning Wei [宁威], "Issues, Challenges, and Measures for Dealing with Relations Between China and ASEAN Against the Backdrop of 'Unprecedented Changes in a Century'" ["'大变局' 视野下中国—东盟关系中的问题、挑战与对策"], *Journal of Yunnan University* (Social Sciences Edition) [云南大学学报(社会科学版)], Vol. 19, No. 1, 2020, p. 133. Cheng is a distinguished professor at the Vietnam Research Institute at Guangxi Normal University in addition to his affiliation with the Collaborative Innovation Center of South China Sea Studies. Ning is a lecturer in the international relations program at the National University of Defense Technology. See also Huang Xingqiu [黄兴球], "Seven Decades of China-Vietnam Relations: Axis and Direction" ["中越关系70 年: 基轴与方向"], *Southeast Asian Affairs* [南洋问题研究], No. 1, 2020.

[439] Cheng Hanping [成汉平] and Ning Wei [宁威], "Issues, Challenges, and Measures for Dealing with Relations Between China and ASEAN Against the Backdrop of 'Unprecedented Changes in a Century'" ["'大变局' 视野下中国—东盟关系中的问题、挑战与对策"], *Journal of Yunnan University* (Social Sciences Edition) [云南大学学报(社会科学版)], Vol. 19, No. 1, 2020, pp. 128–134.

Military Responses

Chinese analysts have rarely cited direct military, paramilitary, or cyber responses to growing U.S.-Vietnam collaboration. However, in 2017, an analyst noted the need to "strengthen China-Russia strategic cooperation, especially defense and security cooperation in the Asia-Pacific region, to ease the military pressure on China from the United States' return" to the region, as well as for China to "strengthen national defense and military building, improve security strategy in [China's] periphery, and improve the ability to respond to security crises in the periphery."[440]

Measures to Manage Escalation

Reports suggest that the Vietnamese Politburo in July 2014 planned to meet to discuss pursuing legal action against China in international fora and making a major foreign policy shift toward actively requesting U.S. support. However, Beijing got wind of the proposal and announced the early withdrawal of the oil rig from Vietnam's EEZ, undercutting proponents of the meeting, which was never held.[441] Chinese and Western analysts also assess that China withdrew the oil rig in advance of the ASEAN Regional Forum meeting in August to undermine potentially strong criticism by the United States and others during the meeting.[442]

Explanations for Chinese Reactions

Overall, Chinese analysts remain confident that ideological ties, geography, and the bilateral balance of power favor China's goal of deepening relations with Vietnam. They are, however, concerned that growing U.S.-Vietnam security relations could complicate Beijing's regional policy, particularly in the SCS.[443] Chinese analysts assess that the United States has encouraged other countries, like Japan, to increase maritime security cooperation with Vietnam, and that growing Japan-Vietnam ties would negatively impact China by encouraging Vietnam to more assertively defend its own claims and interests.[444] Recent Chinese analysis also appears to have

---

[440] Luo Huijun [罗会钧], "U.S.-Vietnam Defense and Security Cooperation and Its Influence on China"

["美越防务安全合作及其对中国的影响"], *Journal of International Security Studies* [国家安全研究], No. 3, 2017, p. 147.

[441] Carlyle A. Thayer, "Vietnam's Foreign Policy in an Era of Rising Sino-U.S. Competition and Increasing Domestic Political Influence," *Asian Security*, Vol. 13, No. 3, 2017, pp. 193–194.

[442] Zeng Yong [曾勇], "South China Sea '981' Oil Platform Stand-Off and Its Impact on Vietnam's South China Sea Policy" ["南海 '981' 钻井平台冲突折射的越南南海政策"], *Journal of Contemporary Asia-Pacific Studies* [当代亚太], No. 1, 2016, pp. 131–132, citing analysis by Carl Thayer.

[443] For an encapsulation of Chinese criticism focused on the U.S. role, see Cheng Hanping, "U.S. Efforts to Cozy Up to Vietnam Won't Work," *Global Times*, March 8, 2020.

[444] Zeng Yong [曾勇], "South China Sea '981' Oil Platform Stand-Off and Its Impact on Vietnam's South China Sea Policy" ["南海 '981' 钻井平台冲突折射的越南南海政策"], *Journal of Contemporary Asia-Pacific Studies* [当

focused on Vietnam's growing military and Coast Guard capabilities over this period, one result of defense sales and transfers from the United States, Japan, and others.[445] A 2015 article republished by the Chinese Defense Ministry went so far as to say that Vietnam is "two-faced," as it "appears to be trying to balance China, the United States, and Russia . . . [and] draw the United States into the South China Sea to check and balance China. . . . The relationship between China and Vietnam is currently in a relatively tranquil period, but we still need to observe its behavior to see whether Vietnam will take action in the future, and China must be prepared."[446]

The crux of Chinese concerns regarding the impact of the 2014 standoff specifically appeared to be that, under the increasingly tense backdrop of Sino-Vietnam relations, any future incidents could lead to an irrevocably deteriorating relationship, as well as a decline in China's overall position in the SCS or even Southeast Asia.[447] Regarding the United States, Chinese analysts lamented Vietnam's "internationalization" of the standoff as well as the U.S. seizure of "international discourse power" to criticize China.[448] One analyst cited U.S. statements by senior State Department officials and a speech by President Obama at West Point, as well as bilateral discussions with senior Chinese foreign and defense officials, as evidence of such U.S. efforts.[449]

代亚太], No. 1, 2016, p. 126; and Derek Grossman and Paul S. Orner, "Tracking Chinese Perceptions of Vietnam's Relations with China and the United States," *Asia Policy*, Vol. 16, No. 2, April 2021, p. 122.

[445] Derek Grossman and Paul S. Orner, "Tracking Chinese Perceptions of Vietnam's Relations with China and the United States," *Asia Policy*, Vol. 16, No. 2, April 2021, pp. 121–122.

[446] "China Is Not Afraid of Making Waves in the South China Sea" ["南海，中国不怕兴风作浪"], *China National Defense News-Military Special Issue* [中国国防报-军事特刊], April 21, 2015.

[447] Zeng Yong [曾勇], "South China Sea '981' Oil Platform Stand-Off and Its Impact on Vietnam's South China Sea Policy" ["南海'981'钻井平台冲突折射的越南南海政策"], *Journal of Contemporary Asia-Pacific Studies* [当代亚太], No. 1, 2016, p. 131; and Wang Zheng [王峥], "The Interaction Between Politics and Security: Perspectives on China-Vietnam Relations Under the South China Sea Disputes" ["政治与安全的互动: 南海争端下中越关系透视"], *Southeast Asian Studies* [东南亚研究], No. 6, 2018, p. 124.

[448] Zeng Yong [曾勇], "South China Sea '981' Oil Platform Stand-Off and Its Impact on Vietnam's South China Sea Policy" ["南海'981'钻井平台冲突折射的越南南海政策"], *Journal of Contemporary Asia-Pacific Studies* [当代亚太], No. 1, 2016, p. 126.

[449] Zeng Yong [曾勇], "South China Sea '981' Oil Platform Stand-Off and Its Impact on Vietnam's South China Sea Policy" ["南海'981'钻井平台冲突折射的越南南海政策"], *Journal of Contemporary Asia-Pacific Studies* [当代亚太], No. 1, 2016, pp. 127–129.

Beyond diplomatic statements, the analyst noted that U.S. reconnaissance aircraft overflew the oil rig area and a U.S. congressional resolution condemned China's actions.[450]

Conclusion

China views growing U.S.-Vietnamese security ties as a threat to its regional influence, particularly its position in the SCS. Cheng Hanping, a scholar at the Nanjing University's state-sponsored Collaborative Innovation Center of South China Sea Studies, summed up the common outlook in 2019: "although U.S. and Vietnam have different strategic considerations, their interaction will have great negative effect on the stability of the South China Sea area."[451] Another expert concluded in 2018 that, "currently, the United States has become the most principal external factor in affecting the situation in the South China Sea."[452] Although Chinese sources typically describe the United States as the most problematic regional actor, it is not the only one—they also often identify Japan and, to a lesser extent, Russia as potential spoilers in Beijing's relationship with Hanoi as well as China's regional influence. In sum, Vietnam's efforts to "internationalize" SCS disputes through international and regional fora and stronger bilateral security relations with other countries appear to be an important driver of Chinese attempts to erode Vietnam's SCS policy. China has sought to do so using a variety of policy carrots and sticks, coupling conciliation with coercion in ways that suggest an implicit sensitivity to escalation risks but a commitment to drawing hard lines against threats to Chinese influence that could affect its regional and even global interests.

---

[450] Zeng Yong [曾勇], "South China Sea '981' Oil Platform Stand-Off and Its Impact on Vietnam's South China Sea Policy" ["南海'981'钻井平台冲突折射的越南南海政策"], *Journal of Contemporary Asia-Pacific Studies* [当代亚太], No. 1, 2016, pp. 130–131.

[451] Cheng Hanping [成汉平], "The Strategic Interaction of U.S. and Vietnam in the South China Sea in the Perspective of Indo-Pacific Strategy: Path, Goal and Effect" ["印太战略视域下美越围绕南海问题的战略互动：路径，目标与影响"], *Asia-Pacific Security and Maritime Affairs* [亚太安全与海洋研究], No. 2, 2019, pp. 3, 72–84.

[452] Wang Zheng [王峥], "The Interaction Between Politics and Security: Perspectives on China-Vietnam Relations Under the South China Sea Disputes" ["政治与安全的互动：南海争端下中越关系透视"], *Southeast Asian Studies* [东南亚研究], No. 6, 2018, p. 121.

Case 6: PRC Response to U.S. Bomber Flights in the South China Sea, 2015 and 2020

Case 6 tests the hypothesis that China is more likely to respond aggressively to U.S. or allied actions or capabilities that it perceives constitute a threat to the PRC regime or physical security. It does so by comparing Chinese responses to U.S. bomber flights in the SCS in 2015 and 2020 and finds that stronger PRC responses to U.S. joint warfighting exercises and training in the SCS in 2020 were likely enabled by growth in China's military capabilities. The case therefore yields mixed support for the hypothesis. There is limited evidence that growing Chinese confidence in PRC military capabilities, which, in theory, should have reduced Chinese concern about the threat posed by the United States, actually made China respond *more* aggressively in 2020. However, it also appears that Chinese aggression could have been driven by Chinese perceptions of the United States' increasingly hostile intent. U.S. policy shifted between 2015 and 2020 to actively countering China in the SCS, and Beijing saw U.S. military operations there as becoming more frequent and sophisticated. In this context, joint bomber and CSG operations conducted during the summer of 2020 may have appeared especially threatening despite the growth in Chinese capabilities.

U.S. Military Activities in the South China Sea

From the 2010s onward, U.S. operations in the SCS were shaped by the broader U.S. rebalance to Asia and recognition that China's incremental advances in the SCS were challenging international norms and altering the regional balance of power.[453] The USAF conducted at least two bomber operations in the SCS in 2015, both involving B-52Hs. One USAF leader indicated that U.S. bomber operations in the Indo-Pacific region became more frequent following the end of the USAF's Continuous Bomber Presence program in April 2020.[454] A Chinese think tank reported that at least 17 operations by B-52H and B-1B bombers

---

[453] For official U.S. policy on maritime security during this era, see DoD, *Asia-Pacific Maritime Security Strategy*, Washington, D.C., 2015.

[454] U.S. bombers conducting missions in the SCS in 2015 and 2020 operated from Andersen AFB in Guam as well as from CONUS and Alaska. From 2004 to April 2020, the Air Force had based strategic bombers outside of the CONUS, including at Guam, as part of the Continuous Bomber Presence program. Bomber Task Force (BTF) missions also took place from the continental United States since 2014, carried out by U.S. Strategic Command's air component, Air Force Global Strike Command. Joint Continuous Bomber Presence and BTF missions were sometimes conducted by aircraft flying out of Guam and CONUS. Until 2017, BTF missions were known as Bomber Assurance and Deterrence missions. In April 2020, the USAF announced the transition away from the Continuous Bomber Presence program to a dynamic force employment model that would enable aircraft to operate from a variety of overseas locations but be based permanently in the United States. See Brian W. Everstine, "Air Force Ends Continuous Bomber Presence in Guam," *Air Force Magazine*, April 17, 2020; Kelley J. Stewart, "B-1B Lancers Return to Indo-Pacific for Bomber Task Force Deployment," Pacific Air Forces, May 1, 2020; and Pacific Air Forces Public Affairs, "U.S., Japan Bomber-Fighter Integration Showcases Alliance, Global Power Projection," U.S. Air Force, February 5, 2020. On the growing frequency of operations, see Brian W. Everstine, "PACAF: China, Russia Have Taken Notice of Increased USAF Bomber Ops," *Air Force Magazine*, November 18, 2020.

took place in the SCS in 2020, of which four operations took off from CONUS and 13 from Guam.[455] Using public sources, we were able to identify 15 operations in 2020, typically conducted by two B-52Hs or (after April) two B-1Bs.[456] These are presented in Table B.3 at the end of this section.

Measures to Manage Escalation

Although the frequency of public USAF bomber operations has grown, the number of aircraft participating in each mission has remained relatively constant from 2015 to 2020 (typically two B-52Hs or B-1Bs). Following an incident during a December 2015 operation in which a B-52 flew within 12 nautical miles of the PRC-held Cuarteron Reef in the Spratly Islands, reportedly due to poor weather conditions, there were no reports of similarly close approaches to PRC-held SCS outposts in 2020.[457]

Chinese Reactions

Chinese responses in both 2015 to 2020 consistently characterized U.S. military operations in the Western Pacific as becoming more frequent, which U.S. sources indicate is accurate, and as driving regional destabilization and militarization.[458] In 2015, China's public responses to U.S. bomber flights involved diplomatic statements conveying disapproval. In 2020, China did not comment publicly on USAF-only bomber operations but leveraged a variety of military and nonmilitary activities to signal its dissatisfaction with joint U.S. bomber and CSG operations in the SCS while demonstrating confidence in PLA capabilities. The most significant and escalatory reactions were during a roughly eight-week period between early July and late August 2020. We did not find evidence of directly related economic or cyber responses in 2015 or 2020.

Political Responses

Following a November 2015 U.S. bomber operation in the SCS, Beijing disclosed that a PLA ground controller in the vicinity warned the aircraft, and the Foreign Ministry spokesperson

[455] SCSPI, *An Incomplete Report on U.S. Military Operations in the South China Sea in 2020*, Beijing: Peking University, March 12, 2021, p. 2. The report states that "most . . . were in dual-bomber formations when operating in the region, with a total of 11 B-52H and 21 B-1B sorties."

[456] Some bomber missions and/or details are likely not publicly disclosed. As one example, the dates referenced in this photo slideshow appear to indicate that during one BTF deployment to Guam, bombers conducted multiple BTF missions between mid-December 2020 and early January 2021. See Pacific Air Forces Public Affairs, "Breaking Barriers: Women of the Bomber Task Force," Pacific Air Forces, January 6, 2021.

[457] Christopher Bodeen, "U.S. Says Bombers Didn't Intend to Fly over China-Held Island," *Military Times*, December 19, 2015; and Fergus Ryan, "South China Sea: U.S. Bomber Angers Beijing with Spratly Islands Flypast," *The Guardian*, December 18, 2015.

[458] For an example of these complaints, see Ministry of National Defense of the People's Republic of China, "Defense Ministry's Regular Press Conference on July 30," July 30, 2015. For a source on the frequency of U.S. operations, see Brian W. Everstine, "PACAF: China, Russia Have Taken Notice of Increased USAF Bomber Ops," *Air Force Magazine*, November 18, 2020.

condemned the flight.[459] Following a December 2015 flight in which a B-52H flew within 12 nautical miles of Cuarteron Reef, the Chinese Defense Ministry called the operation a "serious military provocation" that "threatened the safety of Chinese personnel and facilities as well as peace and stability of the region," suggesting a degree of Chinese concern about the threat posed by U.S. bombers.[460] Additional evidence is provided in the form of Chinese officials who noted that PLA troops stationed on the reef went on high alert and warned the aircraft to leave and, following the incident, China's decision to lodge a formal diplomatic complaint with the United States—which stated that the flight path close to the reef was not intentional.[461]

In 2020, Chinese officials refrained from directly referencing USAF-only bomber operations in the SCS, but after the United States conducted joint operations in the SCS with bombers and two CSGs in early July, the Foreign Ministry denounced the operations.[462] Nonauthoritative Chinese social media accounts directly engaged USN leadership on Twitter to highlight China's arsenal of "carrier killer" anti-ship ballistic missiles in an adaptation of the "wolf warrior diplomacy"–style tactics that have sprung up since Chinese diplomats joined Twitter en masse beginning in 2019.[463] Chinese officials appeared to tacitly endorse publications by think tanks such as the SCSPI to publicly release information about U.S. bomber operations in 2020, including by publicizing operations not previously disclosed by U.S. military sources.[464] This is likely in order to portray U.S. operations as destabilizing to the region while highlighting China's own resolve.

---

[459] Yeganeh Torbati and David Alexander, "U.S. Bombers Flew Near China-Built Islands in South China Sea: Pentagon," Reuters, November 13, 2015.

[460] "U.S. Flight Near Islands 'Serious Military Provocation': Chinese Defense Ministry," Xinhua, December 19, 2015.

[461] "U.S. Flight Near Islands 'Serious Military Provocation': Chinese Defense Ministry," Xinhua, December 19, 2015; Ministry of National Defense of the People's Republic of China, "Defense Ministry's Regular Press Conference on Dec. 31," December 31, 2015; "MND Answers Reporters' Questions About the Entry of U.S. B-52 Bombers into the Adjacent Airspace of the Islands and Reefs of China's Spratly Island Archipelago"
["国防部就美B-52轰炸机进入中国南沙群岛有关岛礁邻近空域答记者问"], Xinhua, December 19, 2015; and People's Republic of China Embassy in Myanmar, "Foreign Ministry Spokesperson Hong Lei's Regular Press Conference on November 13, 2015" ["2015年11月13日外交部发言人洪磊主持例行记者会"], November 13, 2015.

[462] Zhao Lijian, "Foreign Ministry Spokesperson Zhao Lijian's Regular Press Conference on July 6, 2020," Ministry of Foreign Affairs of the People's Republic of China, July 6, 2020.

[463] For more on wolf warrior diplomacy, see Jessica Brandt and Bret Shafer, "How China's 'Wolf Warrior' Diplomats Use and Abuse Twitter," Brookings Institution, October 28, 2020; and Geoff Ziezulewicz, "Two U.S. Aircraft Carriers Are Operating in the South China Sea; Air Force B-52 Joins Them," *Navy Times*, July 6, 2020.

[464] See SCSPI, *An Incomplete Report on U.S. Military Activities in the South China Sea in 2020*, Beijing: Peking University, March 12, 2021. According to a Western analyst, SCSPI has previously leveraged nonpublic data. Greg Poling [@GregPoling], "The 2nd of @SCS_PI's new series on VN fishing/militia activity around Hainan is out an alleges 311 VN boats in February. The problem? None of this is verifiable b/c most of the data appears to be from the Chinese govt, not commercial as the authors claim https://scspi.pku.edu.cn/en/analysis/501624.htm," Twitter post, March 5, 2020.

Economic Responses

We did not find evidence of PRC economic responses directly tied to U.S. bomber operations in the SCS for 2015 or 2020. While both China and the United States each undertook dozens of discrete economic actions during the Trump administration–era trade war amid broader tensions in their bilateral economic relationship, Chinese sources blamed U.S. actions in the economic realm for Beijing's responses.[465]

Military Responses

As described earlier, public reporting on Chinese military responses to U.S. bomber operations in the SCS in 2015 described a very limited response of tactical alerts and a warning provided to U.S. aircraft. Since 2015, the PLA has focused on deploying aircraft, ships, surface-to-air missile systems, anti-ship cruise missiles, jammers, and other equipment to SCS outposts, suggesting a degree of concern about those outposts' vulnerability to attack, as well as by expanding operations by the PLA Navy, Air Force, CCG, and Chinese maritime militia units there.[466] China has also fielded greater numbers of anti-ship ballistic missile systems within its missiles forces, including a medium-range ballistic missile (MRBM) and a new IRBM-range variant.[467] It is not clear whether China has increased its intelligence collection efforts vis-à-vis U.S. bomber activities in the SCS, but growing space-based and other command, control, communications, computers, intelligence, surveillance, and reconnaissance capabilities likely facilitate more-frequent revisit rates and improve the quality of information collected.[468]

In 2020, official PRC government statements described numerous PLA operational responses to U.S. military operations in the SCS and near Taiwan, but we did not find statements disclosing or providing details specifically about the PLA reacting to USAF-only bomber flights there.[469]

---

[465] For a review of U.S.-China bilateral economic actions from 2017 to 2020, see Bonny Lin, Howard J. Shatz, Nathan Chandler, Cristina L. Garafola, Eugeniu Han, Andy Law, King Mallory, and Zev Winkelman, *Bridging the Gap: Assessing U.S. Business Community Support for U.S.-China Competition*, Santa Monica, Calif.: RAND Corporation, RR-A1417-1, 2022.

[466] Bonny Lin, Cristina L. Garafola, Bruce McClintock, Jonah Blank, Jeffrey W. Hornung, Karen Schwindt, Jennifer D. P. Moroney, Paul Orner, Dennis Borrman, Sarah W. Denton, and Jason Chambers, *Competition in the Gray Zone: Countering China's Coercion Against U.S. Allies and Partners in the Indo-Pacific*, Santa Monica, Calif.: RAND Corporation, RR-A594-1, 2022.

[467] Office of the Secretary of Defense, *Annual Report to Congress: Military and Security Developments Involving the People's Republic of China 2020*, Washington, D.C., 2020, p. 56.

[468] On space capabilities, see Office of the Secretary of Defense, *Annual Report to Congress: Military and Security Developments Involving the People's Republic of China 2020*, Washington, D.C., 2020, pp. 61–65, 74.

[469] Official Foreign and Defense Ministry statements of disapproval took place regarding U.S. ship movements in the SCS: "China Warns Off U.S. Destroyer Trespassing in South China Sea: Spokesperson," *China Military Online*, December 22, 2020; U.S. air reconnaissance flights in the SCS: Wang Wenbin, "Foreign Ministry Spokesperson Wang Wenbin's Regular Press Conference on July 28, 2020," Ministry of Foreign Affairs of the People's Republic of China, July 28, 2020; and Wang Wenbin, "Foreign Ministry Spokesperson Wang Wenbin's Regular Press Conference on September 28, 2020," Ministry of Foreign Affairs of the People's Republic of China, September 28,

China's response to SCS flights differs from recent reactions in the ECS, such as a November 2020 flight into China's ADIZ by two B-1B bombers in which PLAAF pilots intercepted the U.S. aircraft and warned them to leave immediately.[470]

However, the PLA demonstrated a variety of capabilities and operations in July and August 2020 following dual U.S. aircraft CSG operations in the SCS, which were accompanied by a B-52H bomber reportedly practicing long-range strikes.[471] After the dual-carrier operations began, PLA fighter aircraft conducted live-fire drills in the SCS, and additional fighters were deployed to the Paracel Islands—around the same time that two B-1Bs conducted a BTF mission in the SCS.[472] Likely after the U.S. bomber operation took place, the PLA Rocket Force launched one anti-ship DF-26 IRBM in an exercise in the SCS, which some Chinese media portrayed as a "quick reaction" to U.S. operations in the SCS.[473] At the end of July, PLAAF and PLAN Aviation bombers drilled over the SCS, though a PLA spokesperson stated that the exercises had been scheduled in advance.[474] On August 26, the Rocket Force launched at least one IRBM- and one MRBM-range anti-ship ballistic missile from different locations in China and may have struck a moving ship target in the waters between Hainan and the Paracels.[475]

2020; and U.S. military activities near Taiwan: "U.S. Flexes Muscles and Stirs Up Trouble in Taiwan Strait: Defense Spokesperson," *China Military Online*, December 31, 2020. During U.S. ship operations in the SCS, for example, the Defense Ministry stated that "the naval and aerial forces of the Chinese PLA Southern Theater Command conducted whole-process tracking and monitoring o[f] the U.S. destroyer and warned it off." See "China Warns Off U.S. Destroyer Trespassing in South China Sea: Spokesperson," *China Military Online*, December 22, 2020. In response to U.S. operations in the Taiwan Strait, the Defense Ministry stated that PLA forces from the Eastern Theater Command "sent naval and air forces to conduct whole-process tracking and monitoring o[f] the U.S. destroyers." See "U.S. Flexes Muscles and Stirs Up Trouble in Taiwan Strait: Defense Spokesperson," *China Military Online*, December 31, 2020. Chinese officials have even reacted more directly and negatively to MQ-9 recon flights in the SCS than they have to USAF bomber flights in the region. See Ministry of Foreign Affairs of the People's Republic of China, "Foreign Ministry Spokesperson Hua Chunying's Regular Press Conference on January 5, 2021," January 5, 2021.

[470] John Feng, "U.S. Warplanes Foray into China Airspace as PLA Jets Disturb Taiwan," *Newsweek*, November 18, 2020.

[471] Mathieu Duchâtel, "China Trends #6—Generally Stable? Facing U.S. Pushback in the South China Sea," Institut Montaigne, August 6, 2020; and Brian W. Everstine, "B-52 Flies with Carrier Strike Groups in South China Sea," *Air Force Magazine*, July 6, 2020.

[472] Minnie Chan, "South China Sea: Chinese Air Force 'Sends Warning' to U.S. Navy with Live-Fire Drills," *South China Morning Post*, July 21, 2020; and Brian W. Everstine, "B-1Bs Fly Through South China Sea Sending Message to Beijing," *Air Force Magazine*, July 23, 2020.

[473] David Lague, "Special Report: Pentagon's Latest Salvo Against China's Growing Might—Cold War Bombers," Reuters, September 1, 2020; and Liu Xuanzun, "PLA Rocket Force Launches DF-26 'Aircraft Carrier Killer' Missile in Fast-Reaction Drills," *Global Times*, August 6, 2020.

[474] Associated Press, "Chinese Long-Range Bombers Join Drills over South China Sea," *Military Times*, July 30, 2020.

[475] David Lague, "Special Report: Pentagon's Latest Salvo Against China's Growing Might—Cold War Bombers," Reuters, September 1, 2020; Kristen Huang, "China Military Fires 'Aircraft-Carrier Killer' Missile into South China Sea in 'Warning to the United States,'" *South China Morning Post*, August 26, 2020; and Joseph Trevithick, "China Tests Long-Range Anti-Ship Ballistic Missiles as U.S. Spy Plane Watches It All," *The Drive*, August 26, 2020.

At the end of the year, PLA counterparts did not attend the virtual Military Maritime Consultative Agreement bilateral meetings, held since 1998 and focused on maritime and air safety, including in the SCS. Instead, the PLA provided procedural explanations that assigned blamed for China's absence on the United States.[476]

Measures to Manage Escalation

Although China appears to have used anti-ship ballistic missile launches to signal its resolve to defend its SCS claims to U.S. audiences and may have potentially demonstrated a new capability by striking a moving target, as described above, anti-ship ballistic missile tests into the SCS are not new. China conducted tests in 2019 that impacted near the Spratlys.[477] There is no public information on whether China informed the United States of the 2020 launches in advance, but China did issue a Notice to Airmen for an area east of Hainan and north of the Paracels prior to the test.[478] In conjunction, this suggests that China likely viewed the escalation risks of anti-ship ballistic missile launches as relatively minimal.

Explanations for Chinese Reactions

Strong PRC responses to U.S. joint warfighting exercises and training in the SCS in 2020 were enabled by growth in China's military capabilities since 2015 that, in turn, was motivated in part by growing Chinese concern over the threat posed by U.S., allied, and partner activities. Between 2015 and 2020, China improved its military capabilities at SCS outposts, allowing the PLA to field a broader array of air and maritime assets throughout the area, while other force modernization efforts enhanced China's overall A2/AD capabilities. The evidence suggests that it did so to defend its position in the SCS against the United States and regional claimants. As a PLAN analyst's assessment from 2015 argues, in order to protect its position in the SCS in the face of hostile maritime and air operations, China needed to strengthen the defensive, reconnaissance, and early warning capabilities based on many of its SCS features and to increase its own maritime patrols of the area with ships and aircraft.[479] In other words, Chinese

---

[476] Phil Stewart, "U.S. Navy Says China Unreliable After Meeting No-Show; Beijing Says U.S. Twisting Facts," *Reuters*, December 16, 2020.

[477] Joseph Trevithick, "China Tests Long-Range Anti-Ship Ballistic Missiles as U.S. Spy Plane Watches It All," *The Drive*, August 26, 2020.

[478] Tyler Rogoway, "China Freaks Out over Supposed U-2 Spy Plane Flight over Its Naval Exercise," *The Drive*, August 25, 2020.

[479] Huang Zijuan [黄子娟], "Expert on Our Military: U.S. B-52 Approaching Islands and Reefs Perhaps Without Live Ammunition Is Just a Show of Force" ["我军专家: 美B52逼近岛礁或未挂实弹只是炫耀武力"], *ChinaNews.com* [中国新闻网], November 13, 2015; for a similar assessment, see Zhang Jingyang [张经洋], "Don't Let Peace Obscure Smoke Signals from Hostile Forces" ["莫让和平遮挡潜在狼烟"], *China Defense News* [中国国防报], August 16, 2018. See also, by a PLAN expert, Zhang Junshe [张军社], "U.S. Military Provocation in

perceptions of the growing threat of U.S. activities around 2015 incentivized it to invest in stronger military capabilities that enabled it to undertake more aggressive responses in 2020.

However, the evidence suggests that China actually acted more aggressively in 2020 because it perceived U.S. activities as still representing a threat in 2020—and perhaps a more significant threat than in 2015. The evidence for this is circumstantial, as there is little information publicly available about decisionmaking by senior Chinese political and military officials around these particular activities. Nonetheless, it is suggested by the overall deterioration in U.S.-China relations between 2015 and 2020 and China's perception of a shift toward assertive confrontation of China in its SCS policy. In 2020, for example, China reacted negatively to both the State Department's July 13 announcement of a revised SCS policy and to an August 24 op-ed written by the Secretary of Defense regarding DoD efforts regarding China.[480] It is also supported by evidence that China viewed U.S. military operations over the latter half of the 2010s, and especially in 2020, as becoming increasingly frequent and sophisticated and thus inherently more threatening. A Chinese think tank report, for example, listed specific concerns about 2020 operations in the SCS, including that bombers conducted joint operations with other U.S. assets.[481] Those concerns align with China's strongest response to SCS bomber operations in 2020, which was to joint bomber and naval operations.

Even with its increased military capabilities and its perception of a growing U.S. threat in the SCS, however, China has by and large chosen not to escalate there in the hopes of remaining under countries' response thresholds, and instead has attempted to defend its interest by leveraging gray zone tactics against fellow dispute claimants.[482] This is in contrast with its recent reactions in the ECS, such as China's forceful response to the November 2020 flight of two U.S. B1B bombers in China's ADIZ;[483] China may have felt a need to respond more strongly in that

---

the South China Sea Is Doomed to Work to No Avail" ["美在南海的军事挑衅注定徒劳无功"], *People's Liberation Army Daily* [解放军报], July 13, 2020.

[480] Zhao Lijian, "Foreign Ministry Spokesperson Zhao Lijian's Regular Press Conference on July 14, 2020," Ministry of Foreign Affairs of the People's Republic of China, July 14, 2020; Xinhua News Agency, "Interview on Current China-U.S. Relations Given by State Councilor and Foreign Minister Wang Yi to Xinhua News Agency," Ministry of Foreign Affairs of the People's Republic of China, August 5, 2020; and Mark Esper, "The Pentagon Is Prepared for China," *Wall Street Journal*, August 24, 2020.

[481] SCSPI, *An Incomplete Report on U.S. Military Activities in the South China Sea in 2020*, Beijing: Peking University, March 12, 2021.

[482] Bonny Lin, Cristina L. Garafola, Bruce McClintock, Jonah Blank, Jeffrey W. Hornung, Karen Schwindt, Jennifer D. P. Moroney, Paul Orner, Dennis Borrman, Sarah W. Denton, and Jason Chambers, *Competition in the Gray Zone: Countering China's Coercion Against U.S. Allies and Partners in the Indo-Pacific*, Santa Monica, Calif.: RAND Corporation, RR-A594-1, 2022.

[483] Kristin Huang, "U.S. Bombers Enter Chinese Air Defence Zone as Beijing's Navy Mounts Massive Exercises," *South China Morning Post*, November 17, 2020.

case to demonstrate its resolve to rapidly challenge U.S. operations within its ECS ADIZ, whereas China does not have an equivalent ADIZ in the SCS.[484]

Conclusion

Chinese perceptions of the threat posed by U.S. bomber flights in the SCS in 2015 contributed to its investments in more-powerful military capabilities that were necessary but insufficient drivers of its more aggressive responses to U.S. SCS joint warfighting exercises and training in 2020. China's perception of the continuing (and possibly growing) threat posed by the United States, however, motivated it to undertake those responses. In other words, new capabilities enabled new Chinese escalatory options, and evidence suggests that Chinese leaders took them in order to respond to what they saw as an intensifying U.S. threat to China's security. As a result, this case provides moderate support for the tested hypothesis.

---

[484] For more on this topic, see Edmund J. Burke and Astrid Stuth Cevallos, *In Line or Out of Order? China's Approach to ADIZ in Theory and Practice*, Santa Monica, Calif.: RAND Corporation, RR-2055-AF, 2017.

Table B.3. Public USAF Bomber Flights in the South China Sea, 2015 (Gray) and 2020 (White)

Date	Aircraft	Mission Location	Notes	PRC Reaction
November 8–9, 2015[a]	2 x B-52H	Took off and returned to Andersen AFB, Guam	Flew near the Spratlys	Foreign Ministry[b]
December 10, 2015[c]	2 x B-52H	[Not clear]	One of the B-52s may have flown off course due to poor weather to within 12 nm of the PRC-held Cuarteron Reef (Spratlys)	Defense Ministry[d]
January 5, 2020[e]	2 x B-52H	Part of Guam Continuous Bomber Presence	Flew near the Paracels	No reference by Foreign or Defense Ministries
March 17, 2020[f]	2 x B-52H	Part of Guam Continuous Bomber Presence		No reference by Foreign or Defense Ministries
March 19, 2020[g]	1 x B-52H	Part of Guam Continuous Bomber Presence		No reference by Foreign or Defense Ministries
April 29–30, 2020[h]	2 x B-1B	CONUS BTF mission (Ellsworth AFB, South Dakota)	Conducted "theater familiarization" training	Possible/indirect Defense Ministry mention[i]
May 8, 2020[j]	2 x B-1B	Part of Guam BTF	Supported PACAF "training efforts and strategic deterrence missions to reinforce the rules-based international order in the Indo-Pacific region"	No reference by Foreign or Defense Ministries
May 18–19, 2020[k]	2 x B-1B	Part of Guam BTF	Nighttime operation	No reference by Foreign or Defense Ministries
May 25–26, 2020[l]	2 x B-1B	Part of Guam BTF	Joint operations with other U.S. aircraft	No reference by Foreign or Defense Ministries
June 17, 2020[m]	2 x B-52H	Other BTF mission (Eielson AFB, Alaska)		No reference by Foreign or Defense Ministries
July 3–4, 2020[n]	1 x B-52H	Took off from Barksdale AFB, Louisiana and landed at Andersen AFB, Guam	Conducted a "maritime integration exercise" with two USN CSGs; "the B-52 aircrew tested and assessed command and control capabilities to inform the development of contested and degraded communication tactics, techniques and procedures to ensure seamless joint interoperability"	Possible/indirect Foreign Ministry mention[o] and no Defense Ministry reaction; but military operational responses (see text)
July 20–21, 2020[p]	2 x B-1B	Part of Guam BTF	Conducted "maritime integration operation with the USS Ronald Reagan CSG in the Philippine Sea"	No Foreign Ministry statement; possible/indirect Defense Ministry statement that does not mention bombers;[q] but military responses (see text)
September 17–23, 2020[r]	4 x B-1B	Part of Guam BTF	Supported the Valiant Shield 2020 joint integration blue-water	No reference by Foreign or Defense Ministries

Date	Aircraft	Mission Location	Notes	PRC Reaction
			training exercise focused on current operational plans	
October 24, 2020[s]	2 x B-1B	Part of Guam BTF	May have flown near Taiwan toward SCS; unclear if entered SCS	Possible/indirect Defense Ministry mention that does not reference the SCS[t]
November 8, 2020[u]	2 x B-1B	Part of Guam BTF	Flew near the Spratlys	No reference by Foreign or Defense Ministries
December 10, 2020[v]	1 x B-1B	Part of Guam BTF	Conducted "stand-off weapons training with the goal of improving coordination with command and control elements"; followed "rapid response training" with two F-22s	No reference by Foreign or Defense Ministries
December 23, 2020[w]	Likely 2 x B-1Bs	Likely part of Guam BTF		No reference by Foreign or Defense Ministries
December 28, 2020[x]	2 x B-1B	Part of Guam BTF	Flew near the Paracels and the Spratlys	No reference by Foreign or Defense Ministries

NOTES: AFB = air force base. Two other potential SCS bomber overflights could not be confirmed. On February 15, 2020, a B-52H traveled from Andersen AFB in Guam to Singapore for an airshow flyover and likely transited the SCS (Aircraft Spots [@AircraftSpots], "FEB 15: USAF B-52H 60-0055 HAWK52 departed Andersen AFB, Guam for a flyover at the Singapore Airshow," Twitter post, February 15, 2020). On September 25, 2020, two B-1Bs departed Guam and may have headed to operate in the ECS or SCS (Aircraft Spots [@AircraftSpots], "USAF B-1Bs KIMBO11 & 12 departed Andersen AFB, Guam heading in a northwest direction, possibly to the East China Sea or South China Sea. USAF KC-135Rs PEARL21 & 22 provided tanker support," Twitter post, September 25, 2020).

[a] Yeganeh Torbati and David Alexander, "U.S. Bombers Flew Near China-Built Islands in South China Sea: Pentagon," Reuters, November 13, 2015.

[b] Yeganeh Torbati and David Alexander, "U.S. Bombers Flew Near China-Built Islands in South China Sea: Pentagon," Reuters, November 13, 2015.

[c] Christopher Bodeen, "U.S. Says Bombers Didn't Intend to Fly over China-Held Island," *Military Times*, December 19, 2015; and Fergus Ryan, "South China Sea: U.S. Bomber Angers Beijing with Spratly Islands Flypast," *The Guardian*, December 18, 2015.

[d] "U.S. Flight Near Islands 'Serious Military Provocation': Chinese Defense Ministry," Xinhua, December 19, 2015; Ministry of National Defense of the People's Republic of China, "Defense Ministry's Regular Press Conference on Dec. 31," December 31, 2015; "MND Answers Reporters' Questions About the Entry of U.S. B-52 Bombers into the Adjacent Airspace of the Islands and Reefs of China's Spratly Island Archipelago" ["国防部就美 B-52 轰炸机进入中国南沙群岛有关岛礁邻近空域答记者问"], Xinhua, December 19, 2015; and People's Republic of China Embassy in Myanmar, "Foreign Ministry Spokesperson Hong Lei's Regular Press Conference on November 13, 2015" ["2015 年 11 月 13 日外交部发言人洪磊主持例行记者会"], November 13, 2015.

[e] Aircraft Spots [@AircraftSpots], "USAF B-52Hs FLAIL01 & 02 flew into the South China Sea specifically near the Paracel Islands upon returning to Andersen AFB, Guam. USAF KC-135Rs PLUG21 & 22 provided tanker support then returned to Guam," Twitter post, January 5, 2020.

[f] Aircraft Spots [@AircraftSpots], "USAF B-52Hs TAINT01 & 02 departed Andersen AFB, Guam en route to the South China Sea. USAF KC-135Rs PIXIE01 & 02 provided tanker support," Twitter post, March 17, 2020.

[g] Aircraft Spots [@AircraftSpots], "Yesterday (March 19th), a single USAF B-52H Stratofortress bomber executed a flight to the South China Sea from Andersen AFB, Guam. This is the second mission this week!" Twitter post, March 20, 2020.

[h] Kelley J. Stewart, "B-1B Lancers Return to Indo-Pacific for Bomber Task Force Deployment," Pacific Air Forces, May 1, 2020; and Pacific Air Forces Public Affairs, "B-1s Conduct South China Sea Mission, Demonstrates Global Presence," Pacific Air Forces, April 30, 2020.

[i] Ministry of National Defense of the People's Republic of China, "Regular Press Conference of the Ministry of National Defense on Apr. 30," May 5, 2020.

[j] River Bruce, "B-1s Conduct Training Mission in South China Sea," Pacific Air Forces, May 8, 2020.

[k] SCSPI, *An Incomplete Report on U.S. Military Activities in the South China Sea in 2020*, Beijing: Peking University, March 12, 2021, p. 10.

[l] SCSPI, *An Incomplete Report on U.S. Military Activities in the South China Sea in 2020*, Beijing: Peking University, March 12, 2021, p. 10; likely the operation described here: Aircraft Spots [@AircraftSpots], "USAF B-1Bs BULLET01

& 02 departed Andersen AFB, Guam en route to the South China Sea USAF KC-135R PEARL11 provided tanker support," Twitter post, May 25, 2020.

[m] Aircraft Spots [@AircraftSpots], "USAF B-52Hs LIMIT96 & 97 are currently returning to Eielson AFB, Alaska following a Bomber Task Force mission through the Sea of Japan, East China Sea and South China Sea," Twitter post, June 17, 2020.

[n] Hailey Haux, "A B-52 Exercises Dynamic Force Employment with Joint Partners in the Indo-Pacific," Pacific Air Forces, July 5, 2020; and SCSPI, *An Incomplete Report on U.S. Military Activities in the South China Sea in 2020*, Beijing: Peking University, March 12, 2021, p. 6.

[o] Zhao Lijian, "Foreign Ministry Spokesperson Zhao Lijian's Regular Press Conference on July 8, 2020," Ministry of Foreign Affairs of the People's Republic of China, July 8, 2020.

[p] Joshua Sinclair, "B-1s Conduct Bomber Task Force Mission in South China Sea," Pacific Air Forces, July 22, 2020. Likely the same operation referenced here: Aircraft Spots [@AircraftSpots], "USAF B-1Bs CLAWS01 & 02 departed Andersen AFB, Guam en route to the South China Sea via the Sulu Sea entrance. USAF KC-135Rs PEARL21 & 22 are providing tanker support," Twitter post, July 20, 2020.

[q] Ministry of National Defense of the People's Republic of China, "Defense Ministry's Regular Press Conference on July 30," July 30, 2015.

[r] "U.S. Indo-Pacific Command Forces Come Together for Valiant Shield 2020," U.S. Indo-Pacific Command, September 11, 2020; and Nicolas Z. Erwin, "28th Bomb Wing Airmen, B-1s Support Valiant Shield," Pacific Air Forces, September 26, 2020.

[s] Aircraft Spots [@AircraftSpots], "USAF B-1Bs HUGE01 & 02 departed Andersen AFB, Guam en route to the South China Sea. USAF KC-135R PEARL11 provided tanker support," Twitter post, October 24, 2020.

[t] Ministry of National Defense of the People's Republic of China, "Defense Ministry's Regular Press Conference on October 29," November 1, 2020.

[u] Aircraft Spots [@AircraftSpots], "On November 8th, USAF B-1Bs DUNK01 & 02 flew round trip from Andersen AFB, Guam to the South China Sea, at one point flying near the Spratly Islands. This flight sends a clear message to China and appeared to be a FONOP operation," Twitter post, November 9, 2020.

[v] Lindsey Heflin, "B-1 Lancers Train with F-22s in South China Sea," Pacific Air Forces, December 10, 2020.

[w] SCSPI, *An Incomplete Report on U.S. Military Activities in the South China Sea in 2020*, Beijing: Peking University, March 12, 2021, p. 8.

[x] Aircraft Spots [@AircraftSpots], "DEC 28: USAF B-1B Lancer bombers MINT11 & 12 from Andersen AFB, Guam conducted a Bomber Task Force mission over the South China Sea flying near Hainan, the Paracel Islands, and the Spratly Islands," Twitter post, December 29, 2020.

Case 7: China Reacts to THAAD Deployment in South Korea

Case 7 tests the degree to which Chinese perceptions of the military threat posed by U.S. or allied capabilities influence its reactions to U.S. activities by analyzing the 2016 deployment of a THAAD battery—a transportable, ground-based missile defense system—to the Korean peninsula. China saw the move as intensifying a variety of military threats, including potentially weakening China's nuclear deterrence, exacerbating regional instability, and providing the United States with valuable intelligence on China's military. However, the case can only provide moderate support for the hypothesis because there are other plausible explanations for Beijing behavior. Most importantly, China considered South Korea's decision to deploy a THAAD battery as an insulting disregard for Beijing's preferences, which may have signaled a decline in Beijing's regional influence. Evidence also suggests that THAAD deployment may have increased Chinese perceptions of the hostile intent of the United States and its allies and suggested that other states did not respect Beijing's resolve to defend its interests. Taken together, it appears that these strategic and military concerns motivated China to respond to THAAD deployment through an aggressive diplomatic, economic, and media campaign. China's military response, however, was relatively restrained; it consisted only of some military exercises and the cancellation of some engagements. Although China failed to persuade South Korea to remove the system, it did extract political pledges to permit China more say over future deployments in exchange for an easing of the pressure.

A Brief History of THAAD Deployment in South Korea

Built by Lockheed Martin, the THAAD missile system is designed to intercept short- and medium-range ballistic missiles up to 200 kilometers away. It is regarded as far superior to other land-based missile defense systems deployed in the ROK. A THAAD battery usually includes an AN/TPY-2 X-band radar with a range of approximately 2,000 kilometers.[485]

After North Korea carried out a satellite launch to test ballistic missile technology in February 2016, South Korea said that it would pursue the system with the United States. In July 2016, the two countries announced the decision to deploy a U.S. THAAD battery in South Korea to defend against the North Korean missile threat. That battery reached initial operating capability on May 2, 2017.[486]

China's reaction was swift. Hours after the July 2016 joint announcement, Beijing issued a demarche to the U.S. and South Korean ambassadors to convey its "firm opposition." PRC officials quickly and regularly issued statements criticizing the deployment. On July 8, 2016, for example, a PRC spokesperson stated that the deployment would "gravely sabotage" the "security

---

[485] Greg Torode and Michael Martina, "Chinese Wary About U.S. Missile System Because Capabilities Unknown: Experts," Reuters, April 3, 2017.

[486] Choe Sang-Hun, "U.S. Antimissile System Goes Live in South Korea," *New York Times*, May 2, 2017.

interests" and "regional balance" of China and other countries.[487] Chinese authorities also issued warnings if South Korea did not reverse course. On July 25, 2016, Foreign Minister Wang Yi urged South Korea to "take China's reasonable and legitimate concerns into serious consideration, carefully weigh the pros and cons, be extra cautious, and think twice before taking actions."[488] Chinese officials and commentators frequently offered threats of retaliation. These threats frequently appeared as warnings that Beijing would "take necessary measures to safeguard China's strategic security and regional strategic balance."[489] From mid-2016 and through early 2017, moreover, China carried out a whole-of-government effort to pressure South Korea into reversing the deployment.

The crisis eased in May 2017, after the inauguration of President Moon Jae-in. The new government made considerable effort to restore the relationship with China. Beijing responded positively, and, on October 31, Beijing and Seoul announced a joint statement on their rapprochement. In the statement, Beijing restated its opposition to THAAD, its concerns about the U.S.-led regional missile defense program, the deployment of additional THAAD batteries, and the U.S.–South Korean–Japanese military cooperation.[490] Seoul did not formally respond to China's concerns in the statement, but a day before the announcement of the joint statement South Korea's Foreign Minister Kang Kyung-wha stated that Seoul had no intention to (1) install additional THAAD batteries, (2) participate in a regional missile defense system, or (3) form a trilateral alliance with the United States and Japan, a position reiterated by President Moon days later. Although Seoul did not remove its THAAD battery, these gestures satisfied Beijing, which agreed to end its economic retribution in return for what became known as Seoul's new "Three No's" policy.[491] Despite resolution of the controversy in 2017, the issue remains sensitive. In May 2020, China's Foreign Ministry responded to reports that U.S. forces had transported THAAD equipment to replace existing missiles by reiterating the country's opposition to the THAAD system's deployment in South Korea. Chinese Foreign Ministry spokesman Zhao Lijian told reporters during a daily briefing that Beijing and Seoul had reached a "clear consensus" on the THAAD issue and said that China hopes that Seoul will "adhere to that agreement."[492]

---

[487] Ministry of Foreign Affairs of the People's Republic of China, "Foreign Ministry Spokesperson Hong Lei's Regular Press Conference on July 8," July 8, 2016.

[488] Ministry of Foreign Affairs of the People's Republic of China, "Wang Yi Meets with Foreign Minister Yun Byung-se of the ROK," July 25, 2016.

[489] Ministry of National Defense of the People's Republic of China, "Defense Ministry's Regular Press Conference," September 29, 2016; and Ministry of National Defense of the People's Republic of China, "Sun Jianguo Meets ROK Defense Minister Han Min-ku" ["孙建国会见韩国国防部长韩民求"], June 4, 2016.

[490] Ministry of Foreign Affairs of the People's Republic of China, "China and South Korea Communicate on Bilateral Relations and Other Issues" ["中韩双方就中韩关系等进行沟通"], October 31, 2017.

[491] Jeongseok Lee, "Back to Normal? The End of the THAAD Dispute Between China and South Korea," *China Brief*, Vol. 17, No. 15, November 22, 2017.

[492] Yew Lun Tian, "China Says Opposes U.S. THAAD Defence System in South Korea," Reuters, May 29, 2020.

Chinese Reactions

China responded to the deployment with a steady whole-of-government effort aimed at compelling South Korea to reverse its decision or make substantive concessions regarding the issue. The reaction consisted primarily of diplomatic, media, and economic pressure. Military responses were limited primarily to the cancellation of bilateral engagements.

Political Responses

As previously noted, China's diplomatic response to the joint U.S.-ROK announcement about THAAD was both forceful and almost immediate. Within hours, China issued a formal protest and publicly criticized the decision.[493] China also ramped up efforts to influence international opinion. On July 9, 2016, Foreign Minister Wang Yi gave an interview to Reuters in which he stated that deployment of the THAAD system goes "far beyond the defense need of the Korean Peninsula." He stated that "any justification to this cannot hold water" and that China had "every reason and right to question the real scheme behind this action." He demanded that the United States "not build its own security on the basis of jeopardizing other countries' security and not to damage other countries' legitimate security interests." In the months that followed, Chinese officials frequently condemned the deployment. According to one study, China's Ministry of Foreign Affairs spoke out on the issue more than 50 times in 2016 and 2017.[494] Chinese media carried many articles criticizing the deployment as well; these themes are discussed in more detail below.

Although it launched many diplomatic actions targeting South Korea, Beijing made few (or no) gestures to reassure Pyongyang, underscoring the point that China's response was driven more by its own security concerns than concern over North Korea. On the contrary, in early 2017, China complied with UN sanctions in response to a North Korean weapons test and cut coal shipments, sparking a furious North Korean denunciation of Beijing. Some observers described the bilateral relationship that year as at its "lowest point" in decades.[495]

In addition to its own unilateral responses, China also coordinated some responses with one of its closest partners, Russia. Throughout 2017, Chinese officials issued multiple joint

---

[493] Ministry of Foreign Affairs of the People's Republic of China, "Foreign Ministry Spokesperson Hong Lei's Regular Press Conference on July 8," July 8, 2016; and Ministry of Foreign Affairs of the People's Republic of China, "Wang Yi Comments on Plan of the U.S. to Deploy THAAD System in ROK," July 9, 2016.

[494] Ethan Meick and Nargiza Salidjanova, *China's Response to U.S.-South Korean Missile Defense System Deployment and Its Implications*, Washington, D.C.: U.S.-China Economic and Security Review Commission, July 26, 2017.

[495] Jane Perlez, "China and North Korea Reveal Sudden, and Deep, Cracks in Their Friendship," *New York Times*, February 24, 2017.

statements with their Russian counterparts expressing opposition to THAAD.[496] Chinese officials and experts argued that THAAD harms the regional "strategic balance."[497]

Economic Responses

China wielded its economic power to punish South Korea through a variety of measures. The THAAD dispute first affected the entertainment industry. Starting around August 2016, Korean celebrities who had enjoyed enormous popularity in China began to lose access. They no longer appeared on commercials and TV shows, and their concerts were suddenly canceled. China also targeted South Korea's dependence on Chinese tourism. In October 2016, authorities instructed Chinese travel agencies to decrease the number of South Korea–bound travelers by 20 percent. Stock prices of major South Korean hotel chains, cosmetics companies, and duty-free shops fell by 7 to 8 percent. Chinese officials singled out the Korean grocer conglomerate Lotte for its decision to provide its golf course in the southeastern county of Seongju as a deployment site. Beijing subjected the retail giant's business in China to extensive tax investigations and safety inspections, eventually forcing 87 out of Lotte's 112 hypermarket stores in China to shut down at the cost of $2.2 billion in losses. Between March and October 2017, hundreds of South Korean companies in China were subjected to various informal punitive measures, such as delayed customs clearances, tightened sanitary inspections, forced removal of products from stores, unilateral cancelation of marketing events, and the refusal of business visas.[498] Beijing's resolve against THAAD cost South Korea at least $7.5 billion in economic losses.[499]

Military Responses

The military response consisted primarily of a freeze in military engagements and military exercises that appeared potentially related to the deployment. PLA experts discussed options about how the PLA could counter the systems in wartime. In November 2016, Beijing suspended high-level defense consultations with Seoul and postponed a planned meeting between defense ministers.[500] In August 2017, the PLA Rocket Force also carried out a combined ballistic and cruise missile exercise in the Bohai Sea, likely with the DF-26B IRBM. The exercise included a

[496] Permanent Mission of the People's Republic of China to the United Nations, "Wang Yi Talks About Current China-Russia Relations," May 26, 2017; and "China, Russia Agree to Further Respond to THAAD Deployment," Xinhua, January 13, 2017.

[497] Ministry of Foreign Affairs of the People's Republic of China, "Foreign Ministry Spokesperson Hua Chunying's Regular Press Conference on March 17, 2017," March 17, 2017; and "China, Russia Sign Joint Statement on Strengthening Global Strategic Stability," Xinhua, June 26, 2016.

[498] Jeongseok Lee, "Back to Normal? The End of the THAAD Dispute Between China and South Korea," *China Brief*, Vol. 17, No. 15, November 22, 2017.

[499] "When China and U.S. Spar, It's South Korea That Gets Punched," *Los Angeles Times*, November 20, 2020.

[500] Ethan Meick and Nargiza Salidjanova, *China's Response to U.S.-South Korean Missile Defense System Deployment and Its Implications*, Washington, D.C.: U.S.-China Economic and Security Review Commission, July 26, 2017.

simulated strike on a THAAD battery and a mock F-22 aircraft, in what appeared to be a message to the United States.[501] Chinese media stated, "The latest weapons test shows that Beijing is proactively improving its capability of defense and counterattack. . . . Never underestimate China's will and strength to safeguard its own security as well as regional peace and stability."[502]

Chinese experts recommended numerous military countermeasures against the THAAD deployment, although the extent to which the PLA considered implementing them remains unclear. Zhao Xiaozhuo, an expert at the PLA's Academy of Military Science, recommended that China employ jamming and EW activities against the THAAD radar in the event of conflict. He also suggested using stealth technology and maneuvering technologies to enable Chinese missiles to evade the defense. He further recommended striking the deployment base with cruise missiles in the event of war. Zhao noted that China's development of hypersonic missiles could render THAAD useless over the longer term."[503]

Finally, China may have directed cyberespionage activity against South Korea as part of its retaliation. On April 21, 2017, John Hultquist, director of cyberespionage analysis at FireEye, a U.S. cybersecurity firm, stated that two cyberespionage groups "linked to Beijing's military and intelligence agencies have launched a variety of attacks against South Korea's government, military, defense companies and a big conglomerate."[504]

Explanations for Chinese Reactions

Analysis of Chinese official statements and commentary suggest strategic and security-related reasons for the strong reaction. The principal drivers stem from strategic fears of a broader regional shift against China, the increasingly hostile intent of the United States and South Korea, and weakening Chinese regional influence manifested in South Korea's disregard for China's preferences. The military threat posed by the THAAD system to China centers principally on the risk that it undermines the latter's deterrence capabilities, that it exacerbates regional instability, and that it enhances U.S. and South Korean intelligence collection.

Chinese officials and commentators frequently invoke the worry that the deployment could signal a regional shift in favor of the United States. On July 11, 2016, a government spokesman

[501] Ankit Panda, "Chinese People's Liberation Army Rocket Force Staged a Massive Missile Drill Against a THAAD Mockup Target," *The Diplomat*, August 3, 2017.

[502] Ai Jun, "New Missile Signals China's Resolve to Counter THAAD," *Global Times*, May 10, 2017; and Deng Xiaoci, "China's Latest Missile Test Shows Country Can Respond to Aircraft Carriers, THAAD," *Global Times*, May 10, 2017.

[503] Ethan Meick and Nargiza Salidjanova, *China's Response to U.S.-South Korean Missile Defense System Deployment and Its Implications*, Washington, D.C.: U.S.-China Economic and Security Review Commission, July 26, 2017, p. 6.

[504] Jonathan Cheng and Josh Chin, "China Hacked South Korea over Missile Defense, U.S. Firm Says," *Wall Street Journal*, April 21, 2017.

explained that by "getting on board with the U.S. [to deploy THAAD], the ROK has involved itself in tipping the scale of regional strategic balance."[505] A 2016 *People's Daily* editorial written under the "Zhong Sheng" byline presented the THAAD decision as highly threatening to both China and Russia, claiming that the deployment's threat to Northeast Asian and "global strategic stability" "could not be underestimated."[506] The article warned that the United States and South Korea would "bear the consequences of their arrogant actions and be responsible for destabilizing the international situation."

Commentators frequently raised the notion of hostile U.S. intent, especially the intent to contain China.[507] Chen Yinde, a researcher at the China Foundation for International Studies, argued that the THAAD deployment would "likely trigger confrontations between major countries." He denounced the move as a "vicious plan" that would "endanger peace and stability on the peninsula and Northeast Asia region." Echoing an argument common in the Chinese press, he dismissed the ostensible purpose of THAAD and said that the "real motive" was to "mitigate the threat from China and Russia," which would allow the United States to "achieve its goal of containing China and Russia."[508] Zhu Chenghu, a professor at the National Defense University, criticized the THAAD deployment as a "severe challenge to the reliability of China's strategic deterrence." He said that it had "nothing to do with North Korea's missile launches or nuclear tests" and was "obviously aimed at containing China."[509] A *People's Daily* commentary published on August 3, 2016, stated that it was "impossible for South Korean leaders not to understand the strategic plans of the United States," which it said was to "contain China."[510]

---

[505] Ministry of Foreign Affairs of the People's Republic of China, "Foreign Ministry Spokesperson Lu Kang's Regular Press Conference," July 11, 2016.

[506] *Zhong Sheng* is a homophone for "voice of the people" and is used for editorials written collectively by the *People's Daily's* international department that typically reflect relatively authoritative sentiments. See Zhong Sheng [钟声], "The U.S. and South Korea Must Understand the Deep Meaning Behind China and Russia's Warnings—Deployment of THAAD Threatens Peace in Northeast Asia" ["美韩须领会中俄严正警告的深意—部署'萨德'威胁的是东北亚和平"], *People's Daily* [人民日报], August 4, 2016.

[507] Ethan Meick and Nargiza Salidjanova, *China's Response to U.S.-South Korean Missile Defense System Deployment and Its Implications*, Washington, D.C.: U.S.-China Economic and Security Review Commission, July 26, 2017, p. 6.

[508] Yin Chengde, "With THAAD, U.S. and South Korea Are Playing with Fire," *China-U.S. Focus*, October 19, 2016.

[509] "Major General Zhu Chenghu: To Respond to THAAD, China Must Be Fully Prepared" ["朱成虎少将: 应对美国'萨德'中国要未雨绸缪"], *Bauhania* [紫荆网], August 2, 2016.

[510] Zhong Sheng [钟声], "China's Security Interests Should Not Be Deliberately Damaged—Deployment of THAAD Threatens Peace in Northeast Asia" ["中国安全利益不容蓄意损害—部署'萨德'威胁的是东北亚和平"], *People's Daily* [人民日报], August 3, 2016.

The frequently encountered criticism in Chinese media of South Korea "stabbing China in the back" reflects the view that South Korea had failed to heed Chinese preferences. Chinese officials and commentators appeared angered by South Korea's decision to weigh as more important the preferences of its U.S. ally over China's preferences, a notion that they regard as infuriating given the country's deep trade ties with China and warm diplomatic relations. Another "Zhong Sheng" commentary in the *People's Daily* compared Seoul's decision to support deployment of THAAD to being "tied to the Northeastern chariot of the United States."[511] It described the decision as one of "dangerous entrapment" that would "inevitably bring dangerous consequences." The article suggested that Seoul should conform to the pattern of rising trade and warming relations with China by relying more on Beijing and less on the United States, favorably contrasting the benefits of a close Beijing-Seoul relationship with that of reliance on a United States "obsessed with hegemony" and intent on using South Korea as a "pawn." An article appearing in the *People's Liberation Army Daily* on July 26, 2016, criticized South Korea for depending on the United States for its security and said that the "only way" to achieve security would be for South Korea to have "good relations" with its "neighboring countries," presumably referring to China.[512] The belief that South Korea should defer more to Chinese preferences given its increasing dependence frequently appears in justifications for retaliation against South Korea. A commentary published in *Global Times* on August 1, 2016, cited Wu Xinbo, Fudan University, who said that South Korea deserved punishment for "failing to properly [take] into account China's interests." He accused Seoul of "stabbing China in the back" despite all the goodwill Beijing had shown through its assistance on the peninsula, warming bilateral relations, and large trade volume. The article cited Zheng Jiyong, an expert in Korean studies at Fudan University, who warned that if China did not "severely punish" South Korea, then other neighboring countries will "challenge China's national interests in the future."[513] Although he did not give examples, his comment could refer to the possibility of other countries, perhaps in Southeast Asia, granting the United States greater access for THAAD or other major combat capabilities and hints at the possibility that Chinese concerns over whether other states might doubt its resolve played a role in its decisionmaking.

The principal Chinese military concern appeared to stem from the THAAD system's X-band radar, which Chinese missile defense experts argue could detect most Chinese missile tests in northeast China and strategic ICBMs in the western part of the country. According to Li Bin, a

---

[511] Zhong Sheng [钟声], "South Korea Needs Composure and Sense of Reality—Deployment of THAAD Threatens Peace in Northeast Asia" ["韩国, 需要基本的清醒和现实感—部署 '萨德' 威胁的是东北亚和平"], *People's Daily* [人民日报], August 1, 2016.

[512] "U.S., ROK Must Stop Deployment of THAAD Missile Battery," *China Military Online*, July 29, 2016.

[513] "How Should China Retaliate Against South Korea for Its Deployment of THAAD?" ["因为 '萨德', 中国应如何 '报复' 韩国"], *Global Times* [环球时报], August 1, 2016.

professor at China's Tsinghua University, the X-band radar allows the United States to detect the radar signature from the back of the warhead and could differentiate between a real Chinese warhead and a decoy, which could imperil China's nuclear deterrent capability.[514]

One of the drivers of China's reaction appears to be the fear that THAAD could expand a missile defense architecture for the United States and its allies, a development that could weaken Beijing's nuclear deterrent capability. The 2021 DoD report on China's military power states that China will have 700 deliverable nuclear warheads by 2027.[515] By contrast, the United States has 1,550 deployed warheads across its delivery platforms and an inventory of 3,750 warheads.[516] China fears that U.S. missile defense capabilities could threaten China's ability to retaliate in the event of a nuclear exchange, leaving the country vulnerable to extensive U.S. nuclear strikes. In March 2017, China's Ministry of Foreign Affairs spokesperson said, "The deployment of THAAD systems in the ROK is a part of the move by the U.S. to boost its global missile defense system and has a bearing on the peace and stability of Northeast Asia."[517]

Other security-related criticisms have centered on the possibility that the deployment could kick off an arms race and exacerbate regional instability. In an October 2016 speech to the UN, Ambassador Wang Qun, Director-General of the Arms Control Department in China's Ministry of Foreign Affairs, stated that the deployment of global missile defense systems by the United States would "impede the nuclear disarmament process, trigger a regional arms race, and escalate military confrontation." He highlighted the deployment of the THAAD system in Korea, which he stated would "in no way" facilitate "denuclearization of the Korean Peninsula and maintain peace and stability on the Peninsula."[518]

Chinese media commentaries and experts have echoed the view made by officials that the THAAD deployment will lead to further escalation of tensions and military buildup. One month after the announced deployment in July 2016, Fan Gaoyue, a retired PLA senior colonel and former researcher at the PLA Academy of Military Science, argued that the system would most benefit North Korea by providing a justification for developing new missiles and speeding up development of its nuclear weapons program, among other things.[519]

---

[514] Li Bin, "The Security Dilemma and THAAD Deployment in the ROK," *China-U.S. Focus*, March 6, 2017.

[515] Office of the Secretary of Defense, *Annual Report to Congress: Military and Security Developments Involving the People's Republic of China 2020*, Washington, D.C., 2020, pp. viii, 90.

[516] See U.S. Department of State, "Transparency in the U.S. Nuclear Weapons Stockpile," fact sheet, October 5, 2021; and U.S. Department of State, "New START Treaty Aggregate Numbers of Strategic Offensive Arms of the United States and the Russian Federation, February 2011–March 2022," fact sheet, March 1, 2022.

[517] Ministry of Foreign Affairs of the People's Republic of China, "Foreign Ministry Spokesperson Lu Kang's Regular Press Conference on March 29, 2017," March 29, 2017.

[518] Wang Qun, "Statement by Ambassador Wang Qun, Director-General of the Arms Control Department of the Ministry of Foreign Affairs of China, at the General Debate of the First Committee of the 71st Session of the UNGA," Ministry of Foreign Affairs of the People's Republic of China, October 10, 2016.

[519] Fan Gaoyue, "ROK: The Biggest Loser of THAAD," *China-U.S. Focus*, August 9, 2016.

Concerns about the intelligence threat posed by the THAAD system appear in Chinese media as well. A commentary on July 29, 2016, dismissed the ostensible purpose of THAAD, stating that "everyone can see that it cannot defend against North Korea's nuclear weapons and missile threat." It alleged that the "real purpose" of the system was to "become an important tool for monitoring the Chinese military."[520]

A minority of experts have expressed a more moderate view. Wang Jisi, a well-known international relations expert, characterized the dispute over the THAAD deployment as just one of many issues that make up a complex relationship between two great powers who both cooperate and compete at the same time.[521]

Conclusion

China's strong reaction to the deployment of the THAAD radar in Korea surprised many observers. Even South Korea seems to have been caught off guard, given its lack of preparation for the retaliation that followed. Some factors that shaped China's response appear self-evident, such as the potential threat that the THAAD system could pose to China's physical security, especially because of its deployment in the context of an already volatile and dangerous security situation on the peninsula. However, in many ways, the THAAD case presents an early and compelling example of China's approach to bilateral relationships in an era of deepening competition with the United States. For Beijing, deepening economic and diplomatic ties carry important implications for the security policy of partner countries, such as South Korea. China's reaction underscores its belief that countries who accept economic and diplomatic benefits from engagement with China should accept a higher level of deference to China's political preferences on contentious issues, including those related to security. Countries that fail to understand the conditions that accompany closer economic and diplomatic relations with China may be exposed to Beijing's fury, as happened to South Korea. Moreover, heightened tensions arising from an intensifying competition with the United States will likely heighten Beijing's sensitivity to U.S. military deployments that carry some potential level of threat and its sensitivity to the strategic significance of any increase in U.S. influence in the region. Militarily, it is true that, in the event of a conflict with the United States, China could fairly easily target the THAAD battery with cruise and ballistic missiles. However, this option would not remove the risk, from Beijing's perspective, that the United States might use THAAD to degrade China's nuclear deterrent before hostilities became widespread, in turn creating pressure on China to act before the United

---

[520] Zhong Sheng [钟声], "Dangerous Action That Warrants Alarm—Deployment of THAAD Threatens Peace in Northeast Asia" ["值得警惕的危险之举—部署 '萨德' 威胁的是东北亚和平"], *People's Daily* [人民日报], July 29, 2016.

[521] "Wang Jisi: A 'New Norm' in U.S.-China Relations" ["王缉思: 中美关系进入一个 '新常态'"], *Global Times* [环球时报], August 19, 2016.

States could do so. From China's perspective, the presence of THAAD and similar systems near its borders therefore creates escalation management challenges for both sides.

Case 8: China and the Philippines, June 2016–Present

This case explores Chinese reactions to the Philippines' Rodrigo Duterte administration to test the hypothesis that China will respond more aggressively to U.S., allied, and partner activities if it perceives them as increasing the threat to China's regional influence. During the Benigno Aquino III administration, from June 2010 to June 2016, the Philippines' ties with the United States grew stronger while those with China grew more contentious. Both trends appear to have changed since Duterte assumed power in 2016, especially over the first few years of his presidency.[522] This plausibly reduced Chinese concern regarding threats to its influence in Southeast Asia—and China behaved less aggressively toward the Philippines over the period in the question. Indeed, there is evidence that China undertook a diplomatic charm offensive in the wake of Duterte's election that included being more forthcoming with aid, military assistance, and praise for Manila's policies. The case therefore provides considerable support for the hypothesis. Notably, however, the softening in China's policies toward the Philippines does not appear to have extended to a relaxation in its SCS military posture. This suggests that China is willing to be less aggressive in one domain if it thinks it can advance its influence but that it is unwilling to sacrifice positions of strength in its territorial disputes, even if doing so undermines those diplomatic efforts.

The Philippines' Accommodating Actions

The Duterte administration came into office with a clear intent to "maintain an independent foreign policy" from the United States.[523] Duterte stated he wanted to "open alliances" with China and Russia;[524] he declared the Philippines' military and economic "separation" from the United States; and he announced that he had "realigned" himself in China's ideological flow and would become dependent on China "for all times."[525] This desire to distance the Philippines from the United States was more than bluster, as it manifested in both military and diplomatic policy.

First, Duterte sought to scale down bilateral military exercises with the United States. In September 2016, he announced that the bilateral Philippines Amphibious Landing Exercise scheduled for October of that year, an amphibious and live-fire training exercise that is combined with humanitarian civic assistance efforts, would be the last military exercise between the

---

[522] Over time, the Duterte administration sought to downplay friction with the United States at the same time it more openly criticized China and took harder positions against Beijing. This chapter focuses only on the first few years to most directly examine the hypothesis under question.

[523] Rodrigo Roa Duterte, *National Security Policy for Change and Well-Being of the Filipino People (2017–2022)*, Manila, Philippines, April 2017, p. 25; and Rodrigo Roa Duterte, "5th State of the Nation Address," Quezon City, Philippines, July 27, 2020.

[524] Manuel Mogato, Enrico dela Cruz, and Arshad Mohammed, "Philippines' Duterte Wants to 'Open Alliances' with Russia, China," Reuters, September 26, 2016.

[525] Rodrigo Roa Duterte, speech delivered at the Philippines-China Trade and Investment Forum, Beijing, October 20, 2016.

Philippines and the United States. He eventually recanted, allowing for smaller exercises but changing the scope to a focus on just humanitarian operations.[526] Making good on this policy, the May 2017 Balikatan exercises, the first conducted under Duterte, were only about half of their previous size and had shifted in focus from combat, through such things as amphibious landings and live-fire drills, to humanitarian and disaster response and CT operations. A few months later, the Kamandag exercise focused on CT and disaster response, although it still includes amphibious landing components.[527]

Diplomatically, shortly after becoming president, Duterte's first major decision was whether and how hard to push Manila's victory over Beijing regarding SCS territorial claims at the Permanent Court of Arbitration, which is explained in greater detail below. Duterte decided not to press Manila's victory over China, declaring that he would "set aside the arbitral ruling" and "not impose anything on China."[528] Instead, the Duterte government publicly suggested bilateral talks with China to settle their SCS dispute. This change in policy came despite the fact that China showed no softening its position and continued to fortify and militarize its artificial SCS islands.[529]

Duterte's moves were a dramatic change not only in Manila's policies vis-à-vis China but also in the Philippines' relations with its U.S. ally. During the Aquino administration, the Philippines sought to balance China's activities in the region. One of the major points of contention between Manila and Beijing had been Chinese island-building.[530] In response, Aquino had sought to shift the military's focus from domestic security to territorial defense, bolster U.S.-Philippine security ties, acquire U.S. military equipment, and seek an explicit security guarantee from Washington under the 1951 Mutual Defense Treaty.[531] Relations with China were so fractious that in 2013 the Aquino administration filed a claim against China with the Permanent Court of Arbitration in The Hague. On July 12, 2016, the tribunal ruled in favor of the Philippines, essentially arguing that China's broad claims were invalid, which thereafter provided the Philippines and the United States ammunition with which to pressure Chinese actions. By contrast, Duterte sought to position the Philippines equidistantly between China and

---

[526] Manuel Mogato, "U.S., Philippines Scale Back Next Month's Military Drills, No More 'War Games,'" Reuters, April 24, 2017.

[527] Seth Robson, "U.S.-Filipino Troops Kick Off New Kamandag Exercise in the Philippines," *Stars and Stripes*, October 2, 2017; and "U.S., Philippines Launch War Games amid Uncertainty over Ties," *DW*, October 4, 2016.

[528] Nestor Corrales, "Duterte Says He'll 'Set Aside' Arbitral Ruling on South China Sea," *Inquirer.net*, December 17, 2016.

[529] Asia Maritime Transparency Initiative, "China's New Spratly Island Defenses," webpage, Center for Strategic and International Studies, December 13, 2016.

[530] Since 2013, China has created 3,200 acres of new land that includes 20 outposts in the Paracel Islands and seven in the Spratly Islands. It has had control of the Scarborough Shoal since 2012. See Asia Maritime Transparency Initiative, "China Island Tracker," webpage, Center for Strategic and International Studies, undated.

[531] Renato Cruz de Castro, "The Duterte Administration's Foreign Policy: Unravelling the Aquino Administration's Balancing Agenda on an Emergent China," *Journal of Current Southeast Asian Affairs*, Vol. 35, No. 3, 2016, p. 139.

the United States, requiring a reduction in U.S.-Philippine military exercises as well as closer cooperation with Beijing for both aid and military equipment. The latter could not be achieved without putting aside the Philippines' victory in the Permanent Court of Arbitration.

Duterte's motivations for the sudden shift in the Philippines' approach are not entirely clear. Some believe that the change is driven by Duterte questioning the level of U.S. commitment to the Philippines, leaving him no choice but to find an independent modus vivendi with China. According to this thinking, Duterte's conciliatory approach to China is based at least partly on the fact that he personally does not trust that Washington will come to the aid of the Philippines over its territorial disputes.[532] Others believe that Duterte believes in the potential benefits that could accrue to the Philippines through closer relations with China. According to this logic, Duterte wanted to prioritize Philippine economic development and sees China as an essential partner in doing so. Support for this statement is visible in Duterte's praise for China and Xi Jinping. For example, during the presidential campaign, Duterte addressed China by saying that if it would "build me a train around Mindanao, build me train from Manila to Bicol . . . build me a train going to Batangas, for the six years that I'll be president, I'll shut up" regarding the SCS disputes.[533] Furthermore, in a separate event, Duterte declared that "what I need from China is help to develop my country" and that, in exchange, he would downgrade security cooperation with the United States and disregard the arbitration court's ruling.[534] It is also possible that Duterte is trying to carefully balance the Philippines between both China and the United States in order to extract the maximum benefits from both sides—getting Chinese development aid and investment while simultaneously getting military support from the United States.[535]

Chinese Reactions

Political Responses

In response to Duterte's actions, China made significant laudatory public statements reaffirming Beijing's welcoming position and encouraging Duterte's movement toward

---

[532] In a media interview in 2015, Duterte described the United States as unwilling to go to war because it sees itself as unable to take the high risks involved to tackle a wide range of problems abroad, citing the example of United States' inability to stop China from building its artificial islands in the SCS that subsequently undermined the Philippines' position. See Michael Sullivan, "Trump and Duterte Could Reset the Shaky U.S.-Philippine Alliance," *NPR*, November 11, 2017; and Prashanth Parameswaran, "Why the Philippines' Rodrigo Duterte Hates America," *The Diplomat*, November 1, 2016.

[533] Richard Javad Heydarian, "How Duterte Turned the Philippines into China's New Play Thing," *National Interest*, February 23, 2020.

[534] Richard Javad Heydarian, "How Duterte Turned the Philippines into China's New Play Thing," *National Interest*, February 23, 2020.

[535] Ralph Jennings, "China or U.S.? Philippines Foreign Policy Plays Both Sides," *Voice of America*, September 3, 2020; and Mark Bryan F. Manantan, "Pivot Toward China: A Critical Analysis of the Philippines' Policy Shift on the South China Sea Disputes," *Asian Politics & Policy*, Vol. 11, No. 4, 2019.

alignment with China's policy positions. Chinese Foreign Minister Wang Yi welcomed the Philippines' more-independent strategic approach, stating that China

> firmly supports the Philippines in pursuing an independent foreign policy and exploring a development path that suits its own national conditions. An independent Philippines will win the Philippines dignity and status in the international arena. A Philippines that is friendly with other countries will open up a broader space for its own development.[536]

China also responded kindly to the Duterte administration's softer tone on the Permanent Court of Arbitration. For example, Foreign Ministry spokeswoman Hua Chunying welcomed Duterte's comments and hoped that Manila could return to bilateral talks, appropriately handle their disputes, and work for the healthy development of bilateral ties.[537] Ministry of Foreign Affairs spokesperson Geng Shuang also struck a congenial tone when asked about fishing activity in the waters of Scarborough Shoal, remarking that

> China and the Philippines have reached consensus on returning to the track of dialogue and consultation on the South China Sea issue. China has also made proper arrangements for Filipino fishermen to go fishing in the relevant waters near Huangyan Island based on friendly feelings. China's sovereignty and jurisdiction over Huangyan Island have not and will not change. We hope that China and the Philippines will strengthen dialogue and cooperation so that the South China Sea issue will become a positive factor in promoting friendship and cooperation between the two sides.[538]

Economic Responses

Beijing rewarded Manila's softer tone economically. During his first foreign trip as president, in October 2016, Duterte visited China. Here, Xi Jinping agreed to provide the Philippines $24 billion in economic pledges and relaxed non-tariff barriers on Filipino fruit exports.[539] Even though it does not appear that China has delivered on these promises, the fact remains that Beijing did not make similar promises during the Aquino period.[540] When Duterte again visited

---

[536] Wang Yi [王毅], "China Firmly Supports the Philippines in Pursuing an Independent Foreign Policy" ["中方坚定支持菲律宾奉行独立自主外交政策"], Ministry of Foreign Affairs of the People's Republic of China, July 25, 2017.

[537] Michael Martina, "China Welcomes Manila's Offer for South China Sea Talks," Reuters, June 1, 2016.

[538] Ministry of Foreign Affairs of the People's Republic of China, "Foreign Ministry Spokesperson Geng Shuang's Regular Press Conference on November 22, 2016" ["2016年11月22日外交部发言人耿爽主持例行记者会"], November 22, 2016.

[539] This included $9 billion in soft loans and economic deals with $15 billion in investments. See Andreo Calonzo and Cecilia Yap, "China Visit Helps Duterte Reap Funding Deals Worth $24 Billion," *Bloomberg*, October 21, 2016; and Richard Javad Heydarian, "Duterte's Uncertain China Gamble," Asia Maritime Transparency Initiative, Center for Strategic and International Studies, November 3, 2016.

[540] Richard Heydarian, "Scepticism Rises in Philippines About Chinese Projects and Duterte's Support of Them," *South China Morning Post*, January 18, 2020; and Melissa Luz Lopez, "China's Loan, Investment Pledges Unlikely to Be Fulfilled Under Duterte's Term—Carpio," *CNN Philippines*, June 8, 2020.

Beijing in 2019, Xi stated that China would continue to invest in Philippine infrastructure as part of its BRI, contributing to industrial parks, telecommunications, and energy, as well as expand Chinese imports of agricultural products. Xi specifically noted that since Duterte had taken office, bilateral relations had continuously upgraded and improved.[541]

Military Responses

In the military domain, China increased its engagement with the Philippines even as the latter reduced its defense cooperation with the United States. For example, following a refusal by Washington to sell the Philippines assault rifles over accusations of human rights violations, China donated 6,000 assault rifles, ammunition, hundreds of sniper rifles, four small patrol boats, and grenade launchers to Manila.[542] It also offered a loan of $500 million for "other equipment" in 2016, but it is unclear what that equipment was and how much has actually been delivered.[543] And on a separate occasion, China pledged to assist the Philippines in countering terrorism, providing both military supplies and supplies for refugees, as well as to provide RMB 20 million in additional emergency relief.[544] One of the most visible differences from the Aquino administration was Duterte's willingness to partner with Chinese forces while trying to limit the scope and number of exercises conducted with the United States. For example, in 2018, Duterte granted PLA aircraft access to air bases in Davao, and the Philippine navy participated in a naval exercise with China—along with other ASEAN states—marking the first time such an exercise was held.[545] Not surprisingly, China reacted positively to these efforts. A Chinese Ministry of Defense spokesperson hailed China's first joint military exercise with ASEAN as a major contribution to cooperation and stability, noting that the exercise "will help enhance mutual understanding and trust between the two sides, deepen China-ASEAN maritime defense and security cooperation, and play a positive role in maintaining peace and stability in the SCS and building a China-ASEAN community with a shared future."[546]

---

[541] Ministry of Foreign Affairs of the People's Republic of China, "Xi Jinping Meets with President Duterte of the Philippines," April 25, 2019.

[542] Manuel Mogato, "China Gives Guns to Philippines to Show It's a Friend, Not a Foe," Reuters, October 5, 2017; and Manuel Mogato, "China Donates Four Small Boats and Grenade Launchers to Philippines," Reuters, July 29, 2018.

[543] Manuel Mogato, "China Offers $14 Million Arms Package to the Philippines: Manila's Defense Minister," Reuters, December 20, 2016.

[544] Wang Yi [王毅], "China Firmly Supports the Philippines in Pursuing an Independent Foreign Policy" ["中方坚定支持菲律宾奉行独立自主外交政策"], Ministry of Foreign Affairs of the People's Republic of China, July 25, 2017.

[545] Patricia Lourdes Viray, "Senate Minority Wants Probe into Chinese Planes in Davao, Chinese Shows on PTV," *Philstar Global*, July 9, 2018; and Priam Nepomuceno "PH Navy Contingent to Sail for ASEAN-China Maritime Drill on Oct. 17," Philippine News Agency, October 16, 2018.

[546] Ministry of National Defense of the People's Republic of China, "Maritime Joint Exercise Exerts Positive Energy for the China-ASEAN Community with a Shared Future" ["海上联演为中国-东盟命运共同体发挥正能量"], October 25, 2018.

Notably, however, Chinese activity around Philippines-claimed geographic features did not show any significant softening except for a slight reduction in activity around Scarborough Shoal during the early days of the Duterte administration. As Case 3 explores in detail, following an April 2012 incident and an ensuing standoff, CCG vessels blocked Philippine fishermen from operating around Scarborough Shoal, and fishermen frequently reported that these CCG vessels would intercept them or employ water cannons to drive them from the area.[547] Under Duterte, in contrast, it appeared that Chinese vessels occasionally tacitly permitted Philippine fishermen to operate in the area, with Duterte crediting warming bilateral ties with this positive development.[548] Despite this, Philippine fishermen continued to report harassment by CCG vessels, with Philippine media releasing a video of Chinese forces boarding Philippine vessels and seizing their catches, and many fishermen claim that they were unwilling to return to the contested waters due to fear of harassment.[549]

At the same time, Chinese forces appear to have become more assertive near other SCS features. In May 2018, a PLAN helicopter attempted to intercept a Philippine resupply mission to the beached *Sierra Madre* at Second Thomas Shoal.[550] A CCG vessel attempted a second intercept of a resupply mission in May 2019, this time succeeding in stopping the mission.[551] Chinese forces also stepped up their presence at Thitu Island. In 2018, likely in response to Philippine efforts to upgrade its facilities on Thitu, CCG and PAFMM vessels "swarmed" the island, with Philippine sources claiming that they identified 600 Chinese vessels in the area during the first quarter of 2019.[552] This trend continues to the present day, with the Philippines observing more than 200 presumed PAFMM vessels at Whitsun Reef in March 2021.[553]

Similarly, Beijing's rhetoric regarding its claims over Scarborough Shoal and the Spratly Islands has remained consistent. As Duterte prepared to take office in 2016, China's Ministry of Foreign Affairs International Law Institute stated, "China has indisputable sovereignty over the islands of the SCS and their adjacent waters. The core of the dispute between China and the Philippines in the SCS is due to the Philippines' illegal occupation of Chinese islands and reefs

[547] Manny Mogato, "Philippines Accuses China of Turning Water Cannon on Its Fishing Boats," *Reuters*, April 21, 2015; and "Philippines Says China 'Fired Water Cannon' on Filipino Fishermen," *BBC News*, February 24, 2014.

[548] Carmela Fonbuena, "Chinese Coast Guard Shoos Away PH Fishermen from Scarborough," *Rappler*, September 27, 2016; and Pia Ranada, "Filipino Fishermen Able to Access Scarborough Shoal—Palace," *Rappler*, October 28, 2016.

[549] Carmela Fonbuena, "Video Captures China Coast Guard Taking PH Fishermen's Catch," *Rappler*, June 8, 2018; and Carmela Fonbuena, "PH Military Encourages Fishermen to Return to Scarborough," *Rappler*, April 25, 2018.

[550] Paterno Esmaquel II, "China Chopper Harasses PH Rubber Boat in Ayungin Shoal—Lawmaker," *Rappler*, May 30, 2018.

[551] "China Coast Guard Blocked Resupply Mission to Ayungin Shoal—DND," *Philstar Global*, September 19, 2019.

[552] J. C. Gotinga, "2019 Year of Rough Seas for PH in the Face of Belligerent China," *Rappler*, December 10, 2019.

[553] Rene Acosta, "Persistent Chinese Maritime Militia Presence off Philippines Raises Concerns in Manila," *USNI News*, April 12, 2021.

in the Spratlys."[554] Similar language was used during Duterte's early time in office. For example, when journalists inquired about upcoming dialogues between China and the Philippines, Ministry of Foreign Affairs spokesperson Hua Chunying stated that China's sovereignty over the Spratly Islands was not up for debate, saying that "China has repeatedly stated that the Spratly Islands are Chinese territory. China's construction on its own territory is to improve the living and working conditions of its stationed personnel, better safeguard its own sovereignty, and at the same time enhance the civil functions and international public welfare service capabilities of relevant islands and reefs."[555] Although not part of the scope of this case study, this language continues to the present. For example, in May 2021, in response to Philippine statements regarding Chinese patrols around Scarborough Shoal, Ministry of Foreign Affairs spokesperson Wang Wenbin reiterated that Scarborough Shoal was Chinese territory and was effectively administered by Chinese law enforcement, saying "China urges the Philippines to honestly respect China's sovereignty and jurisdiction and stop taking actions that complicate the situation."[556]

Philippine Responses to PRC Actions

Manila has responded favorably to China's diplomatic and economic actions. The most notable example that demonstrates this is Duterte's efforts to hollow out an important agreement that allows the United States forces to have temporary access to the Philippines.

On April 28, 2014, the Aquino administration signed EDCA with Washington. It was designed to provide the United States with a rotational presence in the Philippines at five Philippine military bases.[557] EDCA, however, was challenged in court, as some government officials, militant groups, lawyers, and representatives of religious and academic communities questioned its legality, fearing that it would bring the return of a permanent presence of foreign troops to the Philippines.[558] The ensuing court battle took two years. In January 2016, while Aquino was still president, the Philippines' Supreme Court declared EDCA constitutional.

---

[554] Ministry of Foreign Affairs of the People's Republic of China, "The Decision of the Arbitration Tribunal in the South China Sea Arbitration Case Raised by the Philippines Has No Legal Validity" ["菲律宾所提南海仲裁案仲裁庭的裁决没有法律效力"], June 10, 2016.

[555] Ministry of Foreign Affairs of the People's Republic of China, "Foreign Ministry Spokesperson Hua Chunying's Regular Press Conference on March 28, 2017" ["2017年3月28日外交部发言人华春莹主持例行记者会"], March 28, 2017.

[556] Wang Wenbin, "Foreign Ministry Spokesperson Wang Wenbin's Remarks on China-Related Remarks by High-Level Philippine Figures" ["外交部发言人汪文斌就菲律宾高层涉华言论答记者问"], Ministry of Foreign Affairs of the People's Republic of China, May 4, 2021.

[557] United States of America and the Philippines, Agreement Between the Government of the United States of America and the Government of the Republic of the Philippines on Enhanced Defense Cooperation, Quezon City, Philippines, April 28, 2014, pp. 1–2.

[558] Julliane Love De Jesus, "Protest Greets Start of Balikatan War Games," *Inquirer.net*, May 5, 2014; and Eleanor Albert, "The U.S.-Philippines Defense Alliance," Council on Foreign Relations, October 21, 2016.

Duterte showed early on that he was not a strong proponent of EDCA but did not try to change it during the early part of his administration. After years of deteriorating alliance ties, however, in February 2020 Duterte declared that he would end the Visiting Forces Agreement (VFA) with the United States. The VFA, which was signed on February 10, 1998, is a critical pillar of EDCA because it serves as a legal agreement to allow U.S. troops to enter and operate in the Philippines for any activity, including exercises or humanitarian assistance and disaster relief.[559] Although Duterte eventually recanted, his threat would have made operationalizing EDCA difficult because the VFA is needed for U.S. forces to be in the Philippines.

Duterte's changing positions with the United States on EDCA were mirrored in the hardening of his positions against China as the latter continued to push sovereignty claims to the detriment of Manila. Early on in his term, Duterte signaled that he did not intend to contest Chinse actions in the SCS. For example, despite the arbitration court victory, when Duterte made his first official visit to China in October 2016, he stated that territorial disputes would not only "take a back seat" to other issues but also that he would not raise the issue of the SCS unless his Chinese counterparts did so first.[560] As China continued to push its claims over those of the Philippines, however, Manila has gradually adopted a firmer stance. For example, in May 2018, Foreign Minister Cayetano stated that President Duterte was willing to go to war if China attempted to unilaterally develop the resources of the SCS.[561] And in 2019 the Duterte administration began upgrading facilities on Thitu Island, a Philippine-occupied feature that sits across from Chinese-controlled Subi Reef, signaling its intent to reinforce Philippines' claims.[562] After months of deterioration in the bilateral relationship, in 2021 Duterte went so far as to warn regarding the possibility of the Philippines "staking a claim" to energy resources in the SCS using its military that "if we go there to assert our jurisdiction, it will be bloody."[563]

Explanations for Chinese Actions

The record suggests that China responded less aggressively to the Philippines in diplomatic and economic terms when the Duterte administration adopted more conciliatory policies but that this was not accompanied by softening of its military activity or positions on the SCS. There are several possible explanations that may help us understanding why.

---

[559] United States of America and the Philippines, Agreement Between the Government of the Republic of the Philippines and the Government of the United States of America Regarding the Treatment of United States Armed Forces Visiting the Philippines, Manila, Philippines, February 10, 1998.

[560] Ben Blanchard, "Duterte Aligns Philippines with China, Says U.S. Has Lost," Reuters, October 20, 2016.

[561] Ben Westcott, "Duterte Will 'Go to War' over South China Sea Resources, Minister Says," *CNN*, May 29, 2018.

[562] Lucio Blanco Pitlo III, "Philippines Bolsters Posture in South China Sea After Navy Ship Docks at New Spratly Islands Port," *South China Morning Post*, May 27, 2020.

[563] "'It Will Be Bloody': Philippines' Duterte Threatens to 'Stake a Claim' over South China Sea Energy Resources Using Military Ships," *South China Morning Post*, April 20, 2021.

First, China likely responded less aggressively in the wake of the Philippines' changed approach in part to exploit new frictions in the U.S.-Philippine alliance. Seeing the United States' alliances as intended to contain its peaceful rise, China wants to drive a wedge in the U.S.-Philippine alliance to promote alternative regional security frameworks and pull Manila closer to China's strategic orbit.[564]

A second possibility is that China sought to take advantage of Philippine accommodation to rapidly militarize its artificial land features while expanding its deployment of maritime militia forces and coast guard vessels in the SCS to create a new "normal."[565] According to this line of thinking, Beijing saw in Duterte's policies a period of strategic opportunity that could be prolonged through political and economic measures.

A final explanation is that Beijing wanted above all else to downplay the Permanent Court of Arbitration's ruling in order to reduce international criticism of its SCS policy and to normalize its territorial and maritime expansionism.[566] By playing nice with Manila and helping entice it to not press the ruling, Beijing "can easily ignore threats from the United States, the world court or power blocs such as the G7" that try to pressure China into abiding by the court ruling.[567] Should bilateral China-Philippines ties worsen, Manila could reenergize external support for the ruling and thus inflict reputational damage on China.

These explanations, however, do not fully capture the dynamic of Beijing's softening response in the diplomatic and economic domains and continued provocations in the military domain. While any one of these explanations, or a combination of all three, are possible, the likeliest explanation for Beijing's dual approach is rooted in its belief in its indisputable sovereignty over the SCS. As noted above, China sees itself as having sovereignty over much of the SCS and considers its actions to be within the scope of China's sovereignty.[568] As expressed in its position on the 2016 arbitration ruling, Chinese officials maintain that "China has always claimed and enjoyed territorial sovereignty over the entire Zhongsha Islands including Huangyan

[564] Adam P. Liff, "China and the U.S. Alliance System," *China Quarterly*, Vol. 233, March 2018, pp. 137–165; Renato Cruz de Castro, "The U.S.-Philippine Alliance: An Evolving Hedge Against an Emerging China Challenge," *Contemporary Southeast Asia*, Vol. 31, No. 3, December 2009; and Derek Grossman, "China Refuses to Quit on the Philippines," *The Diplomat*, July 22, 2020.

[565] Richard Javad Heydarian, "China Exploits U.S.-Philippine Strategic Weakness," *Asia Times*, March 24, 2021.

[566] Benjamin Herscovitch, "A Balanced Threat Assessment of China's South China Sea Policy," Cato Institute, August 28, 2017.

[567] Ralph Jennings, "China Needs Its Friend the Philippines More Than the Philippines Needs China," *Forbes*, April 20, 2017.

[568] Ministry of Foreign Affairs of the People's Republic of China, "Foreign Ministry Spokesperson Hua Chunying's Regular Press Conference on March 28, 2017" ["2017年3月28日外交部发言人华春莹主持例行记者会"], March 28, 2017.

Island and the entire Spratly Islands including Mischief Reef and eight other islands."[569] This explains Beijing's simultaneous intransigence regarding territorial issues but flexibility toward regional governments that do not challenge the former. China vigorously defends its "core interests," with force if necessary, but is pragmatic and strategically opportunistic elsewhere.

Chinese rigidity on sovereignty issues manifested in forceful declarations of inviolable rights and even more forceful evictions of Filipino fishermen, but willingness to offer economic and diplomatic benefits to rival claimants aligns with this thinking. It suggests that Beijing has been encouraged by the change of tone from Manila, as Duterte's decision to not press the arbitration court's ruling signaled a de facto endorsement of China's claims, or at least a reduction in challenges to one of China's core interests. This, in turn, provided Beijing a "window of opportunity" to expand its strategic space and reputation through largess while maintaining its efforts on territorial issues.[570] Beijing may hope that diplomatic engagement in other areas may help reduce external involvement in its SCS disputes or even lead to international acknowledgment of Beijing's claims.[571] Beijing may also think that it may be able to entice Manila to concede its own counterclaims, or at least show greater deference for Chinese interests, in exchange for Chinese military and economic benefits.

Conclusion

Overall, our analysis of PRC reactions to the behavior of the Philippines under Duterte provides strong support for the hypothesis that China reacts less aggressively when it believes that there may be an opportunity to expand its regional influence, which suggests that China will react *more* aggressively when it believes that its regional influence is at risk. Given that China was more forthcoming with aid, military assistance, and laudatory statements praising Manila's policies, there is evidence to support this argument. However, there was no real softening in China's military actions in the SCS. This suggests that China is willing to be less aggressive in the political and economic domains if it thinks that doing so will help advance its interests but is much less willing to sacrifice its hard power or relax its positions regarding what it sees as core national interests, even at the expense of its diplomatic efforts. China, in other words, is reluctant to budge on territorial issues, even as it responds pragmatically and opportunistically to perceived shifts in its regional influence.

---

[569] Ministry of Foreign Affairs of the People's Republic of China, "The Decision of the Arbitration Tribunal in the South China Sea Arbitration Case Raised by the Philippines Has No Legal Validity" ["菲律宾所提南海仲裁案仲裁庭的裁决没有法律效力"], June 10, 2016.

[570] Zhonglin Li, "The Strategic Posture of China in the South China Sea and Countermeasures" ["中国对南海战略态势的塑造及启示"], *Contemporary International Relations* [现代国际关系], No. 2, 2017, p. 29.

[571] "China Plays Nice Because It Can," *Real Clear Defense*, November 27, 2016.

Case 9: China's Reaction to Developments in the Quadrilateral Security Dialogue

Case 9 focuses on the hypothesis that activities that increase China's perceptions of U.S., allied, and partner hostile intent generate more-aggressive Chinese responses. In recent years, steps toward increased security cooperation undertaken by the United States, India, Japan, and Australia within the framework of the Quad have provoked stern diplomatic protests from China. These reactions stem from Chinese perceptions of an increasingly hostile United States, as well as concerns over the threat posed to China by the geographic position of the Quad member countries, their potential combined military power, and their attendant potential capacity to counter Chinese influence across the Indo-Pacific region. Tensions over the Quad's activities have coincided with an intensification of disputes between Beijing and each of the Quad member states, which likely fuels Chinese threat perceptions regarding the Quad even as it pushes the Quad to cooperate more deeply. The overlapping nature of disputes among the countries complicates efforts to clearly link Chinese reactions to specific aspects or actions of the Quad grouping. Regardless, the case provides significant support for the hypothesis, as there is clear evidence that China's reaction to the Quad's activities is reinforced and aggravated by its reaction to disputes with individual Quad members, which in turn are informed by China's perceptions of the Quad's increasingly hostile intent.

The Growth of the Quad

The Quad, originally founded as a coordinating mechanism for responding to the 2004 Indian Ocean tsunami, advanced to hold a series of multilateral meetings in 2007–2008 and then languished for years with little political or strategic import, due in part to Chinese economic and diplomatic pressure on members.[572] Following increases in tension in the region, as well as increasingly aggressive PRC behavior and pressure tactics against India and Australia in particular, the Quad was "refounded" in 2017.[573] In 2019, senior leaders from all four countries clarified that the revived Quad's purpose was to support "rules-based order in the region that promotes stability, growth, and economic prosperity." They discussed ways to advance cooperation on "counter-terrorism, cyber, development finance, maritime security, humanitarian

---

[572] Richard Rossow and Sarah Watson, "China Creates a Second Chance for the 'Quad,'" Asia Maritime Transparency Initiative, Center for Strategic and International Studies, March 14, 2016; and Evan A. Feigenbaum and James Schwemlein, "How Biden Can Make the Quad Endure," Carnegie Endowment for International Peace, March 11, 2021.

[573] Tanvi Madan, "The Rise, Fall, and Rebirth of the 'Quad,'" *War on the Rocks*, November 16, 2017; and Jeff M. Smith, "Democracy's Squad: India's Change of Heart and the Future of the Quad," *War on the Rocks*, August 13, 2020.

assistance, and disaster response."[574] Since that time, the Quad has grown further in the regularity and importance of its meetings and has expanded into other areas of cooperation. In November 2020, the Quad nations held their first quadrilateral military exercises, the Malabar exercises in the Indian Ocean.[575] In March 2021, they announced a collective plan to produce and distribute large numbers of COVID-19 vaccines throughout Southeast Asia.[576] These developments led many analysts to suggest that the Quad may be emerging as a key diplomatic and strategic force within the Indo-Pacific region and a means of coordinating and mobilizing U.S. allies and partners in a de facto coalition against growing Chinese influence and power.[577]

China's Reactions

China's approach to opposing the Quad builds on its broader efforts to shape Asia's political economy. Since Xi Jinping took power in particular, Beijing has stepped up the use of both incentives to coax countries into cooperating with Beijing and disincentives to raise the cost of opposing Beijing.[578] In the case of the Quad, Beijing has highlighted the potential economic benefits that Quad members gain from cooperating with China to moderate their perceived anti-China activities while signaling the diplomatic and possible economic costs that Quad members could pay if they antagonize Beijing through collaborative activities that appear aimed at stifling China's rise. It has also adopted a range of political and military responses that appear tied directly to the growth of the Quad itself, rather than the actions of its individual member states.

Political Responses

China has denounced the revived Quad with vigorous protests and criticisms in official statements and media commentary, which frequently lambaste the cooperation of Quad member states. Vice Foreign Minister Luo Zhaohui, for example, denounced the Quad in September 2020 as a "mini-NATO" and an "anti-China front line." He warned that "if situation further worsens,

---

[574] U.S. Department of State, "Media Note: U.S.-Australia-India-Japan Consultations ('The Quad')," November 4, 2019.

[575] Manoj Rawat, "Quad 2.0 Is Off to a Good Start—It Must Keep Going," *The Diplomat*, November 23, 2020. For the potential limits on the development of the collective defense aspects of the Quad, see Salvatore Babones, "The Quad's Malabar Exercises Point the Way to an Asian NATO," *Foreign Policy*, November 25, 2020.

[576] David Brunnstrom, Michael Martina, and Jeff Mason, "U.S., India, Japan and Australia Counter China with Billion-Dose Vaccine Pact," Reuters, March 12, 2021; and Teesta Prakash, "The Quad Gives a Boost to India's Vaccine Diplomacy," *The Interpreter*, March 16, 2021.

[577] Michelle Ye Hee Lee and Joanna Slater, "Meeting of Leaders Signals the 'Quad' Grouping Will Become Central Part of the U.S. Strategy in Asia," *Washington Post*, March 13, 2021; Michael J. Green, "Quad Summit's Vaccine Deal Is Biden's Bold First Move in Asia," *Foreign Policy*, March 12, 2021; and Evan A. Feigenbaum and James Schwemlein, "How Biden Can Make the Quad Endure," Carnegie Endowment for International Peace, March 11, 2021.

[578] Yang Jiemian, "China's New Diplomacy Under the Xi Jinping Administration," *China Quarterly of International Strategic Studies*, Vol. 1, No. 1, April 2015.

no country in the region could be spared from its negative impact."[579] One month later, Foreign Minister Wang Yi stated that the Quad "underpinned" the U.S. Free and Open Indo-Pacific Strategy and slammed it as a "so-called Indo-Pacific new NATO." He accused the strategy of seeking to "trump an old fashioned Cold War mentality" and "stoke geopolitical competition" in a bid to "maintain the dominance and hegemonic system" of the United States.[580]

Commentary in the Chinese press has harshly criticized the Quad, albeit with different lines of arguments. Some mocked the Quad, suggesting that the collaboration would bear little fruit, owing to the lack of unity on policies toward China and the inability of the United States to provide a compelling alternative to the economic gains offered by China. For example, a commentary in the party-owned *Global Times* newspaper pointed out that in spite of their cooperation to date, each Quad member had to consider its own economic interests with China, and that this would continue to impede multilateral anti-China efforts. One scholar quoted in the article ridiculed the United States because it "could not offer much to its allies" compared with the economic benefits that Quad members might gain from China.[581] Other media sources took the Quad more seriously, arguing that it could provoke instability in Asia. Responding to an exercise held in late 2020, a commentary in official news agency Xinhua stated that such exercises would "only create tension and confrontation." It warned that the exercise showed that the Quad members appeared to be "mulling military and security cooperation for self-serving reasons." The commentary stated that efforts by Quad members to "stir up rivalry" would "definitely not be accepted" by China and other "major countries in the world."[582]

In addition to criticizing the Quad as a group, tensions remain between China and each of the Quad member states on separate issues. China and the United States, for example, maintain disputes over a range of issues, including trade, technology, Taiwan, and the SCS; China and India's feud over contested border regions boiled over into a bloody brawl; China and Australia have feuded over Chinese influence operations and diplomatic intimidation; and China and Japan maintain a tense standoff in the ECS and toward other issues.[583] In Chinese statements and press,

---

[579] Ministry of Foreign Affairs of the People's Republic of China, "Jointly Safeguarding Peace, Stability and Development in the South China Sea with Dialogue, Consultation and Win-Win Cooperation," September 2, 2020.

[580] "U.S. Indo-Pacific Strategy Undermines Peace, Development Prospect in East Asia: Wang Yi," Xinhua, October 13, 2020.

[581] Zhang Yanping [张燕萍], "Can the U.S., Japan, India and Australia Quad Group Contain China? Expert: There Is Not Much the United States Can Give to Its Allies" ["美日印澳'四方安全对话'牵制中国？专家：美国能给盟国的已经不多了"], *Global Times* [环球时报], February 19, 2021.

[582] "Commentary: Forming Clique and Flexing Muscles Only to Shake Regional Peace, Stability," Xinhua, October 23, 2020.

[583] Barbara Plett Usher, "Why U.S.-China Relations Are at Their Lowest Point in Decades," *BBC News*, July 24, 2020; "Pressure Grows for More Vocal Stance over Chinese Incursions Near Senkakus," *Japan Times*, February 28, 2021; John Ruwitch, "China-Australia Relations Are Quickly Worsening. How Did They Get Bad?" *NPR*,

criticisms of individual country members sometimes also include complaints about anti-China multilateral activity, most likely a reference to the Quad. For example, a March 2021 commentary in the *Global Times* denounced Australia for supporting U.S. restrictions on Huawei and "fabricating groundless conspiracy theory [sic] to frame China as threatening Australia's national security by influencing Australia's politics." It blamed Canberra's "anti-China" behavior on its willingness to become a "pathetic pawn in Washington's power game."[584] Similar messages appear in commentaries about India and Japan as well.[585]

Concern about the Quad could also add impetus to ongoing efforts to bolster ties with states that have antagonistic relationships with Quad members, although this is difficult to prove. China has bolstered ties with countries that have antagonistic relations with the United States, such as Russia and Iran; with countries that frequently oppose India, such as Pakistan; and with those that mistrust Japan, such as the Koreas.[586] China has compelling incentives beyond concerns about the Quad for building such relationships, but the deepening tension over the grouping could add another incentive for Beijing to pursue such ties.

Economic Responses

China has refrained from economic retaliation against the Quad as a grouping, although Beijing has employed economic coercion against individual member countries over separate issues. Chinese commentators warned that Beijing could retaliate economically against Quad countries if the cooperation continued. One commentary in the *Global Times* claimed that China's economic pressure against Australia was an example of the types of instruments that could be employed.[587] Despite the threats by commentators, however, as of early 2021 China had not carried out economic sanctions linked to the developments associated with the Quad. However, complicating the situation is the fact that China has carried out economic coercion against at least one member of the Quad, Australia, since the reinvigoration of the Quad in 2017.[588] While the sanctions appear to have been driven principally by Australia's call for Chinese transparency regarding the COVID-19 pandemic's origins, the possibility that Beijing's irritation over Canberra's embrace of the Quad may have played a factor cannot be discounted.

December 4, 2020; and Rafiq Dossani, "Why Tensions Between China and India Won't Boil Over," *The National Interest*, February 2, 2021.

[584] Chen Hong, "Campbell's Remarks Push Australia Further to the Anti-China Frontline," *Global Times*, March 17, 2021.

[585] Lin Minwang, "What Can India Offer to Turn the US into a 'Pawn'?" *Global Times*, December 24, 2020; and Li Qingqing, "Being US Pawn on SCS Issue Doesn't Serve Japan's Interests," *Global Times*, October 20, 2020.

[586] Jamsheed K. Choksy and Carol E. B. Choksy, "China and Russia Have Iran's Back," *Foreign Affairs*, November 17, 2020; and M. K. Bhadrakumar, "China to Strengthen Military Coordination with Russia," *Asia Times*, December 27, 2020.

[587] Wang Qi, "China Can Retaliate Economically If Red Line Crossed: Experts," *Global Times*, February 18, 2021.

[588] Daniel Hurst, "Australia at Mercy of 'Coercive Trade Warfare' as China and U.S. Continue Rivalry," *The Guardian*, February 15, 2021.

China also has maintained feuds over an array of trade issues with the United States over the same time period, although most of these disputes were initiated by Washington.

China's restraint in the use of economic punishments to directly counter to the Quad may lie in its awareness that such a response is unlikely to break up the group. Moreover, as the much of the public commentary cited above suggests, Beijing likely judges that its strongest counter to an anti-China coalition by Quad members lies in using the promise of economic benefits to entice the Quad members into maintaining cooperative ties with Beijing.[589] The lure of economic benefits may not persuade countries to abandon the Quad, but it could incentivize them to moderate their support for actions against a major economic benefactor. By contrast, Beijing has not hesitated to employ economic coercion in specific bilateral disputes, although experts debate the effectiveness of such measures. For example, Beijing employed economic coercion against Japan in its disputes over the Senkaku Islands in 2010 and has similarly retaliated economically against Australia in disputes over a dispute about China's handling of the COVID-19 response and other issues. In neither case did the target country substantially change the relevant policies.[590]

Military Responses

The PLA recently carried out major exercises that some Chinese press described as a direct response to Quad-related diplomatic activity. In March 2021, the PLAN held major combat-oriented exercises in the North, East, and South China Seas. An article in the *Global Times* reported that sailors participating in the SCS exercise paid respects to "heroes who emerged victorious" in one of China's most recent clashes involving Vietnam in 1988.[591] Chinese media has not been observed to have made similar claims about a PLA response to other Quad activities, such as the Malabar exercises.

Chinese resentment over stronger cooperation related to the Quad has coincided with robust military and paramilitary responses to specific flashpoints involving each of the participants. Chinese naval and paramilitary forces have maintained steady pressure against Japan's Coast Guard near the Senkaku Islands, addressed in more detail in Case 4; in June 2020, as Case 13 explores, Chinese and Indian troops clashed in the first violent confrontation in decades at the cost of at least 20 Indian and four Chinese troops; and in 2021, Chinese authorities clarified conditions under which Chinese forces would be authorized to open fire on other ships in disputed waters.[592] In the SCS, PLA forces continue to carry out frequent military exercises,

---

[589] "Quad Members Fight for Interests with Each Other: Global Times Editorial," *Global Times*, October 20, 2020.

[590] Gloria Xiong, "Beijing Increasingly Relies on Economic Coercion to Reach Its Diplomatic Goals," *Washington Post*, July 23, 2020.

[591] Liu Xuanzun, "China Holds Naval Drills in Three Maritime Areas amid US Military Threats," *Global Times*, March 15, 2021.

[592] Saibal Dasgupta, "China's Move to Empower Coast Guard Stirs Tensions," *Voice of America*, February 11, 2021.

which officials have linked, in part, to U.S. patrols in the region.[593] The consistency of Chinese military activities suggests that Beijing is signaling that it will not be intimidated by Quad members, although they are not necessarily direct responses to the collective Quad's activities.

More indirectly, China has maintained a robust military buildup to defend itself from a variety of capable adversaries, including those of the Quad members.[594] Chinese official documents, such as the 2019 defense white paper, discuss disputes with the United States, India, and Japan in particular when reviewing security threats.[595] China has expanded its arsenal of ballistic missiles, PLAN submarines and surface ships, and combat aircraft, as well as an Eastern Theater Command, in large part to prepare for contingencies involving Japan. China continues to improve its fortifications and force posture on the Indian border and has stepped up naval patrols along the Indian Ocean. Regarding the United States, China continues to develop counterintervention capabilities, including anti-ship ballistic missiles, hypersonic missiles, advanced warplanes and naval ships, and its nuclear inventory. Many of the longer-range missile systems could be employed against targets in Australia as well.[596] Relatedly, under Xi Jinping's leadership, China has stepped up its emphasis on readiness for combat operations. Although previous Chinese leaders have routinely tasked the PLA to improve combat preparations, Xi's calls have had traction to a range of modernization reforms aimed at enhancing the combat effectiveness of the PLA and sustaining an anticorruption drive.[597]

Explanations for Chinese Reactions

China regarded recent developments related to the Quad as threatening for two principal reasons. First, the signs of closer military and diplomatic cooperation stir fears that the United States seeks to contain China and prevent it from achieving the CCP's goal of national revitalization.[598] Chinese official documents also routinely assert that the United States intends to

---

[593] Zachary Haver, "China Begins Month of Military Exercises in South China Sea," *Radio Free Asia*, March 1, 2021.

[594] Office of the Secretary of Defense, *Annual Report to Congress: Military and Security Developments Involving the People's Republic of China 2020*, Washington, D.C., 2020.

[595] State Council Information Office of the People's Republic of China, *China's National Defense in the New Era*, July 24, 2019.

[596] Office of the Secretary of Defense, *Annual Report to Congress: Military and Security Developments Involving the People's Republic of China 2020*, Washington, D.C., 2020.

[597] Liu Zhen, "Xi Jinping Orders China's Military to Be Ready for War 'at Any Second,'" *South China Morning Post*, January 5, 2021.

[598] Such fears are pervasive in Chinese commentaries. See, for example, Zhong Sheng [钟声], "Accumulating Damage to the Strategy to Contain China" ["对华遏制战略蓄患积害"], *People's Daily* [人民日报], August 31, 2020.

maintain its "hegemony," even if that means provoking instability in Asia.[599] Chinese analysts question the Quad members' unity but also recognize that the grouping's economic and military power could pose a serious challenge to China's ambitions.[600] The PLA is larger and, in some respects, of higher quality than the militaries of some Quad member countries, such as Australia and India, but collectively the Quad can muster significantly more hard power than China.[601]

A second, related, factor appears to be the perception that the United States harbors truly malign intentions toward China's security and interests. U.S. success in building a coalition of countries to oppose Chinese power merely serves as a confirmatory manifestation of U.S. hostility. Thus, Chinese apprehension over U.S. intentions arising from the Quad meetings overlaps with apprehension over other U.S. actions that Beijing perceives as malign. The rapid deterioration of U.S.-China relations under President Trump raised Chinese anxieties and fears of hostile U.S. intentions. In this context, the Trump administration's success in rebuilding the Quad confirmed Chinese perceptions of the grouping as a hostile "anti-China" one. Similarly, Chinese officials and commentary routinely criticized U.S. military activity in the SCS as particularly provocative. A typical commentary in the official English newspaper, *China Daily*, denounced the United States for being the "lead provocateur" in the SCS.[602] The combination of a perceived multilateral "containment" effort to stifle China's rise with perceptions of the hostile intent of the United States and other countries that Chinese commentators describe as being "manipulated" by Washington distinguishes China's reactions to the Quad from its more conventional disagreements with the Quad member states. Chinese officials have consistently expressed the view that disagreements and disputes between China and other countries are completely normal and acceptable, so long as they are properly handled. Stepped-up military cooperation and other forms of cooperation among Quad members in recent years signal to Beijing, however, that its feuds with individual countries have escalated into something more ominous—namely, the possible development of a hostile anti-China group of countries committed to undermining and preventing China's national rejuvenation.

The Quad's physical geography provides a third reason for Chinese anxiety. India sits astride a vital oceanic shipping lane and is unavoidably close to other BRI LOCs that, as Case 2 documents, China regards as vital to its development. Japan faces China's vulnerable and

---

[599] State Council Information Office of the People's Republic of China, *China's National Defense in the New Era*, July 24, 2019.

[600] Guo Xiaopeng [郭晓鹏], "Contain China? U.S. Wins over Japan, Australia and India at Planning Summit, but Attitudes Differ Among the Four Countries"
["牵制中国？美拉拢日澳印筹划首脑会，日媒：四国间态度存差异"], *Global Times* [环球时报], February 19, 2021.

[601] International Institute for Strategic Studies, *The Military Balance 2021*, London, February 25, 2021.

[602] Hamzah Rifaat Hussain, "Why the 'Quad Meeting' Should Not Translate into Inflamed Tensions," *China Daily*, October 6, 2020.

prosperous eastern coast. Australia and the United States are more distant but possess military capabilities that could threaten Chinese shipping in the Malacca Strait and elsewhere.

That several of Asia's most powerful nations participate in the Quad provides another reason for Chinese concern. For example, Vietnam, New Zealand, and South Korea joined a recent video conference of the leaders of the Quad countries.[603] Despite Beijing's efforts to bolster its influence across the region, reports indicate that other countries could be interested in cooperating with the Quad grouping. If the trend continued, Beijing could see its regional influence erode and decline, which could worsen its immediate security environment.

At the same time, economic interdependence provides some level of reassurance to Beijing that the Quad's cooperation against China has real limits. Chinese commentators point out that the Quad's members are not unified in their approach to China.[604] Moreover, China remains a top trading partner with each of them. Beijing has emphasized the importance of economic relations with Quad member states, which suggests that it views trade as a powerful restraint on anti-China cooperation, despite the persistence of disputes over a variety of trade issues.[605]

Conclusion

Chinese officials regard Quad members' enhanced cooperation as posing the potential threat of a hostile grouping determined to prevent China's rise. This overlaps with bilateral disputes between China and the Quad's constituent members, aggravating each side's perception of the other side's hostility. China therefore seems determined to demonstrate the limited value of Quad collaboration. It refuses to ease military and paramilitary pressure on any of the flashpoints involving member nations; Chinese forces continue to press their claims along the Indian border, SCS, and Senkaku Islands. While incidents such as the bloody brawl on the Indian border provoked outrage, in no case, other than perhaps U.S. support for Japan in its standoff over the Senkaku Islands, have other Quad members involved themselves. Concern about the combined strength of the Quad countries may also contribute to Beijing's willingness to maintain its robust military modernization effort despite its slowing economy.

This case therefore provides significant support for the hypothesis. China's strident reactions to the Quad's evolution signify the broader struggle to shape the future political economy of the Indo-Pacific. Its pursuit of a regional order defined by norms, values, and principles set by Beijing—manifested in its efforts to lead the regions' economic integration, such as the BRI, the

---

[603] Ralph Jennings, "Vietnam Gets Boost from Western Allies in Its Defense Against China," *Voice of America*, October 31, 2020.

[604] Guo Xiaopeng [郭晓鹏], "Contain China? U.S. Wins over Japan, Australia and India at Planning Summit, but Attitudes Differ Among the Four Countries"
["牵制中国？美拉拢日澳印筹划首脑会，日媒：四国间态度存差异"], *Global Times* [环球时报], February 19, 2021.

[605] "Quad Members Fight for Interests with Each Other: Global Times Editorial," *Global Times*, October 20, 2020.

Asian Infrastructure Investment Bank, and the Shanghai Cooperation Organization—clashes with U.S. support for the established order. A significant and perhaps intractable struggle for influence lies at the core of this dispute.[606] Tensions between China and the Quad member states have intensified in recent years as Beijing has stepped up efforts to realize its vision and prevent the United States from doing the same. China's perceptions of the Quad's increasingly hostile intent feed its bilateral disputes with Quad members and encourage more-aggressive Chinese responses to Quad activities. How regional countries and the Quad grouping itself moderate Beijing and Washington's incompatible visions for the future of the Indo-Pacific region is therefore likely to remain a key factor in shaping China's responses to future Quad's activities.

---

[606] "Biden Should Revamp Asia-Pacific Path, Ditch Indo-Pacific Idea," *Global Times*, November 25, 2020; and "U.S. and China Trade Angry Words at High-Level Alaska Talks," *BBC News*, March 19, 2021.

Case 10: Cross-Strait Chinese Aggression, 2018–2020

Case 10 tests the hypothesis that Chinese perceptions of threats to regime legitimacy make it more likely to respond to U.S. and allied and partner activities aggressively. This case does so by examining a particularly dynamic and tense period in modern cross-strait relations: the second half of the Trump administration. From about 2018 to 2020, Beijing perceived the United States as increasingly belligerent and its intentions as increasingly hostile to China's interests. Although Chinese views of Taiwanese President Tsai Ing-wen and her DPP have been consistently negative, its fear of the DPP's ability to move Taiwan toward greater independence likely increased after her decisive and hard-fought victory in the island's 2020 election. By reducing the likelihood of unification between the mainland and Taiwan, this threatened a key pillar of the CCP's claim to political legitimacy. Perceiving a looming political threat emanating from both Taipei and Washington, Beijing responded to U.S. and Taiwanese actions aggressively, providing strong support for the hypothesis.

Increasing American Support for Taiwan in 2019 and 2020

Congress paved the way for a sharp uptick in American support for Taipei by passing the Taiwan Travel Act in 2018, a law that enabled a flurry of official visitors from Washington to Taipei over the following years.[607] In 2019, Congress passed the TAIPEI Act to counter Beijing's efforts to induce those states that still recognize Taipei as the seat of China's legitimate government to instead recognize Beijing.[608] In 2020, the United States launched an unprecedented series of high-level visits to Taiwan. U.S. Health Secretary Alex Azar made an official trip to Taipei in August 2020, the most senior sitting U.S. official to visit the island since the United States broke off formal relations in 1979.[609] His visit was followed soon after by another official visit from U.S. Undersecretary of State Keith Krach to discuss strengthening economic ties between the island and the United States.[610] Early in 2021, U.S. Ambassador to the United Nations Kelly Craft also paid an official visit to the island.[611]

Perhaps even more infuriating to Beijing, in 2019 and 2020 the United States significantly increased the quantity and quality of arms it sold to Taipei. Arms sales in 2019 totaled more than $10 billion, and those in 2020 totaled more than $5 billion, significantly higher than in 2017 or

---

[607] U.S. House of Representatives, Taiwan Travel Act, H.R. 535, 115th Congress, March 16, 2018.

[608] U.S. Senate, Taiwan Allies International Protection and Enhancement Initiative (TAIPEI) Act of 2019, S. 1678, 116th Congress, March 26, 2020.

[609] Johnson Lai, "Azar Visit to Taiwan Is Fresh Thorn in Prickly U.S.-China Ties," Associated Press, August 10, 2020.

[610] Ben Blanchard, "Factbox: Recent Taiwan Visits by Top U.S. Officials," Reuters, January 7, 2021.

[611] Preeti Jha, "Kelly Craft: U.S. Envoy's 'Last-Minute' Taiwan Visit Angers China," BBC News, January 12, 2021.

2018.[612] In addition to selling an increased volume of military supplies, Trump approved the sale of large weapons platforms that past presidents had refused to sell the island for fear of angering Beijing, including new F-16 fighters.[613] These sales are part of an explicit strategy to create a "fortress Taiwan" that the PLA cannot easily invade, a galling prospect given the fact that Beijing considers the threat of attack to be one of its primary tools in deterring the activity of "independence activists" on the island.[614]

Finally, in 2019 and 2020, the United States significantly increased the frequency of its naval patrols around Taiwan. American warships transited the Taiwan Strait just five times in 2017 and three times in 2018 but nine times in 2019 and 13 times in 2020.[615] Most of these transits were by single destroyers, though they occasionally involved more ships.[616] Case 14 explores Chinese reactions to U.S. FONOPs in 2020 in more detail.

These U.S. actions took place in the context of the heightened cross-strait tensions that followed the electoral victories of Tsai Ing-wen and the DPP in 2016 and 2020. Although Tsai's willingness (or lack thereof) to declare formal independence is debatable, she and her party are often seen in Beijing as "independence activists" working to bring about a permanent separation of Taiwan from the mainland.[617] It should also be noted that after its election in 2016, the DPP's electoral prospects dimmed considerably in 2018 and mid-2019, as the more pro-China Kuomintang Party made significant gains in the 2018 local elections.[618]

---

[612] Ralph Jennings, "U.S. Speeds Arms Sales for Taiwan as Island Revamps China Strategy," *Voice of America*, November 6, 2020; and Ben Blanchard, "Timeline: U.S. Arms Sales to Taiwan in 2020 Total $5 Billion amid China Tensions," Reuters, December 7, 2020.

[613] Ryan Browne and Kevin Liptak, "Trump Admin Gives Green Light for Major Arms Sale to Taiwan," *CNN*, August 16, 2019.

[614] Mike Stone and Patricia Zengerle, "Exclusive: U.S. Pushes Arms Sales Surge to Taiwan, Needling China—Sources," Reuters, September 16, 2020; Liu Xuanzun, "PLA Prepared as US, Secessionists Provoke," *Global Times*, April 8, 2021; and "Attempts to Use Taiwan to Control China or Use Weapons to Prevent Unification Will Fail in the End" ["'以台制华'和'以武拒统'注定难逃失败下场"], *Qiushi* [求是], July 11, 2019.

[615] Lolita C. Baldor, "Sharp Jump in U.S. Navy Transits to Counter China Under Trump," Associated Press, March 15, 2021; and Caitlin Doornbos, "Navy Ties Record with Its 12th Transit Through the Taiwan Strait This Year," *Stars and Stripes*, December 19, 2020.

[616] Caitlin Doornbos, "U.S. Navy Ends 2020 with Another Taiwan Strait Transit," *Stars and Stripes*, December 31, 2020.

[617] "National People's Congress Foreign Affairs Office Issues Statement on the Passage of the '2019 Taipei Act'" ["全国人大外事委员会就美国所谓'2019年台北法案'签署成法发表声明"], *Qiushi* [求是], March 28, 2020; and "PLA Conducts Live Fire Exercises in Taiwan Strait While 2 H-6K Bombers Circle Taiwan" ["解放军台海实弹射击 同时2架轰6K轰炸机绕台飞行"], *Haiwai Net* [海外网], April 19, 2018.

[618] Kharis Templeman, *Taiwan's January 2020 Elections: Prospects and Implications for China and the United States*, Washington, D.C.: Brookings Institution, December 2019, pp. 8–15.

Chinese Reactions

China has reacted to these increased expressions of support in a variety of ways. Any American action in support of Taipei is almost always met with a deluge of condemnation in Chinese official media, and the volume of verbal vitriol seems to have increased somewhat in 2019.[619] In addition to these condemnations, Chinese officials have called on the U.S. government not to implement pro-Taiwan legislation such as the 2019 TAIPEI Act.[620] In 2019 and 2020, the Chinese government also threatened and then levied sanctions on American companies involved in arms sales to Taiwan for the first time.[621] High-level official visits elicited condemnation and occasional military exercises—during the visit of Undersecretary of State Keith in 2020, for example, Chinese warplanes crossed the median line of the Taiwan Strait 40 times in an apparent show of defiance.[622]

China has also significantly increased the frequency and scale of other PLA operations around Taiwan, especially since late 2020. These operations are explicitly meant to convince the island's leaders that the PLA will defeat any attempt at achieving independence and that foreign forces cannot protect them.[623] In 2020, PLA warplanes conducted more flights into Taiwan's ADIZ than at any time since 1996, and by late 2020, such incursions had become an almost daily occurrence.[624] Most of these flights only involved surveillance aircraft, but some consisted of a dozen or more warplanes, including fighters, bombers, and airborne early warning systems.[625] More troubling still, these flights have sometimes been conducted in conjunction with PLAN

---

[619] Jun Sheng [钧声], "Strongly Oppose American Arms Sales to Taiwan" ["坚决反对美对台军售"], *Qiushi* [求是], July 12, 2019. Statements on volume are based on a Baidu search for "site: qstheory.cn 美国台湾" in March 2021, which indicated that the volume of articles in *Qiushi*, the official bimonthly of the CCP Central Committee, mentioning Taiwan and the United States (which were mostly condemnations of American and Taiwanese actions) increased significantly in 2019 relative to 2018 and 2020. A Baidu search for "site: 81.cn 美国 台湾" conducted on March 29, 2021, found similar results in Chinese military publications, although the size of the increase in 2019 relative to 2018 and 2020 was much smaller.

[620] "National People's Congress Foreign Affairs Office Issues Statement on the Passage of the '2019 Taipei Act'" ["全国人大外事委员会就美国所谓'2019 年台北法案'签署成法发表声明"], *Qiushi* [求是], March 28, 2020.

[621] David Brunnstrom, Mike Stone, and Krisztina Than, "China to Impose Sanctions on U.S. Firms That Sell Arms to Taiwan," Reuters, July 12, 2019; and Yew Lun Tian, Gabriel Crossley, and Stella Qiu, "China to Impose Sanctions on U.S. Firms over Taiwan Arms Sales," Reuters, October 26, 2020.

[622] John Xie, "China Is Increasing Taiwan Airspace Incursions," *Voice of America*, January 6, 2021.

[623] Liu Xuanzun, "PLA Prepared as US, Secessionists Provoke," *Global Times*, April 8, 2021; and Jun Sheng [钧声], "Strongly Oppose American Arms Sales to Taiwan" ["坚决反对美对台军售"], *Qiushi* [求是], July 12, 2019.

[624] John Xie, "China Is Increasing Taiwan Airspace Incursions," *Voice of America*, January 6, 2021; Ben Blanchard, "Taiwan Reports Large Incursion by Chinese Air Force," Reuters, January 23, 2021; and "Chinese Incursions Highest Since 1996," *Taipei Times*, January 4, 2021.

[625] Liu Xuanzun, "PLA Carrier, Warplanes Surround Taiwan in Drills, in Show of Capability to Cut Off Foreign Intervention," *Global Times*, April 6, 2021; and Ben Blanchard, "Taiwan Reports Large Incursion by Chinese Air Force," Reuters, January 23, 2021.

carrier operations on the opposite side of the island, demonstrating the PLA's ability to effectively surround Taiwan.[626]

Beijing has also engaged in a wide variety of coercive political and economic actions against Taiwan since Tsai's first election in 2016. These have included restrictions on the number of mainland tourists to Taiwan in 2016, which were strengthened in 2019; sanctions against Taiwanese pineapples in early 2021;[627] the previously noted diplomatic effort to convince countries that still recognize Taiwan diplomatically to switch their recognition to China (both countries claim to be the sole legitimate government of China, and Beijing refuses to establish relations with any country that maintains diplomatic relations with Taipei);[628] and, perhaps most concerningly, a concerted subversion campaign to aid the DPP's rivals in domestic elections.[629]

Explanations for Chinese Reactions

Although there are many possible explanations for China's heightened aggression toward Taiwan during and especially after 2019, Beijing's increasing dismay at what it perceives as growing anti-China hostility in Taipei and Washington is one of the most compelling. The Trump administration was not seen as especially friendly to China in 2016, but many commentators described his politics as no more anti-China than those of a hypothetical Hillary Clinton administration.[630] His late-2017 trip to Beijing also received favorable coverage in the Chinese press.[631] Over the course of 2018 and 2019, however, Trump's prosecution of a Sino-U.S. trade war, as well as his increasingly belligerent rhetoric and policies, soured his image in Beijing, and by 2019 official CCP publications accused him of "seeing China as an enemy in all respects" and driving Sino-U.S. relations to a historical low point.[632]

---

[626] Liu Xuanzun, "PLA Prepared as US, Secessionists Provoke," *Global Times*, April 8, 2021.

[627] "China to Stop Issuing Individual Travel Permits to Taiwan," *BBC News*, July 31, 2019; and Helen Davidson, "Taiwanese Urged to Eat 'Freedom Pineapples' After China Import Ban," *The Guardian*, March 2, 2021.

[628] Nick Aspinwall, "Paraguay Says Chinese Brokers Offered Vaccines for Diplomatic Recognition," *The Diplomat*, March 27, 2021.

[629] Kharis Templeman, *Taiwan's January 2020 Elections: Prospects and Implications for China and the United States*, Washington, D.C.: Brookings Institution, December 2019.

[630] "Trump and Hillary: Who Will Be a More Anti-China President?" ["特朗普和希拉里谁当选美国总统会更反华?"], *China Net* [中华网], November 8, 2016; and "Trump and Hillary: Who Is China-Friendly and Who Is Anti-China?" ["特朗普和希拉里：谁亲华谁反华？"], *Phoenix Media* [凤凰], September 20, 2016.

[631] "Major Consensus Reached at Xi-Trump Summit," Xinhua, November 9, 2017; and "American President Trump Makes Official State Visit to China" ["美国总统特朗普对中国进行国事访问"], Xinhua, 2017.

[632] Zhang Hongyi [张宏毅], "America's Ability to Read China Once Again Put to the Test" ["美国再次面临是否'读懂中国'的考验"], *Qiushi* [求是], November 7, 2019; Yang Jiechi [杨洁篪], "Respecting

Beijing has consistently viewed Tsai and the DPP as enemies of unification and, therefore, as implacable opponents of China and the CCP.[633] Although this view has not changed over the period in question, the DPP's influence over Taiwanese domestic politics (and its therefore power to implement its allegedly separatist agenda) has ebbed and flowed. The DPP took a serious beating in the 2018 midterm local elections, prompting Tsai to step down as the party's leader, and there was widespread speculation that the party might not be able to defeat its more pro-mainland rivals in the 2020 election.[634] It was not until mid-2019 that the party's prospects began to improve, and Tsai's decisive victory in 2020 left her and her party newly emboldened to stand up to Beijing.[635]

Chinese sources suggest that Beijing sees this combination of increased hostility from Washington and Taipei as especially dangerous, and those perceptions could be driving China's responses. The PLA's increasing tempo of operations around Taiwan is often attributed to the DPP's alleged efforts toward Taiwanese independence.[636] Meanwhile, U.S. naval patrols, arms sales, and other actions in support of Taiwan are seen as problematic in large part because they embolden pro-separatist actors, who recognize that they cannot realize their goals without foreign help.[637] An increasingly hostile Washington is seen as happy to provide such

---

History and Looking to the Future, We Must Unswervingly Defend and Stabilize Sino-U.S. Relations" ["尊重历史 面向未来 坚定不移维护和稳定中美关系"], *Qiushi* [求是], August 8, 2020; and Zhang Hongyi [张宏毅], "America's Ability to Read China Once Again Put to the Test" ["美国再次面临是否'读懂中国'的考验"], *Qiushi* [求是], November 7, 2019.

[633] Benjamin Schreer, "The Double-Edged Sword of Coercion: Cross-Strait Relations After the 2016 Taiwan Elections," *Asian Politics and Policy*, Vol. 9, No. 1, January 2017, pp. 50–65; Kharis Templeman, "How Taiwan Stands Up to China," *Journal of Democracy*, Vol. 31, No. 3, July 2020, p. 87; and Ren Chengqi [任成琦], "Playing the 'Taiwan Card' Is a Dangerous Game" ["大'台湾牌'是一场危险游戏"], *Qiushi* [求是], July 10, 2019.

[634] Kharis Templeman, *Taiwan's January 2020 Elections: Prospects and Implications for China and the United States*, Washington, D.C.: Brookings Institution, December 2019.

[635] Lily Kuo, "Tsai Ing-Wen Says China Must 'Face Reality' of Taiwan's Independence," *The Guardian*, January 15, 2020.

[636] Jun Sheng [钧声], "Strongly Oppose American Arms Sales to Taiwan" ["坚决反对美对台军售"], *Qiushi* [求是], July 12, 2019; and Ren Chengqi [任成琦], "Playing the 'Taiwan Card' Is a Dangerous Game" ["大'台湾牌'是一场危险游戏"], *Qiushi* [求是], July 10, 2019.

[637] "National People's Congress Foreign Affairs Office Issues Statement on the Passage of the '2019 Taipei Act'" ["全国人大外事委员会就美国所谓'2019年台北法案'签署成法发表声明"], *Qiushi* [求是], March 28, 2020; Ren Chengqi [任成琦], "Playing the 'Taiwan Card' Is a Dangerous Game" ["大'台湾牌'是一场危险游戏"], *Qiushi* [求是], July 10, 2019; "Attempts to Use Taiwan to Control China or Use Weapons to Prevent Unification Will Fail in the End" ["'以台制华'和'以武拒统'注定难逃失败下场"], *Qiushi* [求是], July 11, 2019; Zhu Ping [王平], "In Traveling Through the U.S., Tsai Ying Wen Courts Controversy in Sensitive Cross-Strait Relations" ["过境美国，蔡英文挑动两岸敏感神经"], *Qiushi* [求实], July 12, 2019; and Ke Mu [枯木], ed., "America Plays the Taiwan

encouragement as part of a broad and nefarious (if somewhat vague) U.S. effort to use Taiwan to "contain" or "control" China.[638] The characters of U.S. and Taiwanese anti-China hostility are not seen as identical—Beijing's Taiwanese foes are usually depicted as being narrowly focused on independence, whereas the United States is generally described as trying to contain or oppose China more broadly.[639] Nevertheless, as Taiwan and Washington are each seen as more hostile, CCP sources describe their mutually reinforcing actions as constituting a growing threat, necessitating ever more aggressive responses and deterrence.[640]

Conclusion

China's perceptions of increased American and Taiwanese hostility toward Chinese interests, and especially of their increasing support for Taiwanese independence, are likely some of the reasons for heightened levels of Chinese aggression toward Taiwan in 2020. Chinese writings indicate that Beijing thought that Trump posed a serious and somewhat surprising threat to its interests in 2019 and 2020. Tsai and the DPP, in contrast, have always been seen as highly hostile, but their perceived ability to put a pro-independence agenda into effect grew as a result of their victory in the 2020 Taiwanese elections. In explaining its own actions and reactions, Beijing often attributes its increasing aggression to necessity: In the face of Taiwanese and American hostility, China has no choice but to behave more aggressively.[641] There are other factors at play as well, of course, including the directness of the threat that Taiwanese

---

Card Again, Punishing Those Who Break Off Relations with Taiwan and Making the DPP Its Lackey" ["美国又打台湾牌，惩罚跟台湾'断交'友邦，民进党成为马前卒"], *Channel News* [海峡要闻], March 24, 2020.

[638] Note that it is not usually explained how exactly greater tensions in the Taiwan Strait or greater boldness by Taiwanese independence activists will benefit Washington. See "Attempts to Use Taiwan to Control China or Use Weapons to Prevent Unification Will Fail in the End" ["'以台制华'和'以武拒统'注定难逃失败下场"], *Qiushi* [求是], July 11, 2019; Zhu Ping [王平], "In Traveling Through the U.S., Tsai Ying Wen Courts Controversy in Sensitive Cross-Strait Relations" ["过境美国，蔡英文挑动两岸敏感神经"], *Qiushi* [求实], July 12, 2019; and Ren Chengqi [任成琦], "Playing the 'Taiwan Card' Is a Dangerous Game" ["大'台湾牌'是一场危险游戏"], *Qiushi* [求是], July 10, 2019.

[639] Ren Chengqi [任成琦], "Playing the 'Taiwan Card' Is a Dangerous Game" ["大'台湾牌'是一场危险游戏"], *Qiushi* [求是], July 10, 2019.

[640] Liu Xuanzun, "PLA Prepared as US, Secessionists Provoke," *Global Times*, April 8, 2021; and Ren Chengqi [任成琦], "Playing the 'Taiwan Card' Is a Dangerous Game" ["大'台湾牌'是一场危险游戏"], *Qiushi* [求是], July 10, 2019.

[641] Liu Xuanzun, "PLA Prepared as US, Secessionists Provoke," *Global Times*, April 8, 2021; Ben Blanchard and Jess Macy Yu, "China Warns of More Action After Military Drills Near Taiwan," Reuters, April 25, 2018; Ren Chengqi [任成琦], "Playing the 'Taiwan Card' Is a Dangerous Game" ["大'台湾牌'是一场危险游戏"], *Qiushi* [求是], July 10, 2019; Zhang Junshe [张军社], "We Strongly Oppose Any Country Developing Military Ties with Taiwan" ["坚决反对任何国家与台开展军事联系"], *Qiushi* [求是], January 16, 2019; and Yang Jiechi [杨洁篪], "Respecting History and Looking to the Future, We Must Unswervingly Defend and Stabilize Sino-U.S. Relations" ["尊重历史 面向未来 坚定不移维护和稳定中美关系"], *Qiushi* [求是], August 8, 2020.

independence poses to CCP legitimacy. The increasing tempo of PLA operations directed against the island is also enabled by the expanding capabilities of the PLA. Even so, the need to counter the perceived increase in hostility from the United States and Taiwan seems to be a key explanatory factor for China's cross-strait behavior.

Case 11: China's Reaction to Closer U.S.-India Security Relations

Case 11 tests the hypothesis that China is more likely to react aggressively to actions that increase its perceptions of the hostile intent of the United States or its allies and partners. To do so, it analyzes China's reactions to the deepening security relationship between the United States and India, particularly since 2018. U.S.-Indian cooperation has exacerbated Chinese fears of the intentions of two of its historical adversaries, and China has responded through a mixture of diplomatic actions, media criticism, and military activities, such as bilateral exercises with Pakistan.[642] Evidence suggests that a violent border brawl that left dozens dead in July 2020—which is examined in greater detail in Case 13 and was the first major clash since the China-India border war in the 1960s—may have been indirectly related to the heightened China-India tensions associated with Chinese perceptions of New Delhi's increasingly hostile intent.[643] This yields moderate support for the hypothesis. Beijing has thus far refrained from economic retaliation against India, however, perhaps in the hope of not foreclosing the possibility that India will support, or at least not vigorously oppose, the BRI. Moreover, China's response has been tempered by an awareness of the limits of U.S.-India cooperation that follow from India's policy of strategic autonomy and desire to maintain good relations with Russia and Iran and China's corresponding desire not to push the United States and India closer together than they already are. The PLA currently appears capable of responding to any land border incursion from India, and although threats to Chinese interests in the Indian Ocean could be more challenging because of limited PLA basing access, China's ongoing naval buildup could mitigate this vulnerability in coming years.[644] That said, greater U.S.-India cooperation could increase Chinese concern over the threat to its southern flank.

Recent Improvements in U.S.-India Security Relations

U.S.-India defense and security relations have deepened substantially over the past two decades, particular since the 2014 electoral victory of Narendra Modi's Bharatiya Janata Party and his subsequent elevation to Prime Minister.[645] Security relations have been built on the 2005 New Framework for Defense Cooperation, renewed in 2015, which has enabled a number of follow-on agreements governing more-specific areas of security cooperation, and in 2016 the

---

[642] Adnan Aamir, "China and Pakistan Ink Military MOU to Counter U.S.-India Pact," *Nikkei Asia*, December 8, 2020.

[643] Steven Lee Myers, "China Acknowledges 4 Deaths in Last Year's Border Clash with India," *New York Times*, March 1, 2021.

[644] Henry Boyd and Meia Nouwens, "Understanding the Military Build-Up on the China-India Border," International Institute for Strategic Studies, June 18, 2020; and Office of the Secretary of Defense, *Annual Report to Congress: Military and Security Developments Involving the People's Republic of China 2020*, Washington, D.C., 2020.

[645] Ashley Tellis, "Narendra Modi and U.S.-India Relations," in Bibek Debroy, Anirban Ganguly, and Kishore Desai, eds., *Making of New India: Transformation Under Modi Government*, New Delhi: Wisdom Tree, 2018.

United States designated India as its first "major defense partner."[646] These agreements have grown hand in hand with a burgeoning arms trade. India has become increasingly concerned with rapid Chinese military modernization, which it perceives as a threat to the security of its own borders with China, and it has turned to imports of weapons from several partners, including the United States, to help address the increasing Sino-Indian military imbalance.[647] Between 2010 and 2016, U.S. arms sales to India totaled roughly $2.6 billion, whereas they reached $3.4 billion in 2020 alone.[648] Diplomatic relations and meetings have also accelerated. U.S. secretaries of the State and Defense Departments have met annually with their Indian counterparts since 2018, and there are now frequent meetings between the U.S. President and the Indian Prime Minister. The overall effect of these efforts has been to substantially strengthen U.S.-India ties. Although disputes over issues such as trade remain between the two countries, the overall trajectory toward a closer partnership on military and security issues appears clear.[649]

Chinese Reactions

China has responded to these developments with diplomatic actions and harsh media commentary. In addition, China has carried out a variety of military activities, including exercises and measures to enhance the security relationship with Pakistan. While Chinese reactions to closer U.S.-India relations have been ongoing for several years, below we focus on a more recent set of tensions.

Chinese officials criticized U.S. cooperation with India but also made gestures aimed at improving their own relations with India. Chinese officials issued a demarche to India's government on several occasions in 2020, mostly in response to the brawl and subsequent developments related to the standoff in the Galwan Valley.[650] Chinese officials also moved quickly to stabilize the situation. On July 6, 2020, the two sides announced an agreement to de-

---

[646] These additional agreements include the Logistics Exchange Memorandum of Agreement in 2016, the 2018 Communications Compatibility and Security Agreement, and the 2020 Basic Exchange and Cooperation Agreement. See T. V. Paul and Erik Underwood, "Theorizing India-U.S.-China Strategic Triangle," *India Review*, Vol. 18, No. 4, 2019, pp. 351–352; Bureau of Political-Military Affairs, "U.S. Security Cooperation with India," fact sheet, U.S. Department of State, January 20, 2021; and Vivek Raghuvanshi, "India, U.S. Sign Intel-Sharing Agreement amid Tension with Neighboring China," *Defense News*, October 28, 2020.

[647] Yogesh Joshi and Anit Mukherjee, "From Denial to Punishment: The Security Dilemma and Changes in India's Military Strategy Towards China," *Asian Security*, Vol. 15, No. 1, 2019.

[648] T. V. Paul and Erik Underwood, "Theorizing India-U.S.-China Strategic Triangle," *India Review*, Vol. 18, No. 4, 2019, p. 352; and "India's Weapons Procurement from the U.S. Jumps to $3.4 Billion in 2020," *The Hindu*, December 9, 2020.

[649] Joshua T. White, "After the Foundational Agreements: An Agenda for U.S.-India Defense and Security Cooperation," Brookings Institution, January 2021. At the same time, U.S.-India cooperation remains constrained by differing strategic and domestic priorities. See, inter alia, Anik Joshi, "Trump Doesn't Love Modi Back," *Foreign Policy*, July 28, 2020.

[650] "Chinese Embassy Urges India to Correct Wrongdoings of Banning Chinese Apps," Xinhua, July 28, 2020.

escalate the Galwan Valley standoff and to ease general tensions.[651] In June 2020, Foreign Minister Wang Yi called on his Russian and Indian counterparts to strengthen communication and coordination within the framework of the UN and "safeguard the overall situation of their relations." He tellingly praised the "strategic independence" of all three countries.[652]

Underscoring a widespread suspicion of U.S. intentions, Chinese media have expressed the view that the United States is purposefully helping India challenge China. A January 7, 2021, commentary in the CCP-owned tabloid *Global Times* described comments by U.S. Ambassador to India Kenneth Juster regarding U.S. "cooperation with India" to "counter 'aggressive' Chinese actions at the Line of Actual Control" as "the first time an official confirmed U.S.-India cooperation" against China over the border standoff. The article noted that the United States had transferred "a lot of equipment" to India, including small arms, cold weather gear, and other items. The commentary stated that the United States "seems to be pushing Indians to the forefront to confront China."[653] A December commentary in the *Global Times* criticized India for going "too far on the path of ganging up with the U.S. against China." It identified various U.S.-India defense agreements as evidence of hostile "anti-China" policies.[654]

An expert from Fudan University cited the U.S.-India agreements as evidence that the two countries appeared headed toward a "quasi-alliance."[655] A commentary in China's official news outlet, Xinhua, warned that India's warming relationship with the United States could be "detrimental to regional stability and India's own development" and could "push India to the cusp of regional conflict." Both sources noted that India's relationship with Russia and Iran would suffer if New Delhi and Washington deepened cooperation.[656]

China has carried out a variety of military measures to counter the closer India-U.S. cooperation. Pakistan has for decades been a close diplomatic and defense partner with China and is an enthusiastic participant in Beijing's BRI. In response to clear signs of a closer U.S.-India relationship, Beijing and Islamabad took steps to deepen their ties. In December 2020, for example, China signed an MOU with Pakistan. The details of the agreement were not made publicly available but reportedly included measures to increase security cooperation, including potential sharing of Pakistani intelligence regarding Indian troop movements along China's

---

[651] "China, India Reach Positive Consensus on Easing Border Situation," Xinhua, July 6, 2020.

[652] "Chinese Foreign Minister Calls on China, Russia, India to Work Together," Xinhua, June 24, 2020.

[653] Liu Zongyi, "Pro-US Strategy May Push India into the Abyss," *Global Times*, January 21, 2021.

[654] Lin Minwang, "What Can India Offer to Turn the US into a 'Pawn'?" *Global Times*, December 24, 2020.

[655] Lin Minwang [林民旺], "India Has Chosen a High Risk Strategic Path" ["林民旺: 印度选择了一条高风险战略路径"], *Global Times* [环球时报], October 27, 2020.

[656] Yang Dingdu [杨定都], "News Analysis: Why Does India Not Catch a Cold from the United States?" ["新闻分析：印度为何对美国拉拢不感冒"], Xinhua, July 13, 2018.

border. Analysts viewed the agreement as a direct response to the Basic Exchange and Cooperation Agreement signed between India and the United States in October 2020.[657]

Chinese authorities also announced in December 2020 that the Pakistani and Chinese air forces would conduct a large joint exercise called Shaheen IX before the end of December. Reports stated that the exercise would surpass in scale and scope the previous iteration of the exercise, Shaheen VIII. In a thinly veiled reference to the recently concluded defense agreements between Washington and New Delhi, Pakistani Chief of Staff of the Army General Qamar Javed Bajwaa stated that the exercise was "vital for both sides amid emerging geo-strategic challenges."[658]

In June 2020, Chinese and Indian troops clashed in the first violent confrontation since the border wars in the 1960s.[659] Many Western and Chinese commentators regarded Beijing's anxiety over an emboldened India, driven in large part by New Delhi's cooperation with Washington, as a key driver of the crisis. Analysts noted that India's location astride China's vulnerable BRI routes, its proximity to vital but vulnerable shipping lanes, and the size and strength of its military increased the risk that it could seriously threaten China's future security and development.[660]

Explanations for Chinese Reactions

China regarded U.S. and Indian diplomatic and security measures as signaling their hostile intent. Chinese media routinely denounced the United States for "anti-China" policies and accused the Washington of seeking to "contain" Beijing through its cooperation with India and other countries.[661] Underscoring its concern about the security implications of closer U.S.-India security cooperation aimed at China, Beijing concluded military cooperation agreements and carried out large-scale exercises with Pakistan that appeared designed, in part, to offset U.S.-India security relations. Evidence for this interpretation includes the conspicuous timing of the China-Pakistan announcements and the contents of both the military-related agreements—which included intelligence-sharing regarding Indian troop movements—and the official statements and

---

[657] Adnan Aamir, "China and Pakistan Ink Military MOU to Counter U.S.-India Pact," *Nikkei Asia*, December 8, 2020.

[658] Chen Lufan, "China-Pakistan Joint Air Exercise 'Shaheen-IX' for Better Interoperability," *China Military Online*, December 21, 2020.

[659] Steven Lee Myers, "China Acknowledges 4 Deaths in Last Year's Border Clash with India," *New York Times*, March 1, 2021.

[660] Yun Sun, "China's Strategic Assessment of the Ladakh Clash," *War on the Rocks*, June 19, 2020.

[661] Zhang Hualong [章华龙], "Will India Cooperate with America to Contain China?"

["印度会配合美国，遏制中国吗?"], *Outlook* [瞭望], October 10, 2019; and "Time for U.S. Anti-China Forces to Cease Regressive Practices: Chinese FM," Xinhua, December 11, 2020.

commentary accompanying them.[662] For example, a December 2020 commentary in the *Global Times* accused India of "getting increasingly closer to anti-China forces, especially the U.S." and concluded that "if cooperation with Pakistan can constitute a certain kind of deterrent toward India, it may be considered as a good approach to balance regional powers."[663] While there is no evidence that Beijing directed local commanders to carry out the violent Galwan Valley border brawl in 2020, Xi Jinping *had* directed a less compromising "bottom line" principle that contributed to the notable hardening of China's stances on dispute issues over the previous years.[664] Moreover, the reliance on violence below the level of armed conflict is consistent with Chinese "gray zone" activities practiced in the other disputed regions, although the brawl differed from the other instances in that it resulted in fatalities.[665]

Indian actions to strengthen its border forces signaled, to China, that the new cooperation with the United States may have emboldened New Delhi.[666] Left unanswered, India could threaten China in two ways. On their mutual land border, Indian troops could carry out incursions that threatened the integrity of Chinese borders. India could also provide support to nonstate pro-independence groups in Tibet, which could imperil Beijing's grip in that region. And China's vulnerability along the Indian Ocean raised the possibility that an emboldened India could menace Chinese ships or coerce neighboring countries into denying China access for its naval ships.

Interestingly, China largely refrained from using economic pressure against India. In many other cases, such as that of the dispute over THAAD in South Korea, Beijing carried out economic coercion to considerable effect.[667] In its dispute with India, however, China favored military means. One possible explanation for China's reluctance to employ economic pressure may be its hope to integrate India into the BRI. Weaponizing trade would reduce India's

---

[662] Zhang Yanping [张燕萍], "Chinese Minister of Defense Visits Nepal and Pakistan Expert: The Practical Significance of Safeguarding the Security Around China's Western Region Is More Prominent" ["中国防长访问尼泊尔巴基斯坦 专家: 对维护中国西部周边安全现实意义更突出"], *Global Times* [环球时报], December 1, 2020.

[663] Lan Jianxue, "India Ridiculous to Clamor About China-Pakistan MOU," *Global Times*, December 2, 2020.

[664] Wang Cong, "China Draws Bottom Line," *Global Times*, June 3, 2019; and Nien-Chung Chang-Liao, "China's New Foreign Policy Under Xi Jinping," *Asian Security*, Vol. 12, No. 2, 2016.

[665] Michael J. Mazarr, *Mastering the Gray Zone: Understanding a Changing Era of Conflict*, Carlisle, Pa.: U.S. Army War College, 2015; and Michael E. O'Hanlon, *China, the Gray Zone, and Contingency Planning at the Department of Defense and Beyond*, Washington, D.C.: Brookings Institution, September 2019.

[666] Li Jian [李剑], Chen Wenwen [陈文文], and Jin Jing [金晶], "The Pattern of Indian Ocean Power and the Expansion of China's Sea Power in the Indian Ocean" ["印度洋海权格局与中国海权的印度洋拓展"], *China's Foreign Policy* [中国外交], 2015; and Christopher K. Colley, "China's Ongoing Debates About India and the United States," *Asia Dispatches*, June 30, 2020.

[667] Ethan Meick and Nargiza Salidjanova, *China's Response to U.S.-South Korean Missile Defense System Deployment and Its Implications*, Washington, D.C.: U.S.-China Economic and Security Review Commission, July 26, 2017.

incentives to join the initiative and perhaps even push it to actively oppose it. Evidence for this may be seen in the statements by Foreign Minister Wang Yi, who called for greater economic cooperation with India even amid tensions over security issues, as well as in China's refusal to respond to India's economic sanctions following the 2020 border brawl.[668] China's willingness to risk more-violent measures to oppose India could also have been informed by India's lack of an alliance with the United States. Chinese commentators frequently pointed out the limits of U.S.-India cooperation and New Delhi's principle of strategic autonomy, as well as its historic friendship with antagonists of the United States, such as Russia and Iran.[669]

While China's perceptions of deepening anti-Chinese U.S.-India cooperation appeared to be an important driver of its diplomatic and military responses, other factors also played significant roles. Tensions between China and India had been growing over the past few years for several reasons. The two countries are historical rivals as Asia's leading powers, and both have experienced substantial recent gains in national power.[670] Moreover, China has long practiced a version of containment against India by closely cooperating with the latter's primary antagonist, Pakistan. China's initiation of the BRI project in 2013 also intensified long-standing Indian fears of Chinese encirclement and encouraged New Delhi to bolster its relations with the United States.[671]

Other factors also affected China's response to the U.S.-India security cooperation. In particular, the rapid deterioration of U.S.-China relations under President Trump and the United States' burgeoning ties with India raised Chinese anxiety over what it saw as increasingly hostile U.S. intentions. An increasingly robust U.S.-Indian political and economic relationship added to these concerns.[672] As shown by the 2+2 meeting in 2019 in which the United States designated India a major defense partner, the governments under President Trump and Prime Minister Modi made substantial efforts to strengthen the bilateral relationship, despite trade tensions.[673]

Although irritated by India's warming ties with the United States, Chinese anxieties were likely alleviated by an awareness of the limits of that cooperation. As Chinese observers

---

[668] "Chinese Foreign Minister Calls on China, Russia, India to Work Together," Xinhua, June 24, 2020.

[669] Wang Shida [王世达], "The Challenge of India-U.S. Security Cooperation to India's Tradition of Strategic Independent" ["印美安全合作对印度战略自主传统的挑战"], *Modern International Relations* [现代国际关系], No. 2, August 7, 2019; and "Will India Further Toss Non-Alignment Policy Under Biden Admin?" *Global Times*, January 28, 2021.

[670] T. V. Paul, ed., *The China-India Rivalry in the Globalization Era*, Washington, D.C.: Georgetown University Press, 2018.

[671] Gulshan Sachdeva, "Indian Perceptions of the Chinese Belt and Road Initiative," *International Studies*, Vol. 55, No. 4, 2018.

[672] For an overview of these concerns, see Christopher K. Colley, "China's Ongoing Debates About India and the United States," *Asia Dispatches*, June 30, 2020.

[673] Bureau of South and Central Asian Affairs, "U.S. Relations with India," U.S. Department of State, January 21, 2021.

frequently pointed out, India maintained a policy of strategic autonomy that it showed no evidence of abandoning. These observers also emphasize that Indian authorities balanced their relationship with the United States with their relationships with long-standing partners Russia and Iran, both of whom remain antagonists of the United States.[674] Other observers pointed out that neither the United States nor India benefited if the other country moved too far toward confronting China, which could drag the other to war, or accommodating China, which could leave the other country vulnerable.[675] Chinese concerns could also be moderated by the awareness of its relatively strong military position. China retained an advantage in the overall strength of its military relative to India, including on the Sino-Indian frontier. However, the PLA's lack of bases and dependence on exposed shipping lanes in the Indian Ocean remained major vulnerabilities. China's naval expansion could help mitigate this vulnerability over time.[676]

Conclusion

China responded firmly to a steady stream of increased U.S.-India security cooperation with primarily diplomatic and military actions. Evidence suggests that anxiety about the threat posed by deepening U.S.-India security cooperation may have been a major factor underpinning Beijing's reaction. U.S. efforts to strengthen its ties with India took place within the context of China's worsening relationship with both states. These broader political and strategic drivers incentivized Beijing to counter U.S.-Indian cooperation by improving its own ties with Pakistan. In a manner consistent with its behavior regarding other flashpoints, moreover, Chinese authorities authorized more-aggressive moves to defend Chinese interests. Although these were below the threshold of armed conflict, they did increase the risk—and, in 2020, contributed to the outbreak—of a violent Sino-Indian confrontation.

---

[674] Wang Shida [王世达], "The Challenge of India-U.S. Security Cooperation to India's Tradition of Strategic Independent" ["印美安全合作对印度战略自主传统的挑战"], *Modern International Relations* [现代国际关系], No. 2, August 7, 2019.

[675] Shiping Tang [唐世平], "China-India Relations in the 'Modi Era'" ["'莫迪时代'的中印关系"], *Modern International Relations* [现代国际关系], No. 21, November 16, 2020.

[676] Office of the Secretary of Defense, *Annual Report to Congress: Military and Security Developments Involving the People's Republic of China 2020*, Washington, D.C., 2020.

Case 12: PRC Activities Against Vietnam at Vanguard Bank

Political scientists have theorized that China could incite a foreign policy crisis to divert attention from domestic instability or to generate a pro-regime "rally around the flag" effect. Case 12 therefore uses China's responses to Vietnam's oil exploration activities near Vanguard Bank, the westernmost reef of the Spratly Islands, in the SCS from May to October 2019 to test the hypothesis that the aggressiveness of Chinese reactions to U.S., allied, and partner activities increases when China is experiencing more domestic instability. Vanguard Bank is a critically important area because it provides 10 percent of Vietnam's energy resources. It is also disputed, as it resides within both Vietnam's EEZ and continental shelf and China's nine-dashed line of SCS maritime claims. Although China did little to push back against Vietnam-backed energy development near Vanguard Bank in 2018, it decided to escalate a dispute in response to a similar Vietnamese effort in 2019. Some analyses suggest that this was because the unrest and protests that erupted in Hong Kong beginning in March 2019 motivated China to act more aggressively. However, there is little support for this conclusion. The evidence actually suggests the opposite: China may have been reluctant to escalate the dispute more than it did out of concern that doing so would embolden Vietnamese or ethnic Vietnamese people in Hong Kong to support the protest movement.

Hong Kong Unrest

From March 2019 through the remainder of the year and into 2020, Hong Kong experienced repeated and intensifying public demonstrations as residents took to the streets in protest of a February 2019 Chinese proposal to amend Hong Kong law to allow the extradition of criminal suspects to China for trial. Afraid that the proposal undermined the "one country, two systems" principle that formed the basis of Hong Kong's pseudo-autonomy, residents took action. Their activism culminated in several major events in 2019, including the June 9 protest that involved half a million people, the July 1 storming of the Hong Kong Legislative Council, and the November occupation and barricading of several university campuses by protesters. The Hong Kong police responded with escalating force, using rubber bullets, tear gas, and water cannons against protesters before using live rounds.[677] China deployed a large contingent of armed police to the mainland city bordering Hong Kong, and many suspected that pro-Beijing forces were behind masked thugs' violent attacks on protesters.[678] By November 2019, and after a key PRC leadership meeting, Beijing asserted that China faced "increasing risks and challenges at home and abroad" and that China remained committed to "maintain lasting prosperity and stability in

---

[677] Karishma Singh, Clare Jim, and Anne Marie Roantree, "Timeline: Key Dates in Hong Kong's Anti-Government Protests," Reuters, November 11, 2019; and "Hong Kong Timeline: A Year of Protests," Associated Press, June 9, 2020.

[678] Lynette H. Ong, "In Hong Kong, Are 'Thugs for Hire' Behind the Attack on Protestors? Here's What We Know About These Groups," *Washington Post*, July 24, 2019.

Hong Kong and Macao," including taking additional steps to tighten control.[679] Beijing specifically blamed the United States for instigating unrest in Hong Kong and, by the end of 2019, had arrested more than 6,500 Hong Kong protesters.[680] While the PRC does not appear to have been significantly concerned that pro-democracy protests in Hong Kong could spread to the rest of China, China's senior leaders were likely worried that unrest in Hong Kong could fuel growing pro-independence sentiment in Taiwan.[681]

Vietnam-Linked Oil Exploration at Vanguard Bank

On May 12, 2019, after the Hong Kong protests were well underway, the Russian oil firm Rosneft—with Vietnamese backing—contracted the Japanese *Hakuryu-5* oil rig to drill in Block 06-01, 370 kilometers (230 miles) southeast of Vietnam and near Vanguard Bank. This activity was not a new one and mirrored drilling conducted the previous year: Rosneft had operated in Block 06-01 in 2018—and similarly contracted *Hakuryu-5* for oil drilling activities.

Chinese Reactions

China viewed *Hakuryu-5* as engaging in unsanctioned activity within its claimed "nine-dashed" line that needed to be stopped in order to uphold China's claims of sovereignty in the area. Its initial reaction in 2019 was limited to political statements, but Beijing later escalated via maritime paramilitary means by sending maritime vessels to the region in mid-June after Vietnam continued to engage in oil exploration activities and the United States engaged in activities to support Vietnam and other SCS claimants, as noted below. Although Beijing responded more forcefully to Vietnam in 2019 than in 2018, China's reactions were relatively restrained when compared with the actions that China took against Vietnam during the 2014 China-Vietnam standoff. A standoff between Chinese and Vietnamese vessels failed to compel Vietnam to halt its oil exploration. Instead, Vietnam twice extended *Hakuryu-5*'s activities, first from end of July to September and then until October. The standoff ended in late October when *Hakuryu-5* completed its operations and left the oil and gas block. The Chinese vessels departed the next day.

---

[679] "19th CPC Central Committee Concludes Fourth Plenary Session, Releases Communiqué," Xinhua, October 31, 2019; see also Chris Buckley, "China Says It Will Roll Out 'National Security' Steps for Hong Kong," *New York Times*, October 31, 2019.

[680] Ministry of Foreign Affairs of the People's Republic of China, "Foreign Ministry Spokesperson Hua Chunying's Regular Press Conference on July 30, 2019," July 30, 2019; and Kong Tsung-gan, "Arrests and Trials of Hong Kong Protestors," *Medium*, December 1, 2019.

[681] For discussion of Taiwan supporting protests in Hong Kong, see Joyu Wang, "Taiwan Rallies for Hong Kong to Resist Beijing's Influence," *Wall Street Journal*, September 29, 2019. Similarly, 2019 also marked the ten-year anniversary of China's harsh crackdown on riots in Xinjiang. It is possible that Beijing was concerned about the risk of increased instability in Xinjiang or the potential that "foreign forces" may use the anniversary to take action or pressure China on Xinjiang similar to what Beijing viewed as occurring in Hong Kong. See Mamatjan Juma, Shohret Hoshur, Kurban Niyaz, and Ekrem Hezim, "10th Anniversary of Urumqi Unrest Brings Protests over Internment Camps, Accountability Demands," *Radio Free Asia*, July 5, 2019.

The following sections first describe China's responses to Vietnam from 2014 to 2018 to provide context and then detail the distinctive features of its responses to Vietnam in 2019.

Historical Context

Prior to 2019, China and Vietnam had experienced periods of tension over energy development in the SCS. The most escalatory recent case involved a standoff between the two countries when China deployed an oil rig in 2014 near the disputed Paracel Islands to engage in energy exploration within Vietnam's EEZ. Vietnam responded forcefully, and both sides quickly massed maritime and air assets near the oil rig, resulting in aggressive maneuvers and at-sea collisions. At the height of the standoff, China reportedly deployed "137 Chinese vessels including military ships such as missile frigates, fast attack missile crafts, anti-submarine patrol ships and amphibious landing ships around the [Chinese] oil rig" and mobilized "helicopters, early warning planes and reconnaissance planes and fighter jets."[682] Both countries also coupled the military and paramilitary responses with significant diplomatic and economic measures targeting the other country—China, for example, limited tourism and reduced trade to Vietnam and there were also rumors of PLA units amassing near the China-Vietnam border.[683]

Similarly, China had publicly opposed Vietnamese activities in and near Vanguard Bank in the past, In July 2017 and March 2018, Chinese threats had caused Vietnam to halt drilling with the Spanish firm Repsol and the United Arab Emirates' state-owned Mubadala Development Company near Block 06-01.[684] In contrast, in 2018 there was limited public Chinese backlash against the Russian state–controlled Rosneft's oil exploration in the same location. Beijing warned Rosneft against engaging in energy exploration and asked "relevant parties"—likely Moscow—to respect Chinese sovereignty claims and rights.[685] However, probably because of the importance of its relationship with Russia, China did not directly threaten Rosneft's operations.[686]

[682] Lye Liang Fook and Ha Hoang Hop, "The Vanguard Bank Incident: Developments and What Next?" *ISEAS Perspective*, No. 69, 2019, p. 6.

[683] Michael Green, Kathleen Hicks, Zack Cooper, John Schaus, and Jake Douglas, "Counter-Coercion Series: China-Vietnam Oil Rig Standoff," Asia Maritime Transparency Initiative, Center for Strategic and International Studies, June 12, 2017; and Bonny Lin, Cristina L. Garafola, Bruce McClintock, Jonah Blank, Jeffrey W. Hornung, Karen Schwindt, Jennifer D. P. Moroney, Paul Orner, Dennis Borrman, Sarah W. Denton, and Jason Chambers, *Competition in the Gray Zone: Countering China's Coercion Against U.S. Allies and Partners in the Indo-Pacific*, Santa Monica, Calif.: RAND Corporation, RR-A594-1, 2022.

[684] Bill Hayton, "The Week Donald Trump Lost the South China Sea," *Foreign Policy*, July 31, 2017.

[685] James Pearson, "Exclusive: As Rosneft's Vietnam Unit Drills in Disputed Area of South China Sea, Beijing Issues Warning," Reuters, May 17, 2018.

[686] Huong Le Thu and Sunny Cao, "Russia's Growing Interests in the South China Sea," *The Strategist*, December 18, 2019; for the growing China-Russia oil relationship and the importance of Rosneft, see Stephen Blank, "Kremlin Ties Rosneft Closer to China," *Eurasia Daily Monitor*, November 8, 2017.

Political Responses

In response to Vietnam's activities in 2019, China did not take any additional significant political responses beyond public statements reaffirming Beijing's diplomatic position and efforts to pressure Vietnam and to encourage the Kremlin to rein in Rosneft, as noted above. On May 20, 2019, seizing the opportunity presented by a U.S. FONOP through waters near Scarborough Shoal, China's Ministry of Foreign Affairs warned that "China has all along respected and protected the freedom of navigation and overflight in the SCS that countries are entitled to under international law. However, China is firmly opposed to actions that undermine its sovereignty and security. . . . China will continue to take all necessary measures to defend national sovereignty and security, and safeguard peace and stability in the South China Sea."[687] Throughout the standoff, China continued to reiterate its position via similar diplomatic statements. In August, on the sidelines of the ASEAN ministerial meeting, Chinese Foreign Minister Wang Yi also reportedly asked his Russian counterpart Sergei Lavrov to stop Rosneft's activities, and Lavrov declined.[688]

Military Responses

In 2019, China's direct military responses involved sending a survey vessel and accompanying Coast Guard vessels to Vanguard Bank to engage in survey activity while also disrupting and facing off against Vietnam-backed exploration activities. In mid-June, CCG vessel *Haijing 35111* began intimidating Vietnamese vessels servicing *Hakuryu-5* (e.g., by conducting high-speed close maneuvers nearby) and sailing close to the oil rig. On July 3, China escalated by dispatching survey vessel *Haiyang Dizhi 8* and two accompanying CCG vessels, *Haijing 37111* and the 12,000-ton *Haijing 3901*, one of China's largest law enforcement vessels. Over time, the *Haijing 3901* was replaced by other CCG vessels, and *Haiyang Dizhi 8* was generally accompanied by four or five Chinese coast guard and maritime militia vessels.[689] Chinese maritime vessels remained around Vanguard Bank from June to late October, with vessels often traveling to Chinese outpost Fiery Cross Reef for resupply. During these months, Vietnamese Major General Nguyen Minh Hoang estimated that 50 Vietnamese and 40 Chinese vessels were active in the area, while other sources suggested that up to 80 different Chinese maritime vessels may have simultaneously operated in the area.[690]

---

[687] Ministry of Foreign Affairs of the People's Republic of China, "Foreign Ministry Spokesperson Lu Kang's Regular Press Conference on May 20, 2019," May 20, 2019.

[688] Carlyle A. Thayer, "A Difficult Summer in the South China Sea," *The Diplomat*, November 2019.

[689] Lye Liang Fook and Ha Hoang Hop, "The Vanguard Bank Incident: Developments and What Next?" *ISEAS Perspective*, No. 69, 2019, p. 2.

[690] Asia Maritime Transparency Initiative, "Update: China Risks Flare-Up over Malaysian, Vietnamese Gas Resources," Center for Strategic and International Studies, December 13, 2019; and Carlyle A. Thayer, "Will Vanguard Bank Ignite Vietnamese Nationalism?" Australian Naval Institute, August 4, 2019.

In addition to activities at Vanguard Bank, China may have also tried to demonstrate its resolve against Vietnam through exercises and military tests in the SCS. China engaged in a two-day military drill around the Paracel Islands in early June followed by a three-day military training again near the Paracels in early August.[691] On July 1, 2019, China for the first time test-launched six anti-ship ballistic missiles from the mainland into two areas in the SCS, one area near Woody Island in the Paracels and one area north of the Spratlys.[692] Analysts speculate that the test was likely intended as a show of force to support China's claims against regional and U.S. activities there, potentially including Vietnam.[693]

Vietnamese Responses to PRC Actions

In response to China's maritime deployments, Vietnam embraced a more cautious response than in 2014. Although Vietnam sent its law enforcement vessels to the region (at times outnumbering the Chinese vessels and even including an advanced naval frigate),[694] Hanoi did not publicize Chinese activities at Vanguard Bank immediately. For example, it observed and tracked the *Haiyang Dizhi 8* for two weeks before issuing vague statements criticizing Chinese activity.[695] Vietnam then proceeded to issue multiple public statements against China.[696]

Unlike in 2014, Hanoi limited domestic coverage of the standoff and discouraged large-scale anti-China public demonstrations in Vietnam.[697] It not only maintained high-level exchanges with China despite tensions at sea (even engaging in a high-level visit to China days after the *Haiyang Dizhi 8* entered Vietnam's EEZ) but also expanded communications with China at all levels, including with Chinese security and defense officials. It continued military cooperation with China as well.[698] Hanoi was also careful to not threaten international legal means against

---

[691] Annabelle Liang, "China Vows Military Action If Taiwan, Sea Claims Opposed," Associated Press, June 2, 2019; and Laura Zhou, "Beijing Starts Military Exercise in Disputed South China Sea as Tensions with Vietnam Rise," *South China Morning Post*, August 15, 2019.

[692] Bill Hayton, "The South China Sea in 2020," statement before the U.S.-China Economic and Security Review Commission, Hearing on U.S.-China Relations in 2020: Enduring Problems and Emerging Challenges, September 9, 2020; and Xavier Vavasseur, "China Launched 6 ASBM into the South China Sea," *Naval News*, July 15, 2019.

[693] Jesse Johnson, "Pentagon Calls Chinese Anti-Ship Missile Test in the South China Sea 'Disturbing,'" *Japan Times*, July 3, 2019.

[694] Lye Liang Fook and Ha Hoang Hop, "The Vanguard Bank Incident: Developments and What Next?" *ISEAS Perspective*, No. 69, 2019.

[695] Carlyle A. Thayer, "A Difficult Summer in the South China Sea," *The Diplomat*, November 2019.

[696] Vietnam repeatedly asked China to immediately end violations and withdraw all vessels from Vietnamese waters. In a rare move, Vietnam also accused China of serious violations of Vietnam sovereignty.

[697] Hanoi still allowed some smaller public protests against China in Vietnam in 2019. See Benedict J. Tria Kerkvliet, "Protesting China: Vietnam's Vanguard," *Southeast Asia Globe*, October 2, 2019; and "Vietnam Activists Stage Rare Anti-China Protest amid Concerns over Survey Ship," *Radio Free Asia*, August 19, 2019.

[698] In late August 2019, for example, the Chinese and Vietnamese militaries participated in an effort to provide free medical treatment in their joint border area. See "Vietnam, China Hold Joint Medical Examination in Border Areas,"

China, such as submitting a dispute with China to the International Tribunal of the Law of the Sea.[699]

At the same time, Hanoi sought broad international support against China and worked with several multilateral institutions.[700] Hanoi had particularly hoped that a combination of key international actors (some exerting influence through their oil companies), including the United States, Russia, and Japan, would discourage a forceful PRC response. The United States issued several unilateral, bilateral, and trilateral public diplomatic statements in support of Vietnam.[701] It also engaged in five different types of military activities in the SCS during the standoff from May to October 2019 that either directly or indirectly supported Vietnam by challenging PRC claims.[702] Japan provided some support and stated that it opposed actions that escalated tensions

Vietnam Net, August 24, 2018; and Zhou Na and Guo Chen, "China-Vietnam Joint Medical Examination in Border Areas Concludes," *China Military Online*, August 29, 2018.

[699] Lye Liang Fook and Ha Hoang Hop, "The Vanguard Bank Incident: Developments and What Next?" *ISEAS Perspective*, No. 69, 2019, p. 6.

[700] Hanoi supposedly briefed the United States, Japan, India, Australia, New Zealand, South Korea, France, Germany, the United Kingdom, and the European Union about dynamics at Vanguard Bank and its attempts to communicate with the PRC. Hanoi also leveraged a range of ASEAN-related fora and an address to the 74th UN General Assembly in September 2019 to raise the situation at Vanguard Bank. See Carlyle A. Thayer, "A Difficult Summer in the South China Sea," *The Diplomat*, November 2019.

[701] In late July and late August, the U.S. Department of State issued statements that criticized PRC activities at Vanguard Bank. The United States, Australia, and Japan also issued a statement expressing serious concern over developments at Vanguard Bank during their Trilateral Security Dialogue in August. This was followed by a statement included in the U.S. and Australia high-level bilateral talks the same month. Beyond U.S. activity, Australian Prime Minister Scott Morrison also traveled to Vietnam in August and issued a joint statement with Vietnamese Prime Minister Nguyen Xuan Phuc that expressed concern over developments in the SCS. Similarly, the European Union's Foreign Affairs and Security Policy issued a statement noting that the unilateral actions in the SCS were contributing to tensions. See Associated Press, "U.S. Concerned over China's 'Interference' in South China Sea," *Voice of America*, July 21, 2019; Morgan Ortagus, "China Escalates Coercion Against Vietnam's Longstanding Oil and Gas Activity in the South China Sea," U.S. Embassy and Consulates in China, August 21, 2019; and Carlyle A. Thayer, "A Difficult Summer in the South China Sea," *The Diplomat*, November 2019.

[702] First, the USS *Ronald Reagan* aircraft carrier conducted a military exercise in the SCS with Japan in mid-June, sailed through the disputed waters in early August, and again conducted operations in the SCS in late September. Second, in mid-August, the Chief of Staff of the USAF, General David Goldfein, and U.S. Pacific Air Forces Commander General Charles Q. Brown both visited Vietnam, marking the first visit to the Southeast Asian country by the Air Chief since the Vietnam War. Both generals reaffirmed Vietnam's right to protect its sovereignty. Third, the United States conducted two FONOPs against Fiery Cross Reef and Mischief Reef in the Spratly Islands in late August and against the Paracel Islands in mid-September. Both FONOPs were targeted at China in support of Vietnam because some of the maritime assets China sent to Vanguard Bank had stopped at Fiery Cross Reef for refueling and Vietnam and China both claim the Paracels. Fourth, between June and when the Vanguard Bank standoff ended in late October, Chinese experts tracked nine U.S. B-52H bombers engaging in operations over the SCS. Of these, China only specified the location of three of them as "to the north of Scarborough Shoal," suggesting that the rest were farther south and could have been close to the Spratlys. Finally, Chinese experts identified the United States as engaging in more than 20 different military exercises and exchanges in or near the SCS between June and late October, of which two involved the Vietnamese military (in mid-August in Singapore and in late September in Vietnam). See Jim Gomez, "U.S. Carrier Sails into Disputed Waters amid New Flare-Ups," Associated Press, August 6, 2019; Jesse Johnson, "Japan-Based U.S. Aircraft Carrier in South China Sea Ahead of Key Chinese Anniversary," *Japan Times*, September 29, 2019; Viet Anh, "U.S. Respects Vietnam's Right to Protect Its

in the SCS, although it did not name China. The Kremlin quickly denied that Rosneft consulted it on drilling but also did not order Rosneft to cease its activity.

Explanations for Chinese Reactions

There are several possible explanations for why China responded to Vietnam in 2019 mainly using military coercion and without highly visible geopolitical or economic measures. First, compared with 2018, China may have escalated in order to place additional pressure on Vietnam and Rosneft to stop its activities at Vanguard Bank, which had now been undertaken for a second consecutive year. Although China may have been more initially cautious and patient with Rosneft because of Beijing's desire to improve relations with Moscow, Beijing had deepened its relations with Russia by 2019 and may have decided that the relationship could withstand increased pressure on Rosneft as a result. In June 2019, Chinese President Xi Jinping traveled to Moscow, and the two countries agreed to upgrade their relationship to a "comprehensive strategic partnership of coordination for a new era."[703]

Indeed, China may have sought to "normalize" PRC efforts to block other SCS claimants from developing energy in its claimed territories by employing its maritime assets in a more sustained fashion while also more privately pressuring claimants.[704] While PRC efforts were not necessarily successful in 2019, Beijing could have decided that instead of making each Chinese effort a costly, high-profile diplomatic and regional crisis involving public demonstrations and economic sanctions, as in the 2014 China-Vietnam standoff, it should instead focus its energy on disrupting its competitors' abilities to operate at sea. Aided by China's ability to operate from developed disputed features it controls in the SCS (such as Subi Reef and Fiery Cross Reef), Chinese maritime actors are increasingly conducting patrols without returning to Hainan for replenishment. PRC actions from 2019 onward support this explanation.[705]

Sovereignty: Generals," *VnExpress*, August 18, 2019; Congressional Research Service, "U.S.-Vietnam Relations," *In Focus*, February 16, 2021, p. 35; Asia Maritime Transparency Initiative, "Update: China Risks Flare-Up over Malaysian, Vietnamese Gas Resources," Center for Strategic and International Studies, December 13, 2019; and SCSPI, *Incomplete Report on U.S. Military Activities in the South China Sea in 2019* [2019年美军南海军事活动不完全报告], Beijing: Peking University, March 28, 2020, pp. 7, 16–23.

[703] "China, Russia Agree to Upgrade Relations for a New Era," Xinhua, June 6, 2019.

[704] Examples of PRC private pressure include China's alleged threat to attack Vietnam's platforms in 2017 to discourage development at Vanguard Bank and the threat of potential significant PRC maritime presence (China had readied 40 naval vessels, including its *Liaoning* aircraft carrier) in 2018. See Bill Hayton, "The South China Sea in 2020," statement before the U.S.-China Economic and Security Review Commission, Hearing on U.S.-China Relations in 2020: Enduring Problems and Emerging Challenges, September 9, 2020.

[705] For example, CCG vessel *Haijing 35111* engaged in provocative actions against Malaysia-linked oil developments efforts near Luconia Shoal in May 2019; several CCG vessels and *Haiyang Dizhi 8* challenged Malaysia's oil exploration efforts near Sarawak from December 2019 to May 2020; a CCG vessel patrolled Vanguard Bank in July and August 2020 to prevent Vietnam-linked exploration activities; and a CCG ship sought to disrupt Vietnamese oil exploration in Block 5-02 in February 2021. See Bill Hayton, "The South China Sea in 2020," statement before the U.S.-China Economic and Security Review Commission, Hearing on U.S.-China

Second, China may have not escalated as much as it did in 2014 because of Vietnam's relatively cautious and restrained approach, as well as the larger geopolitical context—including Vietnam's efforts to internationalize the dispute by involving Russian and Japanese oil companies and also inviting significant U.S. support. China could have assessed that the international reputational costs of a more aggressive approach were too great to be worth it. Also, because Vietnam did not escalate the situation rapidly and as much as in 2014, Beijing may have felt less need to escalate in kind. China was also aware that Vietnam was to assume the chair of ASEAN in 2020 and, as one analysis concludes, "neither China nor Vietnam want[ed] to see a deterioration of their relations to an extent that complicates Vietnam's role as chair."[706] This follows historical patterns, as in the past Beijing has catered to as well as increased pressure on the ASEAN chair to act on its behalf.[707]

Finally, there is little evidence to suggest that events in Hong Kong and Taiwan as well as elevated U.S.-China tensions contributed to China's escalation in 2019.[708] China blamed the United States for the unrest in Hong Kong and supporting Taiwan's "pro-independence" moves and was also on guard for the significant military activity that the United States was taking in the SCS.[709] It is unclear that escalating against Vietnam in the SCS or placing additional blame on Vietnam for unrest in Hong Kong would have given Beijing any additional advantage. Instead, it is possible that Beijing may not have wanted to escalate against Vietnam because China was also simultaneously pushing its maritime claims against the Philippines and Vietnam (in contrast with 2014, when China ramped up pressure on Vietnam but was not as active at the same time against other SCS claimants).[710] China, in other words, may have wanted to avoid overextension.

Finally, China may have sought to discourage Vietnamese support to Hong Kong protesters and discourage additional anti-China Vietnamese protests in Hong Kong on top of the already

---

Relations in 2020: Enduring Problems and Emerging Challenges, September 9, 2020; Ian Storey, "The South China Sea, a Fault Line in China-Russia Relations," *ISEAS Commentary*, October 13, 2020; Duy Nguygen, "Foreign Ministry Spokesperson Opposes China's Intrusion of Vietnam's Waters," *Hanoi Times*, February 25, 2021; Drake Long, "Vietnam Issues Decree Against Illegal Oil and Gas Operations in Its Waters," *Radio Free Asia*, August 31, 2020; and Asia Maritime Transparency Initiative, "Update: China Risks Flare-Up over Malaysian, Vietnamese Gas Resources," Center for Strategic and International Studies, December 13, 2019.

[706] Lye Liang Fook and Ha Hoang Hop, "The Vanguard Bank Incident: Developments and What Next?" *ISEAS Perspective*, No. 69, 2019, p. 7.

[707] For an example of PRC pressure on past ASEAN chairs, see Ernest Z. Bower, "China Reveals Its Hand on ASEAN in Phnom Penh," *CSIS Commentary*, July 20, 2012.

[708] Along with the protests in Hong Kong, Taiwan was gearing up for its presidential election in 2020 and China was worried that the election results may not be favorable. See Lye Liang Fook and Ha Hoang Hop, "The Vanguard Bank Incident: Developments and What Next?" *ISEAS Perspective*, No. 69, 2019.

[709] In July 2019, for example, the United States welcomed a relatively high-profile visit of Taiwan President Tsai Ing-wen, in New York and she also interacted with congressional members. See Ralph Jennings, "Will US First Class Treatment of Visiting Taiwan President Rattle China?" *Voice of America*, July 17, 2019.

[710] Huong Le Thu, "China's Incursion into Vietnam's EEZ and Lessons from the Past," Asia Maritime Transparency Initiative, Center for Strategic and International Studies, August 8, 2019.

tense local dynamics. Vietnamese citizens have in the past staged anti-China protests in Hong Kong, including over sovereignty disputes in the SCS in 2014.[711] In 2014, when there were large-scale protests in Hong Kong as part of the Umbrella Movement, the Vietnamese government did not restrict state-run media coverage of the events in Vietnam, and ethnic Vietnamese people in Hong Kong joined the pro-democracy protests.[712] Although it is difficult to measure the number of Vietnamese tourists and ethnic Vietnamese people in Hong Kong, more than 220,000 Vietnamese asylum seekers either traveled through or stayed in Hong Kong from 1975 to 2000 because of the Vietnam War and because of policies that the subsequent Vietnamese Communist government embraced, so it seems reasonable to believe that Hong Kong's ethnic Vietnamese population is reasonably large.[713] In 2019, there were reports of ethnic Vietnamese people joining the Hong Kong protests and Vietnamese citizens in Hong Kong sharing live feed of local activities via social media to promote the pro-democracy movement.[714] In addition, there is significant sympathy among young Vietnamese people for what Hong Kong protesters seek to achieve, and this was showcased in the demonstrations that the Vietnamese diaspora engaged in against PRC embassies and consulates internationally to support the Hong Kong movement.[715]

What is unexpected and showed CCP concern is that Beijing took steps to mute public blame on Vietnam for the Hong Kong protests. In late July, a delegation of 30-plus youth from the Hong Kong Wanchai District Junior Police Call visited the PRC Consulate General in Ho Chi Minh City, where Chinese Consul General Wu Jun explained China-Vietnam relations, the history of Western colonialism in Southeast Asia, and the origins of the problems in Hong Kong, which he attributed to U.S. and Western intervention.[716] In August, the nationalist PRC newspaper *Global Times* publicly refuted claims that ethnic Vietnamese people in Hong Kong

---

[711] Adam Rose, "Vietnamese Stage Small Anti-China Protest in Hong Kong," Reuters, May 25, 2014.

[712] Marianne Brown, "Hong Kong Protesters 'Inspire' Vietnam Activists," *Voice of America*, October 2, 2014; and Zoe Low, "An Ode to Hong Kong's Extradition Bill Protesters, Penned by Vietnamese-American Dissidents," *South China Morning Post*, July 11, 2019.

[713] Christopher DeWolf, "Fighting Until the End: Hong Kong's Vietnamese Refugees," *Zolima CityMag*, December 12, 2019; Chinese netizens refer to a similar figure of 200,000 ethnic Vietnamese refugees who stayed in in Hong Kong.

[714] "'He Felt I Would Understand,' Hong Kong Protester's Mother Says," *Radio Free Asia*, December 12, 2019.

[715] In Australia, for example, the Vietnamese diaspora had banded together with Uyghurs, Hong Kong residents, and Taiwan citizens to support the protesters. See Julia Barajas and Allison Hong, "Vietnamese Immigrants Rally Behind Hong Kong Protesters Pushing for Democracy in Asia," *Los Angeles Times*, December 15, 2019; and Erin Handley and Iris Zhao, "How Hong Kong's Protest Movement Is Forging Solidary with Australia's Uyghurs and Tibetans," *ABC News*, September 7, 2019. For a discussion from a Vietnamese perspective of why it is natural for Vietnamese people to support Hong Kong's democracy movement, see Trinh Huu Long, "Hong Kong Next-Door Ally," *The Vietnamese*, October 28, 2020.

[716] Consulate General of the People's Republic of China in Ho Chi Minh City, "Consul General Wu Jun Engage in Discussions and Exchanges with Hong Kong Police Wanchai District Junior Youth Call" ["吴骏总领事与香港警务处湾仔警区少年警讯代表团座谈交流"], July 30, 2019.

were to blame for the protests and instead accused the United States and the West of inciting unrest.[717] This article was carried by other PRC media outlets.[718] These Chinese activities suggest that Beijing was at least aware of the possibility that ethnic Vietnamese people and Vietnamese citizens could support the Hong Kong protests and was actively trying to dispel such notions, potentially to prevent pushing them to side with the protesters more.[719] This argues against the hypothesis that Beijing is more likely to be aggressive when China is experiencing internal instability.

Conclusion

Overall, our analysis of PRC reactions to Vietnamese energy development activities at Vanguard Bank does not support the hypothesis that China is more likely to respond aggressively to U.S. or allied/partner actions that occur when China is experiencing increased internal instability. Although China did escalate its activities against Vietnam and Rosneft more in 2019 than in 2018, there is little evidence that this escalation was driven by PRC internal considerations. If anything, China may have wanted to avoid pushing Vietnam too much given the risk that doing so could have encouraged Hanoi (or nationalist Vietnamese citizens or ethnic Vietnamese people abroad) to engage in additional activities to support the pro-democracy protests in Hong Kong.

---

[717] Ling De [凌德] and Li Fengxiang [李风向], "Forgetting Family and Ethnic History, Leading Hong Kong Troublemakers Bring in External Forces" ["忘祖籍抛民族身份，乱港头目成外部势力'带路党'"], *Global Times*, August 21, 2019.

[718] "The Worst HK Troublemakers Are Ethnic Vietnamese? Media Refute Allegations" ["香港闹得最凶的是越南裔？媒体驳斥"], *Sina News*, August 21, 2019.

[719] Related to the PRC concern, we could not find any English or Chinese public statements from the Vietnamese Foreign Ministry affirming Vietnam's support for Hong Kong as internal affairs of China until September 12, 2019, after tensions between Vietnam and China had decreased near Vanguard Bank. This is in contrast with 2014, when Vietnam issued a statement on Hong Kong in early October shortly after massive protests occurred in Hong Kong in late September. It is possible that Hanoi was aware of PRC concerns and wanted to withhold such a statement as leverage against China. See "Vietnam Hopes Situation in China's Hong Kong SAR Back to Normal Soon: Spokesperson," Xinhua, September 12, 2019; and Hai Minh, "Vietnamese Advised to Avoid Protest Sites in Hong Kong," *Socialist Republic of Viet Nam Government News*, October 2, 2014.

Case 13: Hong Kong Protests and the China-India Border Brawl

Like Case 12, Case 13 tests the hypothesis that the aggressiveness of Chinese reactions to U.S., allied, and partner activities increases when China is experiencing more domestic instability by examining whether unrest in Hong Kong in 2019 and 2020 shaped China's external behavior. It focuses on China's apparent decision to provoke a violent brawl with India in June 2020, which resulted in the deaths of 20 Indian and at least four Chinese troops. As in Case 12, a review of the available evidence provides little support for this hypothesis. China's leadership appeared to enjoy strong public support during the Hong Kong protests, and the evidence suggests that the Hong Kong protesters enjoyed little support among the mainland Chinese. Although pressure from domestic disturbances linked to Hong Kong or to other issues such as the COVID-19 pandemic may have indirectly played a role in exacerbating Beijing's suspicions and distrust regarding other international actors, the violence on the China-India border in June 2020 appears to be better explained by broader structural drivers of worsening China-India relations, including worsening incidents and escalating tensions on the disputed border, as well as a broader pattern of more-assertive Chinese behavior regarding its sovereignty flashpoints.

Hong Kong Unrest

As Case 12 describes, on June 9, 2019, protests erupted in Hong Kong over a proposed Chinese law to permit extradition to the mainland. Since the 1997 handover from the United Kingdom, Hong Kong had previously enjoyed a largely separate legal system from the rest of China, which the new law threatened to undermine. The United States and other Western governments condemned the proposed change, which they regarded as an ominous sign of Beijing's tightening grip on the city.[720] In Hong Kong, organizers estimated that about 1 million people participated in peaceful demonstrations.[721] However, an increasingly heavy-handed police response fueled large-scale demonstrations. Protests continued throughout the year, occasionally turning violent. In July 2019, demonstrators broke into the local legislature, and months later students occupied universities for several weeks before the police overcame them. Protests eased with the onset of COVID-19–related restrictions in early 2020, but demonstrations have continued despite brutal police crackdowns, large-scale arrests, and the imposition of strict security restrictions.[722]

---

[720] David Brunnstrom, "U.S. Warns Extradition Law Changes May Jeopardize Hong Kong's Special Status," Reuters, June 10, 2019.

[721] Austin Ramzy and Mike Ives, "Hong Kong Protests: One Year Later," *New York Times*, July 24, 2020.

[722] Austin Ramzy and Mike Ives, "Hong Kong Protests: One Year Later," *New York Times*, July 24, 2020.

China's Reactions

In June 2020, Chinese and Indian troops clashed in their first violent confrontation in decades, resulting in the deaths of 20 Indian troops.[723] Months later, Chinese authorities acknowledged that four PLA troops also died in the encounter.[724] It was the first fatal clash since Chinese troops had killed four Indian soldiers while patrolling disputed territory in 1975. Over the remainder of the summer, troops fought without firearms several additional times, although no deaths were reported in these subsequent encounters. In September 2020, troops on the border fired warning shots—the first time that guns were used on the border in decades.[725] The 2020 clashes therefore represented a dramatic escalation in tensions between the two states along a border that has been formally contested since the British colonial period but had not been a source of violence since the Cold War.

Explanations for China's Reactions

Analysts have considered a number of explanations for the violent brawl. One possibility is that recent Indian actions to strengthen its border forces may have signaled to China that increased cooperation with the United States had emboldened New Delhi.[726] These actions included Indian efforts to strengthen its transportation networks leading to the region. In the weeks leading up to the clash, India added roads and airports in a bid to keep pace with Chinese infrastructure developments. China regarded the infrastructure development as taking place on its territory.[727]

In addition to these changes on the ground, overall tensions between China and India had been growing over the past few years, a phenomenon explored in greater detail in Case 11. The two countries have maintained a historic rivalry as dominant powers in Asia, a rivalry that has only intensified in recent years as both have experienced substantial gains in national power.[728] China has long sought to contain its rival through close cooperation with India's primary

---

[723] Rajesh Roy, "India-China Border Standoff Turns Violent, with 20 Indian Soldiers Dead," *Wall Street Journal*, June 16, 2020.

[724] Nectar Gan, "4 Chinese Soldiers Died in Bloody India Border Clash Last Year, China Reveals," *CNN*, February 20, 2021.

[725] Jeffrey Gettleman, "Shots Fired Along India-China Border for First Time in Years," *New York Times*, September 8, 2020.

[726] Li Jian [李剑], Chen Wenwen [陈文文], and Jin Jing [金晶], "The Pattern of Indian Ocean Power and the Expansion of China's Sea Power in the Indian Ocean" ["印度洋海权格局与中国海权的印度洋拓展"], *China's Foreign Policy* [中国外交], 2015; and Christopher K. Colley, "China's Ongoing Debates About India and the United States," *Asia Dispatches*, June 30, 2020.

[727] Gabriel Crossley and Devjyot Ghoshal, "Explainer: Why Are Chinese and Indian Troops Fighting in a Remote Himalayan Valley?" Reuters, June 17, 2020.

[728] T. V. Paul, ed., *The China-India Rivalry in the Globalization Era*, Washington, D.C.: Georgetown University Press, 2018.

antagonist, Pakistan. China's initiation of the BRI project in 2013 intensified long-standing Indian fears of Chinese encirclement and helped incentivize New Delhi to bolster its relations with the United States.[729]

Chinese perceptions of the United States' activities and intent were also most likely a significant factor in Beijing's handling of both the Hong Kong crisis and border tensions with India. The rapid deterioration of U.S.-China relations under President Trump raised Chinese anxieties and fears regarding the United States. Deepening U.S. military ties to India appeared to confirm these suspicions.[730] However, Beijing's distrust of U.S. intentions also played a role in its view of the Hong Kong protests. Chinese media and commentators routinely blamed the United States for instigating protests and "interfering" in Chinese domestic politics.[731] China's decisionmaking regarding the Indian clash took place in this context of concern over threats of foreign interference in its peripheral territories.

Official Chinese statements and most news commentaries tended to blame incursions by Indian troops on Chinese territory as the main cause of the clash.[732] Other analysts cited China's perception of the growing threat posed by India-U.S. relations, tensions over India's rejection of China's BRI project, friction attendant to Chinese and Indian infrastructure development in contested areas, and other factors related directly to the border dispute or China-India relations more generally.[733] No statements by Chinese officials and no commentary in Chinese press has been observed to have made any link between the Hong Kong protests and the China-India border violence. Indeed, no Chinese source has been found that links concern over domestic instability to foreign policy disputes whatsoever. Chinese sources instead tend to regard the Hong Kong protests and the China-India border issues as separate and distinctly challenges.

Of course, the fact that Chinese media sources do not link the two phenomena does not mean that they are unrelated. Indeed, publicly acknowledging any link might have undermined any "rally around the flag" effect from the clashes, had China sought to precipitate them for this reason. However, there are other reasons to be skeptical of a link. First, the timing is problematic. The Hong Kong protests escalated dramatically in 2019 but ebbed in the beginning of 2020 as the Chinese government clamped down with COVID-19–related restrictions as well as tighter security measures overall. As a result, the level of Hong Kong protests in general was

---

[729] Gulshan Sachdeva, "Indian Perceptions of the Chinese Belt and Road Initiative," *International Studies*, Vol. 55, No. 4, 2018.

[730] Bureau of South and Central Asian Affairs, "U.S. Relations with India," U.S. Department of State, January 21, 2021.

[731] Elizabeth Shim, "China Blames U.S. for Hong Kong Protests," *UPI*, June 10, 2019.

[732] Hu Xijin, "India Lies About Casualties in Border Clash with China," *Global Times*, September 17, 2020.

[733] Yun Sun, "China's Strategic Assessment of the Ladakh Clash," *War on the Rocks*, June 19, 2020.

lower by the summer of 2020 than it had been in 2019.[734] The China-India border clash thus erupted at a time when the Hong Kong situation had quieted considerably from its peak agitation the previous year.

Moreover, there is little evidence that Beijing felt threatened by the Hong Kong protests, even at their height. The city was largely isolated from the rest of the mainland, and the grievances of the city were unique to Hong Kong. All other Chinese cities already operate under the provisions of the "extradition" law, and thus Hong Kong's call for an exception to the country's laws was not likely to inspire much sympathy from Chinese citizens. Anecdotal reporting from Western news agencies generally found that most Chinese citizens opposed the Hong Kong protesters.[735] Although reporters noted occasional private expressions of support for Hong Kong and even evidence that at least a few mainlanders have joined the protests, a consistent theme of Western coverage is that such instances were relatively rare.[736] Observers blamed the lack of mainland support partly on the overwhelmingly negative press coverage of the protests in Chinese media.[737] However, the same sources noted little sympathy for Hong Kong protesters even among well-informed, well-educated Chinese people, which at least one source attributed to a shift in pro-Beijing attitudes and long-standing tensions between Hong Kong and the mainland.[738]

There was also little reason for Beijing to fear that the protests might spread to other cities. Unlike the protests related to Tiananmen Square in 1989 that arose in part due to nationwide economic difficulties, the grievances of the Hong Kong people were fairly specific to the unique arrangements of the city. Moreover, polling generally showed that mainland Chinese citizens supported the central government by large margins, with the caveat that reliable public polling in autocratic countries such as China is problematic.[739] But given what appears to be a solid base of domestic public support, Beijing appears to have had few domestic political incentives to provoke violent clashes with a neighboring country.

The Hong Kong protests stood out as among the most high-profile domestic challenges that confronted Chinese leaders in 2019 and 2020, but they were not the only one. Beginning in late 2019, Chinese leaders also grappled with the domestic and international political consequences of the COVID-19 pandemic, which originated in Wuhan, China. Although the Chinese

---

[734] Primrose Riordan and Nicolle Liu, "Hong Kong Protestors Defy Ban to Show Support for Detained Leaders," *Financial Times*, March 1, 2021.

[735] Karoline Kan, "Mainland Chinese Lack Sympathy for Hong Kong Protestors," *Nikkei Asia*, July 30, 2019.

[736] Li Yuan, "Why Many in China Oppose Hong Kong's Protests," *New York Times*, July 1, 2019.

[737] Ying Ma, "As Hong Kong Protests Face Mainland Pushback, Here's What Chinese Nationalists Misunderstand," *NBC News*, September 9, 2019.

[738] Li Yuan, "Why Many in China Oppose Hong Kong's Protests," *New York Times*, July 1, 2019.

[739] Edward Cunningham, Tony Saich, and Jessie Turiel, *Understanding CCP Resilience: Surveying Chinese Public Opinion Through Time*, Cambridge, Mass.: Ash Center for Democratic Governance and Innovation, July 2020.

government struggled initially to contain the outbreak, by early 2020 its efforts had largely paid off, and official press reports, not surprisingly, trumpeted the success and competence of the Chinese government in its handling of the pandemic.[740] However, China did appear sensitive to the international costs to its reputation for permitting the disease to spread globally. Authorities directed an aggressive overseas propaganda effort to deny any fault by China and promoted disinformation as to the origins of the disease.[741] The shock of the pandemic itself may not have driven Chinese leaders to provoke a clash with India, but tensions with the United States and much of the Western world that arose from the pandemic added to an atmosphere of hostility and resentment that could have indirectly motivated Chinese commanders to act aggressively on the Indian border.

In contrast, the timing of the China-India brawl therefore appears to be closely linked to tensions generated by both sides' efforts to build infrastructure and solidify territorial claims in the disputed China-India border areas.[742] The clash, moreover, followed a series of standoffs, incidents, and near-crises in many Chinese sovereignty and territory-related flashpoints stretching back to the early 2010s, when China and Japan began to intensify their maritime standoff in the Senkakus, China seized Scarborough Reef from the Philippines, and Beijing stepped up its intimidation of Taiwan.[743] Indeed, in 2017, Chinese and Indian military forces endured a 73-day standoff in the Doklam region that many feared might escalate into conflict.[744] Notably, these developments far preceded the eruption of protest and violence in Hong Kong in 2019.

Conclusion

Although strong conclusions are difficult to draw from this case given limited access to high-level PRC thinking and decisionmaking processes, it appears that the domestic crises related to the Hong Kong protests and other issues such as COVID-19 played, at most, an indirect role in encouraging Chinese leaders to overreact to external challenges. The lack of any direct evidence linking the Hong Kong protests and the border clash by itself provides reason to doubt such a hypothesis. Moreover, the deterioration of China-India relations had been gradual; escalating tensions near the China-India border nearly broke out into violence in 2017. Patterns of incidents and near-crises involving sovereignty flashpoints stretching to the early 2010s thus seem to better explain the sudden onset of the China-India violence than proximate internal instability.

---

[740] "China's Achievement of Covid-19 Fight Obvious: Global Times Editorial," *Global Times*, May 10, 2020.

[741] Liu Caiyu and Fan Anqi, "More Evidence Supports Multiple Virus Origins," *Global Times*, November 29, 2020.

[742] Ajai Shukla, "How China and India Came to Lethal Blows," *New York Times*, June 19, 2020.

[743] Office of the Secretary of Defense, *Annual Report to Congress: Military and Security Developments Involving the People's Republic of China 2020*, Washington, D.C., 2020.

[744] Jonathan Marcus, "China-India Border Tension: Satellite Imagery Shows Doklam Plateau Build-Up," *BBC News*, January 26, 2018.

Case 14: Chinese Reactions to U.S. Freedom of Navigation Operations in the Taiwan Strait in 2020

The final case tests the hypothesis that Chinese reactions will be more aggressive to U.S. and allied and partner actions that China perceives as directly threatening its political legitimacy. In 2020, the United States increased the tempo of its transits through the Taiwan Strait. Given the importance of unification with Taiwan to the CCP as a legitimizing policy goal, these transits were probably interpreted by Chinese leaders as threats to their current and future political legitimacy. This helps explain China's decision to mount a range of aggressive military responses and supports the hypothesis. The timing of the acceleration of PLA operations, and especially of Chinese official comments regarding the relationship between American support for Taiwan and "Taiwanese independence forces," suggest that the victory of the DPP in Taiwan's early 2020 elections was also a decisive factor in shaping Beijing's reactions. This was in large part because of the CCP's perception that the DPP posed a clear and present threat to Chinese sovereignty and territorial integrity, two "core interests" the CCP has promised to defend, thus staking the regime's legitimacy on the outcome.

U.S. Escalation of Taiwan Strait Freedom of Navigation Operations

In 2020, the frequency of U.S. transits in the Taiwan Strait increased significantly. American warships transited the strait 13 times that year, up from nine times in 2019 and three times in 2018.[745] Most of these transits were by single destroyers, though they occasionally involved more ships.[746] Such actions are seen as provocative by Beijing because they allegedly challenge China's control over its TW and violate its legally dubious assertion that warships must receive permission before entering those waters.[747] Even more galling for the Chinese, these actions allegedly lend support to "Taiwanese independence activists" who PRC officials fear are pushing for a permanent separation between the island and the mainland.[748] The Chinese National People's Congress denounced U.S. actions such as FONOPs and transits as attempts to "brutally interfere in China's domestic affairs" and embolden Taiwanese separatists, who might lose hope

---

[745] Lolita C. Baldor, "Sharp Jump in U.S. Navy Transits to Counter China Under Trump," Associated Press, March 15, 2021; and Caitlin Doornbos, "Navy Ties Record with Its 12th Transit Through the Taiwan Strait This Year," *Stars and Stripes*, December 19, 2020.

[746] Caitlin Doornbos, "U.S. Navy Ends 2020 with Another Taiwan Strait Transit," *Stars and Stripes*, December 31, 2020.

[747] Ben Werner, "Third Time in Four Months U.S. Warships Transit Tense Taiwan Strait," *USNI News*, January 24, 2019.

[748] "Attempts to Use Taiwan to Control China or Use Weapons to Prevent Unification Will Fail in the End" ["'以台制华'和'以武拒统'注定难逃失败下场"], *Qiushi* [求是], July 11, 2019.

and desist if it were not for the possibility of American assistance.[749] As such, U.S. transits in the Taiwan Strait are problematic for China in both what it sees as its internal affairs, as they provide encouragement to the DPP and its secessionist allies, and its external affairs, as they may embolden other regional actors that are embroiled in maritime territorial disputes with China.[750] It should be noted that this uptick in the frequency of USN transits of the Taiwan Strait came as the United States was increasing its support for Taipei in general, both through legislative action and unprecedented high-level official visits.[751]

Chinese Reactions

The PLA's direct responses to USN transits through the Taiwan Strait were relatively consistent during the Trump presidency and are addressed more broadly in Case 10. Such operations were always roundly condemned in Chinese official statements and media, and the offending ships were often tailed by Chinese vessels or aircraft.[752] The transits were also occasionally followed by PLAN and PLAAF exercises.[753]

In 2020 and early 2021, China also sped up the pace of its own actions in the Taiwan Strait. PLA exercises to intimidate "Taiwanese independence activists" were nothing new, but the size and regularity of these operations increased significantly in 2020. That year, PLA warplanes conducted more flights into Taiwan's ADIZ than at any time since 1996.[754] By late 2020, such incursions had become an almost daily occurrence to the south of the island, between Taiwan and the Taiwan-controlled Pratas Islands.[755] Most of these incursions only involved surveillance aircraft, but they occasionally involved flights of a dozen or more warplanes, including fighters,

---

[749] "National People's Congress Foreign Affairs Office Issues Statement on the Passage of the '2019 Taipei Act'" ["全国人大外事委员会就美国所谓'2019年台北法案'签署成法发表声明"], *Qiushi* [求是], March 28, 2020; and Liu Xuanzun, "PLA Carrier, Warplanes Surround Taiwan in Drills, in Show of Capability to Cut Off Foreign Intervention," *Global Times*, April 6, 2021.

[750] "National People's Congress Foreign Affairs Office Issues Statement on the Passage of the '2019 Taipei Act'" ["全国人大外事委员会就美国所谓'2019 年台北法案'签署成法发表声明"], *Qiushi* [求是], March 28, 2020; and Ren Chengqi [任成琦], "Playing the 'Taiwan Card' Is a Dangerous Game" ["大'台湾牌'是一场危险游戏"], *Qiushi* [求是], July 10, 2019.

[751] Ben Blanchard, "Factbox: Recent Taiwan Visits by Top U.S. Officials," Reuters, January 7, 2021; and Govtrack.us, "Taiwan," search for enacted laws on April 10, 2021.

[752] Ben Blanchard and Reuters Beijing Newsroom, "U.S. Warships Transit Taiwan Strait, China Denounces 'Provocation,'" Reuters, December 30, 2020; and Ben Blanchard and Idrees Ali, "U.S. Warship Sails Through Taiwan Strait, Second Time in a Month," Reuters, April 23, 2020.

[753] Ben Blanchard and Reuters Beijing Newsroom, "U.S. Warships Transit Taiwan Strait, China Denounces 'Provocation,'" Reuters, December 30, 2020; and Ben Blanchard and Idrees Ali, "U.S. Warship Sails Through Taiwan Strait, Second Time in a Month," Reuters, April 23, 2020.

[754] "Chinese Incursions Highest Since 1996," *Taipei Times*, January 4, 2021.

[755] John Xie, "China Is Increasing Taiwan Airspace Incursions," *Voice of America*, January 6, 2021; and Ben Blanchard, "Taiwan Reports Large Incursion by Chinese Air Force," Reuters, January 23, 2021.

bombers, and airborne early warning systems.[756] More troubling still, these air exercises have sometimes been conducted in conjunction with PLAN carrier operations on the opposite side of the island, demonstrating the PLA's ability to effectively surround Taiwan.[757] Figure B.3 contains data on PLA incursions in Taiwan's ADIZ between January 2013 and June 2020.

Figure B.3. PRC Bomber and Fighter Flights Near Taiwan, January 2013 to June 2020

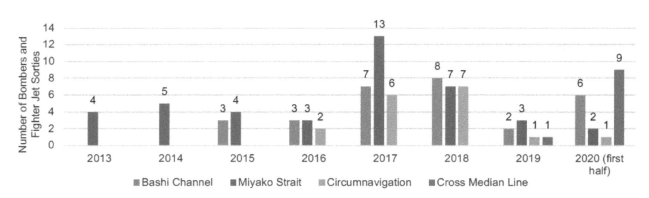

SOURCES: "The Taiwanese Army Is Highly Tense as PLA Fighters Circle Taiwan Again: The Rapid Progress Is Worthy of Vigilance" ["台军高度紧张解放军战机再次绕台: 进步之快值得警惕"], *Sina*, December 19, 2018; Franz-Stefan Gady, "China Flies Su-35 Fighters over Bashi Channel for First Time," *The Diplomat*, May 12, 2018; Franz-Stefan Gady, "China Holds Long-Range Air Combat Drill Near Taiwan," *The Diplomat*, December 20, 2018; Lee Jeong-ho, "Chinese Military Flies Su-30 Fighter Jet, Y-8 Surveillance Plane Close to Taiwan in Latest Show of Strength," *South China Morning Post*, January 23, 2019; Duncan DeAeth, "Chinese Aircraft Transit Miyako Strait Between Taiwan and Okinawa," *Taiwan News*, March 31, 2019; Ankit Panda, "Taipei Slams 'Provocative' Chinese Air Force Fighters Cross Taiwan Strait Median Line," *The Diplomat*, April 1, 2019; other open-source reports; and RAND analysis.

Explanations for Chinese Reactions

China's increasing aggressiveness in 2020 is likely, at least in part, due to the increased threat that U.S. actions posed to CCP legitimacy within the context of Tsai Ing-wen and the DPP decisive victory in the January 2020 general election. For Beijing, Tsai's election was seen as a disaster that it had failed to prevent through a mix of intimidation and subversion.[758] Chinese officials claim that Tsai and her party are constantly seeking to bring about the permanent separation of Taiwan from the mainland.[759] While such moves are not generally described by the

---

[756] Liu Xuanzun, "PLA Carrier, Warplanes Surround Taiwan in Drills, in Show of Capability to Cut Off Foreign Intervention," *Global Times*, April 6, 2021; and Ben Blanchard, "Taiwan Reports Large Incursion by Chinese Air Force," Reuters, January 23, 2021.

[757] Liu Xuanzun, "PLA Prepared as US, Secessionists Provoke," *Global Times*, April 8, 2021.

[758] Kharis Templeman, "How Taiwan Stands Up to China," *Journal of Democracy*, Vol. 31, No. 3, July 2020, pp. 90–93.

[759] Ren Chengqi [任成琦], "Playing the 'Taiwan Card' Is a Dangerous Game" ["大'台湾牌'是一场危险游戏"], *Qiushi* [求是], July 10, 2019.

Chinese themselves as threatening the CCP's legitimacy, they are seen as directly threatening China's territorial integrity and sovereignty, the protection of which is one of the CCP's primary raisons d'être.[760] A failure to deter or prevent Taiwanese independence would mean that the CCP had failed, by its own standards, in its essential task of protecting China's "core interests."[761]

The timing of China's escalation of military exercises near Taiwan suggests that concerns over its legitimacy were a key factor in China's decisionmaking. Although the number of American transits through the Taiwan Strait did increase from 2019 to 2020, it underwent a much larger increase from 2018 to 2019.[762] The greatest accelerations of Chinese air and sea exercises near Taiwan, however, seem to have occurred in 2020.[763] While it is possible that this simply represented a delayed response or the improvement of PLA operational capacity over the course of 2020, it could also have been a response to the changing context in which U.S. operations took place—i.e., following Tsai's reelection and the increase in overt U.S. political support for Taiwan.

That said, the timing between these political events and Chinese reactions is not exact. Although the DPP's more pro-China rivals seemed poised to defeat Tsai for the first half of 2019, as the year progressed polls began to shift more and more in Tsai's favor.[764] PLA operations do not seem to have accelerated until after she won reelection in 2020 and then increased even more significantly in late 2020.[765] This may suggest that American actions in support of Taiwan throughout 2020 (including the increased number of transits, arms sales, and high-level visits) and Tsai's election both played a role. The fact that for most Chinese officials and analysts the problems of American support for Taiwan and Taiwanese separatism are closely linked also supports this view.

The best evidence that China's accelerating military operations are in part a response to the compound threat of American support for Taiwan and the DPP's electoral victories is the fact that Chinese writers have made this link themselves. According to Chinese sources, Taiwanese

---

[760] Ren Chengqi [任成琦], "Playing the 'Taiwan Card' Is a Dangerous Game" ["打'台湾牌'是一场危险游戏"], *Qiushi* [求是], July 10, 2019; Jun Sheng [钧声], "Strongly Oppose American Arms Sales to Taiwan" ["坚决反对美对台军售"], *Qiushi* [求是], July 12, 2019; and Yang Jiechi [杨洁篪], "Respecting History and Looking to the Future, We Must Unswervingly Defend and Stabilize Sino-U.S. Relations" ["尊重历史 面向未来 坚定不移维护和稳定中美关系"], *Qiushi* [求是], August 8, 2020.

[761] Jun Sheng [钧声], "Strongly Oppose American Arms Sales to Taiwan" ["坚决反对美对台军售"], *Qiushi* [求是], July 12, 2019.

[762] Lolita C. Baldor, "Sharp Jump in U.S. Navy Transits to Counter China Under Trump," Associated Press, March 15, 2021.

[763] John Xie, "China Is Increasing Taiwan Airspace Incursions," *Voice of America*, January 6, 2021.

[764] Kharis Templeman, *Taiwan's January 2020 Elections: Prospects and Implications for China and the United States*, Washington, D.C.: Brookings Institution, December 2019.

[765] John Xie, "China Is Increasing Taiwan Airspace Incursions," *Voice of America*, January 6, 2021.

separatists—often a veiled reference to the DPP, or at least the party's more extreme wing—recognize that they cannot hope to stand against the PLA, and so they seek military aid from foreign powers, believing that such protection will give them the cover they need to separate Taiwan from China.[766] Taiwanese leaders are often depicted as obsequiously selling their own country out to foreigners in order to gain such support.[767] The United States is often depicted as more than willing to accommodate the DPP by signaling its support not because they are really committed to Taiwanese democracy but instead because they wish to stoke conflict in the Taiwan Strait to "control" or "contain" China.[768] PLA exercises near Taiwan are seen as needed to deter Taiwanese secessionists, both by reminding them of the consequences of secession and by demonstrating the impotence of foreign powers to save them.[769]

Conclusion

There are many potential explanations for the PLA's increased tempo of operations in the Taiwan Strait over the course of 2020. One is the increasing capabilities of the PLAN and PLAAF: The PLA is able to sustain a higher operational tempo more easily than in the past and has perhaps simply chosen to do so. Since the mid-2010s, the PLAN has added a second aircraft carrier and new destroyers, and the PLAAF has been steadily increasing its comfort and experience with long-range overwater missions since 2013.[770] However, Beijing's *ability* to react

---

[766] "Attempts to Use Taiwan to Control China or Use Weapons to Prevent Unification Will Fail in the End" ["'以台制华'和'以武拒统'注定难逃失败下场"], *Qiushi* [求是], July 11, 2019; Zhu Ping [王平], "In Traveling Through the U.S., Tsai Ying Wen Courts Controversy in Sensitive Cross-Strait Relations" ["过境美国，蔡英文挑动两岸敏感神经"], *Qiushi* [求实], July 12, 2019; Ke Mu [枯木], ed., "America Plays the Taiwan Card Again, Punishing Those Who Break Off Relations with Taiwan and Making the DPP Its Lackey" ["美国又打台湾牌，惩罚跟台湾'断交'友邦，民进党成为马前卒"], *Channel News* [海峡要闻], March 24, 2020; and Liu Xuanzun, "PLA Prepared as US, Secessionists Provoke," *Global Times*, April 8, 2021.

[767] Zhu Ping [王平], "In Traveling Through the U.S., Tsai Ying Wen Courts Controversy in Sensitive Cross-Strait Relations" ["过境美国，蔡英文挑动两岸敏感神经"], *Qiushi* [求实], July 12, 2019.

[768] Note that it is not usually explained how exactly greater tensions in the Taiwan Strait or greater boldness by Taiwanese independence activists will benefit Washington. See "Attempts to Use Taiwan to Control China or Use Weapons to Prevent Unification Will Fail in the End" ["'以台制华'和'以武拒统'注定难逃失败下场"], *Qiushi* [求是], July 11, 2019; Zhu Ping [王平], "In Traveling Through the U.S., Tsai Ying Wen Courts Controversy in Sensitive Cross-Strait Relations" ["过境美国，蔡英文挑动两岸敏感神经"], *Qiushi* [求实], July 12, 2019; and Ren Chengqi [任成琦], "Playing the 'Taiwan Card' Is a Dangerous Game" ["大'台湾牌'是一场危险游戏"], *Qiushi* [求是], July 10, 2019.

[769] Jun Sheng [钧声], "Strongly Oppose American Arms Sales to Taiwan" ["坚决反对美对台军售"], *Qiushi* [求是], July 12, 2019; and Liu Xuanzun, "PLA Prepared as US, Secessionists Provoke," *Global Times*, April 8, 2021.

[770] "China—Navy," *Jane's Sentinel Security Assessment—China and Northeast Asia*, April 1, 2021; and Derek Grossman, Nathan Beauchamp-Mustafaga, Logan Ma, and Michael S. Chase, *China's Long-Range Bomber Flights: Drivers and Implications*, Santa Monica, Calif.: RAND Corporation, RR-2567-AF, 2018, pp. 7, 60–66.

aggressively does not explain its willingness to do so. PLA actions around Taiwan may help the PLA build capabilities necessary to project power into and beyond China's near seas. Beijing may also have wanted to respond to the steady rise in FONOPs challenging its territorial claims in the SCS.[771] Both the desire to build or demonstrate capabilities and to respond to U.S. FONOPs in the SCS, however, were as important in 2019 as they were in 2020. They thus cannot sufficiently account for the sudden jump in PLA activity against Taiwan seen in 2020.

It therefore appears that concern over the growing threat to CCP legitimacy posed by U.S. transits through the Taiwan Strait in 2020 played a major role in driving the aggressiveness of Chinese responses. After the DPP won Taiwan's 2020 elections, Beijing feared that pro-secession leaders now controlled the Taiwanese government and that they might be emboldened to act by U.S. military support.[772] Although the extent to which the DPP is committed to formal independence from China is debatable, the party is perceived in China as constantly and provocatively seeking to increase the political distance between Taiwan and the mainland.[773] Such moves are believed to greatly endanger China's sovereignty and territorial integrity, two "core interests" on which the CCP has anchored its political legitimacy.[774] Because American naval transits and other moves supporting Taiwan are seen as emboldening and enabling pro-independence activists on the island, they struck a particularly acute nerve in China following the DPP's 2020 victory at the ballot box, which helps explain the aggressiveness of PLA actions against Taiwan that year.

---

[771] Jeff M. Smith, "Biden Must Keep Challenging China on Freedom of Navigation," *Foreign Policy*, February 16, 2021.

[772] Zhu Ping [王平], "In Traveling Through the U.S., Tsai Ying Wen Courts Controversy in Sensitive Cross-Strait Relations" ["过境美国，蔡英文挑动两岸敏感神经"], *Qiushi* [求实], July 12, 2019.

[773] Ren Chengqi [任成琦], "Playing the 'Taiwan Card' Is a Dangerous Game" ["大'台湾牌'是一场危险游戏"], *Qiushi* [求是], July 10, 2019.

[774] "National People's Congress Foreign Affairs Office Issues Statement on the Passage of the '2019 Taipei Act'" ["全国人大外事委员会就美国所谓'2019 年台北法案'签署成法发表声明"], *Qiushi* [求是], March 28, 2020.

Appendix C. Example Framework Application

As discussed in Chapter 6, the diversity of different types of U.S. military activities considered in this report led us to develop brief, thumbnail-sketch applications of our framework for a wide range of U.S. military activities. However, the framework developed in the first part of this report also can, and ideally should, be used to more comprehensively assess likely Chinese reactions to different U.S. military activities. This appendix provides a more detailed description of how these "full" applications of the framework would be conducted and includes one detailed application of the framework to a hypothetical specific activity: a series of access and interoperability agreements that the United States might conclude with India.[775]

Steps for Applying the Framework

There are five main steps to applying the complete version of the framework developed in the first part of this report. This section reviews each of these steps in detail. As the prior chapters make clear, this is a complex framework, designed to be nuanced and relatively comprehensive in its assessment of PRC perceptions and reactions. It is not a quick guide that can be utilized by relatively junior analysts or those without substantial knowledge of the PRC and the region. Instead, it is designed to be a supporting tool for analysts with deep prior knowledge of these issues who nonetheless would benefit from a guide that helps them to ensure that they have taken all key issues into consideration. Military planners or others seeking to apply the framework to a potential U.S. military activity should take these requirements into account in deciding when and how best to utilize this framework.[776] For smaller-scale or more-routine activities, they may instead wish to rely on the list of potentially escalatory characteristics highlighted in Chapter 6.

Step 1: Specify Key Characteristics of the U.S. Military Activity

To begin, it is first necessary to specify all of the key characteristics of the proposed military activity, covering the four main categories discussed in Chapter 3: its location, the U.S. allies or partners involved, its capabilities, and its profile. Since the assessments of the military activity as

---

[775] This case was selected for illustrative purposes only. Other than our preference for an activity with a number of different dimensions for which Chinese reactions were not overdetermined to be either extremely escalatory or low/nonreactive, this case could have been substituted for any number of other alternatives.

[776] For example, this framework can be useful for informing various types of assessments on building capabilities and evaluating gaps in security cooperation for regional allies and partners that military planners may be tasked with under Department of Defense Instruction 5132.14, *Assessment, Monitoring, and Evaluation Policy for the Security Cooperation Enterprise*, Washington, D.C.: U.S. Department of Defense, January 31, 2017.

a whole will be dependent on these characteristics, it is important to specify them in detail in advance, even if doing so will require some projections or assumptions. In particular, the profile with which the military activity will be introduced may not be known months or even years in advance of its execution. It is nonetheless important to specify what the analyst's assumptions are about the profile of the military activity, because the resulting analysis may be dependent on them.

Step 2: Identify Relevant Context

Having specified the key characteristics of the military activity, analysts will next need to identify the relevant context that may bear on the assessment. By *relevant context*, we mean prior events and history that relate specifically to the military activity and its key characteristics. It is assumed that analysts will be generally familiar with overarching strategic issues such as the tenor and direction of U.S.-China relations and the overall trajectories of the balance of power in the region. What this step seeks to ensure is that more-specific details that may not be general knowledge are also taken into account. To do so, analysts should consider relevant context that may bear directly on the proposed military activity for each of the six key factors. While the below examples are not comprehensive, they include some of the key questions that analysts should consider when thinking about how context could affect China's responses:

- *Factor 1, China's perceptions of the potential military threat from U.S., allied, and partner capabilities:* Have the military capabilities or defense spending of the U.S. ally or partner involved changed substantially in recent years? Has China demonstrated concern for specific U.S., allied, or partner military capabilities near to or in a similar location to where the military activity is taking place? Has China been conducting military operations against the U.S. ally or partner in recent years, and, if so, what capabilities do those operations rely on?

- *Factor 2, China's perceptions of U.S., allied, and partner hostile intent:* What has been the recent trajectory of PRC relations with the U.S. ally or partner involved? Have U.S.-China relations recently featured any disputes specifically involving this ally or partner? What has been the recent trajectory of U.S. relations with the ally or partner involved, particularly involving defense issues?

- *Factor 3, China's perceptions of threats to its regime legitimacy:* Have there been notable recent U.S.-Taiwan cooperation efforts? Has the ally or partner involved in the U.S. military activity had recent notable statements on or interactions with Taiwan? Has the U.S. ally or partner made other recent statements or initiatives on other areas of separatist concern to Beijing, such as Xinjiang, Tibet, or Hong Kong?

- *Factor 4, China's perceptions of threats to its economic development:* Is the U.S. ally or partner located near any key maritime chokepoints or SLOCs important to China? Does that ally or partner have naval capabilities that could enable it to restrict Chinese shipping, and does it have a history of exercising those capabilities together with the United States? Do the U.S. ally and partner and China have a notable history of shared resource extraction, or is China dependent on the ally or partner for raw materials?

- *Factor 5, China's perceptions of threats to its regional influence:* Does the U.S. ally or partner have a notable role in the region itself? Has it been working to expand its influence? Has China made notable recent efforts to gain influence in the U.S. ally or partner itself?

- *Factor 6, China's perceptions of U.S. commitment to the defense of U.S. allies or partners:* How strong and explicit has the U.S. commitment to defend the ally or partner involved been in the past? What has been the prior history of U.S. basing and security cooperation in the country? Have there been any notable tensions in that bilateral relationship that may have caused China to question the credibility of any U.S. promises to defend the country?

While the relevant context will likely vary considerably across different military activities, these example questions should provide analysts with a starting point for the types of issues to consider.

Step 3: Assess the Linkage Between Activity Characteristics and Key Factors

The next step in applying the framework is to identify which linkages between military activities and key factors, summarized in Table 3.1, apply to this particular military activity. Table 3.1 lists 54 different ways in which posture characteristics may affect the six key factors and, through them, Chinese responses. For a full application of the framework, each of these 47 possibilities should be considered individually (though it is possible to use pieces of the framework to address more-narrow questions). For example, to take the first of these possibilities in the top left of Table 3.1, is the location of the proposed military activity proximate to militarily sensitive areas, bases, or forces of the PRC, adjusted for range? After assessing this question, the analyst would then consider the next: whether the military activity entails the shift of U.S. activity or resources away from militarily sensitive areas, bases, or forces of the PRC, adjusted for range. And so on, through the remainder of the table.

In reviewing all 54 potential linkages between activity characteristics and the key factors, the analyst should also consider what effect the relevant context discussed in Step 2 may have on these linkages. For example, has China expressed prior concern for U.S. military operations in a given location, or has that location been the source of prior tension between the two states? If so, then the importance of the linkage between the location of the military activity and PRC concerns over military threats from U.S. or allied and partner capabilities (Factor 1) may be enhanced. Our framework treats relevant context as a potential multiplier of concern for linkages that apply to a given military activity. That is, while context on its own is unlikely to make an activity characteristic concerning for China, when combined with a clear linkage with a key factor as outlined in Table 3.1, China's concern over that activity characteristic may be enhanced.

Step 4: Aggregate the Overall Effects on PRC Thinking by Activity Characteristic

After assessing all 54 of the potential linkages between activity characteristics and key factors, the next step in our framework is to aggregate overall Chinese concerns, first by each activity characteristic category, and then for the activity as a whole. So, again taking Table 3.1 as a guide, one would first review all of the concerns (and the potential direction of their effects) noted in Step 3 in the "Location" column and consider them together. How substantial do the concerns for all Location linkages assessed in Step 3 appear to be? Do they appear to reflect only minor or limited concerns for China? Or do they instead suggest fundamental threats to Chinese interests likely to be of great concern to Beijing? Or somewhere in between? Furthermore, do some linkages suggest considerations that would reduce PRC concerns or willingness to respond aggressively that may outweigh motivations for more aggressive action?

This process would then be completed for each of the four activity characteristic categories (the columns in Table 3.1) before then further aggregating those into a single assessment for the entire activity. Our framework suggests aggregating PRC concerns by activity characteristic category as an interim step because these characteristics are the levers that U.S. military planners considering a potential activity may wish to alter in response to the results of the analysis. If Chinese concerns with the specific location of an activity are very high, for example, but the specific location is not essential for U.S. goals for the enhancement, which are focused on improving interoperability with the ally or partner, then planners may wish to alter the location in response while maintaining other characteristics.

In the example below, we utilize a simple summarization scheme that borrows the same category names from the PRC reaction typology introduced in Chapter 4 (no or minor, limited, elevated, severe, and maximal) to indicate the approximate aggregate level of PRC concern with a given activity characteristic. While these categories are artificial, they do allow for rough divisions of potential levels of PRC concern, and we believe that choosing five levels strikes an appropriate balance between too few levels, that do not provide an opportunity to reflect real differences, and too many levels, that force analysts into providing a false precision to their assessments.

The process of aggregating PRC concerns is subjective and reliant on the judgment and expertise of the analyst. While in some cases a large number of identified linkages in Step 3 for a given activity characteristic (or column in Table 3.1) may be indicative of elevated Chinese concern, in other cases one or two linkages may on their own be sufficient to indicate an existential area of concern for China. Our framework can help ensure that analysts take into account a fuller range of considerations that may bear on Chinese thinking, but decisions regarding how to weight those considerations, which are more important than others, and how likely each is to push China to consider taking more escalatory responses will ultimately need to rely on the judgment of the analyst applying the framework.

Step 5: Identify Potential PRC Responses

Having assessed an approximate level of PRC concern from the U.S. military activity, the final step in our framework involves identifying the types of PRC actions that could plausibly occur in response. As noted above, our framework suggests aggregating PRC concerns to an approximate level that matches the categories used in the PRC reaction typology summarized in Tables 4.1 and 4.2. The analyst would then review the examples at that intensity level, and those below it, and identify potential responses that would fit the specific circumstances of the activity. The application of the framework below provides an example of this effort.

More challenging, however, is identifying the trade-off between potential near-term and long-term PRC responses. As discussed in Chapter 4, China may decide to respond only in a limited fashion in the near term to U.S. military activities of greater concern while investing substantial resources in longer-term responses that might ultimately be of greater concern to U.S. policymakers. While Chapter 4 provides some guidance regarding when less-visible, longer-term policy changes may be an important aspect of Chinese responses, it may be worth emphasizing here that the higher the level of Chinese concern with a U.S. military activity, the larger the potential for China to undertake a longer-term shift in policy that accompanies its more visible near-term responses. The five steps in our framework are summarized together in Table C.1.

Table C.1. Summary of Framework Application Steps

Steps	Considerations
1. Specify key characteristics of the U.S. military activity	• Location, U.S. ally or partner involved, capabilities, and profile
2. Identify relevant context	• Prior history or events related to activity and key characteristics
3. Assess linkage between activity characteristics and key factors	• Review 54 potential linkages, consider relevant context
4. Aggregate the overall effects on PRC thinking by activity characteristic	• Combination and interaction of PRC concerns by activity characteristic category and for activity as a whole
5. Identify potential PRC responses	• Typology of PRC responses to identify level and type of likely Chinese reactions

Framework Application: Substantial Expansion of Military Access with India

This U.S. military activity, a set of posture enhancements, examines China's potential responses if the United States and India substantially expand military access through a series of agreements that would station U.S. ISR assets along the China-India border; pave the way for the conduct of U.S.-India military exercises in the Himalayas, the Indian Ocean, and with 7th Fleet; and provide the USN greater port access to the Bay of Bengal. We assess that China's reactions to this set of posture enhancements would likely be elevated. China could be motivated to pursue an aggressive response because of concerns over U.S. ISR and forces near disputed border areas and Tibet, as well as the greater capabilities that could be achieved by increased U.S.-India military interoperability and the apparent turn toward joining an anti-China coalition by India. The likelihood that this more-aggressive response could take the form of a direct attack on India would likely be somewhat reduced by the signal that the posture enhancements would send of a stronger U.S.-India defense relationship and the potentially greater willingness of the United States to assist India in defending its border against Chinese incursions. More likely potential Chinese responses could include greater numbers of incursions across the disputed border, more PLAN operations in the Indian Ocean, and a regional diplomatic and messaging campaign to counter U.S. influence.

Posture Enhancement Details

This application of our framework examines China's potential reactions if the United States and India expand their military access agreements.[777] These hypothetical agreements would result in increased U.S. military access at several locations in India, including on the China-India border and at the Visakhapatnam Port on the Bay of Bengal. As part of the agreements, U.S. unmanned aerial systems (UAS) basing would be established near the China-India border, along with an information-sharing and ISR-sharing protocol. The UAS installations would be manned by U.S. military personnel on a small scale, fewer than 20 people. In addition to expanding surveillance along the China-India border, the United States and India would also sign an agreement to hold joint military training exercises in high-altitude areas in the Himalayas with the U.S. Army 10th Mountain Division, although this assessment assumes that those exercises have not yet taken place.

The agreements also have a maritime component, with expanded access for USN ships at Visakhapatnam Port, including regular port calls, fuel storage, and logistics access. In return, the United States agrees to coordinate more activities between the Indian Navy and 7th Fleet, including a regularized schedule of port calls and a series of bilateral and multilateral naval exercises with India and other members of the Quad.

The agreements are announced publicly and accompanied by high-profile senior leader statements and joint appearances, including photos of the agreements being signed by U.S. and Indian leaders. The subsequent statements from U.S. and Indian officials emphasize the two countries' joint interest in protecting against China's coercive actions along the Indian border, as well as China's increasing naval presence in the Indian Ocean. In addition, the United States and

---

[777] For an overview of current U.S.-India defense cooperation efforts, see Bureau of Political-Military Affairs, "U.S. Security Cooperation with India," fact sheet, U.S. Department of State, January 20, 2021.

Indian militaries specify plans for the military exercises to be highly visible and publicized through major U.S. and Indian media channels. While the agreements build on decades of incremental progress in U.S.-India defense ties, the UAS deployment and the joint exercises in the Himalayas illustrate a clear U.S. reorientation toward assisting India with China's border incursions, which would be a new direction for the United States.

Relevant Context

Several areas of prior context would likely inform Chinese reactions to this posture enhancement, including the recent history of border clashes between China and India, India's participation in and support for the Quad, and increases in U.S.-India defense ties. The relevant context is discussed below, organized by each of the six key factors that drive China's reactions to posture enhancements, and is summarized in Table 5.6.

China's perceptions of the military threat posed by increasing U.S. military access with India would likely be affected by the recent increase in Indian military capabilities, particularly along the disputed border areas. Following the clashes along the LAC in 2017, India began a series of efforts to procure weapons, tanks, and planes for its armed forces.[778] India is also in the process of acquiring 30 MQ-9 B Predator drones from the United States to augment surveillance capabilities.[779] These defense acquisitions are aimed at deterring Chinese incursions along the border and would augment China's perception of threat from additional U.S. ISR assets.

For perceptions of hostile intent, China's reactions would likely be informed by the recent China-India border clashes. The most recent conflict began on May 5, 2020, when clashes between Indian and Chinese forces broke out. Within days, these clashes spread to other regions of the LAC, with Chinese and Indian soldiers fighting in the middle LAC along the North Sikkim border.[780] By the end of June 2020, at least 20 Indian and four Chinese soldiers had died in clashes along the LAC, though these numbers are disputed by both sides.[781] Both sides continue to hold talks to de-escalate tensions; however, China would certainly take these crises into account when assessing hostile intent.[782] In addition, closer U.S.-India security cooperation

---

[778] In January 2021, India approved the purchase of 21 MiG-29 and 12 Sukhoi Su-30MKI fighter aircraft from Russia for around $15 billion and an additional 83 Light Combat Aircraft Tejas from India's Hindustan Aeronautics Limited for about $6 billion to bolster its air force. See Sudhi Ranjan Sen, "Defense Stocks Rise as India to Buy $6 Billion Local-Built Jets," *Bloomberg*, January 13, 2021.

[779] Inder Singh Bisht, "India to Finalize MQ-9 B Predator Drone Acquisition," *Defense Post*, July 30, 2021.

[780] Kiran Sharma, "India and China Face Off Along Disputed Himalayan Border," *Nikkei Asia*, May 28, 2020.

[781] Soutik Biswas, "India-China Clash: An Extraordinary Escalation 'with Rocks and Clubs,'" *BBC News*, June 16, 2020.

[782] Anjana Pasricha, "Indian, Chinese Troops Disengage from Himalayan Border Area," *Voice of America*, August 7, 2021.

exemplified by India's participation in the Quad and increased bilateral defense ties also likely enhances China's perceptions of hostile intent.[783]

Chinese perceptions of threats to regime legitimacy might be enhanced by India's ongoing hosting of the Tibetan government in exile; however, New Delhi does not formally recognize it as a government and does not recognize the Dalai Lama as the head of a state.[784] Despite this, Tibet and the Dalai Lama remain an area of sensitivity in China-India relations and might color China's perceptions from this posture enhancement.

Chinese perceptions of threats to economic development are likely to be influenced by the recent expansion of Quad naval activity in the Indian Ocean and near Southeast Asian SLOCs. Though this posture enhancement would not represent a substantial increase in India's or the United States' naval capabilities, it would likely touch on PRC fears of partners that could support the United States in interdicting Chinese shipping in a conflict.[785] China's perceptions of threats to regional influence might also be affected by India's recent efforts to build ties with Southeast Asian states through initiatives such as the Act East policy, which involves building its diplomatic, economic, and military integration with Southeast Asia and represent a counterpoint to Chinese influence efforts.[786] Finally, China's perceptions of U.S. commitment to India's defense would be informed by the strengthening U.S.-India defense relationship and, in particular, the increased emphasis on joint exercises, which potentially illustrate more-robust defense cooperation between the two countries and a greater U.S. commitment to India's defense.[787] Table C.2 summarizes the relevant context for this posture enhancement.

---

[783] "U.S. Indo-Pacific Strategy Undermines Peace, Development Prospect in East Asia: Wang Yi," Xinhua, October 13, 2020. India and the United States have steadily increased their levels of security cooperation over the past several years. See Bureau of Political-Military Affairs, "U.S. Security Cooperation with India," fact sheet, U.S. Department of State, January 20, 2021.

[784] Fiona McConnell, "A State Within a State? Exploring Relations Between the Indian State and the Tibetan Community and Government-in-Exile," Contemporary South Asia, Vol. 19, No. 3, 2011, pp. 299–300.

[785] For example, the Quad's 2020 Malabar exercises involved India, Japan, the United States, and Australia and were conducted in the Indian Ocean. China paid close attention to the exercises, particularly the potential for greater interoperability between participants on counterpiracy and SLOC protection. See Task Force 70 Public Affairs, "India Hosts Japan, Australia, U.S. in Naval Exercise MALABAR 2020," U.S. Navy Office of Information, November 2, 2020; and Harsh V. Pant and Anant Singh Mann, "India's Malabar Dilemma," ORF Issue Brief, No. 393, August 2020.

[786] Dhruva Jaishankar, Acting East: India in the Indo-Pacific, Washington, D.C.: Brookings Institution, October 24, 2019.

[787] For example, the United States and India held their first tri-service military exercise in 2019, Tiger Triumph, which involved the Indian Army, Navy, and Air Force as well the U.S. Navy and USMC. It appears that DoD intends to make this exercise annual and to include both the U.S. Army and Air Force in the future. See Bradley Bowman and Andrew Gabel, "U.S., India Bolster Their Military Partnership in Tiger Triumph Exercise," Defense News, November 13, 2019.

Table C.2. Summary of Relevant Context for Expansion of Military Access with India

Factor PRC Perceptions of:	Summary of Relevant Context
1. Military threat	• Expanding Indian defense capabilities
2. U.S./allied hostile intent	• Recent India-China border clashes • Indian support for Quad • Expansion of U.S.-India defense cooperation
3. Threats to regime legitimacy	• Indian hosting of Tibetan government in exile
4. Threats to economic development	• Expansion of Indian/Quad naval activity in Indian Ocean
5. Threats to regional influence	• History of India's Act East policy/efforts to expand influence in Southeast Asia
6. U.S. commitment to allies/partners	• Increasing U.S.-India defense ties

Effects of Military Activity on PRC Thinking

The following section describes the effects of each of the posture enhancement characteristics (location, U.S. allies and partners involved, capabilities, and profile) on China's level of concern and the likely level of aggressiveness of the PRC response. A summary of these assessments is contained below in Table C.3.

Location

We assess that the location of the access agreements—along the China-India border and in a port on the Bay of Bengal, as well as the exercises in the Himalayas—would affect Chinese levels of concern about this posture enhancement through three of the key factors.

First, China's perceptions of U.S. and allied hostile intent would likely increase due to the locations covered by the access agreements, as they would allow U.S. forces to operate in proximity to disputed regions along the China-India border. The recent China-India border clashes, India's support for the Quad and associated activities, and the recent expansion of U.S.-India bilateral defense cooperation would further heighten China's concerns about expanded U.S. military access to sensitive areas along the border.

Second, the location of some of the agreements could play a role in increasing Chinese perceptions of threats to regime legitimacy. Depending on where the UAS deployment and military exercises were planned for, they could occur in proximity to Tibet or to the Tibetan-exile Central Tibetan Administration in Dharamshala, which could be perceived by China as signaling an enhanced U.S. willingness to involve itself in that dispute. China's prior anxiety over India's support of the Dalai Lama and other Tibetan exiles would further enhance Chinese concerns related to regime legitimacy.

Finally, China's concerns about threats to its regional influence would also likely increase given the location of the access agreements. India allowing U.S. forces and military capabilities to operate close to sensitive Chinese border areas would illustrate that China's military presence and coercive measures along the China-India border had not deterred India from strengthening defense cooperation with the United States, which could highlight a decrease in China's influence in South Asia. Additionally, increased access to the port at Visakhapatnam illustrates potential greater U.S. military involvement and presence in the Indian Ocean region. These concerns could be enhanced by recent Indian efforts to expand influence in Southeast Asia, such as through the Act East policy initiative.

We did not assess that location was relevant to Chinese reactions for Factor 1, as the agreements on their own would not significantly increase the level of U.S. or partner military capabilities along the disputed border areas; Factor 4, as the location of expanded U.S. military access does not threaten Chinese trade routes or other economic interests; and Factor 6, as the location covered by the agreements would not substantially affect China's view of the commitment of the United States to defend India if attacked.

Taken together, we assess that the overall level of Chinese concern stemming from the locations covered by this set of agreements would likely be elevated. Chinese concerns would likely focus on the proximity of U.S. forces and surveillance capabilities to the China-India border, although enhanced U.S. access to the Indian Ocean area would be carefully scrutinized as well.

U.S. Allies/Partners Involved

We assess that expanding access agreements with India would affect Chinese perceptions through five key factors. First, deployment of UAS along the China-India border demonstrates an increase in interoperability and ISR capability between the U.S. and Indian armed forces more broadly, likely increasing China's perception of military threat from this greater integration between its two main competitors. While the specific capabilities enhancements on the border enabled by improved ISR may concern China as well, as discussed in the subsequent section, the more general improvements in U.S.-India interoperability could raise concerns about other threats that could arise if this integration continues and deepens.

Second, Chinese concerns about hostile intent would likely increase as the agreements illustrate a reorientation of U.S.-India defense cooperation toward the disputed border regions, where China would be the only plausible adversary and where the United States had previously avoided direct involvement. In addition, China would be concerned by access agreements that increase U.S. military posture in India and facilitate greater Indian presence in East and Southeast Asia through more interaction with 7th Fleet, as these agreements underscore U.S. efforts to further recruit New Delhi to an anti-China coalition. Chinese concerns would be enhanced by recent, largely successful U.S. efforts to reinvigorate India's role in the Quad.

Third, for Chinese perceptions of threats to economic development, greater interoperability between the U.S. and Indian militaries and more access of U.S. naval assets in Indian ports could increase China's concerns about planned or future U.S. and allied/partner capability to patrol or interdict Chinese ships in key SLOCs in the Indian Ocean region. Recent expansion of the activities of the Quad and an increase in naval exercises between Quad members potentially augment Chinese concerns about the potential for the United States and India to obstruct Chinese shipping in a conflict. However, the fact that China-India economic relations have remained stable despite substantial tensions in the bilateral relationship over the past several years illustrates how both China and India may be cautious before taking steps that threaten their mutually beneficial economic relations.

Fourth, China's concerns about its regional influence might also increase as India's decision to allow greater U.S. military access and posture in India could suggest greater Indian alignment with the United States on weakening China's clout throughout the region, particularly in South Asia and through the Quad. Additionally, India's expanded efforts to build influence in Southeast Asia likely play a role in enhancing Chinese concerns.

Finally, more U.S. military posture in India could potentially indicate a greater willingness on the part of the United States to come to India's defense in the event of a Chinese attack. While these limited steps would likely produce a correspondingly limited shift in Chinese perceptions of any U.S. commitment to defend India—which, of course, has not been made formally—any shift in this direction would certainly be of concern and would likely result in some increase in Chinese caution when contemplating any direct military actions against India.

We did not assess that the involvement of India in this set of access agreements was likely to notably affect China's perceptions of threats to its regime legitimacy, as the Indian military itself does not have strong links with Taiwan—or, for that matter, Tibetan exile groups—that might suggest any direct threats to China over these issues.

Overall, we assess the level of Chinese concern from India's involvement in and support for this posture enhancement to be elevated. China's concerns are primarily related to the increased interoperability and level of ISR capabilities that these agreements would bring to the Indian armed forces more broadly, the apparent shift in focus of U.S.-India defense cooperation efforts to the disputed border, and the signal that these agreements send about India's greater alignment with the United States to form an anti-China coalition and counter China's regional influence. The potential for a direct, aggressive Chinese response against India would likely be slightly mitigated by China's perception of a stronger U.S.-India defense relationship and the greater risk of U.S. military support for India.

Capabilities

The capabilities involved in this posture enhancement would likely affect China's reactions through three key factors. For perceptions of military threat, China's concerns would likely increase as more U.S. and Indian ISR capabilities along the China-India border would somewhat diminish China's surveillance advantage and allow Indian forces to better respond to China's military actions in a future border clash. However, better ISR capabilities along the border might also deter China from aggressive actions, as without the element of surprise China might feel that its actions are too escalatory, particularly if it needs to use larger forces to achieve similar effects to when India had more-limited ISR capabilities. Similarly, Chinese concerns would increase for U.S. and allied hostile intent, as the expanded surveillance capabilities could likely only or primarily be used to detect Chinese actions and forces along the border. The prior context of the recent China-India border clashes and recent expansion of U.S.-India defense cooperation would further heighten China's worries about U.S. and allied and partner hostile intent.

Finally, expanded U.S. and Indian ISR along the border in addition to high-altitude training exercises that demonstrate joint capabilities that could be used against China in the event of a border crisis would also likely demonstrate some enhanced U.S. ability, and willingness, to defend India in the event of a Chinese attack.

We did not assess that the capabilities demonstrated through this set of agreements would be especially relevant to China's perceptions of threats to regime legitimacy, as none of the capabilities in the access agreements would heighten China's concern over Taiwan or, for that matter, realistically, Tibet. The capabilities involved in the agreements would also not be perceived by China as particularly threatening to its economic development, as the ISR is deployed along the Indian border and the port access, while demonstrating increased U.S.-India naval cooperation, does not significantly change the United States' or India's ability to patrol key shipping routes. We also assessed that the capabilities specified in the agreements would not impact China's perception of threats to its regional influence.

Overall, we assess that there would be limited Chinese concern about the capabilities for this posture enhancement. China's primary worries are related to the expanded ISR along its border with India and the potential for those capabilities to be used in a future border clash or to undermine China's surveillance advantage. But the scope and scale of the U.S. or Indian capabilities directly affected by these agreements would be limited, though, as discussed in other sections, the implications they may have for the future trajectory of the U.S.-India relationship or regional dynamics may be more concerning.

Profile

The expanded access agreements would be accompanied by official statements and media publicity, as well as plans to publicize the joint exercises. This relatively high profile would likely affect China's concerns and reactions through three key factors. First, China's concerns regarding U.S. and allied hostile intent would likely increase, as the publicity and statements accompanying the agreements would emphasize the anti-China aspect of the posture enhancement. China would also likely view the publicly stated intent to hold joint military exercises near Tibet and/or sensitive border areas as provocative, particularly given the history of China-India border clashes.

269

Second, China's concerns over threats to its regional influence would also likely increase, as the agreements would be accompanied by statements about augmenting capabilities along the China-India border that challenge PRC claims to the disputed territory and, by extension, China's claim to be an ascendent power in South Asia. India would also likely publish statements emphasizing the closer U.S.-India defense relationship and underscoring U.S. commitment to the region, further undermining Chinese efforts to establish itself as the key player in the region outside of India. These concerns would be heightened by India's recent support for the Quad, itself a substantial concern for Chinese efforts to expand its regional influence.

Finally, U.S.-India joint statements that signal closer alignment of the United States and India as regional defense partners and messages signaling that the access agreements are intended to better defend India from Chinese border aggression would likely affect Chinese perceptions of U.S. willingness to defend its allies and, in this case, partners. This would, in turn, likely be affected by the steady increase in U.S.-India defense ties over the past two decades.

We did not assess that the profile accompanying these agreements was relevant to China's perceptions or concerns about regime legitimacy, as none of the messaging would touch on Taiwan, Tibet, other related issues, or economic development, because the messaging accompanying the agreements would not focus on capabilities to disrupt China's shipping or ability to access maritime chokepoints.

We assess that China would have limited concerns about the profile of this set of posture enhancements. China would likely view the public nature of the agreements and eventual exercises as provocative, particularly given India's support of the Quad and other U.S. efforts to counter China's regional influence. However, the statements would avoid other sensitive areas for China and would further highlight a stronger U.S.-India defense relationship and the public deployment of ISR capabilities to counter China's actions along the border that could also help to deter more directly aggressive PRC responses against India.

Summary of Effects on PRC Thinking and Possible Responses

In aggregate, we assess that expanding military access agreements with India in the manner described would likely have an elevated effect on China's reactions. The main PRC concerns would include the location of U.S. ISR capabilities and personnel along the China-India border, which could be used to detect and target PRC forces in a border crisis; the increase in ISR interoperability and information-sharing between the United States and India and what it implies for their broader relationship; and the reorientation of U.S.-India defense cooperation to focus more on the disputed border areas and what that suggests for U.S. willingness to become involved in those disputes. In addition, Chinese concerns reflect worries about the threat to regional influence as expanded military access agreements, including greater Indian naval access to 7th Fleet resources, signal a stronger anti-China stance by India and a desire for a closer defense relationship with the United States. China is also likely to assess increased risks from any direct attack on India in response to this posture enhancement due to the signals of a stronger

U.S.-India defense relationship and the apparent increased willingness of the United States to come to India's defense, particularly on the disputed border issue.

The typology of PRC reactions in Chapter 4 illustrates some of the responses that China could potentially have in the "elevated" category. For this set of posture enhancements, Chinese responses could include increased PLA incursions, patrols, or surveillance across the LAC along the China-India border, along with large-scale PLA exercises near disputed border areas. In addition, China may decide to increase PLAN patrols in the Indian Ocean in response to India's agreement to provide access to more U.S. naval presence in the Bay of Bengal. China could also engage in a concerted diplomatic and media campaign to push back on the optics of increased U.S. regional influence by branding greater U.S. military presence as destabilizing and meant to contain China. It is also possible that China would engage in limited economic retaliation against India, although this would seem less likely as Beijing has previously sought to preserve China-India economic ties despite tensions in the bilateral relationship.

China's long-term responses to this posture enhancement could consist of accelerating efforts to develop infrastructure, ISR capabilities, and deployments of the PLA to broader swaths of the China-India border. In addition, the PLAN could expand its operations to encompass more of the Indian Ocean region, including allocating more surface ships and submarines to conduct patrols, as well as potentially establishing a naval base or logistics hubs in South Asia or along Africa's eastern coast. Table C.3 summarizes the posture characteristics, scale of Chinese concern, and key effects on Chinese perceptions and reactions stemming from this posture enhancement.

Table C.3. Summary of Effects of Expanding Military Access with India on PRC Thinking

Posture Characteristics	Scale of PRC Concern	Explanation
Location	Elevated	• Increased PRC motivation for aggressive response due to ○ U.S. forces operating near disputed border, Tibet ○ increased U.S. involvement in Indian Ocean region ○ China-India border clashes, India's support for the Quad, hosting of Dalai Lama, expansion of U.S.-India defense cooperation
U.S. allies/partners involved	Elevated	• Increased PRC motivation for aggressive response due to ○ UAS deployment, which illustrates increase in U.S.-Indian military interoperability ○ U.S.-India defense cooperation reorientation to border areas ○ U.S. recruitment of India to anti-China coalition, pushback on China's regional influence ○ India's role in the Quad/Quad naval activities, India's influence building in Southeast Asia • Decreased PRC motivation for aggressive response due to ○ greater U.S. willingness to come to India's defense
Capabilities	Limited	• Increased PRC motivation for aggressive response due to ○ potential to undermine PRC information superiority in event of China-India border clash ○ improved ISR for India in border regions that could be employed versus China ○ prior China-India border clashes, expansion of U.S.-India defense cooperation • Decreased PRC motivation for aggressive response due to ○ demonstrated ISR capabilities that could be used in event of PRC attack on Indian border regions ○ increased visibility of PRC forces, which might deter China, as its actions could be viewed as escalatory
Profile	Limited	• Increased PRC motivation for aggressive response due to ○ highly visible exercise in vicinity of disputed border, Tibet ○ accompanying U.S.-India messaging that demonstrates U.S. staying power, commitment to region ○ U.S. messaging that contains some anti-China statements ○ India's support for the Quad, increased U.S.-India defense ties • Decreased PRC motivation for aggressive response due to ○ messaging that emphasizes that posture enhancement meant to better defend India, particularly along the border ○ statements that signal alignment of the United States and India on security issues

Abbreviations

A2/AD	anti-access/area denial
ACSA	acquisition and cross-servicing agreement
ADIZ	Air Defense Identification Zone
AFB	air force base
AOR	area of responsibility
ASAT	anti-satellite
ASEAN	Association of Southeast Asian Nations
BRI	Belt and Road Initiative
BTF	Bomber Task Force
C-sUAS	counter–small unmanned aerial systems
C-UAS	counter–unmanned aerial systems
C2	command and control
CBPM	continuous bomber presence mission
CCG	China Coast Guard
CCP	Chinese Communist Party
CIA	U.S. Central Intelligence Agency
COIN	counterinsurgency
CONOP	concept of operations
CONUS	continental United States
COVID-19	coronavirus disease 2019
CSG	carrier strike group
CT	counterterrorism
CZ	contiguous zone
DDG	guided missile destroyer
DEFCON	defense readiness condition

DoD	U.S. Department of Defense
DPP	Democratic Progressive Party
ECS	East China Sea
EDCA	Enhanced Defense Cooperation Agreement
EEZ	Exclusive Economic Zone
EW	electronic warfare
FMF	foreign military financing
FMS	foreign military sales
FONOP	freedom of navigation operation
FY	fiscal year
ICBM	intercontinental ballistic missile
IMET	international military education and training
INDOPACOM	U.S. Indo-Pacific Command
IRBM	intermediate-range ballistic missile
ISR	intelligence, surveillance, and reconnaissance
JP	joint publication
LAC	Line of Actual Control
LOC	line of communication
LRHW	long-range hypersonic weapon
MAAG	military advisory and assistance group
MDO	multi-domain operations
MILCON	military construction
MILDEC	military deception
MOU	memorandum of understanding
MRBM	medium-range ballistic missile
NATO	North Atlantic Treaty Organization
NEO	noncombatant evacuation operation
NSC	National Security Council

PACAF	Pacific Air Forces
PAFMM	People's Armed Forces Maritime Militia
PDI	Pacific Deterrence Initiative
PLA	People's Liberation Army
PLAAF	People's Liberation Army Air Force
PLAN	People's Liberation Army Navy
PMC	private military corporation
PRC	People's Republic of China
Quad	Quadrilateral Security Dialogue
R&D	research and development
REFORGER	Return of Forces to Germany
RIMPAC	Rim of the Pacific
ROK	Republic of Korea
S&R	search-and-rescue
SCS	South China Sea
SOFA	status of forces agreement
THAAD	Terminal High Altitude Area Defense
TW	territorial waters
UAS	unmanned aerial systems
UAV	unmanned aerial vehicle
UN	United Nations
USAF	U.S. Air Force
USCG	U.S. Coast Guard
USMC	U.S. Marine Corps
USN	U.S. Navy
USSR	Union of Soviet Socialist Republics
VFA	Visiting Forces Agreement

Bibliography

3rd Marine Division, "Expeditionary Advanced Basing Capabilities on Display During Exercise Noble Fury," *Marines.mil*, October 13, 2020.

"19th CPC Central Committee Concludes Fourth Plenary Session, Releases Communiqué," Xinhua, October 31, 2019.

Aamir, Adnan, "China and Pakistan Ink Military MOU to Counter U.S.-India Pact," *Nikkei Asia*, December 8, 2020.

Acosta, Rene, "Persistent Chinese Maritime Militia Presence off Philippines Raises Concerns in Manila," *USNI News*, April 12, 2021.

Adde, Nick, "Minuteman III Replacement Program Moves Toward Next Phase," *National Defense Magazine*, November 2, 2018. As of September 20, 2021: https://www.nationaldefensemagazine.org/articles/2018/11/2/minuteman-iii-replacement-program-moves-toward-next-phase

Ai Jun, "New Missile Signals China's Resolve to Counter THAAD," *Global Times*, May 10, 2017.

Aircraft Spots [@AircraftSpots], "USAF B-52Hs FLAIL01 & 02 flew into the South China Sea specifically near the Paracel Islands upon returning to Andersen AFB, Guam. USAF KC-135Rs PLUG21 & 22 provided tanker support then returned to Guam," Twitter post, January 5, 2020. As of March 21, 2021: https://twitter.com/AircraftSpots/status/1213894554736136192

———, "FEB 15: USAF B-52H 60-0055 HAWK52 departed Andersen AFB, Guam for a flyover at the Singapore Airshow," Twitter post, February 15, 2020. As of March 21, 2021: https://twitter.com/AircraftSpots/status/1228576751837515777

———, "USAF B-52Hs TAINT01 & 02 departed Andersen AFB, Guam en route to the South China Sea. USAF KC-135Rs PIXIE01 & 02 provided tanker support," Twitter post, March 17, 2020. As of March 21, 2021: https://twitter.com/AircraftSpots/status/1240120954321338369

———, "Yesterday (March 19th), a single USAF B-52H Stratofortress bomber executed a flight to the South China Sea from Andersen AFB, Guam. This is the second mission this week!" Twitter post, March 20, 2020. As of March 21, 2021: https://twitter.com/AircraftSpots/status/1241051883428446210

———, "USAF B-1Bs BULLET01 & 02 departed Andersen AFB, Guam en route to the South China Sea USAF KC-135R PEARL11 provided tanker support," Twitter post, May 25, 2020. As of March 21, 2021:
https://twitter.com/AircraftSpots/status/1265097212033286145

———, "USAF B-52Hs LIMIT96 & 97 are currently returning to Eielson AFB, Alaska following a Bomber Task Force mission through the Sea of Japan, East China Sea and South China Sea," Twitter post, June 17, 2020. As of March 21, 2021:
https://twitter.com/AircraftSpots/status/1273213732609384449

———, "USAF B-1Bs CLAWS01 & 02 departed Andersen AFB, Guam en route to the South China Sea via the Sulu Sea entrance. USAF KC-135Rs PEARL21 & 22 are providing tanker support," Twitter post, July 20, 2020. As of March 21, 2021:
https://twitter.com/AircraftSpots/status/1285340862621216768

———, "USAF B-1Bs KIMBO11 & 12 departed Andersen AFB, Guam heading in a northwest direction, possibly to the East China Sea or South China Sea. USAF KC-135Rs PEARL21 & 22 provided tanker support," Twitter post, September 25, 2020. As of March 21, 2021:
https://twitter.com/AircraftSpots/status/1309345920580943873

———, "USAF B-1Bs HUGE01 & 02 departed Andersen AFB, Guam en route to the South China Sea. USAF KC-135R PEARL11 provided tanker support," Twitter post, October 24, 2020. As of March 21, 2021:
https://twitter.com/AircraftSpots/status/1320026229915807745

———, "On November 8th, USAF B-1Bs DUNK01 & 02 flew round trip from Andersen AFB, Guam to the South China Sea, at one point flying near the Spratly Islands. This flight sends a clear message to China and appeared to be a FONOP operation," Twitter post, November 9, 2020. As of March 21, 2021:
https://twitter.com/AircraftSpots/status/1325711004995477504

———, "DEC 28: USAF B-1B Lancer bombers MINT11 & 12 from Andersen AFB, Guam conducted a Bomber Task Force mission over the South China Sea flying near Hainan, the Paracel Islands, and the Spratly Islands," Twitter post, December 29, 2020. As of March 21, 2021:
https://twitter.com/AircraftSpots/status/1343835094390169601

Albert, Eleanor, "The U.S.-Philippines Defense Alliance," Council on Foreign Relations, October 21, 2016.

Almendral, Aurora, "Philippines Feels Force of China Travel Warning," *BBC News*, October 22, 2014.

Altman, Dan, "The Evolution of Territorial Conquest After 1945 and the Limits of the Territorial Integrity Norm," *International Organization*, Vol. 74, No. 3, Summer 2020, pp. 490–522.

Amador, Julio, III, "National Security of the Philippines Under the Aquino Administration: A Human Security Approach," *Korean Journal of Defense Analysis*, Vol. 23, No. 4, December 2011, pp. 521–536.

"American President Trump Makes Official State Visit to China" ["美国总统特朗普对中国进行国事访问"], Xinhua, 2017.

Anh, Viet, "U.S. Respects Vietnam's Right to Protect Its Sovereignty: Generals," *VnExpress*, August 18, 2019.

Armitage, Richard L., "Remarks and Q & A at the Japan National Press Club," Department of State Archives, February 2, 2004.

Asia Maritime Transparency Initiative, "China Island Tracker," webpage, Center for Strategic and International Studies, undated. As of May 3, 2021: https://amti.csis.org/island-tracker/china/

———, "China's New Spratly Island Defenses," webpage, Center for Strategic and International Studies, December 13, 2016. As of October 1, 2022: https://amti.csis.org/chinas-new-spratly-island-defenses/

———, "Update: China Risks Flare-Up over Malaysian, Vietnamese Gas Resources," Center for Strategic and International Studies, December 13, 2019.

Aspinwall, Nick, "Paraguay Says Chinese Brokers Offered Vaccines for Diplomatic Recognition," *The Diplomat*, March 27, 2021.

Associated Press, "U.S. Concerned over China's 'Interference' in South China Sea," *Voice of America*, July 21, 2019.

———, "Chinese Long-Range Bombers Join Drills over South China Sea," *Military Times*, July 30, 2020.

"Attempts to Use Taiwan to Control China or Use Weapons to Prevent Unification Will Fail in the End" ["'以台制华'和'以武拒统'注定难逃失败下场"], *Qiushi* [求是], July 11, 2019. As of March 19, 2021: http://www.qstheory.cn/llwx/2019-07/11/c_1124737349.htm

Axe, David, "China Is Probing Japan's Defenses over the Disputed Senkaku Islands," *Forbes*, August 19, 2020.

Babb, Carla, "U.S. Adds Rocket Launch Unit in South Korea," *Voice of America*, March 20, 2015.

Babones, Salvatore, "The Quad's Malabar Exercises Point the Way to an Asian NATO," *Foreign Policy*, November 25, 2020.

Baldor, Lolita C., "Sharp Jump in U.S. Navy Transits to Counter China Under Trump," Associated Press, March 15, 2021.

Balestrieri, Brandon, "Reserves Guarantee Continuity to U.S. Operations," *Korea JoongAng Daily*, April 1, 2013.

Barajas, Julia, and Allison Hong, "Vietnamese Immigrants Rally Behind Hong Kong Protesters Pushing for Democracy in Asia," *Los Angeles Times*, December 15, 2019.

Bartnick, Aaron, *Asia Whole and Free? Assessing the Viability and Practicality of a Pacific NATO*, Cambridge, Mass.: Belfer Center, March 2020.

Beauchamp-Mustafaga, Nathan, Derek Grossman, Kristen Gunness, Michael S. Chase, Marigold Black, and Natalia D. Simmons-Thomas, *Deciphering Chinese Deterrence Signalling in the New Era: An Analytic Framework and Seven Case Studies*, Santa Monica, Calif.: RAND Corporation, RR-A1074-1, 2021. As of July 14, 2021:
https://www.rand.org/pubs/research_reports/RRA1074-1.html

Becker, Jeffrey, *Securing China's Lifelines Across the Indian Ocean*, Newport, R.I.: U.S. Naval War College, China Maritime Studies Institute, China Maritime Report No. 11, December 2020.

Bhadrakumar, M. K., "China to Strengthen Military Coordination with Russia," *Asia Times*, December 27, 2020.

"Biden Should Revamp Asia-Pacific Path, Ditch Indo-Pacific Idea," *Global Times*, November 25, 2020.

Bisht, Inder Singh, "India to Finalize MQ-9 B Predator Drone Acquisition," *Defense Post*, July 30, 2021.

Biswas, Soutik, "India-China Clash: An Extraordinary Escalation 'with Rocks and Clubs,'" *BBC News*, June 16, 2020.

Blackwill, Robert D., and Jennifer M. Harris, *War by Other Means: Geoeconomics and Statecraft*, Cambridge, Mass.: Harvard University Press, 2016.

Blackwill, Robert D., and Jeffrey W. Legro, "Constraining Ground Force Exercises of NATO and the Warsaw Pact," *International Security*, Vol. 14, No. 3, 1989, pp. 68–98.

Blanchard, Ben, "Duterte Aligns Philippines with China, Says U.S. Has Lost," Reuters, October 20, 2016.

———, "Timeline: U.S. Arms Sales to Taiwan in 2020 Total $5 Billion amid China Tensions," Reuters, December 7, 2020.

———, "Factbox: Recent Taiwan Visits by Top U.S. Officials," Reuters, January 7, 2021.

———, "Taiwan Reports Large Incursion by Chinese Air Force," Reuters, January 23, 2021.

Blanchard, Ben, and Idrees Ali, "U.S. Warship Sails Through Taiwan Strait, Second Time in a Month," Reuters, April 23, 2020.

Blanchard, Ben, and Reuters Beijing Newsroom, "U.S. Warships Transit Taiwan Strait, China Denounces 'Provocation,'" Reuters, December 30, 2020.

Blanchard, Ben, and Jess Macy Yu, "China Warns of More Action After Military Drills Near Taiwan," Reuters, April 25, 2018.

Blanco Pitlo, Lucio, III, "Philippines Bolsters Posture in South China Sea After Navy Ship Docks at New Spratly Islands Port," *South China Morning Post*, May 27, 2020.

Blank, Stephen, "Kremlin Ties Rosneft Closer to China," *Eurasia Daily Monitor*, November 8, 2017.

Bodeen, Christopher, "U.S. Says Bombers Didn't Intend to Fly over China-Held Island," *Military Times*, December 19, 2015.

Bower, Ernest Z., "China Reveals Its Hand on ASEAN in Phnom Penh," *CSIS Commentary*, July 20, 2012.

Bowman, Bradley, and Andrew Gabel, "U.S., India Bolster Their Military Partnership in Tiger Triumph Exercise," *Defense News*, November 13, 2019.

Boyd, Henry, and Meia Nouwens, "Understanding the Military Build-Up on the China-India Border," International Institute for Strategic Studies, June 18, 2020.

Braesch, Connie, "U.S. Aircraft Inaugural Refueling in India," Defense Logistics Agency, October 29, 2020.

Brandt, Jessica, and Bret Shafer, "How China's 'Wolf Warrior' Diplomats Use and Abuse Twitter," Brookings Institution, October 28, 2020.

Brown, Marianne, "Hong Kong Protesters 'Inspire' Vietnam Activists," *Voice of America*, October 2, 2014.

Browne, Ryan, and Kevin Liptak, "Trump Admin Gives Green Light for Major Arms Sale to Taiwan," *CNN*, August 16, 2019.

Bruce, River, "B-1s Conduct Training Mission in South China Sea," Pacific Air Forces, May 8, 2020.

Brunnstrom, David, "U.S. Warns Extradition Law Changes May Jeopardize Hong Kong's Special Status," Reuters, June 10, 2019.

Brunnstrom, David, Michael Martina, and Jeff Mason, "U.S., India, Japan and Australia Counter China with Billion-Dose Vaccine Pact," Reuters, March 12, 2021.

Brunnstrom, David, Mike Stone, and Krisztina Than, "China to Impose Sanctions on U.S. Firms That Sell Arms to Taiwan," Reuters, July 12, 2019.

Buckley, Chris, "Military Parade in China Gives Xi Jinping a Platform to Show Grip on Power," *New York Times*, September 3, 2015.

———, "China Says It Will Roll Out 'National Security' Steps for Hong Kong," *New York Times*, October 31, 2019.

Bumiller, Elisabeth, and Edward Wong, "China Warily Eyes U.S.-Korea Drills," *New York Times*, July 20, 2010.

Bureau of East Asian and Pacific Affairs, "U.S. Relations with Thailand: Bilateral Relations Fact Sheet," U.S. Department of State, May 4, 2021. As of August 17, 2021:
https://www.state.gov/u-s-relations-with-thailand/

Bureau of Political-Military Affairs, "U.S. Security Cooperation with India," fact sheet, U.S. Department of State, January 20, 2021. As of August 5, 2021:
https://www.state.gov/u-s-security-cooperation-with-india/

Bureau of South and Central Asian Affairs, "U.S. Relations with India," U.S. Department of State, January 21, 2021. As of February 26, 2021:
https://www.state.gov/u-s-relations-with-india/

Burke, Edmund J., and Astrid Stuth Cevallos, *In Line or Out of Order? China's Approach to ADIZ in Theory and Practice*, Santa Monica, Calif.: RAND Corporation, RR-2055-AF, 2017. As of May 3, 2021:
https://www.rand.org/pubs/research_reports/RR2055.html

Burke, Edmund J., Timothy R. Heath, Jeffrey W. Hornung, Logan Ma, Lyle J. Morris, and Michael S. Chase, *China's Military Activities in the East China Sea: Implications for Japan's Air Self-Defense Force*, Santa Monica, Calif.: RAND Corporation, RR-2574-AF, 2018. As of July 12, 2021:
https://www.rand.org/pubs/research_reports/RR2574.html

Butcher, Charity, "Diversionary Theories of Conflict: The Promises and Challenges of an Opportunities Approach," *Oxford Research Encyclopedia of International Studies*, March 25, 2021.

Calonzo, Andreo, and Cecilia Yap, "China Visit Helps Duterte Reap Funding Deals Worth $24 Billion," *Bloomberg*, October 21, 2016.

Cancian, Mark, "U.S. Military Forces in FY 2020: SOF, Civilians, Contractors, and Nukes," Center for Strategic and International Studies, October 24, 2019.

Canyon, Deon, Wade Turvold, and Jim McMullin, "A Network of Maritime Fusion Centers in the Indo-Pacific," *Security Nexus*, Vol. 22, 2021.

Carothers, Thomas, "The Backlash Against Democracy Promotion," *Foreign Affairs*, March/April 2006.

Cebul, Daniel, "US to Remove Several Missile Defense Systems from the Middle East," *Defense News*, September 26, 2018.

Chan, Minnie, "South China Sea: Chinese Air Force 'Sends Warning' to U.S. Navy with Live-Fire Drills," *South China Morning Post*, July 21, 2020.

Chang, Chun-yue, "Study History, Be Close to the People," *China Daily*, July 9, 2013.

Chang-Liao, Nien-Chung, "China's New Foreign Policy Under Xi Jinping," *Asian Security*, Vol. 12, No. 2, 2016, pp. 82–91.

Chen Cihang, "Changes of U.S. Stance on the South China Sea Issue Since 2009," South China Sea Strategic Situation Probing Initiative, May 27, 2021.

Chen, Dingding, and Katrin Kinzelbach, "Democracy Promotion and China: Blocker or Bystander?" *Democratization*, Vol. 22, No. 3, 2015, pp. 400–418.

Chen Hong, "Campbell's Remarks Push Australia Further to the Anti-China Frontline," *Global Times*, March 17, 2021.

Chen Hu [陈虎], "Colonel Chen Hu: China Needs to Have the Ability to 'Resist' Wars," *Tencent Net* [腾讯网], 2010. As of July 14, 2021:
https://news.qq.com/a/20100702/000890.htm

Chen Lufan, "China-Pakistan Joint Air Exercise 'Shaheen-IX' for Better Interoperability," *China Military Online*, December 21, 2020. As of February 23, 2021:
http://eng.chinamil.com.cn/view/2020-12/21/content_9955994.htm

Chen, Yong, "Strengthening Peripheral Bases, Promoting Forward Deterrence—The Analysis and Prediction of Recent U.S. Military Operations in the South China Sea," South China Sea Strategic Situation Probing Initiative, 2019.

Cheng, Dean, "Chinese Lessons from the Gulf Wars," in Andrew Scobell, David Lai, and Roy Kamphausen, eds., *Chinese Lessons from Other Peoples' Wars*, Carlisle, Pa.: U.S. Army War College, 2012.

Cheng Hanping [成汉平], "The Strategic Interaction of U.S. and Vietnam in the South China Sea in the Perspective of Indo-Pacific Strategy: Path, Goal and Effect" ["印太战略 视域下美越围绕南海问题的战略互动: 路径、 目标与影响"], *Asia-Pacific Security and Maritime Affairs* [亚太安全与海洋研究], No. 2, 2019, pp. 3, 72–84.

———, "U.S. Efforts to Cozy Up to Vietnam Won't Work," *Global Times*, March 8, 2020.

Cheng Hanping [成汉平] and Ning Wei [宁威], "Issues, Challenges, and Measures for Dealing with Relations Between China and ASEAN Against the Backdrop of 'Unprecedented Changes in a Century'" ["'大变局' 视野下中国—东盟关系中的问题、 挑战与对策"], *Journal of Yunnan University* (Social Sciences Edition) [云南大学学报(社会科学版)], Vol. 19, No. 1, 2020, pp. 126–134.

Cheng, Jonathan, and Josh Chin, "China Hacked South Korea over Missile Defense, U.S. Firm Says," *Wall Street Journal*, April 21, 2017.

Cheng, Sijin, *Fighting for Reputation: China's Deterrence Policy and Concerns About Credibility*, dissertation, Boston: Boston University, 2014.

Cheung, Eric, and Brad Lendon, "China Sends 77 Warplanes into Taiwan Defense Zone over Two Days, Taipei Says," *CNN*, October 3, 2021.

"China, India Reach Positive Consensus on Easing Border Situation," Xinhua, July 6, 2020.

"China, Russia Agree to Further Respond to THAAD Deployment," Xinhua, January 13, 2017.

"China, Russia Agree to Upgrade Relations for a New Era," Xinhua, June 6, 2019.

"China, Russia Sign Joint Statement on Strengthening Global Strategic Stability," Xinhua, June 26, 2016.

"China Coast Guard Blocked Resupply Mission to Ayungin Shoal—DND," *Philstar Global*, September 19, 2019.

"China Is Not Afraid of Making Waves in the South China Sea" ["南海， 中国不怕兴风作浪"], *China National Defense News-Military Special Issue* [中国国防报-军事特刊], April 21, 2015. As of April 2, 2021:
http://www.mod.gov.cn/intl/2015-04/21/content_4581245_2.htm

"China—Navy," *Jane's Sentinel Security Assessment—China and Northeast Asia*, April 1, 2021.

"The China-Philippine Banana War," *Asia Sentinel*, June 6, 2012.

"China Plays Nice Because It Can," *Real Clear Defense*, November 27, 2016.

"China Responds to Japan's Video on the Senkaku Islands and Urges It to Stop Provocative Words and Actions" ["中方回应日本涉钓鱼岛视频 促其停止挑衅言行"], *Sina*, October 23, 2013.

"China Says U.S. Threatening Peace as Warship Transits Taiwan Strait," Reuters, May 18, 2021.

"China Shifts Its Maritime Strategy," *People's Daily*, July 16, 2012.

"China to Stop Issuing Individual Travel Permits to Taiwan," *BBC News*, July 31, 2019.

"China-Vietnam Joint Announcement" ["中越联合公报"], *People's Daily* [人民日报], January 15, 2017.

"China Warns Off U.S. Destroyer Trespassing in South China Sea: Spokesperson," *China Military Online*, December 22, 2020.

"China's Achievement of Covid-19 Fight Obvious: Global Times Editorial," *Global Times*, May 10, 2020.

"Chinese Embassy Urges India to Correct Wrongdoings of Banning Chinese Apps," Xinhua, July 28, 2020.

"Chinese Foreign Minister Calls on China, Russia, India to Work Together," Xinhua, June 24, 2020.

"Chinese General Says Force an Option to Stop Taiwan Independence," *Nikkei Asia*, May 29, 2020.

"Chinese Incursions Highest Since 1996," *Taipei Times*, January 4, 2021.

"Chinese Mainland to Firmly Handle Chaos at Sea," *Global Times*, May 12, 2021.

Chiozza, Giacomo, and H. E. Goemans, "Peace Through Insecurity: Tenure and International Conflict," *Journal of Conflict Resolution*, Vol. 47, No. 4, 2003, pp. 443–467.

Choe Sang-Hun, "U.S. Antimissile System Goes Live in South Korea," *New York Times*, May 2, 2017.

Choksy, Jamsheed K., and Carol E. B. Choksy, "China and Russia Have Iran's Back," *Foreign Affairs*, November 17, 2020.

Christensen, Thomas J., *Useful Adversaries: Grand Strategy, Domestic Mobilization, and Sino-American Conflict, 1947–1958*, Princeton, N.J.: Princeton University Press, 1997.

———, "The Meaning of the Nuclear Evolution: China's Strategic Modernization and U.S.-China Security Relations," *Journal of Strategic Studies*, Vol. 35, No. 4, 2012, pp. 447–487.

Chubb, Andrew, "PRC Assertiveness in the South China Sea: Measuring Continuity and Change, 1970–2015," *International Security*, Vol. 45, No. 3, Winter 2020/2021, pp. 79–121.

Clare, Joe, and Vesna Danilovic, "Multiple Audiences and Reputation Building in International Conflicts," *Journal of Conflict Resolution*, Vol. 54, No. 6, December 2010, pp. 860–882.

Clarke, Michael, "Beijing's Pivot West: The Convergence of *Innenpolitik* and *Aussenpolitik* on China's 'Belt and Road'?" *Journal of Contemporary China*, Vol. 29, No. 123, 2020, pp. 336–353.

Clinton, Hillary, "Remarks with Japanese Foreign Minister Fumio Kishida After Their Meeting," Washington, D.C., January 18, 2013.

"CMC Opinions on Deepening National Defense and Military Reforms" ["中央军委关于深化国防和军队改革的意见"], Xinhua, January 1, 2016.

Cobble, W. Eugene, H. H. Gaffney, and Dmitry Gorenburg, *For the Record: All U.S. Forces' Responses to Situations, 1970–2000 (with Additions Covering 2000–2003)*, Alexandria, Va.: CNA, 2005.

Cohen, Zachary, "U.S. Cyber Command Expands Operations Against Russia, China and Iran," *CNN*, November 3, 2020.

Cohens-Ashley, Malcolm, "U.S. Army's Only Forward-Stationed Multi-Component Air Defense Task Force," U.S. Indo-Pacific Command, February 7, 2019.

Colley, Christopher K., "China's Ongoing Debates About India and the United States," *Asia Dispatches*, June 30, 2020.

"Commentary: China's Djibouti Base Not for Military Expansion," Xinhua, July 13, 2017.

"Commentary: Forming Clique and Flexing Muscles Only to Shake Regional Peace, Stability," Xinhua, October 23, 2020.

Congressional Research Service, "U.S.-Vietnam Relations," *In Focus*, February 16, 2021.

Consulate General of the People's Republic of China in Ho Chi Minh City, "Consul General Wu Jun Engage in Discussions and Exchanges with Hong Kong Police Wanchai District Junior Youth Call" ["吴骏总领事与香港警务处湾仔警区少年警讯代表团座谈交流"], July 30, 2019.

Cooper, Helene, "U.S. Disinvites China from Military Exercise amid Rising Tensions," *New York Times*, May 23, 2018.

Cooper, Scott, "State-Centric Balance-of-Threat Theory: Explaining the Misunderstood Gulf Cooperation Council," *Security Studies*, Vol. 13, No. 2, December 30, 2003, pp. 306–349.

Corrales, Nestor, "Duterte Says He'll 'Set Aside' Arbitral Ruling on South China Sea," *Inquirer.net*, December 17, 2016.

Cox, Divine, "Andersen Remains Ready," Pacific Air Forces, April 14, 2020.

Crescenzi, Mark J. C., Jacob D. Kathman, Katja B. Kleinberg, and Reed M. Wood, "Reliability, Reputation, and Alliance Formation," *International Studies Quarterly*, Vol. 56, No. 2, June 2012, pp. 259–274.

Crossley, Gabriel, and Devjyot Ghoshal, "Explainer: Why Are Chinese and Indian Troops Fighting in a Remote Himalayan Valley?" Reuters, June 17, 2020.

Cruz de Castro, Renato, "The U.S.-Philippine Alliance: An Evolving Hedge Against an Emerging China Challenge," *Contemporary Southeast Asia*, Vol. 31, No. 3, December 2009, pp. 399–423.

———, "The Duterte Administration's Foreign Policy: Unravelling the Aquino Administration's Balancing Agenda on an Emergent China," *Journal of Current Southeast Asian Affairs*, Vol. 35, No. 3, 2016, pp. 139–159.

Cui Haoran [崔浩然], "The Adjustment of Vietnam's South China Sea Policy Under the New Situation and China's Response Strategy" ["新形势下越南南海政策的调整及中国的应对策略"], *Issues of Contemporary World Socialism* [当代世界社会主义问题], No. 4, 2018, pp. 156–165.

Cummings, Alan, "Hypersonic Weapons: Tactical Uses and Strategic Goals," *War on the Rocks*, November 12, 2019.

Cunningham, Edward, Tony Saich, and Jessie Turiel, *Understanding CCP Resilience: Surveying Chinese Public Opinion Through Time*, Cambridge, Mass.: Ash Center for Democratic Governance and Innovation, July 2020.

Cunningham, Fiona S., and M. Taylor Fravel, "Assuring Assured Retaliation: China's Nuclear Posture and U.S.-China Strategic Stability," *International Security*, Vol. 40, No. 2, October 2015, pp. 7–50.

———, "Dangerous Confidence? Chinese Views on Nuclear Escalation," *International Security*, Vol. 44, No. 2, 2019, pp. 61–109.

Dafoe, Allan, Jonathan Renshon, and Paul Huth, "Reputation and Status as Motives for War," *Annual Review of Political Science*, Vol. 17, 2014, pp. 371–393.

Dai Zheng [戴正] and Zheng Xianwu [郑先武], "China's Security Strategy in the South China Sea Dispute in Recent Years: 'Differential Treatment and a Two-Pronged Approach'" ["中国近年南海争端安全战略: '区别对待，双管齐下'"], *Indian Ocean Economic Studies* [印度洋经济体研究], No. 5, 2019, pp. 106–129.

Dang Cam Tu and Hang Thi Thuy Nguyen, "Understanding the U.S.-Vietnam Security Relationship, 2011–2017," *Korean Journal of Defense Analysis*, Vol. 31, No. 1, March 2019, pp. 121–144.

Daniell, Jonathon, "THAAD Battery Reflags to Align with Air Defense Artillery Brigade in South Korea," U.S. Indo-Pacific Command, October 23, 2017.

Danilovic, Vesna, "The Sources of Threat Credibility in Extended Deterrence," *Journal of Conflict Resolution*, Vol. 45, No. 3, June 2001, pp. 341–369.

Dasgupta, Saibal, "China's Move to Empower Coast Guard Stirs Tensions," *Voice of America*, February 11, 2021.

David, Steven R., "Explaining Third World Alignment," *World Politics*, Vol. 43, No. 2, January 1991, pp. 233–256.

Davidson, Helen, "Taiwanese Urged to Eat 'Freedom Pineapples' After China Import Ban," *The Guardian*, March 2, 2021.

DeAeth, Duncan, "Chinese Aircraft Transit Miyako Strait Between Taiwan and Okinawa," *Taiwan News*, March 31, 2019.

Debs, Alexandre, and Jessica Chen Weiss, "Circumstances, Domestic Audiences, and Reputational Incentives in International Crisis Bargaining," *Journal of Conflict Resolution*, Vol. 60, No. 3, 2016, pp. 403–433.

Defense Security Cooperation Agency, "Monthly Archive," webpage, undated. As of September 12, 2022:
https://www.dsca.mil/major-arms-sales/archive-date

———, *Historical Sales Book: Fiscal Years 1950–2020*, 2020.

Delagarza, Dartanon, "Theodore Roosevelt Carrier Strike Group Conducts Bilateral Exercise with Royal Malaysian Air Force," *America's Navy*, April 7, 2021.

DeLisle, Jacque, and Avery Goldstein, "Introduction: China's Economic Reform and Opening at Forty," in Jacque deLisle and Avery Goldstein, eds., *To Get Rich Is Glorious*, Washington, D.C.: Brookings Institution Press, 2019, pp. 1–28.

Deng Xiaoci, "China's Latest Missile Test Shows Country Can Respond to Aircraft Carriers, THAAD," *Global Times*, May 10, 2017.

Denver, Simon, "China's Scary Lesson to the World: Censoring the Internet Works," *Washington Post*, May 23, 2016.

Department of Defense Instruction 5132.14, *Assessment, Monitoring, and Evaluation Policy for the Security Cooperation Enterprise*, Washington, D.C.: U.S. Department of Defense, January 31, 2017.

DeWolf, Christopher, "Fighting Until the End: Hong Kong's Vietnamese Refugees," *Zolima CityMag*, December 12, 2019.

Diehl, Justin, "Indo-Pacific Deterrence and the Quad in 2030," *Journal of Indo-Pacific Affairs*, Vol. 4, No. 2, Spring 2021, pp. 97–122.

Diehl, Paul F., "Geography and War: A Review and Assessment of the Empirical Literature," *International Interactions*, Vol. 17, No. 1, 1991, pp. 11–27.

Ding, Arthur S., "The Lessons of the 1995–1996 Military Taiwan Strait Crisis: Developing a New Strategy Toward the United States and Taiwan," in Laurie Burkitt, Larry M. Wortzel, and Andrew Scobell, eds., *The Lessons of History: The Chinese People's Liberation Army at 75*, Carlisle, Pa.: U.S. Army War College Press, 2003, pp. 379–402.

Ding Duo, "European Countries Warships in S China Sea Undermine Stability," *China Daily*, March 18, 2021.

DoD—*See* U.S. Department of Defense.

Doornbos, Caitlin, "Navy Ties Record with Its 12th Transit Through the Taiwan Strait This Year," *Stars and Stripes*, December 19, 2020.

———, "U.S. Navy Ends 2020 with Another Taiwan Strait Transit," *Stars and Stripes*, December 31, 2020.

Dossani, Rafiq, "Why Tensions Between China and India Won't Boil Over," *The National Interest*, February 2, 2021.

Downs, Erica, "China's National Oil Companies Return to the World Stage: Navigating Corruption, Low Oil Prices, and the Belt and Road Initiative," in Erica Downs, Mikkal E. Herberg, Michael Kugelman, Christopher Len, and Kaho Yu, *Asia's Energy Security and China's Belt and Road Initiative*, Seattle, Wash.: National Bureau of Asian Research, 2017.

Downs, Erica, Mikkal E. Herberg, Michael Kugelman, Christopher Len, and Kaho Yu, *Asia's Energy Security and China's Belt and Road Initiative*, Seattle, Wash.: National Bureau of Asian Research, 2017.

Downs, George W., and David M. Rocke, "Conflict, Agency, and Gambling for Resurrection: The Principal-Agent Problem Goes to War," *American Journal of Political Science*, Vol. 38, No. 2, May 1994, pp. 362–380.

Doyle, Gerry, "Maritime Patrol Aircraft Seen as Key in Asia, but Buyers Elusive," Reuters, February 28, 2018.

Duchâtel, Mathieu, "China Trends #6—Generally Stable? Facing U.S. Pushback in the South China Sea," Institut Montaigne, August 6, 2020.

Duterte, Rodrigo Roa, speech delivered at the Philippines-China Trade and Investment Forum, Beijing, October 20, 2016. As of May 10, 2021: https://pcoo.gov.ph/oct-20-2016-speech-of-president-rodrigo-roa-duterte-during-the-philippines-china-trade-and-investment-forum/

———, *National Security Policy for Change and Well-Being of the Filipino People (2017–2022)*, Manila, Philippines, April 2017.

———, "5th State of the Nation Address," Quezon City, Philippines, July 27, 2020.

Dziedzic, Stephen, and Andrew Greene, "U.S. Official Urges Australia to Participate in South China Sea Freedom of Navigation Operations," *ABC News*, July 27, 2020.

Eckstein, Megan, "Marines Reach 2011 Goal of 2,500 in Darwin, with Addition of HIMARS Platoon, More to Current Rotation," *USNI News*, July 25, 2019.

———, "Scaled-Back, At-Sea RIMPAC 2020 Exercise Kicks Off Near Hawaii," *USNI News*, August 18, 2020.

———, "Navy Installing More Directed Energy Weapons on DDGs, Conducting Land-Based Laser Testing This Year," *USNI News*, April 7, 2021.

Economy, Elizabeth C., *The Third Revolution: Xi Jinping and the New Chinese State*, New York: Oxford University Press, 2018.

"Editorial: North Korea Reprocesses Plutonium, Let's Ask U.S. and South Korea to Be More Worried" ["社评: 朝鲜提炼核武钚, 请美韩多着着急吧"], *Global Times* [环球时报], August 19, 2016.

Elleman, Bruce A., and S. C. M. Paine, eds., *Naval Coalition Warfare: From Napoleonic War to Operation Iraqi Freedom*, New York: Routledge, 2007.

Embassy of the Philippines, "Newsletter," Washington, D.C., No. 2, 2012. As of April 14, 2021: http://www.philippineshonolulu.org/uploads/embassy%20updates/2012-0813-Newsletter.pdf

Erickson, Andrew S., "The South China Sea's Third Force: Understanding and Countering China's Maritime Militia," testimony before the House Armed Services Committee Seapower and Projection Forces Subcommittee, Washington, D.C., September 21, 2016.

Erickson, Andrew S., "Maritime Numbers Game," *Indo-Pacific Defense Forum*, January 28, 2019.

Erwin, Nicolas Z., "28th Bomb Wing Airmen, B-1s Support Valiant Shield," *Pacific Air Forces*, September 26, 2020.

Esmaquel, Paterno, II, "China Chopper Harasses PH Rubber Boat in Ayungin Shoal—Lawmaker," *Rappler*, May 30, 2018.

Esper, Mark, "The Pentagon Is Prepared for China," *Wall Street Journal*, August 24, 2020.

Everstine, Brian W., "Air Force Ends Continuous Bomber Presence in Guam," *Air Force Magazine*, April 17, 2020.

———, "AFGSC's New Plan to Deploy Bombers Across the Globe," *Air Force Magazine*, April 29, 2020.

———, "B-52 Flies with Carrier Strike Groups in South China Sea," *Air Force Magazine*, July 6, 2020.

———, "B-1Bs Fly Through South China Sea Sending Message to Beijing," *Air Force Magazine*, July 23, 2020.

———, "PACAF: China, Russia Have Taken Notice of Increased USAF Bomber Ops," *Air Force Magazine*, November 18, 2020.

———, "US, South Korea Prepare for Transfer of Wartime Operational Control," *Air Force Magazine*, March 18, 2021.

Fan Gaoyue, "ROK: The Biggest Loser of THAAD," *China-U.S. Focus*, August 9, 2016.

Fang Xiaozhi [方晓志], "A Geo-Security Analysis of U.S. South China Sea Policy" ["对美国南海政策的地缘安全解析"], *Pacific Journal* [太平洋学报], Vol. 20, No. 7, 2012.

———, "U.S.-Australia Expand Military Cooperation: New Variable in Asia-Pacific Security Structure," *Contemporary World* [当代世界], Vol. 11, 2013.

Fearon, James D., "Rationalist Explanations for War," *International Organization*, Vol. 49, No. 3, Summer 1995, pp. 379–414.

———, "Signaling Foreign Policy Interests: Tying Hands Versus Sinking Costs," *Journal of Conflict Resolution*, Vol. 41, No. 1, February 1997, pp. 68–90.

Feigenbaum, Evan A., and James Schwemlein, "How Biden Can Make the Quad Endure," Carnegie Endowment for International Peace, March 11, 2021.

Feng, John, "U.S. Warplanes Foray into China Airspace as PLA Jets Disturb Taiwan," *Newsweek*, November 18, 2020.

Finkelstein, David M., "Breaking the Paradigm: Drivers Behind the PLA's Current Period of Reform," in Phillip C. Saunders, Arthur S. Ding, Andrew Scobell, Andrew N. D. Yang, and Joel Wuthnow, eds., *Chairman Xi Remakes the PLA: Assessing Chinese Military Reforms*, Washington, D.C.: National Defense University Press, 2019, pp. 45–84.

———, "The Chinese View of Strategic Competition with the United States," testimony before the U.S.-China Economic and Security Review Commission, June 24, 2020.

FireEye, *Southeast Asia: An Evolving Cyber Threat Landscape*, Milpitas, Calif., March 2015.

Fonbuena, Carmela, "Chinese Coast Guard Shoos Away PH Fishermen from Scarborough," *Rappler*, September 27, 2016.

———, "PH Military Encourages Fishermen to Return to Scarborough," *Rappler*, April 25, 2018.

———, "Video Captures China Coast Guard Taking PH Fishermen's Catch," *Rappler*, June 8, 2018.

Fook, Lye Liang, and Ha Hoang Hop, "The Vanguard Bank Incident: Developments and What Next?" *ISEAS Perspective*, No. 69, 2019.

Ford, Lindsey W., and James Goldgeier, *Retooling America's Alliances to Manage the China Challenge*, Washington, D.C.: Brookings Institution, January 25, 2021.

Ford, Peter, "China Gives Cool Response to U.S. Military Activity in Australia," *Christian Science Monitor*, November 17, 2011.

Fordham, Benjamin O., "More Than Mixed Results: What We Have Learned from Quantitative Research on the Diversionary Hypothesis," in William R. Thompson, ed., *The Oxford Encyclopedia of Empirical International Relations Theory*, New York: Oxford University Press, 2018.

ForeignAssistance.gov, homepage, 2021. As of October 26, 2022: https://foreignassistance.gov/

Forster, Larissa, *Influence Without Boots on the Ground: Seaborne Crisis Response*, Newport, R.I.: Naval War College Press, 2013.

Fravel, M. Taylor, "Regime Insecurity and International Cooperation: Explaining China's Compromises in Territorial Disputes," *International Security*, Vol. 30, No. 2, Fall 2005, pp. 46–83.

———, "Power Shifts and Escalation: Explaining China's Use of Force in Territorial Disputes," *International Security*, Vol. 32, No. 3, Winter 2007/2008, pp. 44–83.

———, "The Limits of Diversion: Rethinking Internal and External Conflict," *Security Studies*, Vol. 19, No. 2, 2010, pp. 307–341.

Frederick, Bryan, Matthew Povlock, Stephen Watts, Miranda Priebe, and Edward Geist, *Assessing Russian Reactions to U.S. and NATO Posture Enhancements*, Santa Monica, Calif.: RAND Corporation, RR-1879-AF, 2017. As of July 28, 2021: https://www.rand.org/pubs/research_reports/RR1879.html

Fu Mengzi and Liu Chunhao, "Some Thoughts on Building the 21st Century 'Maritime Silk Road'" ["关于 21 世纪'海上丝绸之路'建设的若干思考"], *Contemporary International Relations* [现代国 际关系], No. 3, 2015.

"Full Text of Xi Jinping's Report at the 19th CPC National Congress," Xinhua, November 3, 2017.

Gady, Franz-Stefan, "China Flies Su-35 Fighters over Bashi Channel for First Time," *The Diplomat*, May 12, 2018.

———, "Japan Launches New Guided Missile Destroyer Capable of Ballistic Missile Defense," *The Diplomat*, August 1, 2018.

———, "China Holds Long-Range Air Combat Drill Near Taiwan," *The Diplomat*, December 20, 2018.

———, "U.S. Navy Littoral Combat Ship Arrives in Singapore for Rotational Deployment," *The Diplomat*, July 9, 2019.

Gan, Nectar, "4 Chinese Soldiers Died in Bloody India Border Clash Last Year, China Reveals," *CNN*, February 20, 2021.

Garamone, Jim, "Aircraft Carrier USS *Carl Vinson* Makes Vietnam Port Call," U.S. Department of Defense, March 5, 2018.

Garver, John W., "China's Decision for War with India in 1962," in Alastair Iain Johnston and Robert S. Ross, eds., *New Directions in the Study of China's Foreign Policy*, Stanford, Calif.: Stanford University Press, 2006, pp. 86–130.

———, *Face Off: China, the United States, and Taiwan's Democratization*, Seattle, Wash.: University of Washington Press, 2011.

———, *China's Quest: The History of the Foreign Relations of the People's Republic of China*, New York: Oxford University Press, 2016.

George, Alexander L., and Richard Smoke, *Deterrence in American Foreign Policy: Theory and Practice*, New York: Columbia University Press, 1974.

Gerson, Michael S., *The Sino-Soviet Border Conflict: Deterrence, Escalation, and the Threat of Nuclear War in 1969*, Arlington, Va.: CNA, 2010.

Gettleman, Jeffrey, "Shots Fired Along India-China Border for First Time in Years," *New York Times*, September 8, 2020.

Gilpin, Robert, *War and Change in World Politics*, Cambridge, UK: Cambridge University Press, 1981.

Glaser, Bonnie, "U.S. Pivot to Asia Leaves China Off Balance," *Comparative Connections*, Vol. 13, No. 3, 2011.

Glaser, Charles L., "The Security Dilemma Revisited," *World Politics*, Vol. 50, No. 1, October 1997, pp. 171–201.

Glenshaw, Paul, "Secret Casualties of the Cold War," *Air & Space Magazine*, December 2017.

Goddard, Stacie E., "Uncommon Ground: Indivisible Territory and the Politics of Legitimacy," *International Organization*, Vol. 60, No. 1, Winter 2006, pp. 35–68.

Godwin, Paul H. B., and Alice L. Miller, "China's Forbearance Has Limits: Chinese Threat and Retaliation Signaling and Its Implications for a Sino-American Military Confrontation," *China Strategic Perspectives*, No. 6, Washington, D.C.: Institute for National Strategic Studies, April 2013.

Goldgeier, J. M., and P. E. Tetlock, "Psychology and International Relations Theory," *Annual Review of Political Science*, Vol. 4, 2001, pp. 67–92.

Gomez, Eric, "Are America's East Asia Allies Willing and Able to Host U.S. Intermediate-Range Missiles?" *Asia Pacific Bulletin*, No. 522, August 19, 2020.

Gomez, Jim, "U.S. Carrier Sails into Disputed Waters amid New Flare-Ups," Associated Press, August 6, 2019.

Gompert, David C., Astrid Stuth Cevallos, and Cristina L. Garafola, *War with China: Thinking Through the Unthinkable*, Santa Monica, Calif.: RAND Corporation, RR-1140-A, 2016. As of July 14, 2021:
https://www.rand.org/pubs/research_reports/RR1140.html

Gotinga, J. C., "2019 Year of Rough Seas for PH in the Face of Belligerent China," *Rappler*, December 10, 2019.

Government of the Philippines, *National Security Policy 2011–2016: Securing the Gains of Democracy*, Manila, 2011.

Govtrack.us, "Taiwan," search for enacted laws on April 10, 2021. As of April 10, 2021:
https://www.govtrack.us/congress/bills/subjects/taiwan/6787#sort=introduced_date&congress=115&current_status[]=28

Grady, John, "Biden Admin Wants to Expand Pacific 'Quad' Relationship," *USNI News*, January 30, 2021.

Green, Michael J., "Quad Summit's Vaccine Deal Is Biden's Bold First Move in Asia," *Foreign Policy*, March 12, 2021.

Green, Michael, Kathleen Hicks, Zack Cooper, John Schaus, and Jake Douglas, *Countering Coercion in Maritime Asia: The Theory and Practice of Gray Zone Deterrence*, Washington, D.C.: Center for Strategic and International Studies, May 2017.

———, "Counter-Coercion Series: Scarborough Shoal Standoff," Asia Maritime Transparency Initiative, Center for Strategic and International Studies, May 22, 2017.

———, "Counter-Coercion Series: China-Vietnam Oil Rig Standoff," Asia Maritime Transparency Initiative, Center for Strategic and International Studies, June 12, 2017.

———, "Counter-Coercion Series: Senkaku Islands Nationalization Crisis," Asia Maritime Transparency Initiative, Center for Strategic and International Studies, June 14, 2017.

Greene, Andrew, "Australia Could Soon Host More U.S. Marines in Darwin," *ABC News*, June 10, 2021.

Greitens, Sheena Chestnut, "The U.S.-Philippines Alliance in a Year of Transition: Challenges and Opportunities," working paper, Washington, D.C.: Brookings Institution, May 2016.

Greitens, Sheena Chestnut, Myunghee Lee, and Emir Yazici, "Counterterrorism and Preventive Repression: China's Changing Strategy in Xinjiang," *International Security*, Vol. 44, No. 3, Winter 2019/2020, pp. 9–47.

Grossman, Derek, "China Refuses to Quit on the Philippines," *The Diplomat*, July 22, 2020.

———, "America Is Betting Big on the Second Island Chain," *RAND Blog*, September 8, 2020. As of June 27, 2022:
https://www.rand.org/blog/2020/09/america-is-betting-big-on-the-second-island-chain.html

———, "How U.S.-Vietnam Ties Might Go Off the Rails" *The Diplomat*, February 1, 2021.

Grossman, Derek, Nathan Beauchamp-Mustafaga, Logan Ma, and Michael S. Chase, *China's Long-Range Bomber Flights: Drivers and Implications*, Santa Monica, Calif.: RAND Corporation, RR-2567-AF, 2018. As of May 12, 2021:
https://www.rand.org/pubs/research_reports/RR2567.html

Grossman, Derek, and Paul S. Orner, "Tracking Chinese Perceptions of Vietnam's Relations with China and the United States," *Asia Policy*, Vol. 16, No. 2, 2021, pp. 103–127.

Gunness, Kristen, "The China Dream and the Near Seas," in Roy Kamphausen, David Lai, and Tiffany Ma, eds., *Securing the China Dream*, Seattle, Wash.: National Bureau of Asian Research, 2020, pp. 75–92.

Guo Xiaopeng [郭晓鹏], "Contain China? U.S. Wins over Japan, Australia and India at Planning Summit, but Attitudes Differ Among the Four Countries" ["牵制中国？美拉拢日澳印筹划首脑会，日媒：四国间态度存差异"], *Global Times* [环球时报], February 19, 2021.

Ha Hoang Hop, "The Oil Rig Incident: A Line Has Been Crossed in Vietnam's Relations with China," *ISEAS Perspective*, No. 61, November 18, 2014.

Hafner-Burton, Emilie M., and Alexander H. Montgomery, "Power Positions: International Organizations, Social Networks, and Conflict," *Journal of Conflict Resolution*, Vol. 50, No. 1, 2006, pp. 3–27.

Hagel, Chuck, "Statement on the East China Sea Air Defense Identification Zone," *Real Clear Defense*, November 23, 2013.

Hamilton, Robert E., "Able Archer at 35: Lessons of the 1983 War Scare," Foreign Policy Research Institute, December 3, 2018.

Hammes, T. X., "Offshore Control: A Proposed Strategy for an Unlikely Conflict," *Strategic Forum*, Vol. 278, June 2012, pp. 1–14.

Handley, Erin, and Iris Zhao, "How Hong Kong's Protest Movement Is Forging Solidary with Australia's Uyghurs and Tibetans," *ABC News*, September 7, 2019.

Hao Qing [郝晴] and Li Qi [李琦], "'Cobra Gold-2021' Multinational Joint Humanitarian Assistance and Disaster Relief Exercise Opened" ["'金色眼镜蛇-2021'多国联合演习人道主义救援减灾演习开幕"], Ministry of Defense of the People's Republic of China [中华人民共和国国防部], July 31, 2021. As of August 17, 2021: http://www.mod.gov.cn/action/2021-07-31/content_4890723.htm

Harkavy, Robert E., "Defeat, National Humiliation, and the Revenge Motif in International Politics," *International Politics*, Vol. 37, No. 3, 2000, pp. 345–368.

Harrell, Peter, Elizabeth Rosenberg, and Edoardo Saravalle, *China's Use of Coercive Economic Measures*, Washington, D.C.: Center for a New American Security, June 2018.

Haulman, Daniel, *One Hundred Years of Flight: USAF Chronology of Significant Air and Space Events, 1903–2002*, Maxwell Air Force Base, Ala.: Air University Press, 2003.

Haux, Hailey, "A B-52 Exercises Dynamic Force Employment with Joint Partners in the Indo-Pacific," Pacific Air Forces, July 5, 2020.

Haver, Zachary, "China Begins Month of Military Exercises in South China Sea," *Radio Free Asia*, March 1, 2021.

Hayton, Bill, "The Week Donald Trump Lost the South China Sea," *Foreign Policy*, July 31, 2017.

———, "The South China Sea in 2020," statement before the U.S.-China Economic and Security Review Commission, Hearing on U.S.-China Relations in 2020: Enduring Problems and Emerging Challenges, September 9, 2020.

"'He Felt I Would Understand,' Hong Kong Protester's Mother Says," *Radio Free Asia*, December 12, 2019.

He Qisong [何奇松], "Trump Administration (Missile Defense Assessment)" ["特朗普政府(导弹防御评估)"], *International Forum* [国际论坛], No. 4, 2019.

Heath, Timothy R., Derek Grossman, and Asha Clark, *China's Quest for Global Primacy: An Analysis of Chinese International and Defense Strategies to Outcompete the United States*, Santa Monica, Calif.: RAND Corporation, RR-A447-1, 2021. As of July 12, 2021: https://www.rand.org/pubs/research_reports/RRA447-1.html

Heath, Timothy R., Kristen Gunness, and Cortez A. Cooper III, *The PLA and China's Rejuvenation: National Security and Military Strategies, Deterrence Concepts, and Combat Capabilities*, Santa Monica, Calif.: RAND Corporation, RR-1402-OSD, 2016. As of July 28, 2021: https://www.rand.org/pubs/research_reports/RR1402.html

Heflin, Lindsey, "B-1B Lancers Arrive at Andersen Air Force Base for Bomber Task Force Deployment," Pacific Air Forces, December 6, 2020.

———, "B-1 Lancers Train with F-22s in South China Sea," Pacific Air Forces, December 10, 2020.

Heginbotham, Eric, Michael Nixon, Forrest E. Morgan, Jacob L. Heim, Jeff Hagen, Sheng Tao Li, Jeffrey Engstrom, Martin C. Libicki, Paul DeLuca, David A. Shlapak, David R. Frelinger, Burgess Laird, Kyle Brady, and Lyle J. Morris, *The U.S.-China Military Scorecard: Forces, Geography, and the Evolving Balance of Power, 1996–2017*, Santa Monica, Calif.: RAND Corporation, RR-392-AF, 2015. As of October 1, 2022: https://www.rand.org/pubs/research_reports/RR392.html

Hensel, Paul R., "Charting a Course to Conflict: Territorial Issues and Interstate Conflict, 1816–1992," *Conflict Management and Peace Science*, Vol. 15, No. 1, 1996, pp. 43–73.

———, "An Evolutionary Approach to the Study of Interstate Rivalry," *Conflict Management and Peace Science*, Vol. 17, No. 2, 1999, pp. 175–206.

Hensel, Paul R., and Sara McLaughlin Mitchell, "Issue Indivisibility and Territorial Claims," *GeoJournal*, Vol. 64, No. 4, 2005, pp. 275–285.

Herscovitch, Benjamin, "A Balanced Threat Assessment of China's South China Sea Policy," Cato Institute, August 28, 2017.

Herzinger, Blake, "Reorienting the Coast Guard: A Case for Patrol Forces in the Indo-Pacific," *War on the Rocks*, November 5, 2019.

Heydarian, Richard Javad, "Duterte's Uncertain China Gamble," Asia Maritime Transparency Initiative, Center for Strategic and International Studies, November 3, 2016.

———, "Scepticism Rises in Philippines About Chinese Projects and Duterte's Support of Them," *South China Morning Post*, January 18, 2020.

———, "How Duterte Turned the Philippines into China's New Play Thing," *National Interest*, February 23, 2020.

———, "China Exploits U.S.-Philippine Strategic Weakness," *Asia Times*, March 24, 2021.

Holmgren, Jacob J., "Expanding Cooperative Intelligence, Surveillance, and Reconnaissance with Allies and Partners in the Indo-Pacific," *Journal of Indo-Pacific Affairs*, January 15, 2021.

"Hong Kong Timeline: A Year of Protests," Associated Press, June 9, 2020.

Hornung, Jeffrey W., *Japan's Potential Contributions in an East China Sea Contingency*, Santa Monica, Calif.: RAND Corporation, RR-A314-1, 2020. As of May 4, 2021: https://www.rand.org/pubs/research_reports/RRA314-1.html

"How Should China Retaliate Against South Korea for Its Deployment of THAAD?" ["因为 '萨德', 中国应 如何 '报复' 韩国"], *Global Times* [环球时报], August 1, 2016.

Hu Bo, "Three Major Maritime Security Issues Pose a Test for 'One Belt, One Road'" ["三大海上安全问题考验'一代一路'"], in Zhang Jie, ed., *Assessment of China's Peripheral Security Situation 2016* [中国周边安 全形势评估 2016], Beijing: Social Sciences Academic Press, 2016.

———, "Six Categories of U.S. Military Operations in the South China Sea and Their Tendencies," South China Sea Strategic Situation Probing Initiative, August 29, 2019.

Hu Xijin, "India Lies About Casualties in Border Clash with China," *Global Times*, September 17, 2020.

Huang, Kristen, "China Military Fires 'Aircraft-Carrier Killer' Missile into South China Sea in 'Warning to the United States,'" *South China Morning Post*, August 26, 2020.

———, "U.S. Bombers Enter Chinese Air Defence Zone as Beijing's Navy Mounts Massive Exercises," *South China Morning Post*, November 17, 2020.

Huang Xiaoyong, "Promote Collective Asian Energy Security Through One Belt, One Road" ["以 '一带一路' 促进亚洲共同能源安全"], *Foreign Affairs Observer* [外交观察], August 7, 2015.

Huang Xingqiu [黄兴球], "Seven Decades of China-Vietnam Relations: Axis and Direction" ["中越关系 70 年: 基轴与方向"], *Southeast Asian Affairs* [南洋问题研究], No. 1, 2020, pp. 31–40.

Huang Yingying [黄莹莹], "Meng Xiangqing: Large Breakthroughs Have Already Been Made in Crisis Management and Control on China's Periphery" ["孟祥青: 中国周边危机管控已有大突破"], *International Herald Tribune* [国际先驱导报], November 6, 2012.

Huang Yingying [黄莹莹] and Sun Si [孙思], "Can the 'Scarborough Shoal Model' Be Copied?" ["'黄岩岛模式' 是否可复制"], *International Herald Tribune* [国际先驱导报], April 12, 2013.

Huang Zijuan [黄子娟], "Expert on Our Military: U.S. B-52 Approaching Islands and Reefs Perhaps Without Live Ammunition Is Just a Show of Force" ["我军专家: 美 B52 逼近岛礁或未挂实弹只是炫耀武力"], *ChinaNews.com* [中国新闻网], November 13, 2015.

Hudson, John, "Congressman: Obama Is Letting China Steal U.S. Military Secrets," *Foreign Policy*, June 4, 2013.

Huong Le Thu, "Rough Waters Ahead for Vietnam-China Relations," Carnegie Endowment for International Peace, September 30, 2020.

Hurst, Daniel, "Australia at Mercy of 'Coercive Trade Warfare' as China and US Continue Rivalry," *The Guardian*, February 15, 2021.

Hussain, Hamzah Rifaat, "Why the 'Quad Meeting' Should Not Translate into Inflamed Tensions," *China Daily*, October 6, 2020.

Huth, Paul K., "Extended Deterrence and the Outbreak of War," *American Political Science Review*, Vol. 82, No. 2, 1988, pp. 423–443.

———, "Reputations and Deterrence: A Theoretical and Empirical Assessment," *Security Studies*, Vol. 7, No. 1, 1997, pp. 72–99.

"India's Weapons Procurement from the U.S. Jumps to $3.4 Billion in 2020," *The Hindu*, December 9, 2020.

Information Office of the State Council of the People's Republic of China, *China's National Defense in 2010*, Beijing, March 31, 2011. As of July 14, 2021: http://www.china.org.cn/government/whitepaper/node_7114675.htm

International Crisis Group, *Dangerous Waters: China-Japan Relations on the Rocks*, New York, Asia Report #245, April 8, 2013.

International Institute for Strategic Studies, *The Military Balance 2021*, London, February 25, 2021.

"'It Will Be Bloody': Philippines' Duterte Threatens to 'Stake a Claim' over South China Sea Energy Resources Using Military Ships," *South China Morning Post*, April 20, 2021.

Jaishankar, Dhruva, *Acting East: India in the Indo-Pacific*, Washington, D.C.: Brookings Institution, October 24, 2019.

Japan Coast Guard, "Trends in Chinese Government and Other Vessels in the Waters Around the Senkaku Islands, and Japan's Response" ["尖閣諸島周辺海域における中国海警局に所属する船舶等の動向と我が国の対処"], undated.

"Japan Government 'Reaches Deal to Buy' Disputed Islands," *BBC News*, September 5, 2012.

"Japanese and U.S. Military Work to Improve Interoperability," U.S. Indo-Pacific Command, December 11, 2020.

Japanese Ministry of Defense, *Defense of Japan 2019*, Tokyo, 2019.

Japanese Ministry of Foreign Affairs, *The Guidelines for Japan-U.S. Defense Cooperation*, April 27, 2015. As of May 5, 2021: https://www.mofa.go.jp/files/000078188.pdf

Japanese Ministry of Foreign Affairs, "About the Senkaku Islands," webpage, April 13, 2016. As of May 4, 2021: https://www.mofa.go.jp/region/asia-paci/senkaku/index.html

Japanese Prime Minister's Office, "Meeting of Related Cabinet Officials Regarding the Acquisition and Retention of the Senkaku Islands" ["尖閣諸島の取得・保有に関する関係閣僚会合"], September 10, 2014.

Japanese Prime Minister's Office, "Mutual Agreement Among Related Cabinet Officials Regarding the Acquisition and Retention of the Senkaku Islands" ["尖閣諸島の取得・保有に関する関係閣僚申し合わせ"], September 10, 2014.

Jennings, Ralph, "China Needs Its Friend the Philippines More Than the Philippines Needs China," *Forbes*, April 20, 2017.

———, "Will US First Class Treatment of Visiting Taiwan President Rattle China?" *Voice of America*, July 17, 2019.

———, "China or U.S.? Philippines Foreign Policy Plays Both Sides," *Voice of America*, September 3, 2020.

———, "Vietnam Gets Boost from Western Allies in Its Defense Against China," *Voice of America*, October 31, 2020.

———, "U.S. Speeds Arms Sales for Taiwan as Island Revamps China Strategy," *Voice of America*, November 6, 2020.

Jensen, Johan Skog, "A Game of Chess and a Battle of Wits: India's Forward Policy Decision in Late 1961," *Journal of Defence Studies*, Vol. 6, No. 4, October 2012.

Jervis, Robert, "Cooperation Under the Security Dilemma," *World Politics*, Vol. 30, No. 2, January 1978, pp. 167–214.

———, "Rational Deterrence: Theory and Evidence," *World Politics*, Vol. 41, No. 2, 1989.

———, *The Meaning of the Nuclear Revolution: Statecraft and the Prospect of Armageddon*, Ithaca, N.Y.: Cornell University Press, 1990.

———, "Signaling and Perception: Drawing Inferences and Projecting Images," in K. R. Monroe, ed., *Political Psychology*, Mahwah, N.J.: Lawrence Erlbaum, 2002, pp. 293–312.

———, *Perception and Misperception in International Politics*, Princeton, N.J.: Princeton University Press, 2017.

Jha, Preeti, "Kelly Craft: U.S. Envoy's 'Last-Minute' Taiwan Visit Angers China," *BBC News*, January 12, 2021.

Johnson, Christopher K., *President Xi Jinping's 'Belt and Road' Initiative: A Practical Assessment of the Chinese Communist Party's Roadmap for China's Global Resurgence*, Washington, D.C.: Center for Strategic and International Studies, March 28, 2016.

Johnson, David E., *Doing What You Know: The United States and 250 Years of Irregular Warfare*, Washington, D.C.: Center for Strategic and Budgetary Assessments, 2017.

Johnson, Jesse, "Pentagon Calls Chinese Anti-Ship Missile Test in the South China Sea 'Disturbing,'" *Japan Times*, July 3, 2019.

———, "Japan-Based U.S. Aircraft Carrier in South China Sea Ahead of Key Chinese Anniversary," *Japan Times*, September 29, 2019.

Johnson, Jesse C., Brett Ashley Leeds, and Ahra Wu, "Capability, Credibility, and Extended General Deterrence," *International Interactions*, Vol. 41, No. 2, 2015, pp. 309–336.

Johnston, Alastair Iain, "China's Militarized Interstate Dispute Behaviour 1949–1992: A First Cut at the Data," *China Quarterly*, Vol. 153, 1998, pp. 1–30.

———, "Is Chinese Nationalism Rising? Evidence from Beijing," *International Security*, Vol. 41, No. 3, 2017, pp. 7–43.

Joint Force Space Component Command, "Combined Space Operations Center Established at Vandenberg AFB," July 19, 2018.

Joint Publication 1, *Doctrine for the Armed Forces of the United States*, Washington, D.C.: Joint Chiefs of Staff, July 12, 2017.

Joint Publication 3-0, *Joint Operations*, Washington, D.C.: Joint Chiefs of Staff, October 22, 2018.

Joint Publication 3-16, *Multinational Operations*, Washington, D.C.: Joint Chiefs of Staff, March 1, 2019.

Joint Publication 3-57, *Civil-Military Operations*, Washington, D.C.: Joint Chiefs of Staff, July 9, 2018.

Joint Staff Japan, "About the Emergency Scramble Situation in FY 2014" ["平成２６年度の緊急発進実施状況について"], press release, April 15, 2015.

———, "About the Emergency Scramble Situation in FY 2017" ["平成２９年度の緊急発進実施状況について"], press release, April 13, 2018.

Joshi, Anik, "Trump Doesn't Love Modi Back," *Foreign Policy*, July 28, 2020.

Joshi, Yogesh, and Anit Mukherjee, "From Denial to Punishment: The Security Dilemma and Changes in India's Military Strategy Towards China," *Asian Security*, Vol. 15, No. 1, 2019, pp. 33–35.

Judson, Jen, "US Army Wants to Expand Pre-Positioned Stock in Pacific," *Defense News*, February 4, 2020.

———, "US Army Wants $364 Million for Defender Pacific in FY21," *Defense News*, February 25, 2020.

Juma, Mamatjan, Shohret Hoshur, Kurban Niyaz, and Ekrem Hezim, "10th Anniversary of Urumqi Unrest Brings Protests over Internment Camps, Accountability Demands," *Radio Free Asia*, July 5, 2019.

Jun Sheng [钧声], "Strongly Oppose American Arms Sales to Taiwan" ["坚决反对美对台军售"], *Qiushi* [求是], July 12, 2019.

Jung, Sung Chul, "Foreign Targets and Diversionary Conflict," *International Studies Quarterly*, Vol. 58, No. 3, 2014, pp. 566–578.

Kahn, Joseph, "Chinese General Threatens Use of A-Bombs If U.S. Intrudes," *New York Times*, July 15, 2005.

Kan, Karoline, "Mainland Chinese Lack Sympathy for Hong Kong Protestors," *Nikkei Asia*, July 30, 2019.

Kan, Shirley A., Richard Best, Christopher Bolkcom, Jr., Robert E. Chapman II, Richard P. Cronin, Kerry Dumbaugh, Stuart D. Goldman, Mark E. Manyin, Wayne M. Morrison, Ronald O'Rourke, and David M. Ackerman, *China-U.S. Aircraft Collision Incident of April 2001: Assessments and Policy Implications*, Washington, D.C.: Congressional Research Service, RL30946, October 10, 2001.

Katz, Richard, "Mutual Assured Production," *Foreign Affairs*, July/August 2013.

Kaufman, Alison A., and Daniel M. Hartnett, *Managing Conflict: Examining Recent PLA Writings on Escalation Control*, Arlington, Va.: CNA, February 2016.

Kavanagh, Jennifer, Bryan Frederick, Alexandra Stark, Nathan Chandler, Meagan L. Smith, Matthew Povlock, Lynn E. Davis, and Edward Geist, *Characteristics of Successful U.S. Military Interventions*, Santa Monica, Calif.: RAND Corporation, RR-3062-A, 2019. As of May 17, 2022:
https://www.rand.org/pubs/research_reports/RR3062.html

Ke Mu [枯木], ed., "America Plays the Taiwan Card Again, Punishing Those Who Break Off Relations with Taiwan and Making the DPP Its Lackey" ["美国又打台湾牌，惩罚跟台湾'断交'友邦，民进党成为马前卒"], *Channel News* [海峡要闻], March 24, 2020.

Kelly, Tim, "U.S., UK Conduct First Joint Drills in Contested South China Sea," Reuters, January 16, 2019.

———, "U.S. Navy Commander in Asia Welcomes Japan-Australia Military Pact as Encouraging," Reuters, November 18, 2020.

Kertzer, Joshua D., and Ryan Brutger, "Decomposing Audience Costs: Bringing the Audience Back into Audience Cost Theory," *American Journal of Political Science*, Vol. 60, No. 1, January 2016, pp. 234–249.

Kheel, Rebecca, "Pentagon Pulling 'Certain Forces and Capabilities,' Including Air Defense, from Middle East," *The Hill*, June 18, 2021.

Khong, Yuen Foong, "Power as Prestige in World Politics," *International Affairs*, Vol. 95, No. 1, January 2019, pp. 119–142.

Kimmons, Sean, "South Korea Rotations Give Soldiers Deployment, Cultural Experience," *Army.mil*, August 24, 2018.

Kline, Mikaley, "B-1s Train with JASDF, Return to Andersen Air Force Base for BTF Deployment," Pacific Air Forces, September 11, 2020.

Kong Tsung-gan, "Arrests and Trials of Hong Kong Protestors," *Medium*, December 1, 2019.

Krickovic, Andrej, "Catalyzing Conflict: The Internal Dimension of the Security Dilemma," *Journal of Global Security Studies*, Vol. 1, No. 2, May 2016, pp. 111–126.

Ku, Julian, "Does the U.S. Have a Legal Obligation to Defend the Scarborough Shoal for the Philippines? Not Until It Decides Who Owns It," *Lawfare*, April 27, 2016.

Kuhn, Anthony, "After Being Silent for Decades, Japan Now Speaks Up About Taiwan—And Angers China," *NPR*, August 2, 2021.

Kühnhardt, Ludger, *Region-Building*: Vol. I, *The Global Proliferation of Regional Integration*, New York: Berghahn Books, 2010.

Kuo, Lily, "Tsai Ing-Wen Says China Must 'Face Reality' of Taiwan's Independence," *The Guardian*, January 15, 2020.

LaGrone, Sam, "Pentagon Test Launches Prototype Hypersonic Weapon," *USNI News*, March 20, 2020.

Lague, David, "Special Report: Pentagon's Latest Salvo Against China's Growing Might—Cold War Bombers," Reuters, September 1, 2020.

Lai, Brian, and Dan Slater, "Institutions of the Offensive: Domestic Sources of Dispute Initiation in Authoritarian Regimes, 1950–1992," *American Journal of Political Science*, Vol. 50, No. 1, 2006, pp. 113–126.

Lai, Hongyi, *The Domestic Sources of China's Foreign Policy: Regimes, Leadership, Priorities, and Process*, New York: Routledge, 2010.

Lai, Johnson, "Azar Visit to Taiwan Is Fresh Thorn in Prickly US-China Ties," Associated Press, August 10, 2020.

Laird, Burgess, *War Control: Chinese Writings on the Control of Escalation in Crisis and Conflict*, Washington, D.C.: Center for a New American Security, April 2017.

Lan Jianxue, "India Ridiculous to Clamor About China-Pakistan MOU," *Global Times*, December 2, 2020.

Langfitt, Frank, "In China, Beware: A Camera May Be Watching You," *NPR*, January 29, 2013.

Lardy, Nicholas R., *The State Strike Back: The End of Economic Reform in China?* Washington, D.C.: Peterson Institute for International Economics, 2019.

Larson, Deborah Welch, T. V. Paul, and William C. Wohlforth, "Status and World Order," in T. V. Paul, Deborah Welch Larson, and William C. Wohlforth, eds., *Status in World Politics*, Cambridge, UK: Cambridge University Press, 2014, pp. 3–30.

Larson, Eric V., Gustav Lindstrom, Myron Hura, Ken Gardiner, Jim Keffer, and William Little, *Interoperability of U.S. and NATO Allied Air Forces: Supporting Data and Case Studies*, Santa Monica, Calif.: RAND Corporation, MR-1603-AF, 2003. As of May 17, 2022: https://www.rand.org/pubs/monograph_reports/MR1603.html

Lawrence, Susan, and Wayne Morrison, *Taiwan: Issues for Congress*, Washington, D.C.: Congressional Research Service, October 30, 2017.

Le Thu, Huong, "China's Incursion into Vietnam's EEZ and Lessons from the Past," Asia Maritime Transparency Initiative, Center for Strategic and International Studies, August 8, 2019.

Le Thu, Huong, and Sunny Cao, "Russia's Growing Interests in the South China Sea," *The Strategist*, December 18, 2019.

Lee Jeong-ho, "Chinese Military Flies Su-30 Fighter Jet, Y-8 Surveillance Plane Close to Taiwan in Latest Show of Strength," *South China Morning Post*, January 23, 2019.

Lee, Jeongseok, "Back to Normal? The End of the THAAD Dispute Between China and South Korea," *China Brief*, Vol. 17, No. 15, November 22, 2017, pp. 3–8.

Lee, Michelle Ye Hee, and Joanna Slater, "Meeting of Leaders Signals the 'Quad' Grouping Will Become Central Part of the U.S. Strategy in Asia," *Washington Post*, March 13, 2021.

Lee, Se Young, "Two U.S. Carrier Groups Conduct Exercises in South China Sea," Reuters, February 9, 2021.

Leeds, Brett Ashley, and David R. Davis, "Domestic Political Vulnerability and International Disputes," *Journal of Conflict Resolution*, Vol. 41, No. 6, December 1997, pp. 814–834.

Lema, Karen, and Neil Jerome Morales, "Pompeo Assures Philippines of U.S. Protection in Event of Sea Conflict," Reuters, March 1, 2019.

Lemke, Douglas, and Suzanne Werner, "Power Parity, Commitment to Change, and War," *International Studies Quarterly*, Vol. 40, No. 2, June 1996, pp. 235–260.

Lendon, Brad, "Japan Increases Protection for US Military amid 'Severe Security Environment,'" *CNN*, February 24, 2021.

Lewis, Jeffrey, *Paper Tigers: China's Nuclear Posture*, New York: Routledge, 2015.

Li Bin, "The Security Dilemma and THAAD Deployment in the ROK," *China-U.S. Focus*, March 6, 2017.

Li Chunxia [李春霞], "From Enemy to Comprehensive Partner: Strategic Considerations Regarding Vietnam's Development of Relations with the United States" ["从敌人到全面伙伴: 越南发展对美关系的战略考量"], *International Forum* [国际论坛], Vol. 16, No. 4, 2014.

Li Jian [李剑], Chen Wenwen [陈文文], and Jin Jing [金晶], "Overall Situation of Sea Power in the Indian Ocean and the Expansion in the Indian Ocean of Chinese Sea Powers" ["印度样海权格局与中国海权的印度洋扩展"], *Pacific Journal*, Vol. 22, No. 5, 2014.

———, "The Pattern of Indian Ocean Power and the Expansion of China's Sea Power in the Indian Ocean" ["印度洋海权格局与中国海权的印度洋拓展"], *China's Foreign Policy* [中国外交], 2015.

Li Qingqing, "Being US Pawn on SCS Issue Doesn't Serve Japan's Interests," *Global Times*, October 20, 2020.

Li Xiaokun and Li Lianxing, "U.S. Military Base in Australia Shows 'Cold War Mentality,'" *China Daily*, December 1, 2011.

Li Yuan, "Why Many in China Oppose Hong Kong's Protests," *New York Times*, July 1, 2019.

Li, Zhonglin, "The Strategic Posture of China in the South China Sea and Countermeasures" ["中国对南海战略态势的塑造及启示"], *Contemporary International Relations* [现代国际关系], No. 2, 2017.

Liang, Annabelle, "China Vows Military Action If Taiwan, Sea Claims Opposed," Associated Press, June 2, 2019.

Liff, Adam P., "China and the U.S. Alliance System," *China Quarterly*, Vol. 233, March 2018, pp. 137–165.

———, *China, Japan, and the East China Sea: Beijing's "Gray Zone" Coercion and Tokyo's Response*, Washington, D.C.: Brookings Institution, December 2019.

Lin Minwang [林民旺], "India Has Chosen a High Risk Strategic Path" ["林民旺: 印度选择了一条高风险战略路径"], *Global Times* [环球时报], October 27, 2020.

———, "What Can India Offer to Turn the US into a 'Pawn'?" *Global Times*, December 24, 2020.

Lin Zhiyuan [林治远], "New Changes in U.S. Military Strategy and Combat Theory" ["美国军事战略和作战理论新变化"], *Military Digest* [军事文摘], No. 1, 2019, pp. 7–10.

Lin, Bonny, "U.S. Allied and Partner Support for Taiwan: Responses to a Chinese Attack on Taiwan and Potential U.S. Taiwan Policy Changes," testimony presented before the U.S.-China Economic and Security Review Commission on February 18, 2021, Santa Monica, Calif.: RAND Corporation, CT-A1194-1, 2021. As of August 17, 2021: https://www.rand.org/pubs/testimonies/CTA1194-1.html

Lin, Bonny, Cristina L. Garafola, Bruce McClintock, Jonah Blank, Jeffrey W. Hornung, Karen Schwindt, Jennifer D. P. Moroney, Paul Orner, Dennis Borrman, Sarah W. Denton, and Jason Chambers, *Competition in the Gray Zone: Countering China's Coercion Against U.S. Allies and Partners in the Indo-Pacific*, Santa Monica, Calif.: RAND Corporation, RR-A594-1, 2022. As of August 26, 2022: https://www.rand.org/pubs/research_reports/RRA594-1.html

Lin, Bonny, Howard J. Shatz, Nathan Chandler, Cristina L. Garafola, Eugeniu Han, Andy Law, King Mallory, and Zev Winkelman, *Bridging the Gap: Assessing U.S. Business Community Support for U.S.-China Competition*, Santa Monica, Calif.: RAND Corporation, RR-A1417-1, 2022. As of August 26, 2022: https://www.rand.org/pubs/research_reports/RRA1417-1.html

Lind, Jennifer, and Daryl G. Press, "Markets or Mercantilism? How China Secures Its Energy Supplies," *International Security*, Vol. 42, No. 4, 2018, pp. 170–204.

Ling De [凌德] and Fengxiang Li [李风向], "Forgetting Family and Ethnic History, Leading Hong Kong Troublemakers Bring in External Forces" ["忘祖籍抛民族身份，乱港头目成外部势力'带路党'"], *Global Times*, August 21, 2019.

Liu Caiyu and Fan Anqi, "More Evidence Supports Multiple Virus Origins," *Global Times*, November 29, 2020.

Liu Jifeng [刘戟锋], "Being in a Period of Nonphysical Warfare Is Far from Secure" ["身处非物理战时期远未居安"], *Guangming Daily* [光明日报], March 11, 2015.

Liu Xin and Lin Xiaoyi, "U.S. Supports Separatism in Rivals, Upholds Territorial Integrity in Allies: Report," *Global Times*, November 10, 2020.

Liu Xuanzun, "PLA Rocket Force Launches DF-26 'Aircraft Carrier Killer' Missile in Fast-Reaction Drills," *Global Times*, August 6, 2020.

———, "China Holds Naval Drills in Three Maritime Areas amid US Military Threats," *Global Times*, March 15, 2021.

———, "PLA Carrier, Warplanes Surround Taiwan in Drills, in Show of Capability to Cut Off Foreign Intervention," *Global Times*, April 6, 2021.

———, "PLA Prepared as US, Secessionists Provoke," *Global Times*, April 8, 2021.

Liu Zhen, "Xi Jinping Orders China's Military to Be Ready for War 'at Any Second,'" *South China Morning Post*, January 5, 2021.

Liu Zongyi, "Pro-US Strategy May Push India into the Abyss," *Global Times*, January 21, 2021.

Lohman, Walter, "Scarborough Role for U.S.?" *The Diplomat*, June 2, 2012.

Long, Austin, and Brendan Rittenhouse Green, "Stalking the Secure Second Strike: Intelligence, Counterforce, and Nuclear Strategy," *Journal of Strategic Studies*, Vol. 38, Nos. 1–2, 2015, pp. 38–73.

Long, Drake, "China's Naval Aviation Force Shows Up at Fiery Cross Reef," *Benar News*, May 13, 2020.

———, "Vietnam Issues Decree Against Illegal Oil and Gas Operations in Its Waters," *Radio Free Asia*, August 31, 2020.

Long Xingang [龙心刚] and Dongxing Liang [梁东兴], "On the U.S. Factor in the South China Sea Issue" ["论南海问题中的美国因素"], *Around Southeast Asia* [东南亚纵横], Vol. 9, 2010.

Lostumbo, Michael J., David R. Frelinger, James Williams, and Barry Wilson, *Air Defense Options for Taiwan: An Assessment of Relative Costs and Operational Benefits*, Santa Monica, Calif.: RAND Corporation, RR-1051-OSD, 2016. As of August 17, 2021: https://www.rand.org/pubs/research_reports/RR1051.html

Love De Jesus, Julliane, "Protest Greets Start of Balikatan War Games," *Inquirer.net*, May 5, 2014.

Low, Zoe, "An Ode to Hong Kong's Extradition Bill Protesters, Penned by Vietnamese-American Dissidents," *South China Morning Post*, July 11, 2019.

Löwenheim, Oded, and Gadi Heimann, "Revenge in International Politics," *Security Studies*, Vol. 17, No. 4, 2008, pp. 685–724.

Lubold, Gordon, "U.S. Military Is Offered New Bases in the Pacific," *Wall Street Journal*, September 8, 2020.

Lubold, Gordon, Nancy A. Youssef, and Michael R. Gordon, "U.S. Military to Withdraw Hundreds of Troops, Aircraft, Antimissile Batteries from Middle East," *Wall Street Journal*, June 18, 2021.

Lum, Thomas, *The Republic of the Philippines and U.S. Interests*, Washington, D.C.: Congressional Research Service, April 5, 2012.

Luo Huijun [罗会钧], "U.S.-Vietnam Defense and Security Cooperation and Its Influence on China" ["美越防务安全合作及其对中国的影响"], *Journal of International Security Studies* [国家安全研究], No. 3, 2017.

Lupton, Danielle L., *Reputation for Resolve: How Leaders Signal Determination in International Politics*, Ithaca, N.Y.: Cornell University Press, 2020.

Luz Lopez, Melissa, "China's Loan, Investment Pledges Unlikely to Be Fulfilled Under Duterte's Term—Carpio," *CNN Philippines*, June 8, 2020.

Ma, Ying, "As Hong Kong Protests Face Mainland Pushback, Here's What Chinese Nationalists Misunderstand," *NBC News*, September 9, 2019.

Madan, Tanvi, "The Rise, Fall, and Rebirth of the 'Quad,'" *War on the Rocks*, November 16, 2017.

———, "Emerging Global Issues: China-India Border Dispute and Its Implications," Washington, D.C.: Brookings Institution, September 9, 2020.

Mahadzir, Dzirhan, "Inaugural AUMX Exercise Seeks to Deepen U.S.-ASEAN Maritime Cooperation," *USNI News*, September 3, 2019.

Mahoney, Robert B., Jr., *U.S. Navy Responses to International Incidents and Crises, 1955–1975*: Vol. II, *Summaries of Incidents and Responses*, Arlington, Va.: Center for Naval Analyses, 1977.

"Major Consensus Reached at Xi-Trump Summit," Xinhua, November 9, 2017.

"Major General Zhu Chenghu: To Respond to THAAD, China Must Be Fully Prepared" ["朱成虎少将: 应对美国 '萨德' 中国要未雨绸缪"], *Bauhania* [紫荆网], August 2, 2016. As of February 3, 2021:
http://hk.zijing.org/2016/0802/711051.shtml

Manantan, Mark, "The Cyber Dimension of the South China Sea Clashes," *The Diplomat*, August 5, 2019.

Manantan, Mark Bryan F., "Pivot Toward China: A Critical Analysis of the Philippines' Policy Shift on the South China Sea Disputes," *Asian Politics & Policy*, Vol. 11, No. 4, October 2019, pp. 643–662.

Mansfield, Edward D., and Brian M. Pollins, "The Study of Interdependence and Conflict," *Journal of Conflict Resolution*, Vol. 45, No. 6, 2001, pp. 834–859.

Manyin, Mark E., *U.S.-Vietnam Relations in 2014: Current Issues and Implications for U.S. Policy*, Washington, D.C.: Congressional Research Service, June 24, 2014.

Manyin, Mark E., Stephen Daggett, Ben Dolven, Susan V. Lawrence, Michael F. Martin, Ronald O'Rourke, and Bruce Vaughn, *Pivot to the Pacific? The Obama Administration's "Rebalancing" Toward Asia*, Washington, D.C.: Congressional Research Service, March 28, 2012.

Marcus, Jonathan, "China-India Border Tension: Satellite Imagery Shows Doklam Plateau Build-Up," *BBC News*, January 26, 2018.

"Marine Corps Activates Camp Blaz in Guam," *Marines.mil*, October 1, 2020.

"Marine Littoral Regiment (MLR)," *Marines.mil*, August 2, 2021.

Martina, Michael, "China Welcomes Manila's Offer for South China Sea Talks," Reuters, June 1, 2016.

Martinson, Ryan D., *Echelon Defense: The Role of Sea Power in Chinese Maritime Dispute Strategy*, Newport, R.I.: China Maritime Studies Institute, February 2018.

Mastro, Oriana Skylar, "How China Ends Wars: Implications for East Asian and U.S. Security," *Washington Quarterly*, Vol. 41, No. 1, 2018, pp. 45–60.

Mattis, Jim, *Summary of the 2018 National Defense Strategy of the United States of America*, Washington, D.C.: U.S. Department of Defense, 2018.

Mazarr, Michael J., *Mastering the Gray Zone: Understanding a Changing Era of Conflict*, Carlisle, Pa.: U.S. Army War College Press, 2015.

Mazarr, Michael J., Nathan Beauchamp-Mustafaga, Timothy R. Heath, and Derek Eaton, *What Deters and Why: The State of Deterrence in Korea and the Taiwan Strait*, Santa Monica, Calif.: RAND Corporation, RR-3144-A, 2021. As of July 12, 2021: https://www.rand.org/pubs/research_reports/RR3144.html

Mazarr, Michael J., Joe Cheravitch, Jeffrey W. Hornung, and Stephanie Pezard, *What Deters and Why: Applying a Framework to Assess Deterrence of Gray Zone Aggression*, Santa Monica, Calif.: RAND Corporation, RR-3142-A, 2021. As of July 12, 2021: https://www.rand.org/pubs/research_reports/RR3142.html

McConnell, Fiona, "A State Within a State? Exploring Relations Between the Indian State and the Tibetan Community and Government-in-Exile," *Contemporary South Asia*, Vol. 19, No. 3, 2011, pp. 297–313.

McGregor, Richard, *Asia's Reckoning: China, Japan, and the Fate of U.S. Power in the Pacific Century*, New York: Penguin, 2017.

Mearsheimer, John J., *The Tragedy of Great Power Politics*, New York: W. W. Norton, 2001.

———, *Conventional Deterrence*, Ithaca, N.Y.: Cornell University Press, 1985.

Meernik, James, and Peter Waterman, "The Myth of the Diversionary Use of Force by American Presidents," *Political Research Quarterly*, Vol. 49, No. 3, September 1996, pp. 573–590.

Mehta, Aaron, "New U.S.-Vietnam Agreement Shows Growth, Challenges," *Defense News*, June 1, 2015. As of June 16, 2022:
https://www.defensenews.com/2015/06/01/new-us-vietnam-agreement-shows-growth-challenges/

Meick, Ethan, and Nargiza Salidjanova, *China's Response to U.S.-South Korean Missile Defense System Deployment and Its Implications*, Washington, D.C.: U.S.-China Economic and Security Review Commission, July 26, 2017.

Mercer, Jonathan, "The Illusion of International Prestige," *International Security*, Vol. 41, No. 4, 2017, pp. 133–168.

Metz, Steven, and Douglas V. Johnson II, "Asymmetry and U.S. Military Strategy: Definition, Background, and Strategic Concepts," Carlisle, Pa.: Strategic Studies Institute, U.S. Army War College Press, January 2001.

Miles, Simon, "The War Scare That Wasn't: Able Archer 83 and the Myths of the Second Cold War," *Journal of Cold War Studies*, Vol. 22, No. 3, 2020, pp. 86–118.

Miller, Gregory D., *The Shadow of the Past: Reputation and Military Alliances Before the First World War*, Ithaca, N.Y.: Cornell University Press, 2011.

Mills, Walker, "Deterring the Dragon: Returning U.S. Forces to Taiwan," *Military Review*, September–October 2020.

Minh, Hai, "Vietnamese Advised to Avoid Protest Sites in Hong Kong," *Socialist Republic of Viet Nam Government News*, October 2, 2014.

Ministry of Foreign Affairs of the People's Republic of China, "Statement of the Ministry of Foreign Affairs of the People's Republic of China," September 10, 2012. As of May 4, 2021:
http://www.fmprc.gov.cn/mfa_eng/topics_665678/diaodao_665718/t968188.shtml

———, "Foreign Ministry Spokesperson Hong Lei's Routine Press Conference, April 28, 2015" ["2015 年 4 月 28 日外交部发言人洪磊主持例行记者会"], April 28, 2015.

———, "Foreign Ministry Spokesperson Lu Kang's Regular Press Conference on May 11, 2016," May 11, 2016.

———, "The Decision of the Arbitration Tribunal in the South China Sea Arbitration Case Raised by the Philippines Has No Legal Validity" ["菲律宾所提南海仲裁案仲裁庭的裁决没有法律效力"], June 10, 2016. As of May 21, 2021:
https://www.fmprc.gov.cn/web/zyxw/t1371204.shtml

———, "Foreign Ministry Spokesperson Hong Lei's Regular Press Conference on July 8," July 8, 2016.

———, "Wang Yi Comments on Plan of the U.S. to Deploy THAAD System in ROK," July 9, 2016.

———, "Foreign Ministry Spokesperson Lu Kang's Regular Press Conference," July 11, 2016.

———, "Wang Yi Meets with Foreign Minister Yun Byung-se of the ROK," July 25, 2016.

———, "Foreign Ministry Spokesperson Geng Shuang's Regular Press Conference on November 22, 2016" ["2016 年 11 月 22 日外交部发言人耿爽主持例行记者会"], November 22, 2016.

———, "Foreign Ministry Spokesperson Hua Chunying's Regular Press Conference on March 17, 2017," March 17, 2017.

———, "Foreign Ministry Spokesperson Hua Chunying's Regular Press Conference on March 28, 2017" ["2017 年 3 月 28 日外交部发言人华春莹主持例行记者会"], March 28, 2017.

———, "Foreign Ministry Spokesperson Lu Kang's Regular Press Conference on March 29, 2017," March 29, 2017.

———, "China and South Korea Communicate on Bilateral Relations and Other Issues" ["中韩双方就中韩关系等进行沟通"], October 31, 2017. As of July 13, 2021: http://infogate.fmprc.gov.cn/web/wjb_673085/zygy_673101/kxy_685118/xgxw_685120/t1506044.shtml

———, "Xi Jinping Meets with President Duterte of the Philippines," April 25, 2019. As of May 1, 2021: https://www.fmprc.gov.cn/web/zyxw/t1693011.shtml

———, "Foreign Ministry Spokesperson Lu Kang's Regular Press Conference on May 20, 2019," May 20, 2019.

———, "Foreign Ministry Spokesperson Hua Chunying's Regular Press Conference on July 30, 2019," July 30, 2019.

———, "Jointly Safeguarding Peace, Stability and Development in the South China Sea with Dialogue, Consultation and Win-Win Cooperation," September 3, 2020.

———, "Foreign Ministry Spokesperson Hua Chunying's Regular Press Conference on January 5, 2021," January 5, 2021.

Ministry of National Defense of the People's Republic of China, "Defense Ministry's Regular Press Conference on July 30," July 30, 2015.

———, "Defense Ministry's Regular Press Conference on Dec. 31," December 31, 2015.

———, "Sun Jianguo Meets ROK Defense Minister Han Min-ku" ["孙建国会见韩国国防部长韩民求"], June 4, 2016.

———, "Defense Ministry's Regular Press Conference," September 29, 2016.

———, "Maritime Joint Exercise Exerts Positive Energy for the China-ASEAN Community with a Shared Future" ["海上联演为中国−东盟命运共同体发挥正能量"], October 25, 2018.

———, "Regular Press Conference of the Ministry of National Defense on Apr. 30," May 5, 2020. As of April 23, 2021:
http://eng.mod.gov.cn/news/2020-05/04/content_4864650.htm

———, "Defense Ministry's Regular Press Conference on October 29," November 1, 2020.

Mitchell, Sara McLaughlin, and Brandon C. Prins, "Rivalry and Diversionary Uses of Force," *Journal of Conflict Resolution*, Vol. 48, No. 6, December 2004, pp. 937–961.

"MND Answers Reporters' Questions About the Entry of U.S. B-52 Bombers into the Adjacent Airspace of the Islands and Reefs of China's Spratly Island Archipelago" ["国防部就美B-52轰炸机进入中国南沙群岛有关岛礁邻近空域答记者问"], Xinhua, December 19, 2015.

Mogato, Manuel, "Philippines Accuses China of Turning Water Cannon on Its Fishing Boats," Reuters, April 21, 2015.

———, "China Offers $14 Million Arms Package to the Philippines: Manila's Defense Minister," Reuters, December 20, 2016.

———, "U.S., Philippines Scale Back Next Month's Military Drills, No More 'War Games,'" Reuters, April 24, 2017.

———, "China Gives Guns to Philippines to Show It's a Friend, Not a Foe," Reuters, October 5, 2017.

———, "China Donates Four Small Boats and Grenade Launchers to Philippines," Reuters, July 29, 2018.

Mogato, Manuel, Enrico dela Cruz, and Arshad Mohammad, "Philippines' Duterte Wants to 'Open Alliances' with Russia, China," Reuters, September 26, 2016.

Montgomery, Mark, and Bradley Bowman, "Listen to America's Top Commander in the Indo-Pacific and Fund the Pacific Deterrence Initiative," *War on the Rocks*, March 31, 2021.

Moritsugu, Ken, "AP Interview: China Signals Shift but No Letup in Xinjiang," Associated Press, December 21, 2020.

Morris, Lyle J., "Gray Zone Challenges in the East and South China Sea," *Maritime Issues*, January 7, 2019.

Morris, Lyle J., Michael J. Mazarr, Jeffrey W. Hornung, Stephanie Pezard, Anika Binnendijk, and Marta Kepe, *Gaining Competitive Advantage in the Gray Zone: Response Options for Coercive Aggression Below the Threshold of Major War*, Santa Monica, Calif.: RAND Corporation, RR-2942-OSD, 2019. As of October 1, 2022: https://www.rand.org/pubs/research_reports/RR2942.html

MSCConference, "Maritime Security Challenges Virtual—Session 1—Ms. Nadège Rolland on China's BRI," video, YouTube, October 21, 2020. As of March 24, 2021: https://www.youtube.com/watch?v=MnoTaeuPzfg

Myers, Meghann, "Small Rotations to Far-Flung Southeast Asian Countries Are Likely the Future of INDO-PACOM Assignments," *Military Times*, October 8, 2020.

Myers, Steven Lee, "China Acknowledges 4 Deaths in Last Year's Border Clash with India," *New York Times*, March 1, 2021.

Nakamura, Ryo, "U.S. to Build Anti-China Missile Network Along First Island Chain," *Nikkei Asia*, March 5, 2021.

National Institute for South China Sea Studies, *Report on the Military Presence of the United States of America in the Asia-Pacific Region*, Beijing, November 2016.

————, *The U.S. Military Presence in the Asia-Pacific 2020*, Beijing, June 2020.

"National People's Congress Foreign Affairs Office Issues Statement on the Passage of the '2019 Taipei Act'" ["全国人大外事委员会就美国所谓'2019年台北法案'签署成法发表声明"], *Qiushi* [求是], March 28, 2020. As of March 19, 2021: http://www.qstheory.cn/yaowen/2020-03/28/c_1125780298.htm

Nepomuceno, Priam, "PH Navy Contingent to Sail for ASEAN-China Maritime Drill on Oct. 17," Philippine News Agency, October 16, 2018.

Nguygen, Duy, "Foreign Ministry Spokesperson Opposes China's Intrusion of Vietnam's Waters," *Hanoi Times*, February 25, 2021.

O'Donnell, Sean W., Matthew S. Klimow, and Ann Calvaresi Barr, *Operation Pacific Eagle—Philippines: Lead Inspector General Report to the United States Congress*, Washington, D.C.: U.S. Department of Defense, U.S. Department of State, and U.S. Agency for International Development, July 1–September 30, 2020.

O'Hanlon, Michael E., *China, the Gray Zone, and Contingency Planning at the Department of Defense and Beyond*, Washington, D.C.: Brookings Institution, September 2019.

O'Rourke, Ronald, *Navy Lasers, Railgun, and Gun-Launched Guided Projectile: Background and Issues for Congress*, Washington, D.C.: Congressional Research Service, December 17, 2019.

———, *U.S.-China Strategic Competition in South and East China Seas: Background and Issues for Congress*, Washington, D.C.: Congressional Research Service, March 18, 2021.

Office of the Executive Director for International Cooperation, "U.S.–India Defense Technology and Trade Initiative (DTTI)," U.S. Department of Defense, undated.

Office of the Secretary of Defense, *Annual Report to Congress: Military and Security Developments Involving the People's Republic of China 2019*, Washington, D.C., 2019.

———, *Annual Report to Congress: Military and Security Developments Involving the People's Republic of China 2020*, Washington, D.C., 2020.

———, *Annual Report to Congress: Military and Security Developments Involving the People's Republic of China 2021*, Washington, D.C., 2021.

Office of the Under Secretary of Defense (Comptroller), *Pacific Deterrence Initiative Department of Defense Budget Fiscal Year (FY) 2022*, Washington, D.C., May 2021.

Olson, Wyatt, "U.S. to Give Vietnam Another Coast Guard Cutter amid Rising Tensions in South China Sea," *Stars and Stripes*, November 21, 2019.

———, "A Third Fast-Response Coast Guard Cutter Heads to Guam as Tensions Simmer with China," *Stars and Stripes*, April 22, 2021.

Ong, Lynette H., "In Hong Kong, Are 'Thugs for Hire' Behind the Attack on Protestors? Here's What We Know About These Groups," *Washington Post*, July 24, 2019.

Organski, A. F. K., and Jacek Kugler, *The War Ledger*, Chicago, Ill.: University of Chicago Press, 1980.

Ortagus, Morgan, "China Escalates Coercion Against Vietnam's Longstanding Oil and Gas Activity in the South China Sea," U.S. Embassy and Consulates in China, August 21, 2019.

Owsianka, David, "Dyess Airmen Arrive in Indo-Pacific for Bomber Task Force, Integrate with Koku-Jieitai, U.S. Navy," Pacific Air Forces, October 26, 2020.

———, "Dyess Airmen Participate in Indo-Pacific Joint Exercise," Pacific Air Forces, November 13, 2020.

Pacific Air Forces Public Affairs, "U.S., Japan Bomber-Fighter Integration Showcases Alliance, Global Power Projection," U.S. Air Force, webpage, February 5, 2020.

———, "B-1s Conduct South China Sea Mission, Demonstrates Global Presence," Pacific Air Forces, April 30, 2020.

———, "B2 Spirit Stealth Bombers Deploy to Diego Garcia in Support of Bomber Task Force," *Pacific Air Forces*, August 12, 2020.

———, "Breaking Barriers: Women of the Bomber Task Force," *Pacific Air Forces*, January 6, 2021.

Packham, Colin, "Australia Says U.S. Plans to Build Military Infrastructure," *Reuters*, July 30, 2019.

Pal, Deep, "India-China Relations After Clashes in Ladakh," *National Bureau of Asian Research*, July 10, 2020.

Palwyk, Oriana, "Navy's New Triton Maritime Surveillance Drones Arrive in Guam for 1st Deployment," *Military.com*, February 3, 2020.

Panda, Ankit, "Chinese People's Liberation Army Rocket Force Staged a Massive Missile Drill Against a THAAD Mockup Target," *The Diplomat*, August 3, 2017.

———, "Taipei Slams 'Provocative' Chinese Air Force Fighters Cross Taiwan Strait Median Line," *The Diplomat*, April 1, 2019.

Pant, Harsh V., and Anant Singh Mann, "India's Malabar Dilemma," *ORF Issue Brief*, No. 393, August 2020.

Parameswaran, Prashanth, "U.S. Unveils New Maritime Security Initiatives at ASEAN Defense Meeting," *The Diplomat*, October 2, 2016.

———, "Why the Philippines' Rodrigo Duterte Hates America," *The Diplomat*, November 1, 2016.

Park, Ju-Min, "South Korea, Japan Agree Intelligence-Sharing on North Korea Threat," *Reuters*, November 22, 2016.

Pasricha, Anjana, "Indian, Chinese Troops Disengage from Himalayan Border Area," *Voice of America*, August 7, 2021.

Passeri, Paolo, "Philippines and China, on the Edge of a New Cyber Conflict?" *Hackmageddon*, May 1, 2012.

Patalano, Alessio, "What Is China's Strategy in the Senkaku Islands?" *War on the Rocks*, September 10, 2020.

Paul, T. V., ed., *The China-India Rivalry in the Globalization Era*, Washington, D.C.: Georgetown University Press, 2018.

Paul, T. V., and Erik Underwood, "Theorizing India-U.S.-China Strategic Triangle," *India Review*, Vol. 18, No. 4, 2019.

Pearson, James, "Exclusive: As Rosneft's Vietnam Unit Drills in Disputed Area of South China Sea, Beijing Issues Warning," Reuters, May 17, 2018.

People's Daily [人民网], "China's Core Interests Are Not to Be Challenged" ["中国核心利益不容挑战"], May 25, 2015.

People's Republic of China Embassy in Myanmar, "Foreign Ministry Spokesperson Hong Lei's Regular Press Conference on November 13, 2015" ["2015 年 11 月 13 日外交部发言人洪磊主持例行记者会"], November 13, 2015.

Perlez, Jane, "China and North Korea Reveal Sudden, and Deep, Cracks in Their Friendship," *New York Times*, February 24, 2017.

Permanent Mission of the People's Republic of China to the United Nations, "Remarks of Rebuke Against Japan's Statement on Diaoyu Dao by Ambassador Li Baodong During the General Debate of the 67th Session of the UN General Assembly," October 16, 2012.

———, "Wang Yi Talks About Current China-Russia Relations," May 26, 2017.

"Philippines Says China 'Fired Water Cannon' on Filipino Fishermen," *BBC News*, February 24, 2014.

"Philippines Seeks New Markets amid Sea Dispute with China," Reuters, May 17, 2017.

Pickering, Jeffrey, and Emizet F. Kisangani, "Diversionary Despots? Comparing Autocracies' Propensities to Use and to Benefit from Military Force," *American Journal of Political Science*, Vol. 54, No. 2, April 2010, pp. 477–493.

"PLA Conducts Live Fire Exercises in Taiwan Strait While 2 H-6K Bombers Circle Taiwan" ["解放军台海实弹射击 同时 2 架轰 6K 轰炸机绕台飞行"], *Haiwai Net* [海外网], April 19, 2018. As of March 27, 2020:
http://news.haiwainet.cn/n/2018/0419/c3541093-31301172.html

Poling, Greg [@GregPoling], "The 2nd of @SCS_PI's new series on VN fishing/militia activity around Hainan is out an alleges 311 VN boats in February. The problem? None of this is verifiable b/c most of the data appears to be from the Chinese govt, not commercial as the authors claim https://scspi.pku.edu.cn/en/analysis/501624.htm," Twitter post, March 5, 2020. As of March 21, 2021:
https://twitter.com/GregPoling/status/1235588894265151488

Poling, Gregory B., "Implications and Results: United States–Philippines Ministerial Dialogue," Center for Strategic and International Studies, May 4, 2012.

Pomerleau, Mark, "U.S. Army to Upgrade Bigger Units with New Electronic Warfare Gear," *C4ISRNet*, October 1, 2020.

———, "Special Operations Team in Pacific Will Confront Chinese Information Campaigns," *Army Times*, March 25, 2021.

Pompeo, Michael R., "U.S. Position on Maritime Claims in the South China Sea," press statement, U.S. Department of State, July 13, 2020.

———, "Remarks at the Richard Nixon Presidential Library and Museum: 'Communist China and the Free World's Future,'" U.S. Department of State, July 23, 2020.

Powell, Robert, "War as a Commitment Problem," *International Organization*, Vol. 60, No. 1, Winter 2006, pp. 169–203.

Prakash, Teesta, "The Quad Gives a Boost to India's Vaccine Diplomacy," *The Interpreter*, March 16, 2021.

Press, Daryl G., *Calculating Credibility: How Leaders Assess Military Threats*, Ithaca, N.Y.: Cornell University Press, 2005.

"Pressure Grows for More Vocal Stance over Chinese Incursions Near Senkakus," *Japan Times*, February 28, 2021.

Public Law 115-91, National Defense Authorization Act for Fiscal Year 2018, December 12, 2017.

Purohit, Kunal, "India Joins French-Led Naval Exercise, Revealing Clues About Quad's Plans to Contain China in Indo-Pacific," *South China Morning Post*, April 4, 2021.

Qin Gang, "Foreign Ministry Spokesperson Qin Gang's Routine Press Conference on April 23, 2014" ["2014年4月23日外交部发言人秦刚主持例行记者会"], Ministry of Foreign Affairs of the People's Republic of China, April 23, 2014.

———, "Foreign Ministry Spokesperson Qin Gang's Regular Press Conference on May 27, 2014," Ministry of Foreign Affairs of the People's Republic of China, May 27, 2014.

"Qin Hong: Facing the Philippines, We Have Sufficient Means" ["秦宏: 面对菲律宾我们有足够手段"], Xinhua, May 9, 2012.

Qu, Qingshan [曲青山], "Chinese Communist Party's 100 Year Major Contribution" ["中国共产党百年大贡献"], *Renmin News*, March 30, 2021.

"Quad Members Fight for Interests with Each Other: Global Times Editorial," *Global Times*, October 20, 2020.

Quek, Kai, "Four Costly Signaling Mechanisms," *American Political Science Review*, Vol. 115, No. 2, May 2021, pp. 537–549.

Quinn, Colm, "The U.S. Declared China's South China Seas Claims 'Unlawful.' Now What?" *Foreign Policy*, July 14, 2020.

Raghuvanshi, Vivek, "India, U.S. Sign Intel-Sharing Agreement amid Tension with Neighboring China," *Defense News*, October 28, 2020.

Ramzy, Austin, and Mike Ives, "Hong Kong Protests: One Year Later," *New York Times*, June 9, 2020.

Ranada, Pia, "Filipino Fishermen Able to Access Scarborough Shoal—Palace," *Rappler*, October 28, 2016.

Rawat, Manoj, "Quad 2.0 Is Off to a Good Start—It Must Keep Going," *The Diplomat*, November 23, 2020.

Ren Chengqi [任成琦], "Playing the 'Taiwan Card' Is a Dangerous Game" ["大'台湾牌'是一场危险游戏"], *Qiushi* [求是], July 10, 2019. As of March 19, 2021:
http://www.qstheory.cn/international/2019-07/10/c_1124733332.htm

Rhodes, Andrew, "The Second Island Cloud: A Deeper and Broader Concept for American Presence in the Pacific Islands," *Joint Force Quarterly*, Vol. 95, No. 4, 2019, pp. 46–53.

Riordan, Primrose, and Nicolle Liu, "Hong Kong Protestors Defy Ban to Show Support for Detained Leaders," *Financial Times*, March 1, 2021.

Rivers, Matt, "U.S. and China Conduct Rare Military Drill," *CNN*, November 21, 2016.

Robson, Seth, "U.S.-Filipino Troops Kick Off New Kamandag Exercise in the Philippines," *Stars and Stripes*, October 2, 2017.

Rogoway, Tyler, "China Freaks Out over Supposed U-2 Spy Plane Flight over Its Naval Exercise," *The Drive*, August 25, 2020.

Rolland, Nadège, *China's Vision for a New World Order*, Seattle, Wash.: National Bureau of Asian Research, NBR Special Report, No. 83, January 27, 2020.

Rose, Adam, "Vietnamese Stage Small Anti-China Protest in Hong Kong," Reuters, May 25, 2014.

Ross, Robert S., "The 1995–96 Taiwan Strait Confrontation: Coercion, Credibility, and the Use of Force," *International Security*, Vol. 25, No. 2, 2000, pp. 87–123.

———, "The Domestic Sources of China's 'Assertive Diplomacy,' 2009–2010," in Rosemary Foot, ed., *China Across the Divide: The Domestic and Global in Politics and Society*, New York: Oxford University Press, 2013.

———, "China-Vietnamese Relations in the Era of Rising China: Power, Resistance, and Maritime Conflict," *Journal of Contemporary China*, Vol. 30, No. 130, 2020, pp. 613–629.

Rossow, Richard, and Sarah Watson, "China Creates a Second Chance for the 'Quad,'" Asia Maritime Transparency Initiative, Center for Strategic and International Studies, March 14, 2016.

Roy, Rajesh, "India-China Border Standoff Turns Violent, with 20 Indian Soldiers Dead," *Wall Street Journal*, June 16, 2020.

Russett, Bruce M., "The Calculus of Deterrence," *Journal of Conflict Resolution*, Vol. 7, No. 2, 1963, pp. 97–109.

Ruwitch, John, "China-Australia Relations Are Quickly Worsening. How Did They Get Bad?" *NPR*, December 4, 2020.

Ryan, Fergus, "South China Sea: U.S. Bomber Angers Beijing with Spratly Islands Flypast," *The Guardian*, December 18, 2015.

Saaliq, Sheikh, "India, U.S. to Expand Military Engagement, Defense Ties," Associated Press, March 20, 2021.

Saalman, Lora, "China's Calculus on Hypersonic Glide," Stockholm International Peace Research Institute, August 15, 2017.

Sachdeva, Gulshan, "Indian Perceptions of the Chinese Belt and Road Initiative," *International Studies*, Vol. 55, No. 4, 2018, pp. 285–296.

Sartori, Anne E., *Deterrence by Diplomacy*, Princeton, N.J.: Princeton University Press, 2005.

Schafer, Susanne M., "Reduced REFORGER Exercise Announced," Associated Press, August 7, 1991.

Schelling, Thomas C., *Arms and Influence*, New Haven, Conn.: Yale University Press, 1966.

Schreer, Benjamin, "The Double-Edged Sword of Coercion: Cross-Strait Relations After the 2016 Taiwan Elections," *Asian Politics and Policy*, Vol. 9, No. 1, January 2017, pp. 50–65.

Schrock-Jacobson, Gretchen, "The Violent Consequences of the Nation: Nationalism and the Initiation of Interstate War," *Journal of Conflict Resolution*, Vol. 56, No. 5, 2012, pp. 825–852.

Schuessler, John M., "The Deception Dividend: FDR's Undeclared War," *International Security*, Vol. 34, No. 4, Spring 2010, pp. 133–165.

Scobell, Andrew, "Show of Force: Chinese Soldiers, Statesmen, and the 1995–1996 Taiwan Strait Crisis," *Political Science Quarterly*, Vol. 115, No. 2, 2000, pp. 227–246.

Scobell, Andrew, Edmund J. Burke, Cortez A. Cooper III, Sale Lilly, Chad J. R. Ohlandt, Eric Warner, and J. D. Williams, *China's Grand Strategy: Trends, Trajectories, and Long-Term Competition*, Santa Monica, Calif.: RAND Corporation, RR-2798-A, 2020. As of July 31, 2021:
https://www.rand.org/pubs/research_reports/RR2798.html

Scott, Len, and R. Gerald Hughes, *The Cuban Missile Crisis: A Critical Reappraisal*, New York: Routledge, 2015.

SCSPI—*See* South China Sea Strategic Situation Probing Initiative.

Sechser, Todd S., "Reputations and Signaling in Coercive Bargaining," *Journal of Conflict Resolution*, Vol. 62, No. 2, 2018, pp. 318–345.

Sen, Sudhi Ranjan, "Defense Stocks Rise as India to Buy $6 Billion Local-Built Jets," *Bloomberg*, January 13, 2021.

"Senkaku Islands: Chief Cabinet Secretary Suga 'Rising Tensions Extremely Regrettable,' Chinese Naval Ship Enters Area" ["尖閣諸島 菅官房長官「緊張高め深刻に懸念」中国軍艦入域"], *Mainichi Shimbun*, June 9, 2016.

Serafino, Nina M., "The Global Peace Operations Initiative: Background and Issues for Congress," Washington, D.C.: Congressional Research Service, June 11, 2009.

Sharma, Kiran, "India and China Face Off Along Disputed Himalayan Border," *Nikkei Asia*, May 28, 2020.

Sheng Sai, "Changes and Future Trends in the International Security Situation" ["当前国际大格局的变化、影响和趋势"], Shanghai Institute of International Studies, March 20, 2019.

Shim, Elizabeth, "China Blames U.S. for Hong Kong Protests," *UPI*, June 10, 2019.

Shou Xiaosong [寿晓松], ed., *The Science of Military Strategy* [战略学], 3rd ed., Beijing: Military Science Press [军事科学出版社], 2013.

Shukla, Ajai, "How China and India Came to Lethal Blows," *New York Times*, June 19, 2020.

Siegel, Adam B., *Use of Naval Forces in the Post-War Era: U.S. Navy and U.S. Marine Corps Crisis Response Activity, 1946–1990*, Alexandria, Va.: Center for Naval Analyses, February 1991.

Sinclair, Joshua, "B-1s Conduct Bomber Task Force Mission in South China Sea," Pacific Air Forces, July 22, 2020.

Sinclair, Michael, and Lindsey W. Ford, "Stuck in the Middle with You: Resourcing the Coast Guard for Global Competition," Brookings Institution, October 16, 2020.

Singh, Karishma, Clare Jim, and Anne Marie Roantree, "Timeline: Key Dates in Hong Kong's Anti-Government Protests," Reuters, November 11, 2019.

Smith, Jeff M., "Democracy's Squad: India's Change of Heart and the Future of the Quad," *War on the Rocks*, August 13, 2020.

———, "Biden Must Keep Challenging China on Freedom of Navigation," *Foreign Policy*, February 16, 2021.

Snyder, Glenn H., *Deterrence and Defense*, Princeton, N.J.: Princeton University Press, 1961.

———, "The Security Dilemma in Alliance Politics," *World Politics*, Vol. 36, No. 4, 1983.

South China Sea Strategic Situation Probing Initiative [南海战略态势感知], "2019 U.S. Military Exercises in the South China Sea and Neighboring Areas," December 27, 2019.

———, *Incomplete Report on U.S. Military Activities in the South China Sea in 2019* [2019 年美军南海军事活动不完全报告], Beijing: Peking University, March 28, 2020.

———, "60 Sorties of U.S. Surveillance Planes Flew 'Upwind' to Spy on China in September," October 12, 2020.

———, "U.S. Flying Civilian Contractor Aircraft to Monitor China," November 18, 2020.

———, *An Incomplete Report on U.S. Military Activities in the South China Sea in 2020*, Beijing: Peking University, March 12, 2021.

Stashwick, Steven, "U.S. Destroyer Conducts FONOP Against Russian Claims in Sea of Japan," *The Diplomat*, November 26, 2020.

State Council Information Office of the People's Republic of China, *China's National Defense in the New Era*, July 24, 2019. As of July 13, 2021:
http://eng.mod.gov.cn/news/2019-07/24/content_4846443.htm

———, "China and the World in the New Era," September 27, 2019. As of July 13, 2021:
http://english.scio.gov.cn/2019-09/28/content_75252746_5.htm#:~:text=In%20the%20new%20era%2C%20China%20continues%20to%20pursue,in%20compliance%20with%20national%20security%20and%20development%20interests

State Council of the People's Republic of China, "Xi Jinping with Vietnamese Communist Party's General Secretary and President Nguyen Phu Trong's Mutual Sent Congratulatory Telegrams on the 70th Anniversary of China and Vietnam Establishing Diplomatic Relations" ["习近平就中越建交 70 周年同越共中央总书记、国家主席阮富仲互致贺电"], January 18, 2020. As of May 7, 2021:
http://www.gov.cn/xinwen/2020-01/18/content_5470452.htm

Stewart, Kelley J., "B-1B Lancers Return to Indo-Pacific for Bomber Task Force Deployment," Pacific Air Forces, May 1, 2020.

Stewart, Phil, "U.S. Navy Says China Unreliable After Meeting No-Show; Beijing Says U.S. Twisting Facts," Reuters, December 16, 2020.

Stone, Mike, and Patricia Zengerle, "Exclusive: U.S. Pushes Arms Sales Surge to Taiwan, Needling China—Sources," Reuters, September 16, 2020.

Storey, Ian, "The South China Sea, a Fault Line in China-Russia Relations," *ISEAS Commentary*, October 13, 2020.

Sullivan, Michael, "Trump and Duterte Could Reset the Shaky U.S.-Philippine Alliance," *NPR*, November 11, 2017.

Sun Jianguo, "Use History as a Mirror: Beware the Return of Japanese Militarism" ["以史为鉴：警惕日本军国主义的死灰复燃"], *PLA Daily*, June 23, 2014.

Sun, Yun, "China's Strategic Assessment of the Ladakh Clash," *War on the Rocks*, June 19, 2020.

Swaine, Michael D., "Chinese Leadership and Elite Responses to the U.S. Pacific Pivot," *China Leadership Monitor*, No. 38, Summer 2012.

———, "Chinese Views on South Korea's Deployment of THAAD," *China Leadership Monitor*, No. 52, Winter 2017.

Swaine, Michael D., Zhang Tuosheng, and Danielle F. S. Cohen, eds., *Managing Sino-American Crises: Case Studies and Analysis*, Washington, D.C.: Carnegie Endowment for International Peace, 2006.

"Taiwanese Army Is Highly Tense as PLA Fighters Circle Taiwan Again: The Rapid Progress Is Worthy of Vigilance" ["台军高度紧张解放军战机再次绕台：进步之快值得警惕"], *Sina*, December 19, 2018.

Talmadge, Caitlin, "Would China Go Nuclear? Assessing the Risk of Chinese Nuclear Escalation in a Conventional War with the United States," *International Security*, Vol. 41, No. 4, 2017.

———, "Emerging Technology and Intra-War Escalation Risks: Evidence from the Cold War, Implications for Today," *Journal of Strategic Studies*, Vol. 42, No. 6, 2019, pp. 864–887.

Tang Huaiyu [汤怀宇] and Liu Jie [刘婕], "Media Reports and China's Hypersonic Weapon" ["从媒 体报道看我国高超音速武器"], *Ordnance Knowledge* [兵器知识], No. 5, 2014.

Tang, Shiping, "Reputation, Cult of Reputation, and International Conflict," *Security Studies*, Vol. 14, No. 1, 2005, pp. 34–62.

———, "China-India Relations in the 'Modi Era'" ["'莫迪时代'的中印关系"], *Modern International Relations* [现代国际关系], No. 21, November 16, 2020.

Task Force 70 Public Affairs, "India Hosts Japan, Australia, U.S. in Naval Exercise MALABAR 2020," U.S. Navy Office of Information, November 2, 2020.

Taylor, Phil, "Rush on for Rare Earths as U.S. Firms Seek to Counter Chinese Monopoly," *New York Times*, July 22, 2010.

Tellis, Ashley, "Narendra Modi and U.S.-India Relations," in Bibek Debroy, Anirban Ganguly, and Kishore Desai, eds., *Making of New India: Transformation Under Modi Government*, New Delhi: Wisdom Tree, 2018, pp. 525–535.

Templeman, Kharis, *Taiwan's January 2020 Elections: Prospects and Implications for China and the United States*, Washington, D.C.: Brookings Institution, December 2019.

———, "How Taiwan Stands Up to China," *Journal of Democracy*, Vol. 31, No. 3, July 2020, pp. 85–99.

"THAAD Has Not Been Withdrawn but Instead Upgraded: Is South Korea Stupid?" ["萨德不撤 反升级，韩国傻吗?"], *Global Times* [环球时报], July 20, 2018.

Thayer, Carlyle A., "Vietnam Gradually Warms Up to U.S. Military," *The Diplomat*, November 6, 2013.

———, "China's Oil Rig Gambit: South China Sea Game-Changer?" *The Diplomat*, May 12, 2014.

———, "China-Vietnam Defense Hotline Agreed: What Next?" *The Diplomat*, October 20, 2014.

———, "Obama's Visit to Vietnam: A Turning Point?" *The Diplomat*, May 31, 2016.

———, "Vietnam's Foreign Policy in an Era of Rising Sino-U.S. Competition and Increasing Domestic Political Influence," *Asian Security*, Vol. 13, No. 3, 2017, pp. 183–199.

———, "Will Vanguard Bank Ignite Vietnamese Nationalism?" Australian Naval Institute, August 4, 2019.

———, "A Difficult Summer in the South China Sea," *The Diplomat*, November 2019.

Tierney, Dominic, "The Future of U.S.-PRC Proxy War," *Texas National Security Review*, Vol. 4, No. 2, Spring 2021, pp. 49–73.

"Time for U.S. Anti-China Forces to Cease Regressive Practices: Chinese FM," Xinhua, December 11, 2020.

Tir, Jaroslav, "Territorial Diversion: Diversionary Theory of War and Territorial Conflict," *Journal of Politics*, Vol. 72, No. 2, 2010, pp. 413–425.

Tomacruz, Sofia, and J. C. Gotinga, "List: China's Incursions in Philippine Waters," *Rappler*, August 22, 2019.

Torbati, Yeganeh, and David Alexander, "U.S. Bombers Flew Near China-Built Islands in South China Sea: Pentagon," Reuters, November 13, 2015.

Torode, Greg, and Michael Martina, "Chinese Wary About U.S. Missile System Because Capabilities Unknown: Experts," Reuters, April 3, 2017.

Torreon, Barbara Salazar, and Sofia Plagakis, *Instances of Use of United States Armed Forces Abroad, 1798–2020*, version 31, Washington, D.C.: Congressional Research Service, July 20, 2020.

Trevithick, Joseph, "The Air Force Abruptly Ends Its Continuous Bomber Presence on Guam After 16 Years," *The Drive*, April 17, 2020.

———, "China Tests Long-Range Anti-Ship Ballistic Missiles as U.S. Spy Plane Watches It All," *The Drive*, August 26, 2020.

Tria Kerkvliet, Benedict J., "Protesting China: Vietnam's Vanguard," *Southeast Asia Globe*, October 2, 2019.

Trinh, Huu Long, "Hong Kong Next-Door Ally," *The Vietnamese*, October 28, 2020.

"Trump and Hillary: Who Is China-Friendly and Who Is Anti-China?" ["特朗普和希拉里：谁亲华谁反华？"], *Phoenix Media* [凤凰], September 20, 2016.

"Trump and Hillary: Who Will Be a More Anti-China President?" ["特朗普和希拉里 谁当选美国总统会更反华？"], *China.com* [中华网], November 8, 2016.

United States of America and the Philippines, Agreement Between the Government of the Republic of the Philippines and the Government of the United States of America Regarding the Treatment of United States Armed Forces Visiting the Philippines, Manila, Philippines, February 10, 1998.

United States of America and the Philippines, Agreement Between the Government of the United States of America and the Government of the Republic of the Philippines on Enhanced Defense Cooperation, Quezon City, Philippines, April 28, 2014.

United States Institute of Peace, *Natural Resources, Conflict, and Conflict Resolution*, Washington, D.C., 2007.

"U.S., Chinese Aircraft in 'Unsafe' Encounter over S. China Sea," Associated Press, February 10, 2017. As of August 12, 2021: https://apnews.com/article/04d1a7a84f4648dab7418ab0a69c3d1e

"U.S., Philippines Launch War Games amid Uncertainty over Ties," *DW*, October 4, 2016.

"U.S., ROK Must Stop Deployment of THAAD Missile Battery," *China Military Online*, July 29, 2016.

U.S. Agency for International Development, *U.S. Overseas Loans and Grants: Obligations and Loan Authorizations, July 1, 1945–September 30, 2019*, Washington, D.C., 2021.

"U.S. and China Trade Angry Words at High-Level Alaska Talks," *BBC News*, March 19, 2021.

U.S. Army, *The Army Strategy 2020*, Washington, D.C., 2020.

U.S.-China Economic and Security Review Commission, *2014 Report to Congress*, Washington, D.C., November 2014.

———, "China and the U.S. Rebalance to Asia," in U.S.-China Economic and Security Review Commission, *2016 Report to Congress of the U.S.-China Economic and Security Review Commission*, Washington, D.C.: U.S. Government Publishing Office, November 2016, pp. 475–512.

U.S. Coast Guard Pacific Area, "U.S. Coast Guard Enforces North Korea Sanctions in the East China Sea," U.S. Indo-Pacific Command, March 19, 2019.

U.S. Department of Defense, "Challenges to Excessive Maritime Claims 1 October 2007–30 September 2008," undated. As of April 14, 2021: https://policy.defense.gov/Portals/11/Documents/gsa/cwmd/FY2008%20DOD%20Annual%20FON%20Report.pdf

———, "Challenges to Excessive Maritime Claims 1 October 2008–30 September 2009," undated. As of April 14, 2021:
https://policy.defense.gov/Portals/11/Documents/gsa/cwmd/FY2009%20DOD%20Annual%20FON%20Report.pdf

———, "Challenges to Excessive Maritime Claims 1 October 2009–30 September 2010," undated. As of April 14, 2021:
https://policy.defense.gov/Portals/11/Documents/gsa/cwmd/FY2010%20DOD%20Annual%20FON%20Report.pdf

———, "Challenges to Excessive Maritime Claims 1 October 2010–30 September 2011," undated. As of April 14, 2021:
https://policy.defense.gov/Portals/11/Documents/gsa/cwmd/FY2011%20DOD%20Annual%20FON%20Report.pdf

———, "U.S. Department of Defense (DOD) Freedom of Navigation (FON) Report for Fiscal Year (FY) 2012," January 4, 2013.

———, *Asia-Pacific Maritime Security Strategy*, Washington, D.C., 2015.

———, *Indo-Pacific Strategy Report*, Washington, D.C., 2019.

———, *Counter-Small Unmanned Aircraft Systems Strategy*, Washington, D.C., 2021.

U.S. Department of the Navy, U.S. Marine Corps, and U.S. Coast Guard, *Advantage at Sea: Prevailing with Integrated All-Domain Naval Power*, Washington, D.C., December 2020. As of August 4, 2021:
https://media.defense.gov/2020/Dec/16/2002553074/-1/-1/0/TRISERVICESTRATEGY.PDF

U.S. Department of State, "Joint Statement of the United States–Philippines Bilateral Strategic Dialogue," Washington, D.C., January 27, 2012.

———, "Media Note: U.S.-Australia-India-Japan Consultations ('The Quad')," November 4, 2019.

———, "Transparency in the U.S. Nuclear Weapons Stockpile," fact sheet, October 5, 2021. As of October 25, 2022:
https://www.state.gov/transparency-in-the-u-s-nuclear-weapons-stockpile/

———, "New START Treaty Aggregate Numbers of Strategic Offensive Arms of the United States and the Russian Federation, February 2011–March 2022," fact sheet, March 1, 2022. As of October 25, 2022:
https://www.state.gov/new-start-treaty-aggregate-numbers-of-strategic-offensive-arms-of-the-united-states-and-the-russian-federation-february-2011-march-2022/

U.S. Embassy and Consulate in Vietnam, "U.S.-Vietnam Relations," December 11, 2017.

U.S. Energy Information Administration, "Country Analysis Executive Summary: China," September 30, 2020.

"U.S. Flexes Muscles and Stirs Up Trouble in Taiwan Strait: Defense Spokesperson," *China Military Online*, December 31, 2020. As of April 20, 2021: http://eng.mod.gov.cn/news/2020-12/31/content_4876349.htm

"U.S. Flight Near Islands 'Serious Military Provocation': Chinese Defense Ministry," Xinhua, December 19, 2015.

U.S. Forces Japan, "About USFJ," webpage, undated. As of September 20, 2021: https://www.usfj.mil/About-USFJ/

U.S. Government Accountability Office, "Defense Logistics Agreements: DoD Should Improve Oversight and Seek Payment from Foreign Partners for Thousands of Orders It Identifies as Overdue," Washington, D.C., March 4, 2020.

U.S. House of Representatives, Taiwan Travel Act, H.R. 535, 115th Congress, March 16, 2018.

"U.S. Indo-Pacific Command Forces Come Together for Valiant Shield 2020," U.S. Indo-Pacific Command, September 11, 2020.

"U.S. Indo-Pacific Strategy Undermines Peace, Development Prospect in East Asia: Wang Yi," Xinhua, October 13, 2020.

U.S. Marine Corps, *United States Marine Corps Service Campaign Plan*, Washington, D.C., 2014.

U.S. Navy, "Appendix A," in U.S. Navy, *2007 Program Guide to the U.S. Navy: Sea Power for a New Era*, Washington, D.C., 2007, pp. 181–192.

U.S. Senate, Taiwan Allies International Protection and Enhancement Initiative (TAIPEI) Act of 2019, S. 1678, 116th Congress, March 26, 2020.

Usher, Barbara Plett, "Why U.S.-China Relations Are at Their Lowest Point in Decades," *BBC News*, July 24, 2020.

Van Evera, Stephen, *Causes of War: Structures of Power and the Roots of International Conflict*, Ithaca, N.Y.: Cornell University Press, 1999.

Vasquez, John A., *The War Puzzle*, New York: Cambridge University Press, 1993.

———, "Why Do Neighbors Fight? Proximity, Interaction, or Territoriality," *Journal of Peace Research*, Vol. 32, No. 3, 1995, pp. 277–293.

Vasquez, John, and Christopher S. Leskiw, "The Origins and War Proneness of Interstate Rivalries," *Annual Review of Political Science*, Vol. 4, 2001, pp. 295–316.

Vavasseur, Xavier, "China Launched 6 ASBM into the South China Sea," *Naval News*, July 15, 2019.

Vick, Alan J., David T. Orletsky, Abram N. Shulsky, and John Stillion, *Preparing for U.S. Air Force Military Operations Other Than War*, Santa Monica, Calif.: RAND Corporation, MR-842-AF, 1997. As of May 17, 2022:
https://www.rand.org/pubs/monograph_reports/MR842.html

"Vietnam, China Hold Joint Medical Examination in Border Areas," *Vietnam Net*, August 24, 2018. As of July 13, 2021:
https://english.vietnamnet.vn/fms/government/207434/vietnam--china-hold-joint-medical-examination-in-border-areas.html

"Vietnam, China Issue Joint Communiqué," *Vietnam Plus*, April 8, 2015.

"Vietnam Activists Stage Rare Anti-China Protest amid Concerns over Survey Ship," *Radio Free Asia*, August 19, 2019.

"Vietnam Hopes Situation in China's Hong Kong SAR Back to Normal Soon: Spokesperson," Xinhua, September 12, 2019.

Viray, Patricia Lourdes, "Senate Minority Wants Probe into Chinese Planes in Davao, Chinese Shows on PTV," *Philstar Global*, July 9, 2018.

Volgy, Thomas J., and Stacey Mayhall, "Status Inconsistency and International War: Exploring the Effects of Systemic Change," *International Studies Quarterly*, Vol. 39, No. 1, March 1995, pp. 67–84.

Wakatsuki, Yoko, "Tokyo Governor Outlines Plan to Buy Islands Claimed by China," *CNN*, April 17, 2012.

Walt, Stephen M., *The Origins of Alliances*, Ithaca, N.Y.: Cornell University Press, 1987.

Walter, Barbara F., *Reputation and Civil War: Why Separatist Conflicts Are So Violent*, New York: Cambridge University Press, 2009.

Wang Cong, "China Draws Bottom Line," *Global Times*, June 3, 2019.

Wang, Joyu, "Taiwan Rallies for Hong Kong to Resist Beijing's Influence," *Wall Street Journal*, September 29, 2019.

"Wang Jisi: A 'New Norm' in U.S.-China Relations" ["王缉思: 中美关系进入一个 '新常态'"], *Global Times* [环球时报], August 19, 2016.

Wang Qi, "China Can Retaliate Economically If Red Line Crossed: Experts," *Global Times*, February 18, 2021.

Wang Qun, "Statement by Ambassador Wang Qun, Director-General of the Arms Control Department of the Ministry of Foreign Affairs of China, at the General Debate of the First Committee of the 71st Session of the UNGA," Ministry of Foreign Affairs of the People's Republic of China, October 10, 2016. As of February 3, 2021: https://www.fmprc.gov.cn/mfa_eng/wjdt_665385/zyjh_665391/t1405391.shtml

Wang Shida [王世达], "The Challenge of India-U.S. Security Cooperation to India's Tradition of Strategic Independent" ["印美安全合作对印度战略自主传统的挑战"], *Modern International Relations* [现代国际关系], No. 2, August 7, 2019.

Wang Wenbin, "Foreign Ministry Spokesperson Wang Wenbin's Regular Press Conference on July 28, 2020," Ministry of Foreign Affairs of the People's Republic of China, July 28, 2020.

———, "Foreign Ministry Spokesperson Wang Wenbin's Regular Press Conference on September 28, 2020," Ministry of Foreign Affairs of the People's Republic of China, September 28, 2020.

———, "Foreign Ministry Spokesperson Wang Wenbin's Remarks on China-Related Remarks by High-Level Philippine Figures" ["外交部发言人汪文斌就菲律宾高层涉华言论答记者问"], Ministry of Foreign Affairs of the People's Republic of China, May 4, 2021.

Wang Xiaofeng [王晓枫], "China's Maritime Patrols Cover All of the South China Sea and Maritime Rights Protection Is More Proactive Than in the Past" ["中国海上巡航覆盖整个南海 海上维权更主动"], *People's Daily Online* [人民网], August 27, 2014. As of May 4, 2021: http://military.people.com.cn/n/2014/0827/c172467-25548356.html

Wang Xixin [王西欣], "A Further Discussion on War Control" ["再论控制战"], *China Military Science* [中国军事科学], Vol. 64, 2014.

Wang Yi [王毅], "China Firmly Supports the Philippines in Pursuing an Independent Foreign Policy" ["中方坚定支持菲律宾奉行独立自主外交政策"], Ministry of Foreign Affairs of the People's Republic of China, July 25, 2017. As of July 13, 2021: http://world.people.com.cn/n1/2017/0726/c1002-29429568.html

Wang Zheng [王峥], "The Interaction Between Politics and Security: Perspectives on China-Vietnam Relations Under the South China Sea Disputes" ["政治与安全的互动: 南海争端下中越关系透视"], *Southeast Asian Studies* [东南亚研究], No. 6, 2018, pp. 108–130, 150–151.

Warnock, Timothy A., ed., *Short of War: Major USAF Contingency Operations, 1947–1997*, Maxwell Air Force Base, Ala.: Air University Press, 2000.

Watts, John T., Christian Trotti, and Mark J. Massa, *Primer on Hypersonic Weapons in the Indo-Pacific Region*, Washington, D.C.: Atlantic Council, August 2020.

Watts, Stephen, Bryan Rooney, Gene Germanovich, Bruce McClintock, Stephanie Pezard, Clint Reach, and Melissa Shostak, *Deterrence and Escalation in Competition with Russia: The Role of Ground Forces in Preventing Hostile Measures Below Armed Conflict in Europe*, Santa Monica, Calif.: RAND Corporation, RR-A720-1, 2022. As of May 17, 2022: https://www.rand.org/pubs/research_reports/RRA720-1.html

Weeks, Jessica L., "Strongmen and Straw Men: Authoritarian Regimes and the Initiation of International Conflict," *American Political Science Review*, Vol. 106, No. 2, 2012, pp. 326–347.

Wei Fenghe and Zhang Haiyang, "Diligently Build a Powerful, Informatized Strategic Missile Force" ["努力打造强大的信息化战略导弹部队"], *People's Daily*, December 13, 2012.

Weisiger, Alex, and Keren Yarhi-Milo, "Revisiting Reputation: How Past Actions Matter in International Politics," *International Organization*, Vol. 69, No. 2, 2015, pp. 473–495.

Weiss, Jessica Chen, *Powerful Patriots: Nationalist Protest in China's Foreign Relations*, New York: Oxford University Press, 2014.

———, "How Hawkish Is the Chinese Public? Another Look at 'Rising Nationalism' and Chinese Foreign Policy," *Journal of Contemporary China*, Vol. 28, No. 119, 2019, pp. 679–695.

Werner, Ben, "Destroyer USS *Decatur* Has Close Encounter with Chinese Warship," *USNI News*, October 1, 2018.

———, "Third Time in Four Months U.S. Warships Transit Tense Taiwan Strait," *USNI News*, January 24, 2019.

Werner, Suzanne, "Choosing Demands Strategically: The Distribution of Power, the Distribution of Benefits, and the Risk of Conflict," *Journal of Conflict Resolution*, Vol. 43, No. 6, December 1999, pp. 705–726.

West, Kesha, "Banana Crisis Blamed on Philippines-China Dispute," *ABC News*, June 28, 2012.

Westcott, Ben, "Duterte Will 'Go to War' over South China Sea Resources, Minister Says," *CNN*, May 29, 2018.

"When China and U.S. Spar, It's South Korea That Gets Punched," *Los Angeles Times*, November 20, 2020.

White House, "Joint Statement by President Barack Obama of the United States of America and President Truong Tan Sang of the Socialist Republic of Vietnam," Washington, D.C., July 23, 2013.

———, "Joint Press Conference with President Obama and Prime Minister Abe of Japan," Office of the Press Secretary, April 24, 2014.

———, "U.S.-Japan Joint Statement: The United States and Japan: Shaping the Future of the Asia-Pacific and Beyond," Office of the Press Secretary, April 25, 2014.

———, "Remarks by President Obama and Prime Minister Abe of Japan in Joint Press Conference," Washington, D.C., April 28, 2015.

———, "Remarks by President Obama in Address to the People of Vietnam," Hanoi, Vietnam, May 24, 2016.

———, "Remarks by Deputy National Security Advisor Matt Pottinger to the Miller Center at the University of Virginia," May 4, 2020.

White, Joshua T., "After the Foundational Agreements: An Agenda for U.S.-India Defense and Security Cooperation," Brookings Institution, January 2021.

Wiegand, Krista E., "Militarized Territorial Disputes: States' Attempts to Transfer Reputation for Resolve," *Journal of Peace Research*, Vol. 48, No. 1, 2011, pp. 101–113.

"Will India Further Toss Non-Alignment Policy Under Biden Admin?" *Global Times*, January 28, 2021.

Wolford, Scott, "The Turnover Trap: New Leaders, Reputation, and International Conflict," *American Journal of Political Science*, Vol. 51, No. 4, October 2007, pp. 772–788.

"The Worst HK Troublemakers Are Ethnic Vietnamese? Media Refute Allegations" ["香港闹得最凶的是越南裔？媒体驳斥"], *Sina News*, August 21, 2019.

Wortzel, Larry M., *What the Chinese People's Liberation Army Can Do to Thwart the Army's Multi-Domain Task Force*, Arlington, Va.: Institute of Land Warfare, Land Warfare Paper No. 126, 2019.

Wright, Warren N., "Shiprider Program," *Indo-Pacific Defense Forum*, January 27, 2020.

Wuthnow, Joel, "China's Other Army: The People's Armed Police in an Era of Reform," *China Strategic Perspectives*, No. 14, August 2019.

"Xi Calls for Mended China-Vietnam Ties," Xinhua, August 28, 2014.

"Xi Calls for Powerful Missile Force," *China Daily*, December 5, 2012.

Xi Jinping, "We Need to Do More to Take Interest in the Sea, Understand the Sea, and Strategically Manage the Sea, and Continually Do More to Promote China's Efforts to Become a Maritime Power" ["进一步关心海洋认识海洋经略海 洋推动海洋强国建设不断取得新成就"], *People's Daily*, August 1, 2013.

"Xi Stresses Unity, Striving for National Rejuvenation at PRC Anniversary Reception," Xinhua, September 30, 2019.

Xie, John, "China Is Increasing Taiwan Airspace Incursions," *Voice of America*, January 6, 2021.

Xinhua, "Philippines Claim Illegal—Beijing," *Manila Times*, April 28, 2012.

Xinhua News Agency, "Interview on Current China-U.S. Relations Given by State Councilor and Foreign Minister Wang Yi to Xinhua News Agency," Ministry of Foreign Affairs of the People's Republic of China, August 5, 2020. As of October 1, 2022: https://www.mfa.gov.cn/ce/cefj//eng/sgxw/t1804643.htm

Xiong, Gloria, "Beijing Increasingly Relies on Economic Coercion to Reach Its Diplomatic Goals," *Washington Post*, July 23, 2020.

Xu Bu, "U.S. 'Rebalancing' Is Fishing in S. China Sea's Troubled Waters," *Straits Times*, May 19, 2016.

Xu Liu [刘旭], Weimin Li, Zhipeng Jiang, and Wenjing Song, "Thoughts on Hypersonic Cruise Missile Combat Characteristics and 36 Offense-Defense Model" ["高超声速巡航导弹作战特点及攻防模式思考"], *Cruise Missile* [飞航导弹], No. 9, 2014.

Yang Dingdu [杨定都], "News Analysis: Why Does India Not Catch a Cold from the United States?" ["新闻分析：印度为何对美国拉拢不感冒"], Xinhua, July 13, 2018. As of February 26, 2021: http://www.xinhuanet.com/world/2018-07/13/c_1123122497.htm

Yang Jiechi [杨洁篪], "Respecting History and Looking to the Future, We Must Unswervingly Defend and Stabilize Sino-U.S. Relations" ["尊重历史 面向未来 坚定不移维护和稳定中美关系"], *Qiushi* [求是], August 8, 2020. As of March 23, 2021: http://www.qstheory.cn/qshyjx/2020-08/08/c_1126341617.htm

Yang Jiemian, "China's New Diplomacy Under the Xi Jinping Administration," *China Quarterly of International Strategic Studies*, Vol. 1, No. 1, April 2015, pp. 1–17.

Yew Lun Tian, "China Says Opposes U.S. THAAD Defense System in South Korea," *Reuters*, May 29, 2020.

Yew Lun Tian, Gabriel Crossley, and Stella Qiu, "China to Impose Sanctions on U.S. Firms over Taiwan Arms Sales," *Reuters*, October 26, 2020.

Yew Lun Tian and Sanjeev Miglani, "China-India Border Clash Stokes Contrasting Domestic Responses," *Reuters*, June 23, 2020.

Yin Chengde, "With THAAD, U.S. and South Korea Are Playing with Fire," *China-U.S. Focus*, October 19, 2016.

Yoko, Wakatsuki, "Tokyo Governor Outlines Plan to Buy Islands Claimed by China," *CNN*, April 17, 2012.

Yong Ceng, "Viewing the Trend of China's South China Sea Policy from the 'Huangyan Island Model'" ["从'黄岩岛模式'看中国南海政策走向"], *Forum of World Economics & Politics* [世界经济与政治论坛], No. 5, 2014.

Yong Zhao [赵永], Weimin Li, Chenhao Zhao, and Xu Liu, "U.S. Global Prompt Strike System Development Status and Trend Analysis" ["美国全球快速打击系统发展现状及动向分析"], *Cruise Missile* [飞航导弹], Vol. 1, No. 3, 2014.

Youssef, Nancy A., and Gordon Lubold, "On Iran, White House Criticism Grows, but U.S. Military Posture Recedes," *Wall Street Journal*, October 1, 2018.

Zata, Jonathan V., "National Coast Watch System Moves Forward," *Indo-Pacific Defense Forum*, December 5, 2016.

Zeng Yong [曾勇], "Viewing Trends in China's South China Sea Policy Trends from the 'Scarborough Shoal Model'" ["从'黄岩岛模式'看中国南海政策走向"], *Forum of World Economics & Politics* [世界经济与政治论坛], No. 5, 2014, pp. 127–144. As of May 12, 2021:
https://oversea.cnki.net/KCMS/detail/detail.aspx?dbcode=CJFD&dbname=CJFD2014&filename=SJJT201405009&v=pGUof2I8gfng%25mmd2BJp0gigxj1waPiCL9FMMthUSeGbvV%25mmd2BLZ0O3G6F7eqAtk8DGzCvsi

———, "South China Sea '981' Oil Platform Stand-Off and Its Impact on Vietnam's South China Sea Policy" ["南海 '981' 钻井平台冲突折射的越南南海政策"], *Journal of Contemporary Asia-Pacific Studies* [当代亚太], No. 1, 2016, pp. 124–153, 158–159. As of April 2, 2021:
https://oversea.cnki.net/KCMS/detail/detail.aspx?dbcode=CJFD&dbname=CJFDLAST2016&filename=DDYT201601006&v=f5Dk7dyilXI8B1C1i9nNlXivno7SSZtTwWOYp3lOUN26KkqXxJKr42Aj9OedRGKe

———, "Research on Three Struggles for Rights Protection in the South China Sea Since 2012" ["2012 年来三次南海维权斗争研究"], *Pacific Journal* [太平洋学报], Vol. 27, No. 5, 2019, pp. 40–57. As of May 3, 2021:
https://oversea.cnki.net/KCMS/detail/detail.aspx?dbcode=CJFD&dbname=CJFDLAST2019&filename=TPYX201905006&v=Tl34rk05dNBiKr1Ksr2%25mmd2FpXf4Db%25mmd2B8GJt8dIVwIXbWFiXE%25mmd2Bv5vMppmj6Ufv%25mmd2F1x%25mmd2FIMy

Zeng Yong [曾勇] and Wang Xuefei [万雪飞], "On China's Two Rights Protection Struggles Against the Philippines in the South China Sea" ["论中国两次对菲南海维权斗争"], *Indian Ocean Economic and Political Review* [印度洋经济体研究], No. 5, 2019, pp. 130–152, 156. As of May 12, 2021:
https://oversea.cnki.net/KCMS/detail/detail.aspx?dbcode=CJFD&dbname=CJFDLAST2020&filename=YDYY201905009&v=X%25mmd2B7pTZ6DNgBz2P1RaDWkFuIZVbpGdZjWXelK4vwsbiVu%25mmd2BFl6jLc4AAwiMpFfjAgR

Zhang Hongyi [张宏毅], "America's Ability to Read China Once Again Put to the Test" ["美国再次面临是否'读懂中国'的考验"], *Qiushi* [求是], November 7, 2019. As of March 19, 2021:
http://www.qstheory.cn/llqikan/2019-11/07/c_1125202878.htm

Zhang Hualong [章华龙], "Will India Cooperate with America to Contain China?" ["印度会配合美国，遏制中国吗?"], *Outlook* [瞭望], October 10, 2019. As of March 15, 2021:
http://www.china.com.cn/opinion/think/2019-10/19/content_75318037.htm

Zhang Jie [张洁], "The Scarborough Shoal Model and the Shift in China's Maritime Strategy"

["黄岩岛模式与中国海洋维权政策的转向"], *Southeast Asian Studies* [东南亚研究], No. 4,

June 2013, pp. 25–31. As of May 12, 2021:

https://oversea.cnki.net/KCMS/detail/detail.aspx?dbcode=CJFD&dbname=CJFD2013&filen
ame=DNYY201304004&v=DYBPiBlEg7UEuQmy32vTbVjzgBgg9rgWgIXUeqLMrnGekY
fJOhsQIYtYYqRHXJTy

———, "Regional Security Issues in Constructing 'One Belt, One Road'" ["'一带一路'建设 中

的周边安全问"], *World Affairs* [世界知识], No. 9, 2017.

———, "Assessment of China's Surrounding Security Environment in the New Era" ["新时期

中国周边安全环境评估"], Beijing: Institute of Asia-Pacific and Global Strategy, Chinese

Academy of Social Sciences, February 16, 2019. As of July 13, 2021:

http://niis.cass.cn/xscgnew/ssplnew/201903/P020190314527812828429.pdf

Zhang Jie [张洁], Li Zhifei [李志斐], Zhu Fenglan [朱凤岚], Yang Danzhi [杨丹志], Wu

Zhaoli [吴兆礼], Li Chengri [李成日], Chen Chunhua [陈春华], and Fan Lijun [范丽君],

"Maritime Disputes and Sino-U.S. Contests—China's Peripheral Security Situation" ["海上

纷争与中美 博弈—中国周边安全形势"], *World Affairs* [世界知识], No. 2, 2013, pp. 14–

22. As of May 3, 2021:

https://oversea.cnki.net/KCMS/detail/detail.aspx?dbcode=CJFD&dbname=CJFD2013&filen
ame=SJZS201302009&v=YP65UhToZiLjr%25mmd2BzsAhy%25mmd2Fd9sy7ue5IrUxQL
OjQmURydRz7po%25mmd2BUSQ7IGh9pT9HUvww

Zhang Jingyang [张经洋], "Don't Let Peace Obscure Smoke Signals from Hostile Forces" ["莫

让和平遮挡潜在狼烟"], *China Defense News* [中国国防报], August 16, 2018. As of May 3,

2021:

http://www.mod.gov.cn/jmsd/2018-08/16/content_4822685.htm

Zhang Junshe [张军社], "We Strongly Oppose Any Country Developing Military Ties with

Taiwan" ["坚决反对任何国家与台开展军事联系"], *Qiushi* [求是], January 16, 2019.

———, "U.S. Military Provocation in the South China Sea Is Doomed to Work to No Avail" ["美在南海的军事挑衅注定徒劳无功"], *People's Liberation Army Daily* [解放军报], July 13, 2020. As of May 3, 2021:
http://military.people.com.cn/n1/2020/0713/c1011-31781102.html

Zhang, Ketian, "Cautious Bully: Reputation, Resolve, and Beijing's Use of Coercion in the South China Sea," *International Security*, Vol. 44, No. 1, 2019, pp. 117–159.

Zhang, Xiaoming, *Deng Xiaoping's Long War: The Military Conflict Between China and Vietnam, 1979–1991*, Chapel Hill, N.C.: University of North Carolina Press, 2015.

Zhang Yanping [张燕萍], "Chinese Minister of Defense Visits Nepal and Pakistan Expert: The Practical Significance of Safeguarding the Security Around China's Western Region Is More Prominent" ["中国防长访问尼泊尔巴基斯坦 专家：对维护中国西部周边安全现实意义更突出"], *Global Times* [环球时报], December 1, 2020.

———, "Can the U.S., Japan, India and Australia Quad Group Contain China? Expert: There Is Not Much the United States Can Give to Its Allies" ["美日印澳"四方安全对话"牵制中国？专家：美国能给盟国的已经不多了"], *Global Times* [环球时报], February 19, 2021.

Zhang, Yong-an, "Asia, International Drug Trafficking, and U.S.-China Counternarcotics Cooperation," Washington, D.C.: Brookings Institution, February 10, 2012.

Zhao Beibei, "The South China Sea Issue and Sino-U.S. Relations Under the Background of U.S. 'Return to Asia'" ["美国'重返亚洲'背景下的南海问题与中美关系"], *Journal of the Party School of CPC Jinan Municipal Committee*, Vol. 5, 2014.

Zhao Lijian, "Foreign Ministry Spokesperson Zhao Lijian's Regular Press Conference on July 6, 2020," Ministry of Foreign Affairs of the People's Republic of China, July 6, 2020.

———, "Foreign Ministry Spokesperson Zhao Lijian's Regular Press Conference on July 8, 2020," Ministry of Foreign Affairs of the People's Republic of China, July 8, 2020.

———, "Foreign Ministry Spokesperson Zhao Lijian's Regular Press Conference on July 14, 2020," Ministry of Foreign Affairs of the People's Republic of China, July 14, 2020.

Zhao Minghao, "Washington Adds to U.S.-China Security Dilemma," *Global Times*, July 24, 2016.

Zhao, Suisheng, "Foreign Policy Implications of Chinese Nationalism Revisited: The Strident Turn," *Journal of Contemporary China*, Vol. 22, No. 82, 2013, pp. 535–553.

Zhao, Tong, *Conventional Challenges to Strategic Stability: Chinese Perception of Hypersonic Technology and the Security Dilemma*, Washington, D.C.: Carnegie Endowment for International Peace, 2016.

———, *Practical Ways to Promote U.S.-China Arms Control Negotiations*, Washington, D.C.: Carnegie Endowment for International Peace, October 7, 2020.

Zhao Xiaozhuo, "Expert: THAAD Cannot Enhance U.S. Sense of Security," *China Military Online*, August 1, 2016. As of February 3, 2021:
http://english.chinamil.com.cn/news-channels/pla-daily-commentary/2016-08/01/content_7185003.htm

Zhicheng Wu and Yiyi Chen, "What Is the Difference Between the U.S. Position on Huangyan Island and the Diaoyu Islands Issue?"
["美国在黄岩岛与钓鱼岛问题上的立场缘何不同?"], *Xiandai Guoji Guanxi*
[现代国际关系], No. 4, 2013.

Zhong Sheng [钟声], "Dangerous Action That Warrants Alarm—Deployment of THAAD Threatens Peace in Northeast Asia" ["值得警惕的危险之举—部署'萨德'威胁的是东北亚和平"], *People's Daily* [人民日报], July 29, 2016.

———, "South Korea Needs Composure and Sense of Reality—Deployment of THAAD Threatens Peace in Northeast Asia" ["韩国, 需要基本的清醒和现实感—部署'萨德'威胁的是东北亚和平"], *People's Daily* [人民日报], August 1, 2016.

———, "China's Security Interests Should Not Be Deliberately Damaged—Deployment of THAAD Threatens Peace in Northeast Asia" ["中国安全利益不容蓄意损害—部 署'萨德'威胁的是东北亚和平"], *People's Daily* [人民日报], August 3, 2016. As of February 3, 2021:
http://opinion.people.com.cn/n1/2016/0803/c1003-28605744.html

———, "The U.S. and South Korea Must Understand the Deep Meaning Behind China and Russia's Warnings—Deployment of THAAD Threatens Peace in Northeast Asia" ["美韩须领会中俄严正警告的深意—部署'萨德'威胁的是东北亚和平"], *People's Daily* [人民日报], August 4, 2016. As of July 13, 2021:
http://www.xinhuanet.com/world/2016-08/04/c_129203149.htm

———, "Accumulating Damage to the Strategy to Contain China" ["对华遏制战略蓄患积害"], *People's Daily* [人民日报], August 31, 2020. As of March 16, 2021: http://paper.people.com.cn/rmrb/html/2020-08/31/nw.D110000renmrb_20200831_2-03.htm

Zhou, Laura, "Beijing Starts Military Exercise in Disputed South China Sea as Tensions with Vietnam Rise," *South China Morning Post*, August 15, 2019.

———, "As Coastguard Boats Circle, Vietnam Prepares for Bigger Challenge in South China Sea," *South China Morning Post*, October 12, 2019.

———, "China Warns Japan Against Stoking Military Tensions over Taiwan," *South China Morning Post*, May 21, 2021.

Zhou Na and Guo Chen, "China-Vietnam Joint Medical Examination in Border Areas Concludes," *China Military Online*, August 29, 2018. As of July 13, 2021: http://eng.mod.gov.cn/news/2018-08/29/content_4823562.htm

Zhou, Weifeng, and Mario Esteban, "Beyond Balancing: China's Approach Towards the Belt and Road Initiative," *Journal of Contemporary China*, Vol. 27, No. 112, 2018, pp. 487–501.

Zhu Feng [朱锋], "What Did 'Carl Vinson's' Trip to the South China Sea Reveal?" ["'卡尔·文森'号南海之行透射出什么"], *World Affairs* [世界知识], No. 7, 2018, pp. 30–32.

Zhu Lu-ming and Zhang Wen-wen, "The Causes and Influences of Strengthening the American-Japan Ally Under the Background of the Asia-Pacific Rebalancing Strategy" ["美国'亚太再平衡'背景下美日同盟的强化原因及影响"], *Journal of Lanzhou University of Arts and Science* [兰州文理学院学报], Vol. 4, 2014.

Zhu Ping [王平], "In Traveling Through the U.S., Tsai Ying Wen Courts Controversy in Sensitive Cross-Strait Relations" ["过境美国，蔡英文挑动两岸敏感神经"], *Qiushi* [求实], July 12, 2019. As of March 16, 2021: http://www.qstheory.cn/international/2019-07/12/c_1124743604.htm

Ziezulewicz, Geoff, "Two U.S. Aircraft Carriers Are Operating in the South China Sea; Air Force B-52 Joins Them," *Navy Times*, July 6, 2020.

9 781977 410382